Progress in International Relations Theory

The BCSIA Studies in International Security book series is edited at the Belfer Center for Science and International Affairs at Harvard University's John F. Kennedy School of Government and published by The MIT Press. The series publishes books on contemporary issues in international security policy, as well as their conceptual and historical foundations. Topics of particular interest to the series include the spread of weapons of mass destruction, internal conflict, the international effects of democracy and democratization, and U.S. defense policy.

A complete list of BCSIA Studies appears at the back of this volume.

Progress in International Relations Theory

Appraising the Field

Colin Elman and Miriam Fendius Elman, editors

BCSIA Studies in International Security

MIT Press
Cambridge, Massachusetts
London, England

This book was typeset in Palatino by Teresa Lawson and was
printed and bound in the United States of America.

Library of Congress Cataloging-in-Publication Data
Progress in international relations theory : appraising the field /
Colin Elman and Miriam Fendius Elman, eds.
p.   c.m—(BCSIA studies in international security)
Includes bibliographical references and index.
ISBN 0-262-05068-4 (hc. : alk. paper)—ISBN 0-262-55041-5 (pbk. : alk. paper)
1. International relations—Methodology. I. Elman, Colin. II. Elman, Miriam Fendius.
III. Series.

JZ1242 .P76 2003
327.1'01—dc21   2002032170

Printed in the United States of America

10 9 8 7 6 5 4 3 2 1

We greatly appreciate permission to include previous publications in the following journals:
Chapters 1 and 2 in Colin Elman and Miriam Fendius Elman, "How Not to Be Lakatos
Intolerant: Appraising Progress in IR Research," *International Studies Quarterly*, Vol. 46, No. 2
(June 2002), pp. 231–262; Chapter 4 in Jonathan M. DiCicco and Jack S. Levy, "Power Shifts
and Problem Shifts: The Evolution of the Power Transition Program," *Journal of Conflict
Resolution*, Vol. 43, No. 6 (December 1999), pp. 675–704; Chapter 5 in Andrew Moravcsik,
"Taking Preferences Seriously: A Liberal Theory of International Politics," *International
Organization*, Vol. 51, No. 4 (Autumn 1997), pp. 513–553; Jeffrey Legro and Andrew
Moravcsik, "Is Anybody Still a Realist?" *International Security*, Vol. 24, No. 2 (Fall 1999), pp.
5–55; and Chapter 8 in Robert L. Jervis, "Realism, Neoliberalism, and Cooperation:
Understanding the Dabate," *International Security*, Vol. 24, No. 1 (Summer 1999), pp. 42–63.

On the cover: The Copernican solar system. We gratefully acknowledge permission to
reproduce this illustration from the University of Chicago Press. Redrawn from William D.
Stahlman from Galileo: Dialogue on the Great World Systems, revised, edited, and
annotated by Giorzio de Santillano, University of Chicago Press, © 1953. We also thank
Donna Whipple for research and design assistance.

Contents

Foreword

Thoughts about Assaying Theories

Kenneth N. Waltz

Students sometimes ask, with a hint of exasperation, why I assign Lakatos in seminars on international-political theory. One easily thinks of a number of reasons to omit him: Philosophy of science is a subject that demands clarity and precision; Lakatos's prose is opaque and vague; reading his well-known essay on "Falsification and Research Programmes" provides no clear guide to the evaluation of theories.[1] One certainly is not told just what to do. Yet the answer to why we should take Lakatos seriously is simple: He demolishes the simplistic notions about testing that have been and remain part of the intellectual stock of most students of political science.

How can we assay theories? Karl Popper gave a pleasingly simple answer. First, make a conjecture, preferably a bold one such as *all swans are white*. Then, search for falsifying instances. Thousands or millions of white swans do not prove that all swans are white, but just one black swan proves the conjecture false. Simply multiplying observations that appear to offer confirmation will not do, because one cannot know of the lurking instance that would defeat the "theory." Popper's idea of the "critical" test rests on a distinction between trying to prove truth and being able to demonstrate falsity. Popper believed that the latter is possible; the former, not.

---

1. Imre Lakatos, "Falsification and the Methodology of Scientific Research Programmes," in Imre Lakatos and Alan Musgrave, eds., *Criticism and the Growth of Knowledge: Proceedings of the International Colloquium in the Philosophy of Science*, London, 1965, vol. 4 (Cambridge: Cambridge University Press, 1970), pp. 91–196.

In 1970, Errol Harris published an insightful but little-known book, *Hypothesis and Perception.*[2] His title suggested that the results of tests require interpretation, and his text developed the argument that seemingly critical tests are at best problematic. Tests attempting to falsify a theory are conducted against background information that in its day is taken for granted. How can we know that the background information is valid? Perhaps the black bird one thought a swan was really a turkey. That nothing is both empirical and certain is a proposition established long ago by David Hume and Immanuel Kant.

If the bold conjecture seems to flunk the critical test, the scientist-observer still has decisions to make about the implications that are to be drawn from the outcome. Lakatos takes the problem up at this point. His dictum is that *"we cannot prove theories and we cannot disprove them either."*[3] He was right for this reason among others: Facts are no more independent of theories than theories are independent of facts. The validity of theories does not depend on facts that are simply given. Theory and fact are interdependent. As the English astronomer Sir Arthur Stanley Eddington put it, "We should not put overmuch confidence in the observational results that are put forward until they have been confirmed by theory."[4] A moment's thought reveals the wisdom of his advice. The earth is the center of the universe, and the sun and other heavenly bodies swirl around it: These beliefs were among the "facts" accepted in antiquity and through the Middle Ages. They were easily "verified" by looking around; they conformed to everyday experience. From Copernicus onward, however, new theories changed old facts.

Are these thoughts relevant for today's political scientists? We have to believe so when we read the following statement in a widely consulted manual on the design of social inquiry: "A theory must be consistent with prior evidence about a research question." To drive the

---

2. Errol Harris, *Hypothesis and Perception* (London: Allen and Unwin, 1970).

3. Lakatos, "Falsification and the Methodology of Scientific Research Programmes," p. 100 (emphasis in original).

4. Sir Arthur Stanley Eddington, *New Pathways in Science* (New York: Macmillan, 1935), p. 211.

point home the manual's authors quote Stanley Lieberson's pronouncement that a "theory that ignores existing evidence is an oxymoron."[5] Ironically, these thoughts are recorded in a chapter titled "The *Science* in Social Science."[6] The authors' science, however, is of the medieval variety. Theories, they say, may "emerge from detailed observation, but they should be evaluated with new observations." In this positivist perspective, facts are a source of theories and their arbiters as well. A theory is tested by confronting it with "the hard facts of empirical reality."[7] Yet seeming facts exist in infinite number. Which facts are to be taken as providing evidence for or against a theory? Because of the interdependence of theory and fact, one cannot give a simple answer. As Goethe put it, "The highest wisdom is to realize that every fact is already a theory."[8] According to the manual, a theory must indicate what evidence would show the theory wrong. According to Lakatos, a theory cannot specify the observations that would over-throw it.[9] According to the manual, there is an asymmetry between proving something true and proving something false. The latter is possible; the former, not. Theories are to be tested by trying to falsify them. Yet according to Lakatos, "some of the most interesting experiments result ... in confirmation rather than falsification."[10] Steven

---

5. Gary King, Robert O. Keohane, and Sidney Verba, *Designing Social Inquiry: Scientific Inference in Qualitative Research* (Princeton, N.J.: Princeton University Press, 1994), p. 19.

6. Ibid., chap. 1.

7. Gary King, Robert O. Keohane, and Sidney Verba, "The Importance of Research Design in Political Science," *American Political Science Review*, Vol. 89, No. 2 (June 1995), pp. 475–476.

8. Johann Wolfgang von Goethe, *Wisdom and Experience*, selections by Ludwig Curtius, trans. and ed. with an introduction by Hermann J. Weigand (New York: Pantheon, 1949), p. 94.

9. King, Keohane, and Verba, *Designing Social Inquiry*, p. 19. Lakatos puts his point this way: "*exactly the most admired scientific theories simply fail to forbid any observable state of affairs.*" Lakatos and Musgrave, *Criticism and the Growth of Knowledge*, p. 100 (emphasis in original).

10. Lakatos, "Falsification and the Methodology of Research Programmes," p. 115. Harris argues that among natural scientists, falsification is a seldom used

Weinberg, Nobel laureate in physics, adds that there "is no theory that is not contradicted by some experiment."[11]

Despite all of the difficulties of testing, we need to evaluate theories in order to get rid of the wrong ones. With this thought, both Popper and Lakatos agree. They differ on how to do the evaluation. If, as Lakatos says, no theory can be shown to be either true or false, what are we to do? Rather than solving the problem of testing theory, Lakatos resorts to a displacement. Since no theory can be proved or disproved, he counsels trying to evaluate a series of theories, which he calls "a research programme." He deftly moves from a problem we cannot solve to one we supposedly can. If variations and elaborations of a theory uncover novel facts, research programs gain credence. A research program is based on and takes care to protect the "hard core" of the original theory. Auxiliary hypotheses provide the protection; they explain why seeming anomalies do not count.

Newtonian science provides the model for Lakatos's idea of a research program. A series of theories based on the same concepts and explaining ever more earthly and heavenly phenomena appeared to find confirmation by continuing to turn up novel facts. To Lakatos, the hard core of Newtonian science is the law of gravity and the three laws of dynamics. (Or, we may wonder, might it be the mental picture of the world in which space and time are absolute and the speed of light is relative?) Lakatos's rule is to stick with a research program as long as it produces "novel facts." The accumulation of anomalies (phenomena not accounted for by the theories) may cast the hard core into doubt, but since theories can be neither falsified nor verified, a theory can be overthrown only by a better one.[12]

In the social sciences, unfortunately, theories are scarce and research programs hard to find. The best example of a social science research

---

method. Efforts to confirm theories are much more common. For examples from the work of eminent scientists, see Harris, *Hypothesis and Perception*, pp. 161–178.

11. Steven Weinberg, *Dreams of a Final Theory* (New York: Pantheon Books, 1992), p. 93.

12. Lakatos and Musgrave, *Criticism and the Growth of Knowledge*, p. 119.

program is the elaboration of classical and neoclassical economic theories over a period of more than 150 years, stretching from Adam Smith to John Maynard Keynes. Over the decades, anomalies accumulated and auxiliary hypotheses could no longer defend the hard core. The crucial anomaly was the recurrence of depressions, prolonged to the extent that it became hard to believe that the natural workings of a competitive economy would restore the natural equilibrium of the economy. Hobson showed that economic equilibria can be sustained at a level lower than full employment of the factors of production. When Keynes cast Hobson's ideas in the form of a general theory, macroeconomic theory gained and microeconomic theory lost credence.[13]

Yet one wonders how well the displacement from testing a theory to evaluating a series of theories serves. For a number of reasons, I would say, "not very." First, a research program is not fashioned by the creator of the initiatory theory but by the creator's successors. The original theory may be a good one, but the successor theories weak and defective. If the program should run off the tracks, we would still want to know how good the original theory may be. Second, the problem of evaluating a theory endures, whether or not the theory spawns a succession of theories. Third—an acute problem in the social sciences in applying the "novel facts" test—how are we to decide which facts are to be accepted as novel ones? Some will claim that their theories revealed one or two; others will say, we knew that all along. Fourth, if assaying a theory in itself is not possible, then how can anyone know whether launching a research program is worthwhile? In the end we may be left with Weinberg's thought that the "most important thing ... is not the decision that a theory is true, but the decision that it is worth taking seriously."[14]

Given the problems of Lakatos's methodology of scientific research programs, why, I ask again, should students of politics pay attention to

13. John A. Hobson, *Imperialism: A Study* (London: Allen and Unwin, 1938; originally published 1902); John Maynard Keynes, *The General Theory of Employment, Interest, and Money* (New York: Harcourt, Brace, n.d.).

14. Weinberg, *Dreams of a Final Theory*, p. 103.

it? We should do so for one big reason: Lakatos's assaults crush the crassly positivist ideas about how to evaluate theories that are accepted by most political scientists. He demolishes the notion that one can test theories by pitting them against facts. As he puts it, "no finite sample can ever *disprove* a universal probabilistic theory."[15] One should think hard about why this is true. Paying more attention to Lakatos will help.

In this volume, Colin Elman and Miriam Fendius Elman and the contributors ask whether the field of international relations has made any progress in its efforts to develop theories. The book proceeds from the premise that the work of Imre Lakatos provides useful ways of answering this question. The Elmans review Lakatos's methodology of scientific research programs. The authors of the various chapters then use Lakatosian criteria to assess the contribution of different types of research to the improvement of theory in our field. Such an assessment is overdue, and this book is a good start.

---

15. Lakatos and Musgrave, *Criticism and the Growth of Knowledge*, p. 102.

Acknowledgments

This volume is directly descended from the papers and the discussions at a conference on "Progress in International Relations Theory" that we convened in Scottsdale, Arizona, on January 15–16, 1999. We thank the contributors for their willingness to take time from their very full research agendas to write essays for this book. We are also very grateful for their patience during the volume's long development.

Richard Ashley, Sean Lynn-Jones, Stephen Krasner, and Marie Henehan helped to shape and advance this project by their contributions to the Scottsdale conference. We would also like to thank Akan Malici for his research assistance.

Parts of four of the volume's chapters appeared in earlier versions as journal articles; we thank the editors and publishers of *International Studies Quarterly*, the *Journal of Conflict Resolution*, *International Organization*, and *International Security* for allowing us to reproduce sections of these articles.

We are very grateful to Arizona State University's College of Liberal Arts and Sciences (CLAS), the Department of Political Science, the Graduate College, and the Arizona Foundation for jointly sponsoring the Scottsdale conference. In particular, we would like to express our gratitude to former ASU President Lattie Coor, Senior Vice President and Provost Milton Glick, former CLAS Dean Gary Krahenbuhl, CLAS Dean Milton Sommerfeld, and Stephen Walker and Robert Youngblood, the former Chairs of the Department of Political Science, for their support.

This book project began while we were taking up our respective International Security Fellowships at Harvard University's Belfer Center for Science and International Affairs (BCSIA). We thank Graham Allison, Steven Miller, and Sean Lynn-Jones for inviting us to rejoin BCSIA's outstanding intellectual community, and for their encouragement. We also thank David White and Alex Turrell for their careful proofreading, and John Grennan for his skillfully prepared index. Karen Motley oversaw the final stages of the book's production with her usual care. We are very grateful to consulting editor Teresa Johnson Lawson, whose organizational and editing skills made this a much better book.

Finally, we dedicate this book to Dr. Spiro Latsis, for leading the way.

Colin Elman
Miriam Fendius Elman
Tempe, Arizona

Chapter 1

Introduction

Appraising Progress in International Relations Theory

Colin Elman and
Miriam Fendius Elman

This book investigates how international relations (IR) theorists can equip themselves to determine whether the subfield's work is getting any better; that is, whether it is progressive in the sense of providing cumulative knowledge about hitherto unexplained phenomena. To answer this question, we make use of some well known theories of scientific change. These might seem far removed from the concerns of working practitioners in the subfield, but in science, including political science, there is no "just doing it." Even those working political scientists who loudly declare their indifference to philosophy of science are inevitably using methodological toolkits based on prior, if unconscious, choices about what it means to achieve and to measure progress.[1] Understanding those toolkits gives IR practitioners a better

---

Chapters 1 and 2 draw upon material that appears in Colin Elman and Miriam Fendius Elman, "How Not to Be Lakatos Intolerant: Appraising Progress in IR Research," *International Studies Quarterly*, Vol. 46, No. 2 (June 2002), pp. 231–262. We thank the journal for allowing us to reproduce parts of the article in this book.

---

1. For a convincing argument, "written from a philosopher's point of view," that we also need to pay close attention to ontology, see Alexander Wendt, *Social Theory of International Politics* (Cambridge, UK: Cambridge University Press, 1999), pp. 32, 37. Although Wendt suggests that "IR scholars have been too worried about epistemology," he uses language and evaluative criteria that are consistent with those presented by philosopher of science Imre Lakatos. See ibid., pp. 20, 29, 40, 48, 58, 158, 159.

grasp of the potential and the limits of their selected methodologies, and a greater appreciation of the alternatives.[2] Quite apart from concerns for the accumulation of knowledge, these matters can have surprisingly concrete practical consequences for a scholar's career: professional reputations, research grants, book contracts, and the ability to attract students and followers all hinge on whether one's work is judged positively by others.

We agree with economist Richard Bradley that a refusal to engage in and benefit from methodological debate is to abandon the terrain to intuition, and to the prejudices of whoever has the authority to decide the standards that should be applied.[3] Thus our main interest in this volume is in providing information for IR theorists who perform and assess appraisals within the discipline. We are not suggesting that such evaluations should become the profession's main preoccupation: if everyone spent their time describing and assessing previous scholarship, political science would grind to a halt. However, such appraisals are important and have a long and useful track record in the discipline; when they are done, they should be done well. Meaningful stocktaking requires making explicit and informed selections from among alternative ways to describe and evaluate theories.

While political scientists have often shown an interest in evaluating the state of their discipline,[4] most have relied on partial and subterranean criteria. The international relations subfield is no exception.

---

2. For similar discussions of the importance of philosophical studies to practicing historians, and of the mutual benefits of cross-disciplinary dialogue between historians and philosophers, see Peter Achinstein, "History and Philosophy of Science: A Reply to Cohen," in Frederick Suppe, ed., *The Structure of Scientific Theories*, 2d ed. (Chicago: University of Illinois Press, 1977), pp. 350–360; and I. Bernard Cohen, "History and the Philosopher of Science," in ibid., pp. 308–349.

3. Richard Bradley, "Review of Explorations in Economic Methodology," *British Journal for the Philosophy of Science*, Vol. 50, No. 2 (June 1999), p. 316.

4. See, for example, Terence Ball, "Introduction," in Terence Ball, ed., *Idioms of Inquiry: Critique and Renewal in Political Science* (Albany: State University of New York Press, 1987), p. 1; James Farr, John S. Dryzek, and Stephen T. Leonard, *Political Science in History: Research Programs and Political Traditions* (New York: Cambridge University Press, 1995).

Its practitioners have produced a steady stream of research appraisals. The end of the Cold War and the close of the millennium brought a marked expansion in the number of stock-taking analyses of the subfield.[5] This trend is well represented by Frank Harvey's Call for Papers for the 2000 annual convention of the International Studies Association: titled "Reflection, Integration, Cumulation: International Studies Past and Future," it invited "self-critical, state-of-the-art 'reflection' within epistemologies, perspectives and subfields" and suggested that without such reflection, "the promise of International Studies cannot be fulfilled."[6]

Recent assessments identify theoretical developments in a variety of research areas, and rate those that have proved most and least useful to the study of international relations. They also question why some theoretical orientations—notably neorealism, dependency, and world systems theory—have become less popular, while others—such as rational choice, historical institutionalism, and constructivism—have received increased support. However, in identifying "better" theories, and describing the successes and failures of IR research programs, these field surveys rarely address whether there is a pattern to the fate of specific research agendas, or explain why particular theories of international relations have waxed or waned. More importantly, almost

---

5. See, for example, Richard Ned Lebow and Thomas Risse-Kappen, *International Relations Theory and the End of the Cold War* (New York: Columbia University Press, 1995); Michael W. Doyle and G. John Ikenberry, *New Thinking in International Relations Theory* (Boulder, Colo.: Westview Press, 1997); Tim Dunne, Michael Cox, and Ken Booth, eds., "The Eighty Years Crisis 1919–1999," *Review of International Studies* (special issue), Vol. 24, No. 5 (December 1998); Peter J. Katzenstein, Robert O. Keohane, and Stephen D. Krasner, eds., "*International Organization* at Fifty: Exploration and Contestation in the Study of World Politics," *International Organization* (special issue), Vol. 52, No. 4 (Autumn 1998); and Davis B. Bobrow, ed., "Prospects for International Relations: Conjectures About the Next Millennium," *International Studies Review* (special issue), Vol. 1, No. 2 (January 1999).

6. Similarly, Ada Finifter notes that the millennium makes "critical evaluations and assessments of research traditions and literatures" particularly timely. Ada Finifter, "Editor's Notes," *American Political Science Review*, Vol. 91, No. 4 (December 1997), pp. viii–ix.

none of the recent appraisals adequately engage the question of what measures should be used to determine whether various theoretical moves are progressive.

There is a strong tendency in the subfield to engage in metatheoretic exercises without metatheory; to evaluate theoretical aggregates without using suitable or even necessary toolkits. A good example is the assessment by Jeffrey W. Legro and Andrew Moravcsik of contemporary theoretical developments in realism, an analysis that, although it is cloaked in metatheoretic terms of art, overlooks pertinent epistemology. Legro and Moravcsik argue that "the specification of well-developed paradigms around sets of core assumptions remains central to the study of world politics," and accordingly they describe and evaluate realism as a metatheoretic unit.[7] But they decouple this theoretical aggregate from any underlying metatheory, noting that they "do not mean to imply more with the term 'paradigm'" than they state, and suggesting that the term is interchangeable with "'basic theory,' 'research program,' 'school,' or 'approach'."[8] Legro and Moravcsik insist that their evaluation of realism (and, by implication, of any other body of IR work) does not depend on holding to a specific philosophy of science. Although their statement is more unequivocal than most, this is not an isolated instance. Almost all disciplinary appraisals in the subfield similarly neglect to state the standards by which research is to be judged.

In organizing this volume as an examination of progress in IR theory, we were motivated by the belief that it is impossible to engage in disciplinary appraisals without making explicit selections from among a menu of competing epistemologies. The contributors to this volume follow recent stock-taking efforts by focusing on theoretical approaches that have had significant influence and staying power:

7. Jeffrey W. Legro and Andrew Moravcsik, "Is Anybody Still a Realist?" *International Security*, Vol. 24, No. 2 (Fall 1999), p. 8.

8. Ibid., p. 9, note 5. In note 6, Legro and Moravcsik direct readers' attention to "a fuller account of the desirable criteria" in a working paper that predates their *International Security* essay, but that paper does not address the ambiguity noted above either, and is no more connected to relevant literature on theory appraisal.

realism, liberalism, institutionalism, power transition theory, the democratic peace, and psychological decision making. However, by explicitly grounding these evaluations in metatheory, they go well beyond previous assessments. We asked them to use an influential theory of scientific change—Imre Lakatos's methodology of scientific research programs (MSRP)—as a basis for exploring how we should appraise progress in international relations.[9] Taking Lakatos's metatheory as its starting point, the chapters in this book use his methodology to organize an analysis of major research programs of the last several decades, and make a systematic effort to evaluate them using its criteria for measuring theoretical progress.

This volume has three central goals. First, it lays out a received description of Lakatos's framework for evaluating theoretical and empirical progress. We believe this is necessary and useful because, while many IR scholars have used Lakatos's metric as an "organizing device" and as a means of defending or undermining scholarly contributions, and while Lakatos's 1970 essay is probably one of the most cited methodology texts in the subfield, the great majority of citations appear in boilerplate footnotes, and most of the substantive applications or discussions of the methodology of scientific research programs in IR have proceeded on the basis of popularized, misleading, and incomplete accounts of the metatheory. We argue that decisions whether to employ Lakatos's methodology should be based on what Lakatos and his most thoughtful followers and critics actually say, not on what distant users in the IR subfield have come to believe that they say.

---

9. Imre Lakatos, "Falsification and the Methodology of Scientific Research Programmes," in Imre Lakatos and Alan Musgrave, eds., *Criticism and the Growth of Knowledge* (New York: Cambridge University Press, 1970), pp. 91–196. See also Imre Lakatos, "History of Science and its Rational Reconstructions," in Roger C. Buck and Robert S. Cohen, *Boston Studies in the Philosophy of Science, PSA 1970*, Vol. 8 (Dordrecht: D. Reidel, 1971), pp. 91–136; Imre Lakatos, "Replies to Critics," in ibid., pp. 174–182; and Imre Lakatos, "The Role of Crucial Experiments in Science," *Studies in History and Philosophy of Science*, Vol. 4, No. 4 (1974), pp. 309–325.

Our second goal in this volume is to ask whether Lakatos's methodology is a usable one for evaluating IR theory. Although Lakatos is frequently cited, and there have been some applications of his methodology to particular research programs, there have been no serious attempts to investigate whether the subfield's theoretical developments actually reflect Lakatos's theory of scientific change. In this volume, Lakatos's metric is assessed against an extensive empirical record. The contributors evaluate whether theoretical developments in IR correspond to Lakatos's methodology, and whether his framework offers any useful recommendations as to how we can best promote the growth of knowledge in the subfield. The book thus addresses both descriptive and prescriptive questions: does the methodology of scientific research programs portray how IR research actually develops, and does Lakatos provide the right criteria for assessing the merit of IR theories?[10]

Lastly, this volume has the broader goal of developing debate on the nature of scientific change in the social sciences in general, and in the study of international relations in particular. The methodology of scientific research programs is a useful point of departure, but it is not a philosophical straitjacket that we are committed to advocate or employ. This volume is not produced by a "closed shop of committed Lakatosians" (to borrow Mark Blaug's phrase).[11] Science can progress in more than one way, and none of the authors argue for the unquestioning acceptance or universal application of Lakatos's methodology. Although several of the contributors find that his

---

10. While this book covers some of the major theoretical gambits in the IR subfield, due to obvious space constraints not everything could be included in one volume, and we are aware that we have left out some important areas of research. In particular, our choice of topics reflects research agendas that have had high profiles among scholars in North America, and moreover is heavily weighted toward security issues. A more complete appraisal of recent IR scholarship would also include research agendas that reflect interests from other regions, as well as more on international political economy.

11. See Mark Blaug, "Afterword," in Neil de Marchi and Mark Blaug, eds., *Appraising Economic Theories: Studies in the Methodology of Research Programs* (Brookfield, Vt.: Edward Elgar, 1991), p. 499.

methodology has some utility for the IR subfield, none are Lakatos boosters. Some contributors are quite critical of Lakatos's methodology, and find his metric wanting when compared to competing theories of scientific change offered by other leading philosophers such as Thomas Kuhn, Larry Laudan, and Deborah Mayo.

Why Lakatos?

We argued above that disciplinary appraisals require metatheory: a way to describe and evaluate the trajectory of different theoretical aggregates. In this volume we use as our point of departure Lakatos's methodology of scientific research programs (see "A Brief Guide to Imre Lakatos's Methodology of Scientific Research Programs," pp. 19–20). We do not claim that Lakatos's approach is the best of the alternative philosophies of science. Since IR theorists have largely ignored metatheory, the volume could have broken new ground by beginning with virtually any epistemology. Nonetheless, there are at least four reasons why a more careful study of Lakatos's methodology of scientific research programs is worth the effort.

First, on a variety of grounds, it is an intuitively appealing and powerful candidate metatheory for describing and evaluating research. As we suggest in Chapter 2, it provides a rationalist, pluralist, and tolerant metric that rewards creativity, innovation, and inventiveness. Its descriptions of intellectual trajectories, together with its battery of standards for research programs, are those that many IR scholars acknowledge as logical and consistent with the way they and their colleagues work, or should work. Standards that are consistent with Lakatos's already figure prominently in IR methodology texts, for example, that empirical evidence should be the final arbiter among competing theories, that facts employed in constructing a theory should not be the only ones used to test it, and that good theories should be able to explain facts outside their initial domain of application.[12] Lakatos's central claims transfer well to IR, particularly his advocacy of tolerance and tenacity. IR theorists acknowledge, and tolerate, the existence of competing research programs. Stephen M. Walt, for example, argues that while "scholarship is a competitive enterprise ... the competition that drives progress should be tempered with the recognition that different research traditions can and should coexist."[13] IR scholars also recognize the importance of guiding assumptions and theoretical commitments, and expect scientists who encounter evidentiary discrepancies to fight with tenacity to save their theories.

A second reason for using Lakatos's methodology is that, because it views science not as individual theories but as a series of theories connected by a common core, recent theoretical developments in realism, liberalism, and constructivism are now amenable to Lakatosian appraisal. Several research areas in the subfield have each accumulated a series of theoretical reformulations, and accordingly the metric may now be useful to assess them. By providing a set of rules that enable us to judge what we have learned from developments in IR theory, Lakatos's methodology of scientific research programs helps us to determine whether such iterations offer added value.[14]

Third, consideration of Lakatos's methodology may be particularly timely, given criticisms against much research activity in diverse areas—from the democratic peace to the balancing of power—claiming that it consists of illegitimate theoretical revisions

---

12. See, for example, Gary King, Robert O. Keohane, and Sidney Verba, *Designing Social Inquiry: Scientific Inference in Qualitative Research* (Princeton, N.J.: Princeton University Press, 1994).

13. Stephen M. Walt, "A Model Disagreement," *International Security*, Vol. 24, No. 2 (Fall 1999), p. 130. Although Walt advocates competition and pluralism, he is not a fan of Lakatos. See Stephen M. Walt, "The Progressive Power of Realism," *American Political Science Review*, Vol. 91, No. 4 (December 1997), pp. 931–935.

14. Whether we should view IR research as a series of theoretical aggregates, however, is open to debate. For example, Randall Schweller (Chapter 9 in this volume) insists that Kenneth Waltz's neorealist theory has not been amended, and so neorealism cannot be considered a Lakatosian research program.

accommodating empirical discrepancies. For example, realists typically argue that democratic peace theorists stubbornly shield liberal claims from awkward facts by mere semantic changes, such as reformulating conceptual definitions and causal mechanisms.[15] Critics of realism make similar charges: John A. Vasquez, for instance, recently claimed that contemporary realist theories of balancing are suspect because proponents have reconstructed realism in ways that explain anomalies, but not much else.[16] Similarly, Legro and Moravcsik argue that today's realists are explaining an increasing number of empirical anomalies in a "trivially easy" fashion by softening realism into a loose rationalism indistinguishable from existing liberal and institutionalist theory.[17] Since the methodology of scientific research programs provides explicit guidelines about how scientists should approach empirical counterexamples, and offers conjectures regarding how in practice they do go about dealing with anomalies, a better understanding of Lakatos's ideas might shed light on whether these criticisms are justified. As political scientist Hillard Pouncy puts it, "Lakatosian methodology can be usefully applied in situations in which an evaluator wants to sort out how well a program has defended itself."[18]

---

15. See, for example, David E. Spiro, "The Insignificance of the Liberal Peace," in Michael E. Brown, Sean M. Lynn-Jones, and Steven E. Miller, eds., *Debating the Democratic Peace* (Cambridge, Mass.: MIT Press, 1996), pp. 206–214; and Stephen M. Walt, "Never Say Never: Wishful Thinking on Democracy and War," *Foreign Affairs*, Vol. 78, No. 1 (January/February 1999), pp. 149–150. For an extended discussion of how democratic peace theorists handle anomalous evidence, see Miriam Fendius Elman, "The Never-Ending Story: Democracy and Peace," *International Studies Review*, Vol. 1, No. 3 (Fall 1999), pp. 87–103.

16. John A. Vasquez, "The Realist Paradigm and Degenerative Versus Progressive Research Programs: An Appraisal of Neotraditional Research on Waltz's Balancing Proposition," *American Political Science Review*, Vol. 91, No. 4 (December 1997), pp. 899–912.

17. Legro and Moravcsik, "Is Anybody Still a Realist?" See also Chapter 5 by Andrew Moravcsik in this volume.

18. Hillard Pouncy, "Terms of Agreement: Evaluating the Theory of Symbolic Politics' Impact on the Pluralist Research Program," *American Journal of Political Science*, Vol. 32, No. 3 (August 1988), p. 784.

Finally, a better understanding of Lakatos's methodology is warranted because IR theorists have long noted the utility of his approach. In 1985, Stephen D. Krasner observed that "Lakatos's sophisticated methodological falsification offers a reasonable set of criteria for assessing research.... [It] is an admirable analytic prescription."[19] Over a decade later, Thomas J. Christensen and Jack Snyder similarly noted that "students of international politics should justify their theories in terms of Imre Lakatos's criteria for distinguishing progressive research programs from degenerative ones."[20] Despite these and similar endorsements, most IR theorists have proceeded with only a partial account of the methodology, and without making the predicate choices necessary for its use. Nor have they referred to the voluminous body of work on Lakatos's methodology of scientific research programs that has sought to extend and clarify the method.[21] We aim to provide a more comprehensive and inclusive account.

---

19. Stephen D. Krasner, "Toward Understanding in International Relations," *International Studies Quarterly*, Vol. 29, No. 2 (June 1985), p. 137.

20. Thomas J. Christensen and Jack Snyder, "Progressive Research on Degenerate Alliances," *American Political Science Review*, Vol. 91, No. 4 (December 1997), p. 919.

21. See, for example, Thomas S. Kuhn, "Reflections on my Critics," in Imre Lakatos and Alan Musgrave, eds., *Criticism and the Growth of Knowledge* (New York: Cambridge University Press, 1970), pp. 231–278; Thomas Kuhn, "Notes on Lakatos," in Buck and Cohen, *Boston Studies in the Philosophy of Science*, Vol. VIII, pp. 137–146; Lakatos, "Replies to Critics"; Lakatos, "History of Science and its Rational Reconstructions"; Alan Musgrave, "Logical versus Historical Theories of Confirmation," *British Journal for the Philosophy of Science*, Vol. 25 (1974), pp. 1–23; Alan Musgrave, "Method or Madness? Can the Methodology of Research Programmes be Rescued from Epistemological Anarchism?" in R.S. Cohen, P.K. Feyerabend and M.W. Wartofsky, eds., *Essays in Memory of Imre Lakatos* (Dordrecht: D. Reidel, 1976), pp. 457–491; John Worrall, "Imre Lakatos (1922–1974): Philosopher of Mathematics and Philosopher of Science," in ibid., pp. 1–8; Alan Musgrave, "Evidential Support, Falsification, Heuristics, and Anarchism," in Gerard Radnitzky and Gunnar Andersson, eds., *Progress and Rationality in Science* (Dordrecht: D. Reidel, 1978), pp. 181–201; John Worrall, "The Ways in Which the Methodology of Scientific Research Programmes Improves on Popper's Methodology," in ibid., pp. 45–70; and John

Organization of the Book

In Chapter 2, we describe Lakatos's metric for theory appraisal; discuss and debunk some myths and misconceptions about the methodology of scientific research programs that have become prevalent in the field of international relations; and identify some of the metatheory's weaknesses.

The remainder of the volume is organized into two parts. The first part identifies and evaluates several research programs in the IR subfield. The first five chapters in Part I employ Lakatos's methodology of scientific research programs to judge theoretical and empirical progress in research on institutionalism, power transition theory, liberalism, the democratic peace, and operational code analysis. While applying the methodology, these chapters also discuss its limitations, and suggest alternative ways to evaluate scientific growth. Additional chapters in Part I revisit theoretical developments in realism, neoliberalism, and normative research from a variety of perspectives, not just those of Lakatos. These essays highlight some difficulties with identifying research programs in IR, and demonstrate how such descriptions come to be contested.

In Part II, contributors offer commentaries on the previous chapters, and on the volume as a whole: they assess the applications of Lakatos and the appraisals; discuss the advantages and disadvantages of using Lakatos's methodology; and suggest how IR scholars might move beyond Lakatos's account of scientific development.

In the rest of this introductory chapter, we describe the other chapters of the book in more detail.

Worrall, "Research Programmes, Empirical Support and the Duhem Problem: Replies to Criticism," in ibid., pp. 321–338. For more recent discussions, see Neil de Marchi and Mark Blaug, eds., *Appraising Economic Theories: Studies in the Methodology of Research Programs* (Brookfield, Vt.: Edward Elgar, 1991); Jarrett Leplin, *A Novel Defense of Scientific Realism* (New York: Oxford University Press, 1997); and Roger E. Backhouse, *Explorations in Economic Methodology: From Lakatos to Empirical Philosophy of Science* (New York: Routledge, 1998), pp. 1–71.

PART I: APPLYING LAKATOS: JUDGING THEORETICAL AND
EMPIRICAL PROGRESS IN INTERNATIONAL RELATIONS

In Chapter 3, Robert O. Keohane and Lisa L. Martin describe, in
Lakatosian terms, realist theory and institutional theory, and empirical
developments within the institutional theory research program.
Keohane and Martin argue that institutional theory is a "half-sibling of
realism": it has adopted almost all of the realist hard core, except that it
treats information as a variable. The authors argue that much of the
institutional theory research program has been progressive: supporters
have easily turned challenges such as the relative gains problem into
confirmations of the program, rather than refutations of it. A more
fundamental problem for institutional theory proponents, however, is
how to handle the realist challenge that institutions are endogenous to
structure and are thus epiphenomenal. According to Keohane and
Martin, agency theory may provide institutional theory with the means
to deal with this challenge. They conclude that "although Lakatos's
criteria are ambiguous and his own formulations often contradictory,
thinking about whether research programs are 'progressive' remains, in
our view, a useful way to help us evaluate their relative merits."

In Chapter 4, Jonathan M. DiCicco and Jack S. Levy describe the
power transition research program, and identify the theoretical
amendments that have been degenerative and progressive according to
Lakatosian criteria. DiCicco and Levy argue that power transition
theory incorporates two ideas that differentiate it from balance of
power realism: the importance of changes in power distributions that
result from industrialization, and the stabilizing effects of power concentrations. The peripheral role of alliances in power transition theory
is also a major point of difference: in balance of power realism,
alliances and alignment behavior have a more integral explanatory
role. According to DiCicco and Levy, a better understanding of power
transition theory's hard core makes it easier to see which contemporary
studies aimed at handling refutations and anomalies have constituted
progressive developments within the research program, and which
work is better viewed as a break with the power transition research
program. They conclude that "most theoretical extensions of power
transition principles have generated novel predictions, many of which

have been empirically corroborated." Thus they find that, overall, the power transition research program has many progressive elements.

In Chapter 5, Andrew Moravcsik specifies the elements that distinguish the liberal research program from its realist, institutionalist, and constructivist competitors. Moravcsik argues that liberalism has been, and continues to be, a progressive research program, because it has predicted new facts that have been empirically corroborated, meeting criteria set by Lakatos. In particular, liberalism explains many recent major developments in world politics, even though they were not prevalent during the Enlightenment when liberal theories were initially formulated. In addition, liberalism explains phenomena that contradict, or cannot be predicted by, rival realist theories. Moravcsik argues that, in contrast to liberalism, realism is degenerating. In accounting for empirical anomalies, he asserts, contemporary realists have constructed new versions of realist theory that are blatantly inconsistent with its hard core assumptions and are virtually indistinguishable from competing "background theories," especially liberalism and institutionalism. While Moravcsik concludes that the discipline imposed by Lakatos's approach on theory construction and development offers some benefits, he argues that excessive "Lakatosian thinking" would inhibit scientific progress in the subfield. Moravcsik argues that Lakatos's methodology of scientific research programs fosters a zero-sum competition between all encompassing approaches and would divert attention from rigorous and useful theory synthesis.

In Chapter 6, James Lee Ray reconstructs the democratic peace research program according to Lakatosian guidelines. Ray argues that proponents of the democratic peace proposition have "proven capable of turning anomalies or apparently disconfirming evidence into strengths and corroborating instances." Moreover, Ray argues, research on the democratic peace phenomenon continues to expand the number of dependent variables explained by the theory. These include explanations for why democracies are more likely to trade with each other, form lasting leagues and alliances, obey international laws, and win the wars in which they participate. This expansion attests to progress in a Lakatosian sense, says Ray: a set of scholars is using the theory to predict new facts that they are then empirically corroborating.

Ray provocatively concludes that the democratic peace research program might be said to falsify realism, because it not only explains outcomes that realism successfully explains, but also has "excess empirical power over realism," and is "able to plug a significant gap left by realism ... in a logical, axiomatically-based manner."

In the book's last application of Lakatos's framework, Stephen G. Walker argues in Chapter 7 that, over the past four decades, theoretical emendations and empirical testing in operational code analysis have addressed important anomalies and generated novel facts. For example, an emphasis on self-schemata and self-scripts rather than images of other states accounted for anomalies in previous applications of cognitive theory to foreign policy choices, but only some of these theoretical amendments predicted novel facts that were subsequently corroborated empirically. Walker concludes that while Lakatos's model of scientific change is consistent with the development of research on operational codes, philosopher of science Larry Laudan's criteria for theory appraisal lead to a more accurate description of the evolution of this scientific research program. In particular, the fact that cognitive theory, game theory, and personality theory all combine in operational code analysis is consistent with Laudan's notion of "theory complexes"—sets of theories that complement each other in the solution of common empirical problems.

While the initial chapters in Part I offer descriptions of what applications of the methodology of scientific research programs would look like for particular research programs in IR, the remaining three chapters in Part I focus primarily on better identifying IR research programs and their rivals. In Chapter 8, Robert Jervis discusses the differences between realism and neoliberalism. Like Keohane and Martin, Jervis argues that realism and neoliberalism have much in common. For example, Jervis notes that for both approaches, the differences among leaders have little effect; he further points out that several defensive realist arguments for how to reduce international conflict are compatible with neoliberal prescriptions. He also suggests that many of the factors commonly used to distinguish these two research programs from each other are either "false or exaggerated."

While Jervis's chapter shows how difficult it is to delineate research programs, it also highlights the value of such an exercise.

Of all the chapters in this volume, Chapter 9 by Randall L. Schweller is the most critical of the methodology of scientific research programs. Schweller's "commonsense criteria" for judging progress in IR include aspects that are consistent with Lakatosian metatheory: for example, hypotheses should be supported by evidence, and knowledge should accumulate. Nevertheless, Schweller insists, the determination of which research programs thrive and which ones die "has more to do with what kinds of theories we find intellectually and politically appealing" than the extent to which they are empirically accurate. Using his own set of appraisal criteria, Schweller identifies and defends a new school of political realism that he calls neoclassical or neotraditional realism.

In Chapter 10, Jack Snyder questions how progress in IR should be assessed when theories include normative elements. He argues that Lakatos's framework, and positivist methods more generally, can be used to evaluate the empirical as well as the logical aspects of normative research programs. He also suggests that the intellectual trajectory of several programs he identifies conforms to the description of scientific change laid out in Lakatos's methodology of scientific research programs. For example, Snyder argues that, consistent with Lakatos, the logical structures of many normative research programs in the subfield strive to keep propositions consistent with their hard cores. When scholars who make normative arguments about standards of appropriate international behavior confront empirical anomalies, they have typically fashioned theoretical emendations in order to defend their research programs from falsification. Snyder argues that, "precisely because of the practical stakes in having a sound empirical theory of ethnic peace, the rigorous application of social science standards of falsifiability is especially important in this type of normative research," and that "empirical social science has a great deal to contribute to contemporary debates about multiculturalism, human rights, and virtually every other normative question of international relations."

PART II: COMMENTARIES ON LAKATOS, AND BEYOND

Part II of the volume offers commentaries on the previous applications of Lakatos, and on the book's central question of how we can know whether the international relations subfield of political science is making progress. David Dessler opens this section in Chapter 11 with a discussion of the advantages and disadvantages of employing Lakatos's methodology to appraise theory developments in IR. Dessler argues that "Lakatos's methodology of scientific research programs remains a useful departure point for discussions of progress in international relations" because it helps us to appreciate that research agendas are best considered in "dynamic profile, rather than in static snapshots." He also suggests that Lakatos's notion of a positive heuristic is particularly helpful because it directs scientists to increase the explanatory power of simple models by making them increasingly more complex and realistic. However, Dessler also argues that, if a sufficient condition for scientific progress is explanatory progress, then Lakatos's metric does not provide the means for assessing research programs that depend on historical research. According to Dessler, many of the debates in IR are not theoretical; that is, they do not involve pitting one series of theories against another. Rather, programs such as those investigating the democratic peace, the end of the Cold War, and ethnic conflict involve the development of more accurate descriptions of the historical record. Here progress is measured not just in terms of theory building, but on the "historical side of the ledger." He concludes that although IR research often conforms to the Lakatosian "verificationist" strategy of theory building, applying Lakatos in practice might increase the tendency to continue with research programs that have little or no potential for successful development. Dessler says that Lakatos's work should not be ignored, but we should not downplay the significance of putting hypotheses to "severe" tests, as urged by Karl Popper.

In Chapter 12, Roslyn Simowitz discusses the lessons to be learned from the applications of Lakatos's methodology of scientific research programs, such as those offered by DiCicco and Levy in Chapter 4 and by Snyder in Chapter 10. Simowitz notes that DiCicco and Levy's efforts to apply Lakatosian appraisal criteria to power transition theory reveal a significant drawback to the use of his framework in IR: Lakatos provides no guidance for choosing between competing programs when they each contain progressive and degenerative problemshifts. Net assessments of research programs are likely to prove especially difficult in IR because few of them exhibit evidence of progress across the board. She also disagrees with Snyder that Lakatos's metatheory can be applied to normative arguments: she argues that it is impossible to corroborate or refute normative predictions empirically, and since such corroboration or refutation is essential to Lakatos's theory of confirmation, it is impossible to use his framework when assessing normative research programs. Simowitz concludes that, despite these problems in applying Lakatosian metatheory, its use is justified. Its requirement of a precise statement of hard core assumptions, for example, makes it easier to identify conflicting assumptions and inconsistent predictions in rival programs.

In Chapter 13, John Vasquez argues that Lakatos provides helpful rules for distinguishing legitimate adjustments to theories from ad-hoc reformulations, as when contradictions between a theory and evidence are "resolved" in merely semantic ways. Vasquez notes, however, that the methodology of scientific research programs is one among many standards, and argues that these need not be mutually exclusive. For example, he suggests that scholars interested in making "systematic and rigorous" disciplinary appraisals can usefully combine Kuhnian and Lakatosian perspectives. Vasquez notes, however, that Lakatos's metric is only applicable to IR research that has produced a series of theoretical emendations. To use Lakatosian criteria there must be "a considerable body of research" resulting in anomalies that need to be explained. According to Vasquez, offense-defense theory is an example of an area where, because there has not been a great deal of theoretical innovation in response to discrepant evidence, appraisal criteria other than Lakatos's are more appropriate.

In the final chapter, Andrew Bennett concludes that, while Lakatos's methodology is useful for judging theoretical progress, it provides an imperfect standard that cannot be relied upon exclusively. Reviewing the chapters by Elman and Elman (Chapter 2) and by Dessler (Chapter 11), Bennett contrasts the methodology of scientific research programs with three post-Lakatosian schools of thought: the Bayesian approach associated with John Earman, Colin Howson, and others; the error-statistical school articulated by Deborah Mayo; and the focus on puzzle-solving research traditions advocated by Larry Laudan. He suggests that each of these approaches, along with Lakatos's metatheory, are useful to "guide us toward an answer, or rather many answers, to the nagging question of whether IR has progressed and how we would know if it has."

While this volume does not aspire to convert anyone to a single or dominant method of evaluation, we sympathize with James Lee Ray's observation: "The broader the base of agreement in the field regarding the issue of how we know what we feel we know, the larger and more accommodating will be the platform accessible to all of us for fruitful dialogue." We did not expect, and as the following pages demonstrate, we did not find, consensus on the merits of Lakatos's methodology of scientific research programs. But by using Lakatos's metatheory as a point of departure, the contributors highlight a variety of difficulties common to all theory evaluations, and suggest some preliminary answers to them. Collectively, the chapters corroborate the intuition that was part of the initial impetus for this study: before we can measure progress, we need to decide how.

A Brief Guide to Imre Lakatos's Methodology of Scientific Research Programs

When should one scientific theory replace another? How do we know when one theory or group of theories is superior to another? These questions are addressed by metatheories, which have other theories as their subject matter. A **metatheory** is thus an inquiry at one remove: it is a view <u>of</u> our knowledge of things, as distinct <u>from</u> that knowledge.

One of the most influential statements on the advancement of knowledge is Karl Popper's argument that since science is by definition disprovable, "good" science consists of theories that we attempt to disprove (falsify) but cannot: theories that survive severe tests. (Popper's famous example points out that one could observe any number of white swans, but this would not prove the hypothesis that all swans are white. However, a single black swan can disprove the hypothesis. This concept is known as **falsifiability**.) If empirical data refutes a theory, the theory must be rejected and a replacement sought.

However, Popper, and the philosopher of science who extended his views—**Imre Lakatos**—recognized that scientists are often reluctant to discard their theories. Instead, when confronted by disconfirming evidence, scientists typically use a variety of strategies to save them, including rewriting theories to "cover" discrepancies. Popper and Lakatos both sought to devise rules for deciding when such defensive moves were legitimate.

Lakatos's model of scientific change goes beyond Popper's by shifting the unit of appraisal from individual theories to sequences of theories. He labeled these **scientific research programs** (SRPs); they comprise a series of theories linked by a set of constitutive and guiding assumptions. The **hard core** (or hard core assumptions) comprises the fundamental premises of a scientific research program. (For example, one of the hard core assumptions of the neorealist research program is that states, not sub-state or supra-state actors, are the primary actors in international politics.) The hard core is protected by a **negative heuristic**, which is the rule that forbids scholars within this scientific research program from contradicting its fundamental premises or hard core (e.g., in response to newly discovered evidence that seems to disconfirm the theory). Alteration of the hard core would result in the creation of a new SRP, because the hard core essentially defines the SRP; if it changes, the SRP changes.

A scientific research program also has a **protective belt of auxiliary hypotheses**. These are propositions that are tested, adjusted and readjusted, and replaced as new evidence comes to bear. (For example, in the neorealist research program, scholars typically distinguish two versions of the protective belt: defensive realism, in which states maximize security by defending the status quo; offensive realism, in which they do so by maximizing power.)

→

The replacement of one set of auxiliary hypotheses with another constitutes an **intra-program problemshift**—it is "intra" or within the program because only the protective belt, not the hard core, is changed. Intra-program problemshifts should be undertaken in accordance with the program's **positive heuristic**, a set of suggestions or hints that guide the development of specific theories within the program. (For example, the positive heuristic of the neorealist research program would include the suggestion that scholars make predictions about international political outcomes, e.g., that balances tend to form in the international system, or that multipolar systems will be more war-prone than bipolar systems.)

Despite the negative heuristic, scholars sometimes develop new theories which interfere with the hard core, thus creating a new research program through an **inter-program problemshift**. Both inter-program and intra-program problemshifts face the same problem identified by Popper and Lakatos: how can we tell if these theoretical emendations are just defensive moves designed to cover up discrepant evidence, rather than true progress?

Lakatos argued that to be judged **progressive** new theories must predict **novel facts**. If not, the new theories are merely **ad hoc**, and the research program is **degenerative**. As we detail in Chapter 2, philosophers of science disagree about exactly what this novelty criterion requires: "new" compared to what? One definition—which we prefer—is **heuristic novelty**: the new theory must predict something beyond the anomalous facts used in its construction. (For example, Stephen Walt developed balance of threat theory in part to solve a puzzle for Kenneth Waltz's balance of power theory: western European countries chose to ally with the United States, rather than the Soviet Union, the weaker of the two superpowers. Because balance of threat theory was designed to accommodate this anomaly, solving it cannot count in favor of the new theory. However, Walt's subsequent application of balance of threat theory to explain the connection between domestic revolution and war does count, because that hypothesized relationship was not used to construct the original theory.)

Lakatos's approach is often contrasted with that of **Thomas Kuhn**, whose theory of scientific development sees scientific change as being revolutionary and non-rational, consisting of the wholesale replacement of one dominant view of how the world works (a **paradigm**) by a different one. In contrast to Kuhn, Lakatos rejected the view that a single research program controls a scientific discipline at any given time, or that the decision to reject an old research program and accept a new one was akin to a non-rational "conversion" involving a leap of faith or a "gestalt switch." He argued instead that research programs should be judged on the basis of rational criteria: their ability to successfully generate predictions of novel facts that are subsequently corroborated with empirical evidence.

Chapter 2

Lessons from Lakatos

Colin Elman and
Miriam Fendius Elman

This book explores how to assess theories, and how to decide whether, over time, theories about international relations (IR) are getting any better. We use Imre Lakatos's methodology of scientific research programs (MSRP) as our starting point. Since most applications of the methodology in IR have been based on incomplete or inaccurate accounts, we begin this chapter by laying out a received version of the metatheory. We then debunk several prevalent misconceptions about the methodology, before discussing some of the real problems with applying Lakatos's framework to evaluate progress in IR theory. We conclude the chapter with a call for more discussion on the comparative strengths of various rationalist metrics for appraising theoretical developments, and for more case studies that employ them, in order to judge theoretical developments more rigorously.

Imre Lakatos's Methodology of Scientific Research Programs

In his seminal 1970 essay, "Falsification and the Methodology of Scientific Research Programmes," Lakatos joined the debate between Karl Popper and Thomas Kuhn on how science develops, and how that trajectory should be appraised.[1] Popper argued that "the

---

1. Imre Lakatos, "Falsification and the Methodology of Scientific Research Programmes," in Imre Lakatos and Alan Musgrave, eds., *Criticism and the Growth of Knowledge* (New York: Cambridge University Press, 1970), pp. 91–196. For brief biographical details on Lakatos, see John Worrall, "Imre Lakatos, 1922–1974: Philosopher of Mathematics and Philosopher of Science," in R.S. Cohen, P.K. Feyerabend, and M.W. Wartofsky, eds., *Essays in Memory of Imre Lakatos* (Dordrecht: D. Reidel, 1976), pp. 1–8; Roger E. Backhouse, "Imre Lakatos," in John B. Davis, D. Wade Hands, and Uskali Maki, eds., *The*

development of 'science' is marked by 'progress', whereas 'non-science' evolves without becoming 'better' in any sense of the term."[2] Popper's view was that in order for science to improve, scholars need to frame propositions in ways that allow them to be confronted and falsified with empirical observations.[3] Falsification, however, is not enough to distinguish science from non-science. Popper recognized that scientists could make trivial changes to their propositions so as to avoid contradiction by known empirical evidence, but this did not mean that there had been "progress." Accordingly, he bolstered the criterion of falsification with "methodological rules that forbid what he first called 'ad-hoc auxiliary assumptions,' later 'conventionalist stratagems,' and finally 'immunizing stratagems'."[4]

Handbook of Economic Methodology (Northampton, Mass.: Edward Elgar, 1998), pp. 270–272; Brendan Larvor, *Lakatos: An Introduction* (New York: Routledge, 1998), pp. 1–7; and Jancis Long, "Lakatos in Hungary," *Philosophy of the Social Sciences*, Vol. 28, No. 2 (June 1998), pp. 244–311.

2. Mark Blaug, "Why I am Not a Constructivist: Confessions of an Unrepentant Popperian," in Roger E. Backhouse, ed., *New Directions in Economic Methodology* (New York: Routledge, 1994), pp. 109–110. See also Larvor, *Lakatos: An Introduction*, p. 47.

3. Karl R. Popper, *Conjectures and Refutations: The Growth of Scientific Knowledge*, 5th ed. (London: Routledge, 1989), pp. 36–37, 46. See also Imre Lakatos, "The Role of Crucial Experiments in Science," *Studies in History and Philosophy of Science*, Vol. 4, No. 4 (1974), 310–312; Frederick Suppe, "The Search for Philosophic Understanding of Scientific Theories," in Frederick Suppe, ed., *The Structure of Scientific Theories*, 2d ed. (Chicago: University of Illinois Press, 1977), p. 167; Paul Diesing, *How Does Social Science Work? Reflections on Practice* (Pittsburgh: University of Pittsburgh Press, 1991), pp. 31–32; Mark Blaug, *The Methodology of Economics: Or How Economists Explain* (Cambridge, UK: Cambridge University Press, 1992), p. 14; Arthur Donovan, Larry Laudan, and Rachel Laudan, *Scrutinizing Science: Empirical Studies of Scientific Change*, 2d ed. (Baltimore: The Johns Hopkins University Press, 1992), pp. 4–5; and Jarrett Leplin, *A Novel Defense of Scientific Realism* (New York: Oxford University Press, 1997), p. 38.

4. Blaug, *The Methodology of Economics*, p. 19. See also Bruce J. Caldwell, "The Methodology of Scientific Research Programmes in Economics: Criticisms and Conjectures," in G.K. Shaw, ed., *Economics, Culture and Education: Essays in Honor of Mark Blaug* (Brookfield, Vt.: Edward Elgar, 1991), p. 96.

Thomas Kuhn's 1962 book, *The Structure of Scientific Revolutions*, provided a radically different view of science and scientific progress.[5] He argued that scientific advance does not, as Popper claimed, consist of the gradual accumulation of ever truer theories that, at any given time, have yet to be falsified by failing to pass critical tests. Kuhn suggested that mature sciences were characterized by dominant paradigms, which determined both the trajectory of puzzle-solving "normal science" and provided paradigm-specific criteria for deciding whether such activity is successful or not. In contrast to normal science, said Kuhn, "revolutionary science" occurs when scientific communities switch between paradigms. This is typically triggered when the dominant paradigm becomes mired in increasingly damaging empirical anomalies.[6] Kuhn argued that, because paradigms are based on competing world views, and are consequently incommensurable, the decision to discard one paradigm for another cannot be based on "external" objective criteria. Rather, he wrote, the choice "between competing paradigms proves to be a choice between incompatible modes of community life." For Kuhn, "there is no standard higher than the assent of the relevant [scientific] community."[7]

Popper took an intense, and at least partly political, dislike to Kuhn's view of science.[8] Popper believed that a virtuous society tolerated dissent,[9] and that because a scientific community was characterized by vigorous mutual criticism, it was the finest example of such an open society. This was completely antithetical to Kuhn's

---

5. Thomas Kuhn, *The Structure of Scientific Revolutions* (Chicago: University of Chicago Press, 1962).

6. Suppe, "The Search for Philosophic Understanding of Scientific Theories," pp. 143–144; and Roger E. Backhouse, "Paradigm/Normal Science," in Davis, Hands and Maki, *The Handbook of Economic Methodology*, pp. 352–354, at 352.

7. Kuhn, *The Structure of Scientific Revolutions*, p. 94. See also Suppe, "The Search for Philosophic Understanding of Scientific Theories," pp. 149–150.

8. Karl Popper, "Normal Science and its Dangers," in Lakatos and Musgrave, *Criticism and the Growth of Knowledge*, pp. 51–58, at 52–53. See also Deborah G. Mayo, *Error and the Growth of Experimental Knowledge* (Chicago: The University of Chicago Press, 1996), p. 22.

9. Diesing, *How Does Social Science Work?* p. 34.

suggestion that science was, in effect, nothing more nor less than what the powers-that-be said it was.[10]

Lakatos had similar concerns, and sought to "develop a theory of scientific method which was sufficiently subtle to cope with the detail of the actual history of science and yet sufficiently rationalistic to resist the political dangers presented by Kuhn."[11] Lakatos's solution borrowed elements from both Popper and Kuhn, but both in this juxtaposition, and in its layering of additional features, it provided a different approach to describing and appraising scientific theories.[12]

Although Lakatos's 1970 essay is often considered his definitive statement, it left plenty of room—to put it politely—for his supporters and critics to debate and refine the contents of the methodology. As Mark Blaug notes:

[Lakatos] is not an easy author to pin down to a precise interpretation. His tendency to make vital points in footnotes, to proliferate labels for different intellectual positions, to coin new phrases and expressions, and to refer back and forth to his own writings—as if it were impossible to understand any part of them without understanding the whole—stands in the way of ready comprehension.[13]

---

10. Suppe, "The Search for Philosophic Understanding of Scientific Theories," p. 170; and Larvor, *Lakatos: An Introduction*, p. 45.

11. Larvor, *Lakatos: An Introduction*, pp. 45–46.

12. Interestingly, the resemblance was such that Kuhn would later claim that Lakatos had merely relabeled his approach. See Thomas S. Kuhn, "Reflections on my Critics," in Lakatos and Musgrave, *Criticism and the Growth of Knowledge*, p. 256; Thomas Kuhn, "Notes on Lakatos," in Roger C. Buck and Robert S. Cohen, *Boston Studies in the Philosophy of Science, PSA 1970*, Vol. 8 (Dordrecht: D. Reidel, 1971), pp. 137–146; and Diesing, *How Does Social Science Work?* p. 61. Other scholars who discuss the similarities and differences between Lakatos's approach and Popper's include Mark Blaug, "Methodology of Scientific Research Programs," in Davis, Hands and Maki, *The Handbook of Economic Methodology*, pp. 304–307; and Elie Zahar, "The Popper-Lakatos Controversy," *Fundamenta Scientiae*, Vol. 3, No. 1 (1982), pp. 21–54.

13. Blaug, *The Methodology of Economics*, p. 32, note 24. This lack of clarity has not gone unnoticed by political scientists. Stephen Van Evera, for example, notes that "Lakatos's arguments are well-hidden in tortured prose that gives

Lakatosians and their critics have advanced, restated, and argued at length about the contents of the methodology.[14] Accordingly, its employment requires that scholars first make several predicate choices among the various interpretations of its components. Once these selections have been made, the resulting version of Lakatos's methodology may reflect, but certainly will not exhaust, mainstream Lakatosian understandings. In the remainder of this section we first provide such a customary account, before proceeding to discuss an important area of disagreement.

WHEN DO NEW THEORIES IMPROVE SCIENTIFIC UNDERSTANDING?

Rather than observing and judging science as a sequence of individual theories, Lakatos instead argues that disciplines are best conceptualized as a series of scientific research programs (SRPs). SRPs have four elements: a hard core; a negative heuristic; a positive heuristic; and a protective belt of auxiliary hypotheses (see "A Brief Guide to Imre Lakatos's Methodology of Scientific Research Programs" in Chapter 1 on pp. 19–20). The program's hard core assumptions consist of unchanging content.[15] They are protected by a "negative

---

new meaning to the phrase 'badly written,' and no reading of such abominable writing is ever certain or final." Stephen Van Evera, *Guide to Methods for Students of Political Science* (Ithaca, N.Y.: Cornell University Press, 1997), p. 44, note 55.

14. See, for example, John Worrall, "The Ways in Which the Methodology of Scientific Research Programmes Improves on Popper's Methodology," in Gerard Radnitzky and Gunnar Andersson, eds., *Progress and Rationality in Science* (Dordrecht: D. Reidel, 1978), pp. 45–70; Douglas W. Hands, "Second Thoughts on Lakatos," *History of Political Economy*, Vol. 17, No. 1 (1985), pp. 1–16; and Leplin, *A Novel Defense of Scientific Realism*.

15. Although the elements of a program's hard core may not change, it is generally agreed that they can become better specified over time. See Alan Musgrave, "Method or Madness? Can the Methodology of Research Programmes be Rescued from Epistemological Anarchism?" in Cohen, Feyerabend, and Wartofsky, *Essays in Memory of Imre Lakatos*, pp. 458–467; Henry Frankel, "The Career of Continental Drift Theory: An Application of Imre Lakatos's Analysis of Scientific Growth to the Rise of Drift Theory,"

heuristic," a set of propositions that say that this content cannot be directly challenged or tested. For example, one of the least controversial elements of the hard core of the neorealist SRP is that states are the dominant actors in international relations. It follows that the negative heuristic of the neorealist research program includes a restriction against developing theories that give a decisive causal role to non-state actors such as Greenpeace or the United Nations (if a scientist does so, she is no longer operating within the neorealist scientific research program).

Scientific research programs also have a "protective belt" of auxiliary hypotheses that "bear the brunt of tests and get adjusted and re-adjusted, or even completely replaced, to defend ... the core."[16] As Spiro J. Latsis notes, the "protective belt may consist of various types of propositions [ranging] from specific auxiliary hypotheses, accounting for predictive failure, to redefinitions of the conceptual apparatus."[17] In the neorealist SRP, for example, it is common practice to distinguish between scholars who assert that states are power-maximizing revisionists, and those who contend that states defend the status quo and minimize relative power losses.[18] It is the particular costs and

Studies in History and Philosophy of Science, Vol. 10, No. 1 (1979), pp. 26–28; and Neil de Marchi, "Introduction: Rethinking Lakatos," in Neil de Marchi and Mark Blaug, eds., *Appraising Economic Theories: Studies in the Methodology of Research Programs* (Brookfield, Vt.: Edward Elgar, 1991), p. 12. For the critique that hard cores do not exist in science, see William Berkson, "Lakatos One and Lakatos Two: An Appreciation," in Cohen, Feyerabend and Wartofsky, *Essays in Memory of Imre Lakatos*, p. 52. For the opposite critique that the elements of scientific research programs, including hard cores, are so pervasive in all intellectual endeavors that Lakatos's methodology fails to distinguish science from non-science, see Caldwell, "The Methodology of Scientific Research Programmes in Economics," p. 99.

16. Lakatos, "Falsification and the Methodology of Scientific Research Programmes," p. 133.

17. Spiro J. Latsis, "A Research Programme in Economics," in Spiro J. Latsis, ed., *Method and Appraisal in Economics* (New York: Cambridge University Press, 1976), p. 23.

18. John J. Mearsheimer, 1994/95. "The False Promise of International Institutions," *International Security*, Vol. 19, No. 3 (Winter 1994/95), pp. 5–59, at

benefits suggested by these and other elements of the protective belt, in combination with the unchanging hard core, that lead different realists to predict different state behaviors and international political outcomes.[19]

The SRP's protective belt is developed in accordance with the program's positive heuristic, "a partially articulated set of suggestions or hints"[20] that "guides the production of specific theories within the programme."[21] The positive heuristic of the program contains:

a set of ideas about how to "fill in," make more precise, draw consequences from [statements about the world], and also how to elaborate on them, introduce new assumptions so that they apply to new fields, and how to modify them when difficulties arise.[22]

The neorealist scientific research program's positive heuristic would include the suggestion that scholars develop theories that make

11–12, note 27; Benjamin Frankel, "Restating the Realist Case: An Introduction," *Security Studies*, Vol. 5, No. 3 (Spring 1996), pp. ix–xx, xv–xviii; Joao Resende-Santos, "Anarchy and the Emulation of Military Systems: Military Organization and Technology in South America, 1870–1930," *Security Studies*, Vol. 5, No. 3 (Spring 1996), pp. 193–260, note 34; and Eric J. Labs, "Beyond Victory: Offensive Realism and the Expansion of War Aims," *Security Studies*, Vol. 6, No. 4 (Summer 1997), pp. 1–48.

19. Colin Elman, "Appraising Neorealism as a Scientific Research Program," unpublished manuscript, Arizona State University, 1997.

20. Lakatos, "Falsification and the Methodology of Scientific Research Programmes," p. 135.

21. Worrall, "The Ways in Which the Methodology of Scientific Research Programmes Improves on Popper's Methodology," p. 59.

22. Ibid. See also Latsis, "A Research Programme in Economics," p. 16; and John Worrall, "Research Programmes, Empirical Support and the Duhem Problem: Replies to Criticism," in Radnitzky and Andersson, *Progress and Rationality in Science*, pp. 321–322, 328–329. For a list of the elements one might find in a positive heuristic, see Worrall, "The Ways in Which the Methodology of Scientific Research Programmes Improves on Popper's Methodology," p. 69. For examples of positive heuristics in research programs from economics, see A.W. Coats, "Economics and Psychology: The Death and Resurrection of a Research Program." in Latsis, *Method and Appraisal in Economics*, p. 54; and Latsis, "A Research Programme in Economics," pp. 22–23.

predictions about international political outcomes (for example, that balances tend to form in the international system, or that multipolar systems will be more war-prone than bipolar systems). Scholars are also enjoined to value theoretical leverage, and to use as few variables as possible when making their predictions.

The methodology of scientific research programs is not only a means for describing competing research programs. It also provides criteria for comparing and judging whether theoretical innovations or emendations represent progress or not; Lakatos labels these "problem-shifts."[23] An *intra-program* change or problemshift is one that modifies the protective belt of auxiliary hypotheses of a scientific research program. An *inter-program* problemshift is one that, contrary to the negative heuristic, changes elements of the hard core, thus moving from one program to another.

Lakatos provides explicit rules for determining whether such inter-program and intra-program problemshifts provide added value. Both kinds of problemshifts are degenerative when they are merely ad hoc attempts to deal with apparently disconfirming evidence. Essential to understanding when Lakatosians consider a theoretical adjustment to be ad hoc is the concept of "novel facts." In degenerating research programs, new theories merely save the program from disconfirming evidence, and do nothing else. By contrast, progressive research programs are those that offer additional content by predicting, and empirically corroborating, some hitherto unknown, unexpected, or unused fact.

In determining whether a problemshift is progressive or degenerating, Lakatosians commonly refer to three distinct notions of "ad-hocness": *ad hoc*$_1$ refers to a theoretical move that generates no novel predictions as compared with its predecessor; *ad hoc*$_2$ is used when none of the new theory's novel predictions have been actually verified by empirical evidence; and *ad hoc*$_3$ refers to a situation in which

---

23. Vasquez suggests that by problemshift, Lakatos meant "theoryshift" but did not use that word because it "sounds dreadful." See John Vasquez, *The Power of Power Politics: From Classical Realism to Neotraditionalism* (Cambridge, UK: Cambridge University Press, 1998), p. 244, note 1.

auxiliary hypotheses are modified in ways that do not accord with the spirit of the positive heuristic of the program.[24] Intra-program problemshifts are evaluated on all three ad hoc criteria. Inter-program problemshifts only have to avoid being ad hoc[1] and ad hoc[2]. We now discuss the three kinds of ad-hocness in detail.

Arguably the most important element of Lakatos's methodology is the notion that good science requires more than simply salvaging theories when disconfirming evidence is encountered. Problemshifts must be theoretically progressive, and produce predictions of novel facts or consequences, because "explaining things which were already known is 'cheap success' and counts for nothing."[25] Lakatos requires novel predictions because:

it is easy (and riskless) to make a theory 'testable' ... if one already knows how the tests will turn out.... If a theory T is presently accepted and some new evidence *e* crops up which is not predicted by T, then it is generally trivially easy to use T and *e* to generate a new theory T' which does entail *e*.[26]

---

24. Lakatos, "Falsification and the Methodology of Scientific Research Programmes," p. 175, notes 2 and 3, p. 182; Elie Zahar, "Why Did Einstein's Programme Supersede Lorentz's?" *British Journal for the Philosophy of Science*, Vol. 24 (1973), p. 101; Alan Musgrave, "Logical versus Historical Theories of Confirmation," *British Journal for the Philosophy of Science*, Vol. 25 (1974), p. 20; Richard Nunan, "Novel Facts, Bayesian Rationality, and the History of Continental Drift," *Studies in History and Philosophy of Science*, Vol. 15, No. 4 (1984), p. 272; and Siobhain McGovern, "A Lakatosian Approach to Changes in International Trade Theory," *History of Political Economy*, Vol. 26, No. 3 (Fall 1994), pp. 352, 354. These are only three of many different definitions of "ad hocness" found in the novel fact literature. For additional definitions, see Martin Carrier, "On Novel Facts: A Discussion of Criteria for Non-ad-hoc-ness in the Methodology of Scientific Research Programmes," *Zeitschrift fur allgemaine Wissenschaftstheorie*, Vol. 19, No. 2 (1988), p. 216, note 45.

25. Hands, "Second Thoughts on Lakatos," pp. 6–7; see also Leplin, *A Novel Defense of Scientific Realism*, p. 41.

26. Worrall, "The Ways in Which the Methodology of Scientific Research Programmes Improves on Popper's Methodology," p. 49.

This is not to say that amendments directed to solving anomalies are automatically degenerating. According to Lakatos, there is nothing wrong with problemshifts designed to account for discrepant facts, so long as they *also* produce novel predictions.[27] Thus, new theories that merely try to salvage the research program without predicting any new facts are judged to be *ad hoc₁*.

But problemshifts must do more than just *predict* novel facts. Those predictions must be empirically tested, and if they are not corroborated, the problemshift is judged to be *ad hoc₂*.[28] To be sure, applying this criterion in IR requires the attribution of dates to novel

---

27. See Lakatos, "Falsification and the Methodology of Scientific Research Programmes," pp. 116–118, 124–125, 133, 169–170, 176, 187; Terence Ball, "From Paradigms to Research Programs: Toward a Post-Kuhnian Political Science," *American Journal of Political Science*, Vol. 20, No. 1 (February 1976), pp. 165–166; Mark Blaug, "Kuhn versus Lakatos or Paradigms versus Research Programs in the History of Economics," in Latsis, *Method and Appraisal in Economics*, p. 156; Frankel, "The Career of Continental Drift Theory," p. 23; Hands, "Second Thoughts on Lakatos," p. 4; and McGovern, "A Lakatosian Approach to Changes in International Trade Theory," p. 353. Problemshifts that are not motivated by empirical puzzles can also turn out to have no novel consequences, and hence be *ad hoc₁*. In other words, anomaly solving is only one motive that might produce problemshifts that do not satisfy the need for novelty. As Martin Carrier notes, "the novel fact debate ... is concerned with the legitimacy of *any* theoretical modification, regardless of the reason for its being introduced." Carrier, "On Novel Facts," p. 206.

28. There are at least two ways of structuring inquiry on the *ad hoc₂* criterion, championed by Elie Zahar and by Lakatos, respectively. Zahar characterizes a theory as *ad hoc₂* (at time t) if none of its excess content over its rivals has, at time t, been corroborated. Lakatos, on the other hand, characterizes a theory as *ad hoc₂* if all its excess content has been refuted. See Zahar, "Why Did Einstein's Programme Supersede Lorentz's?" p. 101, note 1. To illustrate, suppose a theory T predicts e, and a subsequent problemshift leads to T' with predictions e, e', e'' and e'''. According to Lakatos, we cannot determine whether the problemshift is *ad hoc₂* until e', e'' and e''' have all been tested. If all are falsified, then the problemshift is *ad hoc₂*. By contrast, Zahar says that if we test for any of e', e'' or e''', and *any* of them are corroborated, we can conclude that the problemshift is non-*ad hoc₂*. As Zahar argues, the single-confirmation method is more in keeping with the tolerant spirit of Lakatos's metatheory than is the complete-falsification method.

predictions, and a decision on how long to wait for the empirical corroboration of at least one of the predicted novel facts generated by the problemshift. Dating the creation of a scientific research program and its series of problemshifts is not, however, always a straightforward exercise. For example, if one were to try to date the inception of a realist research program, one could plausibly argue for circa 400 BC (Thucydides), or 1948 (Morgenthau), or for any number of alternatives in between. With respect to the question of how long to allow for novel facts to be empirically corroborated before declaring the problemshift *ad hoc₂*, it is important to remember that Lakatos's methodology gives theoretically progressive problemshifts some time before deciding whether the novel facts anticipated by the amendment are corroborated. Lakatos notes that we should not be too impatient, nor require instant gratification. Scientists should not quickly characterize problemshifts as degenerative simply because their predicted novel facts have not yet been corroborated.[29]

Lastly, Lakatos's methodology also considers a scientific research program to be degenerating, "if it anticipates novel facts but does so in a patched-up development rather than by a coherent, pre-planned positive heuristic."[30] For Lakatos, then, "theoretical adjustment [must] be governed or constrained by a unified set of principles."[31] This *ad hoc₃* criterion is designed to catch:

unimaginative series of pedestrian "empirical" adjustments which ... may ... make some "novel" predictions and may even conjure up some irrelevant grains of truth in them. But this theorizing has no unifying idea,

---

29. Lakatos, "Falsification and the Methodology of Scientific Research Programmes," pp. 116, 133–134, 151, 155. See also Alexander Rosenberg, "Lakatosian Consolations for Economics," *Economics and Philosophy*, Vol. 2 (April 1986), p. 128.

30. Imre Lakatos, "History of Science and its Rational Reconstructions," in Buck and Cohen, *Boston Studies in the Philosophy of Science*, p. 125. See also de Marchi, "Introduction: Rethinking Lakatos," p. 4.

31. David Moon, "Values and Political Theory: A Modest Defense of a Qualified Cognitivism," *Journal of Politics*, Vol. 39, No. 4 (November 1977), pp. 899–900.

no heuristic power, no continuity. They do not add up to a genuine research programme and are, on the whole, worthless.[32]

This requirement places Lakatos's methodology squarely within the so-called generative tradition, which suggests that new theories are motivated by, and derived from, a body of previous results and guiding principles.[33] According to this view, scientific progress is seldom achieved by boldly striking out into unknown territory. Rather, it arises from concentrated attacks on carefully framed questions and theories generated by extant research programs.

In Lakatos's framework, these three criteria of "ad-hocness" determine whether various theoretical adjustments are legitimate. As shown in Figure 2-1, intra-program problemshifts must be judged on all three criteria, while inter-program problemshifts can only be measured by whether they are *ad hoc$_1$* or *ad hoc$_2$*. That is, shifts from one program to another are judged on the extent to which they produce novel facts that are then corroborated.[34] Shifts *within* programs have the added burden that they must also be undertaken in accordance with the program's positive heuristic; if not, they are *ad hoc$_3$*.[35]

---

32. Lakatos, "Falsification and the Methodology of Scientific Research Programmes," p. 175. For a critique, see Carrier, "On Novel Facts," especially pp. 228–229.

33. Thomas Nickles, "Lakatosian Heuristics and Epistemic Support," *British Journal for the Philosophy of Science*, Vol. 38 (1987), p. 182. According to Nickles, the third ad-hocness rule runs counter to the first two: *ad hoc$_3$* discourages novelty by prohibiting radical departures from the program, while *ad hoc$_1$* and *ad hoc$_2$* demand bold guessing and encourage bold deviations from the current view, no matter how established. See ibid., pp. 191–198.

34. Worrall, "The Ways in Which the Methodology of Scientific Research Programmes Improves on Popper's Methodology," p. 56.

35. Lakatos, "Falsification and the Methodology of Scientific Research Programmes," pp. 175–176.

Figure 2-1. Is a Problemshift Ad-Hoc and Therefore Degenerative, or is it Progressive?

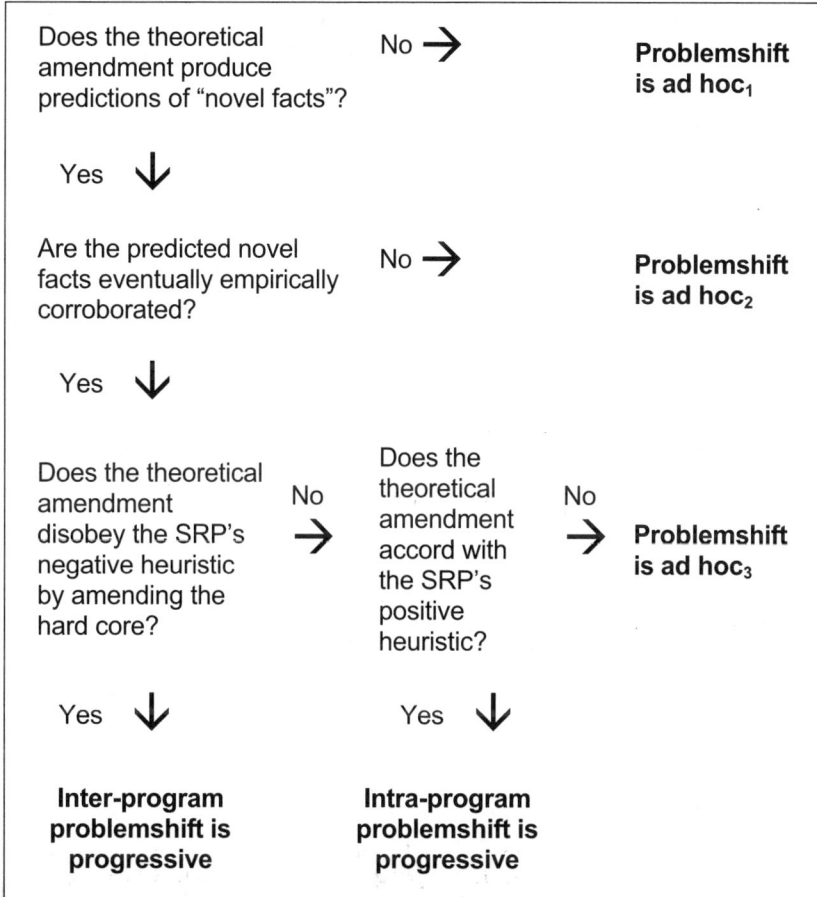

Does the theoretical amendment produce predictions of "novel facts"? No → **Problemshift is ad hoc$_1$**

Yes ↓

Are the predicted novel facts eventually empirically corroborated? No → **Problemshift is ad hoc$_2$**

Yes ↓

Does the theoretical amendment disobey the SRP's negative heuristic by amending the hard core? No → Does the theoretical amendment accord with the SRP's positive heuristic? No → **Problemshift is ad hoc$_3$**

Yes ↓   Yes ↓

Inter-program problemshift is progressive   **Intra-program problemshift is progressive**

IN SEARCH OF NOVELTY: WHAT'S NEW?

Because predicting new phenomena is such an important part of the methodology of scientific research programs, the definition of novelty plays a crucial role. If we change the definition, the outcome of the appraisal is altered; if we confuse or obscure its meaning, the appraisal becomes pointless. While IR theorists are generally aware that predicting novel phenomena is part of the methodology, most are unaware that Lakatosians and others have engaged in an extensive debate as to what constitutes novelty.[36]

The requirement that theories resulting from problemshifts must offer novel predictions follows what philosopher of science Alan Musgrave describes as a "historical approach to confirmation," which "makes the confirmation of a scientific theory somehow dependent upon the historical setting in which that theory was proposed."[37] This suggests that we cannot determine whether evidence supports a theory purely on the basis of the logical relationship between the facts and the theory: we must take "background knowledge" into consideration. Proponents of the various definitions agree that we have to know more about the historical process that uncovered the theory's contents, but they disagree about what facts should be considered indicators of progress.[38] The crucial predicate question for determining whether a theoretical development produces novel predictions is: "novel compared to what?" This section considers four competing categories

---

36. For more on the controversy regarding the definition of novelty, see Michael R. Gardner, "Predicting Novel Facts," *British Journal for the Philosophy of Science*, Vol. 33 (1982), p. 2; Carrier, "On Novel Facts," p. 206; and Nancey Murphy, "Another Look at Novel Facts," *Studies in History and Philosophy of Science*, Vol. 20, No. 3 (1989), p. 385. The debate over the prediction of novel facts as a criterion of theoretical progress predates, and has an importance that extends well beyond, Lakatos's metatheory. For a brief survey, see Roger E. Backhouse, "Novel Facts," in Davis, Hands and Maki, *The Handbook of Economic Methodology*, pp. 339–342.

37. Musgrave, "Logical versus Historical Theories of Confirmation," pp. 3, 7. By contrast, the "purely logical view of confirmation" suggests that, "in deciding whether hypothesis *h* is confirmed by evidence *e*, and how well it is confirmed, we must consider only the statements *h* and *e*, and the logical relations between them. It is quite irrelevant whether *e* was known first and *h* proposed to explain it, or whether *e* resulted from testing predictions drawn from *h*." Musgrave, "Logical versus Historical Theories of Confirmation," p. 2. See also Worrall, "Research Programmes, Empirical Support and the Duhem Problem," pp. 321–338; and Mayo, *Error and the Growth of Experimental Knowledge*, pp. 254–256.

38. Musgrave, "Logical versus Historical Theories of Confirmation," p. 7; and Leplin, *A Novel Defense of Scientific Realism*, p. 43.

of definitions of "novel facts": temporal novelty (Lakatos$_1$), new interpretation novelty (Lakatos$_2$), heuristic novelty (Zahar/Lakatos$_3$), and background theory novelty (Musgrave).

The most straightforward and restrictive way of construing "background knowledge" is: everything known to science at the time a theory was proposed. That is, to be "Lakatos$_1$ novel" a fact must be "improbable or even impossible in the light of previous knowledge."[39] Lakatos subsequently discarded this strict temporal definition as setting a prohibitively difficult standard, and accepted Elie Zahar's criticism that there were some "known" facts that should nevertheless count in support of a problemshift being progressive.[40]

Lakatos also offered a much weaker alternative, arguing that a new theory might explain an "old" fact in a new way, thus converting it into a novel fact.[41] By this measure, "Lakatos$_2$" or "new interpretation novelty," even previously known facts might be considered novel. This definition has been roundly and rightly criticized for being unacceptably permissive. For example, Musgrave suggests that:

---

39. Lakatos, "Falsification and the Methodology of Scientific Research Programmes," p. 118. See also Zahar, "Why Did Einstein's Programme Supersede Lorentz's?" p. 101; Worrall, "The Ways in Which the Methodology of Scientific Research Programmes Improves on Popper's Methodology," pp. 46, and 66, note 7; Frankel, "The Career of Continental Drift Theory," p. 24; Gardner, "Predicting Novel Facts," p. 2; Nunan, "Novel Facts, Bayesian Rationality, and the History of Continental Drift," p. 275; and D. Wade Hands, "Reply to Hamminga and Maki," in de Marchi and Blaug, *Appraising Economic Theories*, p. 96.

40. See Imre Lakatos and Elie Zahar, "Why Did Copernicus' Research Programme Supersede Ptolemy's?" in Robert S. Westman, ed., *The Copernican Achievement* (Berkeley: University of California Press, 1975), p. 376, note 65; and Zahar, "Why Did Einstein's Programme Supersede Lorentz's?" p. 101. See also Worrall, "The Ways in Which the Methodology of Scientific Research Programmes Improves on Popper's Methodology," p. 47; Musgrave, "Logical versus Historical Theories of Confirmation," p. 11; Gardner, "Predicting Novel Facts," p. 2; and Carrier, "On Novel Facts," p. 207.

41. Lakatos, "Falsification and the Methodology of Scientific Research Programmes," p. 118. See also Carrier, "On Novel Facts," p. 206; Nunan, "Novel Facts, Bayesian Rationality, and the History of Continental Drift," p. 275; Musgrave, "Logical versus Historical Theories of Confirmation," p. 11.

Lakatos's watering-down of the notion of a novel fact actually obliterates it altogether. Any deduction of an old fact from a new theory can be said to involve a "reinterpretation" of that fact. And now any ad hoc theory can claim evidential support from the old, but "newly interpreted," facts which it explains.[42]

Since the Lakatos$_2$ definition of novelty would rate almost all problemshifts progressive, it cannot be the basis for a meaningful evaluation.

Zahar suggests a third way to construe "background knowledge," subsequently accepted by Lakatos (hence we label it Zahar/Lakatos$_3$): whether the fact being offered to buttress a theory played some role in that theory's construction.[43] If so, the fact cannot be considered novel, and it thus provides no support for the theory in question.[44] Zahar/Lakatos$_3$ heuristic novelty was endorsed and developed by philosopher of science John Worrall, who argues that Lakatos's methodology of scientific research programs:

---

42. Musgrave, "Logical versus Historical Theories of Confirmation," pp. 11–12. See also Zahar, "Why Did Einstein's Programme Supersede Lorentz's?" p. 102; Noretta Koertge, "Inter-Theoretic Criticism and the Growth of Science," in Buck and Cohen, *Boston Studies in the Philosophy of Science*, p. 171, note 5; Nunan, "Novel Facts, Bayesian Rationality, and the History of Continental Drift," p. 275, note 10; and Carrier, "On Novel Facts," p. 207, note 6.

43. Lakatos and Zahar, "Why Did Copernicus' Research Programme Supersede Ptolemy's?" pp. 375–376. As Zahar and several others have noted, Lakatos$_1$ strict temporal novelty is a subset of Zahar/Lakatos$_3$ heuristic novelty. If a fact is unknown, it cannot have been used in the heuristic process that produced the theory being tested. That is, temporal novelty is a sufficient but not necessary condition for heuristic novelty. See Zahar, "Why Did Einstein's Programme Supersede Lorentz's?" p. 103; Worrall, "The Ways in Which the Methodology of Scientific Research Programmes Improves on Popper's Methodology," pp. 49–50; Hands, "Second Thoughts on Lakatos," p. 7; and Carrier, "On Novel Facts," p. 207.

44. Zahar, "Why Did Einstein's Programme Supersede Lorentz's?" p. 103. See also Musgrave, "Logical versus Historical Theories of Confirmation," pp. 12–13.

embodies the simple rule that one can't use the same fact twice: once in the construction of a theory and then again in its support. But any fact which the theory explains but which it was not in this way pre-arranged to explain supports the theory *whether or not the fact was known prior to the theory's proposal.*[45]

The Zahar/Lakatos$_3$ heuristic novelty approach has been criticized on several grounds. One problem is the extent to which the determination of novelty depends on private, inaccessible biographical knowledge about the scientist or researcher. According to this definition of novel fact, we need to know what facts a scholar had in mind when formulating her initial proposition. Consequently, the contents of a scientist's correspondence and diaries constitute part of the evidential support of her theory, but these are often not available.[46] A second problem is the extent to which the heuristic definition of novelty (Zahar/Lakatos$_3$) makes evidential support of a theory a "person-relative" affair. It risks relativizing novelty to the theorist and thus of introducing a psychological and non-epistemic dimension.[47] For example, we can imagine a situation where two scientists simultaneously devise a theory T. One of them is very well-read and is thus aware that there are two facts that constitute anomalies she would like to resolve, and to which she referred in formulating T: e and e'. By contrast, the second scientist is less well-read, and was unaware of the fact that e' was an anomaly; it thus played no heuristic role in his formulation of theory T. According to the Zahar/Lakatos$_3$ novelty definition, the ignorant second scientist's problemshift is considered progressive, whereas the identical problemshift by the well-read first

45. Worrall, "The Ways in Which the Methodology of Scientific Research Programmes Improves on Popper's Methodology," pp. 48–49 (emphasis in original).

46. Musgrave, "Logical versus Historical Theories of Confirmation," p. 13; see also Carrier, "On Novel Facts," p. 208; Leplin, *A Novel Defense of Scientific Realism,* p. 51; and James Ladyman, "Review of *A Novel Defense of Scientific Realism,*" *British Journal for the Philosophy of Science,* Vol. 50 (1999), p. 183.

47. For an extended discussion, see Leplin, *A Novel Defense of Scientific Realism,* pp. 49–55.

scientist is not.[48] Despite these criticisms, however, the requirement against "double-counting" data—using evidence in both a theory's construction and in its support—has "widespread endorsement" among contemporary philosophers.[49]

Unsatisfied with the temporal, new interpretation, or heuristic definitions of novelty, Musgrave offers a fourth approach, called background theory novelty. He argues that:

in assessing the evidential support of a new theory we should compare it, not with "background knowledge" in general, but with the old theory which it challenges.... According to this view, a new theory is independently testable (or predicts a "novel fact") if it predicts something which is not also predicted by its background theory.[50]

Accordingly, Musgrave suggests that there are two kinds of novel predictions: those that conflict with the predictions of background theories, and those that relate to phenomena about which background theories say nothing. Hence, Musgrave's notion of novelty refers "to facts which could not have been expected from the best rival theory available."[51]

Although Musgrave maintains that this is what Lakatos meant by "novel facts,"[52] we argue that his approach is incompatible with Lakatos's methodology. The central problem that the methodology is designed to address is that:

---

48. Musgrave, "Logical versus Historical Theories of Confirmation," p. 13.

49. Mayo, *Error and the Growth of Experimental Knowledge*, pp. 263–271.

50. Musgrave, "Logical versus Historical Theories of Confirmation," pp. 15–16; see also Alan Musgrave, "Evidential Support, Falsification, Heuristics, and Anarchism," in Radnitzky and Andersson, *Progress and Rationality in Science*, p. 185.

51. Carrier, "On Novel Facts," p. 213. See also Mayo, *Error and the Growth of Experimental Knowledge*, p. 208.

52. Musgrave, "Logical versus Historical Theories of Confirmation," p. 15. Hands observes that Musgrave makes his case by mistakenly citing an earlier work by Lakatos on a different subject, "Lakatos (1968), not Lakatos (1970)";

it is generally possible to modify a theory in a trivial "ad hoc" way so as to entail a correct description of any fact successfully predicted by a rival theory. If, originally, T_1 entails e, but T_2 does not, then it is always possible to produce a T'_2 sufficiently similar to T_2 to be "essentially the same" theory, which does entail e.[53]

The methodology seeks to distinguish between degenerating scientific research programs, which engage in such trivial content-decreasing amendments, and progressive programs, which do not. But Musgrave's definition of novelty renders the distinction between progressive and degenerating meaningless. According to his "background theory" novelty, all anomaly-solving amendments are automatically progressive. If a scholar can come up with a theory that predicts a fact that would have been discrepant evidence for an old theory, then by Musgrave's definition, such a fact is a novel fact, and thus the problemshift is progressive. This is at odds with what Lakatos's methodology was designed to do. Musgrave's background theory novelty is too permissive, allowing virtually any theoretical move to be deemed progressive. Accordingly, although it is not without problems, we submit that the best alternative of the four is Zahar/Lakatos$_3$ or heuristic novelty.[54]

Hands, "Reply to Hamminga and Maki," p. 98. Accordingly, we do not call this definition "Lakatos$_4$."

53. Worrall, "Research Programmes, Empirical Support and the Duhem Problem," pp. 321–322.

54. For a similar view, see D. Wade Hands, "Second Thoughts on 'Second Thoughts': Reconsidering the Lakatosian Progress of *The General Theory*," *Review of Political Economy*, Vol. 2, No. 1 (1990), pp. 70–71. Backhouse implies that the different definitions of novel fact can be used in combination. Roger E. Backhouse, *Explorations in Economic Methodology: From Lakatos to Empirical Philosophy of Science* (New York: Routledge, 1998), pp. 24–25. Our view is that, with the exception of temporal novelty's subsumption by heuristic novelty (see note 43), the definitions are mutually exclusive.

Misconceptions about Lakatos's Methodology

Our strategy of taking the methodology of scientific research programs as the starting point for determining whether international relations scholars' endeavors have been worthwhile runs counter to several widely held views on why Lakatos deserves little or no attention. These arguments—which we find unconvincing—are that IR theorists should leave metatheory to the philosophers; that Lakatos's methodology is outdated and has been superseded; that it does not work for a social science; that employing the methodology of scientific research programs will ignite unproductive "paradigm wars"; and finally and perhaps most importantly, that IR theorists already use Lakatos correctly. We address each of these in turn.

IR THEORISTS SHOULD LEAVE METATHEORY TO THE PHILOSOPHERS

International relations scholars who believe that political science and philosophy of science should go their separate ways often labor under two mistaken, and diametrically opposed, assumptions: that we are trying too hard to be scientists, and that using metatheory is inconsistent with science. The first reproach is that efforts to engage philosophy of science are motivated by "physics envy," a wish to have the subfield's work favorably compared to more "serious" endeavors in the natural or physical sciences. But this critique misstates the nature of the argument, inherent in the application of philosophy of science to political science, that all sciences share similar elements. The assertion of commonality is not the product of envy, but a principled argument for the methodological monist position that, while different sciences have different methods of inquiry, they share the same context of justification.[55] Indeed, most mainstream IR theorists *do* argue that, as social scientists, their work should be described and judged using the rules common to all science.[56] Moreover, taken to its logical extreme,

---

55. Blaug, *The Methodology of Economics*, p. 43.

56. Psychologists Barry Gholson and Peter Barker argue along similar lines in defending applications of Kuhn, Lakatos, and Laudan to various

one could use the "physics envy" argument to forbid political scientists from using any of the procedures employed in the hard sciences, including many of the commonplace practices of our profession such as operationalizing and measuring variables. This is hardly a compelling basis for asserting that the subfield should not be characterized or appraised in metatheoretic terms.

The second critique asserts, to the contrary, that arguing in metatheoretic terms undermines our status as scientists. This line of reasoning seems to be based on an assumption that no self-respecting scientist would be caught dead engaging in philosophical debates. In fact, scholars in all fields—from the humanities and social sciences to the medical, natural, and technical sciences—have seen it as an essential task to reflect upon their priorities and assumptions about how to evaluate scientific knowledge: how one distinguishes the good from the less good, and what comprises a significant theoretical break-through. It is also commonplace for scholars in all of these disciplines to debate metatheory, and particularly to ask whether their discipline displays consistent and enduring theoretical aggregates, and whether changes in them have tended to be incremental and continuous, or revolutionary and disjunctive.[57]

LAKATOS IS PASSÉ
Some argue that the methodology of scientific research programs has been overtaken by subsequent philosophizing, much of which concludes that neither temporal nor heuristic novelty offers useful measures of progress.[58] To be sure, Lakatos has become less popular. At the 1989 Capri conference on research programs in economics, for

---

developments in the history of psychology: "any successful defense of the claim that psychology is a science must show features of psychology that are shared by some other science or sciences." See Barry Gholson and Peter Barker, "Kuhn, Lakatos, and Laudan: Applications in the History of Physics and Psychology," *American Psychologist*, Vol. 40, No. 7 (1985), p. 766.

57. See, for example, T. Hagerstrand, ed., *The Identification of Progress in Learning* (Cambridge, UK: Cambridge University Press, 1985).

58. Stephen M. Walt, "The Progressive Power of Realism," *American Political Science Review*, Vol. 91, No. 4 (December 1997), pp. 931–935.

example, supporters of his methodology were a beleaguered minority: "Of the 37 participants ... only 12 were willing to give Lakatos a further run for his money and of the 17 papers delivered at the conference not more than five were unambiguously positive about the value of Lakatos's methodology of scientific research programs."[59]

While Lakatos's methodology is no longer as favored as it once was, his ideas remain of interest to, and are still engaged by, philosophers of science and methodologists. For example, citing Lakatos, philosopher of science Jarrett Leplin argues that theories should be justified "on the basis of their successful novel predictions."[60] Invoking both heuristic and background theory novelty, Leplin suggests that a successful theory is one that anticipates "experiences of a kind not involved in its development or original application," and that predicts facts that are not accounted for by competing explanations. He shows that the historical records of several theories in physics and astronomy reflect a concern with predictive novelty.[61]

Similarly, philosopher of science Deborah G. Mayo engages at considerable length the "proposed notions of novelty" offered by the "Lakatos-Popper school."[62] She notes that "the question of what counts as novel evidence for a hypothesis" can be restated in terms of the more "general question of what counts as a severe test."[63] Mayo agrees

---

59. Mark Blaug, "Afterword," in de Marchi and Blaug, *Appraising Economic Theories*, p. 500. See also de Marchi, "Introduction: Rethinking Lakatos," pp. 18–19; and Backhouse, *Explorations in Economic Methodology*, pp. 2–4.

60. Leplin, *A Novel Defense of Scientific Realism*, pp. 78, 98–100. See also Ladyman, "Review of *A Novel Defense of Scientific Realism*," p. 183.

61. Leplin, *A Novel Defense of Scientific Realism*, pp. 33, 49, 64, 77, 83–97, 184–185. For additional discussions, see Nickles, "Lakatosian Heuristics and Epistemic Support," pp. 198–204; and Donovan, Laudan, and Laudan, *Scrutinizing Science*, pp. 31, 35–37.

62. Mayo, *Error and the Growth of Experimental Knowledge*, p. 256; see also pp. 251–293.

63. Mayo, *Error and the Growth of Experimental Knowledge*, p. 208. "Severe testing" is central to Mayo's methodology. On the importance of "severe tests," Karl Popper wrote, "The theoretician will ... try his best to detect any false theory among the set of non-refuted competitors; he will try to 'catch' it.

that Lakatosian proponents have an "important kernel of rightness ... [in that] aspects of the hypotheses and data generation procedures need to be taken into account in assessing the goodness of tests. They may be relevant to the error probabilities and so to the severity of the overall experimental tests."[64] In particular, while Mayo insists that not all novel tests are severe tests (or vice versa), she argues that violating the "Zahar-Worrall [criterion] of heuristic novelty" should be avoided if it is likely to diminish the reliability or severity of hypothesis testing.[65]

Scholars in the social sciences also find Lakatos's novelty criteria important indicators of progress. For example, economist Roger E. Backhouse acknowledges that, although there are "problems" with applying Lakatos's methodology to economics, "it nonetheless provides a useful framework for thinking about certain methodological issues."[66] Likewise, Mark Blaug "remains convinced that Lakatos is still capable of inspiring fruitful work in methodology."[67] Sociologists and psychologists have also argued that their theories can be considered scientific because their development and acceptance or rejection follow Lakatos's description of scientific change.[68]

These examples notwithstanding, however, there is no doubt that philosophy of science has moved a considerable distance in the last twenty-five years, and during that time the methodology of scientific

---

That is, he will, with respect to any given non-refuted theory, try to think of cases or situations in which it is likely to fail, if it is false. Thus he will try to construct *severe* tests, and *crucial* test situations." Karl R. Popper, *Objective Knowledge* (Oxford: Clarendon Press, 1972), p. 14. See also Chapter 14 by Andrew Bennett, p. 471.

64. Mayo, *Error and the Growth of Experimental Knowledge*, p. 253.

65. Mayo, *Error and the Growth of Experimental Knowledge*, pp. 253, 259, 275, 278, 292.

66. Backhouse, *Explorations in Economic Methodology*, p. 4.

67. Blaug, "Afterword," pp. 510–511.

68. Gholson and Barker, "Kuhn, Lakatos, and Laudan." See also R. Boudon, "Scientific Advancement in Sociology," in Hagerstrand, *The Identification of Progress in Learning*, pp. 91–114; and Michael Burawoy, "Two Methods in Search of Science," *Theory and Society*, Vol. 6, No. 18 (1989), pp. 759–805.

research programs has become a great deal less fashionable.[69] We readily acknowledge that epistemological advice based on contemporary philosophy of science would be far removed from the international relations subfield's present practices. It is indisputable that mainstream IR is firmly characterized by commitments both to paradigmatism and to the belief that there are generally applicable and rational grounds for distinguishing good and bad theories.[70] Our concern here is not that these practices may be old-fashioned when compared to modern philosophy, but that they have become detached from the metatheories that originally provoked, sustained, and justified them. They have become ingrained habits rather than

---

69. Much of the opposition to the methodology centers on Lakatos's appraisal criteria, especially the emphasis on novel facts. More fundamental criticisms, however, address not only particular elements of the methodology but the predicate question of whether it is possible to make *any* reliable generalizations about scientific change. If science is predominantly irrational, and actual research activities are guided by socialization and internalization, then prestige, propaganda, and polemics will determine which theory wins the day. As Larry Laudan unsympathetically relates, such a skeptical position is reinforced by general arguments of cultural relativism: science is just one set of beliefs among many possible ones, and the West venerates science not because it is more rational but because "we are a product of a culture that has traditionally set great store by science." See Larry Laudan, *Progress and Its Problems: Towards a Theory of Scientific Growth* (Berkeley: University of California Press, 1977), p. 3. According to this view, science is an ideology in which objective, rational preference is impossible and, as Mark Neufeld observes, where the "standards for what constitutes reliable knowledge are human constructs and social conventions." Mark Neufeld, *The Restructuring of International Relations Theory* (Cambridge, UK: Cambridge University Press, 1995), p. 50. We accept that adopting a radically skeptical view would undermine the utility of Lakatos's methodology (ibid., pp. 51, 137–138, note 5). However, it would also entail abandoning almost all mainstream political science.

70. By "paradigmatism" we refer to the position that scientific disciplines are best viewed in terms of durable theoretical aggregates. Disciplinary surveys are structured around these aggregates; theory development and empirical investigations are done in the name of bolstering or undermining them. In IR, paradigmatism is most clearly signaled by the subfield's attachment to the "isms," particularly realism or liberalism.

deliberate, thoughtful choices. In short, while accepting that Lakatos may be unpopular and even discredited in some circles, we maintain that it is nonetheless necessary to undertake a comprehensive reengagement of the epistemological underpinnings of the subfield's attachment to "rational" paradigmatism. As Giovanni Sartori suggests, if "methodological discussions are often reinventing what has been forgotten," rediscovering "the forgotten known is just as important as discover[ing] (anew) an unknown."[71]

LAKATOS'S METHODOLOGY DOES NOT WORK FOR A SOCIAL SCIENCE

A third criticism is that Lakatos's methodology is inappropriate or useless for social sciences. It is true that the methodology was developed by a mathematician, and was first applied in the physical sciences.[72] Lakatos was certainly no fan of the social sciences, and some suggest that he may not have wanted his metatheory to be used to appraise its work.[73] Spiro Latsis, however, describes how he and Lakatos toured the United States recruiting economists and others for a conference to be held in 1974 at Nafplion, Greece.[74] Latsis notes that:

---

71. Giovanni Sartori, "Compare Why and How: Comparing, Miscomparing and the Comparative Method," in Mattei Dogan and Ali Kazancigil, eds., *Comparing Nations: Concepts, Strategies, Substance* (Cambridge, Mass.: Blackwell, 1994), p. 14.

72. On the distinction between the natural and social sciences, and how Lakatos's methodology might apply differently to each, see Michael Nicholson, "Realism and Utopianism Revisited," *Review of International Studies*, Vol. 24, No. 5 (December 1998), p. 70.

73. See, for example, Robert O. Keohane, "Theory of World Politics: Structural Realism and Beyond," in Robert O. Keohane, ed., *International Institutions and State Power* (Boulder, Colo.: Westview Press, 1989), p. 67, note 7.

74. Spiro J. Latsis, "Nafplion Revisited," in Daniel Vaz and Kumaraswamy Velupillai, *Inflation, Institutions and Information: Essays in Honour of Axel Leijonhufvud* (Houndmills: Macmillan, 1996), pp. 24–32. The Nafplion meeting produced two volumes. The first applied the methodology to economics, the second to the physical sciences. See Latsis, *Method and Appraisal in Economics*; and Colin Howson, ed., *Method and Appraisal in the Physical Sciences: The Critical*

[The] idea of holding [the Nafplion] Colloquium was first conceived by ... Lakatos.... Its central purpose was a synoptic examination of Lakatos's new and provocative methodology of scientific research programmes (MSRP) to developments in the physical sciences *and in economics.*"[75]

Some detractors point to Lakatos's harsh evaluation of Marxism and Freudianism, and suggest that this indicates that he did not intend his methodology to be used to appraise social sciences.[76] The more reasonable interpretation, however, is that in using his methodology to appraise the work and adjudge it flawed, Lakatos showed that he thought the criteria *were* applicable.[77] Lakatos also observes, with some sympathy, that those who attempt to falsify everybody else's theories indiscriminately without also creating new knowledge (or "naïve falsificationists") have had a "destructive effect" on budding scientific research programs in the social sciences, implying that they could do better by applying a different set of more tolerant appraisal criteria, such as his own.[78]

Background to Modern Science, 1800–1905 (New York: Cambridge University Press, 1976).

75. Spiro J. Latsis, "Preface," in *Method and Appraisal in Economics*, pp. vii–viii, at p. vii (emphasis added). See also Coats, "Economics and Psychology," p. 43; and Axel Leijonhufvud, "Schools, 'Revolutions', and Research Programmes in Economic Theory," in Latsis, *Method and Appraisal in Economics*, p. 65.

76. On Lakatos's views of Marxism and Freudianism, see Lakatos, "Falsification and the Methodology of Scientific Research Programmes," pp. 175–176; and Worrall, "The Ways in Which the Methodology of Scientific Research Programmes Improves on Popper's Methodology," p. 55.

77. Nor according to Paul Diesing should we take Lakatos's substantive findings on Marxism and psychoanalysis too seriously, since "Lakatos was quite ignorant of the social sciences, as well as quite prejudiced." See Diesing, *How Does Social Science Work?* p. 47; see also Hayward R. Alker, Jr., "A Methodology for Design Research on Interdependence Alternatives," *International Organization*, Vol. 31, No. 1 (Winter 1977), p. 44, note 13.

78. Lakatos, "Falsification and the Methodology of Scientific Research Programmes," p. 179, note 2.

We also note that the problems that Lakatos's methodology addresses are clearly in evidence in political science.[79] For example, scholars often attempt to salvage theories from potentially disconfirming evidence by making trivial amendments that have the effect of decreasing the content of their theories. Descriptions of how the field develops are thus often quite consistent with a Lakatosian perspective. Charles Tilly points to:

a common but logically peculiar ... performance we may call "improving the model." It consists of (1) outlining a widely accepted model of phenomenon A, (2) identifying an instance of A that fails to fit the model in one or more ways, (3) modifying the model so that it now accommodates the previously exceptional instance as well as those instances that previously belonged to its domain.... As a reviewer for professional journals I read a half-dozen drafts each year that follow just such reasoning.[80]

In addition, IR theorists frequently acknowledge that their field consists of enduring theoretical aggregates constituted by different theories with common elements, and most view those aggregates—which could be construed as Lakatosian scientific research programs, Kuhnian paradigms, or Laudanian research traditions, among others—as the most appropriate units of analysis for assessing theoretical growth.

---

79. For the claim that the methodology fails to depict IR theorists' motivations accurately, see William C. Wohlforth, "Measuring Power—And the Power of Theories," in John A. Vasquez and Colin Elman, eds., *Realism and the Balancing of Power: A New Debate* (New York: Prentice Hall, 2003). For the argument that it does not accurately describe how social science research is conducted in general, and that the factors influencing theory choice extend beyond content-increasing efforts in particular, see John S. Dryzek, "The Progress of Political Science," *Journal of Politics*, Vol. 48, No. 2 (May 1986), pp. 301–320.

80. Charles Tilly, "To Explain Political Processes," *American Journal of Sociology*, Vol. 100, No. 6 (May 1995), p. 1597.

EMPLOYING MSRP WILL IGNITE "PARADIGM WARS"

Some critics argue that using the methodology of scientific research programs will encourage an attack of the "isms," inciting scholars to think in terms of mutually exclusive scientific research programs, and to engage in the ungenerous denigration of alternative viewpoints.[81] Our view is that this argument has Lakatos's methodology exactly backwards. Although some level of competition is inevitable and even desirable, it is obviously preferable that scholars maintain a civility of discourse. Since attachments to theories are unavoidable, it is better to employ a metatheory that, like Lakatos's, fosters both tenacity and tolerance: tenacity in defending one's favored scientific research program, and tolerance in accepting that multiple research programs can co-exist at any given time.

The methodology allows for tenacious attachment to a theory because even when a determination is reached that a research program is degenerative, this negative assessment does not result in the automatic rejection of the scientific research program. Lakatos argues that "one may rationally stick to a degenerating programme until it is taken over by a rival *and even after*. What one must *not* do is to deny its poor public record."[82] Worrall notes similarly that:

[Lakatos's methodology] does not predict that, whenever some new programme comes along which it appraises as more progressive than the old one, all scientists will immediately switch to work on the progressive programme. Nor does the methodology pronounce "irrational" those scientists who, in such circumstances, stick to the old programme. Such a scientist may, in perfect conformity with this methodology, agree that the new programme is at the moment superior, but nevertheless declare his intention to work on the old programme in an attempt to improve it so that it becomes even better than the new programme.[83]

---

81. See, for example, Chapter 5 by Andrew Moravcsik in this volume.

82. Lakatos, "History of Science and its Rational Reconstructions," pp. 104–105, emphasis in original.

83. Worrall, "The Ways in Which the Methodology of Scientific Research Programmes Improves on Popper's Methodology," p. 61. Musgrave argues

In part this is because the appraisal of a scientific research program as progressive or degenerating according to Lakatos's methodology is not final. A program may be progressive in one period, then degenerating, later returning to progressiveness. Weak programs can undergo spurts of theoretical or empirical progress and, since scientific research programs tend to progress at different rates, choices between them at any given moment may not be clear-cut.[84] As Gholson and Barker put it: "the revisability of judgment concerning whether a program is progressing or degenerating makes it difficult to supply final appraisals to any contemporary science."[85]

Lakatos's methodology also expects scholars to be tolerant, standing in sharp contrast to the all-or-nothing kind of confrontation anticipated by Kuhn, for whom "paradigm wars" is an oxymoron. Kuhn expects that, most of the time, a single paradigm will be

---

that Lakatos's methodology is capable of giving community-directed advice, and that this counsel will be followed by *most* practitioners, even if every *individual* scientist need not heed this guidance. According to Musgrave "an appraisal like 'This programme has degenerated up till now, while its rival has progressed' can and should lead to heuristic advice of the following kind: 'Science should devote most of its resources to the progressive programme'." See Musgrave, "Method or Madness?" p. 480. See also Rod Cross, "The Duhem-Quine Thesis, Lakatos and the Appraisal of Theories in Macroeconomics," *Economic Journal*, Vol. 92, No. 366 (June 1982), pp. 333–334. Yet Lakatos was very reluctant to comment on contemporary research, arguing that his methodology "presumes to give advice to the scientist neither about how to *arrive* at good theories nor even about which of two rival programmes he should work on." See Imre Lakatos, "Replies to Critics," in Buck and Cohen, *Boston Studies in the Philosophy of Science*, p. 174 (emphasis in original). See also ibid., p. 78; Lakatos, "History of Science and its Rational Reconstructions," p. 125, note 36; Latsis, "Preface," p. viii; and Ian Hacking, "Imre Lakatos's Philosophy of Science," *British Journal for the Philosophy of Science*, Vol. 30 (1979), p. 389. This minimalist position has been questioned by both proponents and critics of the methodology of scientific research programs. Blaug, for example, describes Lakatos's position as amounting to intellectual schizophrenia; see Blaug, *The Methodology of Economics*, p. 37. See also Berkson, "Lakatos One and Lakatos Two," p. 53.

84. Gholson and Barker, "Kuhn, Lakatos, and Laudan," p. 757.

85. Ibid. See also Leplin, *A Novel Defense of Scientific Realism*, pp. 40–41.

dominant. By contrast, Lakatos assumes the simultaneous existence of several research programs. As Musgrave notes, "Lakatos urges ... the necessity of *competing* research programmes, and claims that what Kuhn calls 'normal science' is 'nothing but a research-programme that has achieved monopoly'."[86] Lakatos's methodology also recognizes that scholars can work in more than one scientific research program at any given time, even one to which they hope to prove unhelpful. Finally, as DiCicco and Levy note in Chapter 4, Lakatos's methodology is agnostic about how broadly scientific research programs should be drawn. If they are narrowly described, however, there is no reason to expect intolerance. For example, it is not clear that dividing realist research into narrower defensive and offensive realist scientific research programs—as Robert Jervis suggests in Chapter 7—should inevitably result in the kinds of clashes between worldviews feared by critics who are anxious to avoid sparking unhelpful arguments.[87]

INTERNATIONAL RELATIONS THEORISTS ALREADY USE LAKATOS CORRECTLY, SO NO FURTHER ATTENTION TO MSRP IS REQUIRED

Finally, perhaps the most widespread misapprehension is that nearly all international relations theorists already use Lakatos correctly. They do not. Our point of departure is that IR theorists almost never use metatheory when it is needed, and when they do, they usually get it wrong. This criticism certainly applies to the methodology of scientific research programs, which has been significantly underemployed and misused in the subfield. While IR theorists often pay lip service to

---

86. Musgrave, "Method or Madness?" pp. 482–483. Accordingly, it may be similarly oxymoronic to talk about a "dominant research program." See, for example, Brian Ripley, "Psychology, Foreign Policy, and International Relations Theory," *Political Psychology*, Vol. 14, No. 3 (1993), p. 403; and Randall L. Schweller, "New Realist Research on Alliances: Refining, Not Refuting, Waltz's Balancing Proposition," *American Political Science Review*, Vol. 91, No. 4 (December 1997), p. 927.

87. The downside of Lakatos's emphasis on toleration, however, is that it might permit the continuation of unproductive research programs. See Jonathan DiCicco and Jack Levy, Chapter 4; and David Dessler, Chapter 8 in this volume.

Lakatos's metatheory, they very rarely practice it. There have been few full applications of the methodology that have been consistent with mainstream Lakatosian readings. As the applications of Lakatos's framework in this volume demonstrate, using the methodology of scientific research programs requires a coherent and consistent version of the metatheory, including making necessary predicate choices, such as which definition of a "novel fact" to employ; describing the scientific research program's hard core, negative heuristic, and positive heuristic; specifying and appraising iterations of its protective belt; and determining whether they are $ad\ hoc_1$, $ad\ hoc_2$, or (if an intra-program problemshift) $ad\ hoc_3$.[88] Although some discussions and applications in the IR literature possess some of these virtues, we have seen none that performs well on all of these dimensions.

Indeed, while Lakatos is widely cited throughout the subfield, the great bulk of these references does not signal a comprehensive use of his metatheory. Full-scale and substantive applications or discussions of the methodology in the IR literature are few and far between.[89] This failure is particularly puzzling because IR is, by nature, a "borrowing" subfield: it has imported much of its methodological and substantive content, such as game theory and rational choice, from economics, a discipline that has generated a voluminous literature discussing,

---

88. De Marchi, "Introduction: Rethinking Lakatos," p. 17.

89. For uses in other subfields of political science, many of which mirror the strengths and weaknesses of IR works, see, for example, Mark Sproule-Jones, "Public Choice Theory and Natural Resources: Methodological Explication and Critique," *American Political Science Review*, Vol. 76, No. 4 (December 1982), pp. 790–804; Terence Ball, "Is There Progress in Political Science?" in Terence Ball, ed., *Idioms of Inquiry: Critique and Renewal in Political Science* (Albany: State University of New York Press, 1987), pp. 13–44; Hillard Pouncy, "Terms of Agreement: Evaluating the Theory of Symbolic Politics' Impact on the Pluralist Research Program," *American Journal of Political Science*, Vol. 32, No. 3 (August 1988), pp. 781–795; Will H. Moore, "Rational Rebels: Overcoming the Free-Rider Problem," *Political Research Quarterly*, Vol. 48, No. 2 (1995), pp. 417–454; and Iain S. Lustick, "Lijphart, Lakatos, and Consociationalism," *World Politics*, Vol. 50, No. 1 (1997), pp. 88–117.

debating, and applying Lakatos's methodology much more consistently and rigorously.[90]

Instead, to the extent that metatheoretic criteria are specified at all, an abbreviated and often inaccurate version of Lakatos's methodology is wheeled out to validate favored research and to render a negative assessment of others' research.[91] Regrettably, despite being superficially attracted by its resonance with methods commonly employed in the subfield, most IR theorists have not taken the methodology seriously. Many references simply invoke Lakatos rhetorically, with sympathetic authors promising that what follows amounts to a progressive

---

90. Collaborative efforts by economists at conferences in Nafplion and Capri to examine the relevance of Lakatos's methodology of scientific research programs produced two edited volumes: Latsis, *Method and Appraisal in Economics*; and de Marchi and Blaug, *Appraising Economic Theories*, respectively. See also Joel Jalladeau, "Research Program versus Paradigm in the Development of Economics," *Journal of Economic Issues*, Vol. 12, No. 3 (1978), pp. 583–608; G.C. Archibald, "Method and Appraisal in Economics," *Philosophy of the Social Sciences*, Vol. 9 (1979), pp. 304–315; Douglas W. Hands, "The Methodology of Economic Research Programmes," *Philosophy of the Social Sciences*, Vol. 9 (1979), pp. 293–303; G. Fulton, "Research Programmes in Economics," *History of Political Economy*, Vol. 16 (Summer 1984), pp. 187–206; E. Roy Weintraub, *General Equilibrium Analysis: Studies in Appraisal* (New York: Cambridge University Press, 1985); Elias Khalil, "Kuhn, Lakatos, and the History of Economic Thought," *International Journal of Social Economics*, Vol. 14 (1987), pp. 118–131; J.C. Glass and W. Johnson, "Metaphysics, MSRP and Economics," *British Journal for the Philosophy of Science*, Vol. 39 (1988), pp. 313–329; Roger E. Backhouse, "Lakatosian Perspectives on General Equilibrium Analysis," *Economics and Philosophy*, Vol. 9, No. 2 (1993), pp. 271–282; and Siobhain McGovern, "On a Maze of Second Thoughts and on the Methodology of Economic Methodology," *Journal of Economic Methodology*, Vol. 2, No. 2 (December 1995), pp. 223–237. For the view that Lakatos is "the philosopher who has ... dominated economists' talk of method these past twenty years," see John Maloney, "Economic Method and Economic Rhetoric," *Journal of Economic Methodology*, Vol. 1, No. 2 (December 1994), p. 255.

91. For a similar criticism of IR theorists' employment of metatheory, see Yosef Lapid, "The Third Debate: On the Prospects of International Theory in a Post-Positivist Era," *International Studies Quarterly*, Vol. 33, No. 3 (1989), pp. 247–248.

problemshift, and critics complaining that the scholarship is degenerative. Others seem to aim at proving membership in the social science club, perhaps tipping their hats to the "reviewers-as-bouncers." Apparently, such invocations of Lakatos are meant to lend credence to a supportive or critical appraisal, with a footnote to "appropriate" philosophy of science. Some articles contain a brief discussion of Lakatos's methodology, but these are often so general as to be meaningless. Sometimes such short statements do engage more with the metatheory, although often with an incomplete account of its criteria, as when Alexander Wendt suggests that "degenerating problemshifts are adjustments to a theory that are ad hoc, while progressive shifts are those that have a principled basis in its hard core assumptions."[92] Sometimes the statements are simply unhelpful, as in the observation that "Lakatos's (1970) idea of a progressive auxiliary hypothesis [is] an ad-hoc adjustment to a theory that helps it explain better."[93]

There is unevenness in how IR theorists use Lakatos's methodology, both in the many brief references as well as in the few comprehensive applications and discussions. Some aspects of the metatheory receive more emphasis and are more accurately portrayed than others, in patterns that tend to be repeated. IR theorists tend to recognize and acknowledge that Lakatos's sophisticated methodological falsification-ism stands in opposition to naive falsificationism.[94] They also often

---

92. Alexander Wendt, "Constructing International Politics," *International Security*, Vol. 20, No. 1 (Summer 1995), p. 79. Occasionally such references are made in support of single, isolated arguments, unconnected to the article's main thesis. See, for example, Timothy J. McKeown, "The Limitations of 'Structural' Theories of Commercial Policy," *International Organization*, Vol. 40, No. 1 (Winter 1986), p. 51.

93. Raymond Birt, "Personality and Foreign Policy: The Case of Stalin," *Political Psychology*, Vol. 14, No. 4 (1993), p. 608.

94. See, for example, Friedrich Kratochwil, "The Force of Prescriptions," *International Organization*, Vol. 38, No. 4 (Autumn 1984), pp. 704–705; Stephen D. Krasner, "Toward Understanding in International Relations," *International Studies Quarterly*, Vol. 29, No. 2 (1985), p. 143; David Dessler, "What's At Stake in the Agent-Structure Debate," *International Organization*, Vol. 43, No. 3

note that Lakatos's methodology recommends both tolerance and tenacity. For example, Patrick James suggests that "Lakatos's frame of reference is 'compatible with all theories having false empirical consequences,' hence the toleration of anomalies, which later may be explained."[95] James Rosenau observes that: "Lakatos encourages the idea that knowledge-building is better served through a dialectic method that sustains conflicting theories than through a scientific method that seeks consensual theory."[96] Apart from these areas in which IR theorists do well, other areas are more problematic.

One aspect of the methodology that IR theorists often get wrong is the definition of novel facts. Most users either fail to specify an adequate definition, or employ a meaning that is at odds with the metatheory. With respect to the first group, theorists either say nothing at all, or else ambiguously describe novelty as "increased empirical content," without identifying the class of background knowledge to

---

(Summer 1989), pp. 447, 470; Robert O. Keohane, "International Relations Theory: Contributions of a Feminist Standpoint," *Millennium—Journal of International Studies*, Vol. 18, No. 2 (1989), pp. 249–250; Patrick James, "Neorealism as a Research Enterprise: Toward Elaborated Structural Realism," *International Political Science Review*, Vol. 14, No. 2 (1993), pp. 128–129; Jack S. Levy, "Prospect Theory, Rational Choice, and International Relations," *International Studies Quarterly*, Vol. 41, No. 1 (March 1997), p. 97; Kenneth N. Waltz, "Evaluating Theories," *American Political Science Review*, Vol. 91, No. 4 (December 1997), p. 914; Michael C. Desch, "Correspondence: Isms and Schisms: Culturalism versus Realism in Security Studies," *International Security*, Vol. 24, No. 1 (Summer 1999), p. 173, note 5. For critiques of naive falsificationism, see Gary King, Robert O. Keohane, and Sidney Verba, *Designing Social Inquiry: Scientific Inference in Qualitative Research* (Princeton, N.J.: Princeton University Press, 1994), pp. 100–105; and Bruce Bueno de Mesquita, "Theory and the Advancement of Knowledge About War: A Reply," *Review of International Studies*, Vol. 10, No. 1 (1984), pp. 70–72.

95. James, "Neorealism as a Research Enterprise," p. 129.

96. James N. Rosenau, "A Pre-Theory Revisited: World Politics in an Era of Cascading Interdependence," *International Studies Quarterly*, Vol. 28, No. 3 (September 1984), p. 251. For an example from another subfield, see Ball, "Is There Progress in Political Science?" p. 27: "A Lakatosian perspective ... throws a kinder light on attempts to save a research program from criticism by means of various adjustments to its protective belt."

which the predictions are being compared (which is crucial for determining whether new theories demonstrate progress within or between research programs).[97] In his recent application of Lakatos's methodology to contemporary realist research, for example, John Vasquez provides an ambiguous definition of novel fact, variously "something about the world and its regularities other than what was uncovered by the discrepant evidence"; "new propositions and predictions (or observations) that the original theory did not anticipate"; and facts that "tell us things we did not (theoretically) know before."[98] Although describing "increased content," these definitions do not make it clear what type of novel fact is required. Thus it is difficult to determine whether Vasquez is justified in appraising the realist research program as degenerating in terms of Lakatosian criteria.

To the extent that a definition of novelty is specified, "background theory novelty" is the usual favorite. As we explained, however, this definition reduces Lakatos's methodology to the measurement of anomalies solved, in direct opposition to the metatheory's purposes. For example, Christensen and Snyder argue that by adding security dilemma variables to Waltz's sparse theory, they can account for phenomena on which his theory was silent.[99] In arguing that this is a progressive problemshift, they later claim that Lakatos's criteria include:

---

97. See, for example, Krasner, "Toward Understanding in International Relations," p. 138; James, "Neorealism as a Research Enterprise," p. 129; and Brian M. Pollins, "Global Political Order, Economic Change, and Armed Conflict: Coevolving Systems and the Use of Force," *American Political Science Review*, Vol. 90, No. 1 (March 1996), p. 104. For an example from another subfield, see Virginia Gray and David Lowery, "How Much Do Interest Groups Influence State Economic Growth?" *American Political Science Review*, Vol. 83, No. 4 (December 1989), p. 1305.

98. Vasquez, *The Power of Power Politics*, pp. 244, 246, and 247.

99. Thomas J. Christensen and Jack Snyder, "Chain Gangs and Passed Bucks: Predicting Alliance Patterns in Multipolarity," *International Organization*, Vol. 44, No. 2 (Spring 1990), pp. 137–168.

whether the new theoretical formulation can explain phenomena that the original one cannot. We pass that test, since we explain when chain-ganging occurs and when buck-passing occurs, whereas Waltz only explained that both were more common in multipolarity than in bipolarity.[100]

Similarly, Theo Farrell argues that culturalism is a progressive scientific research program because it explains facts that are not expected and are "unaccounted for" by the rival realist program.[101] Joseph Grieco, in arguing that his "voice opportunities" thesis is a progressive adjustment, uses background theory novelty: he starts with an empirical event (institutional development within the European Union) that is an anomaly for neorealism, amends its protective belt, solves the anomaly, and declares the problemshift progressive by Lakatosian standards.[102] However, unless Grieco's

---

100. Thomas J. Christensen and Jack Snyder, "Progressive Research on Degenerate Alliances," *American Political Science Review*, Vol. 91, No. 4 (December 1997), p. 920. For the argument that Christensen and Snyder's argument can, in fact, be considered progressive in Lakatosian terms, see Dessler, Chapter 11.

101. Theo Farrell, "Correspondence: Isms and Schisms: Culturalism versus Realism in Security Studies," *International Security*, Vol. 24, No. 1 (Summer 1999), p. 168; see also pp. 166–167. For other instances in which scholars mistakenly suggest that Lakatos's methodology regards all theoretical moves aimed at resolving existing anomalies as progressive, see Paul A. Anderson and Timothy J. McKeown, "Changing Aspirations, Limited Attention, and War," *World Politics*, Vol. 40, No. 1 (1987), p. 1; Stephen G. Walker, "The Evolution of Operational Code Analysis," *Political Psychology*, Vol. 11, No. 2 (1990), p. 407; John M. Owen IV, *Liberal Peace, Liberal War: American Politics and International Security* (Ithaca, N.Y.: Cornell University Press, 1997), p. 209; and Mark S. Sheetz, "Correspondence: Debating the Unipolar Moment," *International Security*, Vol. 22, No. 3 (Winter 1997/98), p. 172. For examples where scholars use the understanding of heuristic novelty that we prefer, see Robert Jervis, "Pluralistic Rigor: A Comment on Bueno de Mesquita," *International Studies Quarterly*, Vol. 29, No. 2 (June 1985), pp. 146, 148; and Harvey Starr, "Democracy and War: Choice, Learning and Security Communities," *Journal of Peace Research*, Vol. 29, No. 2 (1992), p. 208.

102. Joseph M. Grieco, "The Maastricht Treaty, Economic and Monetary Union and the Neo-Realist Research Program," *Review of International Studies*, Vol. 21,

change predicts new facts, his theoretical move is not progressive by Lakatosian standards.[103]

This widespread reliance on background theory novelty often goes together with, and its prevalence may be partly explained by, the popularity among IR theorists of Lakatos's much misunderstood observation about "three-cornered fights" between two theories and the facts.[104] It may be that IR theorists' confusion over what Lakatos meant by this phrase has contributed to the mistaken use of background theory novelty. When Lakatos requires that Theory Y should do all that Theory X does and something more, the "something more" cannot just be X's known lacunae.[105]

Occasionally, IR theorists have used an even more problematic definition of novelty: more of the same class of events. Stephen M. Walt, for example, argues that his balance of threat theory predicts novel facts because it can be used to explain alliance behavior in the Middle East, NATO and the Warsaw Pact, 1930s Europe, and Southwest Asia, as well as the grand strategy of the United States in the post–Cold War period and the international consequences of domestic revolutions.[106] Most of the facts on this list, however, predict values of the same dependent variable—alignment behavior—and accordingly cannot be considered novel facts by *any* of the recognizable definitions used in Lakatos's methodology of scientific research

No. 1 (January 1995), pp. 21–40. For a discussion of Grieco's thesis, see Keohane and Martin, Chapter 3. For a spirited argument in favor of background theory novelty criteria, see Moravcsik, Chapter 5.

103. For a potentially heuristically novel application of Grieco's binding hypothesis see John Ikenberry, *After Victory: Institutions, Strategic Restraint, and the Rebuilding of Order After Major Wars* (Princeton, N.J.: Princeton University Press, 2001). Ikenberry uses Grieco's hypothesis to address the question: "what do states that have just won major wars do with their newly acquired power?"

104. Lakatos, "Falsification and the Methodology of Scientific Research Programmes," p. 115.

105. There are, of course, epistemologies that do consider such puzzle-solving as a sign of progress. See, for example, Laudan, *Progress and Its Problems*, pp. 114–118.

106. Walt, "The Progressive Power of Realism," pp. 933–34.

programs.[107] To be sure, repeated tests of the same proposition are valuable because they offer evidence about whether a prediction is empirically accurate. As Robert Jervis notes, "Scholars often look at many cases to see if a proposed generalization fits the data. [But this] is a form of confirmation, not the discovery of new facts."[108] In Walt's list, the only unambiguously novel prediction is the connection between domestic revolutions and international conflict, a fact that we can be fairly certain did not figure into the earlier construction of balance of threat theory, and thus meets the criterion for novelty recommended by Zahar and Lakatos (heuristic novelty).[109]

Hence, IR theorists tend to provide fuller and more accurate accounts of some aspects of Lakatos's methodology than of others. This emphasis, usually inadvertent, sometimes graduates to a deliberately selective employment of elements of the metatheory. For example, Ted Hopf recently argued that he would move "constructivism from the margins by articulating a loosely Lakatosian research program for a constructivist study of international relations."[110] The footnote to this sentence explains:

It is a loose adaptation because, while I adopt Lakatosian criteria for what constitutes a progressive and degenerative shift in a research program, I do not adopt his standards of falsificationism or their associated protective belts of auxiliary hypotheses.

---

107. For a similar use of "more of the same kinds of event" novelty, see Christensen and Snyder "Progressive Research on Degenerate Alliances," p. 920. They suggest that their theory, which adds the perception of the offense/defense balance to Waltz's structural argument, can account for "alliance choices of all the major European powers before both world wars" as well as "nineteenth-century alliance choices." Employment of this novelty criterion is in addition to their use of background theory novelty, described above.

108. Jervis, "Pluralistic Rigor," p. 146.

109. Stephen M. Walt, *Revolution and War* (Ithaca, N.Y.: Cornell University Press, 1996).

110. Ted Hopf, "The Promise of Constructivism in International Relations Theory," *International Security*, Vol. 23, No. 1 (Summer 1998), p. 186.

This deliberate, intentional excision of pieces of the metatheory runs the risk of committing what we call the "sweet shop error": picking and choosing elements, as if Lakatos's methodology were an epistemological candy store. The least important consequence of this error is that the metatheoretic statement offered can no longer be described accurately as "Lakatosian." Much more significant is the fact that the elements that are selected may make no sense in terms of the epistemology being employed, or in the context that they are used.[111]

Some applications of the methodology of scientific research programs are flawed by the inclusion of elements that are incompatible with the metatheory; this might be described as putting epistemology in the great blender. An example of this "Cuisinart" approach is where scholars mix incompatible Kuhnian and Lakatosian metatheories.[112] Some scholars do note the differences between Kuhn and Lakatos, and recognize in particular that, contra Kuhn, the methodology of scientific research programs aspires to provide rational and universal criteria for scientific appraisal.[113] Others, however, engage in the deliberate

---

111. This is not to say that the metatheory cannot be broken down into discrete propositions, or that these cannot be tested individually. For an attempt to make such a list for Kuhn, Feyerabend, Lakatos, and Laudan, see Larry Laudan, Arthur Donovan, Rachel Laudan, Peter Barker, Harold Brown, Jarrett Leplin, Paul Thagard, and Steve Wykstra, "Scientific Change: Philosophic Models and Historical Research," *Synthese*, Vol. 69 (1986), pp. 141–223, especially pp. 199–207.

112. For the view that Lakatos and Kuhn were advancing different epistemologies, see Lakatos, "History of Science and its Rational Reconstructions," p. 120; Blaug, "Kuhn versus Lakatos or Paradigms versus Research Programs in the History of Economics"; Blaug, *The Methodology of Economics*, p. 32; Musgrave, "Method or Madness?" pp. 482–483; and Hands, "Second Thoughts on Lakatos," p. 3. While Lakatos did very occasionally use the terms "research program" and "paradigm" as alternatives, this was usually when referring to metatheoretical units in general. See Lakatos, "Falsification and the Methodology of Scientific Research Programmes," pp. 155, 177–80.

113. See, for example, Friedrich Kratochwil, "Errors Have Their Advantage," *International Organization*, Vol. 38, No. 2 (Spring 1984), p. 314; Krasner, "Toward Understanding in International Relations," p. 137; Jack Snyder, "Richness, Rigor, and Relevance in the Study of Soviet Foreign Policy,"

combination of the two competing approaches, as when Vasquez argues that "any paradigm worth its salt will have more than one ongoing research program" or when Helga Haftendorn questions whether "our present research programs are adequate to construct new paradigms."[114] Since the two epistemologies are, in fact, incompatible, the resulting mélange is inconsistent.[115]

In sum, while firmly wedded to the practice of paradigmatism, IR theorists are not so versed in the epistemologies that justify that choice that they can afford to ignore metatheory in general, or Lakatos's methodology of scientific research programs in particular.

In this section we have described several arguments that we find unconvincing: that IR theorists should leave metatheory to the philosophers; that Lakatos's methodology is outdated and has been superseded; that it does not work for a social science; that employing the methodology will ignite unproductive "paradigm wars"; and that

International Security, Vol. 9, No. 3 (Winter 1984/85), p. 92; Keohane, "Theory of World Politics," p. 37; Roslyn Simowitz and Barry L. Price, "The Expected Utility Theory of Conflict: Measuring Theoretical Progress," *American Political Science Review*, Vol. 84, No. 2 (June 1990), pp. 442–443. For examples from other subfields of political science, see Ball, "From Paradigms to Research Programs"; John G. Gunnell, "Can Political Science History Be Neutral?" *American Political Science Review*, Vol. 84, No. 2 (June 1990), p. 592; and John G. Gunnell, "Realizing Theory: The Philosophy of Science Revisited," *Journal of Politics*, Vol. 57, No. 4 (November 1995), p. 927.

114. John A. Vasquez, "The Realist Paradigm and Degenerative Versus Progressive Research Programs: An Appraisal of Neotraditional Research on Waltz's Balancing Proposition," *American Political Science Review*, Vol. 91, No. 4 (December 1997), p. 902; Helga Haftendorn, "The Security Puzzle: Theory-Building and Discipline-Building in International Security," *International Studies Quarterly*, Vol. 35, No. 1 (March 1991), p. 12. We are not talking here of the practice of using the terms "research program" and "paradigm" interchangeably as, for example, in Krasner, "Toward Understanding in International Relations"; Keohane, "Theory of World Politics"; and Michael Mastanduno, "Preserving the Unipolar Moment: Realist Theories and U.S. Grand Strategy After the Cold War," *International Security*, Vol. 21, No. 4 (Spring 1997), pp. 49–88.

115. For an opposing view that the metatheories can be usefully combined, see Vasquez, Chapter 13.

because IR theorists already use Lakatos correctly, no additional attention to his approach to evaluating science is required. In the next section we consider more serious and substantive difficulties with Lakatos's metric.

Problems with Applying Lakatos's Methodology of Scientific Research Programs in International Relations

There are at least three telling criticisms of the methodology that need to be considered. They are: that it is difficult to identify the hard core and other elements of a research program; that there is controversy over how to define novelty; and that the methodology fails to employ additional or alternative criteria of theory assessment. While none of these problems necessarily prevent the methodology's application, they should, at the very least, frame and limit its employment.

IDENTIFYING THE HARD CORE

In Chapter 3, Keohane and Martin note that "Lakatos does not provide a clear, operational framework for the analysis of research programs." One of the most difficult problems centers on how to define a research program's hard core. As David Dessler has remarked, in an open research setting, it is difficult if not impossible, as Lakatos himself admitted, to identify a complete, unambiguous and unchanging hard core, and thus to distinguish ad hoc from non-ad hoc developments of a theory (i.e., between degenerating and progressive problemshifts). This problem is exacerbated where IR theorists use Lakatos's methodology to appraise current research in which the hard core has yet to harden, and where longevity thus cannot be used as a guide to centrality.

Lakatosians agree that any description of a scientific research program is likely to be contested. As Blaug suggests, "there is no way of writing down once and for all the precise content of the hard core of any SRP ... that would command the universal assent of all the protagonists of that program.... The notion that this is a simple and unambiguous exercise is, surely, naïve."[116] Difficulties are likely to include disputes about the substantive content of the hard core; disagreements on where to draw the line between rival scientific research programs and whether to construe scientific research programs broadly or narrowly;[117] controversies as to whether, within a particular scientific research program, elements belong in the hard core, positive heuristic, or protective belt, and what kinds of definitions, axioms, or assumptions should constitute hard core principles;[118] and debate as to whether theoretical content has to take a particular form (e.g., a mathematical form).[119]

All of these doubts about the certainty with which a scientific research program can be described have relevance for applying Lakatos's methodology to IR theory. For example, in Chapter 9, Randall Schweller relates how scholars have vigorously disagreed about what should be included in the hard core of a realist research program. Andrew Moravcsik in Chapter 5 and James Lee Ray in Chapter 6 show that there are differences of opinion about whether it is more useful and appropriate to delineate and assess a broad liberal scientific research program, or a narrower democratic peace scientific research program.

IR proponents of Lakatos's methodology often underplay the difficulties inherent in describing scientific research programs, trusting that a consensus will form on the correct description of a research program deserving of the name: if scholars offer radically different descriptions of the hard core of any given scientific research program, the controversy surrounding them must indicate that at least one of them is offering a problematic rendition. The problem, however, is that this type of disagreement is ubiquitous: consensuses do not seem to form easily, even on the most popular and widespread IR theories.

---

116. Blaug, "Afterword," pp. 500–501. See also Blaug, "Kuhn versus Lakatos or Paradigms versus Research Programs in the History of Economics," p. 167.

117. De Marchi, "Introduction: Rethinking Lakatos," pp. 12–13; and Backhouse, *Explorations in Economic Methodology*, pp. 3–4, 41.

118. Coats, "Economics and Psychology," pp. 50, 54.

119. Fulton, "Research Programmes in Economics," pp. 191–193.

DEFINING NOVELTY

Some critics argue that the metatheory is paralyzed by the failure to arrive at a single agreed-upon meaning of "novel fact." Indeed, the definition of novelty is one of the most contentious and difficult issues in Lakatosian metatheory.[120] Economic methodologist D. Wade Hands, for example, notes that:

I have spent a great amount of time with the Lakatosian literature and I have *no idea* what Lakatos "really meant" by novel facts. Either Lakatos changed his mind between (and sometimes within) works, or he simply held more than one view simultaneously. The point ... is to contest anyone who has the audacity to argue that there is one "crystal clear" definition of novel facts in Lakatos.[121]

Since different definitions of novel fact will produce contrasting conclusions concerning the progressiveness of the scientific research program under scrutiny, it is impossible to apply Lakatos's methodology without making a choice from among the menu of available meanings.

There are, however, at least two responses to this criticism. The first is that, although there are several definitions of novel fact, each with its own problems, some are clearly better than others. For example, Hands preferred heuristic novelty because "it was the most popular definition in the Lakatosian literature and ... because [Hands] wanted to be as

---

120. Musgrave, "Logical versus Historical Theories of Confirmation"; Murphy, "Another Look at Novel Facts"; Bert Hamminga, "Comment on Hands," in de Marchi and Blaug, eds., *Appraising Economic Theories*, pp. 76–84; Hands, "The Problem of Excess Content"; and Neil Thomason, "Could Lakatos, Even with Zahar's Criterion for Novel Fact, Evaluate the Copernican Research Programme?" *British Journal for the Philosophy of Science*, Vol. 43 (1992), pp. 161–200.

121. Hands, "Reply to Hamminga and Maki," p. 94, emphasis in the original. See also Hands, "The Problem of Excess Content," p. 70. Although at one time Hands was quite enthusiastic about Lakatos's methodology, he later became less so. Compare, for example, Hands, "The Methodology of Economic Research Programs," p. 301, to Hands, "Second Thoughts on Lakatos," and Hands, "Second Thoughts on 'Second Thoughts'."

lenient as possible" with the research he was appraising. In addition, Hands considered background theory novelty to be demonstrably inconsistent with Lakatos's methodology.[122] Second, even if scholars continue to disagree over which definition of novelty to use, so long as they make their decisions in full knowledge of the different candidates' strengths and weaknesses, and insofar as they are explicit about the definition of novelty that they are employing, there is no reason why the novel fact debate should pose an insurmountable obstacle.

FETISHIZING NOVEL PREDICTION

The contributors to this volume note that research programs may be progressive according to Lakatosian standards, and yet nevertheless die out. This, according to Dessler, Schweller, and Vasquez, is because Lakatos's methodology places a disproportionate emphasis on the presence or absence of corroborated novel facts.[123] Hands makes a characteristically straightforward comment on this "novel fact fetishism":

Why would we want to accept the position that the sole necessary condition for scientific progress is predicting novel facts not used in the construction of the theory? Surely humankind's greatest scientific accomplishments have amounted to more than this.... In every other branch of science [we] choose theories because they are deeper, simpler, more general, more operational, explain known facts better, are more corroborated, are more consistent with what we consider to be deeper theories, and for many other reasons.[124]

---

122. Hands, "Reply to Hamminga and Maki," pp. 94–98. By contrast, Moravcsik argues that background theory novelty provides a useful way of assessing progress in the liberal scientific research program: liberalism is progressive because it explains outcomes that were not predicted, and cannot easily be explained, by competing realist theories. See Moravcsik, Chapter 5 in this volume. See also Andrew Bennett, Chapter 13.

123. See also Blaug, "Afterword," p. 500.

124. Hands, "Second Thoughts on 'Second Thoughts'," pp. 77–8. For a similar account of expanded criteria, see Coats, "Economics and Psychology," p. 56.

We agree that novel prediction is not the only valid indicator of success. But Lakatosians are not *only* interested in setting out on hunts for novel facts.[125] An interest in deriving and then corroborating novel facts does not preclude a concern with other criteria of theory appraisal. Although advocates of Lakatos's methodology would argue that accurately predicting novel facts is the most important measure of scientific progress,[126] they welcome the delineation of supplemental appraisal criteria, even as they insist that theoretical and empirical novelty is an indispensable criterion for a progressive problemshift. Thus, while it is clear that more than just excess empirical content enters into scientists' evaluation of theories, Lakatosians suggest that a special emphasis be placed on this criterion. Without theoretical and empirical progress, IR theorists run the risk that their endeavors will produce work that is ultimately empty.[127]

Conclusion: Not "Lakatos or Bust"

This project was motivated by the observation that, while international relations theorists are confirmed paradigmatists who often engage in disciplinary appraisals, they rarely consider the different ways that such evaluations might be made. Lakatos's methodology of scientific research programs is one of many possible places to start. We chose it because it is a consequential and plausible candidate for how to describe and appraise the trajectory of theoretical developments. We like its emphasis on tolerance and on tenacity, and on rewarding innovation. While the contributors to the volume all remain agnostic about whether the methodology of scientific research programs is the best possible alternative, engaging with it proved very helpful in highlighting problems inherent in theory evaluation. The chapters that

---

125. Blaug, "Afterword," p. 502.

126. Ibid.

127. We are grateful to David Dessler for pointing out that this does not, however, provide a decision rule to follow when the novel fact criterion is in opposition to other markers of success.

follow illuminate, in particular, four important lessons that Lakatos teaches about the complexities of theory testing in science.

First, Lakatos's methodology reminds us that straightforward confrontations between theories and data are almost always inconclusive.[128] What is crucial is how a theory fares with respect to its competitors: both its own antecedents and successors within its scientific research program, and against competing research programs. Lakatos gives the sensible advice that no matter how much trouble a theory is in, it should not be abandoned unless there is a better alternative.

Second, the metatheory reminds us not to consider the tenacious defense of theories against evidentiary discrepancies a "crime against science."[129] Good theories are hard to come by, and we should not be too quick to reject them. Their proponents should have tenacity in protecting them, and their critics should be generous even in the face of some contradictory evidence. As Keohane and Martin note in Chapter 3: "By themselves ... anomalies are not particularly disturbing from a Lakatosian perspective. Research programs confront anomalies and seek to resolve them."

Third, the methodology teaches us that unambiguous refutations rarely occur; it is therefore tolerant in its anticipation that at any time a given science will have several extant scientific research programs, not the single monopolistic paradigm expected by Kuhn.

Finally, while encouraging us to preserve pluralistic science, Lakatos rightly insists that we should be unforgiving of anomaly-solving that fails to produce added value. Theoretical adjustments that resolve existing anomalies without predicting anything new are not advances in our understanding. Standards must be imposed on the sorts of theoretical revisions that we treat as legitimate. As Vasquez notes in Chapter 13, without such guidelines, "the danger is to

---

128. Laudan, et al., "Scientific Change: Philosophic Models and Historical Research," p. 158.

129. Ball, "Is There Progress in Political Science?" p. 25. See also Lakatos, "The Role of Crucial Experiments in Science," pp. 316–319, 323; and Moon, "Values and Political Theory," p. 899.

succumb to permitting our political beliefs and prejudices to decide which theory we declare to have been confirmed."

These four cautions notwithstanding, this book does not conclude that our approach to evaluation should be "Lakatos or bust." We agree with Michael Nicholson that "while Lakatos was a remarkably inventive and stimulating philosopher of science, he was not, so far as we know, speaking with the voice of God, and we are entitled to dispute his picture of the advance of science."[130] Indeed, several authors in this volume persuasively argue that other approaches to theory assessment may offer both better prescriptive methodologies (what criteria should be used to promote the growth of knowledge?) and better descriptive methodologies (how have researchers proceeded in practice?). Accordingly, IR theorists should familiarize themselves with other rationalist models of scientific development, with the aim of understanding their problems and potential for studying international relations.[131]

For example, Andrew Moravcsik, Stephen Walker, and Andrew Bennett suggest in Chapters 5, 7, and 14 that closer attention might be paid to Larry Laudan's theory of scientific change, which has emerged as one of the main contenders to Lakatos's methodology.[132] Laudan argues that metatheoretic units generally have malleable hard cores; that research traditions do not "entail" theories, and theories do not entail research traditions, and thus that contradictory theories can belong to the same research traditions, and any given theory can draw its assumptions from different research traditions; and that scholars should "choose the theory (or research tradition) with the highest

---

130. Nicholson, "The Conceptual Bases of *The War Trap*," p. 368.

131. Rationalist accounts, although they are our preference, do not exhaust the possibilities. Philosophers and political scientists have argued that the pattern by which various research waxes and wanes is not wholly driven by objective, scientific merit. See, for example, Kuhn, *The Structure of Scientific Revolutions*; and Robert Jervis, "Realism in the Study of World Politics," *International Organization*, Vol. 52, No. 4 (Autumn 1998), pp. 971–975.

132. See especially Laudan, *Progress and Its Problems*.

problem-solving adequacy."[133] This leads Laudan to accept, as progressive, ad hoc changes that are only capable of solving existing difficulties.[134] These arguments all suggest strategies that are usefully different from those recommended by Lakatos.[135] IR theorists might also follow David Dessler's advice in Chapter 11 and reconsider methods of "severe testing"; Deborah Mayo's method of hypothesis appraisal may prove useful in this endeavor. Arguing against Laudan's (and Lakatos's) view of theory testing in terms of larger metatheoretic units, Mayo suggests that scientific growth consists of subjecting individual hypotheses to severe tests.[136]

While IR theorists need not necessarily use Lakatos's methodology of scientific research programs in their disciplinary appraisals, evaluations of theoretical aggregates must be based on coherent and consistent metatheory. At the very least, all such assessments need a predicate, clear, and public statement of the criteria that are to be employed. Political scientists are not philosophers, and they need not be conversant with every detail of recondite conversations between epistemologists and their critics. But determining whether, over time, new IR theories add to our stock of scientific understanding of international politics cannot be done without metatheory. And deciding which metatheory to use, and then how to use it, is best done with a judgment informed by an appreciation of its contents.

---

133. Ibid., p. 109.

134. Ibid., pp. 114–118.

135. For a useful illustration in political science of Laudan's argument that both definitional precision and consistency with established doctrine strongly influence theory acceptance and rejection, see Albert Somit and Steven A. Peterson, "Rational Choice and Biopolitics: A (Darwinian) Tale of Two Theories," *PS*, Vol. 32, No. 1 (1999), pp. 39–44. For more on Laudan's theory, see Laudan, *Progress and Its Problems*; Ernan McMullin, "Laudan's *Progress and its Problems*," *Philosophy of Science*, Vol. 46, No. 4 (December 1979), pp. 623–644; Paul K. Feyerabend, "More Clothes From the Emperor's Bargain Basement," *The British Journal for the Philosophy of Science*, Vol. 32 (1981), pp. 57–71; and Donovan, Laudan, and Laudan, *Scrutinizing Science*.

136. See Mayo, *Error and the Growth of Experimental Knowledge*.

Part I

Applying Lakatos:

*Judging Theoretical and Empirical Progress
in IR Theory*

Chapter 3

Institutional Theory as a Research Program

Robert O. Keohane and Lisa L. Martin

A generation ago, Imre Lakatos expounded a theory of scientific progress in the natural sciences.[1] Whether he meant his theory to apply to social science or not, it has proved to be a fruitful point of reference for students of international relations seeking to evaluate their own research programs and compare them with rival programs. Yet the Arizona conference, where papers for this volume were discussed, showed that Lakatos does not provide a clear operational framework for the analysis of research programs. As David Dessler convincingly argued, the "hard core" of Lakatos's research program cannot be defined, and we do not know what counts as a "novel fact." It is therefore relatively easy for research programs to avoid being labeled as degenerative. As Dessler also suggested, however, we can tell our stories in Lakatosian terms. Although Lakatos's criteria are ambiguous and his own formulations often contradictory, thinking about whether research programs are "progressive" remains, in our view, a useful way to help us evaluate their relative merits.

It is in this spirit that we engage in the current project. We are not scholars of the philosophy of science, and we are not particularly interested in arcane debates about what Lakatos "really meant" or what he "should have said." However, we find that his criteria for

The authors are grateful for comment on an earlier draft by Colin Elman, Miriam Fendius Elman, Robert Jervis, and John Duffield, and for discussions at the Arizona conference, which led to substantial revisions in the original paper.

1. Imre Lakatos, "Falsification and the Methodology of Scientific Research Programs," in Imre Lakatos and Alan Musgrave, eds., *Criticism and the Growth of Knowledge* (Cambridge, UK: Cambridge University Press, 1970).

progressiveness provide sensible, if not unambiguous, criteria for the evaluation of scientific traditions.[2]

For Lakatos, fruitful research programs must discover novel facts. Even if it is impossible to pin down what constitutes novelty, this criterion is crucial for us as social scientists to keep in mind, since so much work in our field merely relabels old observations with new terms. It may be difficult to ascertain, in international relations, whether a given fact generated by a theory is "novel," but it is easy to identify lots of facts generated by theory that are as old and worn as crumbling books. Like the Philistine in the modern art museum, we know what we do not like—the recycling of geopolitical lore as theory—even though we may have trouble justifying our positive preferences.

At the end of the day, our theories and methods are only as good as the discoveries they help us to make. Generating novel facts requires specifying meaningful propositions that can be tested. For Lakatos, the process of discovering novel facts often occurs through the generation of anomalies. The key test of whether a research program is progressive is how it handles "the ocean of anomalies."[3] It cannot do so by violating its hard core, since this would render the program incoherent. If its practitioners simply try to "patch up" their program with an "arbitrary series of disconnected theories," their research program can properly be regarded as degenerative.[4]

In addition to the hard core, protected by the negative heuristic, research programs, for Lakatos, also contain "positive heuristics," which suggest to scientists what sorts of hypotheses to pursue. In a progressive research program, scientists pursue the positive heuristic of their program in such a way as to resolve anomalies. In the process of

2. Robert O. Keohane, "Theory of World Politics: Structural Realism and Beyond," in Ada Finifter, ed., *Political Science: The State of the Discipline* (Washington, D.C.: APSA 1983), and in Robert O. Keohane, ed., *Neorealism and Its Critics* (New York: Columbia University Press, 1986), p. 161.

3. Lakatos, "Falsification and the Methodology of Scientific Research Programs," p. 135.

4. Ibid., p. 175.

resolving anomalies, progressive research programs are those that discover new facts.

This chapter begins by describing the challenge that institutional theory has since the early 1980s posed to realism, particularly realism as systematized by Kenneth Waltz, and often referred to as "neorealism." We argue that institutional theory adopted almost all of the hard core of realism but that, by treating information as a variable, it was able both to account for extensive cooperation and to show how institutions were linked to such cooperation. The second part of this chapter addresses the challenges to institutional theory posed by realists in the 1980s. The result of these challenges, some of which were more productive than others, was to stimulate efforts at effecting various forms of synthesis between realism and institutionalism. Finally, we take up the most fundamental and difficult challenge posed to institutional theory: the claim that institutions are endogenous to state structure and therefore epiphenomenal. We suggest, using agency theory, that the endogeneity of institutions does not necessarily imply their irrelevance, but that institutional theory needs to deal forthrightly with the endogeneity problem if it is to continue to be progressive.

Institutional Theory as a Partial Challenge to Realism

Institutional theory proceeded roughly as a Lakatosian would suggest. It restated the core of the realist research program; identified and emphasized anomalies facing realism; proposed a new theory to resolve those anomalies; specified a key observational implication of its theory; and sought to test hypotheses based on that theoretical implication, searching for novel facts.

REALISM ACCORDING TO INSTITUTIONALISTS

Institutionalists begin with a restatement of the explicit core assumptions of realism, which can be identified as follows: 1) states are the primary actors in world politics; 2) states behave as if they were rational, in the sense that they assess their strategic situations in light of their environments, and seek to maximize expected gains; 3) states pursue their interests (which prominently include survival), rather than behaving altruistically; 4) states operate in a world of "anarchy," without common government. Different realists claim to hold different assumptions, although the list of four above, including anarchy, is fairly conventional.[5] This list seems consistent with the argument, if not the explicit assumptions, of Kenneth N. Waltz in his classic book, *Theory of International Politics*.[6] Institutional theory fully shares the first three of these assumptions. It also accepts the fourth assumption, that of anarchy, strictly defined as the absence of an external enforcer of agreements. However, institutional theorists are careful to distinguish anarchy in this sense from chaos, and do not accept neorealist assertions that the fact of anarchy has far-reaching negative

---

5. See Joseph Grieco, "The Maastricht Treaty, Economic and Monetary Union, and the Neo-Realist Research Program," *Review of International Studies*, Vol. 21 (January 1995), p. 27. Grieco lists "three assumptions," but one is that actors are "substantively and instrumentally rational," which we interpret as incorporating both assumption 2 and assumption 3, in our formulation. The editors of this volume add the assumption of self-help, which we regard as a derivation from the others, although some have questioned whether this derivation is logically sound.

6. Kenneth N. Waltz, *Theory of International Politics* (Reading, Mass.: Addison-Wesley, 1979). Waltz's systematization of realism is often referred to as "neorealism," but to maintain simplicity of language, we refer throughout to realism, by which we mean the most explicit and systematic variants of that diverse school, in particular those developed by Waltz. Waltz denies that he assumes rationality or anarchy, claiming as he reaffirmed in the Scottsdale conference that he only assumes that "states want to survive." However, this statement contains the assumption that states are key actors, since if they were not actors, they could not "want" anything, even metaphorically, and if they were not key, his theory would presumably focus on the important actors. Furthermore, "want to survive" is a definition of their self-interest, and therefore implies self-interest. As one of us has argued elsewhere, for Waltz's theory to move from desires to actions, the rationality assumption seems essential, since evolutionary selection is not reliable in international relations. Keohane, "Theory of World Politics." It therefore seems evident that Waltz makes the three assumptions that we ascribe both to institutional theory and to realism. Waltz is the scholar who has most popularized the notion of "anarchy," so we regard it as his business, not ours, if he decides that it is not so fundamental after all.

implications for cooperation.[7] Indeed, institutionalists have sought to show that there can be "cooperation under anarchy."[8] From a theoretical standpoint, one of the most striking features of institutional theory, in contrast to the "liberal" international relations theories with which it is often identified, is that it embraces so much of the hard core of realism.

On the basis of such assumptions as the four listed above, Waltz and his followers inferred that states would cooperate little except in response to the prospect of confronting dangerous concentrations of power, or alternatively in response to threat.[9] Institutional theory questions this inference.

IDENTIFYING ANOMALIES IN REALISM

Realism has been confronted with, in Lakatos's phrase, an "ocean of anomalies." Some of these anomalies derive from events that occurred before Waltz's influential 1979 formulation. For instance, Paul Schroeder has pointed out anomalies in Waltz's argument about balancing, and John Vasquez has argued, using standards derived from Lakatos, that "the neotraditional research program on balancing has been degenerating," as a result of ad hoc attempts by realists to respond to such anomalies.[10] Other anomalies have appeared since 1979, either because important regularities seem to have been

---

7. Helen V. Milner, "The Assumption of Anarchy in International Relations Theory: A Critique," *Review of International Studies*, Vol. 17 (January 1991), pp. 67–85; Robert Powell, "Anarchy in International Relations Theory: The Neorealist-Neoliberal Debate," *International Organization*, Vol. 48, No. 2 (Spring 1994), pp. 313–44.

8. Kenneth A. Oye, ed., *Cooperation Under Anarchy* (Princeton: Princeton University Press, 1986).

9. On threat, see Stephen Walt, *The Origins of Alliances* (Ithaca, N.Y.: Cornell University Press, 1987).

10. Paul W. Schroeder, "Historical Reality versus Neorealist Theory," *International Security*, Vol. 19, No. 1 (Summer 1994), pp. 108–48; John Vasquez, "The Realist Paradigm and Degenerative versus Progressive Research Programs: An Appraisal of Neotraditional Research on Waltz's Balancing Proposition," *American Political Science Review*, Vol. 91, No. 4 (December 1997), p. 910.

overlooked earlier, such as that democracies are disinclined to fight one another, or because of new developments such as the fact that non-state actors and issue-networks are becoming more visible and apparently more consequential.[11]

By themselves, these anomalies are not particularly disturbing from a Lakatosian perspective. Research programs confront anomalies and seek to resolve them. From the standpoint of institutional theory, however, one of these anomalies was telling: that international cooperation is extensive and highly institutionalized. Examples include the emergence of a highly rule-oriented trade regime under the General Agreement on Tariffs and Trade (GATT) and then the World Trade Organization (WTO); the significance in managing the global economy of the International Monetary Fund (IMF); the uneven but impressively institutionalized cooperation of the European Union (EU); the invention of a variety of regional and global environmental institutions; and even the robust institutionalization of security cooperation in NATO.[12] To the surprise of realist scholars, such institutionalization has not only continued after the disappearance of the Soviet threat, but has expanded, both in Europe and in the world political economy.[13]

The origins of modern institutional theory can be traced, following a classic Lakatosian pattern, to a disjuncture between established realist theory and the stubborn, persistent fact of extensive, increasing, and highly institutionalized cooperation. Waltz predicted that states would

11. Margaret E. Keck and Kathryn Sikkink, *Activists Beyond Borders: Advocacy Networks in International Politics* (Ithaca, N.Y.: Cornell University Press, 1998).

12. Celeste Wallander and Robert Keohane, "Risk, Threat and Security Institutions," in Helga Haftendorn, Robert O. Keohane, and Celeste A. Wallander, eds., *Imperfect Unions: Security Institutions over Time and Space* (Oxford: Oxford University Press, 1999). Our examples, here and throughout the paper, refer to both formal and informal institutions. Thus both formal organizations and informal sets of rules that make up some regimes or conventions are relevant to institutional theory; we see both as forms of institutions.

13. For one set of realist expectations, see John J. Mearsheimer, "Back to the Future: Instability in Europe after the Cold War," *International Security*, Vol. 15, No. 1 (Summer 1990), pp. 5–56.

be reluctant to engage in forms of cooperation that left them at risk of being taken advantage of by other states. Because security is scarce in international politics, and the environment is highly uncertain, states are forced to behave in a highly risk-averse manner. Thus, realists argued against the likelihood of states engaging in extensive and persistent forms of cooperation. States might cooperate with one another, but only on a short-term, ad hoc basis. Because only these shallow forms of cooperation would arise, there was little need for international institutions in which to structure long-term patterns of cooperation. Realism's predictions about cooperation and institutions were admirably clear: cooperation should be shallow and tenuous, and institutions should be weak and have no observable impact on patterns of cooperation.[14]

The very clarity of Waltz's argument made it difficult to evade the anomaly created by the fact of institutionalized cooperation. Keohane explicitly drew on Lakatosian ideas about research programs to note persistent discrepancies between neorealist predictions and actual state behavior.[15] In particular, he argued that states sometimes engage in deep patterns of cooperation. On issues ranging from economic integration to environmental protection to military alliances, states take steps that put themselves at risk of exploitation in the short term, in exchange for the promise of the longer-term benefits of cooperation. In addition, they have constructed institutions to sustain and enhance these patterns of cooperation. Keohane recognized that these institutions were not "strong," in the sense that many domestic

---

14. Waltz, *Theory of International Politics*. George Downs and David Rocke, *Optimal Imperfection? Domestic Uncertainty and Institutions in International Relations* (Princeton, N.J.: Princeton University Press, 1995), distinguish between deep and shallow forms of cooperation. Deep cooperation involves sunk costs, implying that states can lose if others renege on cooperative arrangements. According to neorealist logic, this risk should strongly inhibit states from engaging in deep cooperation.

15. Robert O. Keohane, "Theory of World Politics: Structural Realism and Beyond," in Ada Finifter, ed., *Political Science: The State of the Discipline* (Washington, D.C.: American Political Science Association, 1983), pp. 503–504; reprinted in Robert O. Keohane, ed., *Neorealism and its Critics* (New York: Columbia University Press, 1986), chap. 7.

institutions are understood to be strong: for example, they had little centralized enforcement power.[16] The puzzle prompted by this observation was: how could institutions facilitate cooperation among states that had conflicts of interest but nevertheless could benefit from cooperation?

INSTITUTIONALIST THEORY

Institutional theory seeks to understand the anomalies facing realist theory by building on, but going beyond, some premises that it has in common with realism. Institutional theory seeks to understand the existence of international institutions, and how they operate. Institutions are defined as "persistent and connected sets of rules (formal and informal) that prescribe behavioral roles, constrain activity, and shape expectations."[17] They can take the form of formal intergovernmental or nongovernmental organizations, international regimes, and informal conventions. Following Douglass North, we conceive of organizations as actors or "players," and institutions as rules that define how the game is played.[18] Regimes are sets of rules and norms that may be formal or informal; conventions are informal understandings.

Early institutional theory sought to show that, even given realist assumptions, international institutions should be seen as significant for the policies followed by states, and thus for the realization of important values in world politics. Such authors as Robert Axelrod and Robert Keohane relied on analysis of mixed-motive games such as the Prisoners' Dilemma to identify factors that would support cooperation, and drew attention to the role of reciprocity and information in allowing states to reach the Pareto frontier of efficient international

16. Below, we note that understandings of domestic institutions have substantially changed in recent years, so that the characterization of them as strong external enforcers of contracts and other agreements is no longer universally accepted.

17. Robert O. Keohane, *International Institutions and State Power* (Boulder, Colo.: Westview, 1989), p. 3.

18. Douglass C. North, *Institutions, Institutional Change and Economic Performance* (New York: Cambridge University Press, 1990), pp. 4–5.

arrangements.[19] These formulations shared the traditional realist conceptualization of states as rational actors pursuing self-interest.

In comparison to the liberal idealism that preceded it, and the constructivism that has followed, institutional theory constituted an incremental modification of realism. Advocates of institutional theory embraced, rather than abandoned, the three core assumptions that it shared with realism; even disagreements over the anarchy assumption were not fundamental to institutional theory. The crucial assumption of realism altered by institutional theory was implicit rather than explicit. Changing this assumption, however, enabled institutional theorists to challenge the validity of the inferences about state behavior that realists had made on the basis of the shared assumptions.

The changed core assumption has to do with the informational environment of international relations. Realism assumes that information about the intentions of other states is pertinent, but of poor quality. States must therefore assume the worst, and thus behave in a defensive, wary manner.[20] More importantly, realists assume that states cannot systematically improve the information conditions in which they operate. This assumption dates back to classical realism, being a major part of the analysis of E.H. Carr, for example.[21] Scarce information, and the inability of states to do anything to improve the situation, force states to adopt worst-case scenarios when choosing their strategies.

---

19. Robert Axelrod, *The Evolution of Cooperation* (New York: Basic Books, 1984); Robert O. Keohane, *After Hegemony: Cooperation and Discord in the World Political Economy* (Princeton, N.J.: Princeton University Press, 1984)

20. Mearsheimer, "Back to the Future"; Waltz, *Theory of International Politics*. Charles Glaser, "Realists as Optimists: Cooperation as Self-Help," *International Security*, Vol. 19, No. 3 (Winter 1994), pp. 50–90, has most directly examined this precept of realism, suggesting that under some conditions information is in fact not scarce, and that states can utilize signaling strategies to inform others of their intentions. He asserts that changing this assumption about information is consistent with realism.

21. Edward Hallett Carr, *The Twenty Years' Crisis, 1919–1939* (New York: Harper & Row, 1939).

info. as
variable

Institutional theory, in contrast, explicitly treats information as a variable. Most important, it treats information as a variable that can be influenced by human action. Institutional theory agrees with realism that scarcity of information will impede the efforts of states to engage in cooperative activities with one another. However, since institutional theory assumes that information can be changed by human agency, it argues that states will take steps to improve the informational environment under these conditions, especially if scarcity of information is impeding the attainment of substantial mutual gains from cooperation. Institutional theory has focused on the role of institutions in improving the informational environment. They can do so in numerous ways, such as by providing information about the intentions and activities of others, by setting standards and identifying focal points, or by providing reliable causal information about the relationship between actions and outcomes. Institutional theory points out that states may be as concerned with providing information about themselves—hence bolstering their credibility and therefore the value of their commitments—as they are with acquiring information about others. States therefore construct institutions to improve both their information about others and their own credibility, to ameliorate the dilemmas and defensive stances otherwise dictated by realism's hard core assumptions.

The shift from realism to institutional theory can be classified, in Lakatos's terms, either as an inter-program problemshift or an intra-program problemshift, depending on whether one views as central the assumption implicit in traditional realist theory that the information content of the system is a constant. We leave that debate to others; in view of the ambiguity of Lakatosian theory and of the scope for argument over realist-institutionalist differences, it is not very important to us to debate whether institutional theory began as a separate research program or merely an attempt to construct what one of the present authors once called "modified structural realism."[22] As we have emphasized, there is much in common between realism and institutional theory, particularly in its early years. Indeed, the closeness

---

22. Keohane, "Theory of World Politics."

of the links between institutional theory and realism is indicated by the fact that institutional theory at the outset adopted realism's unitary actor assumption—although this decision was admittedly taken more for analytical convenience and rhetorical effect than out of deep conviction. It was a tactical decision, later reversed, rather than part of institutional theory's hard core.[23] As we argue below, this adoption of the unitary actor assumption had costs. Whether wise or not, it shows that, for better or worse, institutional theory is a half-sibling of realism. Perhaps their closeness helps to explain the intensity of the disputes that have arisen between them.

SPECIFYING OBSERVABLE IMPLICATIONS

Institutional theory's core assumption, that variations in information could result from human agency, generated an observational implication of its theory: states should devise strategies to construct international institutions that could provide information and reinforce credibility. The positive heuristic of the institutionalist research program, consisting of a "partially articulated set of suggestions or hints," in Lakatos's words, on how to change and develop the refutable aspects of the research program, was aimed at analyzing both institutional growth and state strategies to institute and maintain institutions.[24]

The logic of mixed-motive games combined with the scarcity of information led to specification of a heuristically novel fact: international institutions should engage more heavily in monitoring and information-sharing than in enforcement. In order for reciprocity to work efficiently to sustain cooperation, states required reliable information about other states' preferences and actions. Yet such information was hard to come by in international politics. The key original insight of institutional theory was that institutions could, through monitoring, provide such information. In particular, they

---

23. Keohane and Nye discussed "the limits of systemic explanations" in Robert O. Keohane and Joseph S. Nye, *Power and Interdependence: World Politics in Transition* (Boston: Little, Brown, 1977), pp. 132–137 in the third edition (2001).

24. Lakatos, "Falsification and the Methodology of Scientific Research Programs," p. 135.

could provide information about whether states were living up to their commitments. With this information timely in hand, states could devise strategies of decentralized enforcement that would allow cooperation to emerge as an equilibrium in a repeated game. The key proposition of institutional theory, therefore, was that international institutions should have substantial monitoring and information-sharing authority, while providing for decentralized enforcement by member states themselves.

OBSERVATION: CORROBORATING THE "NOVEL FACT"

Armed with their new theory, institutionalists explored a variety of issue-areas, observing what international institutions did. Investigating economic issues, such as those of the GATT and WTO, environmental regimes,[25] and security institutions,[26] they found ample support for the argument that institutions were significant participants in political processes, and that they provided information as the theory anticipated.

It is important to recognize, however, that the initial tests of institutionalist theory were weak and often methodologically flawed. Institutional researchers have tended to look for confirming evidence that institutions facilitated cooperation in the manner specified in the theory, rather than seeking to refute their theory. Understandably, they wanted to establish an "existence proof" for institutionalized cooperation, and to show how it happened by tracing causal mechanisms. Unfortunately, the result was selection bias in the empirical work on institutional theory, as researchers focused on those cases where it was easiest to make the claim that "institutions mattered." Because the incidence of institutions is not random—states create institutions when they expect them to be useful—looking for

---

25. Peter M. Haas, Robert O. Keohane, and Marc A. Levy, eds., *Institutions for the Earth: Sources of Effective International Environmental Protection* (Cambridge, Mass.: MIT Press, 1993); Ronald Mitchell, *Intentional Oil Pollution at Sea: Environmental Pollution and Treaty Compliance* (Cambridge, Mass.: MIT Press, 1994).

26. Haftendorn, Keohane, and Wallander, *Imperfect Unions*.

patterned variation in the relation between institutions and cooperation suffers from inferential problems.[27]

More generally, institutional researchers confront the problem of endogeneity, always a methodological challenge in a non-experimental science whose observations are not independent of one another. In principle, the investigator would like to discover how significant institutions are, controlling for structure. But it is hard to find enough comparable cases, across which institutional form varies but structure does not, to carry out standard statistical techniques.[28] The experimental alternative is also not available, unless one were to construct a simulation, which has its own validity problems.[29] Only with a very sophisticated simulation could one model the counterfactual world (without institutions) and the actual world (with them) with repeated runs to ascertain what differences the institutions make.

Hence institutional researchers have generally relied on hypothetical counterfactual analysis: imagining what patterns of cooperation and discord would have existed in the absence of institutions, or conversely, what impact a given set of hypothetical institutions might have had. But such imagined counterfactuals can always be challenged, and do not lend themselves to empirical testing.

Another methodological difficulty in the existing institutionalist literature concerns inferences from observed outcomes about non-observable explanatory variables. This is a problem of endogeneity produced not by the real world but by faulty methods. For institutionalists, the growth of institutions is "explained" by the common interests of states in achieving joint gains through institutions. However, where institutions fail to become stronger, this can easily be taken, not as refutation of the theory, but as evidence of the strength of

---

27. See Lisa L. Martin, *Coercive Cooperation: Explaining Multilateral Economic Sanctions* (Princeton, N.J.: Princeton University Press, 1992), for an attempt to identify such variation.

28. For an outstanding attempt to do so, see Page Fortna, "A Peace that Lasts," Ph.D. dissertation (1998), Harvard University, Cambridge, Mass.

29. But see Lars-Erik Cederman, *Emergent Actors in World Politics: How States and Nations Develop and Dissolve* (Princeton, N.J.: Princeton University Press, 1997), for an interesting attempt to begin such modeling.

adverse interests. The key methodological problem here derives from the fact that interests are not directly observed. If interests are inferred from the value of the dependent variable—institutional growth—the test becomes meaningless. A real test of the theory requires *ex ante* rather than *ex post* specification of interests.

Both of these problems can be addressed by more rigorous tests: specifying interests *ex ante*, avoiding selection bias (preferably investigating many cases of a coherent class of events), and investigating difficult as well as easy cases, in an attempt to refute the theory rather than merely to confirm it. There is much room for improvement in the methods used to test institutional theory, but the direction in which these methods should be taken seems clear.[30]

Institutional theory, however, has a methodological strength that derives directly from the endogeneity of institutions to structures. Unless we explicitly consider the intervening role of endogenous institutions, we may be led into false inferences about the relation between structural variables and outcomes. For example, increased intensity of cooperation dilemmas may lead to the creation of stronger institutions and therefore more intense cooperation. If we only considered structural variables and outcomes, we would see an apparently perverse correlation: tougher cooperation problems would be associated with higher (or at least stable) levels of cooperation. We need to consider the role of institutions in order to make sense of observed patterns of behavior.[31]

---

30. For a discussion of methods, many of which are appropriate to the evaluation of institutional theory, see Gary King, Robert O. Keohane, and Sidney Verba, *Designing Social Inquiry: Scientific Inference in Qualitative Research* (Princeton, N.J.: Princeton University Press, 1994). On counterfactuals, see Philip E. Tetlock and Aaron Belkin, eds., *Counterfactual Thought Experiments in World Politics: Logical, Methodological and Psychological Perspectives* (Princeton, N.J.: Princeton University Press, 1996).

31. Recent work by Page Fortna on the effects of peace agreements does an impressive job of examining such effects. She finds that severe conflict between the parties, accompanied by expectations of continued animosities, often leads to more highly institutionalized agreements. Thus the correlation between institutionalization of peace agreements and the duration of subsequent peace

Challenges to Institutional Theory

Until the 1990s, realists had two major responses to the challenge of institutionalist theory, which we characterize as "minimization" and "denial." Often these criticisms were made by the same scholars. During the 1990s, the modal response, from self-described realists and others, has shifted toward synthesis: putting forward interpretations of events that are fundamentally consistent with institutionalist theory, while sometimes giving them different emphases, or different labels. The responses of the 1980s led to what we characterize as short-term challenges that are easily parried by institutional theory. The more synthetic arguments of the 1990s are, in our view, more important and more illuminating.

CHALLENGE AND RESPONSE

Realists in the 1980s sometimes recognized the existence of cooperation in world politics, but minimized its significance, emphasizing that it takes place within the context of power realities that fundamentally shape and limit it. In replying to Robert Keohane's criticisms in 1986, Kenneth Waltz crisply stated this view:

Some states sometimes want to work together to secure the benefits of cooperation. Cooperative projects in the present may lead to more cooperation in the future. But self-help systems do make the cooperation of parties difficult. As Gilpin puts it, "the traditional insights of realism ... help us to explain ... the ongoing retreat from an interdependent world."[32]

Joanne Gowa and Stephen Krasner made similar arguments, recognizing the insights of institutional theory but arguing that it failed to account adequately for the role of power. Gowa praised Robert Axelrod's book, *The Evolution of Cooperation*, for its insights into "the

---

may be negative, even if institutionalization itself has had positive effects. Fortna, "A Peace that Lasts."

32. Kenneth N. Waltz, "Reflections on *Theory of International Politics*: A Response to My Critics," in Keohane, *Neorealism and Its Critics*, p. 336; citing Robert G. Gilpin, "The Richness of the Tradition of Political Realism," in Keohane, *Neorealism and Its Critics*, pp. 301–321.

rationality of cooperation for mutual gain in the long run," but viewed his analysis as "more narrowly bounded than is apparent at first glance."[33] Krasner criticized the argument offered by Keohane in *After Hegemony* for de-emphasizing the role of power even while nominally recognizing its importance:

Neoliberal speculations about the positive consequences of greater information are fascinating.... But they obscure considerations of relative power capabilities, which draw attention to ... ultimately who wins and who loses.[34]

In effect, the minimization critique claimed that the insights of institutional theory could be accommodated within a somewhat broadened version of realism: that institutional theory did not violate realism's hard core. At the Scottsdale conference, this also seemed to be Kenneth Waltz's position. More critical realist arguments attacked key assumptions of institutionalist theory. In 1986, Gowa quoted Waltz as arguing that insecure states, facing the possibility of cooperation for mutual gain, "must ask how the gain will be divided. They are compelled to ask not 'Will both of us gain?' but 'Who will gain more?'"[35] Joseph Grieco pushed this point further.[36] He noted that any cooperative arrangement would give rise to joint gains that could be divided in a multitude of ways among the cooperating parties. Division of these gains would be a matter of intense concern. In any setting, bargaining about the distribution of gains in order to increase

---

33. Joanne Gowa, "Anarchy, Egoism and Third Images: *The Evolution of Cooperation* and International Relations," *International Organization*, Vol. 40, No. 1 (Winter 1986), p. 185; Axelrod, *The Evolution of Cooperation*.

34. Stephen D. Krasner, "Global Communications and National Power: Life on the Pareto Frontier," *World Politics*, Vol. 43, No. 3 (April 1991), p. 366.

35. Gowa, "Anarchy, Egoism and Third Images," p. 177; quoting Waltz, *Theory of International Politics*, p. 105.

36. Joseph Grieco, "Anarchy and the Limits of Cooperation: A Realist Critique of the Newest Liberal Institutionalism," *International Organization*, Vol. 42, No. 3 (Summer 1988), pp. 485–507.

one's absolute gain was to be expected.[37] But in the international arena, the dilemma went even deeper. Because inequalities in the distribution of gains could be transformed into increased inequality in power resources, and because the use of military force was always a possibility in international relations, the deniers argued that states would never engage in cooperation that increased their absolute gains if it meant a relative loss.[38] Once again, the extremely risk-averse nature of states assumed by realism led to a prediction that cooperation would be shallow and infrequent. However, the causal logic that limited cooperation was now specified to be concern for relative gains and losses that could be transformed into a disadvantage during a military confrontation.[39]

In 1991, Robert Powell showed that concerns about relative advantages can be stated in standard absolute-gains terms. There is no need to include a separate term for relative gains that violates the core presumptions of rational-choice approaches. Powell showed that the importance of relative gains was conditional on the system creating "opportunities for one state to turn relative gains to its advantage and to the disadvantage of the other state," particularly through the use or threat of force.[40] The critics who had raised the issue of relative gains

---

37. Jack Knight, *Institutions and Social Conflict* (New York: Cambridge University Press, 1992).

38. Grieco, "Anarchy and the Limits of Cooperation," p. 499.

39. See John J. Mearsheimer, "The False Promise of International Institutions," *International Security*, Vol. 19, No. 3 (Winter 1994/95), pp. 5–49.

40. Robert Powell, "Absolute and Relative Gains in International Relations Theory," *American Political Science Review*, Vol. 85, No. 4 (December 1991), pp. 1303–20, reprinted in David Baldwin, ed., *Neorealism and Neoliberalism: The Contemporary Debate* (New York: Columbia University Press, 1993), p. 1315. It has become very clear over the last decade that it would be a mistake to characterize security issues as necessarily more conflictual than economic ones. Empirically, security relationships between the United States and Japan, or the United States and Germany, have often been less conflictual than their economic relations. Based on institutional theory, we should expect more conflict in economic areas characterized by oligopolistic competition and first-mover advantages than in economic areas characterized by fragmented

were correct that such competition could impede cooperation, but they had overgeneralized their argument. After Powell's clarification, the key question became the empirical one of identifying conditions under which one party could use asymmetrical gains to change the structure of the game to the disadvantage of its partner. Later work by George Downs and his colleagues pointed out that concerns about noncompliance could render cooperation shallow, relative to what would have been optimal in the absence of such concerns.[41]

While the relative-gains debate gave rise to much unproductive argument and research, it did lead to some clarification and development of institutional theory. Although institutional theory depends on common interests, it had never assumed that these interests must be equal or symmetrical.[42] The relative gains debate forced institutional theorists to recognize explicitly that substantially unequal distribution of the benefits of cooperation could provide one partner with the wherewithal to fundamentally change the nature of the game, for example by starting a war. Insofar as this possibility exists, a model such as iterated Prisoner's Dilemma could be faulty. The probability that one partner could fundamentally reshape the nature of the situation must be incorporated into each state's utility function. However, as institutional theory emphasized, the probability that unequal gains would lead to a fundamental restructuring of the game varies; it is often low. Whether actors weigh others' gains positively or negatively is also a variable. Hence the extent to which concerns about others' gains might undermine cooperation must therefore also be treated as a variable—precisely as institutional theory had always prescribed.[43] Institutional theory also responded by noting that an important function of international institutions might be to mitigate relative-gains concerns by assuring a fairly equitable

markets, and we should expect more conflict between potential adversaries than in security communities.

41. George W. Downs, David M. Rocke and Peter N. Barsoom, "Is the Good News about Compliance Good News about Cooperation?" International Organization, Vol. 50, No. 3 (Summer 1996), pp. 379–406.

42. Keohane and Nye, *Power and Interdependence*.

43. Keohane, *After Hegemony*, p. 123.

distribution of the gains from cooperation, particularly where a highly asymmetrical distribution of gains could undermine support for existing institutions by changing the structure of the game. Thus, in spite of some dead ends and fruitless debates, the relative-gains conceptual challenge strengthened institutional theory. In Lakatosian terms, this strengthening occurred because institutional theory was able to respond effectively to the relative gains challenge without altering its hard core.[44]

Some realists also presented an empirical challenge to institutional theory, based on predictions about the future of international institutions in Europe after the Cold War. John Mearsheimer quickly and boldly used Waltz's neorealist theory and Grieco's argument about relative gains to predict increased conflict and even war in Europe.[45] Mearsheimer's logic emphasized that states' concern with security in an anarchic world compelled them to put little confidence in international institutions. Post–World War II institutions rested on the power realities of the Cold War: U.S. dominance of a Western alliance confronting a hostile Soviet bloc. Once these power realities were transformed with the end of the Cold War, intense patterns of conflict among European states would resume, he argued, increasing the chances of major crisis and war in Europe. NATO and the European Community would both be victims of these changes: "It is the Soviet threat that provides the glue that holds NATO together. Take away that offensive threat and the United States is likely to abandon the Continent, whereupon the defensive alliance it has headed for forty years may disintegrate."[46] With the departure of American forces, "relations among the EC [European Community] states will be fundamentally altered. Without a common Soviet threat and without the American night watchman, Western European states will begin viewing each other with greater fear and suspicion."[47]

---

44. The convergence that resulted from this debate supports the call of this volume's editors for tolerance as well as tenacity.

45. Mearsheimer, "Back to the Future."

46. Ibid., p. 52.

47. Ibid., p. 47.

Empirical evidence in the subsequent period did not support Mearsheimer's predictions. The EU has become wider and deeper, and is in most respects stronger than ever, despite struggles associated with the inauguration of European Monetary Union (EMU) and with the "democratic deficit" implied by the weakness of the European Parliament compared to the Council of Ministers and the European Commission. Since international cooperation always arises from discord—and is never harmonious—institutionalists are not distracted by bargaining conflict, but focus on the institutional deepening of the EU during the 1990s.[48] The EMU itself transforms traditional state sovereignty and is entirely inconsistent with the realist vision of a collapsing European Union. NATO, while it experienced wrenching debates and a genuine crisis over intervention in the former Yugoslavia, played a decisive role in bringing the Bosnian war to an end in 1995.[49] In seeking to protect Albanian Kosovars, it extended its scope to offensive warfare, taking on new responsibilities and engaging in a high-risk transformation. Whether NATO's actions were wise or not, this institution is certainly a force to be reckoned with.

Thus, institutional theory has responded effectively to realism, with responses that are theoretically and empirically productive. Its response to the relative gains attack has led to an increased focus on distributional impediments to cooperation, without requiring any changes in the hard core of institutional theory. The response to the empirical challenge did not require even modest changes in the focus of institutional theory. Instead, institutional theory's long-standing claim that established institutions should become especially valuable in the face of increased uncertainty has been borne out by events in Europe. The membership and operating procedures of European institutions have undergone important changes that allow them to respond more effectively to the new realities of European politics. These changes have taken place within the context of well-established, long-lived institutions, which have proven their worth in enhancing

48. See Andrew Moravcsik, *The Choice for Europe* (Ithaca, N.Y.: Cornell University Press, 1998).

49. Richard Holbrooke, *To End a War* (New York: Random House, 1998).

security and providing economic assurances in an increasingly uncertain environment. Thus, by the early 1990s, institutional theory had established itself as a respected "generic approach" to issues of international cooperation.[50] Its key insights about the functioning of international institutions concerned their role in providing information and their reliance on reciprocity as the mechanism for sustaining cooperation.

ATTEMPTS AT SYNTHESIS

In the early 1990s, realism was unable to deny the reality of institutionalized cooperation, but had no theory to explain it. According to an old saying, "you can't beat something with nothing." On the whole, the prevailing response of realists, as represented for instance in the work of Stephen Krasner, has been increasingly to embrace institutionalist arguments while continuing to insist that distributional conflict and power should be emphasized. But there has been at least one valiant attempt, by Joseph Grieco, to construct a distinctively "realist theory" of cooperation.[51] Some of the most compelling critiques of institutional theory have come not from realism but from students of domestic politics, who have challenged the shared states-as-actors assumption of realism and institutional theory, and suggested the need for synthesis of a different sort.

DISTRIBUTIONAL CONFLICT AND INSTITUTIONAL THEORY. As we have seen, Krasner criticized institutional theory for emphasizing attempts to reach the Pareto frontier, at the expense of analyzing distributional conflict along that frontier.[52] James Fearon has more recently argued that problems of distributional bargaining may prevent the formation of agreements, especially if the "shadow of the future" is long: if

---

50. Peter J. Katzenstein, Robert O. Keohane, and Stephen D. Krasner, "*International Organization* and the Study of World Politics," *International Organization,* Vol. 52, No. 4 (Autumn 1998), pp. 645–685.

51. Grieco, "Anarchy and the Limits of Cooperation."

52. Krasner, "Global Communications and National Power."

remote gains and losses loom large.[53] These are important points with which institutional theory must contend.

It is important to note, however, that institutional theory never denied the reality of distributional bargaining. Indeed, in *After Hegemony*, Keohane defined cooperation as mutual adjustment of interests, hence inherently conflictual: "cooperation is typically mixed with conflict and reflects partially successful efforts to overcome conflict, real or potential."[54] The original purpose of institutional theory was to show how, despite the fragmented political structure of international relations, and the pervasiveness of conflicts of interest and discord, cooperation can nevertheless, under some conditions, occur. However, the conflict of interests emphasized by institutional theory was conflict based on the fear that others would renege on cooperative arrangements, rather than conflict over how to distribute the benefits of cooperation. Fear of reneging exists even among identical players; all are properly fearful of receiving the "sucker's payoff." The problem of distributing the benefits of cooperation, in contrast, is more pronounced when the interests of states are asymmetrical, for example when powerful states interact with weaker ones. In this instance, states will have strongly diverging preferences over the form of cooperation, creating a type of conflict of interest that was originally neglected by institutionalist theory. Over time, empirical and theoretical work has shown the importance of such asymmetries.

Institutional theory's treatment of distributional conflict sheds light on its relationship to classic liberalism, as well as to realism. Often institutional theory is viewed as "liberal international relations theory," and liberalism is thought of as an optimistic creed that stresses harmony over conflict. Either of these propositions could be correct, but not both.

There is a form of liberalism—associated with writers such as James Madison, Adam Smith, and Immanuel Kant—that is individualistic

---

53. James D. Fearon, "Bargaining, Enforcement, and International Cooperation," *International Organization*, Vol. 52, No. 2 (Spring 1998), pp. 269–305.

54. Keohane, *After Hegemony*, p. 54.

and rationalistic without being optimistic about human nature or believing in harmony. Madison famously declared government to be "the greatest of all reflections on human nature."[55] Kant wrote of "the evil nature of man."[56] Smith counseled his readers that it is vain to expect help from the "benevolence" of others in society.[57] Anyone who regards these liberals as idealistic utopians has not read their work. All of these writers believed that some individuals are public-spirited, but that, as Madison said, "enlightened statesmen will not always be at the helm."[58] Institutional theory certainly falls within this tradition. It regards people as occasionally empathetic and public-spirited, but builds its theory on the assumption that, in general, while they are rational, they lack general benevolence, altruism, or idealism. Institutional theory has little in common with the optimistic liberal creed caricatured by E.H. Carr or Kenneth Waltz.[59] On the contrary, institutional theory assumes that cooperation derives from conflicts of objectives that are inherent in social life. "Harmony is apolitical.... Cooperation, by contrast, is highly political."[60]

Institutional theory recognizes distributional conflicts but, unlike realism, is not obsessed with them. It has been fairly criticized for not integrating distributional politics into its analysis: for taking such conflict for granted rather than developing theories about it. Issues of distribution were recognized as important, but remained outside of the theory that generated hypotheses about institutions, which relied on the desire of participants to capture potential joint gains more than on their struggle to capture larger shares of the reward. To develop progressively, institutional theory must do a better job of integrating

---

55. James Madison, *The Federalist*, No. 51, originally published 1787–88.

56. Immanuel Kant, *Eternal Peace* (1795), in Carl J. Friedrich, ed., *The Philosophy of Kant* (New York: Modern Library, 1949), p. 442.

57. Adam Smith, *The Wealth of Nations* (1776) (Chicago: University of Chicago Press, 1976), p. 18.

58. Madison, *The Federalist*, No. 10.

59. Carr, *The Twenty Years' Crisis, 1919–1939*; Kenneth N. Waltz, *Man, the State and War* (New York: Columbia University Press, 1959).

60. Keohane, *After Hegemony*, p. 53.

distributional struggles "along the Pareto frontier" with efforts to move that frontier outward.

A REALIST THEORY OF "BINDING." In 1995, Joseph Grieco forthrightly confronted the anomalies facing realism, a theoretical framework to which he was committed.[61] Explicitly employing a Lakatosian framework, Grieco recognized that plans for European Monetary Union (EMU) were anomalous for realism:

The decision by the EC countries to pursue the Maastricht path toward EMU conflicts with neo-realism's auxiliary hypothesis that states do not ascribe importance to institutions. It also conflicts with the neo-realist hypothesis that EC efforts at cooperation have been dependent upon U.S.-Soviet bipolarity.[62]

Grieco deserves great credit for identifying the anomaly that EMU posed for realism, and for trying to deal with it.

Grieco's approach was to identify what he regarded as "auxiliary hypotheses" of realism about international institutions, and to propose their modification:

One is that states find it hard (but not impossible) to work together because of fears about cheating, dependency, and relative gains. Another is that international institutions are unable to dampen these state fears substantially, and therefore states do not ascribe much importance to them.[63]

Grieco's response was a "voice opportunities" thesis, which emphasized the desire of weaker states, under conditions of interdependence, to have a voice in decisions. This thesis "assumes that states favor institutionalized ties with a stronger partner as a way of allowing them to work for mutual gain and to avoid becoming a vassal of the partner."[64] In other words, weak states will use institutions to

61. Grieco, "The Maastricht Treaty, Economic and Monetary Union, and the Neo-Realist Research Program."

62. Ibid., p. 32.

63. Ibid., p. 27.

64. Ibid., p. 34.

bind stronger states. In his article, Grieco briefly applied this theory, which he described as "derived from core realist assumptions," to the negotiations over EMU at Maastricht.

Grieco's honesty is commendable, but the irony of his analysis is equally notable. His "voice opportunities" thesis is institutionalist in all essentials. It incorporates the institutionalist stress on self-interest and mutual gain, and jettisons his earlier argument, which he attributed to realism, that "the fundamental goal of states in any relationship is to prevent others from achieving advances in their relative capabilities."[65] The voice opportunities thesis is no more closely linked to core realist assumptions than is institutionalism: in fact, both arguments share the three key assumptions of realism stated above. To adherents of a research program, there is no support more welcome than that of former adversaries.[66]

INSTITUTIONAL THEORY AND DOMESTIC POLITICS. The most telling recent criticisms of institutional theory have attacked its weakest link: the unitary actor assumption, borrowed from realism. Institutional theory has all the limitations of any research program that takes actors and preferences as given. Scholars such as Andrew Moravcsik and Helen Milner have emphasized that the unitary actor assumption "leads to a neglect of the differences in internal preferences and political institutions within states."[67] Such an assumption also makes it difficult to think about how state institutions, such as legislative arrangements for monitoring international agreements, can be endogenous to patterns of delegation to international institutions. For

---

65. Grieco, "Anarchy and the Limits of Cooperation: A Realist Critique of the Newest Liberal Institutionalism," p. 498.

66. We also found it gratifying that Stephen Krasner emerged as a forceful, eloquent defender of institutionalist theory at the Scottsdale conference, especially emphasizing recent arguments to the effect that institutions may provide critical credibility for states.

67. Helen V. Milner, "Rationalizing Politics: The Emerging Synthesis in International, American and Comparative Politics," *International Organization*, Vol. 52, No. 4 (Autumn 1998), p. 772. See also Andrew Moravcsik, "A Liberal Theory of International Politics," *International Organization*, Vol. 51, No. 4 (Autumn 1997), pp. 513–553.

example, variation in implementation of EU directives by states can be explained well only by taking into account variation in legislative arrangements, which are partly endogenous to the overall patterns of EU delegation.[68]

Institutional theory does help us explain state strategies, since those strategies are affected not only by fundamental preferences but by the constraints and opportunities in their environment, including those provided by international institutions. But institutional theory does not account for more fundamental preferences over outcomes: for instance, for compromising with neighbors who have different values and habits from one's own, or seeking instead to annihilate them or evict them from their homes.

For international relations theory to make really significant progress, it will need to go beyond institutional theory's analysis of institutional strategies to explain variations in state preferences. One way of doing so would be to develop theories with microfoundations: that is, theories that begin with individuals and groups and show how, on the basis of a coherent set of theoretical assumptions, varying preferences emerge.[69] Such theories would build on modern work on domestic institutions. Another approach would be to demonstrate how variations in the social construction of reality, as a result of ideas and identity, account for variations in preferences.[70]

In this broader understanding of international relations, institutional theory—and realism itself—will be important, since one needs an instrumental theory to get from preferences to policies. But they will not be sufficient, since preferences vary in important ways. Constructivists and liberals emphasizing domestic politics seek to "explicate variations in preferences, available strategies, and the nature

---

68. Lisa L. Martin, *Democratic Commitments: Legislatures and International Cooperation* (Princeton, N.J.: Princeton University Press, 1999).

69. Moravcsik, "A Liberal Theory of International Politics"; Lisa L. Martin and Beth Simmons, "Theories and Empirical Studies of International Institutions," *International Organization*, Vol. 52, No. 4 (Autumn 1998); Milner, "Rationalizing Politics"; Martin, *Democratic Commitments*.

70. Alexander E. Wendt, *Social Theory of International Politics* (Cambridge, UK: Cambridge University Press, 1999).

of the players, across space and time," while rationalists try "to explain strategies, given preferences, information, and common knowledge. Neither project can be complete without the other."[71]

The Endogeneity Trap and the Delegation Escape

We have argued that institutional theory was able to turn the relative-gains challenge by realists into a confirmation rather than a refutation of institutional theory. Evidence of hard bargaining and disputes over the distribution of gains is in fact consistent with the conventional utilitarianism accepted by institutional theory, and does not require the additional (and confusing) assumption of concern for relative gains. Indeed, some of the observed activities of international institutions could be interpreted as designed to respond to the danger that asymmetrical bargaining outcomes could undermine states' support for institutions. Furthermore, the empirical predictions that Mearsheimer made in 1990, on the basis of his interpretation of neorealist theory, turned out to be much less consistent with emerging reality than were institutionalist expectations.

However, Mearsheimer raised a deeper theoretical and methodological challenge, although it was largely implicit in his argument. International institutions, he argued, "have minimal influence on state behavior," partly because "the most powerful states create and shape institutions."[72] State security interests, not institutions, account for the cooperation observed during the Cold War; hence, in Mearsheimer's view, international institutions are epiphenomenal.

Mearsheimer's logic drew directly on Waltz's theory and Grieco's application of it, emphasizing the weak nature of international institutions and the need for states to be obsessed with short-term security demands, hence with relative gains. Although he did not use this language, Mearsheimer suggested that international institutions are endogenous to state power and interests. The underlying claim was

---

71. Katzenstein, Keohane, and Krasner, "*International Organization* and the Study of World Politics," p. 682.

72. Mearsheimer, "The False Promise of International Institutions," pp. 7, 13.

that international institutions are endogenous to international structure.

This charge is difficult for institutionalists to disprove, since it closely parallels the claims of institutionalist theory, and indeed may seem to follow directly from institutional theory's "hard core." Recall the five key assumptions of institutional theory, the first four of which are identical with neorealist assumptions: 1) states are the primary actors in world politics; 2) states behave as if they were rational utility-maximizers; 3) states pursue their interests (especially survival) rather than behaving altruistically; 4) no external enforcer of agreements exists; and 5) because they operate in an information-scarce environment, states have incentives to increase both their information about other states' actions, and their own credibility. These assumptions generate a "functional theory of international regimes": that these rational actors will devise institutions that meet their informational demands.[73] But at the limit, this functional theory of international institutions implies complete endogeneity: the theory is strongest when institutions are entirely explained by state interests and strategies.

This endogeneity, which constitutes such a strength from the standpoint of explaining institutions, seems to turn into a weakness in claiming that institutions have significant effects. Insofar as the theory of institutional origins and functions is accepted, the independent explanatory power of institutional theory seems to disappear. The structural factors accounting for institutions also seem to account for outcomes—which should therefore be seen not as effects of the institutions, but of these more fundamental factors.

Institutional theory has not yet responded very well to this fundamental challenge, and needs somehow to confront it in order to continue in a progressive direction. We suggest in this chapter a problemshift designed to resolve this problem, although we do not pursue this argument in detail. The problemshift that we propose makes agency theory central to international institutionalist theory, reconceptualizing the relationship between states and international

---

73. Keohane, *After Hegemony*, chap. 6.

institutions as one of delegation. We think that theories of agency, or delegation, may help provide an answer to the endogeneity conundrum. These theories allow us to take the endogeneity issue seriously, while integrating it in a productive manner into the research program. We characterize such a problemshift as "intra-program," since we retain the hard core of institutionalist theory as specified above.

ENDOGENOUS, YES; BUT EPIPHENOMENAL?

Institutional theory views international organizations as endogenous to state interests and strategies, but this does not mean that their organizational characteristics are irrelevant. Endogenous does not mean epiphenomenal. Thinking about institutions both in terms of organization theory and of agency theory highlights this important point.[74] We focus on organizations rather than on regimes and conventions, since organizations have the capacity to act, and organization theory can be used to analyze how their actions may diverge from the intentions of their founders. Regimes and conventions, being less formal than organizations, cannot rely as heavily on organizational dynamics to explain their persistence.

Three different sets of social science arguments help us to understand how international organizations that are created by, and beholden to, states can still exercise independent influence over events. The first argument concerns the multiple equilibria characteristic of non–zero-sum games; the second draws on organization theory; the third focuses on agency theory. We briefly indicate how each of these arguments may create space for significant action by international organizations.

The existence of multiple equilibria in game-theoretic solutions to virtually all interesting games opens up space for agency: structure, as

---

74. Kenneth Abbott and Duncan Snidal have emphasized the role of international institutions as active organizations, although without using agency theory. Kenneth Abbott and Duncan Snidal, "Why States Use Formal International Organizations," *Journal of Conflict Resolution*, Vol. 42, No. 1 (February 1998), pp. 3–32.

game theory's folk theorem has taught us, is not determining, since rational players can, in equilibrium, pursue quite different strategies.[75] Multiple equilibria are bad for game-theoretic solutions to problems of cooperation, but they are good for institutional theory. If game theory could pinpoint unique equilibria on the basis of structural theory, institutions could be seen simply as these equilibrium solutions.[76] They would not only be endogenous to structure, but epiphenomenal, since structure would be determining. But the existence of multiple equilibria means both that institutional characteristics cannot be predicted reliably from structure and that, once formed, institutions can have a major impact on which equilibria emerge. This impact derives from the tendency of institutions to persist over time, leading to the sort of path-dependence about which Douglass North has written so convincingly.[77] In delegation terms, the implication of multiple equilibria is that states could have an incentive to delegate authority to an agent, if they find a) that they cannot agree on a solution; and b) that the agent will choose a solution that is superior to the status quo for all of them. This is a plausible way to interpret the willingness of states in Europe to agree to the extension of powers of the European Court of Justice.[78]

Organization theory points out that because institutions are costly to construct and change, and because those who design them are often

---

75. The folk theorem shows that in games that are repeated over time, a large number of outcomes can be sustained as equilibria.

76. Randall Calvert, "The Rational Choice Theory of Social Institutions: Cooperation, Coordination, and Communication," in Jeffrey S. Banks and Eric A. Hanushek, eds., *Modern Political Economy: Old Topics, New Directions* (New York: Cambridge University Press, 1995), pp. 216–267.

77. North, *Institutions, Institutional Change and Economic Performance.*

78. Karen J. Alter, "Who are the 'Masters of the Treaty'? European Governments and the European Court of Justice," *International Organization,* Vol. 52, No. 1 (Winter 1998), pp. 177–209; Geoffrey Garrett, R. Daniel Keleman, and Heiner Schulz, "The European Court of Justice, National Governments, and Legal Integration in the European Union," *International Organization,* Vol. 52, No. 1 (Winter 1998), pp. 149–76; Walter Mattli and Anne-Marie Slaughter, "Revisiting the European Court of Justice," *International Organization,* Vol. 52, No. 1 (Winter 1998), pp. 177–209.

risk-averse, we cannot expect institutions to change smoothly in response to changes in structural variables.[79] Like many domestic institutions, international institutions are designed at a particular time to solve a particular problem, but they can then persist and change, in a step-wise fashion rather than smoothly. Sunk costs and risk aversion help to account for the institutional inertia that is often observed. Gaps between the structure and the emerging functions of international institutions may help account for institutional failure. But when institutions remain stable in the face of changes in structural variables, we have an opportunity to observe the independent effect of institutions on state behavior. To take an obvious example, the structure of the United Nations Security Council, with the five victorious allies of World War II or their legal successors holding veto power, reflects the structural reality of 1945, and in some cases the aspirations, but it has had substantial effects on world politics well after that: structural reality has been profoundly altered.

Another aspect of organizational stability is that legally binding actions by international organizations remain valid until they are reversed (unless a time limit has been set). Consider the UN economic sanctions established in 1990 against Iraq. These sanctions remained in place despite widespread loss of support for them after the mid-1990s, as the humanitarian costs to the people of Iraq became obvious and as Saddam Hussein remained unswayed by them. They remained in place because of the so-called "reverse-veto procedure." Since the Security Council voted in favor of sanctions in 1990, the existing status quo throughout the 1990s was a sanctions regime. It would have required an affirmative vote of the Security Council to lift sanctions. Because the Security Council has five members with a permanent veto—most significantly the United States in this instance—one state can effectively maintain sanctions even after they have become unpopular. It would be extremely difficult to understand U.S. policy toward Iraq, or the policies of many other states in the 1990s, without taking into account the specifics of Security Council voting rules. This case also illustrates the stability of institutions. If the UN were created

---

79. Keohane, *After Hegemony*, pp. 100–103.

anew today, it is highly unlikely that veto procedures, or the identity of the states with veto power, would look like the current Security Council procedures. Although the Security Council was certainly created by the great powers to serve their perceived interests, its organizational persistence means that this endogeneity of origins does not imply insignificance of effects.

Agency theory breaks the chain of endogeneity in another way. The initial assumption here is that international organizations are the agents of state interests. The powers and authority that such organizations acquire are the result of delegation of authority from their member states. Hence, the fundamental character of these organizations, when they are founded, can be explained by state interests. However, agency theory also recognizes explicitly that organizations are acting entities with leaders who have institutionally-affected interests of their own—a fact that has often been obscured by the emphasis of institutional theory on structures of rules. Principals often find it useful to endow agents with discretion, and agents typically have superior information, at least about some issues, to that at the disposal of their principals. As a result, there is a potential for "agency slack"—for (admittedly endogenous) international organizations (historically and nominally creatures of states) to act independently, to some significant degree. Hence agency theory agrees with institutional theory's dual assertions: that organizations are endogenous, and that they have effects. Indeed, we think that agency theory can help to show how to transform endogeneity from a liability to an asset for institutional theory.

In institutional theory, as well as in agency theory more generally, agents take actions, which have real effects, within constraints set by their principals, whose support is essential for the agents to exist and to act. In the agency literature, outcomes are brought about jointly by principals and agents. Attention is not directed in agency theory to trying to determine which proportion of the outcomes is caused by each (as if they could be separated), but rather to analyzing the co-determination of outcomes by the rules (constraints and incentives) promulgated by the principals, and by the actions, within those constraints and incentives, taken by the agents. In effect, agency theory focuses on the processes (causal mechanisms) that generate outcomes, and seeks to understand how different conditions, by affecting those processes, affect outcomes. In this theory, endogenous organizations (the agents, coupled with the rules under which they operate) routinely have effects that cannot be reduced to the interests of the principals.

Agency theory thus allows us to direct attention away from the relatively intractable issue of ascertaining the effects of institutions, controlling for structure, toward a different set of questions: what are the conditions that affect the strategically interdependent actions of principals and agents, and therefore the outcomes (in terms of cooperation, institutional characteristics, or other dependent variables) that emerge from an agency relationship?

By turning our attention to theories of agency and delegation, we hope to make three progressive moves in the institutional theory research program. Methodologically, we hope to get around the endogeneity problem, by reframing the question of institutional effects. The issue is not—"what are the effects of institutions, controlling for structure?"—but rather "what institutions emerge endogenously, and how do the resulting agency relationships affect outcomes in world politics?" This question helps to open two theoretical doors. First, it should enable us not to take institutions as given, reified entities, but instead help us to develop a theory of their development.[80] Secondly, using theories of delegation should help us to reintegrate issues of distribution with functional theories that rely especially on the role of information in enabling independent actors to cooperate for joint gains.

The preceding paragraphs indicate why we think that the endogeneity of international institutions does not render institutional theory irrelevant. However, to avoid the endogeneity trap, we weaken the ability of structural factors to predict organizational behavior. Institutionalist theory thereby moves farther from its neorealist roots, putting more emphasis on agency, less on structure.

---

80. See John Gerard Ruggie, "International Regimes, Transactions, and Change: Embedded Liberalism in the Postwar Economic Order," in Krasner, *International Regimes*, pp. 195–231; Cederman, *Emergent Actors in World Politics: How States and Nations Develop and Dissolve*.

The argument of this section has revolved around a difficulty faced by institutional theory. Institutional theory's attempts to explain the origins and functioning of institutions have created an "endogeneity trap": it may seem that endogenous institutions cannot have the independent effects often attributed to them by institutionalists. For institutional theory to continue to be progressive, it must deal forthrightly with this problem. We have argued, on the basis of three different theoretical perspectives, that the endogeneity of international institutions to state power and interests does not render those institutions, and particularly international organizations, epi-phenomenal. Multiple equilibria, organization theory, and agency theories all point to ways in which the characteristics of agents such as international organizations and the choices they make have important effects. We suggest a problemshift (in Lakatos's terms) toward viewing the relationship between states and international organizations as a problem of delegation. By so doing, we expect not only to help resolve the endogeneity anomaly, but also to generate some observable implications (in Lakatos's terms, hypotheses about "new facts") about the form of international organizations.

Conclusions: Institutions as Endogenous and Consequential

In Lakatosian terms, institutional theory shares much of its hard core with realism. However, institutional theory was inspired by the observation of serious anomalies in neorealist theory, and it responded by changing one of the core assumptions of realism. Instead of treating information as a scarce commodity, whose provision is beyond the scope of intentional action, institutional theory treated information as a variable that could be influenced by the activities of states. This change in the hard core led to a change in the positive heuristic, directing researchers' attention to the attempts of states to improve their informational environment via the construction of international institutions.

Institutional theory has survived a number of attacks from skeptics, establishing itself at least initially as a progressive research program. The fact that it takes actors and preferences as given means that it should not be viewed as a comprehensive theory of world politics. Were it to take on such pretensions, it would be vulnerable to a powerful critique, both from theories emphasizing domestic politics and from theories stressing the construction of interests and identities through human choice and human institutions. As compared to its initial rival, realism, institutional theory has empirically held up quite well, helping us to understand how international institutions operate and the kinds of effects they exert. However, even within the limited range of its ambitions, experience over the last two decades reveals some serious methodological and theoretical shortcomings.

Methodologically, institutionalists have often been satisfied with "existence proofs" and weak tests of their information-oriented hypotheses about institutional action. They have found it difficult to distinguish the effects of institutions from the effects of underlying structure. More rigorous analysis that seeks to distinguish these effects is needed if institutionalist theory is to progress.

Three theoretical shortcomings of institutionalist theory are most evident. The first is that although distributional issues have been recognized from the beginning as important, they have not been adequately incorporated into institutionalist theory. This problem is not well-specified by the formulation of "relative gains," but distributional issues lead to important problems of bargaining that shape the form and effects of international organizations. The second shortcoming is that institutional theory has until recently assumed that states are unitary actors. Important work is now being done to show that state preferences can be explained in ways that are consistent with, and that will enrich, institutional theory. Finally, there is the problem of endogeneity. Insofar as structures and functions explain the form and effects of international organizations, their own agency may seem to disappear—and institutionalist theory would seem to be easily folded into a more sophisticated version of structural realism. In this chapter we have relied on game theory, organization theory, and on theories of delegation to show that endogeneity—the fact that international institutions are created and maintained by states to suit their interests—does not reduce international organizations to inconsequentiality. There is space for agency: structures do not determine outcomes.

Our emphasis on organization theory and agency theory clearly refutes any suggestions that institutionalist theory assumes efficient adaptation of institutions to the circumstances of international politics. Such a claim would be inconsistent with a crucial argument of institutional theory: that the sunk costs involved in creating institutions, and the risks involved in discarding old institutions, create tendencies toward persistence of institutions even when circumstances change.[81] It would also be inconsistent with agency theory, which by no means assumes that agents' incentives will be perfectly aligned with those of principals, particularly when there are multiple principals. Taking sunk costs and agency incentives into account means that discrepancies between the "right" institution to solve a problem and the institution that is actually used may appear with some frequency: as circumstances change, institutions adapt in a "path-dependent," step-like manner, rather than smoothly. Recent institutional theory has, following work of Douglass North, clearly adopted the path-dependent rather than the functionalist-determinist position.[82] Structures, and the functions they are designed to perform, do not perfectly predict behavior, as our emphasis in this chapter on agency theory suggests.

Hence, an understanding of contemporary game theory, organization theory, and agency theory allows us to recognize the space between structure and the actions of international organizations. Actions are partially but not entirely endogenous to the power-interest structures in the neorealist sense, and to the institutional arrangements established by powerful states. Institutional design matters: institutions can be designed with built-in incentives for action consistent with designers' intentions, or they can be misdesigned. Rational anticipation ensures that there is likely to be some relationship between cooperation problems and the form of delegation, but organizational and agency

81. Keohane, *After Hegemony*, p. 102.

82. Douglass C. North, *Structure and Change in Economic History* (New York: Norton, 1981); North, *Institutions, Institutional Change and Economic Performance*.

problems make it likely that gaps will appear between problem and form.

In his most important argument, Imre Lakatos emphasized that progressive theories must not only patch up anomalies or apparent contradictions, but predict novel facts. Over the past fifteen years, institutional theory has predicted novel facts about the roles played by international institutions that have to some extent been corroborated. We hope that in the future its extension to politics and institutions within states will lead to further progressive explanation of important patterns of behavior in world politics.

Chapter 4

The Power Transition Research Program

A Lakatosian Analysis

Jonathan M. DiCicco and Jack S. Levy

Although the "paradigm wars" between realism and liberalism have framed much of the discourse in international relations theory over the past two or three decades, realists have recently begun to devote more attention to systematic divisions within their own ranks. Growing dissatisfaction with neorealism has led to a resurgence of interest in classical realism, to a new split between "offensive" realism and "defensive" realism, and to a variety of other efforts to recast realism on a more solid theoretical and empirical foundation.[1]

The authors wish to thank Colin Elman, Miriam Fendius Elman, Ronald Krebs, Jacek Kugler, Douglas Lemke, and Roslyn Simowitz for their helpful comments on drafts of this essay at various stages. The authors also are grateful to participants in the PIRT conference, Scottsdale, Arizona, and the 1999 annual meeting of the Peace Science Society (International) for their suggestions.

---

1. On varieties of realism see Benjamin Frankel, ed., *Realism: Restatements and Renewal* (London: Frank Cass Publishers, 1997); Michael W. Doyle, *Ways of War and Peace* (New York: Norton, 1997); Randall L. Schweller and David Priess, "A Tale of Two Realisms: Expanding the Institutions Debate," *Mershon International Studies Review*, Vol. 41, No. 1 (May 1997), pp. 1–32; Stephen G. Brooks, "Dueling Realisms," *International Organization*, Vol. 51, No. 3 (Summer 1997), pp. 445–477; Gideon Rose, "Neoclassical Realism and Theories of Foreign Policy," *World Politics*, Vol. 51, No. 1 (October 1998), pp. 144–172.

In spite of their differences, these distinct theories within the realist tradition share a common set of assumptions: the key actors in world politics are sovereign states who act rationally to advance their security, power, and wealth in a conflictual international system that lacks a legitimate governmental authority to regulate conflicts or enforce agreements. Realist theories also generate a number of common propositions: that the distribution of power, in the system or within a dyad, is the primary variable that shapes international outcomes; that high concentrations of power in the system generally lead to blocking coalitions and often to war; and that these blocking coalitions, or the anticipation of them, generally work to maintain the sovereign state system and prevent hegemonies from being established and maintained. Thus, classical realism, Waltzian neorealism, offensive and defensive realism, and neoclassical realism are all balance of power theories, although they vary in their specification of exactly who balances, under what conditions, and with what effects.[2]

There are other schools of thought that share basic realist assumptions about the determining role of power in world politics, but reject balance of power theory. Most prominent among these are Organski's power transition theory, Gilpin's hegemonic transition theory, and Modelski and Thompson's theory of long cycles of global leadership and decline.[3] Each of these approaches posits, contrary to balance of power theories, that

---

2. There are many variations of balance of power theory, and whether these constitute a single research program by Lakatosian standards is an interesting question that we do not explore here. For an assessment of the common elements in balance of power theories, see Jack S. Levy, "Balances and Balancing: Concepts, Propositions, and Research Design," in John A. Vasquez and Colin Elman, eds., *Realism and the Balancing of Power: A New Debate* (Englewood Cliffs, N.J.: Prentice-Hall, forthcoming). For a Lakatosian analysis of the realist research program on balancing, see other essays in the Vasquez and Elman volume.

3. A.F.K. Organski, *World Politics* (New York: Knopf, 1958); Robert Gilpin, *War and Change in World Politics* (Cambridge, UK: Cambridge University Press, 1981); Robert Gilpin, "The Theory of Hegemonic War," in Robert I. Rotberg and Theodore K. Rabb, eds., *The Origin and Prevention of Major Wars* (Cambridge, UK: Cambridge University Press, 1988), pp. 15–37; George Modelski and William R. Thompson, "Long Cycles and Global War," in Manus I. Midlarsky, ed., *Handbook of War Studies* (Boston: Unwin Hyman, 1989), pp. 23–54.

hegemonies frequently form, that these extreme concentrations of power are stabilizing rather than destabilizing and contribute to peace rather than to war, and that blocking coalitions do not generally form against dominant states. This variant of realist theory has been referred to as "hegemonic realism," as distinct from "balance of power realism."[4] Because the two approaches share some basic realist assumptions but generate mutually contradictory propositions, we treat them as different research programs within the realist tradition.[5] More specifically, we will argue that power transition theory and other forms of hegemonic theory constitute a break with the "hard core" of assumptions of balance of power realism.[6]

---

4. Jack S. Levy, "The Theoretical Foundations of Paul W. Schroeder's International System," *International History Review,* Vol. 16, No. 4 (November 1994), pp. 725–726.

5. Robert Gilpin, "No One Loves a Political Realist," *Security Studies,* Vol. 5, No. 3 (Spring 1996), p. 6, clearly identifies himself as a realist. Organski and his associates contrast power transition theory with balance of power theory, rarely mention realism, and explicitly reject the realist label. See Organski, *World Politics*; Jacek Kugler and A.F.K. Organski, "The Power Transition: A Retrospective and Prospective Evaluation," in Midlarsky, *Handbook of War Studies*, pp. 172–173; and Jacek Kugler and Douglas Lemke, "The Power Transition Research Program: Assessing Theoretical and Empirical Advances," in Manus I. Midlarsky, ed., *Handbook of War Studies II* (Ann Arbor: University of Michigan Press, 2000), pp. 129–163.

6. This does not imply that the balance of power and hegemonic realist research programs are necessarily incommensurable or mutually exclusive. Bruce Bueno de Mesquita and David Lalman, and Kelly M. Kadera, each try to integrate balance of power theory and power transition theory and to specify the conditions under which the propositions of each are valid. Bruce Bueno de Mesquita and David Lalman, *War and Reason* (New Haven, Conn.: Yale University Press, 1992); Kelly M. Kadera, *The Power-Conflict Story: A Dynamic Model of Interstate Rivalry* (Ann Arbor: University of Michigan Press, 2001). Jack Levy argues that most applications of balance of power theory focus, explicitly or implicitly, on the European system and land-based military power, whereas most applications of power transition theory focus on the global system and measure power in terms of seapower, airpower, or wealth, so that the propositions generated by these theories are not necessarily contradictory. Levy, "Balances and Balancing: Concepts, Propositions, and Research Design." Great powers can simultaneously balance against an aspiring European hegemon and align with a dominant global

One important issue in the application of Lakatosian metatheory—and one on which Lakatos provides inadequate guidance—is how inclusively to define a research program. Although it would be possible to treat hegemonic theory as a single program for the purposes of an assessment based on Lakatos's methodology of scientific research programs,[7] it is more useful to focus our attention on power transition theory as developed by Organski and refined by Organski and Kugler, Kugler and Lemke, and their colleagues.[8] Three generations of scholars have explicitly identified themselves with this research program and continue to refine the theory and test it empirically.[9] This has led to a cumulating body of research, which now constitutes a major research program in the field. If Lakatos's methodology of scientific research programs is not useful for evaluating the evolution of this relatively coherent research program, it is not clear where in the international relations field Lakatosian metatheory could be applied.

power, and this contradicts neither balance of power theory nor power transition theory. This is also an important theme in Karen A. Rasler and William R. Thompson, *The Great Powers and Global Struggle, 1490–1990* (Lexington: University Press of Kentucky, 1994).

7. Imre Lakatos, "Falsification and the Methodology of Scientific Research Programmes," in I. Lakatos and Alan Musgrave, eds., *Criticism and the Growth of Knowledge* (New York: Cambridge University Press, 1970), pp. 91–196. Subsequent citations of Lakatos refer to this chapter; we supply page references in parentheses in the text.

8. Organski, *World Politics*; A.F.K. Organski and Jacek Kugler, *The War Ledger* (Chicago: University of Chicago Press, 1980); Jacek Kugler and Douglas Lemke, eds., *Parity and War: Evaluations and Extensions of "The War Ledger"* (Ann Arbor: University of Michigan Press, 1996); Kugler and Lemke, "The Power Transition Research Program"; Ronald Tammen, Jacek Kugler, Douglas Lemke, Alan Stam III, Mark Abdollahian, Carole Alsharabati, Brian Buford-Efird, and A.F.K. Organski, *Power Transitions* (Chatham, N.J.: Chatham House, 2000).

9. Although we think that self-identification with a line of research is one of several useful criteria for the specification and delimitation of a research program, this criterion may not be perfectly compatible with Lakatosian metatheory. Lakatos aimed to provide objective criteria for the identification and evaluation of research programs. He was less interested in the more subjective criterion of whether a scholar self-consciously identifies with the research program.

We exclude from our analysis a discussion of Gilpin's hegemonic transition theory, Modelski and Thompson's leadership long cycle theory, and Doran's theory of relative power cycles. Although Gilpin's hegemonic transition theory is a theoretically rich and important contribution, and although it shares with Organski's power transition theory many of the same assumptions and arguments, Gilpin does not identify himself with Organski's power transition theory.[10] Moreover, the paucity of subsequent efforts to test Gilpin's theory empirically[11] makes it difficult to apply Lakatosian metatheory, which emphasizes the empirical corroboration of novel facts.[12] Long cycle theory's exclusively systemic orientation (in contrast to Organski's combination of systemic and dyadic elements), its explicit assumption of cycles, and its focus on seapower and leading economic sectors make this line of research sufficiently distinct that it is best examined as a self-contained research program.[13] Finally, although Doran's power cycle theory shares common elements with power transition theory, we exclude it because it includes some nonrationalist elements that are at odds with the rationalist hard core of the power transition research program.[14]

In the pages that follow, we apply Lakatos's methodology of scientific research programs in an effort to evaluate the power transition research

10. Gilpin, *War and Change in World Politics*, p. 94, note 11, cites Organski only once.

11. An exception is K. Edward Spiezio, "British Hegemony and Major Power War, 1815–1939: An Empirical Test of Gilpin's Model of Hegemonic Governance," *International Studies Quarterly*, Vol. 34, No. 2 (June 1990), pp. 165–181.

12. We also exclude "hegemonic stability theory," which seeks to explain stability in the international political economy rather than war. Robert O. Keohane, *After Hegemony: Cooperation and Discord in the World Political Economy* (Princeton, N.J.: Princeton University Press, 1984).

13. William R. Thompson, *On Global War: Historical-Structural Approaches to World Politics* (Columbia, S.C.: University of South Carolina Press, 1988); Rasler and Thompson, *The Great Powers and Global Struggle*.

14. Charles F. Doran and Wes Parsons, "War and the Cycle of Relative Power," *American Political Science Review*, Vol. 74, No. 4 (December 1980), pp. 947–965; Charles F. Doran, "Confronting the Principles of the Power Cycle: Changing

program. First, we describe the theoretical foundations of the research program based on its essential texts. Then we reconstruct the program in Lakatosian terms, identifying its hard core assumptions, its negative heuristic, and its positive heuristic. We then analyze recent developments in power transition research, with particular attention to Douglas Lemke's multiple hierarchy model, Woosang Kim's alliance transition model, and research regarding the timing and initiation of wars associated with power transitions, and we assess whether each of these strands in the research program is progressive or degenerating. We end by reflecting on the preceding analytical exercise, evaluating the utility of Lakatosian metatheory for international relations and for the social sciences in general. We conclude that Lakatos's methodology is useful, but that its application presents some difficult challenges for social scientists. We attribute much of the difficulty to Lakatos's insufficient attention to operational tasks such as identifying the boundaries of a research program, specifying the research program's hard core and whether it evolves over time, evaluating research programs that simultaneously exhibit signs of progress and degeneration, weighing the relative importance of the construction of valid empirical indicators or of multiple corroborations of a hypothesis, and deciding how long to tolerate a struggling research program.

The Foundations of the Research Program: World Politics *and* The War Ledger

The most significant scholarly contribution of A.F.K. Organski's 1958 book *World Politics* was his critique of balance of power theories and his outline of power transition theory as an alternative explanation for the dynamics of international politics and the onset of major war. Organski rejected the argument that an equal balance or distribution of capabilities between adversaries contributes to peace, and argued that balances are more likely

---

Systems Structure, Expectations, and War," in Midlarsky, *Handbook of War Studies II*, pp. 83–110.

to lead to war.[15] He also argued that there is usually a dominant power that sits atop the international hierarchy, positioned above several lesser great powers, other medium and smaller states, and dependencies. The dominant power shapes the "international order" in which relations among states are stable and follow certain patterns and even rules of behavior promoted by the dominant power.[16] Finally, Organski criticized the excessively static character of balance of power theory and its failure to incorporate the changing nature of state power and its implications for the international system. He argued that uneven patterns of growth due to industrialization lead not only to the emergence of a dominant power in the international arena, but also to subsequent challenges to the dominant state's global leadership by great powers undergoing dramatic internal development.

The dominant power achieves its preeminent position in the international hierarchy through a process of rapid economic development that is driven by industrialization. As the boost from industrialization wanes in the dominant state, other contending states industrialize, grow rapidly, and catch up, so that the new distribution of power is no longer commensurate with the existing international order. If a rising power is dissatisfied with its own place in the international hierarchy, it may wish to challenge the existing international order, perhaps using its newly developed military power. Thus the probability of war between the rising challenger and the dominant state peaks near the point of power transition between them. This contrasts with the power parity hypothesis that an equality of power is conducive to peace.

Power transition theory thus incorporates two ideas that have become central in later theories of hegemonic change and war: the importance of changing power distributions in the international system arising from industrialization, and the stabilizing effects of concentrations of power. The theory is centered around two key explanatory variables: relative power, and the degree of satisfaction with the international order (or

---

15. Organski, like many others, often fails to distinguish between dyadic and systemic-level balances or preponderance. The dyadic-level power parity hypothesis is not equivalent to systemic-level balance of power theory.

16. Organski, *World Politics*, pp. 313–16, 326–30.

status quo). The interaction effect between them is the primary determinant of war and peace. States that have insufficient capabilities, no matter how dissatisfied with the status quo, will be fundamentally unable to challenge the dominant power. States that are powerful but satisfied will have little motivation to challenge the dominant state for its preeminent position and for the accompanying ability to shape the international order. Only the powerful and dissatisfied pose a threat.[17]

Organski and Kugler published the first statistical tests of power transition hypotheses in their 1980 book, *The War Ledger*, which focused on the hypothesis that the combination of parity and transition is conducive to major war. Organski and Kugler found that among those states capable of contending for global leadership, no wars take place without a power transition, and that half of the observed transitions were followed by the outbreak of war.[18] Based on these findings, the authors claimed that a power transition among contenders is a necessary but not sufficient condition for major war.[19] Although critics have questioned various aspects of *The War Ledger*'s research design, the book stands as the foundation for the empirical development of the power transition research program.[20]

---

17. Organski, *World Politics*, chap. 12; Organski and Kugler, *The War Ledger*, pp. 19–23, 39; Douglas Lemke, "Toward a General Understanding of Parity and War," *Conflict Management and Peace Science*, Vol. 14, No. 2 (Winter 1995), p. 145; Douglas Lemke and Jacek Kugler, "The Evolution of the Power Transition Perspective," in Kugler and Lemke, *Parity and War*, p. 21. Recent treatments use Most and Starr's language, suggesting that parity provides the *opportunity* for war, and that dissatisfaction with the status quo provides the *willingness* to engage in war with the dominant state. Benjamin A. Most and Harvey Starr, *Inquiry, Logic, and International Politics* (Columbia: University of South Carolina Press, 1989).

18. The findings hinge on the separation of "contenders" from other major powers in the system. Contenders include the dominant state and those states possessing at least 80 percent of the capabilities of the dominant state. If the dominant state is grossly preponderant, the three most powerful states are classified as contenders. Organski and Kugler, *The War Ledger*, pp. 42–45.

19. Organski and Kugler, *The War Ledger*, pp. 50–52; Kugler and Organski, "The Power Transition," p. 179.

20. For recent critiques see John A. Vasquez, "When are Power Transitions Dangerous? An Appraisal and Reformulation of Power Transition Theory," in

A Lakatosian Reconstruction of the Power Transition Research Program

In this section, we reconstruct the power transition research program in Lakatos's terms, identifying the hard core and the negative and positive heuristics.

POWER TRANSITION'S HARD CORE OF IRREFUTABLE ASSUMPTIONS

The central concept of Lakatos's methodology of scientific research programs is the "hard core," which is a set of assumptions considered "'irrefutable' by the methodological decision of its protagonists" and not appropriate for empirical testing (p. 133).[21] Researchers use these assumptions to construct a theoretical system, derive "auxiliary hypotheses" that comprise the "protective belt" around the hard core of the research program, and test those hypotheses empirically. "It is this protective belt of auxiliary hypotheses which has to bear the brunt of tests and get adjusted and re-adjusted" (p. 133). A major contribution of Lakatosian metatheory is to provide criteria for assessing whether the addition of auxiliary hypotheses is "progressive" and enhances scientific knowledge, or instead is degenerating.[22]

Kugler and Lemke, *Parity and War*, pp. 35–56; Randolph M. Siverson and Ross A. Miller, "The Power Transition: Problems and Prospects," in Kugler and Lemke, *Parity and War*, pp. 57–76.

21. Thus Lakatosian metatheory provides a justification for Friedman's famous "as if" assumption. Milton Friedman, "The Methodology of Positive Economics," in Milton Friedman, ed., *Essays in Positive Economics* (Chicago: University of Chicago Press, 1953), pp. 3–43.

22. To be progressive, a theoretical development cannot be ad hoc in either of the following respects: if a problemshift fails to yield predictions of novel facts ("ad hoc_1") or if it predicts novel facts but those novel facts are not empirically corroborated ("ad hoc_2"). Theories that are ad hoc in these senses merely patch up holes in existing theories without providing new theoretical or empirical content. However, it is not perfectly clear what Lakatos (pp. 116–132) means by a "novel fact." For a summary of different interpretations see Elman and Elman's Chapter 2 in this volume. We prefer the concept of "heuristic novelty," which requires that a theory must account for facts that were not used in the construction of the theory.

Although Organski's original statement of power transition theory does not contain an explicit list of assumptions that allows us to specify an unambiguous hard core of the research program, his critique of the assumptions of balance of power theory gives us some leverage for that task. Organski charges balance of power theorists with making two misguided assumptions: "nations are fundamentally static units whose power is not changed from within, and . . . nations have no permanent ties to each other but move about freely, motivated primarily by considerations of power."[23] Organski emphasizes repeatedly that the first assumption fails to hold for the period since 1750. Rather, he argues, the impulses of nationalism and industrialization have transformed international politics such that changes in national power from within drive changes in the relations among states. Internal growth and development has supplanted the constant shifting of alliances as the primary mechanism for reconfiguring international political relationships.[24]

Organski also criticizes the emphasis of balance of power theory on alliance formation and dissolution as the primary mechanism for power redistribution, and on the ease of making and breaking alliances.[25] He

---

This reflects the common methodological injunction that a theory ought not be tested on the same data that were used to construct the theory. As Elman and Elman (Chapter 2, this volume) aptly note, however, this standard can be quite demanding, because in principle it requires information about how the theory was developed. A problemshift is ad hoc in a third sense ("ad hoc$_3$") if it is not in accord with the positive heuristic, in which case it marks a break from the existing research program.

23. Organski uses the term "nations," but plainly he was referring to states. Organski, *World Politics,* p. 287. Note that Organski's critique of the *assumptions* of balance of power theory is inappropriate from the perspective of Lakatosian metatheory, which directs us toward the protective belt. Note too that Waltz makes this critique of Organski, although in non-Lakatosian language. Kenneth N. Waltz, *Theory of International Politics* (Reading, Mass.: Addison-Wesley, 1979), p. 119.

24. Organski, *World Politics,* pp. 287–90, 306–309, 337–38; Organski and Kugler, *The War Ledger,* pp. 24–27; Kugler and Organski, "The Power Transition," p. 173; Lemke and Kugler, "The Evolution of the Power Transition Perspective," pp. 5–10.

25. Organski, *World Politics,* chap. 11.

argues that ties among states in the industrializing period are far less flexible than during the preindustrial era, for three reasons. First, industrialization and the development of a more liberal, free-trade order increased the interdependence of nations, making ties firmer. Second, alliance ties in the modern era require heavy investments—including arms transfers, building and maintenance of bases abroad, and equipment standardization—and consequently alliances are less transitory. Third, the growth of democracy and leaders' appeals to constituents for support of their alignment policies makes it much harder for democratic states to reverse alliance commitments. Economically interdependent, militarily tied, and sentimentally bound nations cannot "switch sides" as easily as the dynastic states of the sixteenth, seventeenth, and early eighteenth centuries, and consequently alliances are not a primary means of enhancing national power.[26]

This discussion, along with more explicit statements in subsequent work,[27] suggests the following set of hard core (HC) assumptions in power transition theory:

(HC-1): states are the primary actors in international politics.[28]

---

26. Organski, *World Politics,* pp. 313–316. Organski implies that the satisfaction of both the dominant state and some other great powers with the status quo may add to the inflexibility of their alliance ties, which reinforce their mutual interests and power.

27. Organski and Kugler, *The War Ledger,* chap. 1; Kugler and Organski, "The Power Transition," pp. 172–175; Tammen, et al., *Power Transitions.*

28. One could imagine the extension of power transition theory to the relations among communal groups within or across state boundaries. In fact, analyses of ethnic conflict that emphasize the impact on the likelihood of conflict or cooperation of changes in the relative power of communal groups, whether driven by demographic change or by other variables, have some striking parallels with power transition theory. See James Fearon, "Commitment Problems and the Spread of Ethnic Conflict," in David A. Lake and Donald Rothchild, eds., *The International Spread of Ethnic Conflict* (Princeton, N.J.: Princeton University Press, 1998), pp. 107–126. The extension of realist theory from states to other actors has an important precedent in the application of the concept of the security dilemma between states to the relations among ethnic groups. Barry R. Posen, "The Security Dilemma and Ethnic Conflict," in Michael E. Brown, ed., *Ethnic Conflict and*

(HC-2): state leaders are rational in their foreign policy choices.[29]

(HC-3): the international order is hierarchically organized under the leadership of a dominant power.

(HC-4): the rules governing the international political system are fundamentally similar to those governing domestic political systems.

(HC-5): internal growth and development of states is the primary source of international change.

(HC-6): alliance ties among states are relatively inflexible, and consequently alliances are not a primary means of enhancing national power.

HC-6 is the most problematic in terms of the identification of the hard core.[30] We could conceivably treat the diminished role of alliances not as a hard core assumption, but rather as a testable hypothesis, and thus as part of the positive heuristic and protective belt of the power transition research program. Although we think that this is how the alliance question *ought* to be treated, this is not how power transition scholars have treated alliances, as there has been virtually no effort to examine empirically the relative impact of alliance ties and internal growth on states' position and influence in the system. The one exception, as we will see, is Kim's work on alliance transition theory, but it is significant that Kim's research thus far has not led other power transition researchers to

---

International Security (Princeton, N.J.: Princeton University Press, 1993), pp. 103–124. Whether such extensions of realist theory in general or power transition theory in particular would constitute intra-program shifts or inter-program shifts raises some difficult issues.

29. The rationality assumption is clear in Organski and Kugler, *The War Ledger,* pp. 39–40; and Kugler and Organski, "The Power Transition," pp. 172–173; and particularly explicit in Tammen et al., *Power Transitions.*

30. Lakatos, "Falsification and the Methodology of Scientific Research Programmes," provides very little guidance on the specific composition of the hard core.

incorporate alliances into their models.[31] This leads us to treat the assumption of the inflexibility of alliances as part of the hard core of the power transition research program, and Kim's work as a break from the hard core.[32]

It is instructive to compare power transition theory's hard core assumptions with those of realist balance of power theories. Although both assume that the key actors in the system are unitary and rational states, they differ in other important respects. Whereas balance of power theories treat both internal growth and alliances as sources of international change, power transition theory excludes alliances and treats internal growth as the only source of power and international change. The peripheral role of alliances in power transition theory is a major point of difference with balance of power realism, where alliances play an indispensable role. In addition, power transition theory is much more explicit about the role of changing power than are balance of power theories.

In contrast to the standard neorealist assumption that anarchy is the key ordering principle of international relations,[33] power transition theory posits a hierarchically organized international order defined both by the

---

31. Woosang Kim, "Power, Alliance, and Major Wars, 1816–1975," *Journal of Conflict Resolution*, Vol. 33, No. 2 (June 1989), pp. 255–273; Woosang Kim, "Alliance Transitions and Great Power War," *American Journal of Political Science*, Vol. 35, No. 4 (1991), pp. 833–50; Woosang Kim, "Power Transitions and Great Power War from Westphalia to Waterloo," *World Politics*, Vol. 45, No. 1 (October 1992), pp. 153–172; Woosang Kim, "Power Parity, Alliance, and War from 1648 to 1975," in Kugler and Lemke, *Parity and War*, pp. 93–106.

32. Admittedly, Organski (*World Politics*, pp. 331–332) occasionally argued that the power parity of international coalitions, or "teams," ought to be associated with a greater danger of major war. But Organski did not sustain this argument, and later power transition theorists eliminated it from their models.

33. Waltz, *Theory of International Politics*; Robert O. Keohane, "Theory of World Politics: Structural Realism and Beyond," in Ada W. Finifter, ed., *Political Science: The State of the Discipline* (Washington, D.C.: American Political Science Association, 1983), pp. 503–540; Helen Milner, "The Assumption of Anarchy in International Relations Theory: A Critique," *Review of International Studies*, Vol. 17, No. 1 (January 1991), pp. 67–85; Barry Buzan, Charles Jones, and Richard Little, *The Logic of Anarchy* (New York: Columbia University Press, 1993).

distribution of power and by the set of rules and common practices imposed by a dominant state. In some respects this distinction is rather thin and reflects merely semantic differences in the meanings that neorealists and power transition theorists attach to the key concepts of anarchy, hierarchy, and authority. Waltz concedes that international politics is characterized by some semblance of order, and power transition and other hegemonic theorists concede that order exists within a nominally anarchic system.[34]

For Waltz, however, order is a systemic effect, not a national strategy. It is a by-product of the "coaction of self-regarding units [i.e., states].... No state intends to participate in the formation of a structure by which it and others will be constrained. International-political systems, like economic markets, are individualist in origin, spontaneously generated, and unintended."[35] In power transition theory, by contrast, order is the intended result of actions taken by a dominant state, which attempts to shape the international order in such ways that advance stability and enhance its own interests.[36] In balance of power theory, a single dominant state almost never arises because the balancing mechanism works to deter potential hegemons or to defeat them if deterrence fails.[37]

In contrast with the Waltzian assumption that states are functionally undifferentiated and have similar goals, Organski argues that because states occupy different positions in the international hierarchy, they may have different goals.[38] Moreover, in contrast to the view often associated with classical realists such as Morgenthau and contemporary "offensive realists" such as Mearsheimer, Organski rejects the argument that all national goals reduce to the maximization of power (though he concedes that every state needs to maintain some minimum level of power to

34. Waltz, *Theory of International Politics*; Lemke and Kugler, "The Evolution of the Power Transition Perspective," p. 21.

35. Waltz, *Theory of International Politics*, p. 91; Robert Jervis, *System Effects* (Princeton, N.J.: Princeton University Press, 1997), p. 132.

36. Organski, *World Politics*, p. 326; Kugler and Lemke, "The Power Transition Research Program."

37. Levy, "Balances and Balancing: Concepts, Propositions, and Research Design."

38. Organski, *World Politics*, pp. 53–57.

survive as a political entity).[39] The assumption of heterogeneous state goals is consistent with Organski's argument that some but not all potential challengers may be satisfied with the existing international order and have no incentive to overturn the hierarchy even if they have the power to do so.[40]

The anarchy/hierarchy distinction is closely related to the question of the similarity of international and domestic political systems. Power transition theory's hard core assumes that the hierarchically-organized international order contains rules similar to those of domestic political systems, "despite the absence of an enforceable code of international law."[41] This breaks from the explicit neorealist assumption that international politics and domestic politics are fundamentally dissimilar because the former is anarchic and the latter is hierarchical.[42] For these reasons we treat the power transition research program as a break with the hard core of balance of power realism.[43]

---

39. Morgenthau, *Politics Among Nations* (New York: Knopf, 1948); and John J. Mearsheimer, *The Tragedy of Great Power Politics* (New York: Norton, 2001).

40. The dominant power often makes a deliberate effort to coopt some potential challengers and win their acceptance of the existing order, often through the construction of institutions that both reinforce the existing order and impose some limits on the leading state. See G. John Ikenberry, *After Victory: Institutions, Strategic Restraint, and the Rebuilding of Order after Major Wars* (Princeton, N.J.: Princeton University Press, 2001).

41. Kugler and Organski, "The Power Transition," p. 172; Lemke and Kugler, "The Evolution of the Power Transition Perspective," p. 8. Gilpin asserts that interstate relationships are ordered within an anarchic international system, and that while domestic and international politics are dissimilar, they share commonalities in their control mechanisms. Gilpin, *War and Change in World Politics*, p. 28.

42. The assumption that international and domestic politics are fundamentally different goes back to Rousseau, which leads Walker to treat Rousseau as the first modern realist. Thomas C. Walker, "Peace, Rivalry, and War" (Ph.D. dissertation, Rutgers University, 2000).

43. Similarly, Keohane argues that Gilpin's hegemonic transition theory represents a break from the hard core of classical realism. Gilpin, *War and Change in World Politics*; Keohane, "Theory of World Politics: Structural Realism and Beyond," pp. 517–520.

POWER TRANSITION'S NEGATIVE HEURISTIC

Lakatos's "negative heuristic" delineates the types of variables and models that ought to be shunned by researchers within a research program because they deviate from the assumptions of the hard core.[44] Power transition's hard core implies that researchers should not develop models that posit the importance of non-state actors, non-rational decision-making, the absence of order or rules in the international system, a sharp distinction between domestic politics and international politics, a static conception of national power, or the significance of alliances as sources of national power. In addition, Organski implies that researchers should avoid explanations that posit homogeneous motivations (including power maximization) across states.

POWER TRANSITION'S POSITIVE HEURISTIC

Lakatos argued that programmatic research is further guided by the positive heuristic, "a partially articulated set of suggestions or hints" regarding the development of increasingly sophisticated models (pp. 134–138). These models generate hypotheses that comprise the protective belt and that should be empirically tested. Lakatos suggested that pioneers of particular research programs anticipate future refutations of some hypotheses derived from the initial model. Although incapable of refining the model at that moment, the researcher should speculate on the types of emendations and changes that would prepare the research program to handle likely refutations and anomalies.

Recognizing that the theory of the power transition would evolve over time, Organski acknowledged that his book, *World Politics*,

contains few "laws" but a great many generalizations and hypotheses which are the first step in the formation of theory. Some of the generalizations are crude and need refinement. Some of the hypotheses are probably downright wrong. The reader is invited to refine and correct wherever he can, for only by

---

44. This suggests that the negative heuristic is redundant because it follows directly from the hard core and provides no additional information.

such steps does knowledge grow. Beginnings must be big and breezy; refinements follow later.[45]

Organski cautioned that power transition theory is not timeless but instead is limited to the period since the Industrial Revolution, stating that, "differential industrialization is the key to understanding the shifts in power in the 19th and 20th centuries, but it was not the key in the years before 1750 or so, and it will not always be the key in the future." Once all states are fully industrialized, he wrote, we will "require new theories."[46]

Organski also provided a detailed discussion of the measurement of national power, which, he argued, comprises six components (ranked in decreasing order of importance): population size, efficacy of political structure, economic development, national morale, resources, and geography. For measurement purposes, Organski collapsed the last two together with population size and economic development, arguing that highly developed and heavily populated states tend to enjoy adequate access to resources and favorable geographic circumstances. He also omitted national morale, which is "virtually impossible to measure objectively," and suggested national income (effectively, gross national product [GNP]) as a quantifiable indicator summarizing population size and economic development.[47]

State political capacity is a key component of national power that was articulated in the formative statement of the power transition research program as part of the positive heuristic. Organski conceded that a good measure of the effectiveness of political institutions had yet to be developed, and he argued that creation of such a measure would be "one

---

45. Organski, *World Politics*, p. 6.

46. Organski, *World Politics*, p. 307. Organski also suggested that all theories are bound by culture and experience, and that theories appropriate to one context are not always applicable to another context. Accordingly, theories require revision, and "one of the most serious criticisms that can be made of the balance of power theory is that it has not been so revised." Ibid., p. 307.

47. Ibid., chap. 8, esp. pp. 203–210; Organski and Kugler, *The War Ledger*, pp. 33–38.

of the major tasks that remains for political scientists to accomplish in the years ahead."[48]

The other key variable in power transition theory, but one that until recently has received less attention than national power, is the degree of satisfaction with the international order or existing status quo. Organski argued that "peaceful adjustment is possible in the case of the challenger who is willing to continue the existing international order and abide by its rules, but is much more difficult, if not impossible, in the case of a challenger who wishes to destroy the existing order."[49] Organski never fully developed the concept or a measure for the degree of satisfaction with the status quo, but clearly the conceptualization and operationalization of this variable is a key element in the positive heuristic of the power transition research program.

Finally, Organski identified four other factors affecting the likelihood that a power transition will result in war. First, the challenger's power potential when beginning its ascent: if a rising state is too small ever to challenge the dominant state, or "so large that its dominance, once it becomes industrial, is virtually guaranteed," war becomes very unlikely.[50] The second factor is the speed of the challenger's rise. The more rapid the challenger's ascent, the greater is the probability of war, for several reasons. The leaders of the dominant state have trouble adjusting to rapid changes; the leaders of the challenger have trouble adapting to a new role in the international order; and a rapid rise "may go to the challenger's head," leaving leaders impatient with the unresponsiveness of the international order to the changing distribution of power.[51] Political

---

48. Organski, *World Politics*, p. 203. For an initial effort to measure political capacity, see Organski and Kugler, *The War Ledger*, chap. 2.

49. Ibid., pp. 325–337.

50. Ibid., pp. 334–337.

51. Ibid., p. 335. This explanation of the effects of a rapid rise of the challenger incorporates certain non-rational psychological processes (see also Doran and Parsons, "War and the Cycle of Relative Power"), and as such it is not fully consistent with the rationalist assumption of the hard core of the research program. Subsequent power transition researchers have incorporated this variable into a rationalist model. Mark A. Abdollahian, "In Search of Structure: The Nonlinear Dynamics of International Politics" (Ph.D. dissertation, Claremont

leaders, seeking to promote extraordinarily rapid growth, might make excessive demands on the populace, which could lead to internal strain and possibly create incentives for the diversionary use of force.[52]

The third factor is the dominant state's flexibility in adjusting to changes in the distribution of power. Especially in conjunction with the rise of a challenger so large as to be assured of dominance in the long run, the ability of the now-dominant state to accommodate the rising challenger through moderate concessions could mitigate the likelihood of war. This is related to the fourth factor, the degree of amity between the dominant power and the challenger. The absence of hostility between the dominant state and the challenger, which may be a function of the similarity of economic or domestic political systems,[53] may reduce the probability of war associated with transitions.[54]

Graduate School, 1996). In any case, propositions about the speed of the challenger's rise have not been central to the research program.

52. In contrast to Organski's argument, Kim and Morrow argue that it is equally plausible that the challenger's leaders will be pessimistic about the ability to sustain extraordinarily rapid growth and will underestimate, not overestimate, their state's eventual position in the international order. Woosang Kim and James D. Morrow, "When Do Power Shifts Lead to War?" *American Journal of Political Science,* Vol. 36, No. 4 (November 1992), pp. 896–922.

53. Organski implied but did not explicitly state that similar domestic institutions facilitate interstate "friendship," which partially anticipates the interdemocratic peace proposition. Organski, *World Politics,* pp. 324, 336–337. Others argue that satisfaction with the status quo could have the same result, and in fact Lemke and Reed argue that power transition theory subsumes the interdemocratic peace. Douglas Lemke and William Reed, "Regime Types and Status Quo Evaluations: Power Transition Theory and the Democratic Peace," *International Interactions,* Vol. 22, No. 2 (1996), pp. 143–164.

54. With the exception of the rapidity of the challenger's rise, Organski explicitly linked these conditions to the peaceful transition between Great Britain and the United States, which he acknowledged as the "one major exception" to the proposed relationship between the rise of a challenger and major war. He discussed a number of possible explanations, but emphasized that "the major reason why England has allowed the United States to take her place without a struggle is because the United States has accepted the Anglo-French international order"—in other words, American satisfaction with the status quo. Organski, *World Politics,* pp. 323–325.

This gives us a characterization of power transition's positive heuristic:

(PH-1): Construct models explaining major war onset during the industrializing era using the interaction of power transitions and degree of satisfaction with the status quo.

(PH-2): Construct quantitative indicators of national power that reflect the intrastate sources of interstate dynamics.

(PH-3): Develop a conceptual and operational definition of political capacity.

(PH-4): Develop a conceptual and operational definition of degree of satisfaction with the status quo.

(PH-5): Where the combination of relative power and degree of satisfaction with the status quo fail to explain the violent or peaceful character of power transitions, incorporate mitigating factors such as the challenger's potential, the speed of the challenger's rise, the dominant power's flexibility, and friendly relations between the dominant power and the challenger.[55]

Three examples from *The War Ledger*, each developed in later work, illustrate how the positive heuristic, rooted in Organski's original formulation of power transition theory, has guided subsequent inquiry. First, Organski and Kugler provided a lengthy discussion of the research design tasks necessary for testing the power preponderance hypothesis (contained in PH-1 and PH-2).[56] Second, they began to develop a quantitative index to measure the effectiveness of political institutions or political capacity (PH-3).[57] Third, Organski and Kugler test a statistical

---

55. The concepts of "friendly relations" and especially "flexibility" are quite vague, and unless they are rigorously defined and operationalized independently of the predicted behavior, they open the way for the introduction of an element of non-falsifiability into power transition hypotheses. In practice, however, power transition theorists have carefully avoided this trap.

56. Organski and Kugler, *The War Ledger*, pp. 33–38.

57. Organski and Kugler do not incorporate their relative political capacity index into the tests of power transition hypotheses on the grounds that the major powers included in the tests are politically developed enough to be roughly on the same

model that incorporates both relative power and the speed of the power transition, in order to explain the likelihood of a peaceful transition (PH-5).[58]

The impact of the positive heuristic is also clear in the development or employment of new measures for key variables. Following Organski, there has been considerable debate, both within and beyond the power transition research program, over the measurement of national power and degree of satisfaction with the status quo.[59] After comparing the Singer-Bremer-Stuckey measure of national capabilities and GNP, Organski and Kugler settled on GNP as a parsimonious indicator of political and economic power for testing power transition theory.[60] Houweling and Siccama, and Lemke and Werner, test power transition hypotheses with Doran and Parsons's relative capabilities index.[61] Recent replications and tests replace GNP with gross domestic product (GDP), and include the Correlates of War composite index of national capabilities as an

---

plane. This rationale raises questions about the utility of the political capacity variable in a theory that is explicitly limited to great power behavior.

58. Organski and Kugler, *The War Ledger*, p. 56. Power transition theorists have recently directed more attention to the speed of transitions. Abdollahian, for example, takes issue with Organski's argument that the faster the transition, the higher the probability of war (PH-5). Abdollahian, "In Search of Structure," pp. 64, 88. Unlike Organski, who suggested that rapid change is dangerous because it disrupts role-perception and generates impatience, or because rapid development might incur domestic unrest, Abdollahian argues that faster transitions are less likely to result in war because the window of opportunity opens and closes more quickly. Slow, prolonged transitions then generate a higher probability of war than do rapid transitions.

59. Organski, *World Politics*, chaps. 5–8, esp. pp. 201–210.

60. J. David Singer, Stuart A. Bremer, and John Stuckey, "Capability Distribution, Uncertainty, and Major Power War, 1820–1965," in Bruce M. Russett, ed., *Peace, War, and Numbers* (Beverly Hills, Calif.: Sage, 1972), pp. 19–48; Organski and Kugler, *The War Ledger*, chap. 1.

61. Henk Houweling and Jan G. Siccama, "Power Transitions as a Cause of War," *Journal of Conflict Resolution*, Vol. 32, No. 1 (March 1988), pp. 87–102; and Douglas Lemke and Suzanne Werner, "Power Parity, Commitment to Change, and War," *International Studies Quarterly*, Vol. 40, No. 2 (June 1996), pp. 235–260; Doran and Parsons, "War and the Cycle of Relative Power."

alternative indicator.[62] Such tests typically demonstrate the robustness of the association between parity and war among the most powerful states in the system over the last two centuries.[63] More recent improvements and applications of a reliable measure of political capacity are summarized in Kugler and Arbetman's *Political Capacity and Economic Behavior.*[64]

Power transition theorists have also made a number of efforts to operationalize the concept of the degree of satisfaction with the status quo and to incorporate it into their models.[65] Kim, for example, operationalizes

62. Indra deSoysa, John R. Oneal, and Yong-hee Park, "Testing Power-Transition Theory Using Alternative Measures of National Capabilities," *Journal of Conflict Resolution*, Vol. 41, No. 4 (August 1997), pp. 509–528; Lemke and Werner, "Power Parity, Commitment to Change, and War."

63. See the findings in, among others, Organski and Kugler, *The War Ledger*; Houweling and Siccama, "Power Transitions as a Cause of War"; Doran and Parsons, "War and the Cycle of Relative Power"; deSoysa et al., "Testing Power-Transition Theory Using Alternative Measures of National Capabilities"; Lemke and Werner, "Power Parity, Commitment to Change, and War." For more complete summaries of the empirical support for power transition theory see Lemke and Kugler, "The Evolution of the Power Transition Perspective," pp. 3–33; and Kugler and Lemke, "The Power Transition Research Program."

64. Jacek Kugler and Marina Arbetman, eds., *Political Capacity and Economic Behavior* (Boulder, Colo.: Westview Press, 1997), building on Jacek Kugler and William Domke, "Comparing the Strength of Nations," *Comparative Political Studies*, Vol. 19, No. 1 (April 1986), pp. 39–69; and Jacek Kugler and Marina Arbetman, "Choosing Among Measures of Power," in Richard J. Stoll and Michael D. Ward, eds., *Power in World Politics* (Boulder, Colo.: Lynne Rienner, 1989), pp. 49–77.

65. These include Werner's and Kugler's indicator of extraordinary military buildups, Kim's alliance profile similarity measure (based on Bruce Bueno de Mesquita, *The War Trap* [New Haven, Conn.: Yale University Press, 1981]), Bueno de Mesquita's money market discount rate measure, and Lemke's and Reed's assessment of the similarity of domestic structures. Suzanne Werner and Jacek Kugler, "Power Transitions and Military Buildups: Resolving the Relationship Between Arms Buildups and War," in Kugler and Lemke, *Parity and War*, pp. 187–210; Kim, "Alliance Transitions and Great Power War," esp. p. 843, note 14; Bruce Bueno de Mesquita, "Pride of Place: The Origins of German Hegemony," *World Politics*, Vol. 43, No. 1 (October 1990), pp. 28–52; Lemke and Reed, "Regime Types and Status Quo Evaluations." For a helpful survey of indicators of status quo evaluations, see Douglas Lemke, *Regions of War and Peace* (Cambridge, UK:

satisfaction in terms of the similarity of the alliance portfolios of the state with that of the dominant power.[66] Although Kim finds little empirical support for the impact of dissatisfaction, others have subsequently used his measure in tests of traditional power transition hypotheses, and this has sparked further debate and concerted efforts to generate a better indicator of degree of satisfaction. Still, no single indicator has gained overwhelming scholarly support. Unsuccessful efforts to improve the measurement of satisfaction have not obstructed the advancement of the power transition research program, but neither have they helped move the program forward.

Some critics might argue that in their haste to construct indicators measuring status quo satisfaction, power transition researchers have neglected several conceptual issues concerning the nature of the status quo. What, exactly, is the status quo, and through what mechanisms does a rising challenger's dissatisfaction with the status quo lead to an increase in the likelihood of a violent confrontation? As Oneal, deSoysa, and Park argue, power transition theorists need to specify exactly "what benefits the international system provides to states and over which they may fight."[67] In the absence of such conceptual refinement, power transition theorists cannot convincingly identify dissatisfied states or demonstrate that the dominant power has constructed an international order that gives it a disproportionate advantage.

There is also a levels-of-analysis question. The status quo can refer to the distribution of benefits in the international system, but also might refer to dyadic or even regional structures or relationships.[68] Not only do

---

Cambridge University Press, 2002), pp. 99–109; for a comparative evaluation of several indicators, see Douglas M. Gibler, "An Assessment of the Validity of Empirical Measures of State Satisfaction with the Status Quo" (unpublished manuscript, University of Kentucky, 2002).

66. Kim, "Alliance Transitions and Great Power War"; Kim, "Power Transitions and Great Power War from Westphalia to Waterloo."

67. John Oneal, Indra deSoysa, and Yong-hee Park, "But Power and Wealth *are* Satisfying: A Reply to Lemke and Reed," *Journal of Conflict Resolution*, Vol. 42, No. 4 (August 1998), p. 518.

68. On dyadic relationships, see Zeev Maoz and Ben D. Mor, "Satisfaction, Capabilities, and the Evolution of Enduring Rivalries, 1816–1990: A Statistical

these analytically distinct categories require different indicators; they also require separate conceptualization. The nature of a distribution of benefits at the level of the international system is hardly equivalent to the nature of the benefits at stake between two states in a dyad, and in fact it is likely that some states will be satisfied with the systemic status quo but dissatisfied with the status quo of a particular bilateral relationship. Greater conceptual refinement of the status quo and states' degree of satisfaction with the status quo is necessary for continued progress within the power transition research program.

Subsequent Development of the Power Transition Research Program

Since Kugler and Organski's 1989 "retrospective and prospective evaluation" of power transition theory, there has been a flurry of activity, both theoretical and empirical.[69] The *Parity and War* anthology, published in 1996, reflects not only new operationalizations of key variables but also extensions of the temporal and spatial domains of power transition theory, continued attempts to merge power transition and other research programs, and formal models of power transition processes.[70] As a result of these developments, the protective belt surrounding power transition's hard core is continually expanding and changing. Although such flux is a normal phenomenon anticipated by Lakatos (p. 137), it makes characterization of the protective belt difficult.

Space limitations prevent us from presenting a comprehensive summary of power transition theory's protective belt, and consequently we focus on three distinct problemshifts: Lemke's multiple hierarchy

Analysis of a Game Theoretic Model," in Frank P. Harvey and Ben D. Mor, eds., *Conflict in World Politics* (New York: St. Martin's Press, 1998), pp. 33–61; on regional patterns, see Lemke and Werner, "Power Parity, Commitment to Change, and War," p. 245, note 11.

69. Kugler and Organski, "The Power Transition"; for reviews see Lemke and Kugler, "The Evolution of the Power Transition Perspective"; Vasquez, "When are Power Transitions Dangerous?"; Siverson and Miller, "The Power Transition"; Kugler and Lemke, "The Power Transition Research Program."

70. Kugler and Lemke, *Parity and War*.

model, Kim's alliance transitions model, and research regarding the timing and initiation of wars associated with power transitions. We also address the lack of attention to the causal mechanisms that lead from power transitions to the outbreak of war, and the role of bargaining in these processes. We present our evaluation of the progress of the power transition research program at the end of this section.

LEMKE'S MULTIPLE HIERARCHY MODEL

Organski's power transition theory focuses almost exclusively on the dyadic interactions among the dominant state and its potential challengers. Scholars have recently moved beyond Organski's exclusive focus on power transitions at the very top of the international hierarchy and have empirically tested power transition hypotheses on data sets that include minor power dyads as well as major powers. The most important of these efforts in terms of power transition theory is Douglas Lemke's multiple hierarchy model, which extends power transition logic to regional subsystems within the overarching international order.[71]

Lemke argues that Organski's international hierarchy is but one of many hierarchies in the global political arena. Nested within it are a number of regional hierarchies, complete with dominant regional powers and regional status quos, and smaller sub-regional hierarchies as well.[72] A minor power might be satisfied with the global status quo (or unable to challenge the globally dominant state), but may nevertheless challenge a locally dominant power for the ability to reshape the regional order.

By extending the basic logic of power transition theory to regional systems, Lemke's problemshift generalizes the theory in important ways. Whether it is an intra-program or inter-program problemshift is difficult to assess because of the ambiguous status of the multiple hierarchy model

71. Douglas Lemke, "Small States and War: An Expansion of Power Transition Theory," in Kugler and Lemke, *Parity and War*, pp. 77–92; Lemke, *Regions of War and Peace*.

72. Lemke's theoretical justification for identifying regional and sub-regional hierarchies hinges on the power projection capacity of minor powers, which is operationalized in terms of a loss-of-strength gradient. Lemke, *Regions of War and*

with respect to the positive heuristic and because of the ambiguity of Lakatosian metatheory on this issue. We believe that the proper criterion is that the problemshift not be inconsistent with the positive heuristic, which is less demanding than the alternative criterion of being explicitly specified in the positive heuristic. Because Lemke's extension of power transition theory is not inconsistent with the positive heuristic, it is not degenerating by this criterion.[73] We argue that it represents an intra-program problemshift that generalizes the logic of power transition theory and contributes the sixth element to the positive heuristic of the research program:

> (PH-6): Construct models that extend the logic of power transition theory to subsystems of states (including dyadic relationships) that are nested within the international order.

Because Lemke's multiple hierarchy model generates hypotheses about the behavior of small states, which were neglected in Organski's original formulation, it clearly yields predictions of novel facts and is consequently not ad hoc_1. Empirical tests of Lemke's hypotheses in some regional contexts have demonstrated significant support for the multiple hierarchy model. Perhaps most strikingly, Lemke's tests demonstrate that in South American regional hierarchies, parity approximates a necessary condition for minor power war.[74] In addition, applications of the model to

---

Peace, chap. 4; Lemke, "Toward a General Understanding of Parity and War"; Lemke, "Small States and War."

73. Although Lakatos (pp. 175–176, 182) sometimes suggests that a problemshift that is not fully in accord with the positive heuristic is ad hoc_3, elsewhere (p. 137) he allows for the positive heuristic to change over time in response to new developments, providing that this change does not violate any hard core assumptions. This suggests that auxiliary hypotheses are ad hoc_3 only if they are inconsistent with the positive heuristic. This is a weaker condition for the classification of a new development as an intra-program shift, for a new emendation need not be explicitly part of the positive heuristic, just not inconsistent with it. This is Zahar's interpretation of Lakatos, and we accept it. Elie Zahar, "Why Did Einstein's Programme Supersede Lorentz's? (I)," British Journal for the Philosophy of Science, Vol. 24 (1973), 101ff.

74. Lemke, "Toward a General Understanding of Parity and War"; Lemke, "Small States and War."

the Middle East and Far East show that conditions of power parity and dissatisfaction with the status quo together markedly increase the probability of war onset in these regions.[75] Thus, many of Lemke's predicted novel facts are empirically corroborated, so the multiple hierarchy problemshift is not ad hoc$_2$. Finally, Lemke and Werner show that the multiple hierarchy model is able to "postdict" (or retrospectively predict) the major wars cited in support of the original power transition theory, satisfying the Lakatosian criterion that the new theory explain not only novel facts but also those predicted by the old theory.[76]

Because Lemke's multiple hierarchy model accounts for the existing empirical content of power transition theory and contains excess content that is not inconsistent with the hard core, and because some of this excess empirical content is empirically corroborated, we argue that the multiple hierarchy model constitutes a progressive, intra-program problemshift.

KIM'S ALLIANCE TRANSITIONS MODEL

Woosang Kim develops a theory of alliance transitions, which he describes as "revised power transition theory," and tests it over the period since 1648. Kim hypothesizes that alliance parity—a balance of capabilities between opposing alliance coalitions—is associated with an increased probability of major war. His statistical tests show that alliance parity is indeed associated with an appreciably higher probability of war, while traditional power transition hypotheses concerning dyadic parity, dyadic transitions, and speed of transition are not empirically supported by the evidence.[77]

---

75. When parity and dissatisfaction are present, the probability of war in Middle Eastern and Far Eastern dyads is at least five times greater than their baseline probability of war (when neither parity nor dissatisfaction is present). Lemke, *Regions of War and Peace*, p. 135.

76. Lemke and Werner, "Power Parity, Commitment to Change, and War."

77. Kim, "Alliance Transitions and Great Power War"; Kim, "Power Transitions and Great Power War from Westphalia to Waterloo"; Kim, "Power Parity, Alliance, and War from 1648 to 1975." Kim includes alliance effects in national capability scores by including expected contributions from other great powers, which he adjusts by weighting the third party's capability by an indicator that reflects the similarity of alliance preferences between the two states in question.

Kim breaks from the main orientation of the power transition research program in two important respects. First, he extends the temporal domain back to 1648. Although Organski asserted that power transition theory does not apply to the preindustrial period, his reliance on industrialization as the primary mechanism for economic growth and consequently international change is unnecessarily restrictive. If we focus on the more general concept of internal growth and uneven rates of growth, extensions of the temporal domain to periods before the onset of industrialization need not violate the hard core assumptions of power transition theory.

More important, Kim relaxes the assumption that internal economic development is the primary means of augmenting national power and argues that alliance formation is a viable alternative.[78] We interpret Kim's argument for relaxing the internal development assumption as a break— albeit a modest one—with power transition's hard core, because it violates the assumption that economic growth within the state, not external affiliations, is the primary means of increasing national power. Thus Kim's alliance transitions model represents an inter-program problemshift, a new theoretical and empirical line of inquiry rooted in, but not fully accepting, the assumptions of the prior research program.

Like intra-program shifts, inter-program problemshifts are judged on their ability to generate novel predictions. Kim's extension of the model to the pre-industrial era generates predictions that were clearly not within the purview of power transition theory, and therefore is not ad hoc$_1$. Statistical testing reveals empirical corroboration of some of the novel predictions; thus Kim's alliance transitions model is not ad hoc$_2$. We conclude that Kim's inter-program problemshift is progressive, and

---

He uses the tau-b statistic to measure alliance similarity, the limitations of which are noted by Signorino and Ritter, who suggest an alternative measure of similarity as a possible corrective for future analyses. Curtis S. Signorino and Jeffrey M. Ritter, "Tau-b or Not Tau-b: Measuring the Similarity of Foreign Policy Positions," *International Studies Quarterly*, Vol. 43, No. 1 (March 1999), pp. 115–144.

78. Kim, "Power, Alliance, and Major Wars, 1816–1975," p. 256; Kim, "Alliance Transitions and Great Power War," pp. 835–836; Kim, "Power Transitions and Great Power War from Westphalia to Waterloo," pp. 155–156.

represents a theoretically and empirically productive offshoot of the power transition research program.

WHO INITIATES WAR, WHEN, AND WHY?

Power transition theory and its associated hypotheses enjoy a substantial record of empirical corroboration. The confluence of a dissatisfied challenger's rise and a dominant state's decline or stagnation is correlated with the onset of major wars. Lemke shows that a similar relationship obtains for minor power wars. One thing that is missing, however, is a specification of which state initiates war, when, and why.

The power transition research program has not fully resolved the question of *timing*: whether war is initiated before transition, at the point of transition, or after transition. Organski originally argued that major wars were initiated by challengers prior to overtaking the dominant state.[79] Organski's subsequent empirical work with Kugler, however, indicates that challengers initiate war *after* overtaking the dominant state, and other studies have generated mixed results.[80]

Organski's and Kugler's first response to the unexpected finding about the timing of war was to argue, based on their empirical findings, that although the challenger initiates war after the *dyadic* transition, it does so before the strength of the challenger's *coalition* has surpassed the dominant state's coalition. They suggest the following tentative explanation:

---

79. Organski, *World Politics*, p. 333. This is theoretically problematic because it implies that the challenger initiates a war while it is still the weaker party and consequently likely to lose the war. See Levy, "Declining Power and the Preventive Motivation for War," *World Politics*, Vol. 40, No. 1 (1987), pp. 82–107, at 83–84.

80. Organski and Kugler, *The War Ledger*, pp. 59–61. Geller provides supporting evidence, but Thompson finds that global wars since 1750 have broken out before the transition point, and Kadera's findings are mixed. Daniel S. Geller, "Relative Power, Rationality, and International Conflict," in Kugler and Lemke, *Parity and War*, pp. 127–44; Thompson, "Succession Crises in the Global System: A Test of the Transition Model," in Albert Bergesen, ed., *Crises in the World System* (Beverly Hills, Calif.: Sage, 1983), pp. 93–116 (see pp. 110–111); Kadera, *The Power-Conflict Story*. Clearly, more work needs to be done on the timing of war onsets during power transitions.

When two nations fight alone, there can be little doubt in the defender's and attacker's minds what their respective positions are and what will be the prospects for each if things are left to drift. On the other hand, when alliances are present the challenger may be in a position to afford to hesitate longer, for there is always hope that some important country will be separated from the rest of the defending coalition, thus tipping the balance. The dominant nation, secure in the support of the stronger coalition, also may tend to procrastinate before it faces up to the necessity of trying to turn back the foe.[81]

This argument is troubling from a Lakatosian perspective. It violates power transition's hard core, for the explanation of the challenger's decision to wait relies on the flexibility of alliance ties, which is explicitly rejected elsewhere (HC-6). In addition, the argument that the dominant state has an incentive to wait because there is "always hope" incorporates an element of wishful thinking, a non-rational factor that runs counter to the assumption (HC-2) that leaders make rational choices.

Another limitation of these analyses of the timing and initiation of war is that they focus only on the behavior of the challenger and ignore the declining dominant power. This is theoretically problematic, for the outbreak of war is a question of strategic interaction between two or more states, and any analysis of the timing and initiation of war must focus not only on the challenger but also on the dominant power and on the strategic interaction between the two. Similarly, in a study of the conditions under which power shifts precipitate war, Kim and Morrow explain, "we do not ask the question of why dominant states do not crush nascent challengers far in advance of their rise to power. The literature, to our knowledge, has never addressed this question, so we do not."[82] This issue is too important to dismiss so easily.

Kugler and Organski anticipate the argument that the dominant power may have an incentive to initiate hostilities, but claim that because the dominant power is satisfied, it "has little incentive" to alter the status quo. "After all, the prevailing international order is controlled by and designed

---

81. Organski and Kugler, *The War Ledger*, pp. 59–61.

82. Kim and Morrow, "When Do Power Shifts Lead to War?" p. 897, note 1. James D. Morrow, "The Logic of Overtaking," in Kugler and Lemke, *Parity and War*, p. 314, makes a similar point.

for the benefit of the dominant power."[83] This argument ignores the fact that the very rise of the challenger constitutes a potential threat to the status quo, and that the declining leader may have an incentive to use force not in order to alter the status quo but to maintain it, by initiating or provoking a "preventive war" to block the rising challenger while the opportunity is still available.[84]

The hypothesized role of the preventive motivation in power transitions draws some support from the empirical literature. Geller finds that wars that break out during power shifts are initiated either by the dominant power before the transition or by the rising challenger after the transition.[85] Copeland, whose dynamic differentials theory merges power transitions with polarity, finds in several cases that "in both multipolarity and bipolarity, it is the dominant and declining state that initiates war."[86]

---

83. Kugler and Organski, "The Power Transition," pp. 187–188.

84. Levy, "Declining Power and the Preventive Motivation for War"; Stephen Van Evera, *Causes of War* (Ithaca, N.Y.: Cornell University Press, 1999), chap. 4. Organski, *World Politics*, pp. 309 and 333, mentions preventive war but questions its employment both on moral grounds and on the basis of historical accuracy, although he cites only anecdotal evidence to support the latter claim. On the problematic nature of the "preventive war" concept, see Jack S. Levy and Joseph R. Gochal, "Democracy and 'Preventive War': Israel in the 1956 Sinai Campaign," *Security Studies*, Vol. 11, No. 2 (Winter 2001–02), pp. 1–49.

85. Daniel S. Geller, "Power Transition and Conflict Initiation," *Conflict Management and Peace Science*, Vol. 12, No. 1 (Fall 1992), pp. 1–16, at p. 14. Because Geller's dependent variable includes disputes short of war, his analysis, while suggestive, does not contradict the finding that *war* occurs after the power transition. In other work that includes initiation of both war and serious disputes, Geller shows that "among contender states, war and dispute initiators are as likely to be inferior to their opponents as they are to be superior in the static balance of relative capabilities." Geller, "Relative Power, Rationality, and International Conflict," p. 138. See also Frank Whelon Wayman, "Power Shifts and the Onset of War," in Kugler and Lemke, *Parity and War*, pp. 145–162.

86. Dale C. Copeland, "Neorealism and the Myth of Bipolar Stability: Toward a New Dynamic Realist Theory of War," *Security Studies*, Vol. 5, No. 3 (Spring 1996), pp. 29–89 (quotation on p. 54); see also Dale C. Copeland, *The Origins of Major War* (Ithaca, N.Y.: Cornell University Press, 2000).

Although power transition theorists continue to reject the hypothesis that under some conditions the declining leader will initiate war for primarily preventive reasons, they have begun to develop some models that incorporate strategic interaction into the power transition research program. After acknowledging the unexpected finding of the post-transition war onset, and after rejecting explanations based on coalitional models and the possibility of faulty measurement of national power, Kugler and Organski emphasize an alternative explanation based on Kugler and Zagare's work on nuclear deterrence, which extends power transition logic by combining it with a game-theoretic framework based on Brams's theory of moves.[87]

Kugler and Zagare's model implies that, given a transition between a dominant state and a dissatisfied challenger, war will not occur prior to the point of transition. War can occur soon after the point of parity or transition only if the declining state is risk-acceptant and if the challenger is either risk-acceptant or risk-neutral.[88] Thus the Kugler and Zagare model can account for the anomalous empirical finding of post-transition war, but only by adding an additional assumption about the risk propensities of states. This is not problematic per se, although for this move to be progressive, additional predictions based on risk orientation would have to be generated and empirically confirmed, as the resolution of existing anomalies is not by itself sufficient. It is puzzling, however, why risk-acceptant actors might go to war after a transition but never before, and a fuller explanation of this puzzle would be helpful.[89]

---

87. Kugler and Organski, "The Power Transition," pp. 183–84; Kugler and Zagare, eds., *Exploring the Stability of Deterrence* (Boulder, Colo.: Lynne Rienner, 1987); Kugler and Zagare, "The Long-Term Stability of Deterrence," *International Interactions*, Vol. 15 (1990), pp. 255–278; Steven J. Brams, *Theory of Moves* (New York: Cambridge University Press, 1994).

88. War can also occur at the exact point of parity, if both states are risk acceptant or if one state is risk acceptant and the other is risk neutral. Kugler and Zagare, "The Long-Term Stability of Deterrence."

89. The Kugler and Zagare prediction is consistent with the fact that in most game-theoretic models, war is not an equilibrium outcome under complete information if actors are risk neutral or risk averse. Bueno de Mesquita and Lalman, *War and Reason*; James D. Fearon, "Rationalist Explanations for War,"

Kugler and Zagare argue further that this explanation accounts for the absence of a superpower nuclear war since 1945, presumably since no challenger has overtaken the United States (*ipso facto*, preserving the conditions of stable deterrence).[90] Thus, they claim to account for the anomaly of post-transition war onset and generate a novel fact—stable nuclear deterrence—that is consistent with the evidence.[91]

Recent dissertations by Alsharabati and Abdollahian deal with the question of the timing and initiation of war, but because this research is unpublished our assessment of it is preliminary and tentative.[92] Although each of these studies is an important step forward in understanding the dynamics of strategic interaction during power transitions, neither goes quite far enough with respect to the question of the role of the declining power.[93] In Alsharabati's game-theoretic model of the strategic interaction between dominant power and challenger, for example, the challenger makes the initial move, leaving the dominant power with a choice between resisting or capitulating. The model does not allow the dominant state to take preventive action to incapacitate the rising power before it has grown powerful enough to challenge the defender. In addition,

---

International Organization, Vol. 49, No. 3 (Summer 1995), pp. 379–414. Most game-theoretic models of international conflict now incorporate the element of incomplete information, and efforts by power transition theorists to subsume their models within a game-theoretic framework probably will have to move in this direction if they are to be successful.

90. See also Kugler and Organski, "The Power Transition," pp. 186–188.

91. Although the prediction of novel facts means that the Kugler and Zagare model is not ad hoc, whether the absence of a U.S.-Soviet war since 1945 constitutes an empirically corroborated novel fact is problematic. Although the long great power peace is consistent with the predictions of Kugler's and Zagare's extension of power transition theory, it is also consistent with many other theories as well, and therefore provides rather weak evidentiary support. Kugler and Zagare, *Exploring the Stability of Deterrence.* Kugler and Zagare concede that "The absence of a superpower war since [1945] ... makes it impossible to test directly the theory of deterrence." Kugler and Zagare, "The Long-Term Stability of Deterrence," p. 256.

92. Carole Alsharabati, "Dynamics of War Initiation" (Ph.D. dissertation, Claremont Graduate School, 1997); Abdollahian, "In Search of Structure."

93. This, of course, is not the only question they are trying to answer.

preliminary empirical tests of the model include variables representing the value of the status quo and the costs of war to the challenger, but not to the defender.[94]

Abdollahian argues that more attention ought to be paid to the dominant power's satisfaction with its dyadic relationship with the challenger.[95] His dynamic differential equations model identifies the structural conditions conducive to stability and instability, and hence in principle can predict the timing of war, but it cannot deal with the question of which specific state initiates war.

Although the question of who initiates war is commonly addressed by scholars both inside and outside the power transition research program, it is actually quite problematic in the context of strategic interaction. If one party has an incentive to initiate a war, its adversary might anticipate this, and act preemptively in order to secure the military advantages of striking first, at least under certain conditions (preemption may also involve diplomatic or domestic political costs). If so, the first state may have an incentive to preempt the preemptor, and so on. This implies that the attempt to identify the initiator may not be analytically useful.[96] On the other hand, the situation is not entirely symmetrical, for both the domestic politics and political psychology of decline may be different from those of ascent (in part because of the overweighting of losses), and these may influence the likelihood of preemption.[97] Moreover, although the infinite regress of preemption is theoretically plausible, on the empirical level there is some evidence that preemption rarely occurs, which undercuts

---

94. Alsharabati, "Dynamics of War Initiation," chaps. 2 and 3.

95. Abdollahian, "In Search of Structure," pp. 63, 84–85.

96. Kadera reaches a similar conclusion via a different logical argument. Kadera, *The Power-Conflict Story*.

97. There is substantial experimental evidence that people respond more strongly to losses than to comparable gains. This suggests another interesting line of research for power transition—to incorporate loss aversion and risk acceptance in the domain of losses. This would be compatible with the hard core of the power transition research program if the actors' reference points were always equated with the current status quo. Jack S. Levy, "Prospect Theory, Rational Choice, and International Relations," *International Studies Quarterly*, Vol. 41, No. 1 (March 1997), pp. 87–112.

the abovementioned arguments that the identification of the initiator is meaningless.[98]

These game-theoretic and dynamic models of the strategic interaction between declining leader and challenger constitute important efforts to put power transition theory in a dynamic and interactive context and to explain the anomalous empirical finding that the onset of war occurs after the point of power transition. Further development of this line of work could help overcome earlier degenerating elements in the research program and might contribute to a progressive intra-program problemshift. At the same time, however, other power transition theorists seem to be moving away from an emphasis on the dynamic nature of power transitions and from the question of the timing of war, and this suggests some ambiguity in the direction of the research program. Werner and Kugler, for example, argue that wars could erupt either prior to or following a transition, and that the condition of parity, not overtake, is the important correlate of war proposed by power transition theory.[99] Similarly, Lemke and Kugler argue emphatically that:

theoretically, it is parity that is important to war initiation. The closer to parity a dyad is, the greater the threat of war. Parity, not actual transitions, is of theoretical importance. For this reason it would have been better if Power *Transition* Theory had been named Power *Parity* Theory.[100]

Arguments for the relative importance of parity, rather than transitions, are puzzling in light of Organski's and Kugler's argument that the onset of war is more consistently associated with the process of transition and overtake than with the condition of parity, and with their finding of exactly zero cases of wars under conditions of parity without transition.[101] Moreover, an emphasis on the condition of parity rather than on the process of transition means that the question of timing of war onset

---

98. Dan Reiter, "Exploding the Powder Keg Myth: Preemptive Wars Almost Never Happen," *International Security*, Vol. 20, No. 2 (Fall 1995), pp. 5–34.

99. Werner and Kugler, "Power Transitions and Military Buildups," p. 204, n. 12.

100. Lemke and Kugler, "The Evolution of the Power Transition Perspective," p. 12 (emphasis in original).

101. Organski and Kugler, *The War Ledger*, pp. 49–52.

is moot, for the classification of the independent variable as parity or non-parity would not be affected by whether war occurred slightly before or slightly after the point of transition. Similarly, whether the dominant power initiates or provokes war would no longer be a central question.[102]

Thus the emphasis on parity over transitions would redirect our attention away from some important questions regarding the causes of war that have interested power transition scholars for years. It would discourage power transition theorists from pursuing important puzzles regarding the timing and initiation of war, and would constitute a major step back from Organski's attempt to construct a dynamic alternative to static balance of power models. We would regard such a shift in the orientation of the power transition research program, if it continued, as degenerating from a Lakatosian perspective.

QUESTIONS OF CAUSAL MECHANISMS AND BARGAINING

The question of who initiates war and when also raises the question of the causal mechanisms through which war occurs. The power transition research program has done a better job of specifying the structural conditions conducive to war than of explaining the causal mechanisms that drive this process. We have ample evidence of a fairly robust correlation between power parity and war, particularly among contenders vying for control of the international or regional order, but we still lack a complete theoretical explanation for this phenomenon.

The central question here concerns bargaining between adversarial states, and particularly why the two adversaries cannot reach a mutually agreeable settlement that avoids war. Unfortunately, power transition

---

102. Geller's recent study is an exception in that he deliberately revisits both Organski's original emphasis on process and the question of which state initiates war. Among enduring rivals engaging in war between 1816 and 1996, dissatisfied challengers are more likely to initiate war than are status quo defenders, but in those cases where defenders do initiate wars with challengers, the dyad in question is almost always experiencing a shift in relative power when war is initiated. Daniel S. Geller, "Status Quo Orientation, Capabilities, and Patterns of War Initiation in Dyadic Rivalries," *Conflict Management and Peace Science*, Vol. 18, No. 1 (Fall 2000), pp. 73–96.

theorists generally neglect this intervening process,[103] although others have addressed it. As Levy has argued,

> There is some level of concessions that the challenger would prefer to grant rather than to fight, particularly since he can always hope to regain those concessions later when he is stronger. Similarly, there is some level of concessions that the declining state would prefer to accept from the challenger rather than to initiate a war. If the challenger's offer matched the declining state's demands, war would not occur. Moreover, if both states agreed on the likely outcome of the war, they would be better off accepting that outcome without incurring the actual costs of war ... [but] the very fact that the declining state knows that the rising adversary will probably be able to regain any concession later makes the former less likely to accept those concessions.[104]

Moreover, the kind of concessions acceptable to the declining state would be those that impeded the further increases in the military power and potential of the rising adversary, but these are often based on internal economic changes that cannot easily be bartered away.

This is generally known as the commitment problem.[105] Along with private information about relative capabilities and resolve, and incentives to misrepresent that information (which generate different expectations by the two adversaries regarding their relative bargaining strength and consequently different incentives to settle), the inability of rising states to commit to refraining from using their power when they achieve a dominant position often makes it difficult for dyads undergoing a shift in relative power to reach a negotiated settlement. Specifying the conditions under which bargaining between a rising state and a declining state leads to a satisfactory settlement and peaceful transition is no easy task, as illustrated by the complexity of Powell's game-theoretic model of

---

103. This is in spite of Organski's hypothesis that the flexibility of the dominant state is an additional variable determining the violent or peaceful character of power transitions (PH-5). Organski, *World Politics*, p. 336.

104. Levy, "Declining Power and the Preventive Motivation for War," p. 96.

105. Fearon, "Rationalist Explanations for War."

bargaining under conditions of shifting relative power.[106] Nevertheless, this is one question to which power transition theorists must devote more attention if they are to construct a more fully developed explanation of the causal paths through which power transitions, combined with status quo evaluations, contribute to the outbreak of war.

Troubling theoretical anomalies are left by the lack of attention to the dominant power and its possible incentives to initiate war, to the problem of strategic interaction and preemption, and to bargaining between leading power and challenger. On the other hand, preliminary efforts to cast power transition theory in a strategic interaction framework and to model the process formally,[107] and thus to incorporate the decisions and incentives of both dominant state and challenger, are useful steps in a more progressive direction.

Summary Evaluation of the Power Transition Program

We have examined several distinct streams of research within the power transition research program, including the initial formulation of the theory by Organski, the refinement of the theory and empirical tests of some of its key propositions by Organski and Kugler, and important extensions of the theory by Kugler and Organski, Lemke, Kim, and others. We have given particular attention to the question of whether these extensions are intra-program or inter-program problemshifts, and whether these problemshifts are progressive or degenerating in a Lakatosian sense. We have argued that in extending power transition theory to regional subsystems, Lemke's multiple hierarchy model subsumes the empirical content of Organski's theory and generates predictions of novel facts that contradict neither the hard core nor the negative and positive heuristics of the research program, and have received some degree of empirical corroboration. Consequently, it constitutes a progressive intra-program problemshift within the power transition research program. We have argued that Kim's alliance

---

106. Robert Powell, *In the Shadow of Power* (Princeton, N.J.: Princeton University Press, 1999).

107. Alsharabati, "Dynamics of War Initiation."

transition theory also builds on the foundations of power transition theory and generates predictions of numerous novel facts that have been empirically confirmed. The focus on alliances, however, breaks from the power transition research program's hard core of assumptions, and we conclude that Kim's project represents a progressive inter-program problemshift.

Finally, with regard to the questions of timing and initiation, we have argued that the power transition research program has exhibited both signs of degeneration and signs of promise. Some attempts to explain anomalies in Organski's initial formulation depart from the program's hard core in significant ways, and are consequently degenerating. Recent efforts to explain the timing and initiation of war in terms of formal models—particularly game-theoretic models capturing strategic interaction—offer considerable promise. This outgrowth of the research program is still at an early stage, however, and several potentially important works have not yet been published. It would therefore be premature to make a definitive judgment whether this work will reverse the earlier trend toward degeneration on the questions of the timing and initiation of war and lead to a progressive problemshift. Lakatos would be the first to urge patience, for he recognized that problemshifts may occur only slowly, and might be discernible as degenerating only with the benefit of hindsight (pp. 154–159).[108]

Because some areas of inquiry within the power transition research program are progressive while others are degenerating, it is difficult to make a summary appraisal of the power transition research program from the perspective of Lakatosian metatheory. One of the limitations of Lakatos's methodology of scientific research programs is its failure to address the problem of how to aggregate judgments about the progressive or degenerating nature of individual projects into an integrated net assessment of the research program as a whole. Nonetheless, we are strongly inclined to argue that the power transition research program is, on balance, progressive. It is a lively and expanding research program that has moved forward in several important substantive directions. Most theoretical extensions of power transition principles have generated novel

---

108. See also Elman and Elman, Chapter 2 in this volume.

predictions, many of which are empirically corroborated, and proponents of the research program have been particularly good at developing improved operational measures of key theoretical concepts.

Scholars working within progressive research programs cannot simply sit back and admire their handiwork, however, for the research program that stops progressing begins to degenerate. We have argued that among the most important tasks for power transition theorists are the conceptual development and operationalization of states' degree of satisfaction with the status quo, the construction of an explanation for the timing of war that is fully consistent with the hard core of the research program, and the better specification of the causal mechanisms leading to war, including the role of bargaining between the dominant state and the rising challenger. Attention to these tasks is essential if the power transition research program is to continue on a progressive trajectory.

Conclusion: The Utility of Lakatos's Methodology for Assessing Progress in International Relations

Having used Lakatos's methodology of scientific research programs as a framework for an analysis of the evolution of the power transition research program, we now reverse gears and consider the lessons we have learned from this exercise for the question of the utility of Lakatosian metatheory for evaluating research in international relations and in social science more generally. Lakatos's framework has been useful in many ways. It shifts our attention from individual theories to a series of theories that make up a research program; it forces us to think critically about both the generation of novel theoretical predictions and their empirical corroboration; and it provides guidelines for assessing whether efforts to resolve anomalies within a research program are scientifically legitimate. Because of space limitations, here we focus primarily on the problems we encountered in applying Lakatosian metatheory.

One very basic problem, for which Lakatos provides little guidance, concerns the "unit of appraisal": how broadly or how narrowly should we define a research program? In our case, should we focus on realism, structural realism, dynamic power theories broadly defined (to include not only Organski's power transition theory but also Gilpin's hegemonic transition theory, Doran's power cycle theory, Thompson's leadership long cycle theory, and Copeland's dynamic realism), or just one particular model of power and change?

In choosing to focus on the power transition research program as developed by Organski, Kugler, Lemke, and their colleagues, we have opted for a somewhat restrictive view of the boundaries of a research program.[109] We have done so deliberately, out of concern that defining research programs too broadly brings with it two related risks. First, by grouping distinct theories together, we run the risk of including internally contradictory assumptions and hypotheses under the same heading. This can generate inconsistencies in the hard core, increase the ambiguity of the testable propositions derived from the hard core assumptions, and consequently diminish the falsifiability of these theories.[110]

A second danger is that the difficulties involved in testing such large, inclusive groups of theories can distract researchers' attention from the empirical evaluation of key hypotheses, and encourage them to engage in more abstract theoretical debates. An example is the "paradigm wars" that have dominated discourse in the international relations field for decades. To minimize these risks, we chose to delimit the unit of appraisal in a restrictive manner, considering only those theories sharing identical or nearly identical assumptions with the works of Organski and his colleagues. The result is a clearly defined research program, but one that is somewhat limited in scope.

---

109. Such a narrow delimitation is consistent with de Marchi's conception of a research program as a connected sequence of models. Neil de Marchi, "Introduction: Rethinking Lakatos," in Neil de Marchi and Mark Blaug, eds., *Appraising Economic Theories: Studies in the Methodology of Scientific Research Programs* (Aldershot, UK: Edward Elgar, 1991), pp. 12–13. A more expansive conception of research programs is reflected in Keohane's argument that classical realism and structural realism are part of the same research program (Keohane, "Theory of World Politics," pp. 506–518), or in Andrew Moravscik's treatment in this volume (Chapter 5) of liberalism as a single research program.

110. On the importance of constructing theories that are both falsifiable and internally consistent, see Gary King, Robert O. Keohane, and Sidney Verba, *Designing Social Inquiry* (Princeton, N.J.: Princeton University Press, 1994), pp. 100–107.

Because the power transition research program is relatively well-defined, and because power transition theorists have used Lakatosian language and identified their work explicitly with the research program, in principle it should be relatively easy to analyze the program through the lenses of Lakatos's methodology of scientific research programs.[111] In fact, delineating the elements of the power transition research program has been very difficult. The most critical task involves the specification of the hard core, which is a prerequisite for all subsequent tasks in Lakatosian metatheory. Lakatos provides few guidelines, however, as to exactly what constitutes the hard core and whether it changes over time. At one point he emphasizes the fact that most Newtonian puzzles were foreseeable and even foreseen in the early phases of Newton's research program, and argues that it is useful to "separate the 'hard core' from the more flexible metaphysical principles expressing the positive heuristic" (pp. 136–137). Elsewhere, however, Lakatos argues that the hard core only emerges over time: the "hard core of a research programme does not actually emerge fully armed like Athene from the head of Zeus. It develops slowly, by a long, preliminary process of trial and error" (p. 133, note 4), and "dramatic spectacular results become visible only with hindsight and rational reconstruction" (p. 179). Most interpreters of Lakatos emphasize this view of the evolving hard core. Neil de Marchi, for example, argues that "the hard core and heuristics evolve and mutually inform each other."[112]

---

111. It is also interesting to note that Organski's own beliefs about what constitutes theoretical progress in international relations are similar to the principles of Lakatos' methodology of scientific research programs. Writing before Lakatos published his famous essay, Organski argued that, "A good theory must be clearly formulated and logically sound, and it must be consistent with the data it seeks to explain. Furthermore, it must explain something about the data that one would not otherwise know, and it must provide a more satisfactory explanation than any other rival theory can offer." Organski, *World Politics*, p. 283. Although not written in the language of Lakatosian metatheory, Organski's remarks are remarkably similar in spirit, emphasizing the issues of empirical testability or falsifiability, prediction of novel facts or excess empirical content, and explanatory capacity exceeding that of competing theories.

112. De Marchi, "Introduction," p. 16. See also Alan Musgrave, "Method or Madness? Can the Methodology of Research Programmes be Rescued from

If the hard core emerges gradually, however, by what criteria do we distinguish between a situation in which a problemshift breaks from the hard core and one in which that same problemshift helps to redefine the hard core? In terms of power transition theory, for example, does Kim's alliance transition theory break with the hard core, as we have argued, or does it broaden the content of the hard core to include alternative elements of national power? The concept of an evolving hard core blurs the distinction between inter-program problemshifts and intra-program shifts.

If the hard core evolves over time, the negative and positive heuristics also evolve and become more difficult to specify with any degree of precision. But even if the hard core is fixed at a certain point in the evolution of a research program, does this mean that the positive heuristic is also fixed, precluding further changes? This strikes us as unrealistic. Research programs evolve in response to theoretical and empirical anomalies that emerge at various stages in the evolution of a research program but that are not necessarily anticipated at the time of the consolidation of the hard core. This leads us to argue that the proper criterion for a progressive problemshift is that it not be inconsistent with the assumptions of the hard core, rather than the more stringent criterion that it be explicitly anticipated by the original positive heuristic. With respect to power transition theory, for example, we treat Lemke's multiple hierarchy model as a progressive intra-program problemshift because it is not inconsistent with the hard core, despite the fact that Organski says nothing about nested multiple hierarchies in his initial formulation of power transition theory.

Although through his discussion of ad hoc emendations Lakatos provides criteria for the classification of research programs as degenerative, his emphasis on tolerance of struggling research programs raises several practical questions, including how long we should wait for the empirical corroboration of novel theoretical predictions and thus for a definitive judgment that a problemshift is or is not degenerating. How

---

Epistemological Anarchism?" in R.S. Cohen, P.K. Feyerabend, and M.W. Wartofsky, eds., *Essays in Memory of Imre Lakatos* (Dordrecht: D. Reidel, 1976), pp. 457–491; Backhouse, "The Lakatosian Legacy in Economic Methodology," p. 176.

much "trial and error" should we tolerate before we conclude that scholars should abandon the research program and shift their efforts in more productive directions? This is similar to the questions that we always ask of our theories: At what point do we conclude that we are wrong? What evidence would convince us to abandon the theory? Lakatos's emphasis on the need to tolerate struggling research programs, if taken to the extreme, runs the risk of undermining objective standards of scientific progress and of failing to discourage attempts to prop up unproductive research programs. One of Lakatos's most important contributions is to provide criteria for assessing what modifications of a research program are scientifically acceptable; excessive tolerance of struggling research programs threatens to undercut this achievement.

Another issue on which Lakatos provides little guidance concerns the fact that most research programs are multidimensional in the sense that they involve several anomalies and several independent efforts to resolve those anomalies. Some of these efforts may be progressive while others may be degenerating, as we found with respect to the power transition research program, and this raises the question of the criteria by which we aggregate these discrete problemshifts and reach an overall judgment of the progressiveness of the research program as a whole. Presumably we should consider the number of novel facts, their centrality to the research program, how many of these have been corroborated and how convincingly, but we have found little discussion of this. To the contrary, much of the secondary literature (though not necessarily Lakatos himself) treats the progressive or degenerative character of a research program as dichotomous categories rather than as a continuum.

Our evaluation of the power transition research program raises several other issues that are related to larger debates over whether Lakatos gives much more emphasis to the generation of novel theoretical predictions than to their empirical corroboration.[113] First, a major strength of the power transition research program—and indeed of many research programs in international relations, particularly those based on large-n research designs—is its constant attention to the development of improved empirical indicators for key theoretical concepts, including

---

113. Elman and Elman, Chapter 2 in this volume.

national power, political capacity, and satisfaction with the status quo. This is an important component of scientific progress because it facilitates empirical testing, but Lakatos fails to give it adequate emphasis or to specify how it should be evaluated. The operationalization of theoretical concepts can presumably be subsumed within the positive heuristic (as we have done here), but it deserves more emphasis than Lakatos gives it.

Another important element of scientific progress to which Lakatos appears to give insufficient attention is the role of multiple corroborations of a single fact through repeated tests based on different empirical domains, different operational indicators, and different research designs. This derives largely from the difficulty of "corroborating" novel facts in international relations and the social sciences more generally, a difficulty that Lakatos appears to underestimate. The recent growth of multi-method research designs is a direct result of the recognition of the difficulty of testing theoretical propositions and the advantages of "triangulation" through the application of different methodologies, each compensating for the weaknesses of others.

Lakatos's emphasis on theoretical progress over empirical progress is also reflected by the tendency to define the hard core exclusively in terms of theoretical assumptions, not methodological assumptions. While our own belief in the utility of multiple methods for testing most theoretical propositions makes us sympathetic toward this perspective, there are a number of important research programs that are closely associated with a specific methodological commitment in addition to certain substantive assumptions. Microeconomics, for example, is dominated by general equilibrium theory and a commitment to mathematical formalism, and has little empirical content.[114] In international relations, some argue that the research program of neoclassical realism includes a commitment to

---

114. E. Roy Weintraub, *General Equilibrium Analysis: Studies in Appraisal* (New York: Cambridge University Press, 1985); Backhouse, "The Lakatosian Legacy in Economic Methodology," p. 176; Mark Blaug, "Why I am Not a Constructivist: Confessions of an Unrepentant Popperian," in Roger E. Backhouse, ed., *New Directions in Economic Methodology* (New York: Routledge, 1994), pp. 115–121.

historical or case study methodologies.[115] Almost every study that we have associated with the power transition research program (beyond Organski's initial formulation of the theory) involves statistical methods. The recent research program on "analytic narratives" is defined by both its theoretical assumptions and its commitment to a particular methodology.[116] These characterizations are not consistent with the common practice of excluding methodological assumptions from the specification of the hard core of a research program.

Despite these problems, we have been able to use Lakatosian concepts as a guide to analyze whether certain problemshifts are progressive or degenerating and whether they remain within a research program or initiate a new research program. We have focused on a single research program. Although our aim has not been to assess the relative merits of competing research programs, we expect that such a task would be far more difficult and that we would receive far less guidance from Lakatos.

Although Lakatos emphasizes the importance of "three-cornered fights between rival theories and experiment," he provides few criteria to evaluate the outcomes of such tests. His well-known injunction—that one theory is falsified if and only if there is a second theory that explains "all the unrefuted content" of the first and in addition predicts novel facts, some of which are corroborated (p. 116)—is of only limited utility in social science. First of all, the only theory that would explain everything another theory does is one that deductively subsumes the first. This generally involves axiomatically-based theories, but these are relatively rare in most of the social sciences outside of economics. More commonly, theory A explains only some of the content of theory B but also explains content that B does not explain, and Lakatos provides no criteria by which we might establish a preference between the two theories. This, of course, resembles the problem that Kuhn raises with his concept of

---

115. Rose, "Neoclassical Realism and Theories of Foreign Policy," p. 166; Schweller, Chapter 9 in this volume.

116. Robert H. Bates, Avner Greif, Margaret Levi, Jean-Laurent Rosenthal, and Barry R. Weingast, *Analytic Narratives* (Princeton, N.J.: Princeton University Press, 1998).

"incommensurable" paradigms.[117] The greater the differences in the assumptions in the hard cores of two different research programs, the less useful is Lakatosian metatheory as a guide for evaluating the respective merits of those research programs.

Let us end with a few remarks about the utility of the collective effort expressed in this volume. Elman and Elman are absolutely correct that most previous applications of Lakatos's methodology of scientific research programs have been based on incomplete understandings of the metatheory, that the assessment of international relations research could be improved by a more informed understanding of Lakatosian metatheory, and that the collection of essays in this volume, which is the first of its kind in political science, makes an important contribution toward that goal. It is necessary to point out, however, that the lessons we can learn from our collective efforts are limited in two respects, each imposed by practical constraints, and that these limitations suggest two potentially useful directions for future investigation.

First, the research programs selected for analysis in this volume are generally those that have endured over time.[118] To the extent that one criterion for a successful research program is that it endures over time, this constitutes a form of "selecting on the dependent variable," in that successful research programs are oversampled relative to unsuccessful research programs. If one of our questions is whether successful research programs tend to evolve in ways that are consistent with Lakatosian criteria for progressive research programs, and another question is whether progressive research programs (in the Lakatosian sense) tend to endure, this selection bias means that we are on more solid ground in answering the first question than the second. It is quite conceivable that there may be other research programs that have generated progressive

---

117. Thomas S. Kuhn, *The Structure of Scientific Revolutions*, 2nd ed. (Chicago: University of Chicago Press, 1970).

118. This is also true of similar anthologies in economics, e.g., Spiro J. Latsis, ed., *Method and Appraisal in Economics* (Cambridge, UK: Cambridge University Press, 1976).

Lakatosian problemshifts but nevertheless die out for other reasons.[119] It would be useful to examine research programs that did not endure and ask whether this was because they failed to satisfy Lakatosian criteria or for some other reason. Possible examples of such "failed" research programs might be applications of Kaplan's balance of power theory or Rummel's framework for the analysis of the relationship between internal conflict and external conflict.[120] Future applications of Lakatos's methodology of scientific research programs should include failed research programs and attempt to explain the sources of failure.

Second, we all recognize that any metatheory has its limitations, and that perhaps the proper question is not the utility of Lakatos's methodology of scientific research programs in any absolute sense, but rather its utility relative to that of alternative metatheories. Ironically, in focusing only on Lakatos's methodology of scientific research programs, this volume as a whole has implicitly adopted a naive falsificationist approach to Lakatosian metatheory, pitting Lakatos in a two-cornered fight against the "data" of the various research programs in this volume rather than a three-cornered fight against these data and rival metatheories. That is, we have applied Popperian criteria, not Lakatosian criteria, to the evaluation of Lakatosian metatheory.[121]

As a first stage in the exploration of the utility of Lakatos's methodology, this is reasonable, because for practical reasons the effort required to gain an adequate understanding of Lakatos could not have been repeated for each of several other metatheories, perhaps including Popper, Kuhn, and Laudan.[122] This suggests, however, that a useful task

---

119. Robert Jervis, "Realism in the Study of World Politics," *International Organization*, Vol. 52, No. 4 (Autumn 1998), pp. 972–975.

120. Morton A. Kaplan, *System and Process in International Politics* (New York: John Wiley, 1957); Rudolph Rummel, "Dimensions of Conflict Behavior Within and Between Nations," *General Systems: Yearbook of the Society for General Systems*, Vol. 8 (1963), pp. 1–50.

121. Karl R. Popper, *The Logic of Scientific Discovery* (New York: Harper and Row, 1959).

122. Popper, *The Logic of Scientific Discovery*; Kuhn, *The Structure of Scientific Revolutions*; and Larry Laudan, *Progress and Its Problems: Towards a Theory of Scientific Growth* (Berkeley: University of California Press, 1977).

for future research would be to examine historical research programs through the conceptual lenses of several distinct metatheories simultaneously in order to evaluate which metatheory most accurately describes how research traditions evolve and provides the best guide as to how they ought to evolve.[123]

123. On the tension between descriptive and prescriptive criteria—that is, between criteria for describing the evolution of scientific research and normative criteria for evaluating and perhaps guiding scientific research—see for example Blaug, "Why I am Not a Constructivist"; Mark Blaug, *The Methodology of Economics*, 2nd ed. (Cambridge, UK: Cambridge University Press, 1992); Latsis, *Method and Appraisal in Economics*; and Roger E. Backhouse, "The Lakatosian Legacy in Economic Methodology," in Backhouse, *New Directions in Economic Methodology*, pp. 173–191.

Chapter 5

Liberal International Relations Theory

A Scientific Assessment

Andrew Moravcsik

This paper advances three arguments. First, there exists a distinct liberal research program in international relations. Section 1 of this chapter proposes three "hard core" assumptions shared by all work within the liberal "scientific research program" in international relations (IR) and introduces three variants of liberal theory—ideational, commercial, and republican liberalism—that share those assumptions.[1] Each type of liberal theory explains interstate politics by tracing the influence of variation in pressure from domestic and transnational societal actors on underlying state preferences.

Second, this liberal research program is "progressive." Section 2 of this chapter assesses the liberal research program using three criteria for novel "excess content" derived from Imre Lakatos's philosophy of science. Judged by these criteria, liberalism has been and continues to be a "progressive" research program. It appears progressive, moreover,

I am grateful to Michael Barnett, Philip Cerny, David Dessler, Colin Elman, Miriam Elman, Stefano Guzzini, Stephen Holmes, Robert Jervis, Peter Katzenstein, Robert Keohane, Stephen Krasner, Jeffrey Legro, Lisa Martin, Robert Paarlberg, Randall Schweller, and Anne-Marie Slaughter for helpful suggestions and comments, and to Marius Hentea for swift and sure research assistance. An earlier version of this paper appeared as Andrew Moravcsik, "Liberal International Relations Theory: A Social Scientific Assessment," *Weatherhead Center for International Affairs Working Paper Series No. 01-02* (Cambridge, Mass.: Harvard University, 2002).

1. A scientific research program, the essential unit of analysis for a Lakatosian analysis of scientific progress, contains a hard core of inviolable assumptions, a positive heuristic, and a resulting "protective belt" of "auxiliary hypotheses."

no matter which received interpretation of empirical fruitfulness we employ, although the most useful, I argue, is "background theory novelty." (This interpretation of Lakatos turns out to be a more rigorous criterion than some, including Elman and Elman in Chapter 2 of this volume, believe it to be.) The progressive nature of the liberal paradigm is particularly evident in comparison with alternative paradigms, notably realism, which has recently tended to "degenerate" (in the strict Lakatosian sense) by borrowing arguments from competing liberal and non-realist paradigms that are incompatible with any plausible realist "hard core."

Third, we should be skeptical about Lakatosian criteria. The tendency of recent realists, including the editors of this volume, to overlook creeping incoherence in the realist paradigm might well lead us to question whether the invocation of Lakatosian philosophy of science provides sufficient incentive to impose logical consistency on IR theories. In Section 3 of this chapter, I highlight—very reluctantly, given how well my favored theory has performed—some limitations of any application of Lakatosian criteria to IR theory. To be sure, Lakatosian philosophy of science usefully highlights the need for consistent assumptions, and the "background theory novelty" criterion for measuring the empirical fruitfulness of assumptions offers a more useful standard for doing so than many believe. Yet the Lakatosian view of theoretical disputes as "fights to the finish" among a few monocausal theories, decided ultimately in favor of the theory that has the greater empirical scope, may impose too constraining a criterion to encourage creative, empirically fruitful social science. There is no reason to believe, at this stage in the development of IR theory, that only the theory with the widest scope is useful. Such a view forgoes two potential benefits of a less conflictual interaction among theories: the delineation of relative explanatory domains and the construction of creative multicausal syntheses. These, I submit, offer more fruitful roads forward for contemporary IR theory than gladiatorial combat among monocausal claims. We should adopt a healthy skepticism towards the doctrinaire application of Lakatosian philosophy of science, narrowly understood, to IR theory—a conclusion broadly consistent with most other contributions to this volume. Overall, this conclusion may well be more consistent with Laudanian than a Lakatosian philosophy of science.[2]

The Liberal Scientific Research Program

This section frames liberal IR theory as a Lakatosian scientific research program, delineating the "hard core" assumptions and "protective belt" of auxiliary propositions.

THE HARD CORE: THREE COMMON ASSUMPTIONS

The liberal scientific research program in IR places state-society relations at the center of world politics. It is based on the fundamental premise that a critical causal factor influencing a state's behavior is the relationship between the state and the domestic and transnational society in which it is embedded. This basic insight can be restated in terms of the three hard core assumptions shared by all liberal theories, which specify the nature of societal actors, of the state, and of the international system.[3] These three assumptions distinguish liberal IR theory from realist, institutionalist, and epistemic (or constructivist) paradigms.

THE NATURE OF THE ACTORS IN INTERNATIONAL POLITICS. The first assumption is that the fundamental actors in international politics are rational individuals and private groups, who organize and exchange to promote their interests. Liberal theory rests on a "bottom-up" view of politics, in which the demands of individuals and societal groups are treated as exogenous causes of the interests underlying state behavior. Socially differentiated individuals define underlying material and

---

2. Larry Laudan, *Beyond Positivism and Relativism: Theory, Method and Evidence* (Boulder, Colo.: Westview Press, 1996).

3. A more detailed and fully cited version of some arguments in Sections 1 and 2 can be found in Andrew Moravcsik, "Taking Preferences Seriously: A Liberal Theory of International Politics," *International Organization*, Vol. 51, No. 4 (Autumn 1997), pp. 513–553. Some material for Section 2 has been drawn from Andrew Moravcsik, "Liberalism and International Relations Theory," *Center for International Affairs Working Paper Series 92-6* (Cambridge, Mass.: Harvard University, 1992/93).

ideational tastes and preferences concerning future "states of the world," and advance them through political exchange and collective action. The central intuition is that we cannot understand the exercise of interstate power or promotion of interstate collective action unless we first understand what fundamental social purposes each state seeks.[4]

Liberal theory thereby rejects the utopian notion of an automatic harmony of interest among individuals and groups in society. Rather, scarcity and differentiation render some competition inevitable. Patterns of political order and conflict result from the variations in the underlying pattern of interaction in pursuit of these preferences for material and ideal welfare. As an empirical matter, societal demands so conflictual that social actors are likely to consider coercion as an acceptable means to promote them tend to be associated with three factors: divergent fundamental beliefs, scarcity of material goods, and

---

4. This assumption should not be controversial. This is tantamount only to saying that relevant domestic groups have some consistent preferences concerning the ultimate goals of foreign policy, based on underlying interests and ideals, and that they are translated into political preferences through individual and group action. Neither the assumption that individuals pursue their preferences instrumentally (shared by many "constructivists"), nor the assumption that the formation of such preferences is exogenous to interstate politics (in any given round of interaction), implies that individual preferences are atomistic. Cultural or sociological arguments that privilege collective social beliefs, either domestic or transnational, as sources of such social preferences, are not excluded. Some metatheoretical discussions between "constructivists" and "rationalists" obscure this potential complementarity between rationalist and cultural explanations, but more recent discussions tend instead to acknowledge it. See, for example, Jeffrey W. Legro, "Culture and Preferences in the International Cooperation Two-Step," *American Political Science Review*, Vol. 90, No. 1 (March 1996), pp. 118–137; Martha Finnemore and Kathryn Sikkink, "International Norm Dynamics and Political Change," *International Organization*, Vol. 52, No. 4 (Autumn 1998), pp. 887–917. Thomas Risse completes the conceptual convergence with his notion of "liberal constructivism." Thomas Risse-Kappen, "Collective Identity in a Democratic Community: The Case of NATO," in Peter J. Katzenstein, ed., *The Culture of National Security: Norms and Identity in World Politics* (New York: Columbia University Press: 1996), pp. 357–399.

inequalities in political power. These three potential motivations define three strands of liberalism—"ideational," "commercial," and "republican" liberalism—described in more detail below.

THE NATURE OF THE STATE. The second assumption of liberal theory is that states (or other political institutions) represent some subset of domestic society, whose weighted preferences constitute the underlying goals ("state preferences") that rational state officials pursue via foreign policy. Representative institutions thereby constitute a critical "transmission belt" by which the preferences and social power of individuals and groups in civil society enter the political realm and are eventually translated into state policy.[5] In the liberal conception of domestic politics, the state is not an actor but a representative institution, constantly subject to capture and recapture, construction and reconstruction, by coalitions of social actors. This pluralist premise assumes neither that all individuals and groups have equal influence on state policy, nor that the structure of state institutions is irrelevant. To the contrary, every government represents some individuals and groups more fully than others—from the ideal-type of a single tyrannical individual, a Pol Pot or Josef Stalin, to broad democratic participation—and thus political institutions can be of decisive importance.[6] Variation in the precise nature of representative

---

5. This assumption does not privilege the nation-state absolutely. Institutions and practices of political representation result from prior contracts, which can generally be taken for granted in explaining foreign policy. This currently privileges existing nation-states, yet where the primary interests and allegiances of individuals and private groups are transferred to a sub-national or supranational institution sufficiently empowered to represent them effectively—as may be true in, say, some aspects of politics in the European Union—a liberal analysis would naturally shift its focus to these levels.

6. Representation, in the liberal view, is not simply a formal attribute of state institutions, but may include other stable characteristics of the political process, formal or informal, that privilege particular societal interests, including informal ties, the form of individual and group rights, the nature of opportunities for exit, or an inegalitarian distribution of property, risk, information or organizational capabilities that establish socioeconomic monopoly power that can be translated into political influence. See Charles

institutions and practices helps define which groups influence the "national interest."

THE NATURE OF THE INTERNATIONAL SYSTEM. The third core assumption of liberal theory is that the configuration of state preferences shapes state behavior in the international system. States require a "purpose"—a perceived underlying stake in the matter at hand—in order to provoke conflict, inaugurate cooperation, or take any other significant foreign policy action. The precise nature of the stakes shapes policy.[7] In a pure liberal explanation, the distribution of capabilities, central to realism, and the distribution of information, central to institutionalism, are thus treated as either fixed constraints or as endogenous to state preferences—or both.[8]

This is not to assert, of course, that each state simply pursues its ideal policy, oblivious of others. Instead, each state seeks to realize its

---

Edward Lindblom, *Politics and Markets: The World's Political Economic Systems* (New York: Basic Books, 1977).

7. Here it is essential to avoid conceptual confusion, given the inconsistency of common usage, by keeping state "preferences" distinct from national "strategies," "tactics," and "policies," that is, the particular transient bargaining positions, negotiating demands, or policy goals that constitute the everyday currency of international politics. States' preferences, as the concept is employed here, comprise a set of fundamental interests defined across "states of the world." They are by definition causally independent of and prior to specific interstate strategic interactions, such as external threats, incentives, withholding of information, or other interstate bargaining tactics. The phrase "Country A changed its preferences in response to an action by Country B" would be an abuse of the term as defined here, implying less than consistently rational behavior. By contrast, strategies and tactics—although they are sometimes termed "preferences" in game-theoretical analyses—are policy options defined across intermediate political aims, as when governments declare an "interest" in maintaining the balance of power, containing or appeasing an adversary, or exercising global leadership. Liberal theory focuses on the consequences for state behavior (and state strategies) of shifts in fundamental preferences, not shifts in the strategic circumstances under which states pursue them. This definition of preferences restricts liberal theory, distinguishing it from a loose intuition that "state interests matter."

8. Liberals also set aside variations in psychology and instrumental beliefs, which lie at the core of epistemic and some constructivist theories.

distinct preferences under constraints imposed by the preferences of other states. In this regard, liberalism is not, in any greater sense than realism or institutionalism, a "domestic" or "second image" theory. All are "systemic" theories, in the strict Waltzian sense, the difference being only that liberals view the distribution of preferences, rather than capabilities (realism) or information (institutionalism), as the systemic characteristic that decisively shapes those strategies. For example, where interstate interaction generates an outcome like trade protection, widely viewed as Pareto sub-optimal, liberals turn first for an explanation to countervailing social preferences and unresolved domestic and transnational distributional conflicts, whereas institutionalists look to the mismanagement of information due to the absence of an appropriate institution, and realists to countervailing considerations arising from the need to manage security competition within the prevailing configuration of political power.

In assuming that state preferences vary exogenously, liberal theory thereby sets aside both the (realist) assumption that state preferences must be treated as if they are naturally conflictual, and the (institutionalist) assumption that they should be treated as if they are conditionally convergent. In their place, liberals assume that the critical theoretical link between varying state preferences, on the one hand, and varying interstate behavior, on the other, is provided by the concept of policy interdependence. Policy interdependence can be described as the set of costs and benefits for dominant social groups in foreign societies (the pattern of transnational externalities) that arise when dominant social groups in a given society seek to realize their own preferences internationally. Liberal theory assumes that this pattern of interdependence among state preferences—"asymmetrical interdependence"—imposes a binding constraint on state behavior.[9]

Following conventional analyses of international strategic behavior, fundamental patterns of policy interdependence can be divided into at least three broad categories, corresponding to the strategic situation

---

9. Robert Keohane and Joseph Nye, *Power and Interdependence: World Politics in Transition* (Boston: Little, Brown, 1977).

(the pattern of policy externalities) that results from unilateral action.[10] First, underlying state preferences may be "zero-sum" or "deadlocked"; that is, an attempt by dominant social groups in one country to realize their preferences through state action necessarily imposes costs (negative externalities) on dominant social groups in other countries. In this case, governments face a bargaining game with few mutual gains and a high potential for interstate tension and conflict. The decisive precondition for costly attempts at coercion, for example, is not a particular configuration of power, as realists assert, or uncertainty, as institutionalists maintain, but configurations of preferences conflictual enough to motivate willingness to accept high cost and risk. In other words, intense conflict presupposes that an "aggressor" or "revisionist" state advance demands to which other states are unwilling to submit.[11]

Preferences need not be conflictual, however. A second category arises where preferences are naturally compatible or "harmonious." Where the externalities of unilateral policies are optimal for others (or insignificant), there are strong incentives for coexistence with low conflict and simple forms of interstate coordination. Still a third category arises where motives are mixed, as when states have an incentive to negotiate institutionalized policy coordination because a shift in expectations, precommitments, or greater information can

---

10. See Lisa Martin, "Interests, Power, and Multilateralism," *International Organization*, Vol. 46, No. 4 (Autumn 1992), pp. 765–792. See also Andreas Hasenclever, Peter Mayer, and Volker Rittberger, *Theories of International Regimes* (Cambridge, UK: Cambridge University Press, 1997).

11. Revisionist preferences—underlying, socially grounded interests in revising the status quo—are distinct from revisionist "strategies," that is, a need to alter the status quo to protect enduring interests under new strategic circumstances. Liberals focus on the former, realists and institutionalists on the latter. Hence while realists and liberals might predict security conflict, they expect it to arise under different circumstances. For example, increased military spending in response to the emergence of a large adversary is a capability-induced change in strategy (with preferences fixed) consistent with realism, whereas increased spending initiated by a new ruling elite ideologically committed to territorial aggrandizement is a preference-induced change in strategy consistent with liberalism.

improve the welfare of both parties relative to unilateral policy adjustment. Further differentiation is possible. As Kenneth Oye, Duncan Snidal, Lisa Martin, and others have argued, games such as Coordination, Assurance, Prisoner's Dilemma, and Suasion have distinctive dynamics, as well as imposing precise costs, benefits, and risks on the parties.[12]

Across and within each of the qualitative categories above, the form, substance, and depth of conflict and cooperation vary according to the precise nature and intensity of preferences. By focusing on this structural element of world politics, liberal theory explores a distinct dimension of the international "system."

AUXILIARY PROPOSITIONS AND THE PROTECTIVE BELT: THREE VARIANTS OF LIBERAL IR THEORY

These three "hard core" liberal assumptions, like those of institutionalism, realism, or any other Lakatosian scientific research program, are relatively "thin" or content-free. While they exclude most existing realist, institutionalist, and epistemic theories, as well as many domestic explanations not based on pluralist and rationalist assumptions, they do not, taken by themselves, define a single unambiguous model or set of theories or hypotheses. This ambiguity is, of course, precisely what the Lakatosian understanding of a "paradigm" leads us to expect. Core assumptions define a paradigm, but auxiliary propositions are required to specify it.

While the core assumptions of liberal theory may appear almost limitless, the empirically and theoretically viable variants of liberal theory are in fact few and focused. There are three such variants of liberal theory: ideational, commercial, and republican liberalism. At the core of each lies a distinct view concerning the sources of the preferences of powerful domestic social groups, the causal mechanisms whereby they are transformed into state preferences, and the resulting

---

12. Kenneth Oye, ed., *Cooperation under Anarchy* (Princeton, N.J.: Princeton University Press, 1983), Martin, "Interests, Power, and Multilateralism"; and Duncan Snidal, "The Game *Theory* of International Politics," *World Politics*, Vol. 38, No. 1 (January 1985), pp. 25–57.

patterns of national preferences in world politics. Let us consider each in turn.[13]

IDEATIONAL LIBERALISM: IDENTITY AND LEGITIMATE SOCIAL ORDERS. Ideational liberalism views the configuration of domestic social identities and values as a basic determinant of state preferences and thus of interstate conflict and cooperation. Drawing on a liberal tradition of political philosophy dating back to John Stuart Mill, Giuseppe Mazzini, and Woodrow Wilson, it defines "social identity" as the set of preferences shared by individuals concerning the proper scope and nature of public goods provision; this in turn specifies the nature of legitimate domestic order by stipulating which social actors belong to the polity and what is owed to them.[14]

Three essential elements of domestic public order often shaped by social identities are geographical borders, political decision-making processes, and socioeconomic regulation. Each can be thought of as a public or "club" good insofar as its provision typically requires that it be legislated universally across a jurisdiction. Recall that for liberals, even the defense of (or, less obvious but no less common, the willing compromise of) territorial integrity, political sovereignty, or national

---

13. For a more detailed discussion, see Moravcsik, "Taking Preferences Seriously."

14. The concept of preferences across public goods employed here is similar to but deliberately more precise than Ruggie's "legitimate social purpose" and Katzenstein's "collective identity." John Gerard Ruggie, "International Regimes, Transactions, and Change: Embedded Liberalism in the Postwar Economic Order," *International Organization*, Vol. 36, No. 2 (Spring 1982), pp. 195–231; and Katzenstein, *The Culture of National Security*. Here is a point of intersection between traditional liberal arguments and more recent constructivist works, which tend to stress the social rather than interstate origins of socialization to particular preferences. Risse-Kappen, "Collective Identity." Liberals take no distinct position on the ultimate origins of social identities, which may stem from historical accretion or be constructed through conscious collective or state action, nor on the question of whether they "ultimately" reflect ideational or material factors—just as long as they are not conceived as endogenous to short-term interstate interaction. The ultimate origin of preferences ("all the way down") is an issue on which IR theorists,

security is not an end in itself, but a means of realizing underlying preferences defined by the demands of societal groups (Assumption 1). Social actors provide support to the government in exchange for institutions that accord with their identity-based preferences and are therefore deemed "legitimate" (Assumption 2). Foreign policy will thus be motivated in part by an effort to realize social views about legitimate borders, political institutions, and modes of socioeconomic regulation. The ultimate consequences of identity-based preferences for IR depend on the resulting patterns of policy interdependence—in other words, on the transnational externalities necessarily created by attempts to realize those preferences (Assumption 3). Hence liberal theory predicts that where national conceptions of legitimate borders, political institutions, and socioeconomic equality are compatible, generating positive or negligible externalities, harmony is likely. Where social identities are incompatible and create significant negative externalities, tension and zero-sum conflict are more likely. Where national claims can be made more compatible by reciprocal policy adjustment, cooperation is likely.

Parallel predictions about international politics follow from each of the three "ideational liberal" sources of societal preferences: national, political, and socioeconomic identity.

The first basic type of social identity concerns the scope of the "nation": specifically, the legitimate location of national borders and the allocation of citizenship rights. Where borders coincide with underlying patterns of identity, coexistence and even mutual recognition are more likely, but where there are inconsistencies between borders and underlying patterns of identity, greater potential for interstate conflict exists. This novel prediction of liberal theory is broadly confirmed. Over the last century and a half, from mid-nineteenth century nationalist uprisings to late twentieth-century national liberation struggles, the desire for national autonomy constitutes the most common issue over which wars have been fought and great power intervention has taken place. The Balkan conflicts

the speculations of constructivists notwithstanding, have little comparative advantage.

preceding World War I and after the Cold War are among the most notorious examples.[15]

The second basic type of social identity comprises the commitments of individuals and groups to particular political institutions. Where the realization of legitimate domestic political order in one jurisdiction threatens its realization in others (a situation of negative externalities), conflict is more likely. This differs from realist theory, which accords theoretical weight to domestic regime type only insofar as it influences the distribution of capabilities, and from institutionalist theory, which accords such influence only insofar as it contributes to the certainty of coordination and commitment. Recent trends in Cold War historiography, as well as political science analysis of the United States and the Soviet Union—both based on Soviet documents heretofore inaccessible to Western scholars—lend weight to liberal predictions about the power of ideology, even in a central area of realist concern.[16]

The third basic type of social identity is the nature of legitimate socioeconomic regulation and redistribution. Modern liberal theory (in contrast to the *laissez faire* libertarianism sometimes labeled as quintessentially "liberal") has long recognized that societal preferences concerning the appropriate nature and level of regulation impose

---

15. Even those such as James Fearon who stress the absence of domestic credible commitment mechanisms or the interaction between ideational and socioeconomic variables in explaining patterns of nationalist conflicts concede the importance of underlying identities. See David Laitin and James Fearon, "Violence and the Social Construction of Ethnic Identity," *International Organization*, Vol. 54, No. 4 (Autumn 2000), pp. 845–877. Remaining dissidents include John Mearsheimer, who bravely asserts that nationalism is a "second-order force in international politics," with a "largely ... international" cause, namely multipolarity. John Mearsheimer, "Back to the Future: Instability in Europe after the Cold War," *International Security*, Vol. 15, No. 1 (Summer 1990), pp. 5–56. This disagreement lends itself to empirical resolution: is violent nationalism more of an international problem in Central and Eastern Europe than in Western Europe, as liberalism predicts, or an equal problem in both areas, as realism predicts? The last decade tends to confirm liberal theory.

16. John Lewis Gaddis, *We Know Now: Rethinking Cold War History* (Oxford: Oxford University Press, 1997); William C. Wohlforth, *Witnesses to the End of the Cold War* (Baltimore: Johns Hopkins University Press, 1996).

legitimate limits on transnational markets. In a Polanyian vein, John Ruggie reminds us that domestic and international markets are embedded in local social compromises concerning the provision of regulatory public goods.[17] Such compromises underlie variation in national policies toward immigration, social welfare, taxation, religious freedom, families, health and safety, environmental and consumer protection, cultural promotion, and many other public goods that have increasingly been the subjects of international economic negotiations. Recent work has confirmed the novel predictions of this model—in particular, the emergence of so-called "Baptist-bootlegger" coalitions around recent regulatory issues.[18]

COMMERCIAL LIBERALISM: ECONOMIC ASSETS AND CROSS-BORDER TRANSACTIONS. Commercial liberal theories seek to explain the individual and collective behavior of states based on the patterns of market incentives facing domestic and transnational economic actors. At its most general, the commercial liberal argument is broadly functionalist: changes in the structure of the domestic and global economy alter the costs and benefits of transnational economic exchange, creating pressure on domestic governments to facilitate or block such exchanges through appropriate foreign economic and security policies. Commercial liberal theory does not predict that economic incentives automatically generate universal free trade and peace—a utopian position often wrongly attributed to it by critics who treat liberalism as an ideology—but instead stresses the interaction between aggregate incentives for certain policies and the obstacles posed by domestic and transnational distributional conflict. Liberal IR theory thereby employs market structure as a variable to explain both openness and closure. The greater the economic benefits for powerful private actors, the greater their incentive, ceteris paribus, to press

---

17. Ruggie, "International Regimes, Transactions, and Change."

18. David Vogel, *Trading Up* (Cambridge, Mass.: Harvard University Press, 1995); John Gerard Ruggie, *At Home Abroad, Abroad at Home: International Liberalization and Domestic Stability in the New World Economy* (Fiesole, Italy: The Robert Schuman Centre at the European University Institute, Jean Monnet Chair Papers, 1995).

governments to facilitate such transactions; the more costly the adjustment imposed by the proposed economic exchanges, the more opposition is likely to arise. The resulting commercial liberal explanation of "relative gains–seeking" in foreign economic policy is quite distinct from that of realism, which emphasizes security externalities and relative (hegemonic) power, or that of institutionalism, which stresses informational and institutional constraints on optimal interstate collective action.[19]

One source of pressure for protection, liberals predict, lies in uncompetitive, monopolistic, or undiversified sectors or factors. These tend to have the most to lose from free trade and thus have a strong incentive to oppose it. Such pressure induces a systematic divergence from *laissez faire* policies—a tendency recognized by Adam Smith, who complained that "the contrivers of [mercantilism are] ... the producers [merchants and manufacturers], whose interest has been so carefully attended to," and echoed by countless liberals since. Recent research supports the view that free trade is most likely where strong competitiveness, extensive intra-industry trade or trade in intermediate goods, large foreign investments, and low asset-specificity internalize the net benefits of free trade to powerful actors, thus reducing the influence of net losers from liberalization. Novel predictions about cross-sectoral and cross-national variation in support for protection have been confirmed.[20]

Commercial liberalism has important implications for security affairs as well. Trade is generally a less costly means of accumulating

19. This body of literature on "endogenous" foreign economic policy theory is exceptionally deep. For a review and discussion of the relationship between commercial and republican liberal theories, see Robert O. Keohane and Helen V. Milner, eds., *Internationalization and Domestic Politics* (Cambridge, UK: Cambridge University Press, 1996).

20. Keohane and Milner, *Internationalization and Domestic Politics*; James Alt and Michael Gilligan, "The Political Economy of Trading States: Factor Specificity, Collective Action Problems, and Domestic Political Institutions," *Journal of Political Philosophy*, Vol. 2, No. 2 (1994), pp. 165–192; Helen Milner, "Trading Places: Industries for Free Trade," *World Politics*, Vol. 40, No. 3 (April 1988), pp. 350–376.

wealth than war, sanctions, or other coercive means, not least due to the minimization of collateral damage. Yet governments sometimes have an incentive to employ coercive means to create and control international markets. To explain this variation, domestic distributional issues and the structure of global markets are critical. Stephen Van Evera argues that the more diversified and complex the existing transnational commercial ties and production structures, the less cost-effective coercion is likely to be.[21] Cost-effective coercion was most profitable in an era where the main sources of economic profit, such as farmland, slave labor, raw materials, or formal monopoly, could be easily controlled in conquered or colonial economies. Economic development, this line of theory predicts, tends to increase the material stake of social actors in existing investments, thereby reducing their willingness to assume the cost and risk of costly coercion through war or sanctions. Again, substantial empirical evidence supports this view.[22]

REPUBLICAN LIBERALISM: REPRESENTATION AND RENT-SEEKING. Where ideational and commercial liberal theory stress, respectively, particular patterns of underlying societal identities and economic interests, republican liberal theory emphasizes the ways in which domestic institutions and practices aggregate such interests, transforming them into state policy. The key variable in republican liberalism is the nature of domestic political representation, which determines whose social preferences dominate policy. While many liberal arguments are concerned with the "capture" of state institutions by administrators (rulers, armies, or bureaucracies), a parallel argument applies to societal groups that capture the state or simply act

---

21. Stephen Van Evera, "Primed for Peace: Europe after the Cold War," *International Security*, Vol. 15, No. 3 (Winter 1990/1991), pp. 7–57.

22. Realist theory, with its assumptions of a unitary state and fixed preferences, simply presumes that the greater the wealth and power of a state, the less the marginal cost of deploying it. Power is thus reduced to capabilities. liberal theory suggests different predictions, and the competing empirical implications are testable.

independently of it.[23] When institutions of political representation are biased in favor of particular groups, they tend to employ government institutions for their ends alone, systematically passing on cost and risk to others.

The simplest prediction of this pluralist view is that policy is biased in favor of the governing coalition or powerful domestic groups, but more sophisticated extensions are numerous. One focuses on rent-seeking. When particular groups are able to formulate policy without necessarily providing gains for society as a whole, the result is likely to be inefficient, sub-optimal policies from the aggregate perspective, of which costly international conflict may be an example. If, following the first assumption, most individuals and groups in society, while acquisitive, tend also to be risk-averse (at least where they have something to lose), the more unbiased the range of domestic groups represented, the less likely it is that they will support indiscriminate use of policy instruments, like war, that impose enormous net costs or risks on a broad range of social actors. Aggressive behavior—the voluntary recourse to costly or risky foreign policy—is most likely in undemocratic or inegalitarian polities where privileged individuals can offload its costs.[24]

Like other strands of liberal theory, republican liberalism is potentially quite complex, yet nonetheless it generates powerful and parsimonious predictions about international conflict in practice. With

---

23. Both possibilities are consistent with Assumption Two, whereby the state represents some weighted subset of societal actors; whether that subset comprises those who direct the state, or those who influence those who direct the state, is secondary.

24. This does not, of course, imply that broad domestic representation necessarily always means international political or economic cooperation, for two reasons. First, in specific cases, elite preferences in multiple states may be more convergent than popular ones. Second, the extent of bias in representation, not democracy per se, is the theoretically critical point. There exist predictable conditions under which specific governing elites may have an incentive to represent long-term social preferences in a way that is less biased than would broad public and elite opinion. This explains the existence of insulated trade policy-making institutions such as "fast track" provisions.

respect to extreme but historically common policies such as war, famine, and radical autarky, for example, broad and fair representation appears to inhibit international conflict. Republican liberal theory thus helps to explain phenomena as diverse as the "democratic peace," modern imperialism, and international trade and monetary cooperation. Given the plausibility of the assumption that major war imposes net costs on society as a whole, it is hardly surprising that the most prominent republican liberal argument concerns the "democratic peace," which one scholar has termed "as close as anything we have to an empirical law in international relations"—one that applies to tribal societies as well as modern states.[25] This line of argument, as James Lee Ray notes in Chapter 6 of this volume, has generated many novel predictions.

Often overlooked is the theoretical obverse of "democratic peace" theory: a republican liberal *theory of war* that stresses abnormally risk-acceptant leaders and rent-seeking coalitions. There is substantial historical evidence that the aggressors who have provoked modern great power wars tend either to be extremely risk-acceptant individuals, or individuals well able to insulate themselves from the costs of war, or both. Jack Snyder, for example, has deepened Hobson's classic rent-seeking analysis of imperialism—in which the military, uncompetitive foreign investors and traders, jingoistic political elites, and others who benefit from imperialism are particularly well-placed to influence policy—by linking unrepresentative and extreme outcomes to log-rolling coalitions.[26] Consistent with this analysis, the

25. Jack S. Levy, "The Causes of War," in Philip E. Tetlock, et al., eds., *Behavior, Society and Nuclear War*, Vol. 1 (New York: Oxford University Press, 1989), p. 270.

26. Jack Snyder, *Myths of Empire: Domestic Politics and International Ambition* (Ithaca, N.Y.: Cornell University Press, 1991). It is indicative of the conceptual confusion that besets metatheoretical labeling in international relations that this argument has been advanced by those often termed "neoclassical realists," including Stephen Van Evera, Stephen Walt, Randall Schweller, and Jack Snyder. For an early critique along these lines by a scholar who subsequently fell into the same trap, see Fareed Zakaria, "Realism and Domestic Politics," *International Security*, Vol. 17, No. 1 (Summer 1992), pp. 177–198. For a

highly unrepresentative consequences of partial democratization, combined with the disruption of rapid industrialization and incomplete political socialization, suggest that democratizing states, if subject to these influences, may be particularly war-prone.[27] While such findings challenge what is sometimes referred to as liberal *ideology*, they are predicted by liberal *theory*.

Precise analogs to the "democratic peace" exist in the area of political economy as well. As we saw in the preceding section, perhaps the most widespread explanation for the persistence of illiberal commercial policies, such as protection, monetary instability, and sectoral subsidization that may manifestly undermine the general welfare of the population, is pressure from powerful domestic groups. The power of such groups may ultimately result from the inherent power of certain business interests in civil society, as argued by pure commercial liberal theory, but might also reflect biases within representative institutions, as republican liberal theory suggests. Where the latter sort of biases exists—and it is seen in most contemporary representative institutions—rent-seeking groups are likely to gain protection through tariffs, subsidies, favorable regulation, or competitive devaluation. Where policy makers are insulated from such pressures, which may involve less democratic but more representative institutions, or where free trade interests dominate policy, open policies are more viable. Recent studies of commercial policy have evolved in this direction.[28]

---

comprehensive critique of the mislabeling and incoherence of attempts to specify a realist paradigm, see Jeffrey Legro and Andrew Moravcsik, "Is Anybody Still a Realist?" *International Security*, Vol. 24, No. 2 (Fall 1999), pp. 5–55.

27. Jack Snyder and Edward Mansfield, "Democratization and the Danger of War," *International Security*, Vol. 20, No. 1 (Summer 1995), pp. 5–38; Jack Snyder, *From Voting to Violence: Democratization and Nationalist Conflict* (New York: Norton, 2000).

28. From this insight follows an entire line of literature about the role of national executives in foreign economic policy. For example, see Stephan Haggard, "The Institutional Foundations of Hegemony: Explaining the

Is Liberal IR Theory a Progressive Research Program?

Assessing whether any given scientific research program—such as the liberal program set forth above—is progressive demands that we ask whether it generates "excess content" in the form of "novel" predicted facts. Chapter 2 provides a helpful discussion of four possible Lakatosian criteria for judging the novelty of facts, of which I will consider three: "strict temporal novelty" (Lakatos$_1$) and "the heuristic definition of novelty" (Lakatos$_3$), considered in the first section below, and "background theory novelty" (Lakatos$_4$), considered in the second section below.[29] The first two I assess with reference to the intellectual history of the liberal scientific research program. The latter I assess with reference to the current research findings of liberal theory and its competitors. No matter which criterion is used, the conclusion is unambiguous, namely, that liberal IR theory is progressive in a Lakatosian sense.

In drawing this conclusion, we learn something about the practical utility of Lakatosian criteria. In contrast to Elman and Elman, I find that the most compelling criterion is "background theory novelty." This is because in practice it proves quite difficult—contrary to what Lakatos and the Elmans both assume—to subsume new empirical results through auxiliary assumptions within the constraints of fixed hard core assumptions. Recent modifications in realism, for example, which have adopted the propositions and assumptions of liberal theories to explain anomalies, demonstrate the difficulty of modifying realism itself. Nonetheless, all three Lakatosian criteria offer some unique insight, and their joint application permits us to draw a consistent and convincing conclusion that the liberal scientific research program in IR is progressive.

Reciprocal Trade Agreements Act of 1934," *International Organization*, Vol. 42, No. 1 (Winter 1988), pp. 91–120.

29. I set aside one of these criteria, namely "new interpretation novelty" (Lakatos$_2$) on the ground, reported by the Elmans, that it has little support in the secondary literature. In Chapter 2, the Elmans use the label "Musgrave" rather than "Lakatos$_4$" for background theory novelty.

TEMPORAL AND HEURISTIC NOVELTY: THE INTELLECTUAL
HISTORY OF LIBERAL IR THEORY

The intellectual origins of a scientific research program are directly relevant to judging consistency with two Lakatosian criteria: temporal and heuristic novelty. Both embody "the simple rule that one can't use the same fact twice: once in the construction of a theory and then again in its support," as John Worrall puts it.[30] "Strict temporal novelty" (Lakatos₁) asks whether the scientific research program successfully predicts facts unknown, "improbable, or even impossible in the light of previous knowledge," while "the heuristic definition of novelty" (Lakatos₃) asks whether the scientific research program successfully predicts facts that did not "play some heuristic role in that theory's construction."[31]

Elman and Elman voice suspicion about these criteria. Strict temporal novelty seems too restrictive, because it treats as "not novel" any "fact that is known to anyone at any time before the theoretical modification"—a criterion they believe is so strict as to "exclude almost any social behavior from ever being counted as a novel fact." While unlikely to code degenerating scientific research programs as progressive, it may overlook some progressive scientific research programs. Elman and Elman side with the second, heuristic novelty, but note that it is difficult to employ, since "the determination of novelty depends on private, inaccessible biographical knowledge about the scientist or researcher."[32]

I submit that, at least at the broadest level, the liberal scientific research program meets the strict temporal and heuristic criteria—and does so in a way that belies some of the Elmans' methodological and pragmatic misgivings about them. The most fundamental hypotheses of modern liberal IR theory were initially advanced by political philosophers and publicists of the eighteenth and nineteenth centuries, who wrote before the independent variables underlying liberal theory

---

30. Quoted in Elman and Elman, Chapter 2 in this volume, p. 37.
31. The first implies the second, of course.
32. Elman and Elman, Chapter 2, p. 37.

(democratization, industrialization, and secular belief systems) were widespread enough (if they existed at all) to generate any consistent record. The critical insights of liberal IR theory in the eighteenth and nineteenth centuries can be found in the writings of the three most prominent philosophers and publicists in this tradition: Immanuel Kant, Adam Smith, and John Stuart Mill. Each was a visionary who predicted the implications for international relations of a social trend that had only just begun when they wrote. To be sure, phenomena of the obverse were visible—wars waged by autocrats, pre-industrial mercantilism for control over fixed resources, and religious fundamentalism. Yet liberal philosophers advanced predictions about the potential for change on the basis of only a small spectrum of historical or geographical variation.

Temporal and heuristic novelty are evident in each variant of liberal theory. Kant advanced a theory about the pacific implications of republican governance for foreign policy at a time when there were no more than a handful of republics in the world.[33] Numerous subsequent thinkers, from Woodrow Wilson to George Kennan to Francis Fukuyama, further developed this view. Adam Smith advanced a firmly grounded theory about socioeconomic and regulatory pressures for free trade and protectionism in a world still governed by great power mercantilism. Subsequent thinkers in this vein included Richard Cobden and John Maynard Keynes. John Stuart Mill advanced systematic conjectures about the implications of collective cultural phenomena—national identity, education, and cosmopolitan values—in an era in which these were only beginning to emerge as a dominant locus of political organization. Subsequent liberal thinkers in this vein included Giuseppe Mazzini and Wilson.

---

33. Kant is often misunderstood in this regard as a global federalist. Yet his movement from the world republic envisioned in "Theory and Practice" of 1793 to the structured relations among republics envisioned in "Toward Perpetual Peace" in 1795 is unambiguous. In the latter, Kant's definitive statement, the internal sovereignty of nations is a constitutive principle of global order. James Bohman and Matthias Lutz-Bachmann, "Introduction," in Bohman and Lutz-Bachmann, eds., *Perpetual Peace: Essays on Kant's Cosmopolitan Ideal* (Cambridge, Mass.: MIT Press, 1997), pp. 6–7.

An assessment of temporal and heuristic novelty requires that we investigate origins, but—it might be objected—perhaps Kant, Smith, and Mill should not be treated as early social scientists, but instead as idealistic visionaries whose predictions just happen in retrospect to have been correct? Since Machiavelli advanced his celebrated distinction between "the effective truth of things" and the "imaginary republics and monarchies that have never been seen or have been known to exist," this has been the attitude of realists. Liberal arguments have been ridiculed as based on idealized notions of enlightened, benevolent individuals inhabiting a state of nature—notions drawn from very limited experience of world politics, if not pure philosophical utopianism. Liberals assume the existence of a perfect harmony of interests, between individuals as between nations, which the spread of education and cosmopolitan values will progressively make known to all. Thus Martin Wight calls the Kantian tradition a "revolutionary" and "utopian" project; Michael Howard criticizes liberals for their naïveté in demanding a Gandhian sense of individual self-sacrifice; and Hans Morgenthau contrasts liberal views with realism's "theoretical concern with human nature as it actually is, and with the historical processes as they actually take place." Arnold Wolfers and Laurence Martin treat it as a narrow doctrine bred of the insularity and unique domestic political legacy of the Anglo-American tradition. Even social scientists sympathetic to the liberal scientific research program have been quick to grant that liberal theories are more philosophy than social science; they cannot meet the standards of rigor set by realism—a remarkable claim in itself!—precisely because their underlying philosophical assertion of the moral worth and independence of the individual introduces, Robert Keohane argues, an ineluctable source of "indeterminacy."[34]

I submit, however, that liberal IR theory, as developed by such philosophers and essayists as Kant, Smith, and Mill, was grounded not in utopian philosophy in what we would term today a distinctive

---

34. Robert O. Keohane, "International Liberalism Reconsidered," in John Dunn, ed., *The Economic Limits to Modern Politics* (Cambridge, UK: Cambridge University Press, 1990), pp. 192–194.

social-scientific analysis of world politics—and thus it should count in favor of temporal novelty. Eighteenth and nineteenth-century liberals did not offer simply a particular ideal of global harmony, but sought to account for variation in international cooperation and conflict. As explained above, distinctive liberal theories of peace beget corresponding liberal theories of war, liberal theories of free trade and cooperation beget liberal theories of protectionism and mercantilism, and liberal theories of ideological conflict beget liberal theories of ideologically-induced consensus. By the time of Smith in Britain, Kant in Germany, and Benjamin Constant, if not Montesquieu, in France, such utopian notions—even if they occasionally reappeared later—had been definitively supplanted by efforts to ground liberal political philosophy in sociological theory. At the risk of gross over-simplification, it could be said that the essential move of modern liberal political philosophy was to place a richly varied society of individuals making choices at the basis of theorizing about political order. Thus the normative claims of subsequent liberal philosophers generally rest on a set of sophisticated claims about the variety of possible relationships between the state and society, of which their ideal prescriptions are simply a limiting case. Modern attempts to assert a normative liberal position must begin by accepting what John Hall has termed a sociological "wager on reason," namely, the assumption that civil society precedes the state and that certain conditions will impel rational individuals in civil society to act politically in predictable ways.[35]

This was as true for classical philosophers as for modern theorists. It is doubtful that even early liberals subscribed to such idealistic views as that their doctrines could be deduced from a mythical state of nature, that societies would harmoniously tend toward progress, or that human beings, once persuaded by liberal arguments, could be trusted to regenerate themselves morally. Sheldon Wolin has observed that:

---

35. John A. Hall, *Liberalism: Politics, Ideology and the Market* (Chapel Hill: University of North Carolina Press, 1987).

Liberalism has repeatedly been characterized as "optimistic" to the point of naïveté; arrogant in its conviction that human reason ought to stand as the sole authority for knowledge and action; bewitched by a vision of history as an escalator endlessly moving upwards towards greater progress; and blasphemous in endowing the human mind and will with a godlike power of refashioning man and society in entirety. For the most part, these criticisms have little or no support in the writings of the liberals.[36]

Kant constructed a plan for movement toward world peace that he asserted would be effective "even in a world of devils."[37] Of Benjamin Constant, Stephen Holmes observed that:

Once again following Montesquieu and other eighteenth-century (particularly Scottish) examples, [Constant] deliberately supplanted the contract myth with the theory of social change. The liberal state is desirable not because it mirrors human nature or respects eternal human rights, but because it is the political arrangement most adequate to solving the problems of European society in its current state of economic, scientific and moral development.[38]

Similarly, Smith made the intellectual journey from a notion that commercial activity could tame or at least successfully oppose the more militant passions, to the notion of a self-regulating society largely independent of the nature of individual norms.[39]

---

36. Sheldon S. Wolin, *Politics and Vision: Continuity and Innovation in Western Political Thought* (Boston: Little, Brown, 1960), p. 305, also pp. 286–294, 305–309. See also Don Herzog, *Without Foundations: Justification in Political Theory* (Ithaca: Cornell University Press, 1985), pp. 204–207; John Dunn, *Rethinking Modern Political Theory: Essays 1979–83* (Cambridge, Mass.: Cambridge University Press, 1985), pp. 154–163; John Gray, *Liberalism* (Minneapolis: University of Minnesota Press, 1986), pp. 45–56.

37. Immanuel Kant, "Perpetual Peace: A Philosophical Sketch," in Hans Reiss, ed., *Kant's Political Writings*, trans. H.B. Nisbet (Cambridge, UK: Cambridge University Press, 1970), pp. 93–130.

38. Stephen Holmes, *Benjamin Constant and the Making of Modern Liberalism* (New Haven: Yale University Press, 1984), p. 32.

39. Albert O. Hirschman, *The Passions and the Interests: Political Arguments for Capitalism before its Triumph* (Princeton, N.J.: Princeton University Press, 1977), pp. 100–112, 120.

The remarkable prescience of early liberal IR theorists, and the resulting ability of liberal theory to meet the criteria of temporal novelty, stands in striking contrast to its realist and institutionalist counterparts. The realist scientific research program emerged from the inductive analyses of Thucydides, Niccolo Machiavelli, Thomas Hobbes, Friedrich Meinecke, and Hans Morgenthau. Here there is little temporal novelty. Each observed, in his era, characteristic realist pathologies of anarchy—an overriding concern for security, the formation of balances of power, the dynamics of deterrence and preventive war—then developed a theory to explain them. (To be sure, much subsequent history confirmed the balance-of-power theory, yet new cases of balancing were far less novel than the emergence and spread of modern republican government.) Similarly, it might be argued that the modern institutionalist scientific research program, which emerged in the 1970s, was developed to explain the success of post–World War II international organizations, which appeared anomalous from a realist perspective, as Robert Keohane and Lisa Martin note in Chapter 3. This is not to say that these research programs have not explained *some* temporally novel facts, only that new facts and major developments in world politics appear to have *preceded* major theoretical innovations in realist and institutionalist scientific research programs to a greater extent than was the case with the liberal scientific research program.

While this speaks well for the liberal scientific research program, I remain unconvinced that temporal or heuristic novelty is an essential criterion for judging scientific research programs. Whether the behavioral regularities that a theory can convincingly explain are known before or after the development of the theory is an entirely secondary consideration. It seems to me that the fact that realist theory was distilled from widespread observation of world politics does not make the evidence of its importance, particularly before the modern period, any less compelling. Despite the Elmans' skepticism, it is in fact far from trivial to develop a coherent theory to unify an extensive set of facts, even if they are fully understood in advance.

Thus whereas I do maintain that liberal theory meets many criteria for theoretical fruitfulness and, accordingly, is unjustly neglected in current theoretical debates, I do not reach this conclusion primarily because liberal theory was derived deductively rather than inductively. More important than novelty, in my view, is performance—confirmed predictions minus confirmed anomalies—as compared to competing scientific research programs. If a particular theory provides a better fit to a specified pattern of facts without generating a greater number of offsetting anomalies, it should be considered more plausible. I turn now to a Lakatosian criterion—"background theory novelty" (Lakatos$_4$)—more consistent with this view.

BACKGROUND THEORY NOVELTY: LIBERALISM AND ITS COMPETITORS IN CURRENT RESEARCH

"Background theory novelty" (Lakatos$_4$), an interpretation of Lakatos proposed by Musgrave, instructs us to assess the excess content of novel facts explained by research programs over time by asking whether the liberal scientific research program "predicts something which is not also predicted by its background theory."[40] This criterion I find more powerful than the alternatives, and according to it, liberal theory is an even more progressive program.

By social-scientific standards, as we have seen, there exists remarkably strong support for key liberal predictions across the board, such as those concerning the democratic peace in the republican liberal tradition, endogenous international trade and monetary policy in the commercial liberal tradition, and the role of societal preferences across public goods in a range of phenomena from nationalist conflict to regulatory harmonization in the ideational liberal tradition. We have seen that liberal theory has generated fruitful new lines of theory in security studies, international organization, and international political economy. Certainly the liberal scientific research program advances a wide range of distinct confirmed predictions not successfully predicted —or in any way derivable from—realist or institutionalist theory.

---

40. Elman and Elman, Chapter 2 in this volume, p. 38, quoting Alan Musgrave. Also see Imre Lakatos and Alan Musgrave, eds., *Criticism and the Growth of Knowledge* (Cambridge, UK: Cambridge University Press, 1970).

Perhaps most important, given the Lakatosian tendency to view inter-paradigmatic conflict as a "three-cornered fight" between two theories and the data, is another point. Recent empirical and theoretical debates demonstrate that non-liberal scientific research programs have a very limited capacity to generate plausible—internally coherent and empirically confirmed—explanations for certain important regularities predicted by liberal theory. Contrary to what Elman and Elman suggest in Chapter 2 about "background theory novelty," it seems in fact quite difficult to generate plausible auxiliary explanations for many phenomena uncovered by competing IR scientific research programs. A comparison of specific areas in which realist and liberal theories have been applied not only generates numerous anomalies where realists have tried and failed to generate satisfactory explanations for confirmed liberal predictions, but also numerous cases in which realists, even in the absence of a direct liberal challenge, have advanced formulations of realism that overtly degenerate toward liberalism, even when we judge "degeneration" according to core definitions that realists themselves have advanced. The next section summarizes the more detailed evidence for this charge.

REALIST ANOMALIES, NOVEL FACTS, AND LIBERAL THEORY. We turn first to areas where realism has failed to propose any detailed explanation for salient phenomena that are well-explained within liberal theory, or where realist explanations for confirmed liberal predictions have, on closer inspection, proved unconvincing. Consider some examples.

Realism provides no explanation for differences in the substantive nature of formally similar orders. What accounts, for example, for differences between Anglo-American, Nazi, and Soviet plans for the post–World War II world? What accounts for the substantial differences between the compromise of "embedded liberalism" underlying Bretton Woods and arrangements under the Gold Standard? divergences between economic cooperation under the European Community and ComEcon? the greater protectionism of agricultural policy of the Organization for Economic Cooperation and Development (OECD), compared to its industrial trade policy? These are realist anomalies. Yet, as John Ruggie and others have shown, there are plausible, parsimonious, and empirically confirmed liberal explanations grounded in the variation in national socioeconomic preferences for each of these novel phenomena.[41]

Another example, the "democratic peace" proposition, remains a robust and significant anomaly for realism. Attempts by Joanne Gowa, David Spiro, Randall Schweller, and others to debunk the "democratic peace" hypothesis advanced by Michael Doyle, Bruce Russett, and others have not succeeded in reversing the strong presumption in its favor.[42] More broadly, realists provide no explanation for the consistent tendency of perceived threats to vary independently of the relative power of the threatener. Why do states tend to provoke war with large states and, more often than not, lose the subsequent war? What explains why U.S. concern about a few North Korean, Iraqi, or Chinese nuclear weapons is greater than that for the larger arsenals held by Great Britain, Israel, and France? The democratic peace hypothesis, as well as theories of ethnic attachment, offer plausible explanations for what are striking realist anomalies.

A third example is the distinct nature of politics among advanced industrial democracies, grounded in reliable expectations of peaceful change, domestic rule of law, stable international institutions, and intensive societal interaction. This is the condition Karl Deutsch terms a "pluralistic security community" and Keohane and Nye term

---

41. Ruggie, *At Home Abroad*; John Gerard Ruggie, "Embedded Liberalism Revisited: Institutions and Progress in International Economic Relations," in Emanuel Adler and Beverly Crawford, eds., *Progress in Postwar International Relations* (New York: Columbia University Press, 1991), pp. 201–234.

42. Joanne S. Gowa, *Ballots and Bullets: The Elusive Democratic Peace* (Princeton, N.J.: Princeton University Press, 1999). The only consistent result of such studies is that under certain extreme specifications—limited periods of time and limited numbers of countries—the relationship between democracy and peace can be reduced to statistical insignificance. Others assert that the democratic peace may not hold in the future. No critique consistently reverses the direction of the causal effect (i.e., democracies go to war more) or proposes a consistently powerful opposing theory to explain the patterns we observe.

"complex interdependence."[43] Whereas realists (and, as discussed below, constructivists) offer no general explanation for the emergence of this distinctive mode of international politics, liberal theory argues that the emergence of a large and expanding bloc of democratic, interdependent, nationally satisfied states has been a precondition for such politics.

Consider, for example, Western Europe since 1989. Unlike realism, liberal theory predicts and explains the absence of competitive alliance formation among West European powers. The lack of serious conflict in the rest of Europe over Yugoslavia—avoiding the "World War I scenario"—reflects in large part a shared perception that the geopolitical stakes among democratic governments are low. Liberalism similarly makes more sense of the sudden reversal of East-West relations, a shift made possible by the widespread view among Russian officials (so interview data reveal) that Germany is ethnically satisfied, politically democratic, and commercially inclined.[44] These facts are novel by both the temporal and the background criteria.

By contrast, John Mearsheimer's realist alternative to democratic peace theory's predictions of peace in post–Cold War Europe has yet to find confirmation. Mearsheimer offers a heroic argument that external threats under multipolarity have triggered nationalist reactions in Yugoslavia. Yet this auxiliary claim fails to explain perhaps the most salient fact about post–Cold War European politics, namely, the disparity between East and West. We observe total peace among the established democracies of Western Europe, yet conflict (and threat of conflict), if sporadic, among the transitional democracies and non-democracies of Central and Eastern Europe. In an effort to account for this, even Mearsheimer is led to invoke the autonomous importance of

43. Karl Wolfgang Deutsch, et al., *Political Community and the North Atlantic Area: International Organization in the Light of Historical Experience* (Princeton, N.J.: Princeton University Press, 1957); and Keohane and Nye, *Power and Interdependence*.

44. Interview data reported in personal communication from Professor Celeste Wallander, Harvard University.

underlying patterns of national identities in the former Yugoslavia.[45] This evolution, which emerged after predictions were on the table in 1990, confirms the novelty of the liberal theory.

Similarly, under the rubrics of hegemonic stability theory and relative gains–seeking, Stephen Krasner, Joseph Grieco, David Lake, and others have posed realist challenges to liberal theories of economic integration and commercial liberalization advanced by Helen Milner, Jeffry Frieden, Ronald Rogowski, John Ruggie, myself, and many others within the now massive literature on endogenous tariff theory. Yet a series of disconfirmations have all but removed hegemonic stability theory from the academic scene. At best, it does not appear robust beyond a single case, that of U.S. policy after World War II.[46] Grieco has offered no convincing answer to criticisms that relative gains–seeking fails to demonstrate a link between security and trade, as well as omitting direct tests with liberal hypotheses.[47] The most that can be said empirically for this line of recent realist work is that some scholars have succeeded in demonstrating the existence of a modest correlation between alliances and trade.[48]

One final example: liberal theory offers a plausible explanation for long-term historical change in the international system, whereas the static quality of both realist and institutionalist theory—their lack of an explanation for fundamental long-term change in the nature of international politics—is a recognized weakness. Global economic development over the past 500 years has been closely related to greater

---

45. Mearsheimer, "Back to the Future."

46. For the best effort at a revival, see David A. Lake, "Leadership, Hegemony, and the International Economy: Naked Emperor or Tattered Monarch with Potential?" *International Studies Quarterly*, Vol. 37, No. 4 (December 1993), pp. 459–489.

47. For criticisms of Grieco, see Robert Powell, "Anarchy in International Relations Theory: The Neorealist-Neoliberal Debate," *International Organization*, Vol. 48, No. 2 (Spring 1994), pp. 313–344.

48. Joanne S. Gowa, "Bipolarity, Multipolarity, and Free Trade," *American Political Science Review*, Vol. 83, No. 4 (December 1989), pp. 1245–1256; and Edward Mansfield, "The Concentration of Capabilities and International Trade," *International Organization*, Vol. 46, No. 3 (Summer 1992), pp. 731–764.

per-capita wealth, democratization, education systems that reinforce new collective identities, and greater incentives for transborder economic transactions. Realist theory accords these changes no theoretical importance. Theorists such as Kenneth Waltz, Robert Gilpin, and Paul Kennedy limit realism to the analysis of unchanging patterns of state behavior or the cyclical rise and decline of great powers and their success in making war.[49] Liberal theory, by contrast, forges a direct causal link between economic, political, and social change and state behavior in world politics. Hence, over the modern period, the principles of international order have been decreasingly linked to dynastic legitimacy and increasingly tied to factors drawn directly from the three variants of liberal theory: national self-determination and social citizenship, the increasing complexity of economic integration, and democratic governance.[50] This is a novel fact—so much so that Michael Howard, a leading realist, was forced to reverse course and concede the limitations of realism in the second edition of his classic critique of liberal IR theory, *War and the Liberal Conscience*.[51]

These examples, each of them involving a significant issue of modern world politics, suggest that liberal theory has, at least in some matters, broader scope than realist theory, and that the latter is accumulating anomalies that are especially visible from the liberal perspective.

REALIST DEGENERATION IN THE DIRECTION OF LIBERAL THEORY. Even more striking than the ability of liberal theory to explain realist anomalies is the increasing tendency of self-styled realists to explain

---

49. Kenneth N. Waltz, *Theory of International Politics* (Reading, Mass.: Addison-Wesley, 1979); Paul Kennedy, *The Rise and Fall of the Great Powers: Economic Change and Military Conflict from 1500 to 2000* (New York: Random House, 1987); Robert Gilpin, *War and Change in International Politics* (Princeton, N.J.: Princeton University Press, 1981).

50. Kalevi J. Holsti, *Peace and War: Armed Conflicts and International Order, 1648–1989* (Cambridge, UK: Cambridge University Press, 1991).

51. Michael Howard, *War and the Liberal Conscience*, 2nd ed. (New Brunswick, N.J.: Rutgers University Press, 1991).

core security relations—patterns of war, alliance formation, arms control, and imperialism—by invoking core assumptions and causal processes drawn from liberal and institutionalist theory, including exogenous variation in societal preferences and transnational information flows through international institutions.[52] A closer examination of this tendency demonstrates not only the power of liberal IR theory, but also the difficulty of explaining anomalies through viable auxiliary assumptions, while retaining the integrity of hard core assumptions. This confirms the utility of Musgrave's conception of "background theory novelty" (Lakatos$_4$), contra Lakatos and the Elmans, who assume it is trivially easy to explain away anomalies in this way.

Jeffrey Legro and I have recently demonstrated that leading self-declared realists—among them Stephen Van Evera, Jack Snyder, Stephen Walt, Charles Glazer, Fareed Zakaria, Randall Schweller, Gideon Rose, William Wohlforth, and Joseph Grieco—have advanced as "realist" theories that water down the hard core of realism to generic assumptions of rationality and anarchy shared by nearly all major IR theories.[53] These self-styled "neoclassical" and "defensive" realists, who dominate modern realist theory, seek to explain the tendency of states to make war and alliance decisions. Some such efforts, to be sure, explain anomalies in a way consistent with a realist "hard core" focused on the resolution of interstate conflict over scarce resources through the application of relative power capabilities—while holding preferences and perceptions constant. Examples of such "progressive" realist shifts include "auxiliary hypotheses" that stress the role of geographical proximity and of offensive or defensive military technology.[54]

---

52. For a detailed summary, see Legro and Moravcsik, "Is Anybody Still a Realist?"

53. Legro and Moravcsik, "Is Anybody Still a Realist?"

54. This applies to the first three of the four elements of Stephen Walt's revised formulation of realism. See Stephen Walt, *The Origins of Alliances* (Ithaca, N.Y.: Cornell University Press, 1987).

Yet most "neoclassical" or "defensive" realists emphasize factors derived from liberal, institutionalist, or sometimes even constructivist core assumptions. Their explanations invoke variations in the transaction-cost-reducing influence of international institutions, misperceptions and belief systems, and (most relevant for an assessment of liberal theory) state preferences—each traditionally seen as fundamentally opposed to realism. The influence of these factors often reverses the empirical predictions of traditional realists. Judged by its core assumptions, rather than its label, recent "realist" literature has done much to strengthen the liberal, institutionalist, and epistemic paradigms.

Legro and I argue that realists have failed to advance a set of distinctive hard core assumptions that subsume these "realist" writings without expanding the "realist" category to include nearly all rationalist theories and causal processes in world politics. This is necessarily so: once realists permit preferences and perception, as well as power, to vary exogenously and influence state behavior, they can invoke as "realist" almost any rational decision-making process. Legro and I argue that the broadest "hard core" that could plausibly be thought of as distinct to realism is one that assumes rational unitary states, fixed conflictual preferences (the element that distinguishes realism from liberalism), and strategic interaction based on relative control over material resources (the element that distinguishes realism from institutionalism).[55] This would, it appears, exclude "neoclassical" realist theories, which would be more properly (i.e., in accord with their core assumptions) categorized as liberal, institutionalist, or epistemic/constructivist.

---

55. Returning to Elman and Elman's definition of neorealism, this analysis implies that the seven assumptions they set forth—states are rational, egotistical, and strategic, possess limited resources, seek security, and act in anarchy—are insufficient even to define neorealism. These assumptions are, at least at the level of generality are stated, entirely consistent with the "democratic peace," theories of interdependence and war, the importance of "security regimes," and many other ostensibly non-realist bodies of theory. Again, either neorealism becomes another word for all rationalist IR theory or it is underspecified.

Most realists who seek to set forth core realist assumptions (surprisingly few do so explicitly) propose instead what Legro and I term a "minimal realist" definition. In this view, realists need only assume that states are rational, unitary, self-interested actors, act in an anarchic setting, and are concerned about security.[56] As a "hard core," this is manifestly inadequate. The only state behaviors it excludes are outright self-abnegating altruism and delegation of power to a world state.[57] Hardly any IR theorist today—certainly no thoughtful regime theorist or liberal theorist—maintains that states are altruistic, irrational, unstrategic, inward-looking, omnipotent, or oblivious of security matters. Nor do many maintain that the international system, even if influenced by international regimes, is anything but an anarchy.[58] Finally, while some liberal theories stress national goals other

---

56. For examples, see Legro and Moravcsik, "Is Anybody Still a Realist?" Schweller's contribution to this volume (Chapter 9) is an example of a realist analysis that crisply and insightfully sets forth the problem, namely that realism cannot progress without sacrificing its essential assumptions of constant underlying conflict of preferences resolved by the applications of material power resources. I find Schweller's diagnosis of the crisis in realist thought, and what needs to be done about it, clearer than that of any other scholar in security studies. Yet he unaccountably concludes that the move from neorealism to theories that do not hold these assumptions about conflict and power—namely "neoclassical realist" theories—constitute a progressive shift. Schweller never resolves the obvious tensions by presenting a Lakatosian "hard core," or some other measure of theoretical coherence, that subsumes both neorealism and neoclassical realism, nor explains why neoclassical realists should not be viewed, as Legro and I argue, as grafting on non-realist arguments. At the very least, Schweller's account leaves us unclear, from a Lakatosian perspective, what any of the theoretical labels mean.

57. This is made very clear in Charles L. Glaser, "Realists as Optimists: Cooperation as Self-Help," *International Security*, Vol. 19, No. 3 (Winter 1995/1996), pp. 50–90.

58. It is true that the liberal hard core assumes that contestation among sub-national actors influences national preferences, but this is employed only to explain variation in preferences. Few liberals deny that states are the major instrumental actors in world politics. Even those who stress the role of non-governmental organizations increasingly focus on their ability to influence states to act in a particular instrumental manner. See, e.g., Margaret Keck and

than security, most liberals see states as placing a preeminent value on security. The democratic peace predicted by liberals, for example, and the formation of arms control regimes predicted under certain conditions by institutionalists, are held together precisely by the high value placed by participating governments on security.[59]

Despite their commitment to Lakatos's concept of a "hard core," Elman and Elman seem to perpetuate this degenerative tendency, as is reflected in the Elmans' own seven-point proposal for a realist hard core ("illustrative specification of the neorealist research program"). They suggest that the neorealist "hard core" might consist of seven assumptions, summarized as that egotistical, rational, strategic states employ limited resources to assure security in an anarchic international system. They conclude with the assertion that "work by structural realists"—by which they clearly mean to encompass far more than Waltzian neorealism—"would share these central and unchanging elements."[60] Yet, having accorded this definition Lakatosian status, Elman and Elman immediately undermine it. They point out that Walt, Van Evera, Snyder, Zakaria, Schweller, Grieco, and Glazer do *not* in fact accept all of these assumptions. Elman and Elman concede that these theorists explain outcomes by invoking exogenous variation in national preferences—what Elman and Elman somewhat misleadingly term "internal factors"—and international institutions. This the Elmans term a paradigm shift from "neorealism" to "neoclassical" (or "neotraditional") realism. Yet they never answer the essential Lakatosian question, left open by their own apparent abandonment of

Kathryn Sikkink, *Activists beyond Borders: Transnational Advocacy Networks in International Politics* (Ithaca, N.Y.: Cornell University Press, 1999).

59. Indeed, as Schweller and Van Evera have argued, a realist world seems to assume the existence of revisionist aggressors, that is, states that seek far more than security. See Randall L. Schweller, *Deadly Imbalances: Tripolarity and Hitler's Strategy of World Conquest* (New York: Columbia University Press, 1998); and Stephen Van Evera, *Causes of War: Power and the Roots of Conflict* (Ithaca, N.Y.: Cornell University Press, 1999).

60. Colin Elman and Miriam Fendius Elman, "Lakatos and Neo-Realism: A Reply to Vasquez," *American Political Science Review*, Vol. 91, No. 4 (December 1997), pp. 923–926.

their seven-part definition, namely: to what core realist propositions do neoclassical realists adhere? Does "neoclassical" realism have a distinctive hard core? These questions must be answered if the Lakatosian approach is to have any meaning at all.

In lieu of setting forth such competing paradigms, Elman and Elman shift to the threadbare "level of analysis" distinction, now nearly a half century old, whereby realist theories—neorealist or not— are said to share a focus on the "external" environment of the state, as opposed to its "internal" environment. This formulation of the level-of-analysis distinction is untenable, precisely because it cannot be reduced to distinct core assumptions. (Indeed, all level of analysis distinctions are probably incoherent.) No rational calculation in world politics focuses entirely on the "external" environment. All such calculations compare instead the attributes of one country to the attributes of others; it is the *relative* position of a country that matters. In this sense, realists, liberals, and institutionalists all assume that states strategize in response to "systemic" imperatives; that is, they make policy by comparing their own internal characteristics with those of foreign states.

In this view, the primary difference between realism, liberalism, and institutionalism lies not in the tendency of some to focus instead on "domestic" or "second-image" variables, but in the particular characteristics of states that they choose to compare in the formulation of national strategy.[61] For realists, it is material power resources. For

---

61. For this reason, I disagree with the suggestion of Stephen Krasner and Robert Jervis at the Progress in International Relations Theory conference (Scottsdale, Arizona, January 1999) that liberal theories simply subsume what were traditionally called "second image" theories. The core liberal claim is not that "domestic politics" is dominant. For liberals, two other conceptual distinctions are fundamental: the first stresses the fundamental sources of differences among states, the second the way in which those differences translate into political behavior. The first is a distinction between the international political system, on the one hand, and civil society (domestic and transnational) on the other. Liberals, in contrast to realists and institutionalists, stress the importance of state-society relations and the ultimate primacy of the societal context. In other words, underlying interdependence among societies, which drives interdependence among policies, is the fundamental force

institutionalists, it is information. For liberals, it is underlying preferences. Once we set aside the misleading "level of analysis" language and focus on assumptions—as Lakatos invites us to do—we find that the realist emperor has no core.

The unwillingness of realists, including Elman and Elman, to confront this issue raises serious concerns both about the integrity of the modern realist paradigm and about the power of Lakatosian language to police the integrity of paradigms in general. The lack of distinctiveness of realist theory is a flaw so fundamental that it transcends debates about the relative virtues of specific philosophies of science proposed by Lakatos, Laudan, and others. If a set of core assumptions is so broad as to be shared by a paradigm and nearly all its recognized competitors, what use is it? In addressing this problem, realists face a difficult choice. They may either define realism narrowly, and thereby admit the existence of increasing numbers of empirical anomalies, or they may water down the hard core to a "minimal realist" foundation, thereby permitting realist theory to degenerate into a loose and generic rationalism consistent with nearly every claim about world politics advanced in the past generation. The Lakatosian framework has the not inconsiderable virtue of making this choice explicit. If it fails to force a choice, as Elman and Elman appear to

---

underlying state behavior. The second distinction, entirely at the interstate level, is between different characteristics of states that might drive policy: the distribution of preferences, resources, information, and beliefs. Liberal analysis stresses the distribution of preferences, and hence all major liberal variables are "systemic," at least insofar as the influence of commercial incentives, national ideals, and regime type on the foreign policy of a given country cannot be assessed in isolation from the corresponding characteristics of other countries. More broadly, this suggests that the level-of-analysis distinction is a hindrance to understanding. The real debate in IR theory is not between second-image and third-image theories, but between different conceptions of the structure of the international system. Is that structure best understood in terms of the distribution of preferences, of resources, or of information? This is consistent with the framework proposed by David A. Lake and Robert Powell, eds., *Strategic Choice and International Relations* (Princeton, N.J.: Princeton University Press, 1999).

believe, then we must surely question whether Lakatos's philosophy has any utility whatsoever in social science.

International Relations: The Limitations of Lakatosian Assessment

In this essay, I have offered a reconstruction of the liberal hard core and the theories that follow from it, and a demonstration that the resulting research program meets the three most important criteria for excess explanatory content: temporal novelty (Lakatos$_1$), heuristic novelty (Lakatos$_3$), and background theory novelty (Lakatos$_4$). An admittedly crude comparison suggests that the liberal scientific research program has generated results at least as progressive as other major scientific research programs within broad domains of state behavior. Most strikingly, recent research has consistently led to the degeneration of other theories into liberal theory, not the reverse.

Let me conclude, however, by turning away from these substantive conclusions about liberal theory to three considerations concerning the topic of this volume, namely the application of Lakatosian philosophy of science to IR theory. Despite the seemingly unambiguous positive result (for a theory I happen to favor), and the clear virtues of forcing social scientists to focus on the explanatory power of distinct core assumptions, my argument suggests some limitations as well as strengths of Lakatosian philosophy as a tool to assess IR theory. Overall, a more pragmatic "problem-solving" approach based on Larry Laudan's philosophy of science seems more appropriate than one based on strict Lakatosian criteria.[62]

THE RIGOR AND UTILITY OF THE "BACKGROUND THEORY NOVELTY" CRITERION

Let us first concede the virtues of the Lakatosian approach. The analysis above suggests the utility of the "background theory novelty" (Lakatos$_4$) criterion. Elman and Elman, we have seen, follow Lakatos's own tendency and reject background theory novelty because they believe that, in the face of anomalies, it remains trivially easy to

---

62. Laudan, *Beyond Positivism*.

develop auxiliary propositions that successfully protect the hard core. One can always add appropriate auxiliary propositions to account for anomalies, without thereby creating additional anomalies.

I see little evidence that this is the case, except in a trivial sense, and the recent failures of the realist research program demonstrate why. It is in fact difficult to explain new facts within a consistent set of hard core propositions without generating overt contradictions. The result, in the case of recent realist writings, has been a transparent appropriation of propositions based on assumptions that—as a matter of intellectual history as well as modern paradigmatic reformulation— are anything but realist. The failure of realism to progress, it is critical to note, is not simply an outside judgment reached by liberals (such as myself) or institutionalists and epistemic theorists defending arbitrarily chosen terrain.[63] Instead, recent realists have taken a position that is *internally* contradictory. Realists find it impossible to match the distinctive and confirmed empirical claims of other paradigms without either violating the traditional realist hard core or loosening it to the point where it no longer has any theoretical power. These conclusions suggest—in the spirit of essays in this volume by Andrew Bennett (Chapter 14) and David Dessler (Chapter 11)—that "background theory novelty" is a more useful criterion than the Elmans' introductory chapter suggests, as well as one that casts the liberal scientific research program in a favorable scientific light.

THEORY SYNTHESIS AND THE LIABILITIES OF LAKATOS

Now the limitations: although the liberal scientific research program appears to be vindicated by the analysis in this chapter, and "background theory novelty" a more useful criterion than Elman and Elman concede, I maintain that we must nonetheless acknowledge

---

63. This is a charge made by our critics. See Legro and Moravcsik, "Is Anybody Still a Realist? The Authors Reply," in "Correspondence: Brother, Can You Spare a Paradigm? (Or Was Anybody Ever a Realist?)," *International Security*, Vol. 25, No. 1 (Summer 2000), pp. 184–193 (critiques by Peter Feaver, Gunther Hellmann, Randall Schweller, Jeffrey Taliaferro, and William Wohlforth).

significant problems inherent in any application (even metaphoric) of Lakatosian philosophy of science to IR theory.

Lakatosian theory is designed to explain the resolution of conflict among a small number of fundamental theories within a uniform field of scientific inquiry. Lakatos and those who have sought to elaborate his approach tend to view theories as claiming plausibly to explain an entire scientific domain. The image is one of a series of discrete conflicts among such theories with ever-expanding empirical scope. While there can be extended failures to agree upon a single paradigm, these tend to be the transitional consequences of the need to assemble and analyze a large body of ambiguous data, rather than fundamental uncertainty about the nature of the microfoundations of the phenomena in question. Under such circumstances, Lakatos expects that conflict among theories will eventually result (or, hypothetically, could ideally result) in the vindication of one, which will subsume the loser by explaining all of its content. This image implies heroic confidence in the universal applicability of some single set of micro-foundational assumptions—confidence that has been vindicated in some areas of the natural sciences.[64]

The study of world politics, by contrast, often manifestly fails to meet these criteria—at least at its current state of development. Even broad scientific research programs such as realism, liberalism, and institutionalism (let alone specific theories such as work on the "operational code" or the democratic peace) do not make any plausible claim to universality, even within a circumscribed domain. It is next to impossible to find any reputable scholar willing to advance such universal claims for liberal, realist, or institutionalist theory. More importantly, there is no *a priori* reason to believe that such a universal claim would be valid. By contrast to the claims advanced by Newton, Einstein, Darwin, and other scientific revolutionaries, which rested on what was arguably a unique and exclusive conceptual foundation, there is little fundamental theoretical reason to assume that war is the

---

64. Anything less would reduce Lakatos's criterion to a pragmatic admonition to seek evidence for competing claims, thus ridding it of almost all distinctive content.

result of, say, the non-democratic governance and underlying social conflict cited by liberals, rather than the perturbations in the balance of power cited by realists or underdeveloped international organization cited by institutionalists. It is not difficult to conceive of sociological and psychological microfoundations (say, a "rationalist" framework of analysis) that encompass all of these.

In this context, the tendency of Lakatosian analysis to focus attention on zero-sum conflict among all-encompassing theories is a liability, most obviously because it poses a manifestly unrealistic standard.[65] No one expects any of these theories, including liberal theory, to supplant or "knock out" its competitors, even within a limited realm.[66] International relations theory without realism or institutionalism strikes me as absurd on its face.

The fundamental problem is that Lakatosian philosophy, even when employed as a heuristic, inhibits full recognition that international relations is ineluctably multi-paradigmatic. Lakatosian philosophy of science tends to block other trajectories of theoretical and disciplinary development. Two are of particular importance for IR theory.

First, Lakatosian thinking inhibits appreciation of the possibility that liberal and other IR theories may be differentially applicable across different specific empirical domains of world politics. Each may have areas of relative power and relative weakness. Keohane and Nye theorized some years ago, for example, that the world of anarchic competition and the world of "complex interdependence" required different theories.[67] In other words, Lakatosian emphasis on maximal claims about the scope of an explanation may blind us to narrower, subtler, and more nuanced conclusions about the conditions under

---

65. This tendency is related to what Keohane and Martin (Chapter 3 in this volume) term the "endogeneity problem."

66. No one except, curiously, defensive realists, who incorrectly attribute this view to Legro and me. See Randall Schweller and Jeffrey Taliaferro in "Brother, Can You Spare a Paradigm? (Or Was Anybody Ever a Realist?)" *International Security*, Vol. 25, No. 1 (Summer 2000), pp. 174–178, 178–182.

67. Keohane and Nye, *Power and Interdependence*.

which particular theories have explanatory power. Such a world of accurate mid-range theories seems closer to our grasp than one with a single dominant theoretical paradigm.

Second and more fundamental, Lakatosian thinking inhibits appreciation of the possibility that paradigms such as realism, institutionalism, and liberalism can usefully be deployed as complements rather than substitutes. From this perspective, the central challenge facing IR today is not selecting the correct philosophy of science most likely to help us develop a universal theory of IR, but selecting frameworks that permit us to engage in rigorous theory synthesis. The central issue here is how analysts should combine major theories into testable explanations of classes of phenomena in world politics, without permitting the resulting empirical analysis to degenerate into a mono-causal approach, on the one hand, or an indeterminate "everything matters" approach, on the other. Each would be deployed to explain different aspects of the same interstate interactions.

The potential complementarity of basic IR theories follows from precisely the aspect that bedevils efforts by "neoclassical realists" to specify a distinct "hard core," namely their shared rationalist assumptions. Within a rationalist world—and most IR theories are predominantly rationalist—there is little fundamental reason to believe that any single theory of the scope of liberalism, realism, or institutionalism could or should triumph. To see why, one need only consider a basic form of rationalist analysis, such as bargaining theory or negotiation analysis as practiced by its leading analysts.[68] In such analyses, it is possible, indeed conventional, to combine preferences (liberalism), coercive resources (realism), and information and norms (institutionalism or constructivism), as well as other factors, into synthetic explanations of bargaining outcomes. Indeed, coherent "bargaining theory" without variation in all these factors seems nonsensical. For the purposes of empirical analysis, separating the

---

68. For an overview, see Howard Raiffa, *The Art and Science of Negotiation: How to Resolve Conflicts and Get the Best out of Bargaining* (Cambridge, Mass.: Harvard University Press, 1982).

problem into competing theories may often be counterproductive. A structured synthesis would be far more illuminating.

An example of structured synthesis, taken from recent empirical research on European integration, places major theories in sequence. In my analysis of major negotiations to create, develop, and amend the treaty structure of the European Union, liberal theory is employed to account for national preferences, rationalist bargaining theory (which could be seen as a non-coercive variant of realism) to account for the efficiency and distributional outcomes of negotiations, and institutionalist theory to account for subsequent delegation.[69] This is only one—although arguably the most general—of many competing generalizable models for synthesizing theories, including qualitative frameworks, multivariate equations, and formal models.[70]

ONTOLOGIES, PARADIGMS, THEORIES: THE PROPER SCOPE OF RESEARCH PROGRAMS

This leads us to a final consideration, namely the proper scope of a paradigm. Some might concede that Lakatosian criteria are inappropriate for theories such as liberalism or realism, yet nonetheless maintain that Lakatosian concepts can nonetheless usefully be employed to evaluate smaller or larger theoretical aggregations: narrower theories or broader "ontologies."

Many of the writers in this volume maintain that Lakatosian criteria are appropriately applied to *narrower* theories, such as democratic

---

69. For a explication and empirical application of this method, see Andrew Moravcsik, *The Choice for Europe: Social Purpose and State Power from Messina to Maastricht* (Ithaca, N.Y.: Cornell University Press, 1998). This is consistent with the implicit model set forth in Lake and Powell, *Strategic Choice and International Relations*.

70. Even if liberal IR theory, to take one element of this proposed synthesis, could be shown to be currently underutilized, of greater power or scope than the alternatives, or analytically prior to other theories (in the sense that the variation in interstate preferences it explains determine the conditions under which these other theories are valid), this would not constitute a valid reason to reject the realist or institutionalist paradigms entirely.

peace theory or theories of international regimes.[71] I do not respond to the full argument of these chapters, but my analysis does suggest caution in accepting such claims. If, as I argue, realism, liberalism, and institutionalism are often complements rather than substitutes, would this not be even more true of narrower hypotheses within these traditions? It is hard to see, for example, why democratic peace theory should plausibly constitute an exclusive theory of war, and thus it is difficult to see what is gained by evaluating its progress and promise within a Lakatosian framework.

Insofar as any theoretical constructions in IR could plausibly advance the type of exclusive claim to explanatory power within a given domain favored by Lakatosian philosophy of science, it must therefore be a theoretical paradigm at a *broader* level, such as what Alexander Wendt terms the "ontological" level of "rationalism" or "sociological theory." An ontology can plausibly make a universal claim across a broad domain, and many believe that such claims are mutually exclusive. One might more reasonably speak of a rationalist research program in IR, with realist, institutionalist, and liberal "paradigms" as leading elements.[72]

There is firm grounding in fundamental social theory for advancing such a claim.[73] Rationalist theories of social interaction, regardless of their substantive scope, tend to isolate three or four basic categories of fundamental causal factors—normally resources, preferences, beliefs, and perhaps information. Hence within a rationalist paradigm, which might perhaps be properly judged using Lakatosian criteria, we should find theories that give causal priority to the international distribution

---

71. This position tends to be held by those who are uncomfortable with the breadth of the liberal paradigm as formulated here. It is important to reiterate that while liberal theory is broad in theory, it tends to be narrow in practice. There are relatively few specifications of each variant—in Lakatosian language, relatively few sets of auxiliary propositions—that can survive empirical testing. The resulting research has therefore been quite focused.

72. Many variants of so-called "liberal constructivism" would be included. Risse-Kappen, "Collective Identity."

73. James S. Coleman, *Foundations of Social Theory* (Cambridge, Mass.: Harvard University Press, 1990); Lake and Powell, *Strategic Choice.*

of resources (realism), preferences (liberalism), information (institutionalism), and beliefs (epistemic or constructivist theory).[74] Future research might profitably assess such meta-paradigms, given how many scholars today seek to reconceptualize international relations theory in terms of a dichotomy between "rationalist" and "sociological" (or "constructivist") theory.[75]

Yet even at this very broad level of abstraction, there remains space for skepticism. The same criticism of Lakatosian analysis advanced above in regard to realism, liberalism, and institutionalism applies equally here. There is no reason to believe that the psychological underpinnings of rationalist or sociological explanation are, in the real world, mutually exclusive. Complex combinations are possible. Few if any serious scholars are willing to assert that only "rational choice" or only "socialization" exists. Recent constructivist efforts to reformulate IR theory as debates between "rationalist" and "sociological" theory are being abandoned by more sophisticated proponents.[76] The constructivist challenge is now focused primarily on the need to forge a structured synthesis between rationalist and sociological theory, rather than demonstrating the dominance of one or the other. Under such circumstances, it is unclear what is to be gained by structuring academic discourse as a battle among mono-causal claims. Second, as Alexander Wendt, Iain Johnston, and others concede, there is only a very loose connection, if any at all, between ontology, at the level of rationalism and constructivism, and concrete testable theory.[77] Many predictions—including realist ones, as Johnston has shown, and liberal

---

74. Moravcsik, "Taking Preferences Seriously."

75. Peter J. Katzenstein, Robert O. Keohane and Stephen D. Krasner, "*International Organization* and the Study of World Politics," *International Organization*, Vol. 52, No. 4 (Autumn 1998), pp. 645–685.

76. Finnemore and Sikkink, "International Norm Dynamics"; and Risse-Kappen, "Collective Identity."

77. Alexander Wendt, *Social Theory of International Politics* (Cambridge, UK: Cambridge University Press, 1998); Alastair Iain Johnston, *Cultural Realism: Strategic Culture and Grand Strategy in Chinese History* (Princeton, N.J.: Princeton University Press, 1995).

ones, as Wendt has demonstrated—are equally consistent with constructivist and with rationalist ontology. Once the connection between ontology and concrete hypotheses has been broken, it becomes unclear exactly how Lakatosian criteria could be employed or what meaning they would have. This suggests not only that a paradigm can be too narrow for Lakatosian assessment, but also that it can be too broad.

In conclusion, the discipline imposed on theory construction and development by the Lakatosian approach—at least in retrospect—is surely a useful reminder of the need for consistent assumptions, rigor, comparative theory testing, and the need to explain patterns in empirical data efficiently. Yet Lakatos's focus on the scope of theories might encourage scholars to advance "universal" and mono-causal claims when it is inappropriate to do so. More appropriate may be a clear specification of proper empirical limits or more subtle theoretical syntheses. Whatever benefits the Lakatosian metaphor may offer, the debates among IR "isms" framed in universal and mono-causal terms that it helps perpetuate can hardly be considered a spur to scientific progress. Overall, the viability of the "background theory novelty" criterion and the more pragmatic "problem-solving" approach adopted here suggests that criteria proposed by Larry Laudan are more appropriate than those of Imre Lakatos.[78] Lakatosian standards—and, for the same reasons, any rigid definitions of paradigms as building blocks for theory development—should be imposed in international relations only with the utmost caution and modesty.[79]

---

78. Laudan, *Beyond Positivism*.

79. Overall, however, this finding is consistent with existing work on IR paradigms that deliberately employs more straightforward criteria, such as distinctiveness and coherence, rather than explicit philosophy of science. See Legro and Moravcsik, "Is Anybody Still a Realist?"; and Moravcsik, "Taking Preferences Seriously."

Chapter 6

A Lakatosian View of the Democratic Peace Research Program

James Lee Ray

The world's need for another review of recent research on the "democratic peace" is not apparent.[1] Another review by this author is particularly prone to redundancy.[2] But this chapter is not intended to provide a comprehensive review of work on the democratic peace; it

This is a revised version of paper presented earlier at the conference on "Progress in International Relations Theory" (PIRT) in Scottsdale, Arizona, January 15–16, 1999, and at the annual convention of the International Studies Association, Washington, D.C., February 16–20, 1999. It was written originally at the invitation of Mimi and Colin Elman, who have provided continual and valuable feedback on earlier versions. Katherine Barbieri, Bruce Bueno de Mesquita, Nils Petter Gleditsch, Bruce Russett, Richard Tucker, and John Vasquez have also provided useful comments. All the participants at the PIRT conference contributed to my education on these matters; Andrew Bennett, Robert Keohane, Steve Krasner, Randy Schweller, and Kenneth Waltz made particularly memorable criticisms. I should also acknowledge that I might have conveniently allowed even more telling comments by others to escape my attention.

1. See, for example, Steve Chan, "In Search of Democratic Peace: Problems and Promise," *Mershon International Studies Review*, Vol. 41, No. 1 (May 1997), pp. 59–91; Bruce Russett and Harvey Starr, "From Democratic Peace to Kantian Peace: Democracy and Conflict in the International System," in Manus Midlarsky, ed., *Handbook of War Studies*, 2d ed. (Ann Arbor, Mich.: University of Michigan Press, 2000), pp. 93–128.

2. James Lee Ray, "The Democratic Path to Peace," *Journal of Democracy*, Vol. 8, No. 2 (April 1997), pp. 49–64; James Lee Ray, "Does Democracy Cause Peace?" in Nelson W. Polsby, ed., *Annual Review of Political Science* (Palo Alto, Calif.: Annual Reviews, Inc., 1998), pp. 27–46; James Lee Ray, "On the Level(s), Does Democracy Correlate with Peace?" in John A. Vasquez, ed., *What Do We Know About War?* (Lanham, Md.: Rowman and Littlefield, 2000), pp. 219–316.

gives particularly short shrift to those who are critical of it. I first review briefly Lakatos's methodology of scientific research programs,[3] pointing out some of its strengths and weaknesses in comparison to its main competitors. Then I turn to a description and analysis of the democratic peace research program, relying on Lakatosian concepts and guidelines. In the process, I focus on a recent innovation or modification of the program focusing on the axiom or basic assumption that all leaders of states (democratic or otherwise) have as a first priority holding onto their positions of leadership. Some of the implications of this basic axiom are considered, as is its potential for making it possible to subsume or even "falsify" more traditional approaches to international politics that rely instead on basic assumptions such as "states seek power," or "states seek security." Finally, having argued that the democratic peace research program does have the potential to "falsify" realism, I conclude with some recognition of the limits to this claim, as well as a discussion of some reasons to be optimistic about the future of this research program.

"Scientific Progress" According to Lakatos

Those of us who might be inclined to cling to the notion of the scientific enterprise as a noble pursuit of "truth" ought to consider, perhaps, the sobering implications of the fact that although Einstein is almost certainly this century's paragon of scientific virtues, even his theories confront potentially debilitating anomalies.[4] All theories face *some* anomalies, and to reject them all would lead to the nihilistic conclusion that no scientific theories are valid. But if one accepts as

---

3. Imre Lakatos, "Falsification and the Methodology of Scientific Research Programmes," in Imre Lakatos and Alan Musgrave, eds., *Criticism and the Growth of Knowledge* (New York: Cambridge University Press, 1970), pp. 91–197.

4. Brian L. Silver, *The Ascent of Science* (New York: Oxford University Press, 1998), p. 441. "Almost every theory in history has had some anomalies or refuting instances; indeed no one has ever been able to point to a single major theory which did not exhibit some anomalies." Larry Laudan, *Progress and Its Problems* (Berkeley, Calif.: University of California Press, 1977), p. 27.

inevitable *some* falsifying evidence pertaining to *all* theories, how much is too much? As Kuhn shows, popular theories, or paradigms, can be impervious to an amount of falsifying evidence that in retrospect seems rather astonishing.[5] So Kuhn, as well as Lakatos, rejects simple falsifiability as the hallmark of scientific theories: "We cannot prove theories and we cannot disprove them either."[6]

If we accept Kuhnian interpretations, transitions between paradigms are at best a-rational, if not downright irrational. According to Kuhn (or at least according to some interpretations of Kuhn),[7] such transitions occur as a result of a gestalt-shift within scientific communities. Taken to its logical extreme, Kuhn's philosophy seems to portray "science" as based on relatively prolonged periods of irrational, dogmatic attachment to predominant paradigms interspersed with equally irrational periods of "revolution" based more on psychological or sociological factors than on sober appraisals of new evidence as it comes along.[8]

Lakatos argues, in contrast, that scientific progress can be based on rational criteria. He "begins by denying that isolated individual theories are the appropriate units of appraisal; what ought to be appraised are clusters of interconnected theories or 'scientific research programs'."[9] While stressing that these research programs cannot and should not be abandoned in the face of single or even multiple examples of contrary evidence, Lakatos is equally insistent that "we

5. Thomas Kuhn, *The Structure of Scientific Revolutions* (Chicago: University of Chicago Press, 1962).

6. Kuhn, *The Structure of Scientific Revolutions*; Lakatos, "Falsification and the Methodology of Scientific Research Programmes," p. 100.

7. "Kuhn changed his views several times. I have come across twenty-five different versions of Kuhn." Paul Diesing, *How Does Social Science Work?* (Pittsburgh, Pa.: University of Pittsburgh Press, 1991), p. 156.

8. John Losee, *A Historical Introduction to the Philosophy of Science*, 3rd ed. (Oxford: Oxford University Press, 1993), p. 228.

9. Mark Blaug, "Kuhn versus Lakatos *or* Paradigms versus Research Programmes in the History of Economics," in Spiro J. Latsis, ed., *Method and Appraisal in Economics* (Cambridge: Cambridge University Press, 1976), pp. 149–180, at 155.

must find a way to eliminate *some* theories. If we do not succeed, the growth of science will be nothing but growing chaos."[10]

To escape this chaos, Lakatos suggests guidelines for moving beyond one research program on to another, more promising one. The candidate research program must not only contain "novel content." It must also account for all of the phenomena explained by its predecessor. In a restatement of this basic principle that has apparently been quite influential within the subfield of international politics, Bruce Bueno de Mesquita asserts that, "I subscribe strongly to the notion that progress is *best* made when one explanation is shown to supplant another.... [K]nowledge in its most stringent sense and in its highest form is gained when one explanation is replaced with another, broader and apparently more accurate one."[11]

As appealing as this idea is on simple, logical grounds, its Lakatosian form creates at least one fundamental problem. As Elman and Elman point out, "it is difficult to identify SRPs [scientific research programs], and to specify the elements of individual SRPs."[12] Latsis explains quite rightly that "a central distinction between [alternative] methodological approaches ... and [Lakatos's methodology of scientific research programs] concerns the *unit of appraisal*."[13] Lakatos attempts to provide a more helpful unit of appraisal than Kuhn's "paradigms."

---

10. Lakatos, "Falsification and the Methodology of Scientific Research Programmes," p. 108 (emphasis in original).

11. Bruce Bueno de Mesquita, "Toward a Scientific Understanding of International Conflict—A Personal View," *International Studies Quarterly*, Vol. 29, No. 2 (June 1985), pp. 121–136, at 123 (emphasis in original).

12. Colin Elman and Miriam Fendius Elman, "Progress in International Relations Theory," prepared for participants in "Progress in International Relations Theory: A Collaborative Assessment and Application of Imre Lakatos's Methodology of Scientific Research Programs," Scottsdale, Arizona, January 15–16, 1998, p. 20.

13. Spiro Latsis, "A Research Programme in Economics," in Latsis, *Method and Appraisal in Economics*, pp. 1–41. "Instead of appraising isolated hypotheses or strings and systems of hypotheses ... we now appraise an organic unity—a research programme." Ibid., p. 14.

Unfortunately, it is not clear that "research programs" can be defined any more clearly or specifically than "paradigms."

A Lakatosian Appraisal of "Democratic Peace"

Lakatos does tell us that "the classical example of a successful research program is Newton's gravitational theory."[14] If we seize upon this definition by example—precisely because it is so much clearer than the abstract definitions provided by Lakatos—we might note with interest that "Newton said three fundamental things about gravity."[15] According to Newton, gravity exists; gravity is a universal force; and $F = (G^*m_1{}^*m_2)/R^2$, where F = gravitational force, G = a gravitational constant, m_1 = the mass of a first body, m_2 = the mass of a second body, and R = the distance between m_1 and m_2.

Is it possible to describe a "democratic peace research program" in roughly analogous terms? One possible argument in the affirmative is that the "hard core" (in Lakatosian terms) of such a program consists at least in part of three stipulations roughly analogous to the core of Newton's gravitational theory. These would be that democracy exists; that its impact is universal; and that $P = (1 - [d_1{}^*d_2])/(R^e + 1)$, where P = the probability of war between two states, d_1 = the degree of democracy in State 1, d_2 = the degree of democracy in State 2, R = the distance between State 1 and State 2, and e = a geographic constant.

Obviously, while Newton's formula includes all of those factors necessary to calculate the gravitational force between two bodies, this formula only specifies the impact of democracy on the probability of war between two states. Nevertheless, democratic peace theorists do argue that democracy has a uniform impact on the conflict-proneness of all states all the time, just as Newton argued that gravity has a universal impact. And while even its most enthusiastic advocates would not argue that the democratic peace proposition constitutes a social-science equivalent to Newton's law of gravity, many do take

---

14. Lakatos, "Falsification and the Methodology of Scientific Research Programmes," p. 133; emphasis added.

15. Silver, *The Ascent of Science*, p. 43.

seriously the assertion that fully democratic states have not and will not fight interstate wars against each other. (This is one implication of the formula for calculating the probability of war between states presented above.) This argument, even in its most categorical form, is clearly an important source of inspiration for many adherents of the democratic peace research program.

For example Babst, widely recognized to have evoked initially the contemporary interest in the democratic peace proposition, concludes in his seminal article that "no wars have been fought between independent nations with elective governments between 1789 and 1941."[16] Rummel asserts that "violence will occur between states only if at least one is non-libertarian."[17] He explains in a later work that this is "an absolute (or 'point') assertion: There will be *no* violence between libertarian states. *One* clear case of violence or war unqualified by very unusual or mitigating circumstances *falsifies* the proposition."[18] Doyle, having conducted a reasonably thorough review of the history of all "liberal" states in the eighteenth, nineteenth, and twentieth centuries, concludes that "constitutionally secure liberal states have yet to engage in war with one another."[19] Having reviewed a list of putative exceptions to this rule, I concluded that "none of those cases is appropriately categorized as an international war between democratic states."[20] In an impressively comprehensive review of all republican

---

16. Dean V. Babst, "A Force for Peace," *Industrial Research,* Vol. 14, No. 4 (April 1972), pp. 55–58, at 55. Earlier, Clarence Streit, *Union Now: A Proposal for a Federal Union of the Leading Democracies* (New York: Harpers, 1938), pointed out the tendency for democratic states to avoid war among themselves, but his book has had little apparent impact on more recent work.

17. R.J. Rummel, *Understanding Conflict and War,* Vol. 4: *War, Power, Peace* (Beverly Hills, Calif.: Sage Publications, 1979), p. 277 <www2.hawaii.edu/~rummel/NOTE13.HTM>.

18. R.J. Rummel, "Libertarianism and International Violence," *Journal of Conflict Resolution,* Vol. 27, No. 1 (March 1983), p. 29.

19. Michael Doyle, "Kant, Liberal Legacies, and Foreign Affairs," *Philosophy and Public Affairs,* Vol. 12, No. 3 (Summer 1983), pp. 205–235, at 213.

20. James Lee Ray, *Democracy and International Conflict* (Columbia: University of South Carolina Press, 1995), p. 125.

states in the history of the world, including ancient Greece, medieval and Renaissance Italy, the Swiss Republics, and the last two centuries,[21] Weart asserts that "the message of this book is that well-established democracies are inhibited by their fundamental nature from warring on one another. I could find no plain counterexample to this rule, even in remote historical locales."[22]

Nevertheless, the proposition at the heart of the hard core (so to speak) of the democratic peace research program in its more widely supported version is probabilistic rather than absolute in character. This proposition or hypothesis is that pairs of democratic states are *less likely* to fight interstate wars against each other than pairs of states that are not both democratic. Rummel was able to evaluate this hypothesis in a limited fashion, categorizing all dyads involved in war from 1816 to 1965 according to regime type, and establishing that none of these dyads was jointly democratic.[23] However, what he did not deal with was the relative *rate* of war involvement (except for a brief period from 1976 to 1980) for jointly democratic states as opposed to pairs of states that included at least one undemocratic state. Maoz and Abdolali were the first to focus on this issue; they are able to show that the absence of wars between democratic states in the time period on which they focus

---

21. Spencer Weart, *Never At War* (New Haven, Conn.: Yale University Press, 1998), p. 293. There are 92 pages of footnotes in Weart's book, almost all of which are devoted not to elaborations on the main text, but simply to a listing of sources consulted.

22. It was this sort of simple, descriptive evidence that evoked from Levy the declaration that "the absence of war between democracies comes as close as anything we have to an empirical law in international relations." Jack S. Levy, "Domestic Politics and War," *Journal of Interdisciplinary History*, Vol. 18, No. 4 (Spring 1988), p. 662. He came to that conclusion before comprehensive statistical analyses regarding this pattern were completed. More recently, Levy observes that "the idea that democracies almost never go to war with each other is now commonplace. The skeptics are in retreat and the proposition has acquired a nearly law-like status." Jack S. Levy, "The Democratic Peace Hypothesis: From Description to Explanation," *Mershon International Studies Review*, Vol. 38, No. 2 (October 1994), p. 352.

23. Rummel, "Libertarianism and International Violence."

(1817 to 1976) is statistically significant.[24] In what Rummel described as "the first book since my volume 4 of *Understanding Conflict and War* (1979) to explicitly test whether democracies don't make war on each other,"[25] Bueno de Mesquita and Lalman analyze all dyads in Europe from 1815 to 1970 that became involved in a "serious dispute."[26] They conclude that "democracies do abhor even low levels of violence toward one another."[27] In the same year, there were two important contributions to the evidence in favor of the democratic peace proposition. Maoz and Russett analyzed 264,819 dyad-year observations from 1946 to 1986; they found that 17,876 of them could be categorized as jointly democratic, and that none of those jointly democratic dyad-years produced an interstate war. They found furthermore that this lack of wars in the jointly democratic category of dyad-years was statistically significant.[28] Similarly, Bremer focused on 199,573 dyad-years from 1816 to 1965, and reported that none of the 21,644 jointly-democratic-year observations revealed an interstate war, again a number "significantly" less than the "expected value."[29]

---

24. Zeev Maoz and Nasrin Abdolali, "Regime Types and International Conflict, 1816–1976," *Journal of Conflict Resolution*, Vol. 33, No. 1 (March 1989), pp. 3–35.

25. R.J. Rummel, *Power Kills* (New Brunswick, New Jersey: Transaction Publishers), p. 36.

26. Bruce Bueno de Mesquita and David Lalman, *War and Reason* (New Haven, Conn.: Yale University Press, 1992). The data they used is described in Charles Gochman and Zeev Maoz, "Militarized Interstate Disputes, 1816–1976: Procedures, Patterns, and Insights," *Journal of Conflict Resolution*, Vol. 28, No. 4 (December 1984), pp. 585–616.

27. Bueno de Mesquita and Lalman, *War and Reason*, p. 152.

28. Zeev Maoz and Bruce Russett, "Alliance, Contiguity, Wealth, and Political Stability: Is the Lack of Conflict Among Democracies a Statistical Artifact?" *International Interactions*, Vol. 17, No. 3 (1992), pp. 245–268.

29. Stuart Bremer, "Dangerous Dyads: Conditions Affecting the Likelihood of Interstate War, 1816–1965," *Journal of Conflict Resolution*, Vol. 36, No. 2 (June 1992), pp. 309–341. Actually, Bremer's data do show one war between democratic states, but this anomaly is easily explained, as Bremer acknowledges, by a kind of coding error brought about by a time lag in the observation of regime type in his analysis.

Translating "Democratic Peace" into Lakatosian Terminology

Assertions about democracy's existence and its power to prevent war between democratic states arguably constitute only the heart of the "hard core" of the democratic peace research program, in the Lakatosian sense of that term. It is possible to infer that a number of other principles are included in this hard core. Since Babst, Rummel, Maoz and Abdolali, Bueno de Mesquita and Lalman, Maoz and Russett, and Bremer all focus their analyses on states as actors, it is fair to conclude that "states are primary actors" in international politics is also a fundamental axiom for this program. States are not, however, the primary units of analysis for its adherents. The hard core of the democratic research program is distinguished from that for other programs by the fact that it calls for analyses focused on *pairs of states*. This is more than a bookkeeping matter or a merely technical adjustment.

One of the major problems with Waltz's (1959) three images and the way the level of analysis problem has been generally conceptualized (Singer 1961) is that they leave out what is turning out to be the most important level.... The missing fourth image ... has been shown to be much more successful in guiding quantitative research than other levels.... Working at the dyadic level ... has been much more productive.[30]

Another principle incorporated into the hard core of the democratic peace research program that can be inferred from many of its early works asserts that "domestic political processes have important impacts on international interactions, and vice versa." Its focus on domestic politics does distinguish the democratic peace research program from neorealism.[31] But Waltz stipulates that he is mainly concerned about the

---

30. John A. Vasquez, *The Power of Power Politics: From Classical Realism to Neotraditionalism* (Cambridge: Cambridge University Press, 1998), p. 194. Citations are to Kenneth Waltz, *Man, the State, and War* (New York: Columbia University Press, 1959; J. David Singer, "The Level of Analysis Problem in International Relations," in Klaus Knorr and Sydney Verba, eds., *The International System: Theoretical Essays* (Princeton, N.J.: Princeton University Press, 1961).

31. Kenneth N. Waltz, *Theory of International Politics* (New York: Random House, 1979).

operation of the international system, not the foreign policies of individual states, and certainly not interactions between pairs of states. And "neoclassical realists" such as Gideon Rose and Randall Schweller do emphasize the impact of "internal factors" on foreign policies.[32] However, there is one more principle at the hard core of the democratic peace research program that distinguishes it from its major competitors, having to do with its treatment of the relationship between domestic and international politics. That additional provision at the hard core of the program is discussed below.

Taking a cue from Elman and Elman, I would define the negative heuristic of the democratic peace research program as an injunction not to abandon or contradict any element of the hard core.[33]

Perhaps the positive heuristic, or rules and guidelines for formulating the protective belt of auxiliary hypotheses, can be inferred from the activities of those defending the hard core of the democratic peace research program. One such guideline would be: "Develop definitions and operationalizations of democracy and war that can be applied consistently to controversial cases." This rule is exemplified in works addressing whether or not there have been historical exceptions to the claim about the absence of wars between democratic states.[34] A larger group of analysts (discussed in more detail below, in a discussion of this program's auxiliary hypotheses) has behaved as if it were adhering to two additional rules that arguably constitute its positive heuristic. One rule is: "develop hypotheses about important differences between democratic and autocratic regimes." The second is "focus those hypotheses on conflict and cooperation in general to deal with the statistical rarity of wars and democracies."

---

32. Gideon Rose, "Neoclassical Realism and Theories of Foreign Policy," *World Politics*, Vol. 51, No. 1 (October 1998), pp. 144–172; Randall L. Schweller, Chapter 9 in this volume.

33. Elman and Elman, "Progress in International Relations Theory"; see also Elman and Elman, Chapters 1 and 2 in this volume.

34. For example, work by Babst, Rummel, Doyle, Ray and Weart.

A LAKATOSIAN RECONSTRUCTION OF THE DEMOCRATIC PEACE RESEARCH PROGRAM

It would be comforting for supporters of the democratic peace thesis to conclude that because of the increasing number of democratic states in the world in the last couple of decades, the statistical rarity of wars and democracies is becoming less problematic. However, it is not clear that such a conclusion is warranted, at least for the time period up to the early 1990s. For the analyses presented in Table 6-1, pairs of states are categorized by regime type according to democracy and autocracy scales ranging from 0 to 10. Specifically, each state's autocracy score for each year is subtracted from its democracy score, and if the result is equal to or greater than 6, that state is categorized as democratic. If each state in the pair has a score of 6 or greater, the pair is categorized as jointly democratic. Each pair of states is also categorized annually according to whether or not one state *initiated* an interstate war against the other during each year observed.

Table 6-1 does indicate that there has been, from 1816 to 1992, a "significant" relationship between the regime type of pairs of states and the likelihood that they will get involved in interstate wars with each other. It further shows that there has been, since 1965 (the end point in time focused on by Bremer), a significant increase in the number of jointly democratic dyad-year observations to work with (even though I have adopted a somewhat more stringent criterion than Bremer did).[35] However, the *proportion* of jointly democratic dyad-years, as well as the proportion of non-zero observations of interstate war, are both somewhat lower than in Bremer's study. So, in spite of the significantly increased number of democratic states in the world and the occurrence of several interstate wars since 1965, Table 6-1 suggests (like Bremer's analysis for a shorter time period) that from 1816 to 1992, there would have been only about nine wars between democratic states had they fought at the same rate as states in general.

---

35. Bremer, "Dangerous Dyads."

Table 6-1. Cross-tabulation of Regime Type and Interstate War Involvement, Standard Dyadic Hypothesis, 1816–1992 (annual observations, all independent states).

Involved in an Interstate War?	Jointly Democratic Dyads		Not Jointly Democratic Dyads	
No	38,878	100.00%	385,723	99.9730%
Yes	0	0.00%	104	0.0269%
	N=424,705	*FET p < .000		

NOTES: Data on regime type are from the Polity III data set as described in Keith Jaggers and Ted Robert Gurr, "Transitions to Democracy: Tracking Democracy's Third Wave with the Polity III Data," *Journal of Peace Research*, Vol. 32, No. 4 (November 1995), pp. 469–482. These date are available in Keith Jaggers and Ted Robert Gurr, *Polity III: Regime Change and Political Authority, 1800–1994* (computer file), 2d ICPSR version (Boulder, Colo., and College Park, Md.: : Keith Jaggers and Ted Robert Gurr, producers, 1995; Ann Arbor, Mich.: Interuniversity Consortium for Political and Social Research (ICPSR), distributor, 1996).

For states involved in an interstate war in a given year, regime scores were taken instead of Polity IIID in order to take advantage of the more specific information regarding the time of regime changes available in that data set. See Sara McLaughlin, Scott Gates, Håvard Hegre, Ranveig Gissner, and Nils Petter Gleditsch, "Timing and Changes in Political Structures," *Journal of Conflict Resolution*, Vol. 42, No. 2 (June 1998), pp. 231–242. Data on war provided by Melvin Small and J. David Singer, *Resort to Arms* (Beverly Hills, Calif.: Sage Publications, 1982); Melvin Small and J. David Singer, *Correlates of War Project: International and Civil War Data, 1816–1992* (computer file), Study no. 9905, 1994, ICPSR version (J. David Singer and Melvin Small, producers, 1993, distributed by ICPSR, 1994).

Correlates of War sources such as Small and Singer (1982) provide only lists of states involved on each side of multilateral wars, rather than information regarding which states on each side were actually involved in military conflict with each other. The data on interstate wars in this table were modified to reflect actual interaction between states involved in multilateral interstate wars on the dyadic level of analysis. See James Lee Ray, "Identifying Interstate War Initiators on the Directed Dyadic Level of Analysis," prepared for delivery at the annual conference of the Peace Science Society, Ann Arbor, Michigan, October 8–10, 1999.

*Fisher's Exact Test, 1-sided.

Thus debates about individual cases will continue to be of some importance to evaluations of the democratic peace research program, because even a small number of wars between democratic states would wipe out entirely the difference between the rate of warfare among democratic states and the rate among states in general. This will be especially true if, as seems likely in the near future, there are interstate wars between such arguably democratic states as Greece and Turkey, Greece and Albania, or India and Pakistan. Ray has provided analyses of crucial cases, as has Owen.[36] Weart's efforts to extend the scope of research for relevant cases far back into history are likely to be quite important to this aspect of the debate regarding the democratic peace research program.[37]

Lakatos points out that when Newton's gravitational theory was first introduced, it was submerged in an "ocean of 'anomalies'," which "Newtonians turned into 'corroborating instances'."[38] Similarly, Einstein's theory of relativity at first produced implications—such as that the universe is expanding—that even "Einstein himself distrusted."[39]

In a roughly analogous fashion, the democratic peace research program has proven capable of turning anomalies or apparently disconfirming evidence into strengths and corroborating instances.

---

36. James Lee Ray, "Wars Between Democracies: Rare, or Nonexistent?" *International Interactions*, Vol. 18, No. 3 (1993), pp. 251–276; Ray, *Democracy and International Conflict*; John M. Owen, "How Liberalism Produces Democratic Peace," *International Security*, Vol. 19, No. 2 (Fall 1994), pp. 87–125; John M. Owen, *Liberal Peace, Liberal War: American Politics and International Security* (Ithaca, N.Y.: Cornell University Press, 1997).

37. Weart, *Never At War*.

38. Lakatos, "Falsification and the Methodology of Scientific Research Programmes," p. 133.

39. Craig J. Hogan, Robert P. Kirshner, and Nicholas B. Suntzeff, "Surveying Space-time with Supernovae," *Scientific American*, Vol. 280 (January 1999), pp. 46–51, at 47. Einstein tried to resolve this anomaly in a manner that appears ad hoc: he added a "cosmological constant" to his system of equations. In retrospect, however, this seems a progressive innovation. Lawrence M. Krauss, "Cosmological Antigravity," *Scientific American*, Vol. 280 (January 1999), pp. 52–59.

Spiro and Ray, for example, pointed out problems with the early evidence regarding peace among democratic states having to do with interdependent observations and the resulting difficulty created for the interpretation of significance tests.[40] Russett crafted an effective early response to this critique with an analysis focused on dyads observed over the length of their existence, rather than yearly, thus eliminating much of the interdependence from observations relied upon to establish the statistical significance of the absence of war between democratic states.[41] Problems with the interdependence of observations (as well as the dichotomous and skewed nature of the dependent variable in many democratic peace analyses) have evoked a series of papers culminating in a paper by Beck, Katz, and Tucker that concludes that, "democracy inhibits conflict ... even taking duration dependence into account."[42]

Farber and Gowa presented an influential critique to the effect that peace among democracies during the Cold War era was produced by the common interests those states had in opposition to Communist states during that prolonged confrontation.[43] Even before Farber and Gowa developed this argument, several studies had shown that even

---

40. David E. Spiro, "The Insignificance of the Liberal Peace," *International Security*, Vol. 19, No. 2 (Fall 1994), pp. 50–86; Ray, *Democracy and International Conflict*.

41. Bruce Russett, "Correspondence: And Yet It Moves," *International Security*, Vol. 19, No. 4 (Spring 1995), pp. 164–175.

42. Nathaniel Beck, Jonathan N. Katz, and Richard Tucker, "Taking Time Seriously: Time-Series-Cross-Section Analysis with a Binary Dependent Variable," *American Journal of Political Science*, Vol. 42, No. 4 (October 1998), p. 1260. Dixon asserts that "the Beck studies have collectively undertaken about two dozen event history or otherwise robust estimations to test the stability of previously published findings supporting the democratic peace, and in every single case these new estimates corroborate earlier results showing that jointly democratic dyads are less likely to engage in militarized conflict." William J. Dixon, "Dyads, Disputes and the Democratic Peace," in Murray Wolfson, ed., *The Political Economy of War and Peace* (Boston, Mass.: Kluwer Academic Publishers, 1998), pp. 103–126, p. 107).

43. Henry S. Farber and Joanne Gowa, "Polities and Peace," *International Security*, Vol. 20, No. 2 (Fall 1995), pp. 123–146.

controlling for "common interests" as reflected in alliance ties, joint democracy exerts a pacifying effect on relationships between states.[44] More recently, Maoz focused even more specifically on this issue and provided systematic empirical evidence that "democracy, rather than alliance, prevents conflict and war. Nonaligned democracies are considerably less likely to fight each other than aligned non-democracies. Two states that share common interests but do not share a democratic system are considerably more likely to fight each other than democracies that do not show an affinity of interests."[45]

On a more intuitive level, proponents of the democratic peace research program pointed out that the Farber-Gowa thesis cannot account for the numerous violent Cold War conflicts and wars among Communist states that also had "common interests," nor three wars during the same period among states in the "Free World" (the Football War in 1969, the clash between Turkey and Cyprus in 1974, and the conflict over the Falkland Islands in 1982 between England and Argentina). None of these conflicts and wars constitutes an anomaly for the democratic peace research program; they are instead corroborating instances.[46]

Perhaps the most visible attack on the democratic peace research program, by Mansfield and Snyder, asserts that while clearly democratic states may not fight wars against each other, states undergoing a *transition* to democracy are disproportionately war-prone.[47] In response,

---

44. Bremer, "Dangerous Dyads"; Maoz and Russett, "Alliance, Contiguity, Wealth, and Political Stability"; Zeev Maoz and Bruce Russett, "Normative and Structural Causes of Democratic Peace, 1817–1976," *American Political Science Review*, Vol. 87, No. 3 (September 1993), pp. 624–638.

45. Zeev Maoz, "The Controversy over the Democratic Peace: Rearguard Action or Cracks in the Wall?" *International Security*, Vol. 22, No. 1 (Summer 1997), p. 176. See also Zeev Maoz, "Realist and Cultural Critiques of the Democratic Peace: A Theoretical and Empirical Re-Assessment," *International Interactions*, Vol. 24, No. 1 (1998), pp. 38–44.

46. Maoz, "The Controversy over the Democratic Peace"; Ray, "Does Democracy Cause Peace?"

47. Edward Mansfield and Jack Snyder, "Democratization and War," *Foreign Affairs*, Vol. 74, No. 3 (May/June 1995), pp. 79–97. Appearing as it did in a

at least one analysis has created some doubt that such a national-level pattern exists.[48] Maoz, however, acknowledges that there is a relationship between regime transitions and conflict, but argues that transitions from autocracy to "anocracy" or from "anocracy" to autocracy are even more likely to produce conflict than changes to or from democracy.[49] These changes bring about conflict because of the response they evoke from states in their immediate environment. Similarly, Oneal and Russett,[50] Oneal and Ray,[51] and Thompson and Tucker[52] all provide evidence that suggests that the national-level relationship between regime transitions and conflict involvement can be subsumed under a dyadic-level pattern brought about by the fact that states undergoing a transition to democracy will experience an increase in conflict only if many or most of their neighbors are undemocratic. It is this increase in "political distance" between themselves and their neighbors, in other words, that may bring about increases in the amount of conflict for states undergoing a transition to democracy. Thus the evidence pertinent to this apparent national-level anomaly regarding democratic transitions and conflict has been shown to conform to and support the idea that regime type has an important impact on inter-state, dyadic relationships.

---

policy-oriented journal, such an argument was obviously intended to discourage policies inspired by the democratic peace proposition that were designed to bring about such transitions.

48. Andrew Enterline, "Driving While Democratizing (DWD)," *International Security*, Vol. 20, No. 4 (Spring 1996), pp. 183–196.

49. Maoz, "Realist and Cultural Critiques of the Democratic Peace," p. 51.

50. John R. Oneal and Bruce M. Russett. "The Classical Liberals Were Right: Democracy, Interdependence, Democracy and International Conflict, 1950–1985," *International Studies Quarterly*, Vol. 41, No. 2 (June 1997), pp. 267–293.

51. John R. Oneal and James Lee Ray. "New Tests of Democratic Peace: Controlling for Economic Interdependence, 1950–1985," *Political Research Quarterly*, Vol. 50, No. 4 (December 1997), pp. 751–775.

52. William Thompson and Richard Tucker, "A Tale of Two Democratic Peace Critiques," *Journal of Conflict Resolution*, Vol. 41, No. 3 (June 1997), pp. 428–454.

Table 6-2. A Sample of Auxiliary Hypotheses Regarding the Impact of Regime Type on Interstate Interactions.

---

1. Democratic pairs of states are less likely to become involved in serious militarized disputes with each other.

> Bremer 1993; Maoz and Russett 1992, 1993; many others

2. Democratic states are more likely to ally with each other.

> Siverson and Emmons 1991; Simon and Gartzke 1996; Weart 1998

3. Democratic states are more likely to join democratic counterparts in ongoing wars.

> Raknerud and Hegre 1997

4. Democratic states are more likely to trade with each other.

> Polachek 1997; Bliss and Russett 1998

5. Democratic states are more likely to form long-lasting "leagues" (permanent intergovernmental organizations [IGOs]).

> Weart 1998

6. Democratic alliances last longer.

> Gaubatz 1996; Bennett 1997; Reed 1997

7. Democratic states in disputes are more likely to accept mediation.

> Dixon 1993; Raymond 1994

8. The probability of peaceful resolution of disputes is proportional to the degree of democracy in the least democratic state.

> Dixon 1994

9. Democratic states are more likely to obey international law.

> Simmons 1998; Slaughter 1995

10. Democratic states are more likely to win wars in which they participate.

> Lake 1992; Stam 1996

Considerable additional evidence regarding the progressivity of the democratic peace research program involves a series of auxiliary hypotheses aimed in part at dealing with the statistical rarity of interstate wars and democracies. A sample of these hypotheses is listed in Table 6-2.

Many studies have analyzed data on militarized interstate disputes generated by the Correlates of War project.[53] Maoz and Abdolali reported that democratic pairs of states are less likely than pairs of states that are not jointly democratic to become involved in these disputes; that basic finding has been reinforced several times over.[54] Confidence in this finding is in turn increased by analysts such as Rousseau, Gelpi, Reiter, and Huth who report that "democratic states are clearly less likely to initiate force against other democracies" within the context of international crises in the twentieth century.[55] It is now "generally accepted" that "pairs of democracies are much less likely than other pairs of states to fight or threaten each other even at low levels of coercive violence.... That is particularly important as war[s] are relatively rare events in international history, and thus present

53. "Militarized interstate disputes are united historical cases of conflict in which the threat, display or use of military force short of war by one member state is explicitly directed towards the government, official representatives, official forces, property, or territory of another state." Daniel M. Jones, Stuart A. Bremer, and J. David Singer, "Militarized Interstate Disputes, 1816–1992," *Conflict Management and Peace Science*, Vol. 15, No. 2 (Fall 1996), pp. 163–213, p. 163.

54. Maoz and Abdolali, "Regime Types and International Conflict, 1816–1976"; Maoz and Russett, "Alliance, Contiguity, Wealth, and Political Stability"; Maoz and Russett, "Normative and Structural Causes of Democratic Peace, 1817–1976"; Stuart Bremer, "Democracy and Militarized Interstate Conflict, 1816–1965," *International Interactions*, Vol. 18, No. 3 (1993), pp. 231–250; Katherine Barbieri, "Economic Interdependence: A Path to Peace or a Source of Interstate Conflict?" *Journal of Peace Research*, Vol. 33, No. 1 (February 1996), pp. 29–40; John R. Oneal, Frances H. Oneal, Zeev Maoz, and Bruce Russett, "The Liberal Peace: Interdependence, Democracy and International Conflict, 1950–85," *Journal of Peace Research*, Vol. 33, No. 1 (February 1996), pp. 11–28; Oneal and Ray, "New Tests of Democratic Peace"; Oneal and Russett, "The Classical Liberals Were Right"; Bruce Russett, John Oneal, and David R. Davis, "The Third Leg of the Kantian Tripod for Peace," *International Organization*, Vol. 52, No. 3 (Summer 1998), pp. 441–467.

55. David L. Rousseau, Christopher Gelpi, Dan Reiter, and Paul K. Huth, "Assessing the Dyadic Nature of the Democratic Peace, 1918–88," *American Political Science Review*, Vol. 90, No. 3 (September 1996), p. 521; Michael

greater difficulty for establishing strong generalizations."[56] This finding is also important because "any theory of war must account for the fact that virtually all wars broke out of militarized disputes."[57] In fact, this is probably the most important auxiliary hypothesis generated by the democratic peace research program.

But there are many others, focusing for example on the impact of regime type on war outcomes. Lake argues that democratic states are more likely to win the wars in which they become involved.[58] Stam seconds that argument.[59] Siverson provides evidence that wars initiated by democratic states tend to be less costly in terms of battle deaths.[60] This in turn suggests that democratic states may be more likely to win wars at least in part because they select their targets more prudently, rather than or at least in addition to the fact that they are better able to mobilize resources (as Lake suggests, as well as Schultz and Weingast), or because their soldiers fight with more determination because of the relative legitimacy of democratic regimes.[61] Perhaps, too, democracies fare relatively well in wars because they have a tendency to cooperate with each other when conflicts or wars break out. According to Bremer, democratic states are more likely to join ongoing

Brecher, Jonathan Wilkenfeld, and Sheila Moser, *Crises in the Twentieth Century, Handbook of International Crises*, Vol. 1 (Oxford, UK: Pergamon, 1988).

56. Russett and Starr, "From Democratic Peace to Kantian Peace."

57. Maoz, "Realist and Cultural Critiques of the Democratic Peace," p. 46.

58. David Lake, "Powerful Pacifists: Democratic States and War," *American Political Science Review*, Vol. 86, No. 1 (March 1992), pp. 24–37.

59. Allan C. Stam III, *Win, Lose, or Draw: Domestic Politics and the Crucible of War* (Ann Arbor, Mich.: University of Michigan Press, 1996).

60. Randolph M. Siverson, "Democracies and War Participation: In Defense of the Institutional Constraints Argument," *European Journal of International Relations*, Vol. 1, No. 4 (December 1995), pp. 481–489.

61. Stam, *Win, Lose, or Draw*; see also Dan Reiter and Allan C. Stam III, "Democracy and Battlefield Military Effectiveness," *Journal of Conflict Resolution*, Vol. 42, No. 3 (June 1998), pp. 259–277; Lake, "Powerful Pacifists"; Kenneth A. Schultz and Barry Weingast, *The Democratic Advantage: The Institutional Sources of State Power in International Competition* (Stanford, Calif.: Hoover Institution, 1996).

wars.[62] They are also more likely to join on the side of their democratic counterparts.[63] These findings are important in general and to the democratic peace research program in particular because they reveal important connections between regime type and conflict. They may also help account for the apparent reluctance of democratic states to initiate wars against other democratic states, for reasons discussed below.

Another strand of research suggesting important linkages between democracy and interaction among states focuses on cooperative behavior outside the context of ongoing serious disputes or wars. Siverson and Emmons assert that democratic states have been more likely to ally with one another than with other kinds of states throughout most of the twentieth century.[64] Simon and Gartzke disagree to some extent; nevertheless their data show that democratic regimes were more likely to ally with each other during the Cold War.[65] Several analysts provide evidence that shows quite convincingly that alliances among democratic states are likely to last longer than

---

62. Stuart Bremer, "Are Democracies Less Likely to Join Wars?" prepared for delivery at the 1992 annual meeting of the American Political Science Association, Chicago, April 6, 1992.

63. Arvid Raknerud and Håvard Hegre, "The Hazard of War: Reassessing the Evidence for the Democratic Peace," *Journal of Peace Research*, Vol. 34, No. 4 (November 1997), pp. 385–404. Also germane to this point would be Babst's emphasis on the fact that none of the sizeable number of democratic pairs of states involved in World War I and World War II fought against each other. Babst, "A Force for Peace." Mousseau shows that democratic states are more likely to collaborate with each other in the initial stages of militarized disputes. Michael Mousseau, "Democracy and Militarized Interstate Collaboration," *Journal of Peace Research*, Vol. 34, No. 1 (February 1997), pp. 73–87.

64. Randolph M. Siverson and Juliann Emmons, "Birds of a Feather: Democratic Political Systems and Alliance Choices in the Twentieth Century," *Journal of Conflict Resolution*, Vol. 35, No. 2 (June 1991), pp. 285–306.

65. Michael W. Simon and Eric Gartzke, "Political System Similarity and the Choice of Allies," *Journal of Conflict Resolution*, Vol. 40, No. 4 (December 1996), pp. 617–635.

alliances between autocratic states, or between autocratic and democratic states.[66]

Alliances can be viewed at least in part as preparation for war (even if they are intended to avoid the war that is being prepared for). Democracies show a tendency to cooperate in broader contexts, too, more divorced from ongoing conflicts and wars, or in preparation for war. Polachek and Bliss and Russett provide evidence that democracies trade more with each other than autocracies, even if such factors as size of economy, distance, and relative costs are controlled for.[67] This and the possible propensity of democracies to be disproportionately likely to ally with each other bring to mind a basic finding from Weart's panoramic, exhaustive review of the history of republics since ancient Greece. One of his most basic conclusions is that "republics and only republics tend to form durable, peaceful leagues."[68] Perhaps the European Union (EU), as well as NATO with its elaborate institutional structure, are exemplary of clear historical tendencies in the behavior of democratic states, rather than unique or idiosyncratic to the Cold War era. Waltz declares that "we must wonder how long NATO will last as an effective organization. As is often said, organizations are

---

66. Kurt Taylor Gaubatz, "Democratic States and Commitment in International Relations," *International Organization*, Vol. 50, No. 1 (Winter 1996), pp. 109–139; D. Scott Bennett, "Testing Alternative Models of Alliance Duration, 1816–1984," *American Journal of Political Science*, Vol. 41, No. 3 (July 1997), pp. 846–878; William Reed, "Alliance Duration and Democracy: An Extension and Cross-Validation of 'Democratic States and Commitment in International Relations'," *American Journal of Political Science*, Vol. 41, No. 3 (July 1997), pp. 1072–78; Weart, *Never At War*, p. 65.

67. Solomon W. Polachek, "Why Do Democracies Cooperate More and Fight Less? The Relationship Between International Trade and Cooperation," *Review of International Economics*, Vol. 5, No. 3 (August 1997), pp. 295–309; Harry Bliss and Bruce Russett, "Democratic Trading Partners: The Liberal Connection," *Journal of Politics*, Vol. 60, No. 4 (November 1998), pp. 1126–47.

68. Weart, *Never At War*, p. 267. He defines a "league" as "an association among several political units with approximately equal privileges and with shared institutions such as a joint treasury and a court or assembly that adjudicates disputes between members under mutually accepted rules or laws." Ibid.

created by their enemies."[69] The jury is still out on this issue, but perhaps the democratic peace research program provides a more valid insight into the bases and prospects for NATO (as well as the EU) than does neorealism.

Thus auxiliary hypotheses related to the democratic peace research program have emphasized the ability of jointly democratic states to avoid serious military conflict, to cooperate in conflicts with autocratic states, and to cooperate with each other on longer-term bases. They have also shown systematic tendencies to resolve the conflicts that do arise among them in a peaceful manner. Dixon, for example, provides evidence that democratic states are more likely to be amenable to third-party mediation when they are involved in disputes with each other.[70] He also shows that the probability that disputes between states will be resolved peacefully is positively affected by the degree of democracy exhibited by the least democratic state involved in that dispute,[71] and that disputes between democratic states are also significantly shorter than disputes involving at least one undemocratic state.[72] Similarly, Mousseau finds that serious militarized disputes between states are more likely to be resolved by compromise if the original disputants are

---

69. Kenneth N. Waltz, "The Emerging Structure of International Politics," *International Security*, Vol. 18, No. 2 (Fall 1993), p. 75; John Mearsheimer expresses similar skepticism about the post–Cold War future of NATO; John J. Mearsheimer, "Back to the Future: Instability in Europe after the Cold War," *International Security*, Vol. 15, No. 1 (Summer 1990), pp. 5–56; John J. Mearsheimer, "The False Promise of International Institutions," *International Security*, Vol. 19, No. 3 (Winter 1994/95), pp. 5–49.

70. William J. Dixon, "Democracy and the Management of International Conflict," *Journal of Conflict Resolution*, Vol. 37, No. 1 (March 1993), pp. 42–68.

71. William J. Dixon, "Democracy and the Peaceful Settlement of International Conflict," *American Political Science Review*, Vol. 88, No. 1 (March 1994), pp. 14–32. This finding is based on data generated by Alker and Sherman rather than the MID data set generated by the Correlates of War project. Hayward Alker and Frank L. Sherman, "International Conflict Episodes, 1945–1979," data file and codebook (Ann Arbor, Mich.: Interuniversity Consortium for Political and Social Research, 1986).

72. Dixon, "Dyads, Disputes and the Democratic Peace."

democratic.[73] Eyerman and Hart provide evidence indicating that one reason for democracy's impact in this regard has to do with the ability of democratic regimes to communicate intent and commitment more effectively.[74] This evidence supports a formal argument by Fearon.[75]

In related research, Raymond reports that democratic states are more likely to agree to arbitration over mediation as a means of resolving disputes.[76] "Arbitration is a method of settling disputes between States in accordance with law, as distinguished from political and diplomatic procedures of mediation and conciliation."[77] These findings point the way, then, toward an emerging strand of research labeled "democratic legalism," based on the thesis that "democracies are more likely to comply with international legal obligations."[78] Some time ago, Henkin argued that "in general ... democracies have tended

---

73. Michael Mousseau, "Democracy and Compromise in Militarized Interstate Conflicts, 1816–1992," *Journal of Conflict Resolution*, Vol. 42, No. 2 (April 1998), pp. 210–230.

74. Joe Eyerman and Robert A. Hart, Jr., "A Empirical Test of the Audience Cost Proposition," *Journal of Conflict Resolution*, Vol. 40, No. 4 (December 1996), pp. 597–616.

75. James D. Fearon, "Domestic Political Audiences and the Escalation of International Disputes," *American Political Science Review*, Vol. 88, No. 3 (September 1994), pp. 577–592.

76. Gregory A. Raymond, "Democracies, Disputes, and Third-Party Intermediaries," *Journal of Conflict Resolution*, Vol. 38, No. 1 (March 1994), pp. 24–42; Gregory A. Raymond, "Demosthenes and Democracies: Regime-Types and Arbitration Outcomes," *International Interactions*, Vol. 22, No. 1 (1996), pp. 1–20.

77. International Law Commission 1952, cited by Raymond, "Democracies, Disputes, and Third-Party Intermediaries," p. 28.

78. Beth A. Simmons, "Compliance with International Agreements," in Nelson W. Polsby, ed., *Annual Review of Political Science* (Palo Alto, Calif.: Annual Reviews, 1998), pp. 75–93; see also Anne-Marie Slaughter, "International Law in a World of Liberal States," *European Journal of International Law*, Vol. 6, No. 2 (Spring 1995), pp. 503–538. "The distinctive contribution of democratic legalism is its expectation of systematic differences between liberal democracies and nondemocracies." Simmons, "Compliance with International Agreements," p. 85.

to observe international law more than do others."[79] Like many other auxiliary hypotheses related to the democratic peace research program, this one has also shown important signs of sparking productive research efforts leading to the generation of systematic and supportive evidence.[80]

One might question the progressivity in the Lakatosian sense of these auxiliary hypotheses on the grounds that they are merely elaborations on the basic point that democratic states have peaceful relationships with each other, or that they point merely to within-path variables that intervene in the process leading from regime type to peace. In short, such an argument would imply that these auxiliary hypotheses fail to provide "novel content" that makes a program progressive, according to Lakatos.

I would argue, however, that these auxiliary hypotheses are more substantial than mere re-statements of the basic point that democratic states avoid interstate war with each other, or trivial assertions focusing on obvious intervening factors. They are all, to be sure, closely related in a logical and theoretical way to the absence of war between democratic states. But these close relationships between the basic democratic peace proposition and auxiliary hypotheses generated by advocates of the democratic peace research program are more fairly viewed as indications of theoretical coherence, I would argue, than of redundancy. The auxiliary hypotheses arising out of the democratic peace research program focus on and provide explanations for a wide variety of international phenomena such as alliances, war outcomes,

---

79. Louis Henkin, *How Nations Behave: Law and Foreign Policy*, 2d ed. (New York: Columbia University Press, 1979), p. 63; cited by Lori Fisler Damrosch, "Use of Force and Constitutionalism," *Columbia Journal of Transnational Law*, Vol. 36, Nos. 1 & 2 (1997), pp. 449–472. See also Lori Fisler Damrosch, "Constitutional Control Over War Powers: A Common Core of Accountability in Democratic Societies?" *University of Miami Law Review*, Vol. 50, No. 1 (October 1995), pp. 181–199.

80. Simmons, "Compliance with International Agreements"; Harold K. Jacobson and E.B. Weiss, "Compliance With International Environmental Accords: Achievements and Strategies," presented at Harvard University Seminar, Law and International Relations, February 5, 1997.

economic integration, trade relationships, compliance with international law, and sub-war conflict resolution. Furthermore, they do this with an emphasis on regime type, and especially the impact of democracy, in a manner that justifies the categorization of many or most of these auxiliary hypotheses as "novel content" in the Lakatosian sense. These relationships escape prediction by neorealism, which tends to de-emphasize internal factors at least on a theoretical level, and even by realism, which can and does take into account domestic factors in some of its incarnations.[81] What neither neorealism nor realism do is emphasize the crucial distinction between democratic and autocratic regimes in the systematic manner characteristic of the democratic peace research program.[82] Just how systematic this emphasis is, at least potentially, is the point to which we now turn.

---

81. Miriam Elman, for example, argues that "realists acknowledge that both domestic and international factors play a role in determining state behavior." Miriam Fendius Elman, ed., *Paths to Peace: Is Democracy the Answer?* (Cambridge, Mass.: MIT Press, 1997), p. 8. Colin Elman even suggests that "where neorealist scholars do see unit-level influences as important, they should take steps to integrate those variables into the neorealist framework in a systematic fashion." Colin Elman, "Horses for Courses: Why *Not* Neorealist Theories of Foreign Policy?" *Security Studies*, Vol. 6, No. 1 (Autumn 1996), pp. 7–53, at 40. See also Rose, "Neoclassical Realism and Theories of Foreign Policy"; and Schweller (Chapter 9 in this volume).

82. Schweller does develop a rather "realist" analysis of power transitions in an account that emphasizes the impact of democracy. Randall L. Schweller, "Domestic Structure and Preventive War: Are Democracies More Pacific?" *World Politics*, Vol. 44, No. 2 (January 1992). However, in so doing he explicitly acknowledges that he has "abandon[ed] the structural-realist assumption that all states react similarly to external pressures," and accepts an "auxiliary second-image hypothesis" regarding the impact of democracy (ibid., p. 267). This work might be categorized either as a degenerative ad hoc shift within the realist program (since Schweller provides no logical or axiomatic basis for his unrealist-like emphasis on the importance of democracy), or a progressive even if rather a-theoretical foreshadowing of tendencies in the democratic peace research program that were still mostly latent at the time his article appeared.

The Hard Core of the Democratic Peace Research Program, Revisited

Although advocates of the democratic peace research program are typically critical of realist approaches to international politics, and the most enthusiastic critics of that program quite often favor a more realist point of view, in fact that program is not at all inalterably or totally opposed to, nor is it entirely inconsistent with, realist principles and ideas. On the contrary, papers central to the development of the democratic peace research program have all generated important evidence regarding the impacts on interstate conflict behavior of such factors as geographic contiguity, alliance ties, major power status, and capability ratios.[83] This feature of the democratic peace research program is so central to its character, in fact, that one of its leading proponents points out that "an amazing ... by-product of the democratic peace research program is that it has generated more empirical support for ... propositions derived from realist perspectives of world politics than any other research program."[84] Obviously inspired by similar notions, Russett, Oneal and Davis declare that "it would be foolish to try to explain the incidence of militarized disputes without also looking at the effects of such *realpolitik* influences as relative power and alliances."[85]

---

83. See, for example, Maoz and Russett, "Normative and Structural Causes of Democratic Peace, 1817–1976"; Bremer, "Dangerous Dyads"; Bremer, "Democracy and Militarized Interstate Conflict, 1816–1965"; Bruce Russett, *Grasping the Democratic Peace* (Princeton, N.J.: Princeton University Press, 1993); Oneal, Oneal, Maoz and Russett, "The Liberal Peace"; Oneal and Russett, "The Classical Liberals Were Right"; Oneal and Ray, "New Tests of Democratic Peace"; and Russett, Oneal, and Davis, "The Third Leg of the Kantian Tripod for Peace."

84. It is important to note, in light of the argument to be developed here, that Maoz also asserts that "realist critiques create the impression that political realism and democratic peace are mutually exclusive. This is hardly the case." Maoz, "The Controversy over the Democratic Peace," p. 193.

85. Russett, Oneal, and Davis, "The Third Leg of the Kantian Tripod for Peace," p. 453.

In addition, "if we analyze the differences between the realpolitik variant of the interaction game presented in *War and Reason* and the domestic variant, we see that they share six basic assumptions.... The *only* difference between the two variants on the level of basic assumptions is reflected in the seventh basic assumption."[86] The domestic variant's seventh assumption incorporated into Bueno de Mesquita and Lalman's interstate interaction game posits that national leaders will attempt to maximize utility within both an international and a national context.[87] (The realpolitik version assumes leaders focus exclusively on the international context.) That seventh assumption in the domestic variant turns out to be an important basis for the derivation of the democratic peace proposition from Bueno de Mesquita and Lalman's model. Related work provides evidence in support of the arguments that regimes that initiate and lose interstate wars are at an especially high risk of being replaced, and that losing a war is a particularly risky proposition for leaders of democratic states.[88]

---

86. Ray, *Democracy and International Conflict*, p. 39 (emphasis in original). According to Keohane, Bruce Bueno de Mesquita, *The War Trap* (New Haven, Conn.: Yale University Press, 1981), is among "the finest work" in the realist genre. Robert O. Keohane, "Theory of World Politics: Structural Realism and Beyond," in Ada Finifter, ed., *Political Science: The State of the Discipline* (Washington, D.C.: American Political Science Association, 1983), pp. 541–78, at 512. Alexander Wendt, "The Agent-Structure Problem in International Relations Theory," *International Organization*, Vol. 41, No. 3 (Summer 1987), p. 351, sees Bueno de Mesquita's 1985 article, "Toward a Scientific Understanding of International Conflict," as "the definitive discussion of the philosophy of science underlying neorealism." In my view, these are both fundamentally erroneous perceptions. Nevertheless, they serve to highlight the potential compatibility of realism and neorealism on the one hand, and the democratic peace research program on the other, that I want to emphasize here.

87. Bueno de Mesquita and Lalman, *War and Reason*.

88. Bruce Bueno de Mesquita, Randolph Siverson, and Gary Woller, "War and the Fate of Regimes: A Comparative Analysis," *American Political Science Review*, Vol. 86, No. 3 (September 1992), pp. 638–646; Bruce Bueno de Mesquita and Randolph Siverson, "War and The Survival of Political Leaders: A Comparative Study of Regime Types and Political Accountability," *American Political Science Review*, Vol. 89, No. 4 (December 1995), pp. 841–853.

All of the auxiliary hypotheses discussed in this chapter rely on the distinction between democratic and autocratic regimes as a key explanatory factor. Most have been examined in a systematic empirical fashion, and have survived such scrutiny. Nevertheless, all of the empirical regularities involving the relationship between democracy and the range of other international political phenomena we have discussed could be of limited theoretical importance. Even considering their weight and scope, a Lakatosian might reasonably argue that those regularities (even the absence of war between democratic states) do not constitute a sufficient condition for categorizing the democratic peace research program as progressive. As Waltz points out, finding anomalies and patching them up, so to speak, by adding additional explanatory factors is not theory construction. "A theory is not a mere collection of variables. If a 'gap' is found in a theory, it cannot be plugged by adding a 'variable' to it. To add to a theory something that one believes has been omitted requires showing how it can take its place as one element of a coherent and effective theory."[89]

A Lakatosian reconstruction of the history of the democratic peace research program can show that it is able to plug a significant gap left by realism (and perhaps by neorealism), and to do so in a logical, axiomatically-based manner.[90] The gap at issue here, having to do with all the systematic differences between democratic and autocratic regimes, can be filled in a theoretically coherent way if we impute a key additional item to the "hard core" of the democratic peace research program. The roots of this additional "hard core" principle in contemporary work on the democratic peace can be traced to Rummel, who postulates that in all states "there are two classes, those with

89. Kenneth N. Waltz, "Evaluating Theories," *American Political Science Review*, Vol. 91, No. 4 (December 1997), p. 916.

90. Laudan, *Progress and Its Problems*, p. 157, points out that Lakatos argues that there need be no resemblance at all between "reconstructed" history as developed by philosophers of science and the "actual exigencies of the case under examination." Laudan, *Progress and Its Problems*, p. 169. My reconstruction clearly attributes more coherence to the development of the democratic peace research program than would a more prosaic, descriptively accurate one.

authoritative roles and those without."[91] Rummel contributes further to the development of the hard core principle proposed here by declaring that "intense violence will occur only if there is an expectation of success."[92] Ray argues that "the basic realist argument that foreign policymakers will make decisions that are in the 'national interest' has always implied a quite 'unrealistic' tendency of national leaders and foreign policymakers to be altruistic."[93] He concludes that it would be "more realistic ... to assume instead ... that 'political elites wish to attain and stay in office',," and that "democracies ... avoid wars against other democratic states not necessarily because of normative convictions about how political conflicts ought to be resolved, nor because they are unable to overcome political, structural obstacles in the way of such policies, but because they feel that fighting such wars might be harmful to their chances of staying in power."[94] A basic assumption of a formal model developed by Bueno de Mesquita and Siverson asserts that "foreign policy leaders, like all politicians, choose actions with an eye toward staying in power."[95]

This assumption is arguably more fundamental than assumptions such as "states seek power," or "states seek security," because it subsumes such assumptions. Obviously the leader of a state is unlikely

91. R.J. Rummel, *Understanding Conflict and War*, Vol. 3: *Conflict in Perspective* (Beverly Hills, Calif.: Sage Publications, 1977), p. 104.

92. Rummel, *Understanding Conflict and War*, p. 263.

93. Ray, *Democracy and International Conflict*, p. 39.

94. Ray, *Democracy and International Conflict*, pp. 39–40.

95. Bruce Bueno de Mesquita and Randolph M. Siverson, "Inside-Out: A Theory of Domestic Political Institutions and the Issues of International Conflict," unpublished manuscript 1996. "In our game, it is common knowledge that each incumbent prefers to retain office above all else." Bruce Bueno de Mesquita and Randolph M. Siverson, "Nasty or Nice? Political Systems, Endogenous Norms, and the Treatment of Adversaries," *Journal of Conflict Resolution*, Vol. 41, No. 1 (February 1997), pp. 175–199, at 183. The implications of this model for the democratic peace research program are discussed more directly in Bruce Bueno de Mesquita, James D. Morrow, Randolph Siverson, and Alastair Smith, "An Institutional Explanation of the

to retain office if the state is invaded, occupied, annexed, or even, as we have seen, simply defeated. So, preserving the territorial integrity, political independence, and power of the state is a pressing concern for all state leaders, as realists and neorealists rightly imply.

But the democratic peace research program does not take this concern into account by anthropomorphizing, reifying, or personifying the state. That the democratic peace assumption about leaders of states is more descriptively accurate than the basic realist or neorealist assumption about states (there is clearly less distortion and abstraction involved in the personification of a person) is a virtue of debatable importance. "In making assumptions about men's (or states') motivations, the world must be drastically simplified.... Descriptions strive for accuracy; assumptions are brazenly false."[96]

What is more clearly useful about this assumption regarding the pervasive desire of political leaders to stay in power is that it emphasizes and provides theoretical purchase on the extent to which leaders involved in international interactions must play a "two-level game."[97] "When national leaders must win ratification ... from their constituents for an international agreement, their negotiating behavior reflects the simultaneous imperatives of both a domestic political game and an international game."[98] According to realism or neorealism, "states" seek power or security. According to democratic peace theory,

---

Democratic Peace," *American Political Science Review*, Vol. 93, No. 4 (December 1999), pp. 791–807.

96. Kenneth N. Waltz, "Realist Thought and Neorealist Theory," *Journal of International Affairs*, Vol. 44, No. 1 (Spring 1990), p. 27. See also Waltz, *Theory of International Politics*, pp. 117–118.

97. "Bueno de Mesquita and Siverson ... outline domestic or endogenous institutional constraints based on the nature of the selectorate and the size of the winning coalition (somewhat akin to Putnam's 1988 argument concerning two level games ...)." Russett and Starr, "From Democratic Peace to Kantian Peace." The reference here is to Bueno de Mesquita and Siverson, "Nasty or Nice?"; Robert D. Putnam, "Diplomacy and Domestic Politics: The Logic of Two-Level Games," *International Organization*, Vol. 42, No. 3 (Summer 1988), pp. 427–460.

98. Putnam, "Diplomacy and Domestic Politics," abstract.

leaders of states are vitally concerned about their state's power and security, but they are *also* fundamentally concerned about their own personal political fortunes. To stay in power, political leaders must deal successfully with their opponents outside the state, *and* inside the state. They continually play a two-level game.

In the Lakatosian view, then, there is another provision at the "hard core" of the democratic peace research program not mentioned above. It is the assumption that a primary goal of leaders of states is to stay in power.

The Advantages and Disadvantages of the Revised Hard Core

One of the potential drawbacks of such an assumption is that it makes the basic democratic peace model more complicated than its realist or neorealist counterparts. This does not necessarily mean, however, that the democratic peace model is less parsimonious. "Parsimony," according to King, Keohane, and Verba, is "a judgment, or even an assumption, about the nature of the world: it is assumed to be simple."[99] This definition of parsimony deviates considerably from common usage of the term. Parsimony as typically discussed by social scientists quite clearly is *not* an assumption about the world. It is rather a characteristic of models shorn of complexity that is unnecessary to accomplish the explanatory task at hand. It is deemed desirable by analysts because of an assumption that the world works in simple ways. It is that assumption which is designated by King, Keohane and Verba, awkwardly in my view, as "parsimony."

While King, Keohane, and Verba are skeptical about the virtues of "parsimony" as they define it, they endorse wholeheartedly the pursuit of "leverage," or "explaining as much as possible with as little as possible."[100] But leverage defined in this way is exactly what is accomplished by parsimonious models, defined as models that are as simple as possible while still accomplishing the explanatory task at

99. Gary King, Robert O. Keohane, and Sidney Verba, *Designing Social Inquiry* (Princeton, N.J.: Princeton University Press, 1994), p. 20.

100. King, Keohane, and Verba, *Designing Social Inquiry*, p. 29.

hand. King, Keohane and Verba tend to use "parsimony" and "simplicity" as synonymous.[101] But if "parsimony" means nothing more than "simplicity," it is a fancy word with no real advantages over the much simpler one, and therefore serves no real purpose.

In other words, to give parsimony a meaning different from "simplicity," and therefore a reason to exist, it should be thought of as effective simplicity, that is, a characteristic of explanatory models that are no more complicated than they need to be. Such a definition implies that a model cannot be *too* parsimonious; if a model is too simple to deal with the phenomena to be accounted for, it ceases to be parsimonious, even though it may be simple.

The assumption about leaders desiring to stay in power, and the resulting necessity to focus on both domestic and international political considerations, is sufficiently complicating that it may be impractical or intractable as a basis for system-level theorizing of the Waltzian type. It may well be better suited to theories regarding pairs of states, or the typically relatively small sets of states involved in conflicts (such as multilateral wars).[102]

---

101. For example, they assert at one point that "to maximize leverage, we should attempt to formulate theories that explain as much as possible with as little as possible. Sometimes this formulation is achieved via parsimony, but sometimes not. We can conceive of examples by which a slightly more complicated theory will explain vastly more about the world." King, Keohane, and Verba, *Designing Social Inquiry*, pp. 104–105.

102. In other words, this writer is not yet persuaded that the democratic peace research program poses a direct challenge to neorealism conceived as a model dealing only with the international political system as a whole as the principal unit of analysis. Several analysts such as Sara McLaughlin, Nils Petter Gleditsch, and Håvard Hegre; Crescenzi and Enterline; and Maoz investigate the relationship between the distribution of regime types and conflict in the international system, but the logical bases of these analyses, or the transfer of basically dyadic-level thinking to the level of the international system, seem problematic. Nevertheless, Bueno de Mesquita, Morrow, Siverson, and Smith may point the way to system-level theorizing in which the distribution of regime types in the system plays an explanatory role similar to that played by the distribution of power in neorealist accounts. Sara McLaughlin, "Endo-geneity and the Democratic Peace," paper presented at the annual meeting of the Peace Science Society, Houston, Texas, October 25–27, 1996; Nils Petter

Another possible objection to the definition of the "hard core" devised here, especially with its emphasis on the assumption regarding the desire of leaders to stay in power, is that it tends to "privilege" rational choice–based structural versions of the democratic peace idea over the approach based on norms and cultural considerations. However, while the democratic peace research program as pictured here may well emphasize structural and rational factors and accounts more than cultural or normative ones, it is not incompatible with the latter arguments.

For example, Spencer Weart, one of the major proponents of the cultural argument regarding the pacifying force of democracy, argues that:

The political culture of republican leaders brings them to follow as a rule of thumb the expectation that in disputes with foreign leaders who share their principles, they will be able to negotiate a satisfactory solution. It is not idealism that makes them follow this practice. Getting objective information about how foreign rivals are likely to behave is so difficult that rules of thumb can be the most efficient way to cut through the clutter of international relations.[103]

Thus culture is seen by Weart as a kind of "signaling" device and a source of information between potentially conflicting states, in a way that is quite consistent with democratic peace arguments within a

Gleditsch and Håvard Hegre, "Peace and Democracy: Three Levels of Analysis," *Journal of Conflict Resolution,* Vol. 41, No. 2 (April 1997), pp. 283–310; Mark J.C. Crescenzi and Andrew J. Enterline, "Ripples from Waves? A Systemic, Time-Series Analysis of Democracy, Democratization, and Interstate War," *Journal of Peace Research,* Vol. 36, No. 1 (January 1999), pp. 75–94; Zeev Maoz, "Democratic Networks: Connecting National, Dyadic, and Systemic Levels-of-Analysis in the Study of Democracy and War," in Zeev Maoz and Azar Gat, eds., *War in a Changing World* (Ann Arbor: University of Michigan Press, 2001), pp. 143–182. Bruce Bueno de Mesquita, James D. Morrow, Randolph Siverson, and Alastair Smith, "Peace Through War? Evolutionary Consequences of Democratic War Behavior," paper prepared for delivery at the Annual Meeting of the Midwest Political Science Association, Chicago, April 23–25, 1998.

103. Weart, *Never At War,* p. 295.

rational choice framework in, for example, Bueno de Mesquita and Lalman.[104]

Maoz points out that findings such as those by Bueno de Mesquita and Lalman, that disputes between democracies are more likely to end in draws or negotiated settlements, can be interpreted as evidence in favor of both cultural and structural arguments.[105] Farber and Gowa argue that norms may in fact be difficult to distinguish from interests, or at least that adherence to norms may be motivated by interests as much as by internalized values.[106] In addition, such prominent proponents of the cultural version of the democratic peace proposition as Oneal and Russett are quite willing to take into account considerations of the "expected utility" of states involved in conflicts, and to develop a theoretical structure based in part on those considerations.[107] "In short, the distinction between the cultural and the structural explanation of democratic peace does not seem either stark or crucial."[108] The reconstruction of the democratic peace research program here may lean in the direction of favoring the structural or strategic version of the democratic peace argument, but it certainly does not discard cultural factors or arguments.

The main advantage of the program as defined (and reconstructed here), especially with the principle added to its hard core that has to do with the priority national leaders give to staying in power, is that it facilitates the incorporation of domestic political considerations into accounts and explanations of interstate interactions. Furthermore, the democratic peace model as construed here takes into account these

---

104. Bueno de Mesquita and Lalman, *War and Reason*; see also Kenneth A. Schultz, "Domestic Opposition and Signaling in International Crises," *American Political Science Review*, Vol. 92, No. 4 (December 1998), pp. 829–844.

105. Maoz, "Realist and Cultural Critiques of the Democratic Peace," p. 13; Bueno de Mesquita and Lalman, *War and Reason*.

106. Farber and Joanne Gowa, "Polities and Peace," pp. 125–126.

107. John R. Oneal and Bruce Russett, "Escaping the War Trap: Evaluating the Liberal Peace Controlling for the Expected Utility of Conflict," paper presented at the annual meeting of the International Studies Association, Toronto, 1997.

108. Ray, *Democracy and International Conflict*, p. 37.

domestic political considerations, as well as the importance of the distinction between democratic and autocratic regimes, not just because they have been found empirically to have important impacts on interstate interactions. The basic principle focusing on the desire of leaders to stay in power allows the integration of domestic and international political considerations affecting interstate interactions *in a theoretically coherent fashion*. That is, the integration of domestic and international factors is provided an axiomatic, theoretical base.

At the same time, this reconstruction of the democratic peace research program does not constitute co-optation of the program by a rational choice approach. It represents instead an attempt to integrate the work of rational choice theorists such as Bruce Bueno de Mesquita with more empirically oriented analysts as Zeev Maoz, John Oneal, and Bruce Russett, as well as such historically minded advocates of the democratic peace proposition as Spencer Weart. I am not in full agreement, certainly, with all of Stephen Walt's criticisms of rational choice approaches. Nevertheless, I do agree with his assertion that the "natural sciences profit from the fruitful collaboration of theoreticians and experimentalists." Such collaboration occurs within the democratic peace research program. Research on international conflict in general can benefit from a closer integration of formal theoretical ideas with an axiomatic basis and statistical analyses of aggregate data.[109]

Conclusion

The central point of Lakatos's essay is that in comparing two research programs, T, and T', if T' "has excess empirical content over T ... explains the previous success of T ... and some of the excess content of T' is corroborated," then T has been "falsified."[110]

The democratic peace research program does provide "excess empirical content" over its realist and neorealist predecessors. The

---

109. Stephen M. Walt, "Rigor, or Rigor Mortis? Rational Choice and Security Studies," *International Security*, Vol. 23, No. 3 (Spring 1999), p. 48.

110. Lakatos, "Falsification and the Methodology of Scientific Research Programmes," p. 116.

finding regarding the absence of war between democratic states is the most central example of this. But the auxiliary hypotheses discussed in this chapter are also based on the distinction between democracies and autocracies in a way that makes most of the patterns they point to unlikely to be discerned or discovered by realist or neorealist approaches. For example, Gelpi and Griesdorf examine serious disputes in the twentieth century, and find, as realists would expect, that relative power has an important impact on the outcomes of such disputes.[111] That is, the more powerful state usually wins such disputes. "But among democracies, relative power has no such effect; the weaker side is more likely to get its way."[112] Similarly, Werner and Lemke analyze the behavior of states that joined ongoing militarized disputes from 1816 to 1986, and report that "power concerns matter only to autocracies: democracies do not seem to base their alignment on the power of the sides in the dispute."[113]

The democratic peace research program also "explains the previous success of T." That is, it takes into account and accommodates important realist (and perhaps neorealist) principles and hypotheses. Its basic assumption—that leaders desire above all to stay in power— recognizes the crucial extent to which this leads them to be vitally concerned about their states' power and/or security. However, at the same time the democratic peace research program offers a basis for establishing priorities among all the diverse policies that might be expected to achieve those "national interests." That is to say, national leaders can be expected to select among that broad array of options that may be perceived to be in "the national interest," and to interact in

---

111. Christopher Gelpi and Michael Griesdorf, "Winners and Losers: Democracies in International Crisis, 1918–1988," paper presented at the annual meeting of the American Political Science Association, Washington, D.C., 1997.

112. Russett and Starr, "From Democratic Peace to Kantian Peace."

113. Suzanne Werner and Douglas Lemke, "Opposites Do Not Attract: The Impact of Domestic Institutions, Power, and Prior Commitments on Alignment Choices," *International Studies Quarterly*, Vol. 41, No. 3 (September 1997), p. 529.

ways that reflect the fact that they are playing the two-level game emphasized by the democratic peace research program.

Thus the democratic peace research program has excess empirical content over realism or neorealism. It has a "hard core" that is compatible with but also capable of subsuming basic realist or neorealist assumptions regarding states seeking power or security. Much of the excess content of the democratic peace research program has been corroborated repeatedly and consistently in all the research devoted to the basic democratic peace proposition and a wide array of auxiliary hypotheses. In other words, according to Lakatosian principles, it would be fair to conclude that realism and/or neorealism have been "falsified."

This is a limited claim. In the Lakatosian sense, strictly speaking, one model or approach or program might be considered "falsified" by another that was only marginally different, as long as the marginal difference allowed that alternative program to develop excess empirical content that could be corroborated. This would not necessarily indicate that the "falsified" program had been fundamentally discredited, by any means. On the contrary, in the type of situation we are envisioning here, the original "falsified" program might still be considered vastly more important for the contributions it has made toward scientific progress and understanding than the program which has "falsified" it. The new program might be an improvement, even if only adjusted in a relatively marginal fashion.

Furthermore, it would arguably be equally reasonable to see what has happened in the still evolving relationship between realism and the democratic peace research program as not necessarily the "falsification" of realism, but a modification of it, or a melding of at least some realist principles with fundamental "liberal" or "neoliberal" ideas leading toward the emergence of some kind of hybrid. Whether this hybrid might be referred to as "realist liberalism," or "liberal realism" is surely more an issue of academic politics than of substance. The extent to which various realists or democratic peace advocates will be comfortable with this hybrid as it is described here will vary widely, and whether or not this hybrid turns out to have lasting importance will depend on developments within the field of international politics in the coming years.[114]

It is especially necessary to be modest in claims that the democratic peace research program has "falsified" realism or neorealism, in light of the argument that realism is a broader approach, and that the democratic peace research program has confined its explanatory efforts to a much narrower range of phenomena. In fact, it could reasonably be argued that the democratic peace approach is too narrow to qualify as a "research program" at all. From this point of view, the claims on behalf of the democratic research program in this paper are made in a fashion too insensitive to Lakatos' dictum that "it is a succession of theories and not one given theory which is appraised as scientific."[115]

In the context of a debate regarding a Lakatosian appraisal of realism or neorealism, Waltz argues that "political scientists generally work from two different paradigms: one behavioral, the other systemic."[116] The term "behavioral" generally connotes or is even equated with the rubric "quantitative." In a comprehensive review of the democratic peace literature, Chan notes that the democratic peace research program "is based on quantitative methods. Indeed, the democratic peace research proposition is arguably one of the most robust generalizations that has been produced to date by this research tradition."[117] In short, it is possible that the "quantitative research program" would be a unit of appraisal more congruent with the notion of "program" as developed by Lakatos. Unfortunately, at this point space limitations (not to mention limitations in time, energy,

---

114. "Lakatos wants to account for science as a rational process, but it turns out that the rationality of choices between rival research programs can be decided only with hindsight." Andrew Belsey, "Review of *Whys and Ways of Science* by Peter J. Riggs," *The British Journal for the Philosophy of Science*, Vol. 47, No. 2 (June 1996), pp. 335–338, at 335. "[Lakatos] denies that anything except retrospective autopsies of long-dead scientific controversies can produce a reliable assessment." Laudan, *Progress and Its Problems*, p. 232.

115. Lakatos, "Falsification and the Methodology of Scientific Research Programmes," p. 132.

116. Waltz, "Evaluating Theories," p. 913.

117. Chan, "In Search of Democratic Peace," p. 60.

knowledge, and inclination) preclude the development of a Lakatosian comparison of the quantitative research program with its competitors.

Instead, let us focus in closing on what this writer would like to believe are two "straws in the wind" that may indicate future trends in research on international politics. In a consideration of the future impact of the expansion of NATO, Bruce Russett and Allen Stam, two prominent proponents of the democratic peace proposition, blend realist and liberal principles in a manner that demonstrates the extent to which they can be integrated, but also the extent to which a democratic peace accounting of this type supersedes a more purely realist analysis.[118] In addition, the prominent advocate of realist analysis, Joseph Grieco, has recently initiated research on a theme suggesting that "democracies may have unique problems in security affairs."[119] In this work, he emphasizes the impact of regime type on interactions between states. At the same time, he stresses the potentially beneficial impact of "force-intensive crisis strategies" in a classically realist manner. These two papers, perhaps, exemplify maturation within the democratic peace research program, as well as its ability to be combined with or possibly even to subsume the realist program.

---

118. Bruce Russett and Allan C. Stam, "Courting Disaster: An Expanded NATO vs. Russia and China," *Political Science Quarterly*, Vol. 113, No. 3 (Fall 1998), pp. 361–382.

119. Joseph M. Grieco, "Democratic States and Repetitive Military Challenges, 1918–1994," poster session materials at the Annual Meeting of the American Political Science Association, Boston, 1998, Abstract.

Chapter 7

Operational Code Analysis as a Scientific Research Program

A Cautionary Tale

Stephen G. Walker

Do leaders matter in world politics? Intuitively, we sense that they do and, as citizens of a democratic society, we act as if they do. However, as scholars we are often confounded by several problems when we try to demonstrate that "who leads matters." As political scientists we study large collectivities that behave in complex ways, and we have difficulty in gaining reliable and valid observations of leaders and establishing connections among them, actions by the state, and political outcomes.

These difficulties have led over the years to the emergence of certain elements of conventional wisdom regarding the nature and importance of political leadership: leadership, it is said, explains relatively little of the variance in the decisions of states, and the linkages between leaders and the outcomes of decisions are even more tenuous. The individual differences between leaders are less important than the common characteristics that they share as members of a culture or society. Leadership in this view involves the tasks, relatively interchangeable among individuals, of articulating shared values, responding to commonly recognized constraints in the environment,

I am grateful to Robert Jervis, Randall Schweller, Andrew Bennett, Kenneth Waltz, Robert Keohane, David Dessler, and the other participants at Arizona State University's "Progress in International Relations Theory" conference in Scottsdale, Arizona, January 14–16, 1999, for their comments on earlier versions of this paper. Alexander George and Ole Holsti were also kind enough to read and comment on the version presented at the annual meeting of the American Political Science Association, Atlanta Georgia, September 1–4, 1999.

and calculating rational choices on the basis of these incentives and constraints. It is important as citizens to be careful, active, and attentive in selecting leaders who are not flawed, but who are instead representative standard-bearers of the dominant culture and who can process information according to the standards of instrumental rationality. However, only rarely and under very restricted conditions are leaders themselves important in explaining political outcomes.

Operational code analysis challenges several of these tenets in a more or less explicit manner by looking for the impact of individual differences on foreign policy decisions and outcomes. The research program originated in a concern shared by academic and policy analysts with the causes of the Cold War and the puzzle presented by Soviet bargaining behavior after World War II. The initial research by Nathan Leites was done under the auspices of the RAND Corporation and represented an extension of the argument in George Kennan's "long telegram," which portrayed the Bolsheviks as revolutionaries with a drive for power that was unusually high by Western standards.[1] Leites himself located the core of Bolshevik strategic conceptions in the cryptic question posed by Lenin, "kto-kovo?" Translated literally as "who-whom," it referred to the political questions, "who (will destroy, will control, will utilize) whom?" and symbolized the preoccupation with conflict and power that characterized the Bolshevik operational code.[2]

The account presented here of the ensuing operational code research program inspired by Leites's seminal study is concerned with an assessment of the theoretical and empirical changes in operational code research as either progressive or degenerative within the context offered by the Lakatosian system for evaluating scientific research programs.[3] Below I explore the elements of the Lakatos model as they

---

1. Nathan Leites, *The Operational Code of the Politburo* (New York: McGraw-Hill, 1951); Nathan Leites, *A Study of Bolshevism* (New York: Free Press, 1953).

2. Leites, *A Study of Bolshevism*, pp. 27–29; see also Leites, *The Operational Code of the Politburo*, pp. 78–81.

3. Imre Lakatos, "Falsification and the Methodology of Scientific Research Programmes," in Imre Lakatos and Alan Musgrave, eds., *Criticism and the*

relate to the evolution of operational code analysis. I begin by identifying the hard core and positive and negative heuristics of the research program from the prototypical study by Leites.[4] Then I present an elaboration of auxiliary hypotheses from two elements in the positive heuristic by Alexander George, which influenced the first generation of operational code analysis as a research program.[5] I turn next to an account of the impact of the cognitive revolution in social psychology on later generations of operational code analysis. These efforts yield a "cautionary tale," one that does not fit the Lakatos account of the growth of scientific progress in all respects. I end with the conclusion that these discrepancies contain some implications for defining theoretical progress and assessing the general pattern of development in the social sciences.

Operational Code Analysis as a Scientific Research Program

The conceptual apparatus that informs this discussion is the operational code construct. As the "construct" label implies, it is a complex set of elements defined initially by Leites in his study of the Soviet elite as "the conceptions of political 'strategy'" in Bolshevik ideology.[6] He identified these conceptions as shared beliefs among Russian communist leaders, which he extracted initially from the texts of public statements by Lenin and Stalin and later related to broader cultural themes found in literary texts by Russian authors.[7] The operational code of the Bolsheviks revealed in this analysis was a mix of different kinds of conceptions—ontological statements, causal attributions, and prescriptive norms—labeled generically as "beliefs,"

Growth of Knowledge (Cambridge: Cambridge University Press, 1970), pp. 91–196.

4. Leites, *The Operational Code of the Politburo*; Leites, *A Study of Bolshevism*.

5. Alexander George, "The 'Operational Code': A Neglected Approach to the Study of Political Leaders and Decision Making," *International Studies Quarterly*, Vol. 13, No. 2 (June 1969), pp. 190–222.

6. Leites, *A Study of Bolshevism*, p. 15.

7. Leites, *The Operational Code of the Politburo*; Leites, *A Study of Bolshevism*.

with overtones of positive and negative "affect" (the feelings and emotions associated with them), and focused on the exercise of power.

This fixation on power became a central part of Leites's explanation for the hostility and intransigence attributed to Soviet leaders in dealing with the West, which contributed to the stalemate and competition associated with the Cold War between the superpowers.[8] As we shall see below, other scholars have employed the operational code construct to explain differences in the negotiating styles of leaders during international crises, the differences in policy preferences between leaders within the same state, and the variations in strategies, tactics, and moves reflected in the foreign policy decisions of different states during periods of protracted conflict.

The Leites analysis of the Bolshevik operational code incorporated the following assumptions, which formed the *hard core* (HC) of the prototypical operational code study:

HC-1. Individuals are the primary actors in politics.

HC-2. The personalities of individuals are coherent systems.

HC-3. Individuals make political decisions under the constraints of "bounded rationality" imposed by environmental uncertainty and idiosyncratic or shared biases in their personality systems.

HC-4. Individuals learn from making and monitoring political decisions: the content and complexity of both their behavior and the beliefs in their personality systems are reinforced or altered as a result of experiential or vicarious knowledge of the environment.

HC-5. Political outcomes are the product of the exercise of power by individuals in different political domains.

Elements of the *negative heuristic* (NH) that can be inferred from the hard core include the following five prescriptions:

NH-1. Do not assume that states are the primary actors.

---

8. Nathan Leites, *Kremlin Moods* (Santa Monica, Calif.: RAND, 1964).

NH-2. Do not assume that all individuals respond to stimuli the same way.

NH-3. Do not assume that individuals process information and make decisions according to principles of rationality that assume complete and perfect information.

NH-4. Do not assume that the future casts a longer shadow than the past or that individuals are "a-historical" in their decision making.

NH-5. Do not assume that environmental constraints, such as the distributions of capabilities, interests, or public opinion, are sufficient to produce decisions or generate outcomes.

Elements of the *positive heuristic* (PH) include the following five prescriptions inferred from the corresponding five assumptions of the hard core:

PH-1. Identify the individuals who are key decision makers: the leaders of states or other political groups.

PH-2. Identify the idiosyncratic or shared elements of a leader's personality that are relevant to the exercise of political power.

PH-3. Identify beliefs in a leader's personality at different points in historical narratives of decision-making episodes.

PH-4. Compare a leader's beliefs over time and across decision-making episodes with the exercise of power attributed to the leader's control.

PH-5. Trace the exercise of political power by leaders to the creation, reinforcement, or alteration of political outcomes.

The elements of the positive heuristic inspired efforts to formulate auxiliary hypotheses about how to conceptualize the relationships among beliefs, the exercise of power, and political outcomes. Alexander George attempted to formalize and simplify the operational code construct so that it could be applied as a general approach to the study of political decision making.[9] He focused on the third and fourth elements of the positive heuristic and recommended that the conceptions of political strategy be identified as a political belief system. George hypothesized that some elements (philosophical beliefs) would guide the diagnosis of the context for action while others (instrumental beliefs) would prescribe the most effective strategy and tactics for achieving political goals.

In doing so, George attempted to isolate the cognitive-strategic dimension of Leites's study of Bolshevik doctrine from its historical and characterological dimensions, which "constituted in some respects a distinct type in social history in the sense that any individual is unique though resembling others in important respects."[10] The analytical strategy for carrying out this task was to identify ten questions about political life suggested by Leites's analysis, and to hypothesize that the answers would capture a leader's "fundamental orientation towards the problem of leadership and action."[11]

Philosophical Beliefs

1. What is the "essential" nature of political life? Is the political universe essentially one of harmony or conflict? What is the fundamental character of one's political opponents?

2. What are the prospects for the eventual realization of one's fundamental values and aspirations? Can one be optimistic, or must one be pessimistic on this score; and in what respects the one and/or the other?

3. Is the political future predictable? In what sense and to what extent?

---

9. George, "The 'Operational Code'."

10. George, "The 'Operational Code'," p. 193.

11. George, "The 'Operational Code'," p. 200. These questions are taken from the discussion on pp. 201–216.

4. How much "control" or "mastery" can one have over historical development? What is one's role in "moving" and "shaping" history in the desired direction?

5. What is the role of "chance" in human affairs and in historical development?

Instrumental Beliefs

1. What is the best approach for selecting goals or objectives for political action?

2. How are the goals of action pursued most effectively?

3. How are the risks of political action calculated, controlled, and accepted?

4. What is the best "timing" of action to advance one's interests?

5. What is the utility and role of different means for advancing one's interests?

While not denying the relationship between political beliefs and either the social-psychological milieu in which they were acquired or the psychoanalytical needs that they satisfied, George argued that a leader's operational code beliefs "can be inferred or postulated by the investigator on the basis of the kinds of data, observational opportunities, and methods generally available to political scientists."[12] The implicit psychological explanation that linked a leader's beliefs and decisions was a theory of cognitive consistency, which had the following basic propositions:[13]

---

12. George, "The 'Operational Code'," p. 195.

13. These propositions are extracted from the discussion in George, "The 'Operational Code'," pp. 205, 216–220. See also Ole Holsti, "The 'Operational Code' as an Approach to the Analysis of Belief Systems," *Final Report to the National Science Foundation*, Grant No. SOC 75-15368 (Durham, N.C.: Duke University, 1977).

An individual's beliefs form an interdependent and hierarchical system whose elements are consistent with one another and resistant to change.

The more interdependent and hierarchically organized the belief system, the more the individual tends to "discount," as the basis for decisions, any new information that is inconsistent with already existing beliefs, particularly central beliefs.

The properties of interdependence and hierarchy make a change in one belief likely to cause a change in others, especially if the initial change is in a belief near or at the center of the hierarchy.

The more interdependent and hierarchically organized the belief system, the greater the consistency between the individual's beliefs and decisions.

The scope conditions for this theory limited its application to leaders rather than masses, because it presumed a different socialization experience for leaders than for their followers. Leaders were assumed to be more politically aware and more informed and interested in political life than the masses, whose lower level of political awareness led them to have vague or poorly structured beliefs and to exhibit inconsistencies between beliefs and preferred political behaviors.[14]

The first generation of operational code studies tended to focus primarily on the first and second propositions stated above. They conducted an exhaustive inventory of a leader's beliefs organized within the framework of George's classification of philosophical beliefs about the political universe and instrumental beliefs about the exercise of political power.[15] These studies were responses to George's call for

---

14. Philip Converse, "The Nature of Belief Systems in Mass Publics," in David Apter, ed., *Ideology and Discontent* (New York: Free Press, 1964), pp. 206–261.

15. See, e.g., Ole Holsti, "The Operational Code Approach to the Study of Political Leaders: John Foster Dulles; Philosophical and Instrumental Belief," *Canadian Journal of Political Science*, Vol. 3, No. 1 (March 1970), pp. 123–157; Stephen Walker, "The Interface Between Beliefs and Behavior: Henry Kissinger's Operational Code and the Vietnam War," *Journal of Conflict*

the content analysis of a decision maker's statements and writings to determine what beliefs were thus revealed, and to assess their consistency with one another and with the leader's diagnosis of incoming information and subsequent decisions.

Ole Holsti reviewed these studies and constructed a typology of belief systems designed to categorize each of the individual leaders within one of the types.[16] The Holsti typology was based on a "master belief" axiom suggested by George to link operational code elements as a construct within the context of cognitive consistency theory.[17] George had argued that a leader's beliefs about the nature of the political universe, and particularly the image of the opponent, constrained the individual's remaining operational code beliefs.[18] Based on the master belief axiom, Holsti constructed a typology of six belief systems. The types were bounded by a 2 x 3 matrix formed by the philosophical beliefs about the permanent or temporary nature of conflict in the political universe and whether the source of conflict was human nature, society, or the international system.[19] In turn, these master philosophical beliefs about the nature of political life constrained the remaining philosophical and instrumental beliefs.

For example, a leader who believes that political conflict is a permanent feature of the political universe is likely to be relatively pessimistic about the prospects for achieving fundamental political values, view the political future as less predictable, believe that control over historical development is relatively low, and assign a higher role to chance in political affairs. On the other hand, a leader who views conflict as temporary is likely to be more optimistic about realizing

---

Resolution, Vol. 2, No. 1 (March 1977), pp. 129–168. An inventory of early studies appears in Stephen Walker, "The Evolution of Operational Code Analysis," *Political Psychology*, Vol. 11, No. 2 (June 1990), pp. 403–418.

16. Holsti, "The 'Operational Code' as an Approach to the Analysis of Belief Systems."

17. George, "The 'Operational Code'."

18. George, "The 'Operational Code'," pp. 202–203.

19. Kenneth Waltz, *Man, the State, and War* (New York: Columbia University Press, 1959).

goals and more confident in the predictability of the future, believe in greater control over historical development, and assign less importance to chance.

According to the logic of cognitive consistency theory, these differences in the diagnosis of the political universe should lead to different prescriptions for political action. The first leader's pessimism is likely to be accompanied by instrumental beliefs that strategy should be limited in its goals, tactics should be flexible, the calculation and control of risks should be cautious and conservative, and force should be a last resort as a means to achieve political ends. The second leader's optimism is more likely to generate beliefs in grand strategic goals, relatively inflexible tactics, long-shot calculations in the assessment of risks, and the utility of force as a tool of statecraft.

Holsti theorized that these internally coherent belief systems remained relatively stable over time and across issue domains for the leaders who hold them. In articulating and testing their respective formalizations of the operational code construct, however, both George and Holsti acknowledged that the Bolshevik belief system and the Holsti typology did not exhaust the rich variety and complexity of political leaders. They might have master beliefs that ranged from zero-sum, through mixed, to non-zero-sum views of the political universe. Nor do all leaders necessarily operate with a single, well-defined set of operational code beliefs; moreover, leaders may change their beliefs over time.[20] Their recipe for operational code analysis placed it within what Philip Tetlock calls the cognitivist research program for explaining world politics.[21]

---

20. George, "The 'Operational Code'"; Holsti, "The 'Operational Code' as an Approach to the Analysis of Belief Systems."

21. Philip E. Tetlock, "Social Psychology and World Politics," in Daniel Gilbert, Susan Fiske, and Gardner Lindzey, eds., *Handbook of Social Psychology* (New York: McGraw-Hill, 1998), pp. 869–912.

The General Cognitivist Research Program

The cognitivist research program assumes Simon's classic principle of bounded rationality: "Policy makers may act rationally, but only within the context of their simplified subjective representations of reality."[22] Tetlock argues that this assumption is based on the following two premises: "1. World politics is not only complex but also deeply ambiguous. Whenever people draw lessons from history, they rely—implicitly or explicitly—on speculative reconstructions of what would have happened in possible worlds of their own mental creation; 2. People—limited-capacity information processors that we are—frequently resort to simplifying strategies to deal with this otherwise overwhelming complexity and uncertainty."[23]

Noting that "cognitivists focus on these simplified mental representations of reality that decision makers use to interpret events and choose among courses of action," Tetlock reviewed and categorized the individual research programs of various scholars under these premises as components of a general cognitivist program.[24] At the same time, he was careful to recognize the considerable disagreement among cognitivists over how to represent these simplified images.

During the 1980s, important research on belief systems within the general cognitivist research program tended to follow two empirical strategies: a focus on belief systems as schemata, and an attempt to identify various forms of cognitive biases and heuristics. Schemata may be about other individuals (person schema), the self (self schema), groups (role schema), or sequences of events (scripts).[25] Depending upon their type, therefore, schemata are hypotheses about the attributes of types of objects and the relationships among their

---

22. Herbert Simon, *Models of Man* (New York: Wiley, 1957); Tetlock, "Social Psychology and World Politics," p. 876.

23. Tetlock, "Social Psychology and World Politics," p. 876.

24. Ibid.

25. Susan Fiske and Shelley Taylor, *Social Cognition*, 2nd ed. (New York: McGraw-Hill, 1991).

attributes. Much of the research by Richard Herrmann, Martha Cottam, Jerel Rosati, and Deborah Larson[26] was based on the hypothesis noted earlier by George and others that the image of the "other" was a master belief, that is, a central schema that influenced the arousal of other schemata as scripts to guide policy decisions.[27]

These examples reflect the spread of the "cognitive revolution" from social psychology to the study of foreign policy decisions.[28] The focus upon cognition and information processing accompanied a shift away from a focus on affect (feelings) as a significant mental phenomenon. The spread of the revolution was due to conceptual and methodological reasons that also accounted for its initial success in social psychology. In contrast to affect, schemata and the processes that generate them lend themselves to relatively precise observation and modeling. The individuals who experience them are more aware of their thoughts than of their feelings. Measurement difficulties and the

---

26. Richard Herrmann, *Perceptions and Behavior in Soviet Foreign Policy* (Pittsburgh, Pa.: University of Pittsburgh Press, 1985); Martha Cottam, *Foreign Policy Decision Making: The Influence of Cognition* (Boulder, Colo.: Westview Press, 1986); Jerel Rosati, *The Carter Administration's Quest for Global Community* (Columbia, S.C.: The University of South Carolina Press (1987); and Deborah Larson, *Origins of Containment* (Princeton, N.J.: Princeton University Press, 1985).

27. George, "The 'Operational Code'"; Alexander George, "The Causal Nexus Between Cognitive Beliefs and Decision-making Behavior: The 'Operational Code'," in Lawrence Falkowski, ed., *Psychological Models in International Politics* (Boulder, Colo.: Westview Press, 1979), pp. 95–124; Ole Holsti, "Cognitive Dynamics and Images of the Enemy," in David Finlay, Ole Holsti, and Richard Fagen, eds., *Enemies in Politics* (Chicago: Rand-McNally, 1967), pp. 25–96; Richard Cottam, *Foreign Policy Motivation: A General Theory and a Case Study* (Pittsburgh, Pa.: University of Pittsburgh Press, 1977).

28. Richard Herrmann, "The Empirical Challenge of the Cognitive Revolution: A Strategy for Drawing Inferences About Perceptions," *International Studies Quarterly*, Vol. 32, No. 2 (June 1988), pp. 175–204.

criterion of parsimony in constructing models led researchers away from affect and toward cognition in their theoretical thinking as well.[29]

Accompanying the introduction of schema as a key analytical tool in the cognitive revolution was the articulation of the concept of heuristics to describe how individuals actually process information. Whereas schemata are hypotheses about the environment, heuristics are the rules by which individuals test the hypotheses in a schema. By extension, heuristics may also be viewed as "content-free" schemata: rules functioning to organize incoming information even in the absence of person, self, role, or event schemata. Cognitive and social psychologists have expended considerable effort to identify different heuristics and trace their implications for making decisions. The main implication for decision-making theory is a better understanding of how misperceptions are formed, which become the basis for making flawed decisions, that is, decisions based upon faulty information processing.[30] The understanding of cognitive processes that emerged was a more complex one than simply the reduction of dissonance and a bias toward consistency. Other cognitive flaws and biases operate as well.

Janice Stein addressed the relationship between cognitive biases and affect through the concept of *motivated bias*.[31] Following Ned Lebow, she argued that motivated biases manifest themselves in forms virtually indistinguishable from cognitive biases.[32] However, the occasion for the use of the heuristic is the occurrence of fears and needs within the individual rather than the existence of an uncertain and complex environment. The introduction of motivated biases enriches the analyst's understanding of how cognitive heuristics are employed

---

29. Philip Tetlock and Ariel Levi, "Attribution Bias: On the Inconclusiveness of the Motivation-Cognition Debate," *Journal of Experimental Social Psychology*, Vol. 18, No. 1 (January 1982), pp. 68–88.

30. Fiske and Taylor, *Social Cognition*.

31. Janice Gross Stein, "Building Politics in Psychology," *Political Psychology*, Vol. 9, No. 2 (June 1988), pp. 245–272.

32. Richard Ned Lebow, *Between Peace and War* (Baltimore, Md.: Johns Hopkins University Press, 1981), cited by Stein, "Building Politics in Psychology," p. 257.

and follows the advice of Jervis who had earlier introduced the cognitive bias literature into the study of world politics.[33] As Stein notes, "Analysis of cognitive biases alone ... cannot establish the likely *direction* of misperception or its *probable occurrence*; the direction of *motivated* errors is far easier to specify."[34] So when a nation faces a potential opponent who is far more powerful, the fear that is generated from this strategic situation makes it more probable that its leaders will overestimate rather than underestimate the threat.

The Evolution of the Operational Code Research Program

In 1979, Alexander George attempted to re-position the operational code construct within the cognitive revolution. He argued that operational code beliefs are schemata, which "refer to generalized principles about social and political life and not, as attitudes presumably do, to predispositions to respond to rather specific or delineated objects.... Operational code beliefs have centrality. Unlike attitudes, they are concerned with fundamental, unchanging issues of politics and political action."[35]

George's subsequent work on decision making in foreign policy tended to follow the strategies associated with the cognitive revolution of focusing on schemata and heuristics and his own conclusions about their most fruitful applications.[36] "One can ... fruitfully define the task of policy science (the task of designing and managing policy-making systems) as that of avoiding, correcting, and/or compensating for

---

33. Robert Jervis, "Perception and Misperception: An Updating of the Analysis," presented at the Annual Meeting of the International Society of Political Psychology, Washington, D.C., 1982; Robert Jervis, *Perception and Misperception in International Politics* (Princeton, N.J.: Princeton Press, 1976).

34. Stein, "Building Politics in Psychology," p. 259 (emphasis added).

35. George, "The Causal Nexus Between Cognitive Beliefs and Decision-making Behavior," pp. 97, 99.

36. For the general implications of a conceptual shift from belief systems to schemata, see Deborah Larson, "The Role of Belief Systems and Schemas in Foreign Policy Decision-making," *Political Psychology*, Vol. 15, No. 1 (March 1994), pp. 17–34.

flaws, errors, and biases of the kind that the policy maker's naïve epistemology introduces into the information processing associated with decision making."[37] He attempted to bridge the cognitive revolution and personality theory by arguing that personality traits have an *indirect* influence on cognitive processes by structuring the bureaucratic channels through which a leader receives and manages information and advice. That is, leaders with differences in cognitive style, orientation toward conflict, and sense of political efficacy construct different advisory systems that, in turn, influence the leader's processing of information and advice.[38]

The *direct* influence of personality on cognition lies in its promise of offering an explanation for similarities in operational code beliefs between leaders who do not share common role-socialization experiences.[39] In his review of the first generation of operational code studies, Holsti hypothesized that two leaders, such as John Foster Dulles and Josef Stalin, may still have the same type of operational code beliefs, even though socialized into roles in quite different

---

37. George, "The Causal Nexus Between Cognitive Beliefs and Decision-making Behavior," p. 99.

38. Alexander George, *Presidential Decisionmaking in Foreign Policy: The Effective Use of Information and Advice* (Boulder, Colo.: Westview Press, 1980); see also Yuen Foong Khong, *Analogies at War* (Princeton, N.J.: Princeton University Press, 1992; Alexander George, "Assessing Presidential Character," in Alexander George and Juliette George, eds., *Presidential Personality and Performance* (Boulder, Colo.: Westview, 1988), pp. 145–198; Alexander George and Eric Stern, "Presidential Management and Styles," in George and George, *Presidential Personality and Performance*, pp. 199–280.

39. Conversely, successful socialization may presuppose a personality disposed toward the acceptance of the norms and values associated with the role. See Ole Holsti, "Foreign Policy Viewed Cognitively," in Robert Axelrod, ed., *The Structure of Decision* (Princeton, N.J.: Princeton, 1976), pp. 18–54. In Leites's initial operational code study, he argued that political beliefs were part of a Bolshevik identity formed by successful socialization into the role of a Politburo member. Leites, *A Study of Bolshevism*; George, "The 'Operational Code'."

political systems with antithetical political ideologies.[40] Holsti did not explain this phenomenon, so much as allow for it by contrasting the very general contents of operational code beliefs with the more specific contents of ideological beliefs.[41] A subsequent analysis of the motivational foundations of the beliefs in Holsti's operational code typology generated an explanation in the form of the following personality theory: [42]

> As a result of early childhood socialization experiences, an individual acquires the dominant motives in his personality prior to adopting a political belief system.

> An individual tends to adopt a political belief system that is compatible with his/her constellation of needs for power, affiliation, and achievement.

> Although an individual's belief system may develop a consistency that is independent from random fluctuations in immediate personal needs,... the activation of these beliefs by environmental stimuli may arouse personal needs embedded in the belief system as the individual uses the various elements of his belief system to interpret a decision-making situation.

> Once aroused, these motives may contribute to the cognitive rigidity of an individual's beliefs and account for the intensity of cognitive dissonance and behavioral intransigence in the face of new information or other stimuli from the environment.

---

40. Holsti, "The 'Operational Code' as an Approach to the Analysis of Belief Systems."

41. See also Alexander George, "Ideology and International Relations: A Conceptual Analysis," presented at the "Ideology and Its Influence on International Politics" Conference at the Leonard Davis Institute of International Relations, The Hebrew University, Jerusalem, Israel 1985.

42. Stephen Walker, "The Motivational Foundations of Political Belief Systems: A Re-analysis of the Operational Code Construct," *International Studies Quarterly*, Vol. 27, No. 2 (June 1983), pp. 179–201. The propositions of this theory are presented here in the same form that they appeared there (p. 189).

In this theory, both operational code beliefs and motivations exist prior to political action. The motivations account for the content of beliefs and also their resistance to change. The evidence for these theoretical amendments was a content analysis of the motivational images in Holsti's typology of operational code belief systems. The results identified overlapping beliefs and underlying motivational foundations that justified the reduction of Holsti's belief systems from six to four: one characterized by power imagery, one with affiliation imagery, and two that shared achievement imagery but differed in the manifestation of power-versus-affiliation imagery.[43]

Self-images formed with the aid of these schemata foreshadow the impending decision, as the decision maker judges what is the appropriate choice. The process produces congruence (or "balance") between the self and the situation: it results in a choice that is consistent with a leader's self-image of how to respond to the situation. This emphasis upon self-schema and self-scripts containing motivational imagery rather than images of others accounted for anomalies in previous applications of purely cognitive theory to foreign policy choices.[44] The self's preferred choice may or may not vary under different circumstances, depending upon the individual's self-schema and self-script. The dimensions of the self are the crucial variables in the equation, although circumstances are not necessarily

---

43. Walker, "The Motivational Foundations of Political Belief Systems"; Stephen Walker and Lawrence Falkowski, "The Operational Codes of U.S. Presidents and Secretaries of State," *Political Psychology*, Vol. 5, No. 2 (June 1984), pp. 237–266; Stephen Walker, "The Evolution of Operational Code Analysis," *Political Psychology*, Vol. 11, No. 2 (June 1990), pp. 403–418; Stephen Walker, "Psychodynamic Processes and Framing Effects in Foreign Policy Decision-Making: Woodrow Wilson's Operational Code," *Political Psychology*, Vol. 16, No. 4, (December 1995), pp. 697–717.

44. Cottam, *Foreign Policy Decision Making*; Harvey Starr, *Henry Kissinger: Perceptions of International Politics* (Lexington, Ky.: University Press of Kentucky, 1984).

spurious in all cases of choice and interact with images of self and other to influence choice.[45]

An example of this dynamic is President Woodrow Wilson's decision making during the ratification debate with the U.S. Senate over the Treaty of Versailles. The conventional accounts of the conflict between the president and the isolationists agree that Wilson's actions contributed heavily to an outcome that was contrary to his avowed goal of ratification. An experienced president and former congressional scholar taking self-defeating actions presents a puzzle that suggests the influence of motivational and cognitive dispositions. A content analysis of Wilson's public statements indicated that Wilson's rhetoric during the Versailles debate was significantly higher in power and achievement imagery than during other decision-making episodes leading up to military intervention in Mexico and declaring war against Germany.[46]

The differences in the distributions of power, affiliation, and achievement are consistent with schemata and scripts that prescribe a rigid, grandiose strategy of conflict toward the U.S. Senate in the Versailles case and a more flexible, restrained strategy of conflict toward opponents in the Mexico and Germany episodes. The president's behavior in the latter two episodes is explicable as a rational response to circumstances without the necessity to refer to the leader's beliefs. However, Wilson's intransigence over the ratification of the Versailles Treaty requires the invocation of individual differences to account for his behavior. The implication is that both his actions and

---

45. Stephen Walker, Mark Schafer, and Michael Young, "Systematic Procedures for Operational Code Analysis," *International Studies Quarterly*, Vol. 42, No. 1 (March 1998), pp. 175–190; Stephen Walker, Mark Schafer, and Michael Young, "Presidential Operational Codes and the Management of Foreign Policy Conflicts in the Post–Cold War World," *Journal of Conflict Resolution*, Vol. 43, No. 5 (October 1999), pp. 610–625.

46. Walker, "Psychodynamic Processes and Framing Effects in Foreign Policy Decision-making," pp. 697–717.

his operational code were indispensable in order to explain the U.S. failure to ratify the Versailles Treaty.[47]

This evidence of alternative "states of mind" for the same decision maker in different contexts prompted the formulation of an amendment to cognitive consistency theory in the form of a "framing effect," linking beliefs, motivations, and actions.[48] A leader may define the situation and identify responses that are more consistent with one ideal type of belief system and then shift toward another ideal type as the situation evolves or as the leader shifts attention from one situation to another. The effect of this theoretical amendment is to make the typology of belief systems dynamic. Depending on the motivations and accompanying beliefs aroused by stimuli, the Holsti typology now represents alternative states of mind for the *same* decision maker rather than *different* decision makers. This re-conceptualization also accounts for the presence of compartmentalized and inconsistent beliefs within the same leader, which become schemata employed under different circumstances and varying degrees of motivational arousal.[49]

Recasting the Holsti typology as a dynamic model of shifting "states of mind" led to the development of quantitative indices to map the changing coordinates of a leader's beliefs to the elements in the operational code construct.[50] The research focus moved to the particular beliefs aroused by the immediate situation or the issue domain in which a state is taking action. Subsequent studies of operational code beliefs in the 1990s identified the particular configuration of cognitive schemata and attribution patterns

---

47. Walker, ibid. See also Fred Greenstein, *Personality and Politics*. Second Edition. (Princeton, N.J., Princeton University Press, 1987).

48. Walker, "Psychodynamic Processes and Framing Effects in Foreign Policy Decision-making," p. 703.

49. Walker, "Psychodynamic Processes and Framing Effects in Foreign Policy Decision-making."

50. Stephen Walker, Mark Schafer, and Michael Young, "Systematic Procedures for Operational Code Analysis"; Stephen Walker, Mark Schafer, and Michael Young, "Presidential Operational Codes and the Management of Foreign Policy Conflicts in the Post–Cold War World."

embedded in the "decision regimes" of U.S. presidential administrations.[51] These investigations looked at presidents' beliefs expressed in two different types of contexts: public sources such as prepared speeches or spontaneous press conferences and interviews from the Carter, Bush, and Clinton administrations; and private sources such as classified documents released subsequently into the public domain for the Kennedy and Johnson administrations.[52]

A formal model of strategic interaction informed by operational code analysis also began to emerge in the early 1990s with the aid of developments in sequential game theory.[53] In this model, the beliefs within the operational code of an individual leader or the shared beliefs of a state's collective decision regime provide a theory of payoffs for the different kinds of strategic interaction games that characterize international relations.[54] Accompanying this shift were attempts to broaden and differentiate the phenomena explained by the operational code research program. Explicit distinctions among

---

51. Charles Kegley, "Decision Regimes and the Comparative Study of Foreign Policy," in Charles Hermann, Charles Kegley, Jr., and James Rosenau, eds., *New Directions in the Study of Foreign Policy* (Boston: Allen and Unwin, 1987), pp. 247–268. "[D]ecision regimes, like operational codes, are composed of cognitive beliefs emerging from a relentlessly political process. Two major types of decision regimes may be identified, although ... they tend to be connected causally. Decision regimes may emerge when there is leadership consensus regarding the substance of policy as well as the process by which it is made. The former are termed *substantive* decision regimes, the latter *procedural* decision regimes." Ibid., pp. 254–255, emphasis in original.

52. The results were published in Mark Schafer, ed., "Symposium on at-a-Distance Psychological Assessment," *Political Psychology*, Vol. 21, No. 3 (September 2000), pp. 511–602.

53. Steven Brams, *Theory of Moves* (Cambridge, UK: Cambridge University Press, 1994)

54. Duncan Snidal, "The Game Theory of International Relations," *World Politics*, Vol. 38, No. 1 (October 1985), pp. 25–87; Stephen Walker, "Game Theory and Foreign Policy Decisions," presented at the Annual Meeting of the American Political Science Association, Washington, D.C. (September, 1991); Stephen Walker, "Interstate and Interpersonal Models of the Persian Gulf Conflict," presented at the Annual Meeting of the International Studies Association, Acapulco, Mexico, 1993.

different levels of decision—behavior, moves, tactics, and strategies—were linked to different elements of the operational code construct. There were also initiatives to apply a general game theory model of strategic interaction informed by operational code beliefs to a broader range of situations than the management of international crises. These efforts have generated predictions of steering, learning, and leadership effects regarding the dynamic relationships between beliefs and different levels of decision, some of which have been corroborated.[55]

Assessing Progress in Operational Code Research

The preceding narrative of theoretical developments in operational code research provides the information to assess whether its trajectory exhibits progress or degeneration as a research program. As Colin Elman and Miriam Fendius Elman note, this distinction hinges on whether theoretical amendments generate *novel facts* without violating the spirit of a research program's positive heuristic.[56] For assessing intra-program progress or degeneration within the operational code research program, two basic assumptions of cognitive consistency theory provide a reference point: (1) beliefs are consistent with one another, and (2) beliefs are consistent with behavior. The subsequent amendments to cognitive consistency theory by George and the re-introduction of motivational personality theory by Walker involved both the modification of these two existing propositions and the addition of others.[57]

---

55. Stephen Walker, "Role Identities and Operational Code Analysis," in Margaret Hermann, ed., *Advances in Political Psychology* (New York and Amsterdam: Elsevier Science, forthcoming); Stephen Walker, Mark Schafer, and Gregory Marfleet, "The British Strategy of Appeasement: Why Did Britain Persist in the Face of Negative Feedback?" in Charles Hermann and Robert Billings, eds., *Responding to Negative Feedback in Foreign Policy Decision Making* (manuscript).

56. Elman and Elman, Chapter 2 in this volume.

57. George, "The Causal Nexus Between Cognitive Beliefs and Decision-making Behavior"; and Walker, "The Motivational Foundations of Political Belief Systems."

Under the influence of the cognitive revolution, George retained a loose version of both assumptions while emphasizing that beliefs are subject to change both in their contents and in their application as decision-making guides in the face of new information from the environment.[58] That is, beliefs are schemata, which are "cold" cognitions that represent working hypotheses about reality, rather than attitudes, which are "hot" cognitions that express needs embedded in the character of the believer. Individuals are scientific problem solvers rather than passionate consistency seekers. These kinds of amendments were local manifestations of the broad impact of the cognitive revolution on the cognitivist research program in world politics.

Did George's theoretical amendments predict novel facts subsequently corroborated empirically by himself or others? Holsti's typology of operational code belief systems was a theoretical attempt to specify schemata that were both very general and consistent with one another.[59] However, subsequent operational code research did not support the hierarchical interdependence between the schemata that represented philosophical and instrumental beliefs, nor was there much subsequent empirical support for the prediction that the first philosophical belief — about the "essential" nature of political life — was important.[60]

These initial results were consistent with a degenerating research program in which novel facts were not corroborated by empirical research based on cognitive consistency theory (T_1). However, the findings did not threaten the hard core that linked beliefs to other features in the leader's personality in the prototypical Leites analysis of the Bolshevik operational code. The re-introduction of a personality theory (T_2) emphasizing the motivational foundations of beliefs

---

58. George, "The Causal Nexus Between Cognitive Beliefs and Decision-making Behavior."

59. Holsti, "The 'Operational Code' as an Approach to the Analysis of Belief Systems."

60. Douglas Stuart, "The Relative Potency of Leader Beliefs as a Determinant of Foreign Policy: John F. Kennedy's Operational Code," University of Southern California Ph.D. dissertation (January 1979); Starr, *Henry Kissinger.*

represented a counter-balancing progressive move because it predicted novel facts, some of which were subsequently corroborated with an empirical analysis of the relationships among a leader's motivations, beliefs, and interpersonal style. Although they did not have belief systems that corresponded to internally consistent ideal types, the beliefs of U.S. presidents and secretaries of state were related to their motivational profiles and interpersonal style.[61]

The findings were also compatible with the valenced attribution theory of "hot" cognition (T_3) guiding current operational code analysis, in which schemata attributed to self and other are tagged with valences of positive and negative affect rather than linked consistently to one another. Although extra-cognitive, personality characteristics remain a focus of study within the operational code research program,[62] there is a clear shift toward identifying the attributions of leaders and simply coding them with affective tags in constructing indices of the leader's philosophical and instrumental beliefs.[63] The scores for key indices are then used to map the leader's image of self and other onto the Holsti typology and classify the leader's operational code. Because the assumption of internal consistency between philosophical and instrumental beliefs no longer organizes these attributions, the type of philosophical beliefs attributed

---

61. Walker and Falkowski, "The Operational Codes of U.S. Presidents and Secretaries of State."

62. See, e.g., Walker, "Psychodynamic Processes and Framing Effects in Foreign Policy Decision-making"; Mark Schafer and Scott Crichlow, "Bill Clinton's Operational Code: Assessing Material Bias," *Political Psychology*, Vol. 21, No. 3 (September 2000), pp. 559–572.

63. David Winter, Margaret Hermann, Walter Weintraub, and Stephen Walker, "The Personalities of Bush and Gorbachev Measured at a Distance," *Political Psychology*, Vol. 12, No. 2 (June 1991), pp. 457–465; Scott Crichlow, "Idealism or Pragmatism? An Operational Code Analysis of Yitzhak Rabin and Shimon Peres," *Political Psychology*, Vol. 19, No. 4 (December 1998), pp. 683–706; Walker, Schafer, and Young, "Systematic Procedures for Operational Code Analysis," pp. 175–190; Walker, Schafer, and Young, "Presidential Operational Codes and the Management of Foreign Policy Conflicts in the Post–Cold War World."

to others may be different from the type of instrumental beliefs attributed to self. [64]

In all three operational code theories (T_1, T_2, T_3), beliefs define the situation and prescribe a leader's response, but the causal mechanisms of cognitive consistency, motivated bias, and valenced attribution are different for each theory. The evolutionary pattern across these causal mechanisms toward re-incorporating affect with the analysis of beliefs via valenced attributions is consistent with a return to the study of "hot" cognition in social and political psychology. [65] The succession of theoretical amendments in the operational code research program has also followed roughly the pattern anticipated by Lakatos in his model of scientific research programs:

Let us take a series of theories T_1, T_2, T_3,... where each subsequent theory results from adding auxiliary clauses to (or from semantical reinterpretations of) the previous theory in order to accommodate some anomaly, each theory having at least as much content as the unrefuted content of its predecessor.... Progress is measured by the degree to which a problem-shift is progressive, [i.e.] by the degree to which the series of theories leads us to the discovery of novel facts. We regard a theory in the series 'falsified' when it is superseded by a theory with higher corroborated content. [66]

Although the theoretical amendments in operational code analysis (T_1, T_2, T_3) have met the requirements of scientific progress in the Lakatos model by generating "novel facts," there is another model of scientific progress that describes more accurately and completely the

---

64. Walker, "Role Identities and Operational Code Analysis"; Walker, Schafer, and Marfleet, "The British Strategy of Appeasement."

65. Fiske and Taylor, *Social Cognition*; Shanto Ayengar and William McGuire, eds., *Explorations in Political Psychology* (Durham, N.C.: Duke University Press, 1993); George Marcus, "Emotions and Politics: Hot Cognition and the Rediscovery of Passion," *Social Science Information*, Vol. 30, No. 2 (June 1991); Tetlock, "Social Psychology and World Politics."

66. Lakatos, "Falsification and the Methodology of Scientific Research Programmes," p. 118. See also Terence Ball, "Is There Progress in Political Science?" in Terence Ball, ed., *Idioms of Inquiry* (Albany: SUNY Press), p. 24.

evolution of operational code analysis as a scientific research program. Larry Laudan offers a more complex image of scientific progress than Imre Lakatos. In Laudan's model, the goal of science is to solve problems rather than to seek novel facts, because solutions in science are approximate and impermanent.[67] According to Laudan, "anything about the natural world which strikes us as odd, or otherwise in need of explanation constitutes an empirical problem."[68] Progress occurs when theories solve empirical problems and minimize internal conceptual problems and anomalies:

If problems are the focal point of scientific thought, theories are its end result.... If problems constitute the questions of sciences, it is theories which constitute the answers. The function of a theory is to resolve ambiguity, to reduce irregularity to uniformity, to show that what happens is somehow intelligible and predictable; it is this complex of functions to which I refer when I speak of theories as solutions to problems.[69]

Laudan counts an empirical problem as solved when a theory solves a research puzzle, even if there are not yet any well-corroborated or confirmed results that support the answer. The standard here is conceptual fruitfulness rather than excess empirical content associated with the corroboration of novel facts. A conceptual problem deals with questions about theories and not about the substantive entities that the theories address. Internal conceptual problems include a vague or inconsistent theory, while external conceptual problems refer to a conflict between two theories where the proponents of one theory believe the other theory to be well-founded.[70]

---

67. Larry Laudan, *Progress and Its Problems: Toward a Theory of Scientific Growth* (Berkeley: University of California Press, 1977).

68. Laudan, *Progress and Its Problems*, p. 15. Earlier (p. 13), he stresses, "I do not believe that 'scientific' problems are fundamentally different from other kinds of problems (though they often are different in degree). Indeed,... the view that I am espousing can be applied, with only a few qualifications, to *all* intellectual disciplines."

69. Ibid., p. 13.

70. Ibid., pp. 11–17.

In Laudan's view, there are three kinds of problems in science: unsolved (no theory solves them), solved (a theory solves them), and anomalies (one theory solves them while another does not). Progress occurs when the first and the third problems are transformed into the second by solving either an empirical or a conceptual problem. Scientists choose between theories by evaluating the number and importance of empirical problems solved minus the number of anomalies and conceptual problems the theory generates.[71]

Another important consideration is the rate of progress exhibited by a theory and its continued acceptability over time. When confronted with two theories, a generally accepted one and a rapidly progressing one, a scientist may invest intellectual efforts in both of them. Diversifying across theories and trying to solve the conceptual problems between them rather than choosing one over the other differentiates Laudan's more complex, non-linear model of scientific progress from Lakatos's sequential model of theoretical progress, in which one theory replaces another in a linear, evolutionary fashion.[72]

Progress in the form of transforming unsolved problems and anomalies into solved problems means that the Lakatosian standard of excess empirical content (predictions and corroboration) is only one criterion for indicating progress. Excess empirical content is progress in the form of "problem inflation," or an increase in the number of solved empirical problems. However, the solution of an anomaly is also counted by Laudan as progress, emphasizing the reduction in a conceptual problem without requiring corroboration. This reduction may be incremental in the form of movement along a continuum from inconsistency or implausibility between theories toward compatibility, reinforcement, or ultimately the "entailment" (derivation) of one theory from another one.[73]

The Laudan account of the growth and development of scientific knowledge seems to capture more precisely the trajectory of the

---

71. Ibid., pp. 17–31.

72. Ibid., pp. 108–114.

73. Laudan, *Progress and Its Problems*, pp. 48–54.

operational code research program. The multiple criteria for defining and detecting progress, i.e., the inflation of solved empirical and conceptual problems and the deflation of conceptual problems, capture important activities within the operational code research program. The solution of conceptual problems is largely ignored in a Lakatosian account of the program's trajectory. Examples of conceptual problem inflation (archetype construction) and deflation (archetype modification) include the construction of the original typology of operational codes by Holsti and its later reduction from six to four types of belief systems by Walker. More generally, there is less flexibility in the Lakatos account for simultaneously investing in several theories, dividing one's intellectual labor across theories, and giving equal weight to the tasks of empirical and conceptual problem-solving. However, Laudan would not be surprised to find cognitive and motivational theories coexisting within the operational code research program and eventually merging into a valenced attribution theory.

These examples of solving conceptual problems within the operational code research program illustrate general forms of both "problem inflation" and "problem deflation" identified by Laudan as important measures of scientific progress. Inflation includes archetype construction and weighting the significance of problems by generality within a theory that is very complex or somewhat vague, in order to clarify its relevance to unsolved problems. Problem deflation (the resolution of anomalies between theories that their respective proponents believe are well founded) includes the dissolution of contradictions due to the clarification of vague or inconsistent elements of a theory, and the deflation of a theory's domain (scope) or the modification of its archetypes.[74]

The coexistence of more than one general theory is another example of a more general feature ignored in the Lakatos account of scientific research programs. According to Lakatos, a general theory and its rival may rest on one or more touchstone theories whose contents are taken as givens; for example, the optical theory of telescopic lenses is taken

---

74. Laudan, *Progress and Its Problems*, pp. 48–69.

as a given in the testing of theories in astronomy.[75] However, the Laudan account more explicitly recognizes that "theory complexes" articulate a research program: sets of theories complement one another in the solution of common empirical problems. Cognitive theory, personality theory, and game theory all combine in the conduct of operational code analysis to produce solved problems. Internal progress is possible by reducing the conceptual problems associated with any of them, because it is logically unclear where to locate praise or blame for their collective successes and failures in solving empirical problems. Much of the effort in the operational code research program has addressed various relationships among these three kinds of theories.

The process of inquiry in the social sciences may also take on characteristics that are more consistent with Laudan's account of progress because of the tendency of scholars to rely on several middle-range theories in the absence of a general theory. In the study of world politics, the use of theory complexes may be more complicated than in the hard sciences, because theories are under-specified. That is, the form of the relationships between variables within each theory has not been worked out. The reasons for this shortfall may be conceptual or empirical: the theorist may not grasp them, or may not know how to measure them precisely enough for modeling purposes.

Social scientists have sometimes employed typologies in an attempt to deal with this problem. Even when the defining dimensions are distinct, a typology does not exhaust all possible combinations of values for each dimension unless they are reduced to a small number of ordinal or nominal categories. This kind of indeterminacy creates two kinds of problems. One is under-specification: the level of measurement precludes a formal mathematical model specifying all possible relationships. The other is the "null set" or "empty cell" problem created by the large number of combinations among the defining attributes of a typology that are logically possible but

---

75. Lakatos, "Falsification and the Methodology of Scientific Research Programs"; Ball, "Is There Progress in Political Science?"

theoretically uninteresting, such as many of the 78 two-person 2 x 2 games with ordinal utility values specified by game theorists.[76]

Social scientists have tended to respond by focusing on intuitively important configurations of the defining attributes, such as the Prisoner's Dilemma game that is prominent in the study of world politics. An extension and generalization of this coping strategy is to focus on such constructs as "social mechanisms," which fall short of covering laws but do explain the relationship between the restricted range of two or more variables by accounting for their connection.[77] This pattern of theoretical thinking characterizes the operational code research program and much of the social psychology on which it rests. Belief systems, schemata, cognitive heuristics, motivated biases, and valenced attributions are all mechanisms of bounded rationality that explain the connection between stimulus and response.

The picture of the theory complex that emerges from this perspective is the interaction of a combination of mechanisms: variable clusters with different combinations of values located at different levels of analysis that interact to explain actions and outcomes.[78] However, the results do not necessarily yield the covering laws expected as markers in standard accounts of scientific progress.[79] Given this tension, the Laudan account is more congenial and has less restrictive expectations than the Lakatos account with respect to this kind of theoretical thinking and empirical inquiry in the social sciences.

---

76. Anatol Rapoport and Melvin Guyer, "A Taxonomy of 2 x 2 Games," *General Systems: Yearbook of the Society for General Systems Research* (Ann Arbor, Mich., 1966), Vol. 11, pp. 203–214; Brams, *Theory of Moves.*

77. Peter Hedstrom and Richard Swedberg, "Social Mechanisms: An Introductory Essay," in Peter Hedstrom and Richard Swedberg, eds., *Social Mechanisms* (Cambridge, UK: Cambridge University Press, 1998), pp. 1–31.

78. George, "The Causal Nexus Between Cognitive Beliefs and Decision-making Behavior."

79. Hedstrom and Swedberg, "Social Mechanisms: An Introductory Essay."

Conclusion

An assessment of progress in operational code analysis depends on the criteria employed. In addition to the generation of novel facts and the solution of conceptual and empirical problems, therefore, it is reasonable to ask whether operational code analysis escapes the "endogeneity trap" and survives "severe testing," two criteria offered by other contributors to this volume.[80] Escaping the endogeneity trap requires that for beliefs to matter, they must be relatively independent of structural features of the decision-making environment and have a significant causal impact on decisions and outcomes.

Jervis argues that beliefs and psychological processes will be more important in the post–Cold War world, because structural external constraints will be less compelling and the range of choice will be greater than during the Cold War era.[81] Walker, Schafer and Young support this argument with evidence that the operational code beliefs of the Bush and Clinton administrations were both significantly independent of the unipolar strategic context following the Cold War and acted as important causes in the explanation of U.S. military interventions in post–Cold War conflicts.[82] This argument is also consistent with Keohane and Martin's conclusion that institutional theory is able to progress and escape the endogeneity trap by placing "more emphasis on agency, less on structure."[83] They note that structures do not lead in a determinate way to outcomes, because of the likelihood of inconsistent and indeterminate relationships among external structure, the domestic preferences of agents and principals,

---

80. Chapter 3 by Robert Keohane and Lisa Martin and Chapter 8 by David Dessler in this volume.

81. Robert Jervis, "Leadership, Post–Cold War Politics, and Psychology," *Political Psychology*, Vol. 15, No. 4 (December 1994), pp. 769–778.

82. Walker, Schafer, and Young, "Presidential Operational Codes and the Management of Foreign Policy Conflicts in the Post–Cold War World."

83. Keohane and Martin, Chapter 3 in this volume, p. 103.

and the multiple equilibrium possibilities for the outcomes of strategic interaction between agents and others.[84]

The growing realization that "beliefs matter" is reflected as well in attempts to meet "severe tests" of corroboration as a criterion of scientific progress. Dessler characterizes the realist research program's incorporation of additional variables in the form of strategic beliefs about the external environment as a progressive move, because it increases the explanatory power of structural realist theory by adding agent-level causal factors and gaining corroboration of additional novel facts.[85] Beliefs, in this account, are independent of external structure, because, for example, the responses of the European powers to a German threat varied by strategic doctrine before 1914 and during the 1930s, in the face of similar multipolar power distributions in the international system.[86] The growing literature on the culture of national security reinforces a recognition of the important role of beliefs in the explanation of strategic interaction by both realist and constructivist theorists.[87]

Just as structural and institutional research programs cannot escape the temptation to incorporate agent-level variables, neither can cognitivist research programs ignore domestic and external contexts in

---

84. Keohane and Martin, Chapter 3.

85. Dessler, Chapter 11, p. 401.

86. See also Thomas Christensen and Jack Snyder, "Progressive Research on Degenerate Alliances," *American Political Science Review*, Vol. 91, No. 4 (December 1997), pp. 919–922.

87. See Alastair Ian Johnston, "Thinking About Strategic Culture," *International Security*, Vol. 19, No. 4 (Spring 1995), pp. 32–64; Peter Katzenstein, ed., *The Culture of National Security* (New York: Columbia, 1996). For reinforcing the importance of this point in their comments on the initial version of this paper, I am indebted to two participants at the Arizona State University conference: Andrew Bennett noted the tendency by realists such as Christensen and Snyder to incorporate beliefs into their theoretical thinking, while Randall Schweller highlighted the emerging study of strategic culture as another manifestation of the importance of beliefs in thinking about national security problems.

subjecting their theories of world politics to severe empirical tests.[88] Each of these general research programs has evolved a pattern of complex relationships with the others, ranging from overt rhetorical rivalry to more subtle relationships of accommodation and assimilation in practice.[89] The lesson from operational code analysis as a scientific research program is that advances in international relations theory may well take the form of a "cautionary tale," in which progress depends on harnessing together fruitful and robust theories from different research programs.

What appears at first glance to be merely a series of amendments within a given research program may actually incorporate theories from other programs with real implications in Lakatosian terms for the program's hard core and the spirit of its positive heuristic.[90] A future examination of these dynamics in more detail may reveal that Laudan's description of research programs as "theory complexes" is more useful, and may thus point the way toward future cooperation rather than rivalry among general research programs in the study of world politics. One should be cautious, therefore, about treating theories as rivals to be either discarded or subsumed after a contest of predicting novel facts. A criterion that emphasizes survival of the fittest rather than tolerance of diversity risks straying from the path of evolutionary progress in international relations theory.[91]

---

88. Walker, Schafer, and Young, "Presidential Operational Codes and the Management of Foreign Policy Conflicts in the Post–Cold War World"; see also Charles Kupchan, *The Vulnerability of Empire* (Ithaca, N.Y.: Cornell University Press, 1994).

89. Robert Keohane, *After Hegemony* (Princeton, N.J.: Princeton University Press, 1984); David Baldwin, *Neorealism and Neoliberalism* (New York: Columbia University Press, 1993); Tetlock, "Social Psychology and World Politics."

90. Elman and Elman, Chapter 2 in this volume.

91. Ball, "Is There Progress in Political Science?"

Chapter 8

Realism, Neoliberalism, and Cooperation

Understanding the Debate

Robert Jervis

The study of international politics often progresses through debates as scholars are forced to re-think their logic and evidence in response to challenges. In fact, debates often lead not to one side winning, but to both sides becoming more sophisticated. For this to happen, however, false issues have to be put aside. There is a real danger of scholarly dispute degenerating into a Woozle hunt, a concept perhaps less familiar to social scientists than the Prisoners' Dilemma, but just as useful. Winnie the Pooh goes searching for the mysterious Woozles and sees a track in the snow. He follows it and to his delight finds that his Woozle has been joined by another. He calls to his colleagues and two of them enroll in the pursuit. Soon they see that the two Woozles have been augmented by three more and so they call in more friends, confident that they are onto something really big—a whole gathering of Woozles. In fact, he and his colleagues have been following their own tracks and are going around in circles. In the same way, scholars often follow each other's prints in producing research, with the fact that someone has used an approach being sufficient justification for others to emulate or criticize it. Of course some research programs wither and others migrate or are expelled, like the psychoanalytic approaches that have moved from the social sciences to the

I am grateful for comments by David Baldwin, Jeffrey Legro, Sean Lynn-Jones, Robert Keohane, Helen Milner, and Andrew Moravcsik. An earlier version of this article appeared as Robert L. Jervis, "Realism, Neoliberalism, and Cooperation: Understanding the Debate," *International Security*, Vol. 24, No. 1 (Summer 1999), pp. 42–63.

humanities. But the possibilities of positive feedback and herd behavior, so prominent in financial markets, should not be discounted in scholarship; we must then be sure we are dealing with issues of real importance.

One of the main functions of a successful research program, at least in political science, may be to point us toward fruitful questions rather than to provide answers. When we look back at many previous debates, we can see that time and energy appear to have been wasted because it is not clear what the argument was about. But in fact the discussion served the useful function of making scholars think more carefully about what actually was in dispute. This is most likely to come about not from the working out of any individual research program, but from the contention between clashing ones. We often think that the success of one such program means that competing ones must be failing. But this may not be the case with the debate between neorealism and neoliberalism. Although I seek to demonstrate that some of the previous conceptions of this argument were misconceived, it is the very attempt to define what is at issue that can make both approaches stronger. Chapter 3 by Robert Keohane and Lisa Martin exemplifies this process. Rather than chase Woozles, they help clarify the important issues at stake in arguments about conflict and cooperation between realists and neoliberal institutionalists.[1] Most students of the subject believe that realists argue that international politics is characterized by high conflict and that institutions play only a small role, and that neoliberals claim that cooperation is more extensive, in large part because institutions are potent.

---

1. Robert Keohane and Lisa Martin, Chapter 3 in this volume, which also says that "institutional theory" is a more descriptive title than "neoliberal institutionalism." For the debate, see John J. Mearsheimer, "The False Promise of International Institutions," *International Security*, Vol. 19, No. 3 (Winter 1994/95), pp. 5–49; Keohane and Martin, "The Promise of Institutional Theory," *International Security*, Vol. 20, No. 1 (Summer 1995), pp. 39–51; Mearsheimer, "A Realist Reply," ibid., pp. 82–93. Also see Lisa L. Martin and Beth Simmons, "Theories and Empirical Studies of International Institutions," *International Organization*, Vol. 52, No. 4 (Autumn 1998), pp. 729–758.

I think this formulation is incorrect and has inhibited intellectual progress. In the first section of this chapter, I argue that the realist-neoliberal disagreement over conflict is not about its extent but about whether it is *unnecessary*, given states' goals. In this context we cannot treat realism as monolithic, but must distinguish between the offensive and defensive variants.[2] In the second section I explain the disagreement in terms of what each school of thought believes would have to change to produce greater cooperation, and use this to understand what is being claimed about the forces that drive conflict.[3]

---

2. My definition of the distinction between offensive and defensive realism can be found below, p. 288. For other discussions, see Jack L. Snyder, *Myths of Empire: Domestic Politics and International Ambition* (Ithaca, N.Y.: Cornell University Press, 1991); Fareed Zakaria, "Realism and Domestic Politics: A Review Essay," *International Security*, Vol. 17, No. 1 (Summer 1992), pp. 177–198; Charles L. Glaser, "Realists as Optimists: Cooperation as Self-Help," *International Security*, Vol. 19, No. 3 (Winter 1994/95), pp. 50–90; Randall L. Schweller, "Neorealism's Status-Quo Bias: What Security Dilemma?" *Security Studies*, Vol. 5, No. 3 (Spring 1996), pp. 90–121; Stephen Brooks, "Dueling Realisms," *International Organization*, Vol. 51, No. 3 (Summer 1997), pp. 445–478; Eric J. Labs, "Beyond Victory: Offensive Realism and the Expansion of War Aims," *Security Studies*, Vol. 6, No. 4 (Summer 1997), pp. 1–49; Andrew Kydd, "Why Security Seekers Do Not Fight Each Other," *Security Studies*, Vol. 7, No. 1 (Autumn 1997), pp. 114–155; and Jeffrey W. Taliaferro, "Security Seeking Under Anarchy," *International Security*, Vol. 25, No. 3 (Winter 2000/01), pp. 128–161. Glaser uses the term "contingent realism," which I think is more descriptive than "defensive realism," but I use the latter term because it has gained greater currency.

3. I use the term "school of thought" because I do not think realism and neoliberal institutionalism can be sharply defined: they are better labeled schools of thought or approaches than theories. Although this vagueness contributes to confusion as scholars talk past one another, a precise definition would be necessary only if either of these approaches really were a tight theory. In that case, falsification of propositions derived from the theory would cast doubt on the entire enterprise. But, for better and for worse, neither of these approaches has the sort of integrity that would permit the use of that logic. For an attempt to formulate a rigorous, but I think excessively narrow, definition of realism, see Jeffrey W. Legro and Andrew Moravcsik, "Is Anybody Still a Realist?" *International Security*, Vol. 24, No. 2 (Summer 1999). Also see Randall L. Schweller, Chapter 9 in this volume; Kenneth N. Waltz, "Realist Thought and Neorealist Theory," in Robert L. Rothstein, ed., *The*

Here disagreements arise about the role of institutions. But these too have often been misunderstood. In the third section I argue that what realists claim is not that institutions lack utility, but that they are not autonomous in the sense of being more than a tool of statecraft. Even if it is true that cooperation and the presence of institutions are correlated, it does not follow that cooperation can be increased by establishing institutions where they do not exist, which is, I think, why most people find the realist-neoliberal debate over cooperation of more than academic interest.

One theme of my analysis is that we should not exaggerate the gap separating realism and neoliberalism. Keohane and Martin are correct to note that "for better or worse, institutional theory is a half-sibling of neorealism."[4] Both realism and neoliberalism start from the assumption that the absence of a sovereign authority that can make and enforce binding agreements creates opportunities for states to advance their interests unilaterally, and makes it both important and difficult for states to cooperate with each other.[5] States must worry that

Evolution of Theory in International Relations (Columbia: University of South Carolina Press, 1991), pp. 21–38; and the exchange between Colin Elman and Waltz in *Security Studies*, Vol. 6, No. 1 (Autumn 1996), pp. 7–61.

4. Keohane and Martin, Chapter 3, p. 83; Robert O. Keohane, *After Hegemony: Cooperation and Discord in the World Political Economy* (Princeton, N.J.: Princeton University Press, 1984), pp. 9, 29, 67; Keohane, *International Institutions and State Power* (Boulder, Colo.: Westview Press, 1989), pp. 7–9. Also see Glaser, "Realists as Optimists," p. 85; Randall L. Schweller and David Priess, "A Tale of Two Realisms: Expanding the Institutions Debate," *Mershon International Studies Review*, Vol. 41, Supplement 1 (May 1997), pp. 1–32; and Martin and Simmons, "Theories and Empirical Studies of International Institutions," pp. 739–740. In the statement quoted, Keohane and Martin refer to neorealism, not realism. For the purposes of this article, I do not need to distinguish between the two; Waltz does so very well in "Realist Thought and Neorealist Theory."

5. The realization that commitment is difficult within states, as well, has led to enormous progress in understanding domestic politics and arrangements among private actors, thus making recent analyses in American and comparative politics appear quite familiar to students of international politics. See Helen V. Milner, "Rationalizing Politics: The Emerging Synthesis among International Politics and American and Comparative Politics," *International Organization*, Vol. 52, No. 4 (Autumn 1998), pp. 759–786. It is often assumed

others will seek to take advantage of them; agreements must be crafted to minimize the danger of double crosses; the incentives that operate when agreements are signed may be quite different when the time comes for them to be carried out; both promises and threats must be made credible. Thus it will take some disentangling to isolate the areas in which there are important disputes between realism and neoliberalism.[6]

In doing this, we should keep in mind the fact that some of the agreement between realism and neoliberalism comes from their both ignoring, if not explicitly rejecting, several other approaches. This is clear from the way Stephen Walker begins Chapter 7: "Do leaders matter in world politics? Intuitively, we sense that they do and, as citizens of a democratic society, we act as if they do."[7] But differences among leaders play little if any role in either realism or neoliberalism. Indeed, almost no modern political science is written as if leaders *do* matter. Part of the fault lies with Kenneth Waltz and his classic *Man, the State, and War*.[8] There is no place in Waltz's levels of analysis for individual differences because "man" is human nature, not the

---

that anarchy and the possibility of the use of force are the same, but this is not correct, as shown by Milner, "The Assumption of Anarchy in International Relations Theory: A Critique," *Review of International Studies*, Vol. 17, No. 1 (January 1991), pp. 71–74; and Robert Powell, "Anarchy in International Relations Theory: The Neorealist-Neoliberal Debate," *International Organization*, Vol. 48, No. 2 (Spring 1994), pp. 330–334.

6. The differences may be sharper in some central issues that I put aside here: the efficacy and fungibility of various forms of power, especially military power; the differences in state behavior when force, coercion, or unilateral solutions are available; and the frequency of such situations. Liberalism and neoliberalism are not comfortable with situations in which one actor can make another "an offer that he can't refuse." For a good discussion, see Lloyd Gruber, *Ruling the World: Power Politics and the Rise of Supranational Institutions* (Chicago: University of Chicago Press, 2000).

7. Stephen G. Walker, Chapter 7 in this volume; Daniel L. Byman and Kenneth M. Pollack, "Let us Now Praise Great Men: Bringing the Statesmen Back In," *International Security*, Vol. 25, No. 4 (Spring 2001), pp. 107–146.

8. Kenneth N. Waltz, *Man, the State, and War* (New York: Columbia University Press, 1954).

characteristics of individual leaders. In fact, individuals may vary both in their bellicosity and their predisposition to perceive conflicts as rooted in the adversary's hostility. Thus it is quite possible that some individual leaders will be much more predisposed to follow conciliatory policies than others and that certain pairs of leaders will be especially prone to cooperate.

In much the same way, arguments about the democratic peace fall outside the ken of realism and neoliberalism, but may be central to cooperation.[9] Like analyses of operational codes, most research on the democratic peace argues or implies that beliefs matter. But this approach homogenizes beliefs within states; leaders of democracies are presumed to think and act differently than authoritarian leaders and a strong socialization effect is postulated, at least within democracies. I have doubts on this score and am skeptical that the effect is universal and overwhelming. Just as some realists err in failing to differentiate between aggressive and status quo states, so the proponents of the democratic peace thesis downplay the possibility of severe conflicts of interest between democracies that could cause them to fight.

Possibilities for Cooperation

Is it true that realism denies the possibility of international cooperation or, less extremely, that realists see less cooperation in world politics than do neoliberal institutionalists? I think the former statement is flatly wrong. The latter also is incorrect, but when properly reformulated points in a productive direction.

FALSE OR EXAGGERATED ISSUES

The affinity between realism and neoliberal institutionalism is not the only reason to doubt the claim that the former has no place for cooperation. This view would imply that conflict of interest is total and

9. James Lee Ray, Chapter 6 in this volume. For a discussion of the propensity of democracies to cooperate with each other, see Michael Mousseau, "Democracy and Compromise in Militarized Interstate Conflicts, 1916–1992," *Journal of Conflict Resolution*, Vol. 42, No. 2 (April 1998), pp. 210–230.

that whatever one state gains, others must lose.[10] This vision of a zero-sum world is implausible. The sense of international politics as characterized by constant bargaining which is central to realism (but not to realism alone, of course) implies a mixture of common and conflicting interests. One can have fighting in a zero-sum world, but not politics.

More worthy of exploration is the less extreme view that realism sees world politics as much more conflictual than does neoliberal institutionalism.[11] For realists, world politics is a continuing if not an unrelenting struggle for survival, advantage, and often dominance. Neoliberals do not deny the existence of cases of extreme conflict, but they do not see them as representative of all of world politics. In many cases and in many areas, states are able to work together to mitigate the effects of anarchy, produce mutual gains, and avoid shared harm.

Although not entirely misguided, this characterization of the difference between realism and neoliberalism is still wrong. To start with, some of the difference reflects the issues that the schools of thought analyze. Neoliberal institutionalists concentrate on international political economy (IPE) and the environment; realists are more prone to study international security and the causes, conduct, and consequences of wars. Thus, although it would be correct to say that one sees more conflict in the world analyzed by realist scholars than in the neoliberal world, this is at least in part because they study different worlds.[12]

---

10. This view is hard even to conceptualize in a multipolar world. Any gain of territory or power by state A would have to come at the expense of some other state, but if it diminishes B or C, this might aid state D, at least in the short run, if D is the rival of B or C. Here the situation is zero-sum (or, more technically, constant sum) overall, but not all actors are hurt, and some may be advantaged, by another's gain.

11. How to measure and even conceptualize conflict and conflict of interest is not easy. See Robert Axelrod, *Conflict of Interest: A Theory of Divergent Goals with Applications to Politics* (Chicago: Markham, 1970).

12. The differences between the issue areas are not inherent, but it is generally believed that the factors such as vulnerability, offensive advantage, and lack of transparency that are conducive to cooperation are more prevalent in IPE than

Similarly, while neoliberal institutionalism is more concerned with efficiency, and realism focuses more on issues of distribution, which are closely linked to power as both an instrument and a stake,[13] it is not clear that this represents different views about the world rather than a difference in the choice of subject matter. Neoliberalism's argument (usually implicit) that distributional conflicts are usually less important than the potential common gains stems at least in part from its substantive concern with issues in which large mutual benefits are believed to be possible, such as protecting the environment, rather than with disputes over territory, status, influence, and dominance.

The related difference between realists and neoliberals on the issue of relative and absolute gains also should not be exaggerated, as recent formulations have explained.[14] To start with, it is not clear whether

in the security arena. See Robert Jervis, "Security Regimes," *International Organization*, Vol. 36, No. 2 (Spring 1982), pp. 358–360; and Charles H. Lipson, "International Cooperation in Economic and Security Affairs," *World Politics*, Vol. 37, No. 1 (October 1984), pp. 1–23.

13. Nonetheless, I think neoliberals were enlightened by Jack Knight's argument that institutions can affect not only the level of cooperation, but who gains more: Knight, *Institutions and Social Conflict* (New York: Cambridge University Press, 1992). Similarly, while neoliberals have drawn heavily on the literature on organizations, they pay little attention to power-laden analyses such as Charles Perrow, *Complex Organizations: A Critical Essay*, 3d ed. (New York: Random House, 1986). Robert O. Keohane acknowledges that he initially underestimated the significance of distributive issues. Keohane, "Institutionalist Theory and the Realist Challenge after the Cold War," in David A. Baldwin, ed., *Neorealism and Neoliberalism: The Contemporary Debate* (New York: Columbia University Press, 1993), pp. 446–447. Also see Keohane and Martin, Chapter 3, pp. 93–94. For a good discussion of distribution and institutions, see Powell, "Anarchy in International Relations Theory," pp. 338–343. For an argument that the shape of domestic institutions affects both the chance of international agreement and the distribution of the benefits, see Helen V. Milner, *Interests, Institutions, and Information: Domestic Politics and International Relations* (Princeton, N.J.: Princeton University Press, 1997).

14. Robert Powell, "Absolute and Relative Gains in International Relations Theory," *American Political Science Review*, Vol. 85, No. 4 (December 1991), pp. 701–726; Powell, "Anarchy in International Relations Theory," pp. 334–338; Glaser, "Realists as Optimists," pp. 74–75; and Arthur A. Stein, *Why Nations Cooperate* (Ithaca, N.Y.: Cornell University Press, 1990), chap. 5. Issues of

neoliberals are arguing that realists are incorrect to assert that states often are concerned with relative gains, or that it is the states that err when they are thus concerned, perhaps because they have been socialized by realist prescriptions. In the latter case, realism would be descriptively correct, although it might share with decisionmakers a misunderstanding of their interests. Substantively, realists never claimed that relative gains were the only thing that mattered—to assert this would be to declare international politics a zero-sum game—and many realists have been sensitive to possibilities of mutual security. Thus, for example, within a few months of the explosion of the first atomic bomb, realist scholars noted that once both sides had a sufficient number of these weapons, little could be gained by further increases and there was little to fear from the other side's increases. The title of the first major book on the subject, *The Absolute Weapon*, indicated quite clearly the radical change from a world in which the greatest form of military power was relative.[15] Indeed, this effect also undercuts much concern over relative gains in the economic area, because their impact on security would be slight.[16] Neoliberals also

---

relative versus absolute gains are not the same as distribution versus efficiency, because an actor can care about distribution even in the absence of concerns about relative gains. It should also be noted that although the main reason for seeking relative gains today is to improve one's absolute situation tomorrow, some goods are inherently positional, such as attaining a top status or ranking or being seen as the best in some category: see the classic and yet underappreciated analysis of Fred Hirsch, *Social Limits to Growth* (Cambridge, Mass.: Harvard University Press, 1976).

15. Bernard Brodie, et al., *The Absolute Weapon* (New York: Harcourt Brace, 1946).

16. When states are allied—and expect to remain so in the future—each may gain "security externalities" from the others' economic gains. See Joanne Gowa, *Allies, Adversaries, and International Trade* (Princeton, N.J.: Princeton University Press, 1994), chap. 3. But relative economic gains can redistribute power within an alliance (as shown by Arthur A. Stein, "The Hegemon's Dilemma: Great Britain, the United States, and the International Economic Order," *International Organization*, Vol. 38, No. 2 [Spring 1984], pp. 355–386), and will be of concern if actors believe that they will influence future wealth. See Robert Jervis, "International Primacy: Is the Game Worth the Candle?" *International Security*, Vol. 17, No. 4 (Spring 1993), pp. 54–59; and John C.

have come to adopt a less extreme position on the absolute-relative gains debate. They initially cast their arguments in terms of absolute gains, but soon acknowledged that it is dangerous for one state to seek absolute gains that would put it at a relative disadvantage *vis-à-vis* an adversary.[17]

AREA OF AGREEMENT: NOT CONFLICT, BUT UNNECESSARY CONFLICT

The disagreements between realism and neoliberalism have not only been exaggerated, but they have also been misunderstood. Neoliberalism does not see more cooperation than does realism; rather, neoliberalism believes that there is much more *unrealized* or *potential* cooperation than does realism, and the schools of thought disagree about how much conflict in world politics is *unnecessary* or *avoidable*, in the sense of actors failing to agree even though their preferences overlap.[18] To put it in a context that frames the next section of this

---

Matthews III, "Current Gains and Future Outcomes: When Cumulative Relative Gains Matter," *International Security*, Vol. 21, No. 1 (Summer 1996), pp. 112–146. Furthermore, despite the existence of nuclear weapons, an extreme gap in the economic health of the United States and West Europe on the one hand and the Soviet Union on the other undermined the latter's security, largely by sapping its self-confidence.

17. The greatest deficiency in the relative/absolute gains literature is that it has remained largely at the level of theory and prescription, with much less attention to when decisionmakers *do* in fact exhibit relative-gains concerns. Thus as noteworthy as the fact that academics employed impeccable logic to demonstrate the irrelevance of relative advantage in a world of mutual second-strike capabilities was the fact that each side's decisionmakers remained unpersuaded, continued to fear that the other side sought nuclear superiority, and sought advantage, if not superiority, for itself. For a related argument, see Glaser, "Realists as Optimists," pp. 86–88. For a good empirical study in the trade area, see Michael Mastanduno, "Do Relative Gains Matter? America's Response to Japanese Industrial Policy," *International Security*, Vol. 16, No. 1 (Summer 1991), pp. 73–113.

18. For a parallel discussion of "real" and "illusory" incompatibility, see Kenneth E. Boulding, "National Images and International Systems," *Journal of Conflict Resolution*, Vol. 3, No. 2 (June 1959), p. 130. This distinction and the one I am making are not without their difficulties, as I discuss below. The move

article, they differ over the changes that they believe are feasible and required to reduce conflict.

When a realist such as Stephen Krasner argues that much international politics is "life on the Pareto frontier," he implies that states already have been able to cooperate to such an extent that no further moves can make all of them better off.[19] For neoliberals, areas without institutions are likely to be far from this frontier, and much of international politics resembles a Prisoner's Dilemma or a market failure in producing sub-optimal outcomes for all concerned. Although neoliberals are strongly influenced by neoclassical economics, they reject the idea that the free play of political forces will capture all possible joint gains.[20] Thus the old joke about two neoclassical economists walking down the street: one sees a $20 bill but before he can bend down to pick it up, his colleague says, "Don't bother; if it were really there someone would have gotten it before us." For neoliberal institutionalists, the world is littered with $20 bills. Because they believe that there are many mutually beneficial arrangements that

---

from conflicting preferences to conflictual behavior is not entirely direct because if information is complete and outcomes are infinitely divisible, the actors should be able to find a way of reaching the outcome that is cheaper than engaging in costly conflict. This is known as the Hicks paradox in economics and was introduced into the international relations literature in James D. Fearon, "Rationalist Explanations for War," *International Organization*, Vol. 49, No. 3 (Summer 1995), pp. 379–414. The subject is important but not central to the issues of concern here.

19. Stephen D. Krasner, "Global Communication and National Power: Life on the Pareto Frontier," *World Politics*, Vol. 43, No. 3 (April 1991), pp. 336–366.

20. This is not to say that all arguments that actors are below the Pareto frontier share neoliberalism's stress on the importance of institutions. Thus Deborah W. Larson's analysis of missed opportunities during the Cold War seeks to demonstrate that, at a number of points, lack of trust and related psychological impediments prevented the United States and the Soviet Union from relaxing tensions and reaching agreements that would have made them both better off. See Larson, *Anatomy of Mistrust: U.S.-Soviet Relations during the Cold War* (Ithaca, N.Y.: Cornell University Press, 1997). Robert McNamara makes a parallel but I think unsustainable argument about Vietnam: Robert McNamara, James Blight, and Robert Brigham, *Argument Without End: In Search of Answers to the Vietnam Tragedy* (New York: Public Affairs, 1999).

states forgo because of the fear that others will cheat or take advantage of them, they see important gains to be made through the more artful arrangement of policies. Like neoclassical economists, some realists doubt this, believing that all available $20 bills have already been picked up. For them, it is unfortunately true that we live in the best of all possible worlds. And if this is the case, distributional issues loom large because they are the only kind that remains, and so it is hard to see how neoliberalist analysis can be brought to bear.[21]

To proceed further, we need to divide realism into offensive and defensive categories. Offensive realists think that few important situations in international politics resemble a Prisoner's Dilemma. This model does not elucidate the most crucial area of the pursuit of security by major powers because mutual security either is not sought or cannot be gained: one or more of the states is willing to risk war to expand, or has security requirements that are incompatible with those of others. Thus for John Mearsheimer, states maximize power (which must be seen in relative terms) either because it is the means by which they can be secure or because they want other values that power is (correctly) believed to bring.[22] For Colin Gray, arms races are a reflection of conflicts of interest, and wars result not because of the mutual pursuit of security but because one side, if not both, is aggressive.[23] For Randall Schweller, it is especially important to "bring the revisionist state back in" because security-seeking states do not get into unnecessary conflicts, as they are able to discern one another's

---

21. For discussion, see Martin and Simmons, "Theories and Empirical Studies of International Institutions," pp. 744–747; and James K. Sebenius, "Challenging Conventional Explanations of International Cooperation," *International Organization*, Vol. 46, No. 1 (Winter 1992), pp. 334–339.

22. John J. Mearsheimer, *The Tragedy of Great Power Politics* (New York: Norton, 2001).

23. Of Gray's voluminous writings, see, for example, Colin Gray, *Weapons Don't Make War: Policy, Strategy, and Military Technology* (Lawrence: University of Kansas Press, 1993); and Gray, *House of Cards: Why Arms Control Must Fail* (Ithaca, N.Y.: Cornell University Press, 1992).

intentions and can move sufficiently quickly to protect themselves if others should become menacing.[24]

Defensive realists disagree, and take a position on the role of unnecessary conflict that has more in common with neoliberals. Scholars such as Charles Glaser, John Herz, Stephen Van Evera, and myself see the Prisoner's Dilemma as capturing important dynamics of international politics, especially through the operation of the security dilemma: the ways in which the attempt by one state to increase its security has the effect (often unintended and sometimes unforeseen) of decreasing the security of others. Often states would be willing to settle for the status quo and are driven more by fear than by the desire to make gains. According to this "spiral model" of international politics, both structural and perceptual reasons conspire to render self-defeating the actions states take to protect themselves. In many cases it is the interactive process among states that *generates* conflict rather than merely revealing or enacting the preexisting differences in goals. Both sides would be satisfied with mutual security; international politics represents tragedy rather than evil, as the actions of states make it even harder for them to be secure. This is not true in all cases, however. Aggressor states are common; security and other interests often create differences that are irreconcilable. In these and only these instances, defensive realists see the conflict as unavoidable.

For defensive realists, the offense-defense balance is particularly important, as Sean Lynn-Jones makes clear.[25] Although the subject is plagued with confusions and disagreements over definition and

---

24. Randall L. Schweller, "Bandwagoning for Profit: Bringing the Revisionist State Back In," *International Security*, Vol. 19, No. 1 (Summer 1994), pp. 72–107; and Schweller, "Neorealism's Status-Quo Bias." Also see Kydd, "Sheep in Sheep's Clothing: Why Security Seekers Do Not Fight Each Other." This is why Charles Glaser sees "realists as optimists": in most circumstances, states that seek security can develop a military posture that signals their benign intentions, thereby minimizing unnecessary conflict. Glaser, "Realists as Optimists," pp. 67–70.

25. Sean M. Lynn-Jones, "Assessing the Progressiveness of Offense-Defense Theory," paper presented at the "Progress in International Relations Theory" conference, Arizona State University, January 15–16, 1999.

method, there is general agreement that some circumstances of geography, technology, and perhaps politics make it relatively easy for states to protect themselves without seriously menacing others. When this is the case, cooperation among status quo powers is within reach because mutual security is a feasible and desired goal. Many of the arguments here are compatible with neoliberalism, as cooperation is facilitated by decreased fear of cheating. Furthermore, it may be possible to transfer the basic idea of offense-defense balance from the military arena to the economic and political realms that are central to neoliberal concerns. In those areas as well, states often seek largely defensive aims, and their ability to reach them cooperatively will be deeply affected by whether they can deploy policies that do not threaten others.

Despite important similarities, three differences make defensive realists less optimistic than neoliberals. First, as noted above, defensive realists believe that only in a subset of situations (size unspecified) is the conflict unnecessary. Second, and related to this, they believe that it is often hard for states to tell which situation they are in. The difficulty that status quo powers have in recognizing one another, in part because of deeply rooted political and psychological biases, is compounded by the high price to be paid for mistaking an expansionist for a partner that seeks mainly security. Third, defensive realists have less faith in the ability of actors to reach common interests than do neoliberals: in some cases mistrust and fear of cheating may be too severe to be overcome. The extent of the differences between the schools of thought are difficult to estimate, however, because realism and neoliberalism have rarely analyzed comparable situations. Unlike defensive realists, neoliberals have concentrated on areas in which the costs of mistakenly believing that the other will cooperate are not prohibitive and in which gains in efficiency are likely to be greater than conflicts over distribution. But it also seems that neoliberals see the restraints that actors can impose on others and themselves as stronger than defensive realists believe them to be. If arrangements to increase cooperation are so feasible, however, the obvious question, which I touch on later, is why they are not employed more often: why are there still $20 bills lying around?

In summary, offensive realists think that the conflict we observe in international politics represents real incompatibility between desired states of the world. The famous example is the reply that Francis I of France gave in the early sixteenth century when he was asked what differences led to constant warfare with Spain's Charles V: "None whatever. We agree perfectly. We both want control of Italy!"[26] At the very least, modeling politics as a Prisoner's Dilemma conceptualizes cooperation as a single alternative, the only one that is better over the long run than mutual defection. In fact, offensive realists note, there are many outcomes better than mutual defection, and these distribute the gains in quite different ways and are inevitable sources of conflict. Neoliberals attribute much conflict to the failure to employ institutions that could move states to the Pareto frontier by facilitating secure and equitable agreements. Defensive realists fall between these views, arguing that a great deal depends on whether the state (assumed to be willing to live with the status quo) is facing a like-minded partner or an expansionist. In the latter case their analysis parallels that of the offensive realists; in the former case it is not unlike that of neoliberals.

Changes Needed for Cooperation

Realists and neoliberals have different perspectives on what would have to change to increase cooperation in a particular situation.[27] These differences can be understood by applying Robert Powell's distinction between preferences over strategies or ways to reach goals, on the one hand, and changes in preferences over goals or outcomes, on the

---

26. Quoted in Frederick L. Schuman, *International Politics*, 7th ed. (New York: McGraw-Hill, 1953), p. 283.

27. A particularly insightful use of counterfactuals to explore changes that could have avoided a major war is Paul Schroeder, "Embedded Counterfactuals and the Case for World War I as an 'Unavoidable' War," in Richard Ned Lebow, Philip E. Tetlock, and Geoffrey Parker, eds., *Unmaking the West: Exploring Alternative Histories of Counterfactual Worlds* (forthcoming). I am concerned here with short-run changes that could reduce a current conflict, not with changes like instituting a world government, making all states democratic, or using future DNA technology to alter human nature.

other.[28] Neoliberals are more optimistic than realists because they believe that changes in preferences over strategies usually are sufficient to produce mutual benefit. Much of this change can come by more and better information: information about the situation, information about what the other side has done and why it has done it, and information about what the other side is likely to do in the future.[29] States can cooperate by reducing transaction costs (the costs and risks associated with reaching and carrying out agreements), and the successful reduction of such costs can in turn facilitate cooperation. Institutions can play a large role here, and this helps explain why institutionalized cooperation can continue even when the initially propitious conditions have disappeared.[30] But it is hard to see how changes in information can be effective when changes in preferences over outcomes are required. Thus neoliberals do not discuss how states do or should behave when vital interests clash: there are no neoliberal analyses of the Cold War, the diplomacy of the 1930s, or relations between the United States and Iraq, and the approach could have helped in Kosovo only if there were some outcomes acceptable to Serbs and Kosovars absent changes in power.

Offensive realists see little room for increasing cooperation. Aggressors may be deterred or defeated, but given that the security dilemma is irrelevant or intractable, additional information cannot lead to conflict-reducing changes in preference over strategies. Furthermore,

---

28. Powell, "Anarchy in International Relations Theory," pp. 318–321.

29. Thus reputation plays a central role in neoliberalism parallel to its role in deterrence theory. But what little empirical research we have casts grave doubt on the standard deductive claims for how reputations form and operate. See Ted Hopf, *Peripheral Visions: Deterrence Theory and American Foreign Policy in the Third World, 1965–1990* (Ann Arbor: University of Michigan Press, 1994); and Jonathan Mercer, *Reputation and International Politics* (Ithaca, N.Y.: Cornell University Press, 1996). Also see Robert Jervis, "Signaling and Perception: Drawing Inferences and Projecting Images," in Kristen Monroe, ed., *Political Psychology* (Mahwah, N.J.: Lawrence Erlbaum Associates, 2002), pp. 293–312.

30. Keohane, *After Hegemony*; also see Celeste A. Wallander, *Mortal Friends, Best Enemies: German-Russian Cooperation after the Cold War* (Ithaca, N.Y.: Cornell University Press, 1998), pp. 19–34.

changes in preferences over outcomes may be out of reach if all states seek to dominate. Altering the incentives that states face may be effective, but this will benefit one side only. Although changes in relative power drive much of international politics, they too alter what each state gains, but they do not bring mutual benefit. Increasing the costs of war may reduce violent conflict, but rarely can cooperation be increased by changing beliefs and information about the other or the world.

For defensive realists, much depends on the nature of the situation, because the changes required when a status quo power faces an expansionist power are very different from the changes that could increase cooperation among status quo powers that fear one another. When dealing with aggressors, increasing cooperation is beyond reach, and the analysis and preferred policies of defensive realists differ little from those of offensive realists; when the security dilemma is the problem, either or both sides can seek changes in preferences over strategies (both their own and those of the other) in the form of implementing standard "cooperation under anarchy" policies. In these cases, both defensive realists and neoliberals embrace the apparent paradox that actors can be well advised to reduce their own ability to take advantage of others now and in the future. Both agree that cooperation is more likely, or can be made so, if large transactions can be divided up into a series of smaller ones, if transparency can be increased, if the gains from cheating and the costs of being cheated on are relatively low, if mutual cooperation is or can be made much more advantageous than mutual defection, and if each side employs strategies of reciprocity and believes that the interactions will continue over a long period of time.[31]

---

31. Kenneth A. Oye, ed., *Cooperation under Anarchy* (Princeton, N.J.: Princeton University Press, 1986), includes essays by defensive realists and neoliberals. These arguments were developed in works that formed the basis for the Oye volume: Robert Axelrod, *The Evolution of Cooperation* (New York: Basic Books, 1984); Robert Jervis, "Cooperation under the Security Dilemma," *World Politics*, Vol. 30, No. 2 (January 1978), pp. 167–214; and Keohane, *After Hegemony*. It is not true, however, that a long "shadow of the future" by itself increases cooperation. When an agreement is expected to last for a long time, the

Thus for defensive realists, diagnosis of the situation and the other's objectives is a critical and difficult step, which explains why analysts of this type come to different policy prescriptions when they have different views of the adversary.[32] For example, much of the American debate over how to respond to North Korea's nuclear program turns on beliefs about whether that country is driven by insecurity and seeks better relations with the United States on acceptable terms, or whether its goal is to push the United States off the peninsula and dominate South Korea, in which case North Korea would not refrain from developing atomic bombs in return for a reasonable agreement and instead would respond only to coercion.[33]

Often more fine-grained distinctions about preferences are required to understand what needs to change in order to increase cooperation. Because states have hierarchies of means-ends beliefs, some preferences over outcomes are, from a broader perspective, preferences over strategies. Thus many conflicts can be seen as both an avoidable

---

incentives to bargain harder are greater; James D. Fearon, "Bargaining, Enforcement, and International Cooperation," *International Organization*, Vol. 52, No. 2 (Spring 1998), pp. 269–305. Similarly, when what is at stake are actors' reputations for standing firm, as was true in many Cold War interactions, then issues of little intrinsic importance produce very high conflict. Much of the relative gains problem turns on the expectation that the outcome of the current interaction will strongly affect the actors' future well-being; states often fight at a given time because they fear that otherwise they will be at a greater disadvantage in the future. Neoliberals argue that these effects can be minimized by institutions.

32. For the importance of diagnosis, see Alexander L. George, *Bridging the Gap: Theory and Practice in Foreign Policy* (Washington, D.C.: U.S. Institute of Peace Press, 1993). Also see Robert Jervis, *Perception and Misperception in International Politics* (Princeton, N.J.: Princeton University Press, 1976), chap. 3. In many cases, contemporary policymakers or later analysts may not be clear as to whether they are disagreeing about the nature of the situation the state is in, or instead about the policies that are appropriate for that situation.

33. Leon V. Sigal, *Disarming Strangers: Nuclear Diplomacy with North Korea* (Princeton, N.J.: Princeton University Press, 1998). For a different analysis that also calls for diplomatic engagement with North Korea, see Victor D. Cha, "Hawk Engagement and Preventive Defense on the Korean Peninsula," *International Security*, Vol. 27, No. 1 (Summer 2002), pp. 40–78.

security dilemma and as the product of irreconcilable differences. For example, it can be argued that at bottom what Japan sought in the 1930s was security: dominance over the "Greater East Asia Co-prosperity Sphere" was desired not as an ultimate value or even for national wealth but as a source of autonomy and protection. This in turn was needed not because Japan was under immediate Western pressure—this was an effect, not a cause, of Japan's policy—but rather because of the expectation that eventually the West would menace Japan. Cooperation would have been possible if the United States and Great Britain had been able to reassure Japan of their continuing goodwill (so long as Japan did not engage in military adventures), but this was difficult if not beyond reach for states in anarchy. Although Japan's ultimate goals would not have to have changed to produce cooperation, "mere" alterations in images of the other side and the deployment of conflict-reduction strategies could not have kept the peace. Similarly, even if the United States and the Soviet Union ultimately sought security during the Cold War, deep internal changes were a prerequisite for far-reaching cooperation, because each believed that the other would be a menace as long as its domestic system was in place.

INSTITUTIONS AND COOPERATION

As their name suggests, neoliberal institutionalists stress the role of institutions, broadly defined as enduring patterns of shared expectations of behavior that have received some degree of formal assent.[34] Here too it is important to understand the disagreement with

---

34. Similar definitions are found in Knight, *Institutions and Social Conflict*, pp. 2–4; Douglass C. North, *Institutions, Institutional Change, and Economic Performance* (New York: Norton, 1990), pp. 4–5; and Celeste A. Wallander, Helga Haftendorn, and Robert O. Keohane, "Introduction," in Haftendorn, Keohane, and Wallander, eds., *Imperfect Unions: Security Institutions over Time and Space* (New York: Oxford University Press, 1999), pp. 1–2. Despite its roots in economics, neoliberalism's treatment of institutions pays scant attention to principal-agent problems and the ways in which institutions and their leaders can maximize their own self-interests at the expense of the interests of the principals.

realists, which is not over the existence of institutions or the fact that they are found where cooperation is high, but over the claim that they are more than instruments of statecraft and have an independent impact, a life of their own.[35] The obvious threat to the latter argument is the assertion of endogeneity: if it is predictable that certain kinds of institutions will produce increased cooperation, then actors will establish such arrangements when and only when they want this outcome, which is likely to be consistent with realist analysis.[36] As Charles Glaser puts it, institutions are "the product of the same factors—states' interests and the constraints imposed by the system—that influence whether states should cooperate."[37] Neoliberals think that establishing an institution can increase cooperation. Realists believe that this is not so much a false statement as a false remedy, because the states will establish an institution if and only if they seek the goals that the institution will help them reach.

---

35. Keohane and Martin, Chapter 3, agree that the question is posed correctly, although answered incorrectly, in Mearsheimer, "The False Promise of International Institutions." Also see Martin and Simmons, "Theories and Empirical Studies of International Institutions" and, from a different perspective, Michael Barnett and Martha Finnemore, "The Politics, Politics, and Pathologies of International Organizations," *International Organization*, Vol. 53, No. 4 (Autumn 1999), pp. 699–732. For the finding that joint membership in international organizations is negatively correlated with conflict, see Bruce M. Russett, John R. Oneal, and David R. Davis, "The Third Leg of the Kantian Tripod for Peace: International Organizations and Militarized Disputes, 1950–1985," *International Organization*, Vol. 52, No. 3 (Summer 1998), pp. 441–468. The recent literature on the role of institutions in domestic politics is very large: recent surveys are Peter A. Hall and Rosemary Taylor, "Political Science and the Three New Institutionalisms," *Political Studies*, Vol. 44, No. 5 (April 1996), pp. 936–957; and Ira Katznelson, "The Doleful Dance of Politics and Policy: Can Historical Institutionalism Make a Difference?" *American Political Science Review*, Vol. 92, No. 1 (March 1998), pp. 191–197.

36. Keohane and Martin, "Institutional Theory, Endogeneity, and Delegation." This is consistent with Keohane's "functional theory regimes" in Keohane, *After Hegemony*, chap. 6.

37. Glaser, "Realists as Optimists," p. 85. Also see Kenneth Waltz, "Structural Realism after the Cold War," *International Security*, Vol. 25, No. 1 (Summer 2000), pp. 18–27.

The contrast between realist and neoliberal views can be brought out by differing interpretations of Page Fortna's finding that cease-fires are more likely to be maintained when devices such as buffer zones, inspections, and arms limitations are involved.[38] Even though this conclusion holds when situational variables are held constant, the endogeneity problem arises as it must with any study comparing the outcomes of cases in which policymakers make different choices, and this allows neoliberals and realists to make different interpretations.[39] A neoliberal would argue that the efficacy of these arrangements shows their independent impact and implies that they would produce some good effect if they had been employed in other cases. Realists see the finding as a demonstration of the importance of statecraft but are skeptical of the implications for other cases, arguing that no set of control variables can capture all the factors that go into decisionmakers' judgments. There are likely to be good reasons why certain arrangements are adopted in some cases and not in others: if states had wanted to make it more difficult to break the cease-fire in the latter cases and if technology, terrain, and third-party influences had permitted this, then they would have done so. The cease-fires that broke down were thus not instances of mutually undesired and unnecessary conflict, and the arrangements were reflections of the actors' preferences over outcomes.

This kind of reasoning leads realists to argue that the key errors of reformers after World War I were the belief that the war had been caused by a lack of mechanisms for conflict resolution and the inference that the path to peace was to establish such an organization

---

38. Page V. Fortna, *Peace Time: Cease-Fire Agreements and the Durability of Peace* (Princeton, N.J.: Princeton University Press, forthcoming). Also see Caroline A. Hartzell, "Explaining the Stability of Negotiated Settlements to Intrastate Wars," *Journal of Conflict Resolution*, Vol. 43, No. 1 (February 1999), pp. 3–22; and Barbara Walter, "Designing Transitions from Civil War: Demobilization, Democratization, and Commitments to Peace," *International Security*, Vol. 24, No. 1 (Summer 1999), pp. 127–155.

39. For further discussion of the methodological issues involved, see Robert Jervis, *System Effects: Complexity in Political and Social Life* (Princeton, N.J.: Princeton University Press, 1997), pp. 81–87.

even in the absence of shifts in the goals of the states. Similarly, realists believe that while the multilateral security institutions that have developed in post–Cold War Europe serve important functions, they reflect the states' desires not to threaten each other and to work together. These institutions may be part of the solution to Europe's problems, but it would be a mistake to believe that similar arrangements could bring peace to other parts of the world.

THREE TYPES OF INSTITUTIONS

To analyze the role played by institutional arrangements and the links among interests, policies, and cooperation, we need to distinguish among the functions that institutions perform: what can be called standard institutions, those that are more innovative, and those that operate in ways that alter preferences. What is crucial is whether the arrangements "merely" further established interests, or whether they change preferences over outcomes, thereby permitting forms and degrees of cooperation that could not be reached through the provision of more information and the deployment of standard ways of giving actors confidence that agreements will be maintained. It is when institutions are autonomous in this sense that neoliberal analysis makes its most distinctive contribution.

INSTITUTIONS AS STANDARD TOOLS: BINDING AND SELF-BINDING. The first set of institutions consists of well-known instruments of statecraft such as alliances and trade agreements. Neoliberals have argued that realists cannot explain why these agreements have any impact, given the realists' strong arguments about anarchy and the difficulties of making credible commitments. Although neoliberals have added to our knowledge of the mechanisms involved, in fact they are consistent with defensive realism's analysis of how actors can overcome Prisoner's Dilemmas, as noted earlier. Furthermore, there is no dispute that these institutions are reflections of states' preexisting interests.

Many institutions that make it more difficult and costly for states to defect in the future, and so modify anarchy, similarly embody preferences over outcomes. Realists are likely to stress the desire to bind others to keep their commitments; neoliberals are more sensitive to the fact that it can be equally important for actors—indeed, for powerful ones, more important—to bind themselves.[40] But the difference is in emphasis only, and a defensive realist would not be surprised by a German official's explanation of his support for strong European institutions: "We wanted to bind Germany into a structure which practically obliges Germany to take the interests of its neighbors into consideration. We wanted to give our neighbors assurances that we won't do what we don't intend to do anyway."[41]

Although realists see binding as somewhat more difficult and less likely to be desired than do neoliberals, they do not deny that states can take themselves out of anarchy if they choose to cede much of their sovereignty to a central authority, as the thirteen American colonies did. It is probably true that neoliberals see the "web of inter- dependence" among countries as stronger than realists do, in part

---

40. Compare, for example, Joseph Grieco, "State Interest and Institutional Rule Trajectories: A Neorealist Interpretation of the Maastricht Treaty and European Economic and Monetary Union," in Baldwin, *Neorealism and Neoliberalism*, pp. 116–169; and Andrew Moravcsik, *The Choice for Europe: Social Purpose and State Power from Messina to Maastricht* (Ithaca, N.Y.: Cornell University Press, 1998). Also see G. John Ikenberry, "Institutions, Strategic Restraint, and the Persistence of American Postwar Order," *International Security*, Vol. 23, No. 3 (Winter 1998/99), pp. 44–45, 55; Ikenberry, *After Victory: Institutions, Strategic Restraint, and the Rebuilding of Order after Major Wars* (Princeton, N.J.: Princeton University Press, 2001); and Kenneth W. Abbott and Duncan Snidal, "Why States Act through Formal Organizations," *Journal of Conflict Resolution*, Vol. 42, No. 1 (February 1998), pp. 3–32. This emphasis on commitment is consistent with the past generation of research that has argued that the crucial role of governments in economic development is their willingness and ability to maintain domestic order while guaranteeing that they will not confiscate property and wealth, and the quite different work on intertemporal games explaining why and how individuals might bind themselves to do what they would otherwise not do in the future. For the former, the classic study is Douglass C. North and Robert D. Thomas, *The Rise of the Western World: A New Economic History* (Cambridge: Cambridge University Press, 1973). For a brief summary of the literature in the latter area, see Partha Dasgupta, "Trust as a Commodity," in Diego Gambetta, ed., *Trust: Making and Breaking Cooperative Relations* (New York: Basil Blackwell, 1988), pp. 54–55.

41. Quoted in Jane Perlez, "Blunt Reasoning for Enlarging NATO: Curbs on Germany," *New York Times*, December 7, 1997, p. 18.

because they believe that elites and members of the public place greater value on economic values as compared to security, status, and self-assertion. But these differences are elusive because they are matters of degree. No one thinks that unifying processes are irreversible: even states such as Yugoslavia, Czechoslovakia, and the Soviet Union that once shared common institutions and were economically integrated have come apart in the face of strong conflicts, and the United States was held together only by force in its civil war. No one argues that institutions cannot be broken without incurring any costs—indeed, these costs are what gives each actor some confidence that others will continue to respect them. But what is crucial here is that, irrespective of their strength, these arrangements are instituted because national leaders want them to have the binding effects. The institutions can then be important, but even if they involve giving power to autonomous actors such as the United Nations Secretary General or the World Trade Organization, they are *not* autonomous in the sense of overriding or shaping the preferences of those who established them.

INSTITUTIONS AS INNOVATIVE TOOLS. The second set of institutions comprises those that are potential tools but remain outside the realm of normal statecraft because leaders have not thought of them or do not appreciate their effectiveness. Here there is an area of unrealized common interest, and greater cooperation could be secured by increasing information and knowledge.[42] Because people learn from experience, problems that could not have been solved in the past may be treatable today. Furthermore, scholars can discover the efficacy of neglected instruments. For example, Keohane and Martin not only argue that it can be in the interest of states to delegate authority to unbiased bodies, but imply that this is not apparent to all decisionmakers. Thus increased understanding could allow them to

---

42. There is some overlap here with the arguments for the potential role of greater knowledge. See, for example, Ernst B. Haas, *When Knowledge Is Power* (Berkeley: University of California Press, 1990); and Peter J. Haas, ed., "Knowledge, Power, and International Policy Coordination," special issue on epistemic communities, *International Organization*, Vol. 46, No. 1 (Winter 1992).

cooperate more. Similarly, when defensive realists called for arrangements that decreased the "reciprocal fear of surprise attack" and developed the theory of arms control, they implied that a fuller and more accurate appreciation of crisis instability as a cause of war could lead to corrective measures and greater cooperation.[43]

As is the case with other analyses that are simultaneously descriptive and prescriptive,[44] however, there is tension between the claim that academics have ignored some kinds of institutions and the argument that it is states that have neglected them. To the extent that scholars can show that their peers have not appreciated a range of devices that states have in fact utilized, they undercut the claim that this finding can increase cooperation. My sense is that academics generally underestimate the ingenuity of skilled practitioners, although they may play a role in spreading such skill. For example, the recent settlement of the long-standing border dispute between Peru and Ecuador created "peace parks," including a square kilometer that was the site of the last Ecuadorian stand against Peru in 1995 and the grave of twelve Ecuadorian soldiers. Although this land is in Peru and will remain under Peruvian sovereignty, it will be under Ecuadorian control.[45] Arrangements like these are well worth studying and

---

43. Thomas C. Schelling, *The Strategy of Conflict* (Cambridge, Mass: Harvard University Press, 1960), chap. 9; Schelling and Morton H. Halperin, *Strategy and Arms Control* (New York: Twentieth Century Fund, 1961); and Robert Jervis, "Arms Control, Stability, and Causes of War," *Political Science Quarterly*, Vol. 108, No. 2 (Summer 1993), pp. 239–253.

44. For further discussion, see Jervis, "Hans Morgenthau, Realism, and the Scientific Study of International Politics," *Social Research*, Vol. 61, No. 4 (Winter 1994), pp. 859–860; Jervis, "Security Studies: Ideas, Policy, and Politics," in Edward D. Mansfield and Richard Sisson, eds., *Political Knowledge and the Public Interest* (Columbus: Ohio State University Press, forthcoming).

45. Anthony Faiola, "Peru, Ecuador Sign Pact Ending Border Dispute," *Washington Post*, October 27, 1998, p. A20; "Peru and Ecuador Sign Treaty to End Longstanding Conflict," *New York Times*, October 27, 1998, p. 3; Luigi Einaudi, "The Ecuador-Peru Peace Process," in Chester A. Crocker, Fen Osler Hampson, and Pamela Aall, eds., *Herding Cats: Multiparty Mediation in a Complex World* (Washington, D.C.: U.S. Institute of Peace Press, 1999), pp. 405–429.

neoliberals could perform a major service by pointing to underutilized institutions or inventing new ones. But because these instruments would still reflect underlying interests, realist claims would not necessarily be disturbed.

INSTITUTIONS AS CAUSES OF CHANGE IN PREFERENCES OVER OUTCOMES. The case is different, however, with institutions that change preferences over outcomes. Realists say that in a system of self-help, institutions cannot stop states from fighting "when push comes to shove." Neoliberals reply that even if this is correct, it misses the more important point that institutions can make it less likely that push will come to shove by providing information, altering the consequences of shoving, and diminishing the desire to push. But if we are to classify the institutions as more than instruments of underlying interest, these changes must be unanticipated by the actors.

Borderline cases are attempts at what might be called "deep self-binding." For example, the German effort discussed earlier can be seen as an attempt to shape not only future German behavior, but also future German preferences over outcomes. Just as Gary Becker argues that individuals may act in a certain way to influence what their later tastes will be,[46] so today's German leaders may want to strengthen European ties to ensure that later Germans would not even contemplate independent military action or the pursuit of security policies that could endanger other European countries. If international institutions serve these functions, they can increase cooperation and, more important, shape the future, but they still are serving the goals envisaged by the current decisionmakers.

This is not true if the changes that occur are unforeseen and unintended. The classic example is described in Ernst Haas's analysis

---

46. Gary S. Becker, *Accounting for Tastes* (Cambridge, Mass: Harvard University Press, 1996), Part 1. For more subtle treatments, see Amartya Sen, "Rational Fools: A Critique of the Behavioral Foundations of Economic Theory," *Philosophy and Public Affairs*, Vol. 6, No. 4 (Summer 1977), pp. 317–344; and Albert O. Hirschman, "Against Parsimony: Three Easy Ways of Complicating Some Categories of Economic Discourse," in Hirschman, *Rival Views of Market Society and Other Recent Essays* (New York: Viking, 1986), chap. 6.

of the spillover processes of regional integration, in which decision-makers seek limited cooperation, but the policies they adopt for this purpose trigger changes in laws, incentives, interest group strategies, and eventually loyalties that lead to much greater integration.[47] The great diminution of national sovereignty that we have seen, the delegation of significant power to supranational bodies, and the development of some degree of popular identification with Europe rather than with individual nations were not what most of the European leaders sought at the start, but rather were the product of the institutions they established.[48] The institutions had "a life of their own" not only in binding the states more than the founders foresaw, but in changing beliefs about what is possible and desirable: they shaped as much as they reflected interests. When these processes operate, people are instruments of institutions rather than the other way around.

47. The literature on regional integration is enormous. See, for example, Karl W. Deutsch, *Political Community at the International Level* (Garden City, N.Y.: Doubleday, 1954); Ernst B. Haas, *The Uniting of Europe* (Stanford, California: Stanford University Press, 1958); Leon N. Lindberg and Stuart A. Scheingold, eds., "Regional Integration," special issue of *International Organization*, Vol. 24, No. 4 (Autumn 1970) ; Ernst B. Haas, *The Obsolescence of Regional Integration Theory* (Berkeley: Institute of International Studies, University of California, 1975); and Wayne Sandholtz, *High-Tech Europe: The Politics of International Cooperation* (Berkeley: University of California Press, 1992). For a related argument about rules for regulating the environment, see Marc Levy, "European Acid Rain: The Power of Tote-Board Diplomacy," in Peter M. Haas, Robert O. Keohane, and Marc A. Levy, eds., *Institutions for the Earth* (Cambridge, Mass.: MIT Press, 1993), pp. 75–132. For objections and rebuttals to Haas's argument, see Stanley Hoffmann, "Obstinate or Obsolete? The Fate of the Nation-State and the Case of Western Europe," *Daedalus*, Vol. 95, No. 3 (Summer 1966), pp. 862–915; Alan S. Milward, *The European Rescue of the Nation-State* (London: Routledge, 1992); and Milward, Ruggero Ranieri, Frances Lynch, F. Romero, and Vibeke Sorensen, *The Frontier of National Sovereignty: History and Theory, 1945–1992* (London: Routledge, 1993). The most thorough liberal account is Moravcsik, *The Choice for Europe*, which argues that few unintended processes were at work.

48. For a brief discussion of both the intended and unintended creation of identities, see James G. March and Johan P. Olsen, "The Institutional Dynamics of International Political Orders," *International Organization*, Vol. 52, No. 4 (Autumn 1998), pp. 960–964.

Less dramatically, arrangements developed for one purpose can be put to uses that were not originally contemplated. Thus Lisa Martin shows that Great Britain gained European support for economic sanctions against Argentina during the Falklands War by using the coordinating mechanisms and forums of the European Community.[49] These institutions had been developed to facilitate economic integration within Europe; no one had thought that they would assist one European Community member in its security policy against an outsider. But this did turn out to be the case, and their utility may have increased the faith that members (especially Great Britain) placed in them. Similarly, the consortium established to build nuclear reactors in North Korea as part of the bargain that ended the crisis with the United States in 1994 became an important venue for direct and quiet talks between North and South Korea.[50] Processes of biological evolution work in this way: many new features of plants and animals are highly adaptive when they are fully developed but, like wings on birds, they can rarely appear all at once and complete. If they are to arise, then, they must serve other functions in their half-way stages.[51]

---

49. Lisa L. Martin, "Institutions and Cooperation: Sanctions during the Falkland Islands Conflict," *International Security*, Vol. 16, No. 4 (Spring 1992), pp. 143–178. For the general argument that the development of institutional capabilities can produce unforeseen changes in behavior and preferences, see March and Olsen, "The Institutional Dynamics of International Political Orders," pp. 964–968. Martin and Simmons see unanticipated consequences (which they correctly note may not be the same as unintended ones) as a puzzle for institutional theory rather than as its strength; Martin and Simmons, "International Institutions," pp. 750–751.

50. Sigal, *Disarming Strangers*, p. 203.

51. Stephen Jay Gould, "Not Yet a Wing," *Natural History*, Vol. 94, No. 10 (October 1985), pp. 12–25. Institutions, like evolution, can also "lock in" arrangements that are sub-optimal or that advantage one party. There is also a parallel in the argument that "social capital," in the form of dense networks of groups and voluntary associations, has the unintended effect of facilitating a wide range of political and economic activities. The most prominent works are Robert D. Putnam, *Making Democracy Work: Civic Traditions in Modern Italy* (Princeton, N.J.: Princeton University Press, 1993); and Putnam, *Bowling Alone: The Collapse and Revival of American Community* (New York: Simon & Schuster,

According to Thomas Knock, Woodrow Wilson's conception of how the League of Nations would function provides a good example. He kept some of the most important provisions vague not only to defang the opposition, but also because he thought that the organization (and world politics) would evolve as problems arose and were dealt with. "The administrative constitution of the League must *grow* and not be made.... In the very process of carrying out [agreements] ... from time to time a machinery and practice of cooperation would naturally spring up which would in the end produce ... a regularly constituted and employed concert of nations."[52] The North Atlantic Treaty Organization may have developed in this manner. Although its functioning during the Cold War did not transform its members and it still retains much of its original purpose of "keeping the Russians out, the Americans in, and the Germans down,"[53] its operation has influenced beliefs and preferences at all levels of the respective governments, from the members of the bureaucracy who have a stake in its success, to foreign office officials who gained a potent new tool of joint action, to political leaders who would lose domestic or international support if they act unilaterally rather than through the institution.

More broadly, institutions can generate many different kinds of powerful feedback. For example, the Anglo-French Entente of 1904 created a dynamic that greatly increased cooperation between these

---

2000). For critical reviews of the literature, see Robert W. Jackman, "Social Capital and Politics," *Annual Review of Political Science*, Vol. 1 (Palo Alto, Calif.: Annual Reviews Press, 1998), pp. 47–74; Alejandro Portes, "Social Capital: Its Origins and Applications in Modern Sociology," *Annual Review of Sociology* (Palo Alto, Calif.: Annual Reviews Press, 1998), Vol. 24, pp. 1–24; special issue of *Political Psychology*, Vol. 19, No. 3 (September 1998).

52. Wilson quoted in Thomas Knock, *To End All Wars: Woodrow Wilson and the Quest for a New World Order* (New York: Oxford University Press, 1992), pp. 147, 127.

53. Furthermore, post–Cold War developments show the continuing importance of national conflicts and American power. Robert J. Art, "Why Western Europe Needs the United States and NATO," *Political Science Quarterly*, Vol. 111, No. 1 (Spring 1996), pp. 1–39; and Waltz, "Structural Realism after the Cold War."

countries and also between them and Russia in ways that were not initially foreseen or desired (and, as both a cause and an effect of these changes, increased Anglo-German hostility).[54] In other cases the institutions can erode the power of those who played the dominant role in establishing them by giving voice, legitimacy, and forms of influence to weak or new actors, as has proven the case with important international organizations such as the International Civil Aviation Organization and, to some extent, the UN General Assembly.[55]

Perhaps the most important path by which institutions can change preferences is through domestic politics. Drawing on liberalism, neoliberalism holds that states are not all alike and that preferences in part arise internally. To the extent that this is correct, international arrangements can alter the power, beliefs, and goals of groups in society in ways that will affect foreign relations. Thus arms control agreements can strengthen the hands of "doves"; lowered tariff barriers can drive out inefficient producers and bolster the power of advocates for still lower tariffs; and one of the less foolish arguments in favor of expanding NATO was the claim that this would give reformers in East Europe greater influence.[56]

I think we have underestimated the importance of these dynamic effects of institutions. Although the instruments of diplomacy, including institutions of the first two kinds (standard and innovative), are

---

54. Jervis, *System Effects*, pp. 146–165, 243–52.

55. Stephen D. Krasner, *Structural Conflict: The Third World against Global Liberalism* (Princeton, N.J.: Princeton University Press, 1985).

56. Helen V. Milner, *Resisting Protectionism: Global Industries and the Politics of International Trade* (Princeton, N.J.: Princeton University Press, 1988); Scott C. James and David A. Lake, "The Second Face of Hegemony: Britain's Repeal of the Corn Laws and the American Walker Tariff of 1846," *International Organization*, Vol. 43, No. 1 (Winter 1989), pp. 1–29; and Lars S. Skalnes, "From the Inside Out: NATO Expansion and International Relations Theory," *Security Studies*, Vol. 7, No. 4 (Summer 1998), pp. 44–87. Also see Keohane, "Institutional Theory and the Realist Challenge after the Cold War," p. 295. I think Martin and Simmons are too harsh when they say that "institutionalists have generally neglected the role of domestic politics." Martin and Simmons,

adequate for realizing some degree of cooperation, they are fragile and leave the world full of conflict unless they produce or are accompanied by deeper changes in what the actors want and how they conceive of their interests.[57] Many of these effects may not be expected at the time because, although states often seek to bind others and even themselves to behave in certain ways in the future, only rarely will they consciously seek to alter their own values and preferences over outcomes. So it is perhaps the unintended consequences of institutions that are not only the most interesting, but also the most powerful. This raises an obvious question for scholars, however: if we teach decisionmakers that institutions can have unintended effects, and that small steps toward cooperation may lead to limitations on national sovereignty and broad changes in politics, preferences, and values, will they hasten onward or, forewarned, instead refrain from taking these steps?

Conclusions

I have sought to clear away some of the underbrush obscuring the differences between realist and neoliberal schools of thought. Realism,

---

"Theories and Empirical Studies of International Institutions," p. 747. I am grateful to Robert Keohane for discussion on this subject.

57. Thus my analysis of the Concert of Europe that is based on defensive realism denies or at least ignores the deeper changes that Paul W. Schroeder argues had occurred. See Schroeder, "Did the Congress of Vienna Rest on a Balance of Power?" *American Historical Review*, Vol. 97, No. 3 (June 1992), pp. 683–706; and Jervis, "A Political Science Perspective on the Balance of Power and the Concert," ibid., pp. 716–724. For a fuller presentation of Schroeder's views, see Schroeder, *The Transformation of European Politics, 1763–1848* (New York: Oxford University Press, 1996). For a discussion of how international institutions can sometimes socialize their members, see the exchange between Robert Jervis and Randall L. Schweller in *International Security*, Vol. 27, No. 1 (Summer 2002); also see Alastair Iain Johnston, "Treating International Institutions as Social Environments," *International Studies Quarterly*, Vol. 45, No. 4 (December 2001), pp. 487–516. Those who stress the contrast between neorealism and social constructivism sometimes overlook Waltz's discussion of socialization, although for him it is the international system rather than institutions that are exerting this influence; Waltz, *Theory of International Politics* (Reading, Mass.: Addison-Wesley, 1979), pp. 74–76.

especially in its defensive variant, does not deny the possibility of cooperation. Cooperation does need to be explained, but it is a puzzle that needs to be explored rather than an anomaly that challenges its core, to use Kuhn's terms.[58] The existence of cooperation is not necessarily inconsistent with the realist approach, any more than the existence of conflict disconfirms neoliberalism. But neoliberals see more conflict as unnecessary and avoidable than do realists. The contrast is greater with offensive realists, who believe that the compelling nature of the international environment and the clash of states' preferences over outcomes put sharp limits on the extent to which conflict can be reduced by feasible alternative policies. Defensive realists believe that a great deal depends on the severity of the security dilemma and the intentions of the actors, which leads these scholars to a position that is not only between the other two camps but is also contingent, because prescriptions depend heavily on a diagnosis of the situation.

It is useful to ask whether changes in preferences over strategies would be sufficient to produce greater cooperation. Neoliberalism argues that this is often the case and, more specifically, that institutions are efficacious instruments for this purpose. But this raises two related questions. If institutions can bring such mutual benefit, why have states not employed them more often? Second, are institutions effects or causes? The answer to the first question may turn on a response to the second: realists usually argue that institutions are largely effects and are established when and only when decisionmakers believe that there are mutual benefits to be gained. They are tools of statecraft— important ones to be sure—but mainly a reflection of state interest. If leaders have not fully appreciated the role that institutions can play, however, scholarly research and ingenuity can lead to their deployment in situations in which they would have otherwise been neglected. Even more interestingly, when the actors have limited foresight, institutions can be autonomous not only in the sense of helping actors limit the pernicious effects of anarchy, but in more

---

58. Thomas S. Kuhn, *The Structure of Scientific Revolutions* (Chicago: University of Chicago Press, 1962).

deeply affecting actors' preferences over outcomes. They may thus shape what actors seek and want, usually in ways that were not contemplated at the start. This, it seems to me, is a very fruitful area of research, as is the related question of what our theories assume about the knowledge and expectations of the actors we are studying, whose sophistication we should not underestimate.

Chapter 9

The Progressiveness of Neoclassical Realism

Randall L. Schweller

There is no unifying, grand theory of international relations (IR), and there is little hope of ever constructing one. I am not even sure what such a theory would look like. Kenneth Waltz, whose ideas have most shaped the discipline, claims that such a theory would have to unite domestic and international politics to explain "the behavior of states, their interactions, and international outcomes." He points out that "no one has even suggested how such a grand theory can be constructed, let alone developed one."[1] No one has attempted such a task because it is an impossible one. Who can imagine a theory that would explain the origins and settlements of crises and war, as well as issues of international trade and finance; one that could be usefully applied to explain the Nazi-Soviet pact of August 1939, as well as the European Community's agricultural policy reform?

Leaving aside the problem of its comprehensiveness, a unified IR theory would have to specify necessary causes of international outcomes and national behavior, not merely sufficient ones. No IR theory even remotely fits this description, even for specific issue-areas within the subfields of the discipline. Consider, for instance, the issue of war and peace. There are competing theories about the causes of war at every level of analysis. This is as it should be. For just as there are many sufficient causes of death but no necessary ones, there is no single cause of war, and no one should bother searching for one.

---

1. Kenneth N. Waltz, "International Politics Is Not Foreign Policy," *Security Studies*, Vol. 6, No. 1 (Autumn 1996), p. 57. For a more sanguine view, see Colin Elman, "Horses For Courses: Why *Not* Neorealist Theories of Foreign Policy?" in ibid., pp. 7–53.

With no realistic chance of creating anything approaching a unified theory of international relations, the field is instead composed of islands of theory on various matters residing within the immense domain of world politics: alliances, trade and monetary relations, supranational institutions, polarity and war, economic inter-dependence, crisis diplomacy, deterrence, etc.[2] While this fragmented state of the discipline is not ideal, it is not entirely unsatisfactory either: it avoids the risks (and they are significant ones) of having all our IR eggs in one theoretical basket. Moreover, progress—defined as "an increasing ability to explain and connect complex phenomena"—can still be made.[3] There is every reason to expect that some of these small islands of theory will someday be tied together into more definitive and broader explanations. Indeed, progress in IR theory can be measured in precisely this way: by how far the discipline moves from these tiny islands to larger bodies of land, perhaps even to continents of theory. But no matter how much progress is made, there will always be vast oceans separating even the most fully developed areas of theory.[4]

The question then becomes: how do we know when an attempt to move from an island to a continent has been successful? If theoretical progress in the discipline is the development of more powerful theories that have greater explanatory range with little sacrifice of parsimony and elegance, can Lakatos's methodology of scientific research programs be usefully applied to IR theory? For several

---

2. The "islands of theory" metaphor is borrowed from Harold Guetzkow, "Long Range Research in International Relations," in John A. Vasquez, ed., *Classics of International Relations*, 3rd ed. (Upper Saddle River, N.J.: Prentice Hall, 1996), pp. 70, 73.

3. John S. Dryzek, "The Progress of Political Science," *The Journal of Politics*, Vol. 48, No. 2 (May 1986), p. 301.

4. Harold Guetzkow, writing in 1950, was fairly optimistic about the field's ability "to construct an integrated set of theories about international relations." Indeed, he envisioned a central program administered by an "integrating team," whose task it was to coordinate and bring together the research of specialized centers into a developing global theory. Guetzkow, "Long Range Research," p. 73.

reasons, I think not. First, there are many facts in international relations, but little agreement about their causes, even within so-called research programs. Second, there is little consensus on what constitutes an IR research program. Is neorealism a research program? What about classical realism, neoliberal institutionalism, constructivism, and neoculturalism? What are their hard cores, positive and negative heuristics, and protective belts of theories, in Lakatos's terms? Does anyone reasonably believe that a fieldwide consensus can be reached on these issues? With the possible exception of Waltzian neorealism and John Mearsheimer's offensive realism, none of the field's various "isms" represents a fully articulated theory of international relations.[5] They are, instead, vaguely conceptualized "perspectives" or political philosophies rooted in and guided by beliefs about "what matters" and what requires explanation in international affairs. As a result, they tend to focus on very different types of issues.

Even Waltz's neorealist theory, though extraordinarily important to the development of the field, may not qualify as a research program. This is because Waltz brilliantly said everything that can be usefully said about neorealism; there is no way to improve or amend Waltz's theory without violating its structural-systemic nature and, in so doing, confounding the theory's highly deductive and internally consistent logic. For this reason, neorealism has never been, as is commonly assumed, a fertile research program. There cannot be any theoretical reformulations of neorealism, only extended applications of its logic to various historical cases. The problem here, however, is that neorealism's causal variable (polarity) has changed only twice: the system moved from multipolarity to bipolarity in 1945, and from bipolarity to unipolarity in 1989, a change the theory does not predict because unipolarity is a non-balance-of-power system. This severely limits its applicability to historical cases. Moreover, the theory cannot explain specific events or foreign policy. There is nothing left for neorealists to do that Waltz has not already done.

---

5. As presented in Kenneth N. Waltz, *Theory of International Politics* (Reading, Mass.: Addison-Wesley, 1979); John J. Mearsheimer, *The Tragedy of Great Power Politics* (New York: Norton, 2001).

Third, how do we decide what constitutes a novel fact in IR theory, and which of the several definitions of a novel fact should be used to make this determination?[6] Fourth, lacking any external, objective criteria and measures of what constitutes a successful research program, how do we decide whether a research program is progressing or degenerating, and who decides? In practice, as Robert Jervis points out, research programs "are notoriously difficult to confirm or disconfirm": the relevant judgments are influenced by (1) "our perspectives and interests (in both senses of the term)," (2) current events and the social context that define the empirical problems for political inquiry, and (3) "our general political orientations." Ultimately, which research program thrives and which one dies on the vine has more to do with what kinds of theories we find intellectually and politically appealing—often because they reaffirm our preexisting beliefs about the world—than "the extent to which it produces propositions that anticipate and fit with empirical facts."[7]

Finally, it is useless (if not pointless) to judge research programs by Lakatosian standards, for, as John Dryzek avers, "it is clear that none of the major existing perspectives in political science truly meets the standards of a successful Lakatosian research program. That is, none of

---

6. For an insightful discussion and review of this issue, see Colin Elman, "Neocultural Progress? A Preliminary Discussion of Lakatos's Methodology of Scientific Research Programs," paper presented at the 1997 Annual Meeting of the American Political Science Association, Washington, D.C., August 28–31, 1997. Also see Elman and Elman, Chapters 1 and 2 in this volume.

7. Robert Jervis, "Realism in World Politics," in Peter J. Katzenstein, Robert O. Keohane, Stephen D. Krasner, eds., "*International Organization* at Fifty: Exploration and Contestation in the Study of World Politics," a special issue of *International Organization*, Vol. 52, No. 4 (Autumn 1998), pp. 972–73, 975. Similarly, Dryzek argues that progress, defined as a series of stable, rational choices between competing theories, research programs, or research traditions within a discipline, "cannot occur in political science because any comparisons among research traditions can only proceed in the context of a set of empirical problems which are socially determined. Political scientists have a say in this determination—but so does the larger society in which political science is embedded. The rationality of any choice among research traditions is therefore historically contingent." Dryzek, "The Progress of Political Science," p. 301.

these perspectives has yielded a series of theories of increased empirical explanatory power, with each theory incorporating its predecessor in the series and predicting novel facts."[8]

Is Neoclassical Realism a Progressive Research Program?

Setting aside Lakatos's methodology of scientific research programs, four commonsense criteria may be used to judge whether a particular piece of IR scholarship or an entire research program represents progress or not. First, does the research ask interesting and important questions, raising, for example, new theoretical or empirical puzzles? Second, are plausible and compelling answers to these questions provided, that is, are the hypotheses and the theory or research program in which they are embedded reasonably supported by the evidence? Third, is the methodology employed consistent with the broad canons of evidence and argument in the social sciences? In the absence of precise operational details, this criterion is rather tricky to apply, especially with regard to post-positivist and related forms of critical theory.[9] Nevertheless, scientific progress cannot be achieved without widely accepted methods of evaluating the truth of statements. And fourth, when evaluating an entire research program or body of theory, we must ask a basic Lakatosian question: is the research program producing cumulative knowledge? After all, cumulative knowledge is the *sine qua non* of scientific progress.

In practice, even these relatively weak demands might be too stringent: simply raising extraordinarily important questions may be enough to qualify as progress. Indeed, classic works in political science typically advanced new and important theoretical questions and just as

---

8. Dryzek, "Progress in Political Science," p. 304.

9. For a lucid discussion of these issues, see Ted Hopf, "The Promise of Constructivism in International Relations Theory," *International Security*, Vol. 23, No. 1 (Summer 1998), pp. 171–200.

often failed to offer persuasive explanations for these puzzles.[10] Surely, some of these classic works contributed to progress in IR theory.

In this vein, a new school of realism, variously called neoclassical or neotraditional realism, has attempted to place the rich but scattered ideas and untested assertions of early realist works within a more theoretically rigorous framework. In his recent review of the neoclassical realist literature, Gideon Rose offers the following characterization of the school:

It explicitly incorporates both external and internal variables.... Its adherents argue that the scope and ambition of a country's foreign policy [are] driven first and foremost by its place in the international system and specifically by its relative material power capabilities. This is why they are realist. They argue further, however, that the impact of such power capabilities on foreign policy is indirect and complex, because systemic pressures must be translated through intervening variables at the unit level. This is why they are neoclassical.[11]

There are several reasons for neoclassical realism's emergence, but the primary one is that structural realism (Waltzian neorealism) is

---

10. A good example of this is Edward Hallett Carr, *The Twenty Years' Crisis, 1919–1939: An Introduction to the Study of International Relations* (London: Macmillan, 1939). Despite its lack of a coherent overarching theory, Carr's book remains one of the most important works in the field because of its many innovative but theoretically undeveloped insights about the problems associated with international order and peaceful change. Another example is Frank L. Klingberg's compelling discovery of alternating U.S. foreign policy mood swings from introversion, lasting roughly 22 years, to extroversion, lasting 27 years, which he could not explain. See Klingberg, "The Historical Alternation of Moods in American Foreign Policy," *World Politics*, Vol. 4, No. 2 (January 1952), pp. 239–273. For an attempt to explain these Klingberg cycles of U.S. foreign policy, see Brian M. Pollins and Randall L. Schweller, "Linking the Levels: The Long Wave and Shifts in U.S. Foreign Policy, 1790–1993," *American Journal of Political Science*, Vol. 43, No. 2 (April 1999), pp. 431–464.

11. Gideon Rose, "Neoclassical Realism and Theories of Foreign Policy," *World Politics*, Vol. 51, No. 1 (October 1998), p. 146. Rose refers to Thomas Christensen, Aaron Friedberg, Randall Schweller, William Wohlforth, and Fareed Zakaria as neoclassical realists; this essay adheres to Rose's list, which seems correct to me.

strictly a theory of international politics, which, accordingly, makes no claim to explain foreign policy or specific historical events. Recognizing this limitation, a new breed of realist scholars has embraced the richer formulations of traditional, pre-Waltzian realists, who focused more on foreign policy than systemic-level phenomena. While not abandoning Waltz's insights about international structure and its consequences, neo-classical realists have added first and second image variables (e.g., domestic politics, internal extraction capacity and processes, state power and intentions, and leaders' perceptions of the relative distribution of capabilities and of the offense-defense balance) to explain foreign policy decision making and intrinsically important historical puzzles.

Using the commonsense criteria listed above, the new school of neoclassical realism represents progress within the realist research tradition. Neoclassical realists emphasize problem-focused research that (1) seeks to clarify and extend the logic of basic (classical and structural) realist propositions, (2) employs the case-study method to test general theories, explain cases, and generate hypotheses, (3) incorporates first, second, and third image variables, (4) addresses important questions about foreign policy and national behavior, and (5) has produced a body of cumulative knowledge.

A partial list of theoretical questions explored by neoclassical realism includes: Under what conditions do nations expand their political interests abroad?[12] What is the relationship between a nation's external behavior and its domestic mobilization?[13] How do political elites perceive and think about power in world politics?[14] How do

---

12. Fareed Zakaria, *From Wealth to Power: The Unusual Origins of America's World Role* (Princeton, N.J.: Princeton University Press, 1998).

13. Thomas J. Christensen, *Useful Adversaries: Grand Strategy, Domestic Mobilization, and Sino-American Conflict, 1947–1958* (Princeton, N.J.: Princeton University Press, 1996).

14. William C. Wohlforth, *The Elusive Balance: Power and Perceptions During the Cold War* (Ithaca, N.Y.: Cornell University Press, 1993).

states assess and adapt to changes in their relative power?[15] How do states respond to threats and opportunities in their external environment, and do different kinds of states respond in different ways?[16] What explains variation in state alliance strategies, whether they choose to balance, buck-pass, bandwagon, chain-gang, or avoid alliances altogether?[17]

In their examinations of these questions, which lie outside the scope of neorealist theory, neoclassical realists have not rejected systemic theory but instead incorporated its insights. As Zakaria suggests, "a good account of a nation's foreign policy should include systemic, domestic, and other influences, specifying what aspects of policy can be explained by what factors."[18] Likewise, Jack Snyder writes: "Theoretically, Realism must be recaptured from those who look only at politics between societies, ignoring what goes on within societies. Realists are right in stressing power, interests, and coalition making as the central elements in a theory of politics, but recent exponents of

---

15. Aaron L. Friedberg, *The Weary Titan: Britain and the Experience of Relative Decline, 1895–1905* (Princeton, N.J.: Princeton University Press, 1988); Zakaria, *From Wealth to Power*. Friedberg investigates this question from the perspective of a declining power, while Zakaria studies a rising power.

16. Randall L. Schweller, *Deadly Imbalances: Tripolarity and Hitler's Strategy of World Conquest* (New York: Columbia University Press, 1998), chap. 3; and Aaron L. Friedberg, *In the Shadows of the Garrison State: America's Anti-Statism and its Cold War Grand Strategy* (Princeton, N.J.: Princeton University Press, 2000).

17. Thomas J. Christensen and Jack Snyder, "Chain Gangs and Passed Bucks: Predicting Alliance Patterns In Multipolarity," *International Organization*, Vol. 44, No. 2 (Spring 1990), pp. 137–168; Thomas J. Christensen, "Perceptions and Alliances in Europe, 1865–1940," *International Organization*, Vol. 51, No. 1 (Winter 1997), pp. 65–98; Randall L. Schweller, "Bandwagoning For Profit: Bringing the Revisionist State Back In," *International Security*, Vol. 19, No. 1 (Summer 1994), pp. 72–107.

18. Fareed Zakaria, "Realism and Domestic Politics: A Review Essay," *International Security*, Vol. 17, No. 1 (Summer 1992), p. 198. For further elaboration, see Jennifer Sterling-Folker, "Realist Environment, Liberal Process, and Domestic-Level Variables," *International Studies Quarterly*, Vol. 41, No. 1 (March 1997), pp. 1–25.

Realism in international relations have been wrong in looking exclusively to states as the irreducible atoms whose power and interests are to be assessed."[19]

In Waltz's eyes, theories that combine systemic and sub-systemic causal variables tend to be reductionist in the sense that they rely on national or sub-national attributes or processes to explain international outcomes. While this may be true, one cannot explain international outcomes (let alone foreign policy) solely by reference to systemic-level variables. Such a theory would have to posit strict situational determinism—a "straitjacket" or "single exit" notion of international structure—that leaves actors with no other choice but to act as they did, such that no outcome can occur other than the one predicted by the theory.[20]

Waltz clearly does not subscribe to such a view. Instead, international structure (anarchy and the systemwide distribution of capabilities) provides only "a set of constraining conditions" for state action. The external environment, in Waltz's words, "can tell us what pressures are exerted and what possibilities are posed by systems of different structure, but it cannot tell us just how, and how effectively, the units of a system will respond to those pressures and possibilities."[21] Thus, "each state arrives at policies and decides on actions according to its own internal processes, but its decisions are shaped by the very presence of other states as well as by interactions with them."[22]

The key point is that Waltzian neorealism makes no assertions about what domestic processes look like, where they come from, and how they influence the way nations assess and adapt to changes in their environment; this is precisely why, as Jennifer Sterling-Folker astutely observes, it "is realist systemic theory, and not liberal systemic

[handwritten margin note: Waltz on role of the stok]

19. Jack Snyder, *Myths of Empire: Domestic Politics and International Ambition* (Ithaca, N.Y.: Cornell University Press, 1991), p. 19.

20. Spiro J. Latsis, "Situational Determinism in Economics," *British Journal for the Philosophy of Science*, Vol. 23 (1972), pp. 207–245.

21. Waltz, *Theory of International Politics*, p. 71.

22. Ibid., pp. 73, 65.

theory as is commonly assumed, that can incorporate domestic-level processes as causal variables in a consistent and rigorously deductive manner."[23] In other words, because "the anarchic environment does not automatically induce effective imitations of seemingly successful processes," Sterling-Folker points out, "systemic realism incorporates process-based theorizing without raising any deductive inconsistencies."[24] Her logic is straightforward: "While the anarchic environment encourages the goal of survival and comparative assessments of process, it is domestic process that is responsible for the ability of states to emulate the processes of others. Thus it is domestic process that acts as the final arbiter for state survival within the anarchic environment."[25]

Rather than inferring the conditions of international politics from the internal composition of states, which would indeed be reductionist as Waltz claims, neoclassical realists explore the "internal processes" by which states "arrive at policies and decide on actions" in response to the pressures and opportunities in their external environment.[26] By incorporating insights and propositions derived from realist systemic theory, neoclassical realism conforms to the traditional view of scientific progress by accumulation, whereby "theories are formulated, verified, and then added to the accumulated stockpile of true theory."[27]

Theories of International Politics and Foreign Policy

Theories of international relations are typically categorized according to "levels of analysis" or the location of the independent variable: whether the unit of analysis of the causal variable is the international system, nation-state, bureaucracy, or individual decision maker. IR

---

23. Sterling-Folker, "Realist Environment," p. 22.

24. Ibid., p. 19.

25. Ibid., pp. 19, 21.

26. For an insightful discussion of systemic realism and the deductive underpinnings for domestic theorizing, see ibid., pp. 16–22.

27. Dryzek, "The Progress of Political Science," 302.

theories may also be classified according to their dependent variables, or the type of phenomena they seek to explain. Here, the most fundamental distinction is between theories of international politics, sometimes called systems theories, and those of foreign policy. In Waltz's view:

Systems theories explain why different units behave similarly and, despite their variations, produce outcomes that fall within expected ranges. Conversely, theories at the unit level tell us why different units behave differently despite their similar placement in a system. A theory of foreign policy is a theory at the national level. It leads to expectations about the responses that dissimilar polities will make to external pressures. A theory of international politics bears on the foreign policies of nations while claiming to explain only certain aspects of them. It can tell us what international conditions national policies have to cope with.[28]

A theory of international politics can explain the outcomes of international events and account for the results, often unintended, of nations' efforts, "but not the motives of nations; it must instead make assumptions about them," notes Fareed Zakaria. By contrast, a theory of foreign policy explains why different states, or the same state at different historical moments, have different intentions, goals, and preferences toward the outside world.... [It] sheds light on the reasons for a nation's efforts."[29]

This neat conceptual division between theories of international politics and theories of foreign policy is virtually unchallenged within the discipline. However, it obstructs opportunities for further advances in knowledge; moreover, it is unsustainable on logical grounds, and it has been a primary source of confusion about theory evaluation and testing. It is unproductive and illogical because, to move beyond mere correlational observations, theories of international politics must specify the hypothesized linkages between purported systemic-level causes and the alleged unit-level responses to such external stimuli. Lamenting the problem of underspecified causal linkages that has

---

28. Waltz, *Theory of International Politics*, p. 72.
29. Zakaria, *From Wealth to Power*, p. 14.

need to show links between systemic conditions + system behavior

plagued systems theories, J. David Singer declares that "unless one can illuminate the decisional links between the environmental conditions and the behavior of the nations making up that system, any model of systemic effects on the incidence of war must remain less than complete."[30]

The division between theories of international politics and theories of foreign policy creates problems with theory testing and evaluation, because our confidence in an explanation rests on its fit with the actual behavior of states under the conditions specified by the theory. Thus, even systems theories must investigate historical cases of state behavior and foreign policy to see if the actors spoke and acted in the manner predicted by the explanation, the case unfolded and events occurred in the order predicted, and the details of the case conform to the explanation's predictions.[31]

Classical Realism and Neorealism: Similarities and Differences

There are many theories, competing and complementary, within the realist perspective, each derived from the same first principles and basic set of assumptions.[32]

---

30. J. David Singer, "System Structure, Decision Processes, and the Incidence of International War," in Manus I. Midlarsky, ed., *Handbook of War Studies* (Boston: Unwin Hyman, 1989), p. 8.

31. Even though the purpose of systems theory is to explain unintended consequences, this method of evaluation is still appropriate and necessary: to say that an outcome was unintended or the result of structural constraints requires specification of what the state actually intended to accomplish in the first place or would have desired had it not been structurally constrained.

32. For recent discussions of the core assumptions and basic principles of realism and of the distinctions between the various strands of realism (e.g., defensive, offensive, classical, neoclassical, and structural), see Jeffrey W. Taliaferro, "Security Seeking Under Anarchy: Defensive Realism Revisited," *International Security*, Vol. 25, No. 3 (Winter 2000/01), pp. 128–161; Randall L. Schweller and David Priess, "A Tale of Two Realisms: Expanding the Institutions Debate," *Mershon International Studies Review*, Vol. 41, Supplement 1 (May 1997), pp. 1–32; Stephen G. Brooks, "Dueling Realisms," *International Organization*, Vol. 51, No. 3 (Summer 1997), pp. 445–477; Rose, "Neoclassical

Broadly speaking, realism is a political philosophy or worldview that is profoundly pessimistic about the human condition, moral progress, and the capacity of human reason to create a world of peace and harmony. Accordingly, realist first principles assert that: (1) humankind cannot transcend conflict through the progressive power of reason to discover a science of peace;[33] realists of all stripes "share a skeptical attitude toward schemes for pacific international order";[34] (2) politics are not a function of ethics—morality is instead the product of power and material interests;[35] and (3) necessity and reason of state trump morality and ethics when these values conflict.[36] Unlike Kantians (liberal universalists) or Grotians (legal institutionalists), realists believe either that foreign policy takes place in a moral and legal vacuum, or that moral behavior in foreign policy resides in the state's self-assertion. As a normative theory of state behavior, realism prescribes "that power considerations indeed should lie at the heart of policy; that things go wrong when these crucial factors are ignored or not given the weight they deserve."[37]

Realism and Theories of Foreign Policy"; and Jeffrey Legro and Andrew Moravcsik, "Is Anybody Still a Realist?" *International Security*, Vol. 24, No. 2 (Fall 1999), pp. 5–55. Also see Benjamin Frankel, ed., "Realism: Restatements and Renewal," special issue of *Security Studies*, Vol. 5, No. 3 (Spring 1996); Daniel Deudney, "Dividing Realism: Structural Realism versus Security Materialism on Nuclear Security and Proliferation," *Security Studies*, Vol. 2, Nos. 3/4 (Summer 1993), pp. 117–136; Michael E. Brown, Sean M. Lynn-Jones, and Steven E. Miller, eds., *The Perils of Anarchy: Contemporary Realism and International Security* (Cambridge, Mass.: MIT Press, 1995).

33. Hans J. Morgenthau, *Scientific Man vs. Power Politics* (Chicago: The University of Chicago Press, 1946), chap. 8, pp. 90–95.

34. Michael W. Doyle, *Ways of War and Peace: Realism, Liberalism, and Socialism* (New York and London: Norton, 1997), p. 43.

35. Carr, *The Twenty Years' Crisis*, pp. 63–64.

36. Arnold Wolfers, "Political Theory and International Relations," in Wolfers, *Discord and Collaboration: Essays on International Politics* (Baltimore: Johns Hopkins Press, 1962), p. 244.

37. Marc Trachtenberg, "Peace and the Pursuit of Power: Book Review of Paul W. Schroeder, *The Transformation of European Politics, 1763–1848*," *Orbis*, Vol. 40, No. 4 (Winter 1996), p. 159.

These recurrent pessimistic themes, more than any specific proposition or testable hypothesis, make it possible to speak of a tradition of realist thought that includes Thucydides, Machiavelli, Hobbes, Hegel, Rousseau, Weber, Aron, Kissinger, Waltz, and Mearsheimer.[38] Rejecting the notion of a natural harmony of interests in human and international affairs, all political realists, whether philosophers or scientists, are cynical about the prospect of developing more peaceful relations among humans and nation-states than has been characteristic of the past.[39]

Realism's hard core of assumptions do not—contrary to conventional wisdom—include rationality. Indeed, both Hans Morgenthau and Kenneth Waltz, considered the preeminent theorists of modern-day realism, reject the claim that states necessarily act rationally to achieve intended goals, which themselves may not be rational in terms of the actual opportunities and constraints presented by the external environment in which they are embedded.[40] Neorealism is *not* a rationalist theory of state behavior.[41] Waltz explicitly asserts that his "theory requires no assumptions of rationality" because structure affects state behavior primarily through

38. See Michael Joseph Smith, *Realist Thought From Weber to Kissinger* (Baton Rouge: Louisiana State University Press, 1986).

39. Specifically, realists see international politics as a perpetual struggle for security, prestige, and power and influence, that is, control over territory, the behavior of other states, and the world economy. See Robert Gilpin, *War and Change in World Politics* (New York: Cambridge University Press, 1981), pp. 23–25.

40. For the mistaken notion that basic realist theory assumes rationality, see Legro and Moravcsik, "Is Anybody Still a Realist?"; Robert O. Keohane, "Theory of World Politics," in Robert O. Keohane, ed., *Neorealism and Its Critics* (New York: Columbia University Press, 1986), pp. 164–165; and Joseph M. Grieco, "Realist International Theory and the Study of World Politics," in Michael Doyle and G. John Ikenberry, eds., *New Thinking In International Relations Theory* (Boulder, Colo.: Westview Press, 1997), chap. 7.

41. Robert Keohane's widely accepted claim that rationality is one of three key assumptions that define the "hard core" of the "Classical Realist research program" is simply incorrect. Keohane, "Theory of World Politics," pp. 164–65.

the processes of socialization and competition.[42] In Waltz's words, "one cannot expect of political leaders the nicely calculated decisions that the word 'rationality' suggests."[43] Likewise, Morgenthau's writings are conspicuous for their heated rejections of both rationalist inquiry and the possibility of creating a political "science."[44]

What, then, are realism's core assumptions? I propose three fundamental assumptions, which, I believe, distinguish realism from all other IR perspectives and are common to all realist theories: that conflict groups are the key actors in world politics; that power is the fundamental feature of international politics; and that the essential nature of international politics is conflictual.

CONFLICT GROUPS ARE THE KEY ACTORS IN WORLD POLITICS

In Robert Gilpin's words: "The essence of social reality is the group. The building blocks and ultimate units of social and political life are not the individuals of liberal thought nor the classes of Marxism [but rather] 'conflict groups'."[45] These conflict groups—states, city-states,

---

42. Waltz, *Theory of International Politics*, 118. This point is also made by Miles Kahler, "Rationality in International Relations," *International Organization*, Vol. 52, No. 4 (Autumn 1998), p. 925.

43. Kenneth N. Waltz, "Reflections on *Theory of International Politics*: A Response to My Critics," in Keohane, *Neorealism and Its Critics*, 330–31. In fact, Waltz's balance of power theory makes only two basic assumptions: that states are the primary actors in international politics, and that states are unitary actors. Anarchy is not an assumption but rather a scope condition, that is, an initial condition required for his theory to work. In addition, Waltz claims that balance of power politics requires that the anarchic order be populated by some units (more than one) wishing to survive. See Waltz, *Theory of International Politics*, p. 121.

44. For insightful discussion of this point, see Ashley J. Tellis, "Reconstructing Political Realism: The Long March to Scientific Theory," *Security Studies*, Vol. 5, No. 2 (Winter 1996), pp. 39–51.

45. Robert Gilpin, "The Richness of the Tradition of Political Realism," in Keohane, *Neorealism and Its Critics*, pp. 304–305; and Gilpin, "No One Loves a Political Realist," *Security Studies*, Vol. 5, No. 3 (Spring 1996), p. 7.

tribes, principalities, etc.—are assumed to be unitary, but not necessarily rational, actors.[46]

POWER IS THE FUNDAMENTAL FEATURE OF INTERNATIONAL POLITICS

Power is required to secure any national goal, whether world mastery or simply to be left alone. Estimates of relative power are the currency of diplomatic bargaining and, for that matter, the whole of international politics. Consequently, all war aims are simply varieties of power. As Geoffrey Blainey crisply observes: "The conflicting aims of rival nations are always conflicts of power. Not only is power the issue at stake, but the decision to resolve the issue by peaceful or warlike methods is largely determined by assessments of relative power."[47]

THE ESSENTIAL NATURE OF INTERNATIONAL POLITICS IS CONFLICTUAL

Realists envision a world of continual positional competition among groups under conditions of general scarcity, whether it be material

---

46. Unlike Legro and Moravcsik, I do not believe that conflict groups must have sovereign control over a given territorial jurisdiction to be properly viewed as realism's units of analysis (or primary actors). Legro and Moravcsik argue, in other words, that conflict groups that do not possess a monopoly of legitimate force within specified territorial jurisdictions (e.g., competing ethnic groups or warlords in a stateless society) are inconsistent with realism's assumption of who the primary actors are in the theory. See Legro and Moravcsik, "Is Anybody Still a Realist?" Legro and Moravcsik's formulation of realism's "conflict group" assumption severely limits the scope of realist theory, preventing it, for instance, from being applied to domestic group conflicts; they provide no compelling theoretical or conceptual justification for making group sovereignty a core realist assumption. Realist concepts such as the security dilemma have recently been applied with great success to ethnic conflicts sparked precisely by conflicting sovereignty claims among rival groups. See Barry R. Posen, "The Security Dilemma and Ethnic Conflict," in Michael E. Brown, ed., *Ethnic Conflict and International Security* (Princeton, N.J.: Princeton University Press, 1993), pp. 103–124.

47. Geoffrey Blainey, *The Causes of War*, 3rd ed. (New York: Free Press, 1988), p. 150.

resources, security, or social resources such as prestige, leadership, and status.[48] This is not to say that realism denies the possibility (or the existence) of international cooperation; politics, by definition, must contain elements of both common and conflicting interests, of collaboration and discord. Instead, the realm of international politics is characterized by persistent distributional conflicts that are "closely linked to power as both an instrument and a stake."[49] It is in this sense that realism describes an essentially zero-sum world of positional competition. By positional I mean that what counts is not the actors' absolute skills or capabilities but how they perform relative to their opponents. In such situations, a change in the absolute capability of any actor (holding constant the remaining actors' capabilities) has important effects not only for that player but also for the other competitors.[50] By competition I mean that the constitutive units of the system engage in—indeed they cannot avoid—strategic interaction, which, in turn, shapes their goals and strategies.

Realists disagree, however, over the precise nature of these state interests. It is now standard practice to divide realists into two camps—offensive (or aggressive) realists and defensive realists—

---

48. "A world without struggle would be a world in which life had ceased to exist." Nicholas John Spykman, *America's Strategy in World Politics: The United States and the Balance of Power* (New York: Harcourt, Brace and Company, 1942), p. 12. For a discussion of realism and social scarcity, especially prestige, leadership, and status concerns, see Randall L. Schweller, "Realism and the Present Great Power System: Growth and Positional Conflict Over Scarce Resources," in Ethan B. Kapstein and Michael Mastanduno, eds., *Unipolar Politics: Realism and State Strategies After the Cold War* (New York: Columbia University Press, 1999), chap. 2.

49. Robert Jervis, "Realism, Neoliberalism, and Cooperation: Understanding the Debate," *International Security*, Vol. 24, No. 1 (Summer 1999), pp. 44–45; also see Robert Jervis, Chapter 8 in this volume.

50. See Thomas C. Schelling, "Hockey Helmets, Daylight Saving, and Other Binary Choices," in Schelling, *Micromotives and Macrobehavior* (New York: Norton, 1978), chap. 7; and Robert H. Frank, "Positional Externalities," in Richard J. Zeckhauser, ed., *Strategy and Choice* (Cambridge, Mass.: MIT Press, 1991), pp. 25–47.

according to their views on this point.[51] Offensive realists claim that, because security and survival can never be assured and others' intentions can never be known for certain and, even if they could, can change over time, anarchy compels states to attempt to maximize their relative power and influence (thereby climbing the ladder of power) at all times and in all places whenever the benefits of doing so outweigh the costs. In this view, all states harbor revisionist intentions with hegemony as their ultimate goal; only hegemons, which are quite rare in history, are satisfied, status-quo powers.[52] In contrast, defensive realists argue that states are less concerned to make relative gains and to maximize their power than they are to avoid relative losses (to maintain their position within the hierarchy of power) and to maximize their security: states are said to be "defensive positionalists" who seek to preserve the existing balance of power.[53] Notwithstanding

---

51. The terms "aggressive" realism and "defensive" realism first appeared in Jack Snyder, *Myths of Empire*, pp. 11–12. For insightful overviews of offensive and defensive realism, see Benjamin Frankel, ed., "Restating the Realist Case: An Introduction," special issue of *Security Studies*, Vol. 5, No. 3 (Spring 1996), pp. xiv–xx; Frankel, "The Reading List," in Frankel, "Realism: Restatement and Renewal," pp. 186–88; Colin Elman, "Horses for Courses"; Sean M. Lynn-Jones, "Realism and America's Rise: A Review Essay," *International Security*, Vol. 23, No. 2 (Fall 1998), pp. 170–78; and Sean M. Lynn-Jones and Steven E. Miller, "Preface," in Brown, Lynn-Jones, and Miller, *The Perils of Anarchy*, pp. ix–xii.

52. The definitive work on offensive realism is Mearsheimer, *The Tragedy of Great Power Politics*. Other examples of offensive realism include John J. Mearsheimer, "Back to the Future: Instability in Europe after the Cold War," *International Security*, Vol. 15, No. 1 (Summer 1990), pp. 5–56; Randall L. Schweller, "Neorealism's Status-Quo Bias: What Security Dilemma?" *Security Studies*, Vol. 5, No. 3 (Spring 1996), pp. 90–121; Samuel P. Huntington, "Why International Primacy Matters," *International Security*, Vol. 17, No. 4 (Spring 1993), pp. 68–83; Zakaria, *From Wealth to Power*; and Eric J. Labs, "Beyond Victory: Offensive Realism and the Expansion of War Aims," *Security Studies*, Vol. 6, No. 4 (Summer 1997), pp. 1–49.

53. Joseph M. Grieco coined the term "defensive positionalists"; see Grieco, *Cooperation Among Nations: Europe, America, and Non-tariff Barriers to Trade* (Ithaca, N.Y.: Cornell University Press, 1990). Examples of defensive realism include Robert Jervis, "Cooperation Under the Security Dilemma," *World*

their differences regarding state interest and motivation, both offensive and defensive realists agree that the systemic imperatives of anarchy require states to view their gains and losses in relative, not absolute, terms. Therefore, I argue, both camps essentially posit a world of positional competition (a claim that is obvious for offensive realists, but admittedly less so for defensive realists). Consider, however, that the theoretical foundation for defensive realism is the security dilemma, which asserts that efforts to increase a state's security often decrease the security of others. Is this not zero-sum positional competition *par excellence*?

In summary, all self-described realists share the conviction that anarchy is a persistent condition that cannot be transcended, and that states (the primary conflict group in the modern epoch of world politics) will continue to struggle, as they have always done, for material capabilities, political influence, security, prestige, and other scarce material and social resources. Seen in this light, political realism is not only a predictive and explanatory theory about international politics but also a prescriptive theory of "pragmatic" foreign or external policy. Realism tells us how the "competitive" state or other conflict group can best advance its interests, whether economic, territorial, security, ideological, or political in nature. These interests are largely a function of the relative power and placement of the given conflict group in either the international or domestic realms.[54]

Politics, Vol. 30, No. 2 (January 1978), pp. 167–214; Stephen Van Evera, *Causes of War: Power and the Roots of Conflict* (Ithaca, N.Y.: Cornell University Press, 1999); Van Evera, "Offense, Defense, and the Causes of War," *International Security*, Vol. 22, No. 4 (Spring 1998), pp. 5–43; Stephen M. Walt, *The Origins of Alliances* (Ithaca: Cornell University Press, 1987); Walt, *Revolution and War* (Ithaca, N.Y.: Cornell University Press, 1996); Snyder, *Myths of Empire*; Charles L. Glaser, "Realists as Optimists: Cooperation as Self-Help," *International Security*, Vol. 19, No. 3 (Winter 1994/95), pp. 50–90; and Taliaferro, "Security Seeking Under Anarchy."

54. Exemplars of this realist approach include Machiavelli's *The Prince* and *The Discourses*; Weber's concern for the character and quality of leadership, which runs through all of his work; and Henry Kissinger's *A World Restored* and *Diplomacy*, in which he draws attention to the need for creative diplomacy to preserve international equilibrium and legitimacy. Niccolo Machiavelli, *The*

Disagreements within the realist tradition arise from basic philosophical differences, from placing emphasis on different assumptions or, more often, from varying interpretations of the preceding assumptions. Six major differences divide classical realists and neorealists.[55] First, there is philosophical disagreement about the roots of realism. Specifically, which discipline(s) should realist theory be grounded in and draw most heavily from? Traditional realism is rooted in sociology and history (with some attention to psychology, theology, and economics); neorealism borrows most heavily from microeconomics.[56] Second, traditional realists view power as an end in itself; states define their interests in terms of power and seek to maximize power as well as their security.[57] Neorealists believe that security is the highest end.[58] Third, the basic causal variables are not the same for traditional realists and neorealists. Traditional realists posit that power and the interests of states (whether they seek to revise or instead to preserve the status-quo order) drive national behavior; neorealists examine only anarchy and the distribution of capabilities.

Prince and the Discourses, trans. Christian Detmold (New York: Modern Library, 1950). For illuminating discussions of Weber's work, see David Beetham, *Max Weber and the Theory of Modern Politics* (London: George Allen and Unwin, 1974); Raymond Aron, "Max Weber and Power Politics," in Otto Stammer, ed., *Max Weber and Sociology Today* (New York: Harper Torchbooks, 1971); and Smith, *Realist Thought from Weber to Kissinger*, chap. 2. See Henry A. Kissinger, *A World Restored: Metternich, Castlereagh, and the Problems of Peace, 1812–22* (Boston: Houghton Mifflin, 1957); and Kissinger, *Diplomacy* (New York: Simon and Schuster, 1994). For recent realist works on foreign policy, see Elman, "Horses For Courses"; and Zakaria, *From Wealth to Power*.

55. These distinctions are discussed in detail in Schweller and Priess, "A Tale of Two Realisms," pp. 7–8.

56. See, for example, the discussion of this point in Martha Finnemore and Kathryn Sikkink, "International Norm Dynamics and Political Change," *International Organization*, Vol. 52, No. 4 (Autumn 1998), pp. 889–90.

57. See Hans J. Morgenthau, *Politics Among Nations: The Struggle For Power and Peace*, 6th ed. (New York: Alfred A. Knopf, 1985), p. 5; Gilpin, *War and Change in World Politics*, p. 6.

58. Waltz, *Theory of International Politics*, p. 126.

The fourth and fifth differences center on the meaning of "capability." Classical realism is a theory of foreign policy, focusing on the relative distribution of capabilities (balances and imbalances) between specific pairs of states or coalitions of states, not on the systemwide distribution of capabilities or the polarity of the system. "The historically most important manifestation of the balance of power," Morgenthau observed, is "in the relations between one nation or alliance and another alliance."[59] Traditional realists understood capability to be neither a unit nor structural attribute but rather a relationship between states, such as the potential outcome of military interaction. Seen as a product of unit interactions, capability is a process variable that describes the effects of dyadic or coalitional capability disparities on interstate behavior and strategic interactions.[60]

In contrast, neorealism is a theory of international politics, focusing on the systemwide distribution of capabilities, that is, on the polarity of the system as measured by the number of great powers, not the relative inequalities of power among them. Neorealists conceptualize capability as a unit-level property, indicated by a state's inventory of military forces and those resources that can be transformed into military forces; this concept is then raised to the system level to yield the main explanatory variable of neorealism: system polarity, a structural property that is largely ignored by traditional realists.[61]

Sixth, the two camps disagree over the meaning of "system." A system refers to "an arrangement of certain components so interrelated as to form a whole" or "sets of elements standing in interaction."[62] For

---

59. Morgenthau, *Politics Among Nations*, p. 201.

60. See Glenn H. Snyder, "Process Variables in Neorealist Theory," *Security Studies*, Vol. 5, No. 3 (Spring 1996), pp. 167–192. I suspect that Waltz would not approve of Snyder's extension of his theory, however. By attempting to incorporate process variables within a neorealist framework, Snyder violates the purely structural nature of Waltz's theory and winds up with a theory of foreign policy rather than one of international politics. Snyder's process theory is logically sound and progressive, in my view, but it is not a neorealist theory.

61. Waltz, *Theory of International Politics*, p. 126.

62. George J. Klir, "The Polyphonic General Systems Theory," in George Klir, ed., *Trends in General Systems Theory* (New York: Wiley Interscience, 1972), p. 1;

classical realists, the international system is composed of units, interactions, and structure. "Interaction is crucial to the concept of system, for without it, the term system has no meaning," as Barry Buzan points out.[63] The inclusion of interaction in the definition of a system allows process variables (such as institutions, norms, or rules) as well as structural variables to define the nature of world politics and to have an effect on their operation and dynamics.[64]

In neorealism, such process variables are not considered system attributes. Although Waltz defines a system as composed of a structure and of interacting units, his distinction between reductionist theories (those based on unit attributes and interactions) and systemic theories (those based on structural causes) and "his usage of terms such as 'systems theory' and 'systems level' makes the term *system* effectively a synonym for structure."[65] In Waltz's words, "definitions of structure must leave aside, or abstract from, the characteristics of units, their behavior, and their interactions."[66]

Changes in the Balance of Power: Assessment and Response

Realists of all stripes claim that central decisionmakers take their cues from changes, underway or anticipated, in the structure of the international system, which "encourage[s] states to do some things and to refrain from doing others."[67] Indeed, the most basic realist proposition is that states recognize and respond to shifts in the balance of power. For instance, how a state defines and redefines its interests

---

Ludwig von Bertalanffy, *General System Theory: Foundations, Development, Applications* (New York: George Braziller, 1968), p. 38.

63. Barry Buzan, Charles Jones, and Richard Little, *The Logic of Anarchy: Neorealism to Structural Realism* (New York: Columbia University Press, 1993), p. 29.

64. Snyder, "Process Variables."

65. Buzan et al., *The Logic of Anarchy*, p. 28.

66. Waltz, *Theory of International Politics*, 79.

67. Kenneth N. Waltz, "Evaluating Theories," *American Political Science Review*, Vol. 91, No. 4 (December 1997), p. 915.

(or, in game-theoretic terms, its preferences and payoffs, or expected effects of actions) is a function of its relative power and placement in the international system. For this reason, Waltz claims that similarly placed units, despite variations in their internal qualities, behave similarly and produce outcomes that fall within expected ranges.[68]

Despite its vital importance to the realist approach, the actual distribution of capabilities (or "real" balance of power) has remained an elusive concept. Recognizing the inherent ambiguity of all power calculations, classical realists "subscribed to Francis Bacon's warning that 'there is nothing among civil affairs more subject to error than the forming of a true and right valuation of the power and forces of an empire'."[69] Thus, Hans Morgenthau asserted,

uncertainty of power calculations is inherent in the nature of national power itself. It will therefore come into play even in the most simple pattern of balance of power; that is, when one nation opposes another. This uncertainty is, however, immeasurably magnified when [the pattern of power] is composed not of single units but of alliances.[70]

Likewise, Wolfers noted, "Neither the difficulties nor the importance of accuracy in the estimates of power can be exaggerated."[71] The problem with classical realism on this issue is that, as Aaron Friedberg observes, "when it comes to explaining how statesmen actually do their difficult job, the classical realists appear to lose interest and move on to other, more tractable subjects."[72]

How do neorealism and neoclassical realism handle the issues of how states assess and adapt to changes in their own and others'

---

68. The converse is also true: similar units behave differently if they are differently placed in the system. See Waltz, *Theory of International Politics*; and Kenneth N. Waltz, "The Origins of War in Neorealist Theory," in Robert I. Rotberg and Theodore K. Rabb, eds., *The Origin and Prevention of Major Wars* (Cambridge, U.K.: Cambridge University Press, 1989), p. 43.

69. Wohlforth, *The Elusive Balance*, p. 9.

70. Morgenthau, *Politics Among Nations*, p. 225.

71. Wolfers, *Discord and Collaboration*, p. 112.

72. Friedberg, *The Weary Titan*, p. 11.

relative power? At first glance, it may appear that neorealism posits a process of accurate assessments and smooth, continuous adaptations to changes in relative power; that is, changes in state behavior are assumed to move in lockstep with actual shifts in the distribution of capabilities across the system. This would not be a correct impression, however. As a theory of international politics, neorealism simply does not address unit-level matters of foreign policy and internal decision making. Accordingly, the theory is unconcerned with and cannot account for specific state responses to external stimuli, whether or not such responses are characteristic or anomalous, prudent or reckless. In Waltz's words: "Because states coexist in a self-help system, they are free to do any fool thing they care to, but they are likely to be rewarded for behavior that is responsive to structural pressures and punished for behavior that is not."[73]

Neorealism simply claims that balances of power, once disrupted, will be restored. How quickly or efficiently the balancing process unfolds in any particular case is beyond the scope of the theory. Historical cases of delayed and inefficient balancing, such as occurred prior to World War II, do not, therefore, constitute evidence that contradicts Waltz's theory. So long as a balance is eventually completed, one must infer that the actions of states brought the system into balance, whether intended or not, and Waltz's theory is thereby confirmed. Here it is worth pointing out that, if a balance of power is in fact intended by the actors, Waltz's systems-theory approach is less compelling than if the outcome is an unintended consequence of system structure. We do not need a systems theory to explain outcomes produced by straightforward intentional actions.

Having re-stated Waltz's views on the matter and made the case the way I believe Waltz himself would make it, I argue that the logic of neorealism belies the substance of the argument. Waltz's theory implies that great powers are those states that are especially adroit at assessing changes in the balance of power and adapting their behavior accordingly. One could reasonably argue, in fact, that his theory requires these abilities of great powers, defining them as *the* actors

---

73. Waltz, "Evaluating Theories," p. 915.

most capable of adapting to systemic exigencies and change. All that is required for Waltz's theory to work, however, is that at least one great power excels at these tasks, even if the others do not. But—and this is important—polar status can only be achieved and maintained by accurately perceiving and anticipating momentous changes in the distribution of capabilities and responding in an appropriate manner to them, which often entails taking a long-run view of future international challenges.

Consider, for instance, Waltz's discussion of emulation and the "sameness effect." His theory maintains that contending states—those wishing to become great powers or that have achieved such status and desire to maintain it—will imitate the successful military, economic, and diplomatic practices "contrived by the country of greatest capability and ingenuity."[74] Given the pressures of a competitive, self-help system, "those who do not help themselves, or who do so less effectively than others, will fail to prosper, will lay themselves open to dangers, will suffer.... If some do relatively well, others will emulate them or fall by the wayside."[75] Accordingly, the international system induces a "sameness effect" among the great powers, which imitate each other and become socialized to their era's system, "conforming to common international practices even though for internal reasons they would prefer not to."[76]

This is important because Waltz's theory "is written in terms of the great powers"; states that fail to maintain their great-power status forfeit their ability to "set the scene of action for others as well as for themselves" and generate the structure of the system through their interactions with other states.[77] So, while the theory allows states to do "any fool thing they care to," the theory's logic assumes that polar powers—neorealism's primary actors and its unit of analysis—are especially good at assessing and adapting to changes in their own and

---

74. Waltz, *Theory of International Politics*, p. 127.

75. Ibid., p. 118.

76. Ibid., p. 127.

77. Ibid., p. 72.

rationality in Waltz

others' relative power. In Waltz's own words, "competitive systems are regulated, so to speak, by the 'rationality' of the more successful competitors. What does rationality mean? It means only that some do better than others—whether through intelligence, skill, hard work, or dumb luck."[78]

In contrast, neoclassical realists highlight the problems that decisionmakers experience in both assessing and adapting to structural-systemic changes. Generally speaking, their theoretical insights have not contradicted the propositions of structural or classical realism but have instead complemented and extended them by specifying and further developing the non-structural arguments, causal processes, and linkages at the domestic and international levels implied by (structural) realist theories of balance of power and hegemonic rivalry.

Greater specification of the causal nexus between domestic and international factors and policy challenges not only represents theoretical progress in IR but is indispensable for testing and refining core realist propositions about the effects of international structure on nation-state behavior. "Given the insufficient determinacy of Waltz's original approach for analyzing foreign policy," Christensen writes, "additional assumptions about actors' rationality in responding to the international system are necessary if we are to argue from the international distribution of capabilities to the security strategies of particular nation-states."[79]

ASSESSMENT

Neoclassical realists treat national net assessments as an intervening variable between international structure and the behavior of states. Their claim is an obvious but important one: "Foreign policy choices are made by actual political leaders and elites, and so it is their perceptions of relative power that matter, not simply relative quantities

---

78. Ibid., pp. 76–77.
79. Christensen, *Useful Adversaries*, p. 12.

of physical forces in being."[80] To the extent that leaders misperceive the actual distribution of capabilities, their behavior will not conform to the predictions of balance-of-power theory. Along these lines, Thomas Christensen writes:

If leaders misperceive the distribution of capabilities, they may stand aside at crucial junctures in a conflict, overreact to insignificant threats, or even assist the wrong side in a war. If leaders mistake stronger states for weaker ones, they may even join the side of the mighty, thereby behaving more like bandwagoners than balancers.[81]

Similarly, Zakaria claims that a purely materialist version of realism cannot explain the *reasons* for a nation's efforts, which are determined, instead, by political elites' perceptions of power: "Statesmen, not states, are the primary actors in international affairs, and their perceptions of shifts in power, rather than objective measures, are critical."[82] Distinguishing between national power and state power, defined as "that fraction of national power that the state apparatus can extract for its purposes,"[83] Zakaria reformulates the classical realist hypothesis that "nations expand their interests abroad when their relative power increases" as follows: "Nations try to expand their political interests abroad when central decisionmakers *perceive* a relative increase in state power."[84] In this way, Zakaria's "state-centric" realism incorporates both domestic mobilization processes and elites' perceptions of their state's extractive capacity (the ability of the state to extract material and human resources from society for whatever purposes state elites determine are in the nation's or, more narrowly, the regime's interests) relative to that of other nations as causes of state expansion and isolation.

---

80. Rose, "Neoclassical Realism," p. 147.

81. Christensen, "Perceptions and Alliances In Europe," p. 68.

82. Zakaria, *From Wealth to Power*, p. 42.

83. Ibid., p. 35.

84. Ibid., p. 42 (emphasis added; entire sentence is emphasized in original).

In his study of British decline during the decade of 1895–1905, Aaron Friedberg finds that official assessments of relative power were based on simplistic self-images and distorted beliefs about other countries, which were typically derived from a single measure of power. These simple indicators, which "narrowed attention to a very small range of familiar, countable factors" and "conveyed a stylized, flattened picture" of multidimensional processes, were "invested with a symbolic significance that far exceeded their actual usefulness," obscuring "the significance of major political, doctrinal, economic, and technological developments" and "making it more difficult for those who used them to reach a realistic appreciation of on-going shifts in the distribution of relative national power."[85]

Changes in perceptions of power may be completely unrelated to actual material capabilities. In his study of how Soviet political elites conceptualized and perceived power in world politics during the Cold War, Wohlforth found that "perceptions of power are more dynamic than measurements of material relationships. Rapid shifts in behavior may be related to perceived shifts in the distribution of power which are not captured by typical measures of capabilities."[86]

Even when power shifts can be captured by standard measures, Christensen finds that "misperceptions of the balance of power are most likely during radical shifts in the distribution of power, when traditionally powerful states are overtaken by formerly weaker ones."[87] This dynamic may explain why Stalin misperceived the actual balance of power in Europe prior to the Second World War and therefore chose, disastrously, to bandwagon with Germany rather than balance against it. If Stalin had presented Hitler with the prospect of a two-front war, he would have undermined Hitler's strategy, perhaps causing it to be abandoned. But Stalin mistakenly perceived Europe as a tripolar, not a bipolar, system, with France and Britain as the third pole; he therefore expected a war of attrition in the West. That expectation was abruptly

---

85. Friedberg, *The Weary Titan*, p. 284.
86. Wohlforth, *The Elusive Balance*, p. 294.
87. Christensen, "Perceptions and Alliances In Europe," p. 92.

dissolved by the fall of France, which ended Stalin's dream of easy conquests in an exhausted postwar Europe.[88]

Aside from leaders' misperceptions, mistakes in estimates of the relative distribution of power also arise from the fragmented nature and organization of the net assessment process. Although possessing both the resources and the incentives to try to make accurate relative power calculations, great powers have typically not had a single office with unified responsibility for generating official assessments, achieving broad intragovernmental consensus about them, and coordinating national responses to them.

For example, at the turn of the century, in neither Great Britain nor its great-power contemporaries were government estimates "the product of a single mind or agency," writes Aaron Friedberg.

Instead the assessment process was fragmented, both intellectually and bureaucratically. People did at times think and talk in terms of "national power" writ large but they tended for the most part to concentrate on the different forms that the nation's power was assumed to take, whether economic, financial, naval, or military.[89]

Friedberg concludes that the widespread use of simple indicators of national capabilities such as trade returns, numbers of battleships, absolute government spending figures, and infantry reinforcements "seems likely to inhibit rather than to promote recognition of changes in relative power."[90]

In summary, by exploring the details of the decision-making processes of both rising and declining powers, neoclassical realists have identified many of the domestic, bureaucratic, and perceptual causes that underlie Morgenthau's "typical errors of evaluation":

Of all the errors that nations can commit in evaluating their own power and the power of other nations, three types are so frequent and illustrate

---

88. On this point, see Schweller, *Deadly Imbalances*, p. 168; also see Rose, "Neoclassical Realism," p. 161.

89. Friedberg, *The Weary Titan*, p. 280.

90. Ibid., p. 285.

so well the intellectual pitfalls and practical risks inherent in such evaluations that they deserve some further discussion. The first disregards the relativity of power by erecting the power of one particular nation into an absolute. The second takes for granted the permanency of a certain factor that has in the past played a decisive role, thus overlooking the dynamic change to which most power factors are subject. The third attributes to one single factor a decisive importance, to the neglect of all the others.[91]

Further, by specifying how leaders typically conceptualize and misperceive relative power, neoclassical realists are able to explain "outlier" cases that appear to defy realist logic, that is, cases in which national behavior deviated from the predictions of balance-of-power theory.

POLICY ADAPTATION

How do states adapt to changes in the international distribution of capabilities and what obstacles do they confront in doing so? Realism predicts that states will pursue internal and external balancing policies to redress unfavorable shifts in their relative power and to prevent long-term imbalances of power that pose potential threats to their national security. In his evaluation of the "balancing predominates" view of neorealism, however, Wohlforth found that, in practice, many if not most states have historically not behaved in this manner: "If the balance of power has laws, then they are laws with loopholes big enough to drive a superpower through. If states show a tendency to balance against power, it is a weak one."[92] Elsewhere I have also challenged neorealism's "balancing prevails" position: I find that unthreatened revisionist states (ignored by Waltzian neorealism and Stephen Walt's balance-of-threat theory) often bandwagon with the stronger revisionist state or coalition for opportunistic reasons. In fact, balancing is an extremely costly activity that most states would rather

---

91. Morgenthau, *Politics Among Nations*, p. 174.

92. Wohlforth, *The Elusive Balance*, p. 299. Also see Paul Schroeder, "Historical Reality vs. Neo-Realist Theory," *International Security*, Vol. 19, No. 1 (Summer 1994), pp. 108–148.

not engage in; sometimes, however, they must, in order to survive and to protect their values. In contrast, bandwagoning rarely involves costs and is typically done in the expectation of gain, and for this reason, bandwagoning is more common than Walt or Waltz suggest. [93]

A key component of national power and a *sine qua non* for effective internal balancing is, as Waltz recognizes, a "state's political competence and stability."[94] Hans Morgenthau similarly argued that domestic political factors, such as "morale" and "the quality of government," are "the most important ... components of national power" but also "the most elusive" ones to measure.[95] Pointing out that non-material factors such as governmental skill and national unity are elements essential to the determination of national power and to the functioning of balance-of-power processes is, however, not the same as *explaining* how to measure these bases of power. Instead, what we need are theories that tell us precisely how these types of domestic factors (such as social cohesion, elite politics, and elite-mass linkages) impede or further states' efforts to conform their behavior to the predictions of the theory. Simply put, we need a theory about how various inputs at the domestic level may either constrain or enhance the ability of states to build arms and form alliances when threats and opportunities emerge in their external environment.[96]

Along these lines, three neoclassical realists—Christensen, Zakaria, and Friedberg—have specifically addressed the issue of how state power and national political power affect the process of adapting to shifts in relative power, examining cases of both rising nations, such as the United States, 1865–1908, and China, 1947–1958, and declining states such as Britain, 1895–1905, and the United States, 1947–58. In each case, the author successfully applies his own amended version of

---

93. See Schweller, "Bandwagoning For Profit," p. 93; Schweller, *Deadly Imbalances*, esp. chap. 3.

94. Waltz, *Theory of International Politics*, p. 131.

95. Morgenthau, *Politics Among Nations*, p. 224.

96. I am currently working on such a theory. See Randall L. Schweller, "Unanswered Threats: Domestic Constraints on the Balance of Power," unpublished manuscript, June 2002.

classical realism to explain what had previously appeared, from a purely structural-realist perspective, to be anomalous (that is, irrational) state behavior.

Christensen

Christensen develops the concept of national political power, "defined as the ability of state leaders to mobilize their nation's human and material resources behind security policy initiatives."[97] He uses the concept to highlight the problems that leaders face in choosing a grand strategy to meet real but not immediate security threats. Because the general public "does not have the time or expertise to understand the subtleties of balance-of-power politics,"[98] tends to have a higher discount rate than state leaders regarding distant and indirect international threats, and has an incentive to ride free on the sacrifices of others for national-security objectives, even politically secure leaders typically face significant domestic political obstacles ("hurdles to mobilization") when attempting to implement new and expensive grand strategies. This is particularly true when the international climate is a peaceful one, but leaders nonetheless fear that the state may confront a long-run challenge from potentially harmful changes in the future distribution of capabilities, either in the region or globally.[99] To generate public support under such conditions for new and costly grand strategies they believe are essential to national security, leaders might rationally adopt policies that appear to scholars as "overly aggressive, ideological, or otherwise wasteful of resources and alliance opportunities."[100]

Christensen offers a "two-level" domestic mobilization model that posits "the height of political hurdles to mobilization faced by otherwise politically secure state leaders" as an intervening variable between the independent variable—international challenges that

---

97. Christensen, *Useful Adversaries*, p. 11.

98. Ibid., p. 17.

99. For an excellent recent discussion of this problem, see Thomas J. Christensen, "Posing Problems without Catching Up: China's Rise and Challenges for U.S. Security Policy," *International Security*, Vol. 25, No. 4 (Spring 2001), pp. 5–40.

100. Christensen, *Useful Adversaries*, p. 3.

require massive mobilization drives (extensive internal balancing)—and the dependent variable, the security strategies (over-active, optimal, or under-active) adopted by the state to meet those challenges. His study "concentrates on cases of apparent overreactions to the international environment that are rooted in state leaders' need to overcome high, but surmountable, hurdles to mobilization."[101]

In the same spirit as Christensen's state mobilization model, Zakaria's state-centric version of neoclassical realism shifts the unit of analysis from the nation to the state. What matters to political leaders confronting the international system is not the nation's aggregate capabilities but rather state power—the government's ability to extract national resources for its own ends. Treating the variable of state power as a continuum measured along several dimensions, Zakaria defines strong states as cohesive, autonomous, wealthy, and maximal in the scope of their responsibilities; weak states, in contrast, are divided, society-penetrated, poor, and minimal in their scope.[102] Zakaria concludes that nations expand their political interests abroad when statesmen perceive a relative increase in state power. Thus, only strong states expand; weak states are inward-looking, adopting isolationist policies even when their aggregate national power is dramatically increasing relative to that of other nations. Zakaria calls this phenomenon "imperial understretch" and claims that a weak American state explains why the United States failed to expand from 1865 to 1889, when its national power rose substantially relative to the other great powers.

Friedberg concludes that a broad intergovernmental consensus is a necessary precondition for a coordinated response to national decline. More specifically, the case of British decline at the turn of the century suggests to Friedberg that there are:

three general prerequisites for an integrated, national response to decline: internal consensus on the existence, nature, and extent of unfavorable changes, not just in one area but in several simultaneously; agreement

---

101. Ibid., p. 14.
102. Zakaria, *From Wealth to Power*, pp. 38–39.

inside the government on the appropriate set of responses to such changes; and finally, the ability to implement the various parts of a planned response, assuming that one can be agreed upon. Countries in which power is concentrated, both in the state and inside the national government, seem, in theory at least, to have a better chance of responding in a coordinated, centrally directed way to early inklings of relative decline. It would not be surprising, therefore, if liberal democracies failed to do particularly well in this regard.[103]

In general, the work of neoclassical realists suggests that the behavior of weak and incoherent states does not conform to the logic of balance of power theory; they do not systematically balance against external threats or take advantage of opportunities to expand when they can.

Conclusions

If one judges the success of a research program by its popularity among scholars working within the discipline and by its impact on the field, then neoclassical realism is in very good health. The books produced by neoclassical realists have been published by the top university presses in the field, and have been widely cited and well-received. They generated a review article in *World Politics* and a forum in the *American Political Science Review*.[104]

My guess is that neoclassical realism will flourish in the coming years because it straddles diplomatic history and international relations theory and thereby satisfies the discipline's thirst for both richness and rigor.[105] Just as important, neoclassical realism is

---

103. Friedberg, *The Weary Titan*, p. 290.

104. See John A. Vasquez, "The Realist Paradigm and Degenerative versus Progressive Research Programs: An Appraisal of Neotraditional Research on Waltz's Balancing Proposition," *American Political Science Review*, Vol. 91, No. 4 (December 1997), pp. 899–912; and the responses by Kenneth Waltz, Thomas Christensen and Jack Snyder, Colin Elman and Miriam Fendius Elman, Randall Schweller, and Stephen Walt.

105. See Colin Elman and Miriam Fendius Elman, *Bridges and Boundaries: Historians, Political Scientists, and the Study of International Relations* (Cambridge, Mass.: MIT Press, 2001). Also see Colin Elman and Miriam Fendius Elman,

essentially the only game in town for the current and next generation of realists.[106] Aside from Waltz's theory, the only realist alternatives to neoclassical realism are highly abstract, purely structural-systemic theories: Mearsheimer's offensive realism and Dale Copeland's dynamic differentials theory.[107] Offensive realism, like Waltz's neorealism, suffers from too much success: Mearsheimer has said everything that can be usefully said about the theory and applied it to the history of the great powers. What is left to be done? As for dynamic differentials theory, while I find much to admire in Copeland's theory

"Diplomatic History and International Relations Theory: Respecting Difference and Crossing Boundaries," *International Security*, Vol. 22, No. 1 (Summer 1997), pp. 5–21; and the other contributions to the "Symposium: History and Theory" in that issue. For the richness and rigor trade-off, see Jack Snyder, "Richness, Rigor, and Relevance in the Study of Soviet Foreign Policy," *International Security*, Vol. 9, No. 3 (Winter 1984/85), pp. 89–108.

106. To illustrate this point, among the very best and brightest young scholars in the field are three up-and-coming stars whose work is consistent with neoclassical realism: Jason Davidson, David Edelstein, and Kevin Narizny. See Jason W. Davidson, "The Roots of Revisionism and Status-Quo Seeking: Opportunities and Pressures at the International and Domestic Levels" (Ph.D. diss., Georgetown University, June 2001); David M. Edelstein, "Choosing Friends and Enemies: Perceptions of Intentions in International Relations," Ph.D. diss., University of Chicago, August 2000; Kevin Narizny, "The Political Economy of Alignment: Great Britain's Commitments to Europe, 1905–1939," unpublished manuscript, January 2002; and Narizny, "Both Guns and Butter, or Neither: Class Interests in the Political Economy of Rearmament," unpublished manuscript, June 2002.

107. As presented, respectively, in Mearsheimer, *The Tragedy of Great Power Politics* and Dale C. Copeland, *The Origins of Major War* (Ithaca, N.Y.: Cornell University Press, 2000). Readers may be wondering why I have not included "defensive realism" as an alternative. In my view, and it is shared by many others, defensive realism is simply neorealism supplemented by the offense-defense balance—a dubious theoretical concept about which there is no consensus regarding its definition, conceptualization, operationalization, or measurement and which has failed most empirical tests. See, for example, correspondence among James W. Davis, Jr., Bernard I. Finel, Stacie E. Goddard, Stephen Van Evera, Charles L. Glaser, and Chaim Kaufmann in "Taking Offense at Offense-Defense Theory," *International Security*, Vol. 23, No. 3 (Winter 1998/99), pp. 179–206.

as presented in his book, *The Origins of Major War*, I agree with Robert Kaufman's overall assessment: *"The Origins of Major War* offers a cautionary tale of the bad things that can happen when international relations theory strives to achieve a level of elegance and prediction beyond what the subject matter will admit. Granted, a more qualified version of dynamic differentials theory than Copeland's may contribute to our understanding of why some, if not all, major wars occur."[108]

In theory and practice, all three of these structural-systemic alternatives—neorealism, offensive realism, and dynamic differentials theory—can and should be used by neoclassical realists as a first cut, providing a baseline expectation for state behavior. Only when behavior and outcomes deviate from these structural-systemic theories' expectations should unit-level variables associated with neoclassical realism be added to these theories to explain why.[109] The problem is that Copeland, like Waltz, seems to bristle at the suggestion that his parsimonious theory should be supplemented (sullied would be a more accurate word, in his and Waltz's view) with additional causal variables to give it more explanatory and predictive accuracy and range.[110]

Let me conclude with a general point about neoclassical realism and its connection with the aims of this volume. With its stress on power

---

108. Robert G. Kaufman, "On the Uses and Abuses of History in International Relations Theory," *Security Studies*, Vol. 10, No. 4 (Summer 2001), p. 209.

109. In addition, neoclassical realist variables should be added to these theories when the phenomena being explored are not addressed by structural-systemic theories. This problem often arises because the explanatory range of structural-systemic theories is extremely limited; for example, Waltzian neorealism cannot explain foreign policy.

110. For example, see Jeffrey W. Taliaferro's suggestion of incorporating prospect theory into dynamic differentials theory and Copeland's response in their recent exchange along with Robert Kaufman in *Security Studies*, Vol. 10, No. 4 (Summer 2001), in a section entitled: "Fear of Falling: Debating Dale Copeland's *The Origins of Major War.*" The specific titles are: Jeffrey W. Taliaferro, "Realism, Power Shifts, and Major War," pp. 145–178; and Dale C. Copeland, "Theory and History in the Study of Major War," pp. 212–239.

and the "necessity of state," realism, more than any other IR perspective, is about politics writ large. One of the main contributions of neoclassical realism is that it has brought back in the warp and woof of domestic politics, which was expunged by Waltz's theory. To be sure, the political process is a messy and complex business, but it is the subject matter that we have chosen to study and theorize about. I am concerned that too much fascination with the scientific foundations of IR theory may obscure this essential ingredient from realist theory and, more generally, the study of political science. There is no logical reason for such a tradeoff. Nevertheless, it seems that, as the discipline becomes more self-conscious about its status as a science, it produces less interesting and more apolitical work. It is my hope that this volume contributes to a healthier balance between "politics" and "science" than the discipline presently enjoys.

Chapter 10

"Is" and "Ought"

Evaluating Empirical Aspects of Normative Research

Jack Snyder

Everyday debates about politics, such as those in the op-ed pages of newspapers, are a jumble of claims about facts, assertions about causes, and arguments about norms. In a conscious attempt to escape from the conflation of moralistic and empirical reasoning that are characteristic of these debates, most American scholars of international politics have sought to keep "is" and "ought" separate in their research agendas.[1] Realists, for example, insist on a particular approach to achieving this separation, hard won in their foundational battles with the so-called idealist tradition in American foreign policy. First, they say, one should study the reality of international relations, and only then (usually in the last two pages of any publication) weigh the possibilities for achieving ethically-informed objectives, given the constraints imposed by power politics.

In contrast, a growing number of international relations scholars, many of them arguing that social reality is constructed through discourse about norms, call for a reuniting of research on "what 'is' and what 'ought to be'."[2] They see narrowly conceived research on what "is" as yielding a myopic form of "problem-solving"—a rearranging of the deck chairs on the *Titanic* that ignores the underlying forces of change in international relations. At its worst, they see narrowly empirical research in a realist vein as helping to reproduce an ideology

---

1. Martha Finnemore and Kathryn Sikkink, "International Norm Dynamics and Political Change," *International Organization*, Vol. 52, No. 4 (Autumn 1998), p. 889.

2. Ibid., p. 916.

of power politics that props up the system of war and human rights abuses.[3] Instead of separating empirical research from normative issues, more scholars are now carrying out research at the nexus of normative political theory and international relations that seeks to show "how the 'ought' becomes the 'is'."[4]

Favoring the reunification of normative and empirical scholarship need not, however, imply abandoning rigorous, scientific criteria for evaluating arguments. Indeed, as empirical arguments become more bound together with normative elements, special methodological care will be required to prevent scholarship from becoming indistinguishable from the tendentious jumble of facts and assertions found on the op-ed page. But how can progress in international relations theory be assessed, if it includes normative as well as empirical arguments?

A long philosophical tradition contends that "the force of the better argument," whether normative or empirical, is best assessed in a free and open contest of opinions, in which the logical and empirical assertions of both sides receive systematic public scrutiny. Most of John Stuart Mill's examples of the advantages of free speech in *On Liberty* pertain to the evaluation of normative arguments, such as claims about how society *ought* to be organized or how people *ought* to behave, if they are moral. Oliver Wendell Holmes likewise had in mind the free contestation of normative arguments when he coined the term "marketplace of ideas." Their intellectual descendant, Jürgen Habermas, similarly applies his notion of the ideal speech condition to discussions of normative as well as empirical truths.[5]

---

3. Robert Cox, "Social Forces, States, and World Orders: Beyond International Relations Theory," *Millennium*, Vol. 10, No. 2 (Summer 1981), pp. 126–155; Richard Ashley, "The Poverty of Neorealism," *International Organization*, Vol. 38, No. 2 (Spring 1984), pp. 225–286; Alexander Wendt, *Social Theory and International Politics* (New York: Cambridge, 1999), p. 368.

4. Finnemore and Sikkink, "International Norm Dynamics and Political Change," p. 916.

5. John Stuart Mill, *On Liberty* (Cambridge, UK: Cambridge University Press, 1989; original ed., 1859), part 2; Jürgen Habermas, *The Structural Transformation of the Public Sphere* (Cambridge, Mass.: MIT Press, 1989).

In this spirit, I explore how conventional social-science methods for assessing the persuasiveness of an argument can contribute to evaluating research agendas on normative questions in the field of international politics. Standard social-science methods (often called the positivist method) judge arguments by their logical consistency and by their ability to explain or predict empirical outcomes or to trace the workings of causal mechanisms with accuracy.[6] While the evaluation of normative arguments cannot be reduced *only* to this, these methods are indispensable for assessing key logical and empirical elements of some common kinds of normative arguments.

As the other contributions to this volume show, the evaluation of progress in scientific research programs raises thorny epistemological issues, even in the domain of strictly empirical arguments. A number of these contributions employ Imre Lakatos's methodology for assessing how the force of the better argument should be evaluated in debates among a community of scientists. Although Lakatos accepted that no single experiment could disconfirm a theory, he explained how scientists should and do discriminate between progressive and degenerative research paradigms on the basis of their ability to predict new facts and account for apparent anomalies in theoretically

---

6. By positivism, I mean the view that the task of social science is to show the logical coherence of "if, then" generalizations and to test them systematically against empirical evidence. For a baseline statement of standard positivist social-science methods of inference, see Gary King, Robert Keohane, and Sidney Verba, *Designing Social Inquiry: Scientific Inference in Qualitative Research* (Princeton, N.J.: Princeton University Press, 1994); for criticisms of King, Keohane, and Verba that remain nonetheless within the mainstream of what I mean by positivist social science, see articles in the *American Political Science Review*, June 1995. For the purposes of the present discussion, I see my arguments as applying equally to the methods of King, Keohane, and Verba and to their positivist critics. I set aside the question of how non-positivist methods might contribute to the evaluation of normative research programs. When I use the term positivism in this discussion, I do *not* mean the completely unrelated legal theory that is also called positivism. On causal mechanisms, see Jon Elster, *Nuts and Bolts for the Social Sciences* (Cambridge, UK: Cambridge University Press, 1989), chapter 1.

satisfying ways.[7] Here, I also use some of Lakatos's concepts to assess progress in the logical and empirical aspects of normative research programs.[8]

Most of my illustrations are taken from arguments about ethnic conflict, ethnic minority rights, and punishment for genocide or other human rights abuses against minorities. These topics have been central to recent normative debates about world politics. At least some of these lines of argument (for example, those of Arend Lijphart about "consociational" powersharing) have enough of a track record of longevity, conceptual elaboration, and empirical testing that they qualify as research programs in Lakatos's sense. Consequently, they are particularly suitable for examining the interplay of "is" and "ought."

In exploring these themes, my aims are to show how the logical and empirical methods of social science can play a valuable role in assessing normative claims about politics, and in particular to show how normative arguments may depend on claims about empirical causal relationships. First, I define terms, then I discuss the evaluation of the logic of normative arguments, and finally I turn to the assessment of empirical aspects of normative arguments.

Distinguishing Normative from Empirical Arguments

By normative arguments, I mean claims about standards of appropriate behavior that are or should be morally or legally binding.[9] By empirical arguments, I mean claims about facts or about relationships between facts, including causal and correlational generalizations. By empirical aspects of normative arguments, I mean factual or causal claims that

7. Imre Lakatos, "Falsification and the Methodology of Scientific Research Programmes," in Imre Lakatos and Alan Musgrave, eds., *Criticism and the Growth of Knowledge* (New York: Cambridge University Press, 1970), pp. 91–196.

8. For an attempt to apply Lakatos to normative issues, see J. Donald Moon, "Values and Political Theory: A Modest Defense of a Qualified Cognitivism," *Journal of Politics*, Vol. 39, No. 4 (1977), pp. 877–903.

9. Finnemore and Sikkink, "International Norm Dynamics and Political Change," p. 891.

are advanced in support of a normative claim. By logical aspects of normative arguments, I mean logical deductions that are offered in support of a normative claim. While social-science methods cannot judge the value-laden starting point of a normative argument, they can help scrutinize the logical and empirical elements of a reasoning chain that traces implications of this moral or legal criterion in a particular context or for a particular problem.

In the real world, political arguments almost always include both normative and empirical elements. People make arguments in order to convince others to do something. In a purely bargaining relationship, one side may be able to convince the other to do what it wants through the modalities of carrots and sticks, without invoking any normative arguments. However, in most political discourse, it is advantageous and indeed necessary to argue that the proposed course of action is morally correct, legally obligatory, or at least collectively beneficial for the group making the decision. At the same time, almost all political arguments—even normative ones—invoke some factual or causal claims. For example, human rights activists typically argue not only that genocide must be punished as a matter of absolute law and morality, but also that a particular action, such as the 1994 slaughter in Rwanda, was indeed a genocide and that punishing the killers will deter future genocides.[10]

In academic political science, normative and empirical arguments are more likely to be addressed separately, though not entirely so. In the field of international security affairs, for example, the typical journal article starts with a policy problem (given objective Y, what action X will achieve it?), then turns to an empirical analysis of the causal relations between X and Y, and finally returns to some inferences about what ought to be done, in light of this causal knowledge. In contrast, the field of political theory primarily emphasizes working out the logic of normative arguments; there, however, empirical claims often come into play in describing the problem to be addressed, delimiting the scope of feasible actions, or asserting likely

10. Samantha Power, *"A Problem from Hell": America and the Age of Genocide* (New York: Basic, 2002).

consequences of ethical choices. For example, a normative theorist might assert that it is reasonable to assume that holding genocide trials might deter future perpetrators, and then debate the international community's moral obligation to hold such killers accountable despite the self-interested considerations that often lead to shirking such duties. Finally, political scientists also make arguments about promoting the development of norms, which can involve causal hypotheses about the emergence of norms as well as evaluative claims about the desirability of certain norms. For example, scholars offer "if, then" empirical arguments about the role of activist organizations in spreading norms against the use of land mines, and they also offer normative arguments that banning land mines will lead to good outcomes.[11] Thus, in political science, as in real politics, normative arguments are bound up with empirical claims in varied ways.

Political science generally does a worse job at systematically evaluating the empirical aspects of normative arguments than it does in testing non-normative research programs. Political theorists are usually quite casual in supporting many of their empirical assertions, and empirical social scientists typically fail to fill this gap because they rarely see normative evaluation as part of their job. Although I discuss this mainly with reference to arguments among political scientists, my analysis also pertains to non-academic political discourse, since it too mixes semi-supported empirical claims with normative arguments.

The Logic of Normative Arguments

In a positivist framework, propositions should follow logically from theoretical assumptions. In Lakatosian terms, propositions should be logically consistent with the hard core of the research program. Empirical findings that do not seem to fit the predicted pattern are not allowed to change the hard core; instead they are explained away by auxiliary hypotheses about how core variables are to be measured,

---

11. Richard Price, "Reversing the Gun Sights: Transnational Civil Society Targets Land Mines," *International Organization*, Vol. 52, No. 3 (Summer 1998), pp. 613–44.

how core variables interact with other variables, conditions under which the theory does or does not apply, and so forth. These auxiliary hypotheses cannot, however, be ad hoc; they must be consistent with the core logic of the theory.

The logical structure of many normative research programs in the field of international politics strives to conform to the same rule. Consider the norms governing the international trade regime, together with the research program that seeks to understand their workings.[12] The hard core of this normative system is the principle of reciprocity of openness to trade between states, based on most-favored-nation status and multilateral tariff reduction agreements. General norms of the regime ban cheating on agreements or discriminating against the goods of particular countries that adhere to the regime. Of course, countries sometimes do take actions that, on their face, seem to violate agreements, or they discriminate in ways that seem to be at odds with the core principles, such as those of the World Trade Organization (WTO). Yet states hardly ever concede that their actions violate the normative hard core of the trade regime; rather, they invoke excuses that they claim are consistent with the basic principles. They claim, for example, that their trade restrictions are not really violations, because they are just enforcing domestic product safety laws, or that the other state is dumping goods at prices that are lower than the cost of production, or that the other state has a distribution system biased against foreign goods. Indeed, they may claim that their defection is good for the WTO's norms: if they retaliate, the other state will become a better norm-follower.

Thus, normative international regime theory has what Lakatosians might call a hard core, a deductive logical structure, a protective belt, and negative and positive heuristics.[13] Moreover, it resembles a research program in the sense that its abstract principles confront empirical challenges that "test" the ability of the normative structure to

---

12. Stephen Krasner, ed., *International Regimes* (Ithaca, N.Y.: Cornell University Press, 1983).

13. For elaboration of these concepts, see the introductory chapters to this volume by Colin Elman and Miriam Elman.

accommodate anomalies, and that could lead to a "progressive problemshift" in that structure by redefining the positive heuristic (e.g., the creation of new rules for handling disputes about countervailing tariffs, structural barriers to trade, or non-tariff barriers). Unlike typical positivist theories, such normative programs are about norms and the relationship between norms and facts, not about the relationship between some facts and other facts. Nonetheless, there is enough of a structural resemblance that some Lakatosian concepts are relevant to evaluating normative programs.

Some normative arguments about ethnic politics follow a similar pattern. For example, Will Kymlicka's books on liberalism and multiculturalism try to show that granting rights to culturally defined groups is consistent with the hard core of liberal theory.[14] Grounding his argument in the hard core liberal assumption that the aim of politics should be to create conditions in which individuals can make autonomous decisions about their own life-plans, Kymlicka contends that a culturally secure frame of reference is a precondition for making such choices. Under conditions where strict adherence to an individual-rights framework would destroy that precondition, Kymlicka argues that defending group rights against some claims to individual rights is not only consistent with liberal theory, but necessary for the meaningful implementation of liberal principles. Through such arguments, he justifies measures that bar private ownership of land by members of certain Native American tribes, prevent non-tribal members from buying land, and deny access to free public education solely in the majority language for members of ethnic minorities living in areas reserved for minorities.

Against this view, Jeremy Waldron argues that Kymlicka's arguments constitute what Lakatosians might call a degeneration of

---

14. Will Kymlicka, *Liberalism, Community and Culture* (Oxford: Oxford University Press, 1989); Will Kymlicka, *Multicultural Citizenship: A Liberal Theory of Minority Rights* (Oxford: Clarendon, 1995).

liberal theory.[15] Like Kymlicka, Waldron sets his arguments in the context of John Rawls' liberal theory of justice; Rawls defined fairness in terms of the choices that individuals would make about the organization of society if they had no knowledge of the position that they themselves would occupy in the society.[16] Citing Rawls on the hard core of liberal theory, Waldron acknowledges that the choice of a life-plan presupposes some cultural basis for devising and evaluating potential alternatives. Waldron argues, however, that it violates liberal principles to claim that such choices must be made with reference to a single, integral culture. Rather, people can (and do) devise and assess possible life-plans by drawing on whatever cultural materials they have at hand, including those drawn from traditional minority culture, minority culture as adapted to changing circumstances, majority culture, snippets from other cultural sources, or hybridized, cosmopolitan cultural variants: what he calls "cultural bricolage." Viewed in this way, says Waldron, recognizing the cultural underpinnings of choice requires no deviation from a strict individual-rights perspective. Interestingly, this debate is in part about whether Kymlicka's argument is in principle a logical degeneration of liberal reasoning, and in part about the empirical consequences of the strategy of cultural bricolage for members of some minority groups. I save discussion of the empirical dispute for a later section.

Does applying a positivist yardstick introduce an inherent bias against nationalist norms or group-rights reasoning? Contemporary positivist social science, including Lakatosian criteria, is mainly about the testing of generalizations, whereas the arguments of nationalists themselves seem on their face to be particularistic. Thus, the argument that "Serbs died defending Kosovo five hundred years ago, therefore Serbia ought to own it now," sounds preposterous within a generalizing framework, but it seems to make perfect moral sense to many Serbs.

---

15. Jeremy Waldron, "Minority Cultures and the Cosmopolitan Alternative," in Will Kymlicka, ed., *The Rights of Minority Cultures* (Oxford: Oxford University Press, 1995), pp. 93–122.

16. John Rawls, *A Theory of Justice* (London: Oxford, 1971).

Despite this, I think a generalizing bias for evaluating normative arguments is acceptable, even within the domain of nationalist discourse. Johann Herder did not argue that only Germans deserved a state that reflected their distinctive culture; he argued that all nations deserved this. Even turn-of-the-century militarist Social Darwinists such as Friedrich von Bernhardi did not argue that Germans deserved to conquer other peoples simply because they were Germans; rather, he argued that culturally superior peoples should dominate, and that Germany had cultural superiority.[17] Thus, what looks like a particularistic argument is justified by a general covering law, whose logical and empirical foundations can in principle be assessed through a common discussion.

If members of one group care about persuading members of other groups, they will have to offer arguments that are at least general enough to encompass the normative presumptions of the two communities, if not all of humanity. Even rules governing in-group persuasion must generalize at least to the extent of encompassing the normative perspectives of all in-group members. Thus, Slobodan Milosevic had to argue that his policies were "good" at least from a Serbian perspective, and not just good for his self-serving clique.

Positivist truth claims rarely take the form of unqualified, universal generalizations. Instead, they specify the domains in which they do or do not apply. Similarly, normative claims can be assessed with reference to a circumscribed domain, so long as the reason for the circumscription is consistent with the hard core logic of the argument and is not degenerative or ad hoc. Thus, the argument that democracies are (and should be) pacific with respect to each other, but not with respect to authoritarian states, makes perfect sense in terms of the hard core of normative democratic peace theory.

A social-science perspective on assessing normative arguments should lead to skepticism about overgeneralized claims that fail to state the domain in which they apply. An example of such a claim is that by

---

17. F.M. Barnard, *Herder's Social and Political Thought* (Oxford: Clarendon, 1965); Friedrich von Bernhardi, *Germany and the Next War* (New York: Longmans Green, 1914).

many proponents of international human rights, who have argued against pragmatic amnesties for atrocities committed in civil strife in such places as Mozambique, El Salvador, and Angola, even though amnesties have often been essential to the negotiation of ceasefires that are prerequisite to establishing the institutional and material basis for enforcing the rule of law.[18] This stance abandons context-sensitive social-science criteria for assessing the empirical presuppositions of normative arguments in favor of a morally absolutist universalism, and thus offers a prescription that is more likely to damage human rights than to improve them.

Empirical Aspects of Normative Arguments

Empirical claims enter into normative arguments in many ways. In order to show how positivist methods might play a role in evaluating the empirical assumptions that underpin normative arguments, I discuss three of them: (1) simple consequentialist arguments about norms; (2) arguments that focus not on direct consequences, but on consequences for the long-run strengthening of norms, which I call "norms consequentialist" arguments;[19] and (3) empirical assumptions that frame normative debates.

SIMPLE CONSEQUENTIALISM

Some consequentialist arguments make a clear separation between their normative and their empirical parts. For example, they might argue that Y is a just, fair, or morally desirable outcome, and that we

---

18. Priscilla B. Hayner, *Unspeakable Truths: Confronting State Terror and Atrocity* (New York: Routledge, 2001), p. 187; Margaret Popkin, "El Salvador: A Negotiated End to Impunity?" in Naomi Roht-Arriaza, ed., *Impunity and Human Rights in International Law and Practice* (New York: Oxford University Press, 1995), pp. 198–217.

19. The term "norms-consequentialism" occurred to me by analogy to Jon Elster's term "rights-consequentialism" in Elster, "Coming to Terms with the Past: A Framework for the Study of Justice in the Transition to Democracy," *European Journal of Sociology* (Archives européenes de sociologie), Vol. 39, No. 1 (1998), pp. 7–48, esp. 37–38.

should adopt policy X, because it will produce this outcome. Or in a close variation, they might argue that we are morally or legally obligated to work to cause outcome Y, if and only if our efforts can achieve it, and therefore we should adopt policy X, which will cause Y. For example, some key UN officials argued that military intervention to stop the Rwanda genocide would be morally obligatory only if there were feasible military options that would actually protect the threatened population.[20]

The assessment of such arguments can proceed on two largely separate tracks. On the first track, philosophers and lawyers can debate whether Y is indeed good or obligatory; on the second track, social scientists can debate whether X would indeed bring it about. Work on the second track can proceed in exactly the same manner as if the task were simply to verify a hypothesis of positive social science. Indeed, work on the second track would proceed no differently if the proposition on the first track were: "Y is great for us, because it will make us richer and stronger than our blameless neighbors, whom we hate and envy."

Some of the most widely debated work on ethnic relations is of this simple consequentialist type. For example, Arend Lijphart and Donald Horowitz agree that designing political institutions to mitigate ethnic violence is a worthy enterprise. There is no difference between them on track one. However, on track two, they make some diametrically opposite arguments about how to accomplish this shared objective.[21] Lijphart argues that ethnic peace in culturally divided societies requires powersharing between reified cultural groups, including internal self-

---

20. For a discussion of debates inside the UN Secretariat on this during the Rwanda genocide, see Michael Barnett, *Eyewitness to a Genocide: The United Nations and Rwanda* (Ithaca, N.Y.: Cornell University Press, 2002).

21. Arend Lijphart, *Democracy in Plural Societies* (New Haven: Yale University Press, 1977); Lijphart, "The Power-Sharing Approach," in Joseph V. Montville, ed., *Conflict and Peacemaking in Multiethnic Societies* (New York: Lexington, 1991), pp. 491–510; Donald Horowitz, *A Democratic South Africa? Constitutional Engineering in a Divided Society* (Berkeley: University of California Press, 1991); Horowitz, "Making Moderation Pay," in Montville, *Conflict and Peacemaking in Multiethnic Societies*, pp. 451–476.

rule, guaranteed proportional representation in legislatures and bureaucracies, and the right to group vetoes of policies that affect the group's core interests. In contrast, Horowitz argues for electoral schemes that create incentives to break up the politicization of cultural groups and that encourage cross-cultural political alignments. Thus, Lijphart seeks to draw district lines so that each group is concentrated in its own district, whereas Horowitz recommends drawing lines in ways that split up each group to form heterogeneous districts. Lijphart favors a parliamentary system and proportional representation, whereas Horowitz sees advantages in presidentialism and in single-member-district electoral systems that provide for distributing second-preference votes for losers between the two leading candidates.

Although this is a policy debate with a normative agenda, it can be adjudicated as a straightforward Lakatosian competition between two competing research programs. Indeed, a Lakatosian sensibility is very useful in tracing how these two authors and their schools of thought have tried to protect the hard core of their theories from falsification.[22] Since human history is lacking in a long list of consociational success stories, Lijphart has had to engage in concept-stretching, calling India a *de facto* consociational regime insofar as it provides access to power for religious and cultural minorities, although it lacks most of the formal arrangements that he prescribes for inter-group bargaining, guaranteed representation, internal self-rule, and formal group veto rights.[23] This comes close to measuring the independent variable by reasoning backward from the observed outcome, and is arguably a sign of degeneration.

In another Lakatosian move, Lijphart has argued that powersharing is sometimes, in effect, the worst solution except for all the rest. Even in hard cases where unfavorable conditions make powersharing an uncertain strategy, Lijphart says that it is nonetheless superior to all the

22. Ian Lustick, "Lijphart, Lakatos, and Consociationalism," *World Politics*, Vol. 50, No. 1 (October 1997), pp. 88–117.

23. Arend Lijphart, "The Puzzle of Indian Democracy," *American Political Science Review*, Vol. 90, No. 2 (June 1996), pp. 258–268; Lustick, "Lijphart, Lakatos, and Consociationalism," pp. 113–117.

alternatives. Thus, like the battered, degenerating Ptolemy and Newton, Lijphart may continue to hold sway in policy debates until some Copernicus or Einstein shows how powersharing can be superseded.

A Lakatosian critique by Ian Lustick argues that Lijphart's prescriptive commitment to powersharing has led him to Teflon-coat his theory, making it so vague and slippery that no empirical criticism can possibly stick to it.[24] Yet, precisely because of the practical stakes in having a sound empirical theory of ethnic peace, the rigorous application of social-science standards of falsifiability is especially important in this type of normative research.

Horowitz's research program that centers on cross-ethnic alliances also suffers under close scrutiny. Logically, his scheme for second-preference voting is identical to the French run-off system, which has the same majority-inflating properties of single-member-district electoral rules. Empirically, there are very few cases where Horowitzian electoral schemes have been tried, and hardly any where it has achieved the desired results.[25] Just after Sri Lanka adopted second-preference voting, Tamil-Sinhalese violence escalated in the early 1980s.

Moreover, Horowitz's claims for "success cases" such as Nigeria and Malaysia suffer from omitted variable bias. The omitted variable is authoritarian control over political outcomes. It is true that Nigeria had less ethnic conflict after it redistricted from three ethnically concentrated regions to thirty districts that broke up these concentrations, but Nigeria has mainly been a military dictatorship since that change, so it is unclear how electoral districting can be credited with causing ethnic peace. Likewise, Malaysia has seen ethnic peace and some cross-ethnic political alliances, but these are enforced by government coercion, restraints on free speech and political organizing, and economic side-payments wielded by a largely

---

24. Lustick, "Lijphart, Lakatos, and Consociationalism," p. 108.

25. Arend Lijphart, "The Alternative Vote: A Realistic Alternative for South Africa?" *Politikon: The South African Journal of Political Science*, Vol. 18, No. 2 (June 1991), pp. 91–101.

unaccountable leader, not by the spontaneous workings of a system of electoral incentives.

As these cases imply, there is a contradiction at the heart of Horowitz's scheme: it would rely on democratic institutions to shape behavior in societies where democratic institutions are extremely weak. If Horowitz's theory were qualified by limiting its scope to countries with strong democratic institutions, it might retain its relevance for understanding the political dynamics of Canada, Belgium, and the UK, and it might even work for India. However, it would no longer apply to most of the countries that Horowitz studies and cares about.

In summary, the Lijphart-Horowitz debate shows how positivist and Lakatosian criteria can usefully be applied to normatively-driven policy research programs. However, not every consequentialist debate is so easily sorted out. For example, the debate over ethnic partition between Chaim Kaufmann and Radha Kumar might seem to be a simple consequentialist debate of the Lijphart-Horowitz kind, where the protagonists agree on the goal of inter-ethnic peace but disagree in their causal theories of how to achieve it.[26] In fact, that is only part of the story.

Kaufmann argues that, once ethnic groups have been subjected to intense violence at each other's hands, the only way to prevent future outbreaks of violence is to partition the groups into separate states and to organize population transfers. Conversely, Kumar argues that partition reifies the groups as each other's enemy and causes conflict that would otherwise not occur. In their debate, Kaufmann appropriately sets up a protective belt around his hard core, looking for logically consistent explanations for partitions that were associated with high numbers of deaths. Thus, he explains the violence in post-partition Ireland as a result of the incompleteness of the partition: too

---

26. Chaim Kaufmann, "Possible and Impossible Solutions to Ethnic Civil Wars," *International Security*, Vol. 20, No. 4 (Spring 1996), pp. 136–175; Radha Kumar, "The Troubled History of Partition," *Foreign Affairs*, Vol. 76, No. 1 (January/February 1997), p. 26; Kaufmann, "When all Else Fails: Ethnic Population Transfers and Partitions in the Twentieth Century," *International Security*, Vol. 23, No. 2 (Fall 1998), pp. 120–156.

many Catholics were left under the thumb of the Protestants in the North. Likewise, he explains the 800,000 deaths during the partition of India as a result of the way the partition was implemented (without police supervision or administrative coordination), in a way that is consistent with his core framework of anarchy and the ethnic security dilemma. He also argues that even more Indians would have died if partition had not occurred. The latter argument, however, seems to be contradicted by the relatively moderate death toll over the past half century among the numerous Muslims remaining in post-partition India. This fact Kaufmann explains by arguing that the remaining Muslim community is too small and dispersed to constitute a substantial security dilemma. Since this argument is a generalization that can be deduced from his core logic, this adjustment should count as progressive if the hypothesis accurately predicts outcomes in other cases. In contrast, Kumar argues that the announcement of the policy of partition caused many deaths that otherwise would not have occurred. Indeed, it seems true that Britain's divide-and-quit policy spurred fears among Muslims and created opportunities for land-grabbers to exploit the turmoil through violence.[27]

Much of this argumentation between Kaufmann and Kumar reflects the healthy practice of normal empirical science. Kaufmann in particular has worked systematically to flesh out the protective belt of his theory under the guidance of its positive heuristic and in light of evidence from hard empirical tests. One problem in the debate, however, is that the two research programs do not entirely share the same dependent variable; to put it in a more normative way, they disagree about the normatively desired outcome as well as about the means to achieve it. For example, Kumar codes Cyprus as a failed partition, because the two sides remain hostile to each other and have not renounced the use of force to settle their continuing disagreement.[28] In contrast, for Kaufmann, the partition of Cyprus counts as a success, since the number of deaths ascribed to ethnic violence since 1974

---

27. H.V. Hodson, *The Great Divide* (London: Hutchison, 1969); Anup Chand Kapur, *The Punjab Crisis* (New Delhi: S. Chand, 1985).

28. Kumar, "Troubled History," p. 29.

remains in single digits. Kaufmann sees mutual wariness as a widespread characteristic of politics in anarchy, and thus considers it an acceptable outcome if the two sides are effectively deterred, even if they remain latently hostile. It is possible that this aspect of their disagreement reflects a purely normative difference in their views (e.g., Kumar's belief that this kind of "peace" is not good enough), which is not subject to empirical adjudication. However, it also seems to reflect a difference in their underlying causal theories, such as Kumar's belief that the peace of armed camps is unstable even when fences are high, in contrast to Kaufmann's willingness to accept a level of wariness as inevitable.

In sum, one task for social scientists is to clarify the relationship between the normative and empirical aspects of simple consequential-ist arguments, such as those between Horowitz and Lijphart and between Kaufmann and Kumar.

NORMS CONSEQUENTIALISM

A variant of consequentialism that might be called norms consequentialism holds that the strengthening of good social norms is a precondition for achieving good outcomes. Therefore, instead of simply calculating the immediate consequences of an action in a given case, actors should give great weight to the effects of their actions on the long-run strengthening or weakening of such norms. Norms consequentialism contrasts with, for example, the argument that a simple consequentialist might make, that the establishment of an international war crimes tribunal made nationalist Bosnian Serbs less willing to surrender their positions of power, and therefore had bad consequences for ethnic harmony.[29] In contrast, norms consequential-ists would argue that what counts more is the long-run impact on the general norm that war crimes and crimes against humanity must not

---

29. For an argument of that kind, see Tonya Putnam, "Human Rights and Sustainable Peace," in Stephen John Stedman, Donald Rothchild, and Elizabeth Cousens, eds., *Ending Civil Wars: The Implementation of Peace Agreements* (New York: Lynne Rienner, 2002).

go unpunished.[30] One attempt to reconcile these two perspectives argues that the short-run backlash against attempts to enforce human rights norms is merely an early phase in a multi-step process that will, eventually, lead to the widespread entrenchment of human rights norms.[31]

This type of argument is also amenable to positivist evaluation. However, testing of norms consequentialist arguments can become unnecessarily difficult when their proponents conflate such arguments with norms-absolutist arguments and with simple consequentialist arguments. For example, advocates of war crimes tribunals tend to claim that punishing war criminals is (1) an absolute moral and legal imperative, regardless of consequences (a norms-absolutist argument), (2) a cause of social catharsis, without which the specific post-conflict society in question will not be politically stable (a simple consequentialist argument), and (3) a step toward the establishment of a strong norm of always punishing war crimes, which in the long run will reduce the incidence of this evil (a norms consequentialist argument).[32] Perhaps because the absolutist element in the argument

---

30. See, for example, the op-ed by the communications director of Human Rights Watch, Carroll Bogert, "The Pinochet Precedent," *New York Times*, December 2, 1998, p. A27.

31. Thomas Risse and Kathryn Sikkink, "The Socialization of International Human Rights Norms into Domestic Practice," in Thomas Risse, Stephen Ropp, and Kathryn Sikkink, eds., *The Power of Human Rights: International Norms and Domestic Change* (Cambridge, UK: Cambridge University Press, 1999), pp. 23–24.

32. For some examples of these arguments and related debates about other problems of transitional justice, see various chapters in Neil Kritz, ed., *Transitional Justice*, Vol. I (Washington, D.C.: U.S. Institute of Peace, 1995); Aryeh Neier, *War Crimes: Brutality, Genocide, Terror, and the Struggle for Justice* (New York: Times Books, 1998); Neil Kritz, "Coming to Terms with Atrocities," *Law and Contemporary Problems*, Vol. 59, No. 4 (Fall 1998). For positivistic assessments of this issue and related literature, see Elster, "Coming to Terms with the Past"; the chapters by Samuel Huntington and by David Pion-Berlin in Kritz, *Transitional Justice*; and especially Carlos Santiago Nino, *Radical Evil on Trial* (New Haven: Yale University Press, 1996), chapter 3. Thanks to Leslie Vinjamuri for discussion of these issues.

makes the case as a whole non-falsifiable by evidence, this may reduce the motivation of both proponents and opponents to subject the norms consequentialist element to separate testing.[33] In principle, however, there is no reason why this should be more difficult than other forms of scientific testing.

Indeed, the logical structure of norms consequentialist arguments is similar to that of other social-science arguments about reputational effects or purportedly self-reinforcing (positive feedback) processes. For the purpose of testing a norms consequentialist hypothesis, attempts to enforce a norm can be treated as behavioral variables. Of course, international relations scholars are aware that norms are "counterfactually valid."[34] That is, behavior in violation of a norm does not falsify or revoke the existence of the norm as a standard of morally or legally appropriate behavior. The existence of murder—even the existence of widespread murder—does not revoke the injunction "thou shalt not kill" nor make homicide legal. Nonetheless, the proposition that attempts to enforce a norm against a proscribed behavior in one instance will deter similar behavior in a future instance is a straightforward causal hypothesis. To test it, the social scientist must simply identify the causal mechanism at work and look for the predicted co-variation between cause and effect, controlling for perturbing influences.

Proponents of international tribunals envision several causal mechanisms linking the establishment of tribunals in one case to the prevention of war crimes and crimes against humanity in future cases. The most obvious is deterrence. If potential war criminals and torturers see that past evil-doers suffered severe and certain punishment, they may hesitate to act. At present, however, what potential perpetrators

---

33. On the danger that "bare assertions" may be substituted for "reasoned arguments" when advocates adopt "the language of rights," see Richard Primus, *The American Language of Rights* (Cambridge, UK: Cambridge University Press, 1995), p. 8.

34. Friedrich Kratochwil and John Ruggie, "International Organization: A State of the Art on the Art of the State," *International Organization*, Vol. 40, No. 4 (Autumn 1986), esp. pp. 763–771.

actually see is that justice is applied unevenly, most perpetrators go free, and punishments are sometimes light. As a result, deterrence is weak. The existence of a war-crimes tribunal for the former Yugoslavia did not deter further atrocities there. Given the mixed track record of enforcement, proponents of tribunals can always explain away continuing transgressions by arguing that the normative regime is not strong enough yet, and that (QED) it must be strengthened by having more prosecutions. For that reason, simple co-variation tests cannot under present conditions determine decisively whether this norms consequentialist research program is progressive or degenerating.

Moreover, deterrence is not the only purported mechanism at work. Some argue that holding tribunals will strengthen international legal institutions and cadres, as well as the justice institutions of transitional states, even if there are few prosecutions of war crimes and crimes against humanity. Others argue that some political figures and influential social groups in transitional states want to copy the accepted practices of powerful states, and therefore they will establish laws and legal infrastructure that strengthen international norms even if the short-run effect of prosecutions is unimpressive.[35]

In principle, these sorts of norms consequentialist hypotheses should be no harder to test than are hypotheses about falling dominoes or snow-balling deterrence failures in other settings. Many of the empirical questions are analogous. Does standing firm in one case make aggression less likely in the next? Does the creation of an institutionalized alliance deter aggression and encourage band-wagoning with the alliance? If so, does it work by facilitating policy coordination among those who might resist the aggression, or does it work by altering calculations of outcome probabilities in the mind of the would-be aggressor?

Especially pertinent to norms consequentialist arguments about the deterrence of war crimes and crimes against humanity are Robert Jervis's arguments about the importance of context in drawing

---

35. This is by analogy to the arguments of John Meyer, as developed in Martha Finnemore, *National Interests in International Society* (Ithaca, N.Y.: Cornell University Press, 1996).

inferences about past behavior. Arguing that many U.S. cold-warriors erred in their overgeneralized fear that retreats would be taken as an invitation to aggression, Jervis points out that it makes sense only to draw inferences from similar cases. The reputational version of the domino theory held that a failure to fight for Vietnam would cast doubt on the willingness of the United States to fight for Germany. But it is hardly obvious that observers will draw inferences from behavior in cases where no vital interests are at stake and apply them to cases where interests *are* vital. Arguably, such reputational over-generalizations make sense only if the defender creates the problem by announcing that the former case should be taken as a precedent for behavior in the latter.[36]

Norms consequentialist arguments about deterring crimes against humanity should be tested in a way that is similarly sensitive to context. One might find that the ability of the international community and of individual states to punish atrocities is much more predictable in some contexts (e.g., East German border guards) than in others (e.g., mass genocide in Rwanda, heavily-armed Serbian thugs, warlord bands in Sierra Leone). There are many societies where legal precedents *do* make a difference in shaping behavior, because legal institutions are reasonably effective, key political actors identify with accepted international practices, and potential evil-doers calculate that the risks of violating international norms are great. Conversely, in other contexts, the prospect of international justice is likely to be so remote that it has little impact on pragmatic calculations. One might even find that unsuccessful attempts to apply the norm to areas where it is unworkable would tend to undermine adherence to the norm in areas where it might otherwise have held firmly, just as artificially linking U.S. credibility to the case of Vietnam may needlessly have raised questions about deterrence in Europe.

---

36. Robert Jervis, "Domino Beliefs and Strategic Behavior," in Robert Jervis and Jack Snyder, eds., *Dominoes and Bandwagons: Strategic Beliefs and Great Power Competition in the Eurasian Rimland* (New York: Oxford University Press, 1991), pp. 20–50, esp. 26–29.

If so, this empirical finding would have implications for the normative part of the norms consequentialist case: one could conclude that human rights activists, in order to increase their effectiveness, ought to distinguish between those political and institutional contexts in which international norms can be predictably enforced, and those where they cannot.

Such empirically-informed reasoning is sometimes undercut by the common practice of intermingling norms absolutist and norms consequentialist arguments. In norms absolutism, the basic line of action is never in doubt. No evidence can lead to the conclusion that the norm should not be applied. For example, during the 1995 Dayton negotiations with Slobodan Milosevic, then a potential target for indictment, the Hague Tribunal's prosecutor Richard Goldstone told journalists that "we are interested in building up a body of legal evidence, regardless of the political consequences."[37]

In this perspective, empirical research is undertaken only to help answer the question of how to apply a norm, not whether to apply it. This orientation is prevalent in much of the activist, legal, and even scholarly writing on the former Yugoslavia. For example, Neil Kritz of the U.S. Institute of Peace acknowledges that the effect of Serb and Croat media reporting on the Yugoslav war crimes tribunal has been to "lionize every member of that group accused of war crimes, automatically portraying them as heroes and martyrs regardless of the facts." Instead of concluding, however, that the tribunals are thereby contributing to a backlash against international norms, Kritz recommends that "a program of media training on the process of justice be undertaken" to overcome this backlash effect.[38] An even more counterintuitive argument is advanced by José Alvarez, who acknowledges that the trials produce a backlash, not deterrence, but claims that this is a good thing, because it spurs intense debate in the

---

37. Quoted in *The Washington Post*, November 10, 1995.
38. Kritz, "Coming to Terms with Atrocities," p. 138.

former Yugoslavia on the important topic of international criminal justice.[39]

I think it would be wrong to classify these as norms consequentialist arguments that are degenerating in a Lakatosian sense. Rather, I think they reflect an activist research agenda driven by underlying norms-absolutist views. Here, the question for empirical research is not *whether* to advance an uncompromising normative agenda, but *how* to do it. "How to" empirical research on international human rights, driven by explicitly normative concerns, is becoming increasingly important in the literature on international politics. For example, Martha Finnemore and Kathryn Sikkink close their influential essay on the international norms research program with this manifesto:

For decades now IR research has been divorced from political theory on the grounds (implicitly, if not explicitly, articulated) that what "is" in the world and what "ought to be" are very different and must be kept separate, both intellectually and in policy. However, contemporary empirical research on norms is aimed precisely at showing how the "ought" becomes the "is." ... Understanding where these "oughtness" claims come from, how they are related to one another, which ones will be powerful, and what their implications are for world politics is vital, but it is an inquiry which can only be undertaken at the nexus of political theory and IR.[40]

The kind of research that Finnemore and Sikkink advocate overlaps substantially with the positivist or Lakatosian approaches that I discuss in this chapter. Among the issues that concern them is the quintessentially positivist question of what kinds of norms are likely to emerge under what kinds of conditions. Part of their research program is aimed at discovering "if, then" laws about the effect of given constraints on normative outcomes. However, there is also a

---

39. José Alvarez, "Rush to Closure: Lessons of the Tadic Judgment," *Michigan Law Review*, Vol. 96, p. 2084. For a similar argument made at a more general level, see Risse and Sikkink, "The Socialization of International Human Rights Norms into Domestic Practice," p. 27.

40. Finnemore and Sikkink, "International Norm Dynamics and Political Change," p. 916.

transformational aspect to their endeavor, which seeks to understand how activists can overcome such constraints. Thus, they look at the role of "norm entrepreneurs" in reframing problems, persuading actors to follow norms, institutionalizing international norms, and setting off normative tipping processes, even in cases where a theory of constraints would predict that normative change is unlikely. For example, a research project organized by Thomas Risse, Stephen Ropp, and Kathryn Sikkink studied attempts to persuade human-rights-abusing dictators to accommodate to international norms.[41] Guided by the positive heuristic of their normative theory, their research focused on "how to" questions: e.g., what tactics are most effective at what stage of the process of normative persuasion, and whether pressure for normative change can work even in very poor countries with very bad dictators.

In many respects, this study is exemplary social science. It pays close attention to deductive theorizing, traces causal processes in detail, and looks for patterns of co-variation through paired cases of more successful and less successful normative change. It empirically assesses and casts doubt upon competing materialist explanations for normative change, such as great power coercion and economic modernization.[42]

Nonetheless, even this exemplary study reveals some potential dangers of activist-inspired "how to" research, especially those that stem from the pitfall of teleology. The outcome to be caused (the activist's objective) is taken as a given, and research asks how it can be achieved. This diverts attention from other possible outcomes that are off the desired path, including the unintended consequences of the activists' own strategies.

Failures to make substantial progress in changing norms and behavior could be chalked up, erroneously, to insufficient effort or to not having found the right tactics yet. Worse still, backlash against

41. Risse, Ropp, and Sikkink, *The Power of Human Rights*.

42. Thomas Risse and Stephen Ropp, "International Human Rights Norms and Domestic Change: Conclusions," in Risse, Ropp, and Sikkink, *The Power of Human Rights*, pp. 267–270.

pressures to enforce international human rights standards might be seen as confirmation of the theory's predictions (viz., it is just a predicted phase of resistance to rights norms and debate over them), thus underscoring the political necessity of trying harder (those increasingly terrible atrocities must be squelched). For example, in Burundi in 1993 and Rwanda in 1994, pressures from international donors and human rights activists for powersharing, press freedom, democracy, and accountability for past ethnic mayhem triggered a dramatic intensification of the killing by guilty elites who, hard-pressed, gambled on maintaining their positions through violence. Yet in the wake of these disasters, groups like Human Rights Watch tended to call for redoubling exactly the same kinds of policies that helped trigger the escalation in violence.[43] Risse, Ropp, and Sikkink did not include these cases in their study, introducing a selection bias that protected their hypothesis from disconfirming evidence.

In addition to the risk of classifying negative outcomes as confirming the activists' theory, there is a danger that a teleological, activist research orientation will count ephemeral positive outcomes too heavily in the theory's favor. For example, although transitions to democracy can happen at almost any level of per-capita income, in poorer states such regimes almost always slip back into autocracy.[44] Likewise, activist pressures for lip service to human rights norms or even prosecutions may lead to short-run successes that are unsustainable in places where underlying conditions are not favorable.[45]

---

43. Jack Snyder, *From Voting to Violence: Democratization and Nationalist Conflict* (New York: Norton, 2000), chap. 6.

44. Adam Przeworski and Fernando Limongi, "Modernization: Theories and Facts," *World Politics* , Vol. 49, No. 2 (January 1997), pp. 155–183.

45. Sieglinde Gränzer, "Changing Discourse: Transnational Advocacy Networks in Tunisia and Morocco," in Risse, Ropp, and Sikkink, *The Power of Human Rights*, pp. 126–130.

Because of the risk of the backlash effects described above, "how to" research agendas must also study "when and how *not* to."[46] Most important, narrow-focus activist research must constantly question itself in dialogue with basic research that challenges fundamental assumptions by assessing them in the broadest possible context.

EMPIRICAL ASSUMPTIONS FRAMING NORMATIVE PROBLEMS

Very little normative work of interest to nationalism scholars has an entirely hypothetical starting point, with the debaters standing behind a veil of ignorance with no data to shape the questions that they ask. Instead, most normative debates about ethnicity and human rights are framed by a set of empirical presumptions. Typical is the dispute between Kymlicka and Waldron, which is heavily driven by their differing empirical assumptions about culture and individual choice. This is not to say that there is no normative difference between them. Nonetheless, if their empirical assumptions were not dramatically different, their normative argument might seem rather inconsequential.

Kymlicka comes at the problem of group rights from the rather extreme example of some threatened Native American cultures which, he says, cannot function unless they are isolated from devastatingly corrosive contacts with majority culture. When individual-rights principles are rigidly applied to Native Americans, he claims, these individuals are stripped of their culture, deprived of a basis for making meaningful choices about their lives, and often wind up with disintegrated lives that nobody would ever consciously choose. Waldron comes at the same problem from the opposite but equally extreme example of the cosmopolitan, trans-national, culturally-eclectic intellectual class, which lacks firm roots in any particular traditional culture, yet makes rewarding life choices from a rich, ever-changing array of possibilities.

---

46. Showing awareness of this issue are Michael Barnett and Martha Finnemore, "The Politics, Power, and Pathologies of International Organizations," *International Organization*, Vol. 53, No. 4 (Autumn 1999), pp. 699–732.

Thus, each is arguing from a favorable, extreme case, and trying to make this the basis for a general argument about multiculturalism and group rights that, each says, should be applied to a broader range of cultural groups. While readers steeped in normative political theory might see this as mainly a normative debate, readers of an empirical bent might see this mainly as a debate that should be put in perspective by more data. Is it true that Francophones in Quebec, Hungarians in Slovakia, or Russians in Estonia will be bereft of a cultural basis for meaningful life-choices unless the state protects their culture through the granting of group rights that sometimes trump individual rights, as Kymlicka's argument implies? Or would an equitably constructed individual rights system actually enhance the range of choice for minorities as well as majorities in such cases, as Waldron's implies? These are questions that can be answered by research.

I posit that David Laitin's highly empirical book on language-learning choices by Russian minorities in the post-Soviet "near abroad" reveals more about the issue that Kymlicka and Waldron are debating than do their normative extrapolations from the extreme cases that they use to frame their dispute. It shows that Russians do make individual life-plan calculations across the whole menu of cultural options available to them (as Waldron would expect), yet it also shows that their strongest inclination is to construct a transformed Russophone identity that is mainly grounded in their prior cultural repertoire (as Kymlicka would expect). As a result, Laitin favors a fluid identity regime that might include some group rights, but tries to avoid reification of the cultural group, and creates incentives for beneficial cross-group interactions.[47]

Some of the questions that Waldron and Kymlicka debate seem to be strictly normative, not empirical. However, even these turn out to have empirical aspects. Waldron argues, for example, that failing cultures that cannot survive the jostling and struggles of real life have no value as a basis for individual life-choices. Here, the question is not whether the culture will disintegrate, or even whether individuals in

---

47. David Laitin, *Identity in Formation* (Ithaca, N.Y.: Cornell University Press, 1998), esp. pp. 344–345.

that culture will face an exceedingly rough adjustment, but even in cases where this is stipulated to be true, whether the state should respond by shoring up the existing culture or instead by facilitating adjustment to a more viable culture. Even here, empirical questions are relevant, if not dispositive: would protective cultural isolation cost more and have a higher probability of success across the population of affected individuals than would cultural-adjustment assistance?

One reason that so many of the issues dividing Kymlicka and Waldron turn out to be empirical is that both are liberals arguing from Rawlsian principles. In Lakatosian terms, they agree on the normative hard core. Thus, they are mainly debating different ways to protect the core from empirical anomalies, that is, situations in which the application of liberal principles seems to lead to results that are normatively disastrous in the liberals' own terms. Issues dividing liberals from communitarians, who have adopted a different hard core, could not be addressed so easily through empirical research.

Rethinking the Relationship between "Ought" and "Is"

I have argued that many normative questions in the social sciences can profitably be broken down into their logical and empirical components, many of which may be tractable to positivist research techniques. Naturally, I do not mean to argue that social scientists, or anybody else, can magically derive "ought" statements directly from "is" statements. Indeed, we should be wary of those who purport to do so. It is a transparent fallacy for Serbian politicians to argue that, because Serbia fought for Kosovo five hundred years ago, therefore Serbia ought to own Kosovo today.

Yet even here there are gray areas to explore: in customary international law, for example, "ought" does sometimes emerge from "is"; however, it has to emerge in a way that custom considers legally binding. The right of a state to control a piece of territory typically derives from certain facts: that it has done so for a long time, that this has gone unchallenged, and that other states tacitly accept this control as a matter of the state's sovereign right. However, "is" gets transformed into "ought" only because the specific case is embedded in a more general set of covering norms governing the legal relations between states. That a state or a people fought for a valley five hundred years ago does not count as a valid basis for an "ought" claim, but holding it continuously for the last five hundred years usually does.

My point is that the relationship between normative and empirical arguments is considerably more complex than the usual view taken by most empirical social scientists, who stick strictly to the "is" and leave the "ought" to political theorists, op-ed writers, and non-governmental organization (NGO) activists. I agree with the manifesto of Finnemore and Sikkink that this division is unhealthy and unnecessary. Empirical social science has a great deal to contribute to contemporary debates about multiculturalism, human rights, and virtually every other normative question of international relations.

Part II

Commentaries on Lakatos, and Beyond

Chapter 11

Explanation and Scientific Progress

David Dessler

Lakatos developed his "methodology of scientific research programs" in response to two questions that were central to the philosophy of science in the 1960s.[1] The first of these was the "demarcation" question: what distinguishes science from non-science? Why, for example, do we consider astronomy, but not astrology, a science? The second question concerned the rationality of scientific change. Do the deep ruptures and radical discontinuities that occasionally occur in science, in which the conceptual framework of a discipline is thrown aside in favor of an altogether new set of terms, definitions, models, and concepts, suggest that science is not altogether a rational enterprise? How can scientists choose rationally between theoretical frameworks when the frameworks are so different as to be "incommensurable"?

The demarcation question had been given prominence, and answered influentially, by Karl Popper in the 1930s, while the rationality question was pushed to the fore by Thomas Kuhn in the early 1960s.[2] It was Kuhn's work that drew Lakatos's attention and motivated his work in the philosophy of science from the mid-1960s on. (Previously, Lakatos had worked only in the philosophy of mathematics.) Kuhn argued in essence that scientific change—at least during times of "revolution"—was not rational. Lakatos rejected this conclusion, and drew on Popper's earlier work to attack Kuhn,

---

1. Imre Lakatos, "Falsification and the Methodology of Scientific Research Programmes," in Imre Lakatos and Alan Musgrave, eds., *Criticism and the Growth of Knowledge* (Cambridge: Cambridge University Press, 1970); Imre Lakatos, *The Methodology of Scientific Research Programs*, Vol. 1 of *Philosophical Papers* (Cambridge: Cambridge University Press, 1978).

2. Karl R. Popper, *Objective Knowledge* (Oxford: Clarendon Press, 1972).

effectively fusing answers to the demarcation and rationality questions in a single argument. Popper had argued that what made a theory scientific was its falsifiability. Lakatos's strategy was to adopt this demarcation criterion but to shift the unit of appraisal from the individual theory to *sequences* of theories. "It is a succession of theories and not one given theory which is appraised as scientific or pseudo-scientific," Lakatos asserted.[3] Lakatos labeled such a succession of theories a "research program." He argued that research programs could be judged as either "progressive" or "degenerating," and that, on this basis, rational decisions between rival programs could be made. In this way, Lakatos meant to refute Kuhn's influential thesis concerning growth and change in scientific knowledge.

For Lakatos, progress in science "is measured by the degree to which the series of theories leads us to the discovery of novel facts."[4] Vibrant research programs that, over time, explain new facts, and in addition "overtake" lagging programs, are rationally preferable to the latter. Lakatos illustrated this understanding of scientific rationality with the story of Einstein's overthrow of the Newtonian paradigm:

Einstein's theory is better than—that is, represents progress compared with—Newton's theory *anno* 1916 ... *because* it explained everything that Newton's theory had successfully explained, and it explained also to *some extent* some known anomalies and, in addition, forbade events like transmission of light along straight lines near large masses about which Newton's theory had said nothing but which had been permitted by other well-corroborated theories of the day; moreover, *at least some* of the unexpected excess Einsteinian content was in fact *corroborated* (for example, by the eclipse experiments).[5]

While this basic idea is simple, and the intuition behind it appealing, efforts by practicing scientists to *use* Lakatos's ideas in their own work—that is, to use the scheme laid out in Lakatos's

---

3. Lakatos, "Falsification and the Methodology of Scientific Research Programmes," p. 132; also pp. 118–119.

4. Ibid., p. 118.

5. Ibid., p. 124, emphasis in original.

methodology of scientific research programs to adjudicate ongoing debates over the relative status of competing theories and approaches within a discipline—must come to grips with three fundamental weaknesses in Lakatos's work.

First, Lakatos fails to specify criteria for delineating the various elements of a scientific research program. He tells us that a scientific research program comprises a "hard core," a "positive heuristic," a "negative heuristic," and a "protective belt of auxiliary hypotheses." And though Lakatos characterizes each of these elements in general terms, he offers no insight into the process by which an analyst can non-arbitrarily specify them for particular research programs. In his historical reconstructions of scientific growth and change, Lakatos simply stipulates the constitutive elements of various research programs. He makes no attempt to justify or explain his judgments. For example, he asserts that the hard core of the Newtonian program consisted of "the three laws of dynamics and [the] law of gravitation."[6] Lakatos offers no discussion of Newton's views on space and time, which were central to the Newtonian framework and considered by Newtonians to be as "irrefutable" as any of Newton's laws of motion. Nor does he justify including the third law of motion, which nineteenth-century Newtonians were prepared to abandon in their efforts to assimilate work on electromagnetism to the underlying mechanistic paradigm. The reader is given no guidance on the question of determining the adequacy of any particular characterization of a research program's hard core or heuristics. Indeed, we are given no indication that Lakatos gave serious thought to this central problem.

Second, although Lakatos makes the prediction of "novel facts" the very condition of the progressivity (and indeed the scientificity) of a research program, his discussion of novel facts is riddled with ambiguities and inconsistencies. A "novel fact" is defined variously as: a future event, a new interpretation of an "old fact," a phenomenon not explained by rival theories, and a phenomenon not used as guidance in

---

6. Ibid., p. 133.

extending one's own theory.[7] The practicing scientist who wishes to use Lakatos's methodology of scientific research programs is left in the dark not only with regard to the question of identifying novel facts, but more fundamentally with respect to the underlying logic of judging claims to progressivity made on behalf of any particular research program. Lakatos clearly understood that he had not worked out this aspect of his methodology of scientific research programs; one of the reasons that we have at least four definitions of "novel fact" is that he kept revising his account to cope with deficiencies of earlier versions. But he never resolved the question, leaving open the critical issue of just what logic of confirmation or corroboration Lakatos thought scientists should affirm in their efforts to predict novel facts.

Third, and finally, Lakatos is guilty of a severe "selection bias" in the aspects of science he considers in articulating and defending the methodology of scientific research programs. Scientific inquiry has two sides, theoretical and historical. Theoretical research aims to characterize fundamental entities and their relationships, enduring causal structures, and the like, in abstraction from particular circumstances. Historical analysis is focused on past and present states of affairs: actual events, located in space and time, featuring observable (namable) entities and structures. The bias in Lakatos's work is that his concerns are drawn exclusively from the theoretical side of science. Indeed, he defines a scientific research program as a *series of theories*. But many research programs are heavily historical; for example, the massive research program on the so-called K-T extinction event that occurred about 65 million years ago has generated nearly 3,000 publications to date.[8] Some are simply descriptive, such as the Human

---

7. Colin Elman and Miriam Fendius Elman, "Progress in International Relations Theory," prepared for participants in "Progress in International Relations Theory: A Collaborative Assessment and Application of Imre Lakatos's Methodology of Scientific Research Programs," January 15–16, 1999, Scottsdale, Arizona, pp. 12–18. See also Elman and Elman, Chapter 2 in this volume.

8. Considerable research has gone into attempts to discover the reasons for the mass extinctions that took place at the "K-T boundary," the end of the Cretaceous Period and the beginning of the Tertiary Period, when the

Genome Project. The balance between theory and history varies across disciplines. While some sciences are heavily historical in research orientation (e.g., evolutionary biology, geology), others are more purely theoretical (e.g., classical physics, quantum mechanics). If our guiding question is whether, as a result of "all the theorizing and empirical research in the international relations subfield, ... we now know and understand *more* about international relations?" as Elman and Elman have suggested, and if we recognize that knowledge of international relations includes *historical* as well as theoretical knowledge, Lakatos's scheme again leaves the practicing scientist without needed guidance. (We return to the problem of historical progress below.)

Despite these difficulties, Lakatos's methodology of scientific research programs remains a useful departure point for discussions of progress in international relations, for two reasons. The first is widely appreciated: to make comparative judgments in any scientific debate, we need to look at research programs in dynamic profile, rather than in static snapshots. Lakatos's rejection of "instant rationality" is convincing. A second reason for appealing to Lakatos's work is rarely articulated: if we are to understand and judge scientific progress, a commitment to epistemological realism (or "metaphysical realism," in Popper's terminology) is necessary. Lakatos articulates a relatively clear and straightforward epistemological realism, not only in his essay framing methodology of scientific research programs, but in the wider corpus of his work. His views on this topic are valuable in sorting through debates over progress in science, particularly when discussion turns to the nature or structure of scientific theory.

The question remains, however, how the practicing scientist is to handle the inconsistencies, ambiguities, and gaps in Lakatos's methodology of scientific research programs. In this chapter, I propose that we use the concept of explanation to clarify some of the main claims of Lakatos's philosophy. Oddly, nowhere in his writings does Lakatos detail his understanding of scientific explanation. He does not even explicitly acknowledge explanation as a central goal of science. In

---

dinosaurs were killed off, along with 75 percent of marine life and almost all land animals weighing more than 50 pounds.

this paper, I outline a widely-accepted model of scientific explanation—roughly, a positivist one—and use it to clarify and extend some of Lakatos's main claims about progress in science. In what follows, I assume that a sufficient condition for scientific progress is explanatory progress. That is, if researchers in a discipline or subfield are, over time, producing more explanations, or better explanations, or both, we can consider that area of research "progressive."

In the following section I defend the claim that we confirm theories by showing that their explanatory power increases with their "verisimilitude" (net truth content). This claim is implicit in Lakatos's vision of scientific progress, I argue, and I draw on his writings to illustrate it.

A Model of Scientific Explanation

The model of explanation outlined here is one formalized by twentieth-century philosophers that most modern social scientists would label "positivist," including Karl Popper, Carl Hempel, and Ernest Nagel. It is a widely-used model, and indeed is relied upon (if only implicitly) even by social scientists who would consider themselves anti-positivist. The model has four elements: theories, laws, initial conditions, and events. The two foci or objects of explanation are *laws* and *events*. According to this positivist model, a law or event is explained when it is shown to be something that is or was to be expected in the circumstances where it is found. As Carl Hempel put it, when we construct an explanation, we look for information that "affords good grounds for believing that the phenomenon to be explained does, or did, indeed occur. This condition must be met if we are to be entitled to say: 'That explains it—the phenomenon in question was indeed to be expected under the circumstances!'"[9]

---

9. Carl Hempel, *Philosophy of Natural Science* (Englewood Cliffs, N.J.: Prentice-Hall, 1966), p. 48.

THE EXPLANATION OF EVENTS

An event is a concrete occurrence or happening at a particular place and time. To explain an event one must appeal to one or more laws, since without a knowledge of regularities and recurring patterns in the world, we would have no reason to expect particular happenings at particular times. Event-explanation also requires a description of the conditions or the setting in which the event occurred. A particular event is explained by showing that it is the kind of event one would expect in the concrete circumstances that prevailed, given known laws.

A simple example illustrates this logic. Suppose we wish to explain the observed rise of mercury in a thermometer at a particular place and time. To do so, we must adduce information that enables us to see this event as something that was to be expected in the circumstances that prevailed. For example, we might point to the thermometer's immersion in hot water (initial conditions) and cite the regularity that mercury expands when heated (a law). The regularity tells us that we should expect the mercury to rise in any thermometer that is heated. The initial conditions establish that this particular thermometer was, at the given time and place, heated. The law and the initial conditions together offer conclusive reasons (through the logic of deduction) for believing that the mercury in the thermometer did in fact rise at this time. Insofar as the mercury's rise is expected, it is explained.

The positivist model yields two distinct research strategies for the explanation of events. The first is a generalizing strategy, according to which researchers treat the event to be explained as an instance of a certain *type* of event, which is then shown to accompany or follow regularly from conditions of a specified kind. The example of the thermometer immersed in warm water, where the rise in mercury is explained by showing it is just the kind of event one would expect under the circumstances, illustrates this explanatory approach. An example in the study of world politics is Jack Snyder's account of why the Cold War's end was peaceful.[10] He focuses on the Soviet Union and

---

10. Jack Snyder, "Myths, Modernization, and the Post-Gorbachev World," in Richard Ned Lebow and Thomas Risse-Kappen, eds., *International Relations*

argues that "a state's foreign policy is shaped by the myths it holds about how to achieve security." Expansionist myths (which hold that a state's security is enhanced by aggressive expansion) are held in check in democracies, but can "run rampant" in polities that feature logrolling among highly concentrated interest groups. The state's domestic political structure is, in turn, shaped by the timing of its industrialization. Note that these are all type-level generalizations; to use them to explain the USSR's peaceful acquiescence at the end of the Cold War, we must describe the concrete conditions of that case. According to Snyder, Russia's historic economic backwardness shaped Soviet political modernization, which in turn created a political constituency for a foreign policy of peace and international economic integration. This constituency developed the legitimating ideas needed to mobilize support for the policy, and these ideas were determinative at the Cold War's end. The laws and initial conditions set forth in this account suggest that the peaceful collapse of the Soviet empire was, while unprecedented, something to be expected, under the circumstances. The event is in this way explained.[11]

The second strategy is a particularizing one, in which the researcher explains an event by detailing the sequence of happenings leading up to it. In this approach, which aims at accurate historical reconstruction, there is no attempt to place the phenomenon in question into a larger class. The event is explained as the end-point of a concrete historical sequence, not as an instance of a particular type. In Hempel's words, this type of explanation "presents the phenomenon under study as the final stage of a developmental sequence, and accordingly accounts for the phenomenon by describing the successive stages of that sequence."[12] Like a generalizing or covering-law account, a particularizing or reconstructive explanation necessarily relies upon

Theory and the End of the Cold War (New York: Columbia University Press, 1995).

11. Snyder, "Myths, Modernization, and the Post-Gorbachev World," quotations from pp. 109–110.

12. Carl Hempel, *Aspects of Scientific Explanation* (New York: Free Press, 1965), p. 447.

laws, but these are component laws rather than covering ones, in that each pertains to only a segment of the pathway leading up to the event to be explained. Of course, each component law can be considered a covering law for the segment of the pathway that it explains, but the event itself is explained by the *sequence* of happenings leading up to it, and typically this sequence is not law-governed. (If the sequence is law-governed, a single covering law can be constructed to explain the outcome.) Like any sound positivist explanation, reconstructive accounts explain by showing that the event in question was to be expected in the circumstances in which it occurred.

William Wohlforth's account of the Soviet Union's peaceful collapse exemplifies the reconstructive approach.[13] Wohlforth does not attempt to "cover" Soviet behavior with type-level generalizations that show it to be the kind of behavior we would expect in the circumstances. Rather, he details the sequence of events leading up to Soviet collapse, and shows how the behavior to be explained emerges from it. In the early 1980s, Wohlforth argues, Soviet economic decline and geopolitical vulnerability brought the issue of reform to the fore of Soviet policymaking. New ideas for change in foreign and domestic policy began to percolate up to the top leadership. Under Gorbachev, starting in 1985, reform was a trial-and-error learning process that brought Soviet leaders new evidence of the Soviet Union's perilous situation. These leaders made concessions to the West in arms control negotiations between 1986 and 1988 in the hope that decreased international tension and lowered security costs would shore up the Soviet position; and so on. Wohlforth's reconstruction explains the Soviet Union's peaceful collapse by showing it to be the expected "last step" in the sequence. This expectation emerges from the logic of the narrative, itself filled with contingency as well as predictability. Unlike generalizing accounts, where covering laws carry the explanatory burden, in reconstructive accounts it is history that "drives" the explanation.

---

13. William C. Wohlforth, "Realism and the End of the Cold War," *International Security*, Vol. 19, No. 3 (Winter 1994/95), pp. 91–129.

These two strategies, and the explanations they yield, are equally positivist. Each fully meets the requirements of positivist explanation. Yet they lead to quite different ways of framing questions in research. In the generalizing or covering-law approach, an event is identified, and the researcher asks: what is this a case of? The logic of inquiry proceeds "outward" from the consideration of single events to the analysis of classes of events. In the particularizing or reconstructive approach, the researcher asks of the event to be explained: from what historical pathway did this event emerge? Inquiry then moves "inward" to a detailed reconstruction of the actual sequences, causal conjunctions, and contingencies that led, step by step, to the outcome in question.

Note that the law or laws used in an event-explanation must be theoretically-grounded. That is, we must be able to show that the laws can be derived from deeper regularities and structures, that they identify the operation of causal capacities and do not simply represent accidental conjunctions of event-types. Often, in explaining an event, the scientist will not only cite the relevant covering or component laws, but will suggest or point to the theoretical warrant for them. It is the latter that provides the explanatory understanding that is often sought in explaining an event. For example, returning to the above example, when we explain the mercury's rise in the thermometer by citing the law that mercury expands when heated, we recognize this law as explanatory because (and only insofar as) we can derive it from our understanding of the causal structure of metals. To say "X happened because X is just the kind of event that regularly happens in these circumstances" will be an unsatisfactory explanation if it is not clear why the regularity itself should hold. Laws that lack theoretical grounding will not yield satisfying explanations. This brings us to the issue of explaining laws.

THE EXPLANATION OF LAWS

A law is a regularity, or repeating pattern, that describes a causal relationship between two or more factors. Like events, laws are to be explained by fitting them into larger patterns, by appealing to other, possibly higher or more encompassing, laws. All positivist explanation, whether of events or laws, is thus "nomic," or reliant on laws. Hempel concludes that "all scientific explanation ... seeks to provide a systematic understanding of empirical phenomena by showing that they fit into a nomic nexus."[14] Science teaches us that when, say, this thing over here moves in one way (say, a tree falls), that thing over there will move in another (say, the car parked most unfortunately under the tree is crushed). We can learn more about what to expect from falling trees by observing them in yet more conditions. In this way, the positivists argue, science builds up a "nomic nexus" (an interconnected set of claims showing things of the world moving this way and that, and doing so by showing *why* we should expect these movements to be interconnected as they are.) To explain something, for the positivist, is just to fit it into the nomic nexus: when we come upon the car to find it flattened after a big storm, we say, well, yes, this is just the sort of outcome we should have expected—a flattened car—given that the tree fell on it.

A theory is a description of causal structure within a bounded domain of activity. It posits "basic entities and processes" governed by "basic theoretical laws, or theoretical principles."[15] A theory consists of "substantive paradigmatic claims ... about what types of things exist and the manner of their existence."[16] It is a representation, partly idealized, of a bounded domain of entities and of interconnections among them. "A theory is a picture, mentally formed, of a bounded realm or domain of activity. A theory is a depiction of the organization of a domain and of the connections among its parts."[17] Theories convey causal information. They provide answers to such questions as, "Why does this occur? How does that thing work? What causes what? How does it all hang together?"[18]

---

14. Hempel, *Aspects of Scientific Explanation*, p. 488.

15. Hempel, *Philosophy of Natural Science*, p. 70.

16. John G. Gunnell, "Realizing Theory: The Philosophy of Science Revisited," *The Journal of Politics*, Vol. 57 (November 1995), pp. 923–940, at 926.

17. Kenneth N. Waltz, *Theory of International Politics* (Reading, Mass.: Addison-Wesley, 1979), p. 8.

18. Ibid.

Theories have truth value, but because they are complex structures or networks of statements, they cannot be judged simply "true" or "false." Some of the statements that a theory comprises are true, and others, being idealizations or distortions of one type or another, are not. Different theories thus have different degrees of truth, or *verisimilitude*.[19] In Popper's formulation, "a theory T_1 has less verisimilitude than a theory T_2 if and only if (a) their truth contents (or their measures) are comparable, and either (b) the truth content, but not the falsity content, of T_1 is smaller than that of T_2, or else (c) the truth content of T_1 is not greater than that of T_2, but its falsity content is greater."[20] Lakatos, following Popper, characterizes the verisimilitude of a theory as its "truth-content minus falsity-content."[21]

Theories explain laws by showing them to be the products of an underlying causal structure. In Hempel's characterization,

Theories are usually introduced when previous study of a class of phenomena has revealed a system of uniformities that can be expressed in the form of empirical laws. Theories then seek to explain those regularities and, generally, to afford a deeper and more accurate understanding of the phenomena in question. To this end, a theory construes those phenomena as manifestations of entities and processes that lie behind or beneath them, as it were.[22]

---

19. This is where the commitment to epistemological realism is important. Epistemological realists believe that theories, which describe an independent if sometimes inaccessible reality, have truth-value. Anti-realists do not. For example, instrumentalists hold that theories are simply devices for prediction, and are to be judged in terms not of their truth-value but of their practical utility. Both Popper and Lakatos, along with most other mid-twentieth century positivists (e.g., Hempel, Nagel, Braithwaite), are realists. Lakatos discusses his scientific epistemology in Lakatos, "Popper on Demarcation and Induction," Lakatos, *The Methodology of Scientific Research Programs*, pp. 139–167; see esp. 154–159.

20. Popper, *Objective Knowledge*, p. 52.

21. Lakatos, *The Methodology of Scientific Research Programs*, p. 156; also Lakatos, "Falsification and the Methodology of Scientific Research Programmes," p. 114, fn 3.

22. Hempel, *Philosophy of Natural Science*, p. 70.

Hempel offers this example: "The kinetic theory of gases offers explanations for a wide variety of empirically established regularities by construing them as macroscopic manifestations of statistical regularities in the underlying molecular and atomic phenomena."[23]

Laws, like events, are explained when we can show that the regularities or associations they describe are just the ones we should expect, given the causal structure of the world. Hempel stresses that the "assumptions made by a scientific theory about underlying processes must be definite enough to permit the derivation of specific implications concerning the phenomena [i.e., the laws] that the theory is to explain." We must be able to say, argues Hempel, "On the basis of these theoretical assumptions, this is just what was to be expected—the theory explains it!"[24] However, because laws are not "happenings" but relations between types of entities and factors or properties, their explanation requires no appeal to initial conditions. Laws are explained by other laws and theoretical principles, without reference to any particular conditions.

Laws explain other laws in two schemas: genus-species and part-whole.[25] "Some regularities are simply species of others. For example, the regularity captured by the law, 'Wood floats on water' is a species of the regularity captured by the law, 'A solid body with a specific gravity less than that of a given liquid will float in that liquid.' The relata of the genus regularity are more comprehensive that the relata of the species."[26] In the part-whole example, a regularity is "a *manifestation* of several other regularities." For example, "the regularity captured by the statement, 'Car radiator crackings are regularly connected with certain (specified) conditions of temperature, radiator content, etc.' is explained by showing it to be a manifestation or convergence of several other different kinds of regularities (some

23. Ibid., p. 71.

24. Ibid., pp. 71–2.

25. Joyce Kinoshita, "How Do Scientific Explanations Explain?" in Dudley Knowles, ed., *Explanation and Its Limits* (Cambridge: Cambridge University Press, 1990), pp. 301–303.

26. Ibid., p. 301.

concerning the behavior of water at the freezing point, others accounting for the brittleness of the metals that radiators are made of, and so on)."[27]

In the study of international politics, Jack Snyder gives a clear example of the genus-species type of theoretical explanation:

The hypothesis that offensive advantage causes conflict even among status quo powers is just one application of the more general Prisoners' Dilemma theorem in game theory. According to a strictly mathematical proof, rational players in a single-play Prisoners' Dilemma, by the logic of their situation, are constrained to compete even though they end up worse off than if they had cooperated. Offensive advantage increases the incentive for competitive play by magnifying the gains that arise from exploiting one-sided cooperation in a single play of the game, and by magnifying the losses that arise from being exploited. If international politics is like a Prisoners' Dilemma, and if offensive advantage makes it resemble a single-play contest, then, by logical deduction, offensive advantage should promote conflict.[28]

I am aware of no clear examples of the part-whole schema of theoretical explanation in the study of world politics. It is probable, however, that should a phenomenon as complex as (say) the democratic peace be convincingly explained theoretically, the explanation will draw on several component laws that combine and interact at various levels, rather than simply showing this regularity to be a species of a wider genus covering associations of this type.

Dimensions of Explanatory Progress

Scientists do not just develop theory; they also explain history. In this section, we take up some of the issues concerned with the relation between these two categories of scientific research.

---

27. Ibid., pp. 301–302.

28. Jack Snyder, "Science and Sovietology: Bridging the Methods Gap in Soviet Foreign Policy Studies," *World Politics*, Vol. 40, No. 2 (January 1988), p. 169–193, at pp. 172–173.

EXPLANATORY PROGRESS THROUGH HISTORICAL RESEARCH

Because Lakatos defines a scientific research program as "a series of theories," his methodology of scientific research programs equates scientific progress with *theoretical* progress, failing to acknowledge even the possibility that scientific knowledge can grow through historical research. Consider, for example, the research program focused on the mass extinction at the K-T boundary. In 1980, a proposal by a Berkeley physicist named Walter Alvarez transformed the study of this event and mass extinctions more generally. Alvarez proposed that the K-T extinction was caused by the impact of a meteorite. As a result of publication of this proposition, "career goals have been refocused, dormant areas of research rejuvenated, tacit assumptions hastily re-examined, and scientists in widely separated fields swept into an unprecedented array of collaborative efforts. Ingenious experiments, field studies, and the development of new instruments now undergird an effort to resolve the many questions raised in these far-flung debates."[29]

What deserves emphasis here is that the apparatus of Lakatos's methodology of scientific research programs is incapable of grasping the advances in knowledge that this research program has generated. While Lakatos's concern is exclusively with theoretical progress, the Alvarez hypothesis is a purely historical one: it asserts that a meteorite hit the Earth 65 million years ago and that this impact caused a mass extinction. Its chief rival is the "volcanism hypothesis," which attributes the extinction to massive volcanic activity. The debate is not theoretical; it does not involve the pitting of one series of theories against another, which is the only kind of debate Lakatos's methodology of scientific research programs can comprehend. Knowledge of this episode has been gained by using existing theories and laws, and acquiring a more precise characterization of the initial conditions and the event itself. In other words, scientists have developed better, more accurate, more complete explanations of the

29. William Glen, "What the Impact/Volcanism/Mass-Extinction Debates Are About," in William Glen, ed., *The Mass-Extinction Debates: How Science Works in a Crisis* (Stanford: Stanford University Press, 1994), pp. 7–8.

various aspects of the complex K-T episode because they have acquired more and better historical knowledge. In terms of the explanatory model outlined above, we conclude that explanatory progress on this topic has resulted from research directed toward the concrete particulars of the event in question, rather than on the theories and laws that are drawn upon in pulling together the overall explanation.

For a program to be as purely historical as this one, of course, researchers must have a good deal of reliable theory at hand. Otherwise, the improved knowledge of initial conditions they generate would not lead to improved explanations. K-T extinction researchers rely upon well-confirmed theories in physics, biology, and geology to construct their explanatory accounts. By comparison, theories in the study of world politics are weak, and research programs are unlikely to be as one-sidedly historical as the one on the K-T mass extinction. Instead, they will typically include a significant theoretical component. But that does not necessarily make these programs simply a *series of theories*, which is the only kind of research effort that concerns Lakatos. Many programs—for example, those concerning the "long peace," the end of the Cold War, the democratic peace, and ethnic conflict—will measure their progress not just in terms of theory-building, but on the historical side of the ledger as well, generating more accurate and appropriate descriptions of the relevant historical conditions. To the extent that these improved descriptions contribute to more powerful or more detailed explanations, they constitute scientific progress.

EXPLANATORY PROGRESS THROUGH THEORETICAL RESEARCH

In this section I defend the claim that we confirm theories by showing that their explanatory power increases with their verisimilitude (net truth content). This claim is implicit in Lakatos's epistemology, and I draw on his writings to illustrate it.

To explain this thesis, let us return to the example of the kinetic theory of gases mentioned above. A typical textbook in physical chemistry discusses the "gas laws" (the regularities governing the behavior of gases under various conditions), beginning with a treatment of "perfect" or "ideal" gases. An ideal gas consists of small molecules in ceaseless random motion. These molecules have perfectly elastic collisions with one another, but they do not otherwise interact. The size of these molecules is very small in comparison to the average distance traveled between collisions. Given these properties (stipulated as the underlying theoretical assumptions), an ideal or perfect gas can be expected to exhibit certain patterns of behavior. For example, at constant temperature, the pressure of a fixed amount of an ideal gas varies inversely with the volume it occupies. More precisely,

$$p = nRT/V$$

where p stands for pressure; n for the amount of gas; R for a constant; T for temperature; and V for volume. When put in the form

$$pV = \text{constant (at fixed } n, T)$$

the equation is known as Boyle's Law. It is a regularity we explain by appealing to the underlying model. "The molecular explanation of Boyle's Law can be traced to the fact that if the volume of a sample is reduced by half, there are twice as many molecules per unit volume. Twice as many molecules strike the walls [of the container holding the gas] in a given period of time, and so the average force they exert is double."[30]

Of course, the molecules making up any real gas *do* interact. We can make the gas model more realistic by modeling the attractive and repulsive forces between the molecules. "The repulsive interactions between molecules are taken into account by supposing that they cause the molecules to behave as small but impenetrable spheres. The non-zero volume of the molecules implies that instead of moving in a volume V they are restricted to a small volume $V-nb$, where nb is approximately the total volume taken up by the molecules themselves."[31] At the same time, with the molecules occupying such a small volume, the forces between them serve to lessen the velocity of these particles striking the surface of the container, thus lowering the

---

30. P.W. Atkins, *Physical Chemistry*, 4th ed. (New York: W.H. Freeman, 1990), p. 9.

31. For the actual equation, see Atkins, *Physical Chemistry*, p. 17.

observed pressure. The picture has become rapidly complicated because we have introduced intermolecular forces, which are ignored in the ideal gas law. But this gives us a more realistic model (a theory with higher verisimilitude), which in turn yields a more precise rendering of the gas law, known as the van der Waals equation.[32] Note what has happened here: by relaxing some of the unrealistic assumptions of the ideal gas law, and building a more realistic model, we have generated a more complex equation that explains the behavior of gases more fully. And the models are connected just as we would expect: for example, if we move from a highly compressed gas (where almost all the space in the box is occupied by gas molecules) to a gas without much compression (where just a few molecules are sharing the wide open spaces), the van der Waals equation makes the same prediction that the ideal gas law did. The van der Waals model thus explains what the ideal gas model does and more. It thereby represents, using Lakatos's terminology, *theoretical* progress; as it is corroborated in testing, it represents *empirical* progress as well.[33]

This example of theoretical progressivity offers insight into the role and implications of "as-if assumptions" in theory-building. Scientific theories are built on assumptions that are partly true and partly false. The parts that are true supply the theory with its explanatory leverage; the components that are false (the "as-if" assumptions) determine the conditions under which the leverage can be used. For example, in the ideal gas model, the gas is said to behave *as if* the molecules occupy no volume and have no interactions. These are idealizations. They are useful because they lay bare the essential workings of a gas, showing us how to conceptualize a gas's temperature in terms of the energy of the molecules, its pressure in terms of the force with which the molecules hit the walls of the container holding it, and so forth. The idealizations also restrict the model's range of applicability: while the ideal gas law explains well the behavior of a gas where few molecules occupy a large box, it accounts poorly for the behavior of a highly

32. Ibid.

33. Lakatos, "Falsification and the Methodology of Scientific Research Programmes," p. 118.

compressed gas, where the molecules are crammed together. Thus the idealizations are effective and constructive. This comes as no surprise. If a small amount of gas occupies a large volume, its molecules will on average be widely separated, and they will not much affect one another's motion through attractive and repulsive forces. Under such conditions, Boyle's Law offers a good explanatory account. On the other hand, if a gas is highly compressed, the interactions between the molecules become significant. In this case we need a more detailed equation, like the van der Waals, to explain behavior. The theory's explanatory power increases as its false assumptions are "relaxed"— that is, as the assumptions' distorting, idealizing, or simplifying effects are removed. At each step in the process, it is the assumptions that are true that carry the explanatory burden.[34] To the extent the theory remains false, its range and power are restricted.

Lakatos defines the "positive heuristic" of a theoretical research program as the "instructions" that scientists follow in making relatively simple and unrealistic models more complex, realistic, and powerful. Lakatos defines "model" as "a set of initial conditions (possibly together with some of the observational theories) which one knows is *bound* to be replaced during the further development of the program."[35] "The positive heuristic," he writes, "sets out a program which lists a chain of ever more complicated *models* simulating reality."[36] The example he gives, paralleling the one just described concerning the kinetic theory of gases, is drawn from Newton's work.

Newton first worked out his program for a planetary system with a fixed point-like sun and one single point-like planet. It was in this model that he

---

34. An instrumentalist, being uninterested in explanation, is uninterested in a theory's truth. After all, if predictive capacity is all that matters, the truth or falsity of a theory's assumptions are irrelevant. Milton Friedman, "The Methodology of Positive Economics," in Friedman, *Essays in Positive Economics* (Chicago: University of Chicago Press, 1953). But if we are interested in *explanation* as well as prediction, the truth of theories becomes an issue.

35. Lakatos, "Falsification and the Methodology of Scientific Research Programmes," p. 137 (emphasis in original).

36. Ibid., p. 136 (emphasis in original).

derived his inverse square law for Kepler's ellipse.... The model had to be replaced by one in which both the sun and the planet revolved around a common center of gravity.... Then he worked out the program for more planets as if there were only heliocentric but no interplanetary forces. Then he worked out the case where the sun and the planets were not mass-points but mass-*balls*."[37]

Lakatos's point in this section is that Newton constructed this sequence of increasingly complicated models by following the internal logic of his research program (its positive heuristic), initially setting aside any concerns about data that needed accommodation. But ultimately what justifies this process is that the increasingly realistic models explain more data, or explain them better (e.g., with more precision), or both. In other words, the point is to show that increasing verisimilitude leads to greater explanatory power.

In this way Lakatos is able to reverse Popper's "negativism"—that is, Popper's exclusive focus on falsifiability—and show how the *positive* corroboration of *more detailed, more realistic* models justifies the research program to which these models give shape. Lakatos defines "verification" as "a corroboration of excess content in the expanding program." He argues that "it is the *'verifications'* rather than the refutations which provide the contact points with reality.... It is the 'verifications' which keep the program going."[38] He makes this "verificationism" the feature that distinguishes his "sophisticated methodological empiricism" (i.e., methodology of scientific research programs) from "dogmatic falsificationism":

For the dogmatic falsificationist, learning about a theory is learning whether it is refuted or not; about confirmed theories one learns nothing (one cannot prove or probabilify anything), about refuted theories one

---

37. Ibid., p. 135 (emphasis in original).

38. Lakatos, "Falsification and the Methodology of Scientific Research Programmes," p. 137 (emphasis in original).

learns they are disproved. For the sophisticated falsificationist, learning about a theory is primarily learning which new facts it anticipated.[39]

Two examples from the December 1997 *APSR* symposium on Lakatos's methodology of scientific research programs illustrate this approach to theory-confirmation. First, Thomas Christensen and Jack Snyder take Waltz's simple structural model as a starting point and extend it to explain additional phenomena. Waltz's model, they note, leaves a puzzle: "alliance patterns before the two world wars were very different, in fact opposite, yet the polarity of the international system, as defined by Waltz, was very similar."[40] They note that "additional causal factors" must be added to Waltz's model, if the variance in alliance patterns is to be explained. The variable they add is that of "leaders' perceptions of the strategic environment," specifically, perceptions or beliefs about the relative efficacy of offensive and defensive military doctrines. They find that this more realistic model explains additional data: in this case, the fact that "the European powers chain-ganged as a response to the German threat before 1914 and buck-passed in the face of a similar threat in the 1930s, despite the similar multipolar configurations of power."[41]

Second, Randall Schweller notes that "contemporary realists, such as Waltz and Walt, treat *all* states as if they were satisfied, status-quo powers that seek primarily to maximize their security rather than their power."[42] This assumption about states is a simplification or idealization that Schweller sets aside to construct a more realistic model. "My balance-of-interests theory," Schweller writes, "includes *both* revisionist states (those that seek to increase their power) and status-quo states (those that seek merely to keep what they already

39. Lakatos, "Falsification and the Methodology of Scientific Research Programmes," p. 123.

40. Thomas J. Christensen and Jack Snyder, "Progressive Research on Degenerate Alliances," *American Political Science Review*, Vol. 91, No. 4 (December 1997), pp. 919–922, at p. 919.

41. Ibid.

42. Randall Schweller, "New Realist Research on Alliances," *American Political Science Review*, Vol. 91, No. 4 (December 1997), pp. 927–930, at p. 929.

possess). By relaxing neorealism's assumptions that all states value what they possess more than what they covet, my theory allows for the full range of state interests."[43] With this more detailed and comprehensive model, Schweller aims to explain why "great powers typically bandwagon with rising dissatisfied challengers," a regularity for which the simpler realist models cannot account.[44]

Christensen's and Snyder's work and Schweller's research both exemplify the Lakatosian "verificationist" approach to theory-building. A simple model is identified; it is extended by relaxing an unrealistic assumption; and the new, more complicated model is corroborated by showing that it accounts for data that the simpler, less realistic model cannot explain. Where increasing verisimilitude leads to greater explanatory power in this fashion, theories gain corroboration.

Conclusion

The explanatory model summarized in this chapter stabilizes Lakatos's discussion of "novel facts" in theoretical research programs. To "predict new facts" with a theory means to explain additional phenomena with more complex and more realistic models. In other words, it shows how new facts can be fitted into the network of what the positivist philosophers like Hempel called "the paradigm of nomic expectability" (the network of expectations we have about how things work and what is connected to what in the world). What matters in this process is "excess corroboration," that is, the confirmation of additional explanatory power with the greater realism of the theory.[45] A "novel" fact is an additional fact; it need not be temporally or heuristically novel. Note that "facts" include not just events but laws. A novel fact, in other words, is any new *explanandum* (object to be explained).

---

43. Ibid.

44. Ibid., p. 928.

45. Lakatos, "Falsification and the Methodology of Scientific Research Programmes," p. 123.

Of course, to establish the progressivity of a research program, not just any theoretical extension and empirical corroboration will do. Lakatos introduces the technical apparatus of his methodology of scientific research programs (the hard core, heuristics, etc.) at least in part to distinguish between *ad hoc* extensions of a theory (which represent degeneration of a research program) and non–*ad hoc* extensions (which represent progressivity). However, as noted in the introduction to this chapter, the constitutive components of a research program are difficult to specify non-arbitrarily. This leaves us with the problem of handling potentially *ad hoc* hypotheses. Those who ponder this problem might do well to keep in mind Popper's general approach, which rests on the idea of *severe tests*. Popper writes:

The theoretician will ... try his best to detect any false theory among the set of non-refuted competitors; he will try to "catch" it. That is, he will, with respect to any given non-refuted theory, try to think of cases or situations in which it is likely to fail, if it is false. Thus he will try to construct *severe* tests, and *crucial* test situations.[46]

Lakatos, although he follows Popper on many other points, downplays the significance of severe testing. He explicitly rejects the idea of crucial tests "if these are meant to be experiments which can *instantly* overthrow a research program."[47] Lakatos recommends leniency toward new research programs, arguing that "we should not discard a budding research program simply because it has so far failed to overtake a powerful rival."[48] All theories, in any case, "are born refuted and die refuted," in Lakatos's view.[49] His methodology of scientific research programs is an impassioned plea for tolerance toward theories that face disconfirming evidence, even over long periods of time.

---

46. Popper, *Objective Knowledge*, p. 14.

47. Lakatos, "Falsification and the Methodology of Scientific Research Programmes," p. 173 (emphasis in the original).

48. Ibid., p. 157.

49. Lakatos, *The Methodology of Scientific Research Programs*, p. 5.

Lakatos's pleas for tolerance are well taken, but they create a potential problem if his criteria for determining the constitutive elements of a scientific research program remain incomplete or ambiguous. Unless we can identify, for any research program under examination, a *complete, unambiguous* and *unchanging* hard core, it will be impossible to distinguish *ad hoc* from non–*ad hoc* developments of a theory, and hence between progressive and degenerating problem-shifts. For under these conditions there will be little to stop researchers from tweaking the hard core in order to immunize a new hypothesis against the charge of being *ad hoc*. If Lakatos's real purpose is to distinguish theories that pass severe tests from those that do not (and often this seems to be the case, as when he praises theories that correctly make "undreamt of" predictions, and condemns "theories that are fabricated only in order to accommodate known facts"[50]), our discussion might focus fruitfully on the structure and logic of such testing. Intuitively, a test of a theory is severe if it has a high probability of "flunking" a false theory. Severity is analogous to what many statisticians traditionally call the "power" of a test: the probability of correctly rejecting a mistaken hypothesis.[51]

None of this means that Lakatos's methodology of scientific research programs should be abandoned. Rather, it means that in working through the various problems that Lakatos has left behind—particularly the difficulty of identifying the elements of a scientific research program, and sorting out the ambiguities of the role that "novel facts" play in theory confirmation—we should keep in mind Lakatos's Popperian roots, and remember that, in the short run at least, our aim should be to seek the best and most severe tests of our theories that we can construct.

---

50. Lakatos, *The Methodology of Scientific Research Programs*, p. 5.

51. These statisticians are most closely associated with the Neyman-Pearson tradition. Ronald Giere, "Testing Theoretical Hypotheses," in John Earman, ed., *Testing Scientific Theories* (Minneapolis: University of Minnesota Press, 1983), p. 292.

Chapter 12

Measuring Intra-programmatic Progress

Roslyn Simowitz

Exploring why scientists have switched their allegiance from one research program to a rival program has been a major bone of contention among philosophers and historians of science. Lakatos believed that shifting allegiances from one research program to another was a rational process in which scientists chose the progressive program over its degenerating rival.[1] Thomas Kuhn, on the other hand, regarded this process of shifting loyalties and commitments to be largely grounded in psychological and sociological factors, making these shifts primarily nonrational.[2] Kuhn referred to these shifts by scientists as revolutionary science, leading to completely different terms, conceptual definitions, and problems to be investigated.

Unlike the criteria for choosing between competing theories, philosophers and historians of science have largely agreed upon the criteria for measuring progress within a single research paradigm. Lakatos and Popper, for example, both emphasize the ability of successive theories to predict novel phenomena.[3] Both Popper and Kuhn emphasize increased generality, precision, and simplicity as indicative of intra-programmatic progress.[4] Lakatos's concept of progressive shifts within a research program includes, among other things, increased generality.

---

1. Imre Lakatos, "Falsification and the Methodology of Scientific Research Programmes," in Imre Lakatos and Alan Musgrave, eds., *Criticism and the Growth of Knowledge* (Cambridge: Cambridge University Press, 1970).

2. Thomas Kuhn, *The Structure of Scientific Revolutions* (Chicago: University of Chicago Press, 1970).

3. Karl Popper, *Conjectures and Refutations: The Growth of Scientific Knowledge* (New York: Basic Books, 1963).

4. Karl Popper, *The Logic of Discovery* (New York: Basic Books, 1959).

Eliminating logical inconsistencies as well as resolving methodological problems such as inappropriate statistical tests are measures of intra-programmatic progress for both Kuhn and Laudan.[5]

Scholars in international relations appear to be in agreement, as well, regarding measures of progress within a single research program. In the past, for example, Rudolph Rummel, J. David Singer, and Harold Guetzkow argued that their respective research programs were progressive because, among other reasons, they tested more precise, more general, or simpler propositions as research in their programs evolved.[6] More recently, Kugler and Organski and Bruce Bueno de Mesquita have claimed that their research programs were more progressive than rival programs because their respective programs met Lakatosian standards for progress while rival programs did not.[7] Prior to this volume, however, international relations scholars have not clearly defined or operationalized Lakatos's measures of progress so that they could be systematically applied to different bodies of literature in international

5. Larry Laudan, *Progress and Its Problems* (Berkeley: University of California Press, 1977).

6. Rudolph Rummel, "The Dimensionality of Nations Project," in Francis W. Hoole and Dina A. Zinnes, eds., *Quantitative International Politics: An Appraisal* (New York: Praeger, 1976), pp. 149–154, 219–243; J. David Singer, "The Correlates of War Project: Continuity, Diversity, and Convergence," in Frank W. Hoole and Dina A. Zinnes, eds., *Quantitative International Politics: An Appraisal* (New York: Praeger, 1976), pp. 21–42, 128–145; Harold Guetzkow, "An Incomplete History of Fifteen Short Years in Simulating International Processes, " in Hoole and Zinnes, *Quantitative International Politics*, pp. 247–258; Harold Guetzkow and William Ladd Hollist, "Some Instructive Experiences Gained in Simulating International Processes, 1959–72," in Hoole and Zinnes, *Quantitative International Politics*, pp. 328–346.

7. A.F.K. Organski and Jacek Kugler, "The Power Transition: A Retrospective and Prospective Evaluation," in Manus I. Midlarsky, ed., *Handbook of War Studies* (Winchester, Mass.: Unwin Hyman, 1989), pp. 171–194; Bruce Bueno de Mesquita, "The Contribution of Expected Utility Theory to the Study of International Conflict," in ibid.; Bueno de Mesquita, "Toward a Scientific Understanding of International Conflict: A Personal View," *International Studies Quarterly*, Vol. 29, No. 2 (June 1985), pp. 121–136.

relations. Elman and Elman are among the first scholars to clarify and define Lakatos's measures precisely.[8]

In this volume, DiCicco and Levy and Snyder examine how generally applicable Lakatos's criteria are to the variety of research programs found in the international relations literature. DiCicco and Levy use these measures to assess progress within the power transition research program, while Snyder asks whether it is also possible to apply Lakatosian measures to normative research programs that do not use a positivist methodology. Positivism involves applying scientific methods to evaluate specific theoretical predictions. Both positivist research programs (such as the power transition program) and nonpositivist programs involve making empirical claims about reality. But positivist research programs test their empirical claims employing scientific methodology, whereas nonpositivist programs do not.

In reviewing the studies by DiCicco and Levy and Snyder, three questions are addressed. The first question is whether Lakatos's criteria can be applied in a systematic way to positive research programs in international relations. The answer to this question is a qualified yes. Although DiCicco and Levy show that it is possible to identify and differentiate progressive problemshifts from degenerative ones, because of several ambiguities in Lakatos's methodology it is not always possible to identify all types of problemshifts.

The second question that arises is whether employing Lakatos's criteria can help us in determining whether a particular program is degenerative or progressive. I argue that Lakatos's criteria cannot help us in making this determination. Although it is possible to distinguish between progressive and degenerative problemshifts, Lakatos does not provided us with the means to aggregate these shifts into a single assessment of progressivity. Additionally, Lakatos's criteria for progress are much too narrow in determining whether a particular research program is progressive or degenerative. Lakatos's criteria for progress fail to include many scientific activities that are regarded by the scientific community as rational and progressive pursuits.

---

8. Colin Elman and Miriam Fendius Elman, Chapters 1 and 2 in this volume.

The third and final question addressed here is whether it is possible to apply Lakatosian standards to measure progress within normative research programs. I argue that because the empirical claims of these programs are irrefutable, it is impossible to apply Lakatos's criteria to them. Although Lakatos's measures cannot be used to assess the progressivity of normative research programs, I argue that, nonetheless, there are a number of advantages to be obtained by applying his criteria to ongoing research programs.

The Power Transition Research Program

DiCicco and Levy do an excellent job of describing the power transition research program, identifying the fundamental elements of Lakatos's methodology of scientific research programs, and assessing problemshifts for evidence of progress and degeneration. Moreover, by describing difficulties they encountered in their application, they are able to identify several ambiguities in Lakatos's metatheory, thereby raising questions about the general applicability of his appraisal criteria. After identifying the fundamental components of Lakatos's methodology, DiCicco and Levy identify both progressive and degenerative problemshifts. They find mixed results. Lemke's work on hierarchical systems is regarded as a progressive intra-program problemshift,[9] while Kim's study of alliances is judged to be a progressive inter-program problemshift.[10] In contrast,

---

9. Douglas Lemke, *Multiple Hierarchies in World Politics* (Ph.D. diss., Vanderbilt University, 1993); Lemke, "Toward a General Understanding of Parity and War," *Conflict Management and Peace Science*, Vol. 14, No. 2 (Winter 1995), pp. 143–162; Lemke, "Small States and War: An Expansion of Power Transition Theory," in Jacek Kugler and Douglas Lemke, eds., *Parity and War: Evaluations and Extensions of* The War Ledger (Ann Arbor: University of Michigan Press, 1996), pp. 77–92; Lemke, "Peace and War in the Far East: An Application of the Multiple Hierarchy Model," paper presented at the annual meeting of the International Studies Association, Toronto, 1997; Douglas Lemke and Suzanne Werner, "Power Parity, Commitment to Change, and War," *International Studies Quarterly*, Vol. 40, No. 2 (June 1996), pp. 235–260.

10. Woosang Kim, "Power, Alliance, and Major Wars, 1816–1975," *Journal of Conflict Resolution*, Vol. 33, No. 2 (June 1989), pp. 255–273; Kim, "Alliance Transitions and Great Power War," *American Journal of Political Science*, Vol. 35, No.

studies on the timing of war—whether wars occur prior to, during, or after transitions, and who initiates war and why—appear to exhibit degenerative tendencies. DiCicco and Levy conclude that more work is needed in these areas.

DiCicco and Levy's rigorous efforts to apply Lakatos's criteria to the power transition research program enable them to identify more general problems in applying Lakatosian criteria. Finding evidence of both progressive and degenerative problemshifts, DiCicco and Levy point out that Lakatos fails to suggest how to aggregate these shifts into one overall assessment of the research program. Although Lakatos intended his criteria to be used to assess rival programs, it is easy to conceive of competing programs where each exhibits both progressive and degenerative problemshifts. Here too, Lakatos provides no guidance or rational grounds for choosing between competing programs where each contains progressive and degenerative problemshifts.

DiCicco and Levy also note difficulties in identifying the hard core, and question whether the core can be assumed to evolve over time. If we can assume the latter, it becomes difficult if not impossible to distinguish between intra-program and inter-program problemshifts. Likewise, if the positive heuristic is also assumed to evolve, we cannot distinguish "ad hoc_3," degenerating adjustments from progressive intra-program problem-shifts.[11]

DiCicco and Levy conclude their assessment of Lakatosian metatheory by claiming that Lakatos's definition of progress is overly restrictive, although they do not discuss their reasons for this claim. I also find Lakatos's definition of progress too narrow. This is because there is a significant amount of scientific activity that would not be viewed as progressive from a Lakatosian perspective. The most obvious examples involve work done in the development and refinement of measures of key

---

4 (November 1991), pp. 833–850; Kim, "Power Transitions and Great Power War from Westphalia to Waterloo," *World Politics*, Vol. 45, No. 1 (October 1992), pp. 153–172; Kim, "Power Parity, Alliance, and War from 1648 to 1975," in Kugler and Lemke, *Parity and War*, pp. 93–106.

[11] See Elman and Elman, Chapter 2 in this volume, for a discussion of the varieties of ad hoc adjustments.

variables. Unless these operationalizations save the theory from refutation and lead to the prediction and corroboration of novel information, these activities would not be regarded as progressive. The same claim can be made for testing the robustness of propositions. Many researchers test the robustness of a single proposition by varying operationalizations of variables, time periods, and domains. But these tests do not involve predicting and corroborating novel phenomena and would therefore not be categorized as progressive using Lakatosian criteria. In short, Lakatos's definition of progress is not in accord with what many scientists do and with what they identify as rational and progressive pursuits.

Given these various problems in applying Lakatosian metatheory, are there any justifications for continuing to employ it? I believe the answer is affirmative for several reasons. First, the requirement of a precise statement of the hard core in a given research program may facilitate detection of conceptual ambiguities and inconsistencies. To demonstrate this, I turn to Lemke's study of hierarchical systems. By viewing regional systems nested within the global system as hierarchically ordered, Lemke is able to predict wars between regional challenger and dominant nations. According to one of power transition theory's core assumptions, the dominant global power imposes its order throughout the global system. In doing so, the dominant global nation would also be imposing order within its nested subsystems. If this interpretation is correct, then the regional challenger might not only challenge the order imposed by the dominant regional power, but also the order imposed by the dominant global power if the latter wishes to maintain the regional status quo. Under these circumstances, the regional challenger would then be initiating war in spite of a significant power differential between itself and the dominant global nation. Although this interpretation may shed light on the tendency of dominant global nations to intervene in regional wars, it also contradicts the relationship between parity and war predicted by power transitionists.

While this interpretation of Lemke's work may be inaccurate, it emanates in part from the ambiguity of the concept "order." A failure to identify the rules, practices, and interactions prescribed and prohibited by dominant global powers may result in inconsistencies between theoretical assumptions and predictions.

Another example where an application of Lakatosian metatheory may facilitate the identification of inconsistencies involves the timing of war and who initiates. As DiCicco and Levy note, these issues have been a source of controversy among power transitionists. Organski originally argued that war was initiated by the challenger prior to the transition.[12] However, in subsequent work, Organski and Kugler argued that the challenger initiated war after the transition.[13] In the latter argument, it appears that the rational calculations of dominant global powers are being seriously overlooked, with little (if any) attention given to the possibility that dominant global nations might initiate preventive wars. Initiation of preventive war by dominant global powers prior to transitions would appear to be their most rational strategy. In requiring an explicit statement of the hard core assumptions of the power transition research program, Lakatosian metatheory highlights the failure of Organski and Kugler to take into account the rationality of dominant global powers.

A second advantage of applying Lakatosian metatheory to research programs is that it may also facilitate the identification of inconsistent predictions between rival programs. In their identification of the hard core, for example, DiCicco and Levy describe two assumptions of power transition theory that conflict with assumptions of balance of power theory. According to power transitionists, the international system is ordered in ways that reflect the interests of dominant global powers. Balance of power theorists, on the other hand, emphasize the anarchic nature of the international system and view any semblance of order as an unintended consequence. Because power transitionists see the system as ordered, they also assume a great deal of similarity between domestic and international systems. In contrast, balance of power theorists see a great deal of dissimilarity between the two. Although these are clearly contradictory assumptions, their implications for international outcomes are, to a large extent, unspecified. What are the different predictions implied by assumptions of order versus anarchy, and similarity versus dissimilarity? Applying Lakatosian metatheory makes us more cognizant

---

12. A.F.K. Organski, *World Politics* (New York: Knopf, 1958).

13. A.F.K. Organski and Jacek Kugler, *The War Ledger* (Chicago: University of Chicago Press, 1980).

of conflicting assumptions in rival research programs by requiring an identification of their hard cores. In also requiring an identification of their positive heuristics and protective belts of auxiliary statements, we are more attuned to the propositions requiring modification or adjustment to derive additional, and in this case, contradictory implications. If the implications of these conflicting assumptions were identified and tested, we might have a more rational basis for choosing between competing research programs.

Although DiCicco and Levy demonstrate that it is indeed possible to apply Lakatosian standards in a systematic way, they also show that these standards cannot be used to assess whether or not a specific research program is progressive or degenerative. This is because Lakatos provides no guidance for how we aggregate the degenerative and progressive problemshifts evidenced within a single program. Likewise, the inability to aggregate progressive and degenerative problemshifts also renders it impossible to choose between rival research programs. Furthermore, ambiguities surrounding several of Lakatos's key concepts make it difficult to distinguish between intra- and inter-programmatic progress as well as between ad hoc$_3$ degenerating problemshifts and progressive intra-program problemshifts. It is also evident that Lakatosian criteria fail to include many of the pursuits that scientists themselves consider progressive.

Despite these flaws, applying Lakatosian metatheory to evaluate scientific progress is superior to most of the evaluations currently found in the international relations literature. Most appraisals of progress rely upon ambiguous or even unstated measures that are not systematically applied to the studies under review. Because Elman and Elman provide clear and precise definitions of Lakatos's measures, DiCicco and Levy have been able to apply them in a consistent and systematic way to the power transition research program. Although DiCicco and Levy were unable to provide an overall assessment of the progress made in this research program, they were able to distinguish between progressive and degenerative research strategies employed by those scholars working within it.

Applying Lakatosian Measures to Normative Research Programs

Snyder argues that it is also possible to subject the empirical predictions of normative arguments to scientific testing and Lakatosian standards for appraising progress. This is an intriguing issue because, as Snyder points out, although normative arguments contain empirical claims, international relations scholars have rarely tested these claims in a scientific way. Contrary to Snyder, however, I argue that it is virtually impossible to test normative claims scientifically or to assess progress in normative programs using Lakatosian standards. Although the empirical claims found in normative arguments are falsifiable in principle, they are nonfalsifiable in practice, as I argue below. Therefore it is impossible to employ scientific methodology in testing them. Because Lakatosian standards can only be applied to theories or arguments whose derived propositions are falsifiable, I find it impossible to apply Lakatosian measures to evaluate progress within normative research programs.

To assess Snyder's argument, it is first necessary to distinguish between using positivist methods and using Lakatosian methodology. Positivism involves applying scientific methods to evaluate specific theoretical predictions. Lakatosian methodology, on the other hand, is a metatheoretic system for appraising progress in a series of scientific theories. Consequently, two distinct questions must be addressed: (1) can normative arguments be subjected to the scientific methodology of positivism? and (2) can normative research programs be subjected to Lakatosian criteria?

I begin by addressing the first question: can empirical claims in normative arguments be subjected to scientific tests? Snyder describes the empirical claims found in positivist theories as stating relationships between facts. Normative arguments, on the other hand, stipulate relationships between norms and facts. From the examples Snyder provides, norm-fact relationships are typically presented in the following way: states should behave in specific ways in order to achieve X, where X is the desired norm. The conditional statement resulting from this argument is simply that if nations behave in such and such ways, X will result. In the examples Snyder provides, both antecedent and consequent clauses in these conditional statements are, in principle, observable.

Although the antecedent and consequent clauses of these norm-fact propositions are observable and falsifiable in principle, unfortunately, they are nonfalsifiable in practice. To be falsifiable in practice, the antecedent clauses describing national behavior must be refutable. But the antecedent clauses of these propositions describing national behavior are, for all practical purposes, vacuous. This is because nations rarely, if ever, behave in the hypothesized ways described by the antecedent clauses. Therefore, these conditional propositions expressing a relationship between national behaviors (or facts) and norms are irrefutable. The only way these propositions can be refuted or falsified is when their antecedents are corroborated while their consequent clauses are refuted. But in these types of propositions, the antecedent clauses can never be corroborated if they are almost always vacuous. Therefore, these conditional propositions relating national behaviors to norms are rendered nonfalsifiable.

To illustrate this point, I turn to some of the specific examples provided by Snyder. One way in which empirical claims enter normative arguments is through what Snyder calls "simple consequentialism." Someone might, for example, argue that X is a just or fair outcome and we should therefore adopt policy Y to achieve X. Snyder refers to work on ethnic relations by Lijphart and Horowitz as representative of this type of argument.[14] Both want to reduce the amount of inter-ethnic violence, but they disagree on the political institutions that would achieve this objective. Their hypotheses are of the following form: if certain political processes were instituted, a reduction in ethnic violence would result. These hypotheses look, in fact, very much like the empirical claims found in many positivist theories. The problem here, however, is that there are too few instantiations of the conditions in the antecedent clauses to warrant the use of scientific methods for testing these hypotheses. In other

---

14. Arend Lijphart, *Democracy in Plural Societies* (New Haven, Conn.: Yale University Press, 1977); Lijphart, "The Power-Sharing Approach," in Joseph V. Montville, ed., *Conflict and Peacemaking in Multiethnic Societies* (New York: Lexington, 1991), pp. 491–510; Donald Horowitz, *A Democratic South Africa: Constitutional Engineering in a Divided Society* (Berkeley: University of California

words, if one wanted to use inferential statistical procedures to test these hypotheses, the antecedent clauses would be, for all practical purposes, vacuous. However, the only way to falsify or refute these hypotheses is by corroborating their antecedent clauses while refuting their consequents.

Snyder identifies a second type of normative argument with empirical claims as "norms consequentialism." These are claims about the effects that actions have on the long term weakening or strengthening of norms. The example given here involves war crime tribunals. Advocates of these tribunals argue that if punishment is certain and severe, future war criminals will be deterred. But once again, this antecedent condition, although observable in principle, is vacuous in reality, thereby rendering the hypothesis nonfalsifiable. In this example Snyder acknowledges that "co-variation tests under present conditions cannot reveal whether this norm's consequentialist program is progressing or degenerating." But prior to assessing progression or degeneration in this research program, it is necessary to acknowledge that its major empirical claim cannot be tested using scientific methods.

I turn now to the second issue Snyder raises: can Lakatosian criteria be used for assessing progress in normative research programs? Snyder believes it may be feasible to apply Lakatosian criteria to assess progress in normative programs, and in fact he employs some Lakatosian concepts in his examples. However, given that, as I have just argued, their empirical claims are nonfalsifiable, it is impossible to apply Lakatosian criteria to assess the progressiveness of normative research programs.

As Snyder argues, because normative research programs make claims about observable phenomena, it is interesting to see whether these programs can be subjected to scientific testing and Lakatosian standards for measuring progress. Although Snyder concludes that these endeavors are feasible, I do not. Because Snyder demonstrates that the claims made in normative arguments are in principle observable, he believes they can therefore be subjected to scientific testing as well as Lakatosian standards of appraisal. I argue, however, that if the phenomena described by a proposition are rarely (if ever) observable in the real world, that

---

Press, 1991); Horowitz, "Making Moderation Pay," in Montville, *Conflict and Peacemaking in Multiethnic Societies*, pp. 451–476.

proposition cannot be scientifically tested. Thus normative research programs cannot be subjected to Lakatosian standards of appraisal. The falsifiability of propositions is a necessary condition for applying Lakatos's methodology of scientific research programs.

Conclusion

DiCicco and Levy demonstrate convincingly that it is possible to apply Lakatos's criteria in a systematic way by identifying progressive and degenerative problemshifts in the power transition research program. However, Snyder's argument is less convincing; I argue that it is impossible to subject the empirical claims of normative research programs to scientific testing or to an application of Lakatos's measures of progress.

The significant question is whether Lakatosian methodology can be used to assess the overall progressivity of research programs in international relations. Lakatos's criteria cannot be applied to normative research programs due to the irrefutable nature of their claims. Moreover, although Lakatos's criteria can be applied in a systematic way to scientific research programs, I believe it is impossible for these criteria to provide us with an overall measure of a particular research program's progressivity. This is largely a result of our inability to aggregate opposing problemshifts into one net assessment of progressivity. To my knowledge, Lakatos does not address this problem. To provide such an assessment, it would be necessary to weigh the number, significance, and generality of the phenomena explained by the program's progressive problemshifts as well as the simplicity of those shifts. It would also be necessary to compare how persistent were its degenerating shifts and the significance of the phenomena the research program fails to explain. The phenomena repeatedly resistant to progressive problemshifts and the significance of these phenomena would then have to be subtracted from the significance and array of phenomena the program explains. If this task of ascribing weights could be done, it might be possible to use Lakatos's criteria to provide a net assessment of a specific research program's progressivity. However, Lakatos intended his criteria to serve as a comparative metric for choosing between competing research programs. Applying Lakatos's criteria for choosing between competing programs, however, may prove impossible if the phenomena explained by each are incomparable. Relying solely on Lakatos's criteria would in all likelihood provide an inadequate assessment of a research program's progressivity, because many activities commonly pursued by scientists and regarded by them as progressive—such as eliminating conceptual ambiguities, providing better operationalizations of key concepts, and applying more appropriate statistical tests—are not incorporated in Lakatos's measures of progress. To obtain an overall assessment of a research program's progressivity, these activities would have to be appraised in conjunction with use of Lakatos's criteria. Showing that it is possible to define, operationalize, and systematically apply Lakatos's measures, Elman and Elman provide us with hope that it may be possible to operationalize and systematically apply these other criteria as well.

In pointing out the limitations of Lakatos's criteria to assess the progressivity of research programs, I do not mean to imply that an application of Lakatos's measures is without merit. It could help us to detect conceptual ambiguities and inconsistencies in a particular research program. It could also facilitate an identification of inconsistent predictions between rival research programs. Such an application could serve to focus our attention on those propositions in need of modification or adjustment in order to eliminate a program's inconsistencies or contradictory implications. Most significantly, Lakatos's criteria, as clarified by Elman and Elman, applied in a consistent and uniform manner to research programs in international relations, would most definitely provide more systematic evaluations of research in the field.

Chapter 13

Kuhn versus Lakatos?

The Case for Multiple Frames in Appraising International Relations Theory

John Vasquez

Progress, and the idea of it, has been since the time of the Enlightenment a cherished tradition, although of late it has produced its skeptics.[1] This chapter juxtaposes two different ideas of progress that are used in this book—the conventional Enlightenment idea of the cumulation of knowledge and the more technical criterion of progressive problemshifts outlined in recent discussions of philosophy of science—and assesses their implications for appraising theory in international relations. Assessing progress in international relations (IR) involves appraising theory in a rigorous fashion; however, there are multiple ways in which theory can be appraised. This chapter compares the relative merits of using the frameworks offered by Imre Lakatos and Thomas Kuhn.[2] Two research programs—offense-defense theory and neoclassical realism—are briefly reviewed to illustrate the

My thanks to the editors and to Marie T. Henehan for useful comments. The sole responsibility for the article remains mine, however.

1. Michel Foucault, *Power/Knowledge*, ed. by C. Gordon (New York: Pantheon, 1980); Richard K. Ashley, "At the Impasse: Epistemology and the Scientific Evaluation of Foreign Policy," in John Vasquez, ed., *Evaluating U.S. Foreign Policy* (New York: Praeger, 1986), pp. 159–204.

2. Imre Lakatos, "Falsification and the Methodology of Scientific Research Programmes," in Imre Lakatos and Alan Musgrave, eds., *Criticism and the Growth of Knowledge* (Cambridge: Cambridge University Press, 1970), pp. 91–196; Thomas S. Kuhn, *The Structure of Scientific Revolutions*, 2nd ed., enl. (Chicago: University of Chicago Press, 1970).

relevancy and limits of Lakatos's framework and some of the key issues at stake in theory appraisal.

The term progress, even as used in this volume, has its ambiguities. The conventional meaning refers to the idea that there will be an advancement in knowledge, at least in terms of knowing things that one did not know or solving puzzles. The promise and hope of the Enlightenment is that inquiry will increase knowledge and that this knowledge can be used to improve the lot of humanity.

The field of international relations is no stranger to this sentiment, even though it is a latecomer to the social sciences. Born in the aftermath of the First World War, the field was created by scholars and supported by idealists in the political arena in order to apply human reason to solve the problem of war and, in effect, end it.[3] The failure of the League of Nations to live up to this promise led to the overthrow of idealism as the dominant paradigm within international relations inquiry and the ascendance of realism.[4] The idea of progress, then, not only helped give birth to the field but was the main motivation behind its first paradigm shift, in that the obvious failure to prevent war led to the demise of the dominant paradigm of idealism.

The conventional Enlightenment meaning of progress has been at the heart of international relations inquiry, and no doubt part of the attention the idea receives in this book and others like it stems from the role it continues to play in the field.[5] There is, however, a second

---

3. See Grayson Kirk, *The Study of International Relations in American Colleges and Universities* (New York: Council on Foreign Relations, 1947), pp. 3–4; William T.R. Fox, "Interwar International Relations Research: The American Experience," *World Politics*, Vol. 2, No. 1 (October 1949), pp. 67–79, p. 68; Brian Porter, ed., *The Aberystwyth Papers: International Politics 1919–1969* (London: Oxford University Press, 1972); John Vasquez, *The Power of Power Politics: A Critique* (New Brunswick: Rutgers University Press, 1983), pp. 13–14.

4. William C. Olson, "The Growth of a Discipline," in Porter, *The Aberystwyth Papers: International Politics*, pp. 1–29; Vasquez, *The Power of Power Politics* (1983), pp. 15–19; Steve Smith, "The Self-Images of a Discipline: A Genealogy of International Relations Theory," in Ken Booth and Steve Smith, eds., *International Relations Theory Today* (Cambridge, U.K.: Polity Press, 1995), pp. 1–37.

5. See, e.g., Emmanuel Adler and Beverly Crawford, eds., *Progress in Postwar International Relations* (New York: Columbia University Press, 1991). For a non-

meaning and referent to the term. This is the idea of "progressive versus degenerating problemshifts" that was developed by Imre Lakatos.[6] This idea of progress underlies all of the chapters in this book, and it is important to distinguish it from the more conventional meaning of progress because the two are quite different, and using them interchangeably, as is sometimes done, can lead to ambiguity and needless miscommunication.

Lakatos developed the idea of "progressive problemshifts" to deal with a very specific problem in philosophy of science in reaction to Kuhn's criticism of Popper—namely, that theories are not falsified by discrepant evidence but reformulated.[7] Lakatos points out that there can be an endless number of reformulations that, in effect, produce a violation of Popper's rule of falsifiability.[8] Since working scientists do not falsify theories the way Popper thought they *should*, does this make scientific inquiry irrational? Lakatos concedes to Kuhn and later post-positivists that there are no logically compelling grounds on which to prevent theory reformulation, but he offers a decision rule that he argues is reasonable (although one is not logically compelled to use it). He argues that since Popper's procedure does not offer "a suitable guide for a rational reconstruction of the history of science, we may just as well completely rethink our approach. Why aim at falsification at any price? Why not rather *impose* certain standards on the theoretical adjustments by which one is allowed to save a theory?"[9]

Lakatos's replacement standard—that of progressive problem-shifts—is derivative of his more important idea of what constitutes a degenerating research program. He apparently understands the indicators of the problem he is trying to solve better than the indicators

---

IR treatment, see James B. Rule, *Theory and Progress in Social Science* (Cambridge: Cambridge University Press, 1997).

6. Lakatos, "Falsification and the Methodology of Scientific Research Programmes."

7. Kuhn, *The Structure of Scientific Revolutions*, 2nd ed.; Karl Popper, *The Logic of Scientific Discovery* (London: Hutchinson, 1959).

8. Lakatos, "Falsification and the Methodology of Scientific Research Programmes," pp. 116–117.

9. Ibid., p. 117, emphasis added.

of a successful research program, since his indicators of what constitutes a degenerating research program appear a bit clearer, at least to this reader. Nevertheless, the key point is that Lakatos's criterion is much more technical and deals with a very specific problem in research that is not present in all research programs, unlike the conventional idea of progress, which is widely applicable. For Lakatos, the idea of a degenerating or progressive research program only arises in light of research that has produced a considerable body of evidence. If this research has produced a number of anomalies that are not easily explained away and results in a *series* of theories that constantly shift the stipulated body of evidence that would falsify it, this raises the question whether this is a degenerating research program. (In the absence of a series of theoretical emendations, it is unlikely that the question would arise: the question of a progressive research program is only likely to be raised in comparison to a research program that is thought by some to be degenerating.) The main point is that without a considerable body of research, it is premature and hence inappropriate to apply Lakatos's technical criterion to a research program. In such a case, looser and more general ideas of progress, or some entirely different criteria, might be applied.

Some discussions in this volume slip from Lakatos's technical definition of progress to the broader conventional Enlightenment definition. This tends to happen when, instead of looking at whether a research program avoids being degenerating or actually appears to be progressive, authors appraise a program on the very general terms of whether we have learned anything, without dealing with the specific indicators of what constitutes a progressive or degenerating problemshift. In other places, Lakatos's technical criterion is applied to situations where it is inappropriate: to situations where there has not been much research at all and there are, therefore, no anomalies to explain away in a degenerative or progressive fashion.

This chapter explores how these two ideas of progress apply to appraising international relations theory. Theory appraisal is an important task within any field, and particularly one like IR, where debates over paradigms and contending theories frequently come to the fore. To appraise the adequacy of theories and paradigms, it is necessary to have a set of standards by which they can be compared and evaluated. These standards will be most useful if all sides agree on their importance and their relevance.

THEORY APPRAISAL AND THE DESIRABILITY OF MULTIPLE FRAMES

The thesis of this chapter is that there are a variety of useful ways of conducting a theory appraisal and a number of different criteria that can be applied. So long as the appraisal is rigorous and the criteria are specific, any systematic effort is probably going to be more useful than the typical review of the literature that substitutes for serious appraisal in the field, or the occasional ranting across paradigm boundaries. This is not to say that literature reviews and open debates are unimportant, only that appraisals of theories and paradigms can, and should, be done in a more systematic and rigorous fashion.

To achieve this end, it is necessary to indicate on what basis a theory can satisfy or fail to satisfy a particular criterion. The criteria themselves should be justified on some epistemological foundation. The most powerful frames for appraisal are those that explicitly address the major questions of philosophy of science, and those that are embedded in theoretical explanations of the development and history of science.[10] Two widely used frames that fit these characterizations are those of Thomas Kuhn and Imre Lakatos.[11] Each has different strengths. Alternative frames are those of Laudan and Foucault, as well as Alker, who reviews Kuhn and Lakatos in terms of the possibility of using a dialectical frame for theory appraisal.[12]

While it is difficult for practicing social scientists to make original contributions to philosophy of science and epistemology, and unlikely

10. See David Dessler, Chapter 11 in this volume.

11. Kuhn, *The Structure of Scientific Revolutions*; Lakatos, "Falsification and the Methodology of Scientific Research Programmes."

12. Larry Laudan, *Progress and Its Problems: Towards a Theory of Scientific Growth* (Berkeley: University of California Press, 1977); Michel Foucault, *The Archaeology of Knowledge* (New York: Pantheon, 1972); Hayward R. Alker, Jr., "Logic, Dialectics, Politics: Some Recent Controversies," *Dialectical Logics for the Political Sciences*, Vol. 7 of *Poznan Studies in the Philosophy of the Sciences and the Humanities* (Amsterdam: Rodopi, 1982), pp. 65–94.

that any frame we could construct would be as strong as one we could borrow, it becomes quickly obvious that some aspects of existing frames are more easily applied, appear more relevant, and are less procrustean than other aspects. This is true of all frames, even those provided by Kuhn and by Lakatos.

The case for using multiple frames is based on the assumption that no single frame is perfect: that no one epistemology has solved the problem of truth. Some scholars have a misplaced confidence in their ability to develop a perfect epistemology or research design. Given the history of inquiry and of philosophy, it is reasonable to build safeguards into any theory appraisal, in case the foundation upon which it is based turns out to be wrong. We are all seekers of the truth, but we dwell in Plato's Cave and not in the Open Light of the Forms. There are those who think they have found a path out of the Cave—that it is possible to distinguish clearly correct epistemologies from those that are wrong. Yet the history of philosophy and epistemology is one of constantly finding logical and other flaws, indeed cracks, in the foundation of knowledge. In such circumstances, it is best to apply different frames and see what they tell us about the field and its search for truth.

Different frames are apt to tell us different things about our own endeavors and uncover different strengths and weaknesses. The strongest theories should be able to satisfy the differing criteria of various frames, and the weakest and most muddled are likely to find it difficult to satisfy any of them. A field characterized by epistemological pluralism, as IR now is, should at least apply the frames it has and see if they make a difference in how competing theories or paradigms are evaluated.

For example, realism in its various forms is, in my view, so flawed in certain areas that it will not do well except with frames that have ambiguous criteria that just about any theory or paradigm would be able to satisfy. The criteria embodied in Kuhn's and Lakatos's frames are not of this sort. I have derived six criteria from standard philosophy of science, drawing upon Popper, Kuhn, and Lakatos, for appraising empirical theory, and seven criteria, drawn from other sources, for appraising practical theory.[13] The criteria for appraising empirical theory are: empirical accuracy, falsifiability, explanatory power, progressive versus degenerating problemshifts, consistency with what is known, and parsimony. All of these criteria have widespread adherence within mainstream IR and political science, as they do in the physical sciences.[14] My appraisal of neotraditional research on Waltz's balancing-of-power hypothesis employed only Lakatos's degenerating versus progressive problemshift criterion, which for the sake of convenience I will refer to here as Lakatos's criterion of progressivity.[15] This attracted widespread attention, giving rise to a Forum in the *American Political Science Review* with replies by Kenneth Waltz, Thomas Christensen and Jack Snyder, Colin Elman and Miriam Fendius Elman, Randall Schweller, and Stephen Walt and then a book edited by Vasquez and Colin Elman with several new contributions to the debate.[16] However, this was only one of four inter-related theory

---

13. John Vasquez, *The Power of Power Politics: From Classical Realism to Neotraditionalism* (Cambridge: Cambridge University Press, 1998), chap. 10; Popper, *The Logic of Scientific Discovery*; Kuhn, *The Structure of Scientific Revolutions*, p. 199; Lakatos, "Falsification and the Methodology of Scientific Research Programmes."

14. See Kuhn, *The Structure of Scientific Revolutions*, p. 199.

15. Kenneth N. Waltz, *Theory of International Politics* (Reading, Mass.: Addison-Wesley, 1979); John Vasquez, "The Realist Paradigm and Degenerative versus Progressive Research Programs: An Appraisal of Neotraditional Research on Waltz's Balancing Proposition," *American Political Science Review*, Vol. 91, No. 4 (December 1997), pp. 899–912. By "neotraditional research," I mean research that tends to eschew quantitative analysis and emphasizes comparative case studies, historical analysis, and theoretical argumentation.

16. Kenneth N. Waltz, "Evaluating Theories," *American Political Science Review*, Vol. 91, No. 4 (December 1997), pp. 913–917; Thomas J. Christensen and Jack Snyder, "Progressive Research on Degenerate Alliances," ibid., pp. 919–922; Colin Elman and Miriam Fendius Elman, "Lakatos and Neorealism: A Reply to Vasquez," ibid., pp. 923–926; Randall L. Schweller, "New Realist Research on Alliances: Refining, Not Refuting, Waltz's Balancing Proposition," ibid., pp. 927–930; Stephen M. Walt, "The Progressive Power of Realism," ibid., pp. 931–935; and John Vasquez and Colin Elman, eds., *Realism and the Balancing of Power: A New Debate* (Upper Saddle River, N.J.: Prentice-Hall, 2003).

appraisals I conducted on the realist paradigm, each of which employs different criteria.[17]

Colin Elman and Miriam Fendius Elman describe my use of multiple frames and criteria as a "sweet shop error" in their tongue-in-cheek fashion (or perhaps it is a hard-candy-in-the-cheek manner?).[18] Why it is an error to select different pieces of candy when going to a sweet shop eludes me, but I think they mean to say that one should apply a single frame and not embrace eclecticism. They also object to mixing metrics, which they refer to as the "Cuisinart" error.[19] Eclecticism is a well-known response to the quandary of having to adopt a philosophy when one finds all existing philosophies having some flaws but, at the same time, some elements worthy of adopting. This is the situation in all of the social sciences when we find ourselves confronting the fields of epistemology and philosophy of science. It is perfectly permissible to select one frame and apply it systematically, but given that there is no one single flawless frame, there is no reason that would logically prohibit the use of other frames as well. This strategy would also have the utilitarian benefit for those who are risk-averse by allowing the hedging of bets if one of the frames were subsequently overturned by philosophers. If the different frames produced the same appraisal, then this would simply add to the weight of the argument. If they produced different appraisals, then this might provide the basis for discerning what aspects of a theory or paradigm were adequate and what aspects might be flawed. Thus, even in the "worst case" scenario in which different frames produce different appraisals, one need not be reduced to relativism.

While it is difficult to argue against providing more information by employing multiple frames, it is easier to make the argument against mixing different metrics. If the criteria and metrics used to measure whether a theory or paradigm is adequate or increasing knowledge are

---

17. Vasquez, *The Power of Power Politics* (1998).

18. Elman and Elman, Chapter 2 in this volume.

19. Ibid.; also see Colin Elman and Miriam Fendius Elman, "How Not to be Lakatos Intolerant: Appraising Progress in International Relations Theory," *International Studies Quarterly*, Vol. 46, No. 2 (June 2002), pp. 231–262, at 244–245.

based on different epistemologies, then simply bootlegging different criteria may in fact be throwing in vegetables with fruits without regard to whether they will taste good together. Criteria of adequacy should fit together; they should complement one another in terms of the whole picture they provide. The question is whether mixing Kuhn and Lakatos, as I have, has been done in a way that mixes metrics rather than uses multiple frames to complement one another. Put another way, is it a case of Kuhn versus Lakatos, as often put by post-positivists, or can the two be synthesized at some level?

Even though Kuhn and Lakatos are different in two important respects—they differ in their understanding of how inquiry and research unfold within a discipline and in their underlying epistemological predispositions—there is a basis for synthesis. The main contributions of each can, in fact, complement those of the other. Kuhn's major contribution is to provide a theoretically-informed history of science that seeks to uncover general patterns. He is less concerned with how science should work than he is with how practicing scientists actually do work. Lakatos's main contribution is within philosophy of science. He wants to provide a justification and reconstruction of the logic of the scientific method so that we can have confidence that it is producing knowledge. Kuhn is dealing with empirical matters; Lakatos with epistemological questions. This difference in purpose is a basis for synthesis.

Kuhn better understands the empirical history of a science. Several of his concepts provide important insights about scientific inquiry, including the concept of "paradigm" and the ideas of "normal science" and "crisis and scientific revolution." Lakatos ignores these concepts in his description of inquiry. Instead, he develops his own conceptual framework of "research programs" with a "hard core" and "negative and positive heuristics." Some of these concepts are more easily applied than others, as the chapters in this book make abundantly clear. The idea of a positive heuristic provides insight into how a research program unfolds its own logic (which any student of Hegel can appreciate). The idea of a negative heuristic is more elusive, and finding the hard core of a research program (and sometimes the research program itself) is not always as obvious as one would think, reading the abstract Lakatos. The end result is that sometimes (but not always) trying to apply his scheme to write a history or even a description of a field like IR appears to be a procrustean effort.

While this is more than just an inelegance with Lakatos's empirical understanding of science, the real problem is that he has jettisoned Kuhnian concepts that provide insights about science that we did not have before. Gone is the idea of a paradigm and the role it plays in science, and with it the insight that specific theories and research within a field can be guided by an overarching fundamental view of the world that scholars share. This view of the world is provided by the field's exemplar, like Newton's *Principia*, which provides certain fundamental assumptions that guide inquiry.[20] Theory construction for Kuhn is paradigm articulation, and research becomes a matter of solving puzzles initially posed by the exemplar to produce a cumulation of knowledge.[21] This is the long "normal science" phase of inquiry. Only when research produces repeated anomalies do individual scientists begin to question and challenge the assumptions of the paradigm. Then the paradigm may be overthrown and displaced by a new paradigm in the period of crisis and scientific revolution, which occurs infrequently.[22] The process then repeats itself.

Nowhere in Lakatos do we see this kind of history. In particular, the idea of the interconnection among various theoretical schools is lost, and is replaced with the idea of almost atomistic research programs that are highly coherent within themselves but have little relation to each other. Fields do not appear, in Lakatos, as coherent disciplines that integrate and guide a plethora of research programs, and the reason they do not is that he does not identify any equivalent to the paradigm concept.[23] One can use Lakatos's idea of research programs to get an

20. Kuhn, *The Structure of Scientific Revolutions*, p. 10.

21. Ibid., p. 33.

22. Ibid., pp. 52–53.

23. For a defense and reformulation of the paradigm concept in light of criticism of it, see Kuhn, "Postscript—1969," *The Structure of Scientific Revolutions*. Using this reformulation by Kuhn, I define paradigm as "the fundamental assumptions scholars make about the world they are studying." Vasquez, *The Power of Power Politics* (1983), p. 5.

idea of what kinds of questions specific communities of scholars are addressing and how successful they have been in coming up with answers, as is done in the main substantive chapters of this book. But missing in this sort of analysis is a sense of the field as a whole and what, if anything, is guiding its overarching purpose. Fields guided by a paradigm or that have major paradigmatic debates, as IR has, will not have their history adequately served by Lakatos's framework.

It was for this reason that when I first endeavored to write an intellectual history of international relations inquiry, I turned to Kuhn and not to Lakatos.[24] Nevertheless, for anyone interested primarily in theory appraisal and paradigm evaluation, Kuhn can be unsettling. His description of paradigm displacement extols images of revolution and appears to give more force to sociological factors than to reason in the shifting from one paradigm to another. Lakatos, like others, was very disconcerted by this, for it undermined the rationality of science. Kuhn's theory-informed description of science raised both an empirical and a logical problem with Karl Popper's reconstruction of scientific inquiry. Kuhn showed that falsification did not occur, and his history showed, even though Kuhn himself did not dwell on this point, that while falsification of a given hypothesis might falsify a specific narrowly defined theory, it did not prevent a theory from being slightly reformulated. Thus, a series of theories or a family of theories, which in effect is what a paradigm consists of, can go on almost endlessly. Theories and, more importantly, paradigms are not logically falsified by research tests, but psychologically displaced when researchers become disenchanted with reformulating them, or the community as a whole becomes impatient with a proliferation of theories that are simply variations on a theme, all claiming to be the authentic theory.

Lakatos did not like the arbitrary non-rational flavor of all this and sought to reformulate the rejection of theories on a firmer basis. In the end, however, he is willing to concede the point that theories and research programs are not logically falsified. He is prepared to grant that the decision to reject a theory is not logically compelled; however,

24. Vasquez, *The Power of Power Politics* (1983).

this does not mean that there is no rational basis for rejecting a theory.[25] Lakatos develops the idea of a degenerating (as opposed to progressive) problemshift as a way of saving the rationality of science. For him a problemshift is the construction of a new theory that is no longer inconsistent with discrepant evidence that has been uncovered. For this reason, the term "theoryshift," which Lakatos entertained using, makes it clearer precisely what must be evaluated—the new theory—in appraising whether a shift is progressive or degenerating.[26]

It is the introduction of this idea that is the major contribution of Lakatos. The conceptual framework that is meant to describe the history of a field is ancillary and not so logically integrated with the criterion that it cannot be replaced. In fact, Lakatos's criterion makes most sense, and is most useful, less for evaluating and comparing theories within a research program than for comparing paradigms in terms of their relative success at producing adequate theories.[27] Using Lakatos's terms, an inadequate paradigm produces theories that have degenerating research programs, whereas a successful one produces theories with progressive research programs.

The contributions of Lakatos, then, are useful for comparing paradigms. However, they are only applicable for a very specific problem, namely, the construction of a series of theories that are being formulated and reformulated because research has uncovered discrepant evidence, rather than evidence consistent with the theory's expectations. His contributions are most relevant when a theory has been extensively tested.

This situation may not always be present in every research program in a field, and in those cases Lakatos's frame would not necessarily be the most relevant. There are two obvious cases where this might occur: when there has not been much systematic research (and differences occur because of different theoretical assumptions about how the world works), and when research produces evidence that is always

25. Lakatos, "Falsification and the Methodology of Scientific Research Programmes," p. 117.

26. Ibid., p. 118, note 3.

27. See Vasquez, The Power of Power Politics (1983), pp. 9–12.

consistent with the theory's expectations and thus does not require any theory reformulation. In such circumstances the applicability of Lakatos is more limited.

Does such a situation mean that there are no other criteria upon which to appraise theories and the paradigm that underlies them? Obviously not; Kuhn even said in his reply to critics that he never meant to suggest that standard criteria for evaluating theories, namely, "accuracy, simplicity, fruitfulness, and the like" should be abandoned.[28] These conventional criteria still have a place within both the physical sciences and the social sciences. When the problem of repeated theoretical emendation in light of discrepant evidence does not occur, then the other criteria, particularly that of empirical accuracy, need to be applied.[29]

Of the various research programs within international relations that have been guided by the realist paradigm, I have argued that the one for which Lakatos's analysis is most pertinent is the neotraditional research on Waltz's power-balancing proposition.[30] This does not mean that all research programs or all aspects of the realist paradigm are degenerating. Each program or theory needs to be evaluated on its own merits, as Elman and Elman rightly point out.[31] However, Lakatos's criterion is the most pertinent for this research program, and applying his criterion shows that the core hypothesis of structural realism appears to be a degenerating rather than a progressive research program.

---

28. Kuhn, *The Structure of Scientific Revolutions*, p. 199.

29. Waltz, for example, in his reply to my evaluation of his balancing proposition, essentially argues that his proposition is true and has not encountered extensive discrepant evidence. Waltz, "Evaluating Theories"; Vasquez, "The Realist Paradigm and Degenerative versus Progressive Research Programs." Therefore, the criterion of empirical accuracy can be employed, if an agreement can be reached as to what test or tests are valid; see John Vasquez, "The New Debate on Balancing Power: A Reply to My Critics," in Vasquez and Elman, eds., *Realism and the Balancing of Power: A New Debate*, chap. 8.

30. Vasquez, "The Realist Paradigm and Degenerative versus Progressive Research Programs."

31. Elman and Elman, "Lakatos and Neorealism."

In addition, it should not be assumed that where Lakatos's criteria are inapplicable, this means that all is well with other realist theories or research programs. They, too, must be evaluated in terms of appropriate criteria. For this reason, I have applied other criteria to other aspects of the realist paradigm, namely, the criteria of empirical accuracy, explanatory power, and policy relevance to neorealist explanations of war and peace, Mearsheimer's analysis of multipolarity and institutions, and the debate over the end of the Cold War.[32]

The Research Programs of Offense-Defense Theory and Neoclassical Realism

Since I have discussed elsewhere at length where the Lakatos frame is relevant by applying it to one research program, here I discuss briefly his more general applicability by looking at two other research programs: one—offense-defense theory—where he is not relevant, but where he still might provide us with insights and alert us to potential dangers that might materialize if discrepant evidence were encountered, and a second—neoclassical realism—where he appears more relevant, even though the research program is still in its early stages.

OFFENSE-DEFENSE THEORY

Sean Lynn-Jones concluded, in his review of the offense-defense research program, that it is too soon to tell whether it is progressive or degenerating.[33] This is a conclusion that most appraisers would reach, and the reason is that, while the research program has had some fertile discussions and a variety of theoretical emendations, it has not been widely tested. Even Van Evera's extensive review of the historical record must be seen as a preliminary empirical probe.[34] We do not have

---

32. Vasquez, *The Power of Power Politics* (1998), chap. 9, 11, 12, 13.

33. Sean M. Lynn-Jones, "Assessing the Progressiveness of Offense-Defense Theory," paper presented at the Conference on "Progress in International Relations Theory," Arizona State University, January 15–16, 1999.

34. Stephen Van Evera, "Offense, Defense, and the Causes of War," *International Security*, Vol. 22, No. 4 (Spring 1998), pp. 5–43.

a situation where the research has produced discrepant evidence resulting in theoretical emendations in response. Hence, this is not a case in which Lakatos's criterion is most appropriate.

Other criteria are more appropriate for appraising work in this research program. One would be to see whether the logic (or hard core) of the approach produces one explanation or several. One of the problems facing the offense-defense research program is which of the various possible explanations is really the best embodiment of the logic(s) underlying the theory. If there is no single one or a fairly finite number, then the theory is in danger of being indeterminate in its predictions. This reflects negatively on its explanatory power and raises questions about its logical consistency.

A second criterion that would be more appropriate than Lakatos's criterion of progressivity is that of empirical accuracy. The empirical claims of the approach must be investigated and tested to see how much evidence is consistent with it. The early works of Snyder and Van Evera and the more recent Van Evera provide such initial evidence, but obviously much more needs to be done.[35] When more extensive evidence becomes available, then it will be possible to see if the research program is degenerating. This will only be necessary, however, if the evidence is seriously discrepant with the theory's hypotheses, and if the theory is repeatedly emended in an ad hoc fashion to discount such evidence.

The case, then, is still very much open for the offense-defense research program, but that does not mean that all is well with it. Lakatos's criterion might be useful in pointing out some potential problems that might develop if analysts are not careful in how they

35. Jack Snyder, *The Ideology of the Offensive* (Ithaca, N.Y.: Cornell University Press, 1984); Jack Snyder, "Perceptions of the Security Dilemma in 1914," in Robert Jervis, Richard Ned Lebow, and Janice Gross Stein, eds. *Psychology and Deterrence* (Baltimore: Johns Hopkins University Press, 1985), pp. 153–179; Stephen Van Evera, "The Cult of the Offensive and the Origins of the First World War," *International Security*, Vol. 9, No. 1 (Summer 1984), pp. 58–107; Stephen Van Evera, "Offense, Defense, and the Causes of War," *International Security*, Vol. 22, No. 4 (Spring 1998), pp. 5–43; Stephen Van Evera, *The Causes of War* (Ithaca, N.Y.: Cornell University Press, 1999).

treat discrepant evidence. Let me point out some of these potential problems and, in passing, how an awareness of Lakatos would be useful to scholars trying to avoid these problems.

One of the problems that could become very severe is that the concept of offense and defense may be so elastic that it becomes a "catch-all" for a variety of variables, rather than just a single variable or a narrow set of closely intertwined variables. When the offense-defense balance refers to the technology of weapon systems, battlefield strategies, military doctrine, and similar variables, it is already referring to different things, but these are, at least, somewhat inter-related. If the concept is broadened further, however, to include such things as nationalism, alliances, collective security, and diplomacy, as has been suggested by Van Evera, then the concept is subsuming a number of different variables that might better stand alone.[36]

Subsuming is a problem because the concept becomes more ambiguous in that it has several distinct empirical referents. This makes measurement more difficult. As it is, even the narrow concept has proven difficult to measure. Levy questioned whether it is always possible to distinguish whether offense or defense has the advantage.[37] Much of the current debate on the utility of the concept and hence of the entire theoretical approach turns on whether the concept can be measured.[38] If it cannot, then the research program and its theory are not going to get very far. This sort of problem is much more relevant and immediate than Lakatos's criterion of progressivity.

36. Van Evera, "Offense, Defense, and the Causes of War"; see also the critiques by James W. Davis, Jr., "Correspondence: Taking Offense at Offense-Defense Theory," *International Security*, Vol. 23, No. 3 (Winter 1998/99), pp. 179–182; and Bernard I. Finel, ibid., pp. 182–189.

37. Jack S. Levy, "The Offensive/Defensive Balance of Military Technology: A Theoretical and Historical Analysis," *International Studies Quarterly*, Vol. 28, No. 2 (June 1984), pp. 219–238.

38. Charles L. Glaser and Chaim Kaufmann, "What is the Offense-Defense Balance and How Can We Measure It?" *International Security*, Vol. 22, No. 4 (Spring 1998), pp. 44–82; Stacie E. Goddard, "Correspondence: Taking Offense at Offense-Defense Theory," *International Security*, Vol. 23, No. 3 (Winter 1998/99), pp. 189–195; Stephen Van Evera, "Correspondence," ibid., pp. 195–200; Charles L. Glaser and Chaim Kaufmann, "Correspondence," ibid., pp. 200–206.

Subsuming is also problematic in that it probably mis-specifies and exaggerates the role that the offense-defense balance plays. The narrow concept and variables are, at best, intervening variables. To try to make a full-blown theory of war out of them, as Van Evera does, is not going to be easy.[39] Weapon systems do not cause war; they may increase the probability of war in conjunction with other variables, but they do not appear to be fundamental. States do not fight because they have certain weapons; rather they acquire certain weapons because they fear or anticipate fighting.

The potential problem is that if future empirical tests show that the narrow empirical referents of the concept do not play the role delineated for them, then the other variables that have been subsumed in the concept can be used to "save" the theory and the approach from this discrepant evidence. Having a variety of indicators of the concept that are really different variables permits the research program to take a "tag-team" approach to testing, where failure by one member of the conceptual team is prevented by another member taking over. When such a procedure occurs, there is a danger that the research program will take on degenerating characteristics, and Lakatos's criterion becomes useful in making practitioners and outside appraisers aware of this danger.

Nevertheless, Van Evera's preliminary empirical investigation and theoretical analysis is promising in that the evidence he marshals is consistent with his explanation's predictions, and he provides insights and information about the past that are not part of the current literature on war.[40] The bottom line, however, is whether the explanation can pass more detailed and rigorous testing. In this sense, the criterion of empirical accuracy is still more appropriate. In the interim, one could certainly say that Van Evera's analysis conforms to the more conventional idea of progress, as an advance in our theoretical knowledge and insight.

A second potential problem is that the concept of offense-defense can rest either on the effect of its material basis or the effect of perceptions

---

39. Van Evera, "Offense, Defense, and the Causes of War."
40. Ibid.

about that material basis. This discrepancy can be a potential source of ad hoc explanations, although they do not have to be ad hoc. For example, if offensive material conditions do not increase the probability of war, then it is very tempting to say that this is because one or more sides did not perceive the balance as offensive. Likewise, if defensive material conditions result in war, then it is tempting to say that one or more sides misperceived it as offensive. Conversely, if the appropriate material conditions result in the expected outcome, then perceptions may never be examined. Such a set of collective predictions (by different scholars) benefit the approach as a whole by making it more difficult to falsify and thus less likely to be falsified. At the same time, however, such a collective set of tests makes it more difficult to know if we are really testing our claims, since the body of evidence that would falsify the theory has not been specified in advance, as Popper would demand.[41] The different variables become a rich (and perhaps endless) source of ad hoc propositions. In other words, some research programs may have the potential for a degenerating research program already "built in" from the start.

Any theory that has both perceptual and material versions of its variables is susceptible to this problem. Using the material conditions, as opposed to perceptions, of the narrowly defined technological and related military variables is going to make it less likely that theorists will fall into an "ad hoc trap." The way to avoid the problem when both kinds of variables are used is to specify clearly which is more important. Is the theory about material conditions or is it about beliefs? We would expect in IR that realist theories should be about material capability, and that psychological or constructivist theories should be about beliefs. When the former resorts to perceptions and the latter resorts to material conditions, then such moves should become suspect, especially if this is done after the fact.

The problem becomes most acute when theorists may want to mix these variables assuming, which is perfectly reasonable, that sometimes it is the material condition and sometimes the perceptual that is important. The only way to avoid making such a theory non-falsifiable

---

41. Popper, *The Logic of Scientific Discovery*.

in this circumstance is to specify clearly in advance the conditions under which the effects of these two variables are expected to occur. If one waits until after the evidence is reviewed to make the specification, then one has to recognize that such historical information is not evidence that has tested the theory, but rather information that has been used to construct the theory. In other words, such "inductive" theories still need to be tested by other bodies of evidence before we have any confidence in their empirical accuracy. Even Elman and Elman agree that one cannot use the same body of evidence twice—once to construct a theory and again as confirmatory evidence.[42] Lakatos's analysis of ad hoc explanations makes us aware of this problem; those in the early stage of theory construction, as scholars in the offense-defense research program are, would do well to incorporate his advice on this problem.

Using perceptual variables can also be a problem in terms of determining whose perceptions are important. It is obviously an anthropomorphic error to speak of a state's perceptions, as in "France perceived." One usually takes this to mean that the official foreign policy decisionmakers "perceived." However, it may be the case, as Christensen shows, that different domestic decisionmakers have different perceptions of the offense-defense balance.[43] This can result in a very idiographic analysis, and once one goes in that direction, then a potentially large body of ad hoc propositions is available to save an explanation from discrepant evidence.

To date, however, these potential problems have not materialized, and my point is not to say that they will, but only to warn that they are possible. Nor is this to say that scholars are unaware of such problems.[44] Whether problems will or will not develop depends very much on how analysts handle and interpret test results.

---

42. Elman and Elman, "Lakatos and Neorealism," p. 924, note 1.

43. Thomas J. Christensen, "Perceptions and Alliances in Europe, 1865–1940," *International Organization* Vol. 51, No. 1 (Winter 1997), pp. 65–97.

44. See Snyder's early discussions in Snyder, *Ideology of the Offensive*, chap. 1; and Snyder, "Perceptions of the Security Dilemma in 1914."

It must be pointed out, however, that even though a particular research program, like offense-defense balance, is not in and of itself exhibiting any degenerating tendencies, that does not mean that explanations from this theory cannot be brought into another research program (or brought to bear on a separate proposition) to "save" it from discrepant evidence, and thereby provide a ready-made ad hoc explanation that gives the appearance of theoretical insight.[45] The key question, as Lakatos puts it, is whether this importation is a new insight and hence a progressive problemshift, or really a linguistic reinterpretation and semantic hiding of discrepant evidence.[46]

My complaint about Christensen and Snyder's use of offense-defense balance is that they import the idea of offense-defense balance to explain away the periodic failure of balancing to occur in multipolarity.[47] To me, the evidence that balancing does not regularly occur in multipolarity is a clear violation of Waltz's proposition that "balance-of-power politics prevail wherever two and only two requirements are met: that the order be anarchic and that it be populated by units wishing to survive."[48] To admit that balancing goes less smoothly in multipolarity[49] already says that the proposition does not apply to most of history, since multipolarity is the modal condition in international relations after the decline of the ancient empires.

---

45. It is important to point out that here I differ from Lynn-Jones, "Assessing the Progressiveness of Offense-Defense Theory," in his characterization of offense-defense theory as part of the broader neorealist research program. I see it as a separate research program with its own logic (positive heuristic) and literature that is distinct from the Waltzian research program on balancing.

46. Lakatos, "Falsification and the Methodology of Scientific Research Programmes," p. 119.

47. Thomas J. Christensen and Jack Snyder, "Chain Gangs and Passed Bucks: Predicting Alliance Patterns in Multipolarity," *International Organization*, Vol. 44, No. 2 (Spring 1990), pp. 137–168; Vasquez, "The Realist Paradigm and Degenerative versus Progressive Research Programs," pp. 906–907.

48. Waltz, *Theory of International Politics*, p. 121.

49. Christensen and Snyder, "Progressive Research on Degenerate Alliances," p. 920.

The danger of *ex post facto* theory construction is that if there is no balance, one can always say that this was because the defensive balance dominated or that perceptions of the defensive predominated. Similarly, if there is a balance, then one can say that the offense, or perceptions of it, were present. Alternatively, if one finds balancing, one can say that Waltz is right and never even look at the offense-defense balance. My objection to Christensen and Snyder's move of incorporating offense-defense is not that the concept, in principle, is degenerating, but that because the concept is not clearly measurable we cannot just automatically take this move as a progressive problemshift.[50] In combination with other moves that they make, it does seem that Christensen and Snyder are at pains to explain away discrepant evidence. When researchers go to great lengths to explain away discrepant evidence, this is one indicator that the research program may be degenerating. Whether it is or not depends very much on whether the theoretical emendation they make falls into one of Lakatos's three types of ad hoc explanation.[51]

My complaint is not that Snyder and Christensen are neorealists— they are not[52]—but that they do not explicitly recognize the extent to which the evidence they provide on alliances is highly discrepant with Waltz's proposition on balancing, and that their introduction of the concepts of offense-defense, buck-passing, etc. is an ad hoc explanation aimed at saving Waltz's proposition from falsifying evidence.[53]

How the concepts of a research program, in this case offense-defense theory, are used in another research program is a separate question, however, from whether the program itself has degenerative tendencies. For offense-defense theory, it is much too early to apply Lakatos's criterion of progressivity. At best, he is useful for pointing out

---

50. Christensen and Snyder, "Chain Gangs and Passed Bucks."

51. Lakatos, "Falsification and the Methodology of Scientific Research Programmes," pp. 175, 182. Also see Elman and Elman, Chapter 2 in this volume.

52. Christensen and Snyder, "Progressive Research on Degenerate Alliances," p. 919.

53. See Vasquez, "The New Debate on Balancing Power."

potential problems that can be fixed or addressed. Let me now turn to the emerging research program of neoclassical realism, particularly as it is represented by the work of Randall Schweller.

NEOCLASSICAL REALISM

The emergence of what Gideon Rose labels "neoclassical realism" has rightly attracted attention within the community concerned with international relations theory.[54] Here, I concentrate on aspects of this school, particularly as it is reflected in the work of Randall Schweller.[55] The question is whether the work of this school represents progress, and if so, what implications this has for the debate over the adequacy of the realist paradigm.

Schweller, having eschewed Lakatos's methodology of scientific research programs, sets out his own criteria for progress.[56] These are reasonable and easily justified in terms of the conventional definition of progress as cumulation of knowledge. His three criteria are: does a program ask theoretically interesting questions; does it provide answers to these questions; and is the methodology employed consistent with the discipline's rules for evidence. He makes a good case that neoclassical realism and his own work satisfy these criteria. Indeed, even critics of neorealism and the broader realist paradigm find this school's re-introduction of domestic politics variables and global institutions into IR theory a more empirically accurate and

---

54. Gideon Rose, "Neoclassical Realism and Theories of Foreign Policy," *World Politics*, Vol. 51, No. 1 (October 1998), pp. 144–172.

55. Schweller, Chapter 9 in this volume; Randall L. Schweller, "Bandwagoning for Profit: Bringing the Revisionist State Back In," *International Security*, Vol. 19, No. 1 (Summer 1994), pp. 72–107; Randall L. Schweller and David Priess, "A Tale of Two Realisms: Expanding the Institutions Debate," *Mershon International Studies Review*, Vol. 41 (May 1997), pp. 1–32. Because I cannot do justice to it in this short space, I will not discuss in any detail Schweller's book on the Second World War. Randall L. Schweller, *Deadly Imbalances: Tripolarity and Hitler's Strategy of World Conquest* (New York: Columbia University Press, 1998). For two different views, see Rose, "Neoclassical Realism and Theories of Foreign Policy"; and Jeffrey Legro and Andrew Moravcsik, "Is Anybody Still a Realist?" *International Security*, Vol. 24, No. 2 (Fall 1999), pp. 5–55.

56. Schweller, Chapter 9 in this volume.

complete explanation than neorealism. Likewise, his call and that of others for a theory of foreign policy to supplement Waltz is welcome.[57] In this manner, the school is an advance over structural realism, if for no other reason than providing insight about the role of non-systemic factors.

It also helps to advance the debate over the realist paradigm in that it sets out some common ground between defenders of the realist paradigm and its critics. It identifies at least three sets of variables and propositions that both neoclassical realists and critics of realism see as essential for explaining world politics: 1) that domestic politics play a crucial role in determining foreign policy—in particular, that the role of two-level games must be given a central place in analyses of foreign policy;[58] 2) that international institutions are important; and 3) that perceptions and beliefs cannot be ignored. Their disagreement is two-fold: first, over whether such variables are more usefully studied within the perspective of the realist paradigm or some other paradigm, and second and less fundamental, how important each of these variables is in explaining world politics and specific dependent variables such as the onset of war. Nevertheless, common ground permits some agreement as to what has been "left out" of at least one important theory of the realist paradigm and what needs to be put in. Common ground also permits research to go forward to answer empirical disagreements or fill in details where patterns have not been documented.

What can Kuhn and Lakatos tell us about this development in the intellectual history of the field? The conventional idea of progress as cumulation of knowledge is best seen as what drives normal science. Normal science finds problems, gaps, or puzzles in dominant theories, and then produces new theories to provide a more detailed picture of

---

57. E.g., Colin Elman, "Horses for Courses: Why *Not* Neorealist Theories of Foreign Policy?" *Security Studies*, Vol. 6, No. 1 (Autumn 1996), pp. 7–53.

58. Robert D. Putnam, "Diplomacy and Domestic Politics: The Logic of Two-Level Games," *International Organization*, Vol. 42, No. 3 (Summer 1988), pp. 427–60.

the world scholars are studying.[59] This is precisely what Schweller and others have done; they have recognized that Waltz does not provide a theory of foreign policy, and then they take a bold step forward and argue that there must be such a theory if realism is to continue to flourish and "progress."[60] For Kuhn, this is the kind of theory construction one would find in normal science.[61]

It is not fundamentally different from what Waltz did in advancing what we now call classical realism by introducing structural realism. Waltz borrows from structuralism the insight that the system will be the primary determinant of individual member behavior, identifies the structure of the international system as anarchic, and then tries to explain what he sees as the modal behavior of system members as a result of anarchy (balancing).[62] Later, Buzan, Jones, and Little progress upon Waltz by finding gaps and puzzles in his analysis of anarchy and "correcting" them.[63] Kuhn sees this as a fundamental pattern in the history of science.[64] Reading him helps us understand our own history because the way intellectual change has unfolded seems to conform to his idea of normal science.

The conventional idea of progress is fine so long as one takes a normal-science perspective. In light of Kuhn's analysis of scientific crisis and paradigm debates, and Lakatos's critique of Popper and

---

59. Kuhn, *The Structure of Scientific Revolutions*, pp. 23–24; Vasquez, *The Power of Power Politics* (1983), pp. 38–39.

60. Compare Kenneth N. Waltz, "International Politics is Not Foreign Policy," *Security Studies*, Vol. 6, No. 1 (Autumn 1996), pp. 54–57.

61. Kuhn, *The Structure of Scientific Revolutions*, pp. 35–39.

62. Waltz, *Theory of International Politics*; see Vasquez, "The New Debate on Balancing Power."

63. Barry Buzan, Charles Jones, and Richard Little, *The Logic of Anarchy: Neorealism to Structural Realism* (New York: Columbia University Press, 1993).

64. Kuhn, *The Structure of Scientific Revolutions*; see also Stephen Toulmin, "Conceptual Revolutions in Science," in R.S. Cohen and M.W. Wartofsky, eds., *Boston Studies in Philosophy of Science*, Vol. 3 (Dordrecht, Holland: D. Reidel, 1967), pp. 331–47; Stephen Toulin, "Does the Distinction Between Normal and Revolutionary Science Hold Water?" in Lakatos and Musgrave, *Criticism and the Growth of Knowledge*, pp. 39–47.

Kuhn, however, it can become much more problematic. This is especially the case when a paradigm debate emerges in a field, as it has in international relations.

Lakatos has much more stringent criteria for theory appraisal, especially for the kind of theory development or "proliferation" represented by neoclassical realism. Lakatos, as I argue elsewhere in detail, provides a set of rules for comparing the relative worth of competing theories derived from different paradigms.[65] Can the conventional broader criteria outlined by Schweller do that? The answer is no.

The main reason they cannot is that any paradigm able to dominate a field in the first place is going to be able to produce at least one theory (and more likely several) that can satisfy his three criteria, especially if rules for evidence are loose or in contention, as they are in IR. To expect otherwise is to expect that the normal science stage of inquiry is rare, rather than modal. Some may think that this situation is a good thing, but they forget that the history of the physical sciences shows that even empirically inaccurate theories can sometimes satisfy these criteria. This indicates that these criteria are insufficient and can potentially deceive scholars about the empirical utility of a theoretical approach.

To avoid this problem, we need the more rigorous appraisal provided by Lakatos. At a certain stage, normal science is fine and so are many of the emendations Schweller reviews, but are they progressive "theoryshifts" in Lakatos's sense?[66] Do they reflect progressive theoryshifts that demonstrate the fruitfulness of the paradigm, or are they nothing but a series of ad hoc emendations that explain away, evade, and hide discrepant evidence to avoid displacement?

These questions are too complicated and too serious to be answered here, but let me, as a way of elucidating the utility and importance of Lakatos, briefly outline the case against neoclassical realism as a progressive theoryshift. First, it is not so much a shift forward as it is a

---

65. Vasquez, *The Power of Power Politics* (1983), pp. 9–12.

66. Schweller, Chapter 9 in this volume; Lakatos, "Falsification and the Methodology of Scientific Research Programmes," p. 118, n. 3.

retro-shift back to the exemplar—Morgenthau's *Politics Among Nations*.[67]

This raises the problem of the temporal ordering of emendations: When are explanations made? In what context of the intellectual history of a field are they made? These questions are pertinent to establishing whether the emendations are what Lakatos calls an ad hoc[1] explanation.[68] At the most basic level, neoclassical realism's theoryshift is not uncovering novel facts. Why then do neoclassical realists now emphasize factors that have long been in the exemplar? Is it that an important set of variables in Morgenthau has been lost in Waltz's structuralist perspective? Or is it that these factors were always marginal to realism, and now are only made more central because critics of realism have used more recently developed evidence to explore the deficiencies of the realist paradigm as a whole?[69] If it is the latter, then this is not a progressive theoryshift, but is simply hiding this discrepant evidence by arguing that these factors were mentioned in the exemplar.[70] As Legro and Moravcsik make clear, introducing such variables cannot be justified by pointing out that they make cameo appearances in the intellectual history of realism, but only by showing how they are derived from the logic of the theory.[71] Similarly,

---

67. Hans J. Morgenthau, *Politics among Nations: The Struggle for Power and Peace*, 1st and 3rd ed. (New York: Knopf, 1948, 1960).

68. Lakatos, "Falsification and the Methodology of Scientific Research Programmes," p. 175, notes 2, 3; see Elman and Elman, Chapter 2 in this volume.

69. These critics include: Richard Ned Lebow, "The Long Peace, the End of the Cold War, and the Failure of Realism," *International Organization*, Vol. 48, No. 2 (Spring (1994), pp. 249–77; Janice Gross Stein, "Political Learning by Doing: Gorbachev as Uncommitted Thinker and Motivated Leader," *International Organization*, Vol. 48, No. 2 (Spring 1994), pp. 155–183; Charles W. Kegley, Jr., and Gregory A. Raymond, *When Trust Breaks Down* (Columbia: University of South Carolina Press, 1990), as well as the early criticism by Robert O. Keohane, *After Hegemony* (Princeton, N.J.: Princeton University Press, 1984).

70. Of course, what is relevant here is not the motivations of those making the theoryshift, but the effect of their emendations on discourse.

71. Legro and Moravcsik, "Is Anybody Still a Realist?" p. 31.

Waltz insists that variables can be introduced only if they are deduced from a theory's assumptions.[72]

While it is the case that domestic politics and international institutions play a role in Morgenthau's analysis, it is also true that a dual criticism of Morgenthau is that his theory is a single-factor analysis exaggerating the importance of power (as an explanatory concept) and that his concept of national power is a kitchen-sink theory of power. The grand tautology of realism is arguing that power explains everything and arguing everything has an impact on power. It is not surprising that Schweller and others find a role for international institutions and domestic politics in Morgenthau's classical realism; if one spells out the ripple effects of power far enough, one can find a role for almost anything. This does not mean that these factors are central to the logic (or positive heuristic) of classical realism, however. Indeed, one could argue that unless capability remains the fundamental determinant and has a fairly immediate impact, then such emendations undercut the theory.[73]

---

72. Waltz, "International Politics is Not Foreign Policy," p. 57.

73. Walt, "The Progressive Power of Realism," seems to miss this point when he sees balancing of threat as not a very great deviation from balancing of power. For both Waltz and Morgenthau, superior power always forms a potential threat and therefore must be of concern to a state, whether or not it is actualized as an explicit threat. Waltz accepts this logic when he predicts that eventually other states will balance against the United States in the post–Cold War era because it is too powerful. Kenneth N. Waltz, "The Emerging Structure of International Politics," *International Security*, Vol. 18, No. 2 (Fall 1993), pp. 44–79. For Waltz (and Morgenthau), superior power will always pose a threat. This is because the superior power is apt to be exercised, but even if it is not, rational actors must deal with the possibility that it might be; otherwise they are relying on the good will of others, rather than their own prudence. Walt, "The Progressive Power of Realism," also neglects the fact that balancing of threat may be discrepant if perceptions of threat are produced by something other than differences in material capability (or even perceptions of it). In an important critique of Walt's *Origins of Alliances*, Michael N. Barnett shows that among Arab states, it is their construction of identity and order, not shifts in power, that shapes alliance behavior. Stephen M. Walt, *The Origins of Alliances* (Ithaca, N.Y.: Cornell University Press, 1987); Michael N. Barnett, "Identity and Alliances in the Middle East," in Peter J. Katzenstein, ed., *The Culture of National*

This raises a second and more important problem, namely, that the "innovations" (or new variables) of neoclassical realism are really borrowed from competing paradigms or non-realist mid-range theories and not derived from the logic of realism (either the logic of power or the logic of anarchy). This is what Lakatos would call an ad hoc[3] explanation, a type of ad hoc explanation that Elman and Elman rightly see as important. It lies at the heart of Legro and Moravcsik's question, "Is Anybody Still a Realist?"[74]

The argument is that incorporating these factors and accepting the evidence on the role they play is a *de facto* recognition of the inability of the heart of the realist paradigm to explain international relations. Realists of all stripes must accept that for their paradigm, the key, fundamental, most important (and never the second-most important) factor is power.[75] Otherwise, they are not really realists. What early critics argued is that other factors were often more important.[76] On these grounds, Mearsheimer's position on international institutions is

Security: Norms and Identity in World Politics (New York: Columbia University Press), pp. 400–447. Barnett's points are made even more explicit in Michael N. Barnett, "Alliances, Balances of Threats, and Neo-Realism: The Accidental Coup," in Vasquez and Elman, eds., *Realism and the Balancing of Power*, chap. 8.

74. Lakatos, "Falsification and the Methodology of Scientific Research Programmes," p. 175, notes 2, 3; Elman and Elman, "Lakatos and Neorealism"; Elman and Elman, Chapter 2 in this volume; Legro and Moravcsik, "Is Anybody Still a Realist?"

75. Legro and Moravcsik, "Is Anybody Still a Realist?" p. 18.

76. Robert O. Keohane and Joseph S. Nye, Jr., eds., *Transnational Relations and World Politics* (Cambridge, Mass.: Harvard University Press, 1971, 1972); John W. Burton, A.J.R. Groom, Chris R. Mitchell, and A.V.S. de Reuck, *The Study of World Society: A London Perspective*, Occasional Paper No. 1, International Studies Association (1974); Richard W. Mansbach, Yale Ferguson, and Donald Lambert, *The Web of World Politics* (Englewood Cliffs, N.J.: Prentice-Hall, 1976); and Richard W. Mansbach and John A. Vasquez, *In Search of Theory: A New Paradigm for Global Politics* (New York: Columbia University Press, 1981); Vasquez, *The Power of Power Politics* (1983).

more authentically realist because he says institutions merely reflect the power of states (a position shared by Krasner).[77]

A similar criticism can be made about Jervis's, Snyder's, and Christensen's use of perceptions, and what is generally called "defensive realism."[78] As one moves away from capability to other variables, then one may be borrowing the logic of other paradigms and their view of the world; in the case of perceptions, cognitive psychology is providing the paradigmatic perspective. From the perspective of realism's critics, such emendations cannot save realism, because they are ad hoc$_3$ explanations. The new variables are not derived from the logic of power nor the logic of anarchy, but borrowed.[79] Such borrowing implies that studying the world through different lenses might improve our ability to generate propositions that

77. John J. Mearsheimer, "The False Promise of International Institutions," *International Security*, Vol. 19, No. 3 (Winter 1994/95), pp. 5–49; Stephen D. Krasner, comments at the 1999 Conference on "Progress in International Relations Theory."

78. Robert Jervis, *Perception and Misperception in International Politics* (Princeton, N.J.: Princeton University Press, 1972); Snyder, *The Ideology of the Offensive*; Jack Snyder, *Myths of Empire: Domestic Politics and International Ambition* (Ithaca, N.Y.: Cornell University Press, 1991); Christensen, "Perceptions and Alliances in Europe, 1865–1940." For the definitions of "defensive realism," see Snyder, *Myths of Empire*, pp. 11–12; Mearsheimer, "The False Promise of International Institutions," p. 11, note 27.

79. Legro and Moravcsik, "Is Anybody Still a Realist?" pp. 6, 31. The logic of power is derived from Morgenthau, *Politics among Nations*, and the paradigm's assumption that the world of international relations is fundamentally a struggle for power and peace. Thus, the realist logic of power is not simply an assumption that strategic thinking occurs in states' interactions, but that states are engaged in a constant life-and-death struggle to get and keep power. Morgenthau, *Politics among Nations*, pp. 23, 27–28, 38. See Vasquez, *The Power of Power Politics* (1983), pp. 18–19, 28–30 for a discussion and justification of this assumption as one of the three fundamental assumptions of the realist paradigm. Morgenthau, *Politics among Nations*, p. 33, especially note 5, sees this struggle as emanating from a drive for dominance. Waltz, on the other hand, sees it flowing out of anarchy and a need for security; Kenneth N. Waltz, "The Origins of War in Neorealist Theory," in Robert I. Rotberg and Theodore K. Rabb, eds., *The Origin and Prevention of Major Wars* (Cambridge: Cambridge University Press, 1989), pp. 39–52, p. 40.

pass empirical tests. It also implies that theorists who see such factors as important should consider breaking with the realist paradigm rather than trying to repair it from within by using one or more "foreign" logics. Breaking with the dominant paradigm is what many of those interested in political psychology have done, as have conflict resolution theorists.[80]

Such a decision, of course, is not logically compelled, but rather a decision about risk in terms of where one wants to place one's research bets to maximize success. Although it is unlikely that neoclassical realists or defensive realists will abandon the realist label, their work helps establish agreement on what factors other than material power play key roles in world politics. By doing so they provide more of a consensus on the "facts," even though we still disagree about the theoretical and paradigmatic significance of these facts.

Although the disagreement is primarily over interpretation, there are still significant differences of opinion about just how discrepant the facts are with realist propositions. Schweller admits that neoclassical realists, including Christensen, Zakaria, and Friedberg, have identified cases that "appeared to be anomalous (irrational) state behavior from a purely structural-realist perspective."[81] Nevertheless, he thinks of these cases as basically exceptions to a general pattern:

---

80. Lebow, "The Long Peace, the End of the Cold War, and the Failure of Realism"; Stein, "Political Learning by Doing"; Burton, et al., *The Study of World Society*; Dean G. Pruitt and Jeffrey Z. Rubin, *Social Conflict: Escalation, Stalemate and Settlement* (New York: Random House, 1986).

81. Schweller, Chapter 9 in this volume; Thomas J. Christensen, *Useful Adversaries: Grand Strategy, Domestic Mobilization, and Sino-American Conflict, 1947–1958* (Princeton, N.J.: Princeton University Press, 1996); Fareed Zakaria, *From Wealth to Power: The Unusual Origins of America's World Role* (Princeton, N.J.: Princeton University Press, 1998); Aaron L. Friedberg, *The Weary Titan: Britain and the Experience of Relative Decline, 1895–1905* (Princeton, N.J.: Princeton University Press, 1988).

neoclassical realists are able to explain "outlier" cases that appear to defy realist logic; that is, cases in which national behavior deviated from the predictions of balance-of-power theory.[82]

In Lakatos's frame, this is clearly an instance of discrepant evidence that produces a progressive theoryshift (as Schweller would view it if he adopted the Lakatos frame). An empirical disagreement that I have with Schweller is that I do not regard these cases as outliers that deviate from a well-documented pattern. First, the pattern has not been documented, and second, if Waltz's balancing proposition were systematically tested, I and other critics would expect that these "outliers" or anomalous cases would be sufficiently frequent to make the hypothesis statistically insignificant.[83] This is an empirical disagreement based on a criterion of empirical accuracy that is separate from whatever disagreement we may have about whether the theoryshifts of neoclassical realism are progressive.

One of the advantages of volumes like this is that they permit scholars to come together to specify just what their intellectual disagreements are and how they might be resolved. In this case, research within the balancing program would be advanced if adherents and critics of Waltz's explanation could come together to identify the testable differences between their positions and then agree on a research design to see which side, if any, has accurately described the empirical pattern that is under contention. Elsewhere, I have elaborated such a research design for the balancing proposition in detail.[84] This might spur useful research that would provide more

---

82. Schweller, Chapter 9 in this volume, p. 30.

83. Some other critics of realism, for example, Legro and Moravcsik, "Is Anybody Still a Realist?" p. 5, are too quick to agree that balancing occurs. The empirical point is not that balancing does not ever occur or does not play a role in decision making (as in George H.W. Bush's willingness not to topple Saddam Hussein during the Persian Gulf War because he wanted to maintain an Iraq capable of "balancing" Iran), but that balancing does not occur frequently enough under the two conditions Waltz (*Theory of International Politics*, p. 121) specifies for it to be considered a "law," even a probabilistic law or regularity of international politics.

84. Vasquez, "The New Debate on Balancing Power."

agreement about the "facts" and thereby expand the common ground that does exist.

Regardless of whether the above substantive points about the realist paradigm are seen as having merit, the more relevant question here is that these points become meaningful only in light of Kuhn and Lakatos. Utilizing the insights of each of these thinkers has made the discourse in IR more rigorous and sophisticated. They also frame the debate in a way that links what happens in our field to what occurs in other disciplines in both the social and physical sciences. In this way, they prove the point that borrowing from philosophy of science is more fruitful than trying to create our own framework for theory appraisal from scratch.

Conclusion

The preceding discussion shows that Lakatos's criteria are not always the most appropriate frame to evaluate a research program or a particular aspect of a paradigm, but at the same time it demonstrates that, even in such instances, drawing upon Lakatos can provide important insights and early warning signals about potential pitfalls. When Lakatos's criterion of progressivity is the most appropriate to apply, its real utility becomes clearer.

Lakatos's two main contributions are, first, to provide a set of "good reasons" for not permitting an endless and hence non-falsifiable set of theoretical reformulations in light of discrepant evidence, and second, a set of rules for determining when theoretical emendations are acceptable (and hence progressive) or degenerating (and hence not acceptable). The most important rules for the latter are his identification of three types of ad hoc explanations and his discussion of what constitutes a "novel fact."[85] In addition, his contrast between research under a progressive program and research under a degenerating program provides some idea of what the output of each should look like.

---

85. Elman and Elman, "Lakatos and Neorealism: A Reply to Vasquez," pp. 923–924; Elman and Elman, Chapter 2 in this volume.

The set of rules and indicators that demark degenerating from progressive problemshifts is not always the easiest to apply. Labeling them as theoryshifts would help immensely to point out that what must be evaluated is whether the theoretical emendation is a legitimate move under the rules. Theoretical emendations try to take discrepant evidence and make it part of the theory's predictions after the fact by explaining why the new theory would expect this behavior or experimental outcome. By this process, the new theory, T', can claim that the evidence is not discrepant with it, but only with the old theory, T. The question is whether the theoretical emendation (shift to T') is simply a linguistic reinterpretation that resolves the contradiction "in a merely semantical unscientific way" as Lakatos states it, and hence an ad hoc explanation, or whether instead it is truly a progressive theoryshift that adds to the research program's understanding.[86]

These are not easy questions to answer, but applying criteria in a variety of situations is often not easy. For instance, it is not always easy to apply the laws of the criminal justice system of a given country to a particular case at hand. Even when all parties agree that the accused actually killed the person in question, it may be difficult to determine whether this is a case of second degree murder, negligent homicide, reckless endangerment, justifiable self-defense, or none of the above. The difficulty in applying criteria is sometimes because the rules are not sufficiently precise, sometimes because the evidence is not clear, and sometimes a combination of both. While Lakatos's rules are not as precise as we may like, they are probably the most precise that we have for the specific problem he delineated. They are certainly more precise than what Kuhn provided, which are simply the standard rules and do not by themselves resolve the problem Kuhn raised with Popper's falsification program. They also appear much more precise than Laudan's criterion of progress, which rests very much on common-sense ideas of progress with few specific indicators of how one is to tell whether progress has been achieved.[87]

---

86. Lakatos, "Falsification and the Methodology of Scientific Research Programmes," p. 119.

87. Laudan, *Progress and Its Problems*, pp. 115–120.

As international relations scholars, we must realize that, whatever criteria of adequacy we adopt, these are normative choices that we collectively impose to appraise the quality of our own theories in order to evaluate whether they are making a contribution to knowledge.[88] Theory appraisal requires that we make certain assumptions—namely, that knowledge can be defined, and that we can perceive whether something has produced knowledge and something else is in error. Epistemological skeptics and those who enjoy playing the role of the sophist will deny that knowledge is possible. Nevertheless, if we believe, for a variety of good reasons, that it is important to choose among empirical theories, then some criteria are needed.

The foundation of these criteria can be of two sorts—instrumental or epistemologically realist (see Toulmin and Nagel, respectively).[89] The instrumental is easier to defend against epistemological skeptics in that it rests its case on the claim that whether something is useful depends on whether it produces hypotheses that, when researched and tested, produce strong findings. Such an approach can rely on Tarski's semantic conception of truth to say that knowledge is what is produced by following certain procedures.[90] An epistemological realist wants to go a step further and say that science is not just the production of what is useful for generating findings, but the production of a body of knowledge that we can take to be true. Nagel's position is that the disagreement between these two schools does not affect the working community of scientists and thus need not be resolved.[91] In a sense, either side is free to interpret its activities as it sees fit. My own sensibilities move me to prefer the position of the epistemological

88. See Kuhn, *The Structure of Scientific Revolutions*, pp. 199–200; Lakatos, "Falsification and the Methodology of Scientific Research Programmes," p. 117.

89. Stephen Toulmin, *Philosophy of Science: An Introduction* (New York: Harper and Row, 1953); Ernest Nagel, *The Structure of Science* (New York: Harcourt, Brace, and World, 1961).

90. Alfred Tarski, "The Semantic Conception of Truth," in Herbert Feigl and Wilfrid Sellars, eds., *Readings in Philosophical Analysis* (New York: Appleton-Century-Crofts, 1949), pp. 52–84; Vasquez, *The Power of Power Politics* (1983), pp. 11–12.

91. Nagel, *The Structure of Science*, pp. 117–118, 141–152, 196.

realists, but the instrumental position provides an adequate foundation for scientific empirical research.

A number of post-modernists have raised the question of theoretical pluralism and denied the necessity of having to choose among theories. This position makes more sense for normative and ethical theories and less for empirical ones or the empirical aspects of normative theories. Even with purely normative theories, however, it may be desirable or necessary to have criteria for choosing between them—say between Nazism's program of racial purity and any of the other competing political philosophies of the 1930s. My position with regard to empirical matters is that relativism is neither necessary nor desirable.[92] The world, including the human world, is not so chaotic that we cannot know how it works, not so determined that it can only work one way, nor so undetermined that any construction can be placed on it.

Nevertheless, post-modernists provide a much-needed breath of fresh air to the social science proclivity to see everything in terms of Pareto-optimality, rather than one of several equally possible choices; this proclivity has become even more self-righteous with the triumph of capitalism and democracy in the post–Cold War era and the widespread liberal belief that the end of history has been reached. The danger that social science would produce a single homogenized world that Ashley warned against is much greater now than when he wrote just a few short years ago.[93] It is important, therefore, that we be epistemologically modest in our efforts at theory appraisal.

We must recognize that theory appraisal criteria are guidelines for our collective decision making about the truth (albeit truth with a small "t"). As such, they are the acts of power that Foucault so well described.[94] Nevertheless, explicit rules and criteria prevent these

---

92. For a full discussion, see John Vasquez, "The Post-Positivist Debate: Reconstructing Scientific and IR Theory After Enlightenment's Fall," in Booth and Smith, eds., International Relations Theory Today, pp. 217–240.

93. Richard K. Ashley, "The Eye of Power: The Politics of World Modeling," *International Organization*, Vol. 37, No. 3 (Summer 1983), pp. 495–535.

94. Foucault, *The Archaeology of Knowledge*.

decisions about truth from being arbitrary.[95] This is particularly the case in science, which regards its knowledge as a process of attaining the truth rather than a particular end product known for all time. The alternative is to use some non-empirical criterion for determining the acceptance of theories; the danger is to succumb to permitting our political beliefs and prejudices to decide which empirical theory we declare to have been confirmed.

In modern democratic government there are today many "spin doctors" who process information and are more interested in winning adherents to their position than searching for the truth. In the modern academy, we do not yet have many "spin academics." Science is a system of values and decision rules.[96] It permits those with differing political beliefs to test the empirical aspects of their beliefs on the basis of a common set of criteria of adequacy and the assumption that the truth is the highest relevant value for their decision. Acceptance of such a foundation not only is an intrinsic good, but makes us a *discipline* in both the good and negative senses set forth by Foucault.[97] Whether we ground theory appraisal on a realist epistemology or an instrumental one, or whether we use Lakatos, Kuhn, Laudan, or some other frame, is less important than an agreement on what theory appraisal entails and on the need for its systematic application to the paradigm debate by which the field is now once again deeply gripped. Such debates, although sometimes tiresome, still add a vibrancy and direction to our scholarship missing from other fields.

---

95. Stephen Toulmin, *The Place of Reason in Ethics* (Cambridge: Cambridge University Press, 1950).

96. Vasquez, *The Power of Power Politics* (1998), pp. 228–229.

97. Foucault, *The Archaeology of Knowledge*.

Chapter 14

A Lakatosian Reading of Lakatos

What Can we Salvage from the Hard Core?

Andrew Bennett

The editors of this volume deserve the gratitude of every teacher of international relations for addressing two vexing questions that our students frequently pose. The first, raised by graduate students, is whether there is an article or book chapter that gives a concise and intelligible summary and critique of Imre Lakatos's famous but rather impenetrable essay on the methodology of scientific research programs. The second, innocently posed by undergraduates, is whether international relations theory has made demonstrable progress since Thucydides. The essays herein by Colin and Miriam Elman (Chapters 1 and 2) and David Dessler (Chapter 11) admirably answer the first question and will find their way onto many graduate syllabi. In so doing, however, these essays intensify the challenge of judging progress in international relations theory by thoroughly critiquing Lakatos's proposed methodological standards of theoretical progress. If there is no nonarbitrary way to distinguish between the hard core and outer belt of theories, as Dessler and the Elmans persuasively argue, does this mean that a theory's ability to generate and verify "novel facts" is also an arbitrary standard for judging progressivity? If so, are there other reliable criteria for assessing the progressivity of theories?

In this chapter, I argue that the novel facts criterion is a salvageable and useful standard for judging theoretical progress. At the same time, it is an imperfect criterion and it is not the only standard for assessing progress. Standards for judging theoretical progress must be applied

The author gratefully acknowledges the insightful suggestions of David Dessler, Colin Elman, and Miriam Fendius Elman.

with greater attention to three distinctions. First, it is important to attend to differences among the theoretical units in question: schools of thought, law-like theories, puzzle or problem-driven research programs, or causal mechanisms acting in isolation or joined in combinations. Here, Lakatos's distinction between the hard core and outer belt, while a useful metaphor, is rather arbitrary and insufficiently fine-grained. Second, as David Dessler argues, in judging progress it is necessary to specify which of the potential epistemic aims of a theory or research program is being assessed: law-like generalizations, historical explanations of events, or contingent generalizations about the conditions under which causal mechanisms have specified effects. Third, in devising standards for theoretical progress, we must make distinctions among the kinds of theories that are possible in the social sciences and those that are possible in the biological and physical sciences. The physical sciences are, notably, the basis of most of Lakatos's thinking and examples, just as they are the basis of much of the philosophy of science, but these sciences differ in fundamental ways from the social sciences.

Drawing on these three distinctions, theoretical progress in international relations may consist of advances in puzzle-driven research programs, increasingly complete and convincing historical explanations, and theories that are stronger at explaining social behavior than at predicting it. Lakatos notwithstanding, progress is not limited to the development of general theories or schools of thought with greater validity, scope, and predictive capability, as desirable as these kinds of progress may be. Much of the seeming lack of progress in international relations theory results from an excessive focus on the "isms" in judging progress, or on the broad schools of thought of (neo) realism, (neo) liberalism, and constructivism, rather than on analytically distinct puzzle-driven research programs such as those on the democratic peace or the end of the Cold War. Moreover, international relations theory and the social sciences more generally have at times suffered from the wholesale adoption of philosophies of science developed with a focus on the physical sciences, and hence from an over-emphasis on nomological generalization at the expense of the goals of historical explanation and contingent generalization. Finally, there is arguably a rational as well as a sociological basis for judging progress in terms of the development of a consensus among scholars who began with diverse and conflicting starting points, and also in terms of their increasing confidence in the instruments being used for measurement and testing. By all these measures, the democratic peace research program discussed by James Lee Ray in Chapter 6 of this volume provides clear examples of demonstrable theoretical progress in the last fifteen years, even though this research program still remains largely a collection of empirical findings in search of a widely accepted theory or set of theories. The other international relations research programs addressed herein also show signs of progress, though not as unambiguous, dramatic, or rapid. Thus, after taking into account the different elements that go into judgments about scientific progress, there is much that is useful in Lakatos, and in the philosophy of science more generally, to help convince our students and ourselves that there has indeed been progress in theories and historical explanations of international relations.

A single essay cannot critique Lakatos and his successors, do full justice to the three distinctions noted above, and address all the exemplar chapters in the book. In this chapter, therefore, I attempt only to convey the broad outlines of the first two subjects and to use the other chapters for illustrative purposes. Thus, this chapter first critiques the essays by Colin and Miriam Elman and David Dessler. It then puts these essays in context by very briefly outlining three post-Lakatosian schools of thought on scientific change: the Bayesians, the "error-statistical" school, and the "naturalists." Next, it analyzes the theoretical units and epistemic aims of international relations theory, and the differences between the study of the physical sciences and that of international relations and the social sciences more generally. I conclude that, judged on the basis of a variety of standards from different schools of thought in the philosophy of science, international relations theory has indeed made demonstrable progress.

Getting MSRP on the Table, Putting IR Theory on the Couch

The chapters by the Elmans and by David Dessler clearly and concisely summarize Lakatos's methodology of scientific research programs and obviate the need for doing so here. It is useful, however, to consider the key points of agreement and disagreement between these two essays, and it is illuminating to situate these two essays in the context of ongoing debates among post-Lakatosian schools of thought in the philosophy of science. I argue that this comparison leads to the conclusion that judging theoretical shifts by their ability to generate and confirm "novel facts" is useful, even if the distinction between the Lakatosian hard core (negative heuristic) and outer belt (positive heuristic) of research programs is necessarily arbitrary when applied to any particular program.

As a means of making the subsequent discussion of these issues more intelligible, it is worthwhile to consider three episodes from the history of science that provide useful frames of reference. In the first, two biologists and a physicist set out to explain the puzzling fact, first noted in the 1930s, that many characteristics of living creatures—life spans, pulse rates, energy burn rates, muscle strength—vary with body mass according to precise mathematical formulae. For example, mice, elephants, and every species of mammal in between have roughly the same number of heartbeats (about one billion) during an average life span. Analogous regularities hold for plants. The biologists and the physicist sought to explain these regularities by deductively working out a theory centered on the fractal geometrical properties of living beings' internal networks for distributing nutrients.

At first, the model worked beautifully for plants but not at all for mammals. Later, after corrections for hydrodynamic differences between the distribution of blood and that of plant nutrients, the model worked extremely well for both plants and animals. One Friday, however, the physicist was at home "playing with his equations when he realized to his chagrin that the model predicted that all mammals must have about the same blood pressure," which he felt could not be true.[1] After an uneasy weekend, he called one of his biologist collaborators, who informed him that mammals do indeed have roughly the same blood pressure.

In the second episode, a team of scientists set out to devise an explanation for schizophrenia based on brain chemistry. Once they had derived such a model, they uncovered the unexpected result that the brain chemicals in which, their model suggested, schizophrenics were deficient were the same chemicals affected by the process of smoking cigarettes. Hence, the brain chemistry model was consistent with the well-known but puzzling fact, which this model had not set out to explain, that many schizophrenics are chain smokers. These schizophrenics, the model now suggested, were using smoking to compensate for their brains' inadequacy at producing certain chemicals.

The third and best-known episode concerns the "confirmation" of Einstein's General Theory of Relativity (GTR), which is one of Lakatos's central examples. Einstein worked out GTR at a time when a central anomaly for physics was that Mercury's orbit did not fit the prediction of the Newtonian model. The common version of the story is that GTR was "confirmed" when its prediction about the curvature of light around the sun was "corroborated" during the solar eclipse of 1916. Some historians of science argue, however, that physicists at the time found GTR's mathematical explanation of Mercury's orbit more convincing than the eclipse experiment.[2] In fact, some of the photographic plates used in the eclipse experiment in Africa did not exactly fit the predictions of GTR, and it was only after the results of

---

1. George Johnson, "Of Mice and Elephants: A Matter of Scale," *The New York Times*, January 12, 1999, p. F1.

2. John Earman, *Bayes or Bust? A Critical Examination of Bayesian Confirmation Theory* (Cambridge, Mass.: MIT Press, 1992), p. 119, citing an "exhaustive survey of the literature" by Stephen G. Brush, "Prediction and Theory Evaluation: The Case of Light Bending," *Science*, No. 246 (1989), pp. 1124–1129.

these plates were changed to account for warping from heat that they were consistent with GTR.[3]

These examples, chosen not to represent all of science, but to illustrate some of its features, help to ground the discussion below of several of the most challenging issues in the philosophy of science. The Elmans' essay (Chapter 2) greatly clarifies how Lakatos's dense opus is relevant to these and other episodes in the history of science. In addition to analyzing the critiques of Lakatos's methodology of scientific research programs and applying the results to research in international relations, the Elmans outline the different kinds of "ad-hocness" in theory shifts and the different conceptions of "novel facts." Particularly useful is the Elmans' clear articulation of the distinction between "heuristic novelty," sometimes called "use novelty"—whereby only facts not used in the construction of a hypothesis can be considered novel for that hypothesis—and background theory novelty, whereby a fact is novel if it "could not have been expected from the best rival theory available."[4] In the above examples, the constancy of mammalian blood pressure, the chain-smoking of schizophrenics, and the curvature of light around the sun all had heuristic novelty: they were not used to derive or develop the theories in question. The physicist did not know of the constancy of mammalian blood pressure, and although some of the scientists studying schizophrenia were presumably aware of its link to chain-smoking, they did not use this link to devise their theory. All three theories satisfy the criterion of background theory novelty by explaining puzzling anomalies for which there had been no other accepted theoretical explanation.

It is important to emphasize, as the Elmans do, that novelty does not attend only to the prediction of future events or of universally

---

3. For a detailed account of the 1919 eclipse tests of Einstein's Law of Gravitation, see Deborah Mayo, *Error and the Growth of Experimental Knowledge* (Chicago: University of Chicago Press, 1996), pp. 278–292.

4. Martin Carrier, "On Novel Facts: A Discussion of Criteria for Non-ad-hoc-ness in the Methodology of Science Research Programs," *Zeitschrift fuer allgemeine Wissenschaftstheorie*, Vol. 19, No. 2 (1988), p. 213, quoted in Elman and Elman, Chapter 2.

unknown facts. A future event can have both heuristic novelty and background novelty, as did the bending of light around the sun circa 1915: no one had previously observed this phenomenon, and none of the extant theories save GTR could account for it. But a future event can also lack both kinds of novelty, as, for example, a theory predicting that the sun will rise tomorrow. A past event or well-observed phenomenon, such as constant mammalian blood pressure, can also have both heuristic and background novelty for some researchers. This raises the problem that heuristic novelty can be person-dependent. This is a problem for logical approaches to theory confirmation, but it is worth noting that the person-dependency of heuristic novelty is not necessarily a problem for the Bayesian approach to theory testing, discussed below, which allows for differences in the subjective prior probabilities that individuals assign to the truth of theories. Thus, in the Bayesian view, the same evidence can revise one individual's estimate of a theory's likely truth more radically than another's.

Despite these complexities, the Elmans clearly favor the criterion of heuristic novelty, arguing that background theory novelty is too permissive. They state that background theory novelty cannot be made consistent with Lakatos's distinction between the hard core and the outer belt, and thus it admits trivial ad hoc theory shifts and progressive theory shifts in equal measure. The Elmans also argue that we should not commit the "sweet shop" error of arbitrarily picking and choosing those parts of the methodology of scientific research programs that we find most congenial.

My own view is rather different. I emphasize first that, as in the examples above, the most powerful source of confidence in a new theory is the *combination* of heuristically novel facts *and* the explanation of either "old" anomalies or new predictions not accounted for by extant background theories. This is evident in the passage of Lakatos, quoted by Dessler, stating that Einstein's theory was progressive because it explained "to *some extent* some known anomalies [background novelty] and, in addition, forbade events like transmission of light along straight lines near large masses about which Newton's theory had said nothing [heuristic novelty with an element of background novelty]."[5]

Second, the hard question is whether we would accept background novelty alone as a measure of progress: if the elegant mathematics of GTR had "explained" only Mercury's orbit, but predicted nothing else then observable in the universe, would the physicists have accepted GTR as progressive? The Elmans appear to answer no; Larry Laudan, discussed below, would in my reading answer yes; Lakatos is characteristically ambiguous. If pressed, I would answer yes but I would first try to weasel out by saying that there is almost always some other observable and testable implication to a theory, whether it concerns future outcomes or past processes.[6]

Third, if the criterion of background novelty cannot be made consistent with the core-belt distinction, why should we downplay the role of background theory novelty rather than that of the core-belt distinction? After all, it is the core-belt distinction that the Elmans, Dessler, and many philosophers of science find to be weak and arbitrary even if it serves as a useful metaphor. Indeed, the strongest point of agreement among all of the participants at our Arizona conference was that there is no non-arbitrary means of achieving a consensus on what constitutes the hard core and outer belt of any particular research program. More difficult is the question of whether the failure of this distinction also undercuts the value of the heuristic and background novelty criteria.

David Dessler's main contribution, to which I return below, is in distinguishing between the explanation of events and the explanation of laws, and including both as important components of explanatory

---

5. David Dessler, Chapter 11 in this volume, p. 382.

6. A relevant example here is string theory, an approach in theoretical physics that posits ten or eleven dimensions, rather then the usual four, to explain anomalies in the inflationary theory of the "big bang" at the start of the universe. String theory has attracted many proponents even though it has not yet made any verifiable use-novel predictions. Even here, scientists may yet be able to devise new instruments to test the theory's novel predictions about the very first moments after the "big bang." See Susan Okre, "New Theory of Universe Goes Beyond the Bang," *Washington Post*, May 13, 2002, p. A6.

progress. Dessler also appears to concur with my view that background novelty is useful: most of the examples he cites from the history of science involve the explanation of anomalies, which take shape only against the failure of existing theories. In these examples, heuristically novel facts often emerge only after the proposal of theories built to address known anomalies. Another difference between Dessler and the Elmans is Dessler's reminder that we need not swallow either Popper's or Lakatos's philosophies whole. The Elmans also point out that we need not say "Lakatos or bust," but at the same time they warn against the "sweet shop error" of picking and choosing parts of Lakatos's methodology of scientific research programs. Neither essay addresses head-on what I take to be the key issue here: can we separate and rescue the standard of novel facts from our inability to delineate non-arbitrarily between the hard core and outer belt?

A Lakatosian reading of Lakatos confirms that we need not swallow Lakatos's methodology whole. To do so would be to privilege all of his methodology of scientific research programs as if it were an immutable hard core. Instead, we should differentiate the hard core of Lakatos's methodology from its outer belt: what are the logically necessary relations among elements of the methodology of scientific research programs, and what elements or connections are peculiar to Lakatos's own reading of the history of science? Interestingly, Larry Laudan and others have outlined a list of assertions about science made by Lakatos, Thomas Kuhn, and others; indicated which propositions are more widely accepted and which are more contested; and suggested that these propositions about the history and development of science should be subjected to empirical tests just like scientific theories themselves.[7] I have not carried out such a full-scale empirical test, and an evaluation of any metatheory must proceed on logical grounds (how can science work?) and normative grounds (how should

---

7. Larry Laudan, Arthur Donovan, Rachel Laudan, Peter Barker, Harold Brown, Jarred Leplin, Paul Thagard, and Steve Wykstra, "Scientific Change: Philosophical Models and Historical Research," *Synthese*, Vol. 69, No. 2 (November 1986), pp. 141–223.

scientists work?) as well as historical and empirical grounds (how have scientists worked?). However, drawing upon Lakatos's critics, I argue that the Lakatosian hard core that moves science forward is the novel facts criterion, despite its complexities and ambiguities, whereas the hard core/outer belt distinction, while a useful metaphor for guarding against naive falsification, is not a necessary component of progress. If I propose a theory, for example, it is not necessary for others to agree with the way in which I have delineated my theory's hard core and outer belt in order for them to agree whether certain facts satisfy heuristic novelty and/or background novelty for my theory. In addition, drawing on several post-Lakatosian philosophies of science, I argue that background theory novelty is more fundamental to progress than heuristic novelty.[8] It is the contestation over background novelty that brings us back to Popper's notion, discussed by Dessler, of severe tests.

To develop these conclusions, I review three post-Lakatosian schools of thought in the philosophy of science: the "Bayesian" approach associated with John Earman, Colin Howson, Peter Urbach, Geoffrey Hellman, and others; the "error-statistical" school articulated by Deborah Mayo largely as a critique of the Bayesians; and the "naturalist" approach advocated by Larry Laudan and Philip Kitcher.[9] All three claim to have resolved the problem that motivated Lakatos to develop his methodology of scientific research programs: the Duhem-Quine thesis, which maintains that when a theory confronts an anomaly, there is no logical standard for deciding whether the anomaly undercuts the theory or rather the theory's (often implicit) "auxiliary"

---

8. In practice, many progressive problemshifts arise from background theory novelty in the form of explaining "deviant cases" that were not predicted by and cannot easily be explained by existing theories. Stephen Van Evera, *Guide to Methods for Students of Political Science* (Ithaca, N.Y.: Cornell University Press, 1997), pp. 30–34; and Alexander L. George and Andrew Bennett, *Case Studies and Theory Development* (Cambridge, Mass.: MIT Press, forthcoming).

9. Tomas Bayes proposed his theory of probability in Bayes, "Essay towards Solving a Problem in the Doctrine of Chances," published in the *Philosophical Transactions of the Royal Society of London* in 1764.

hypotheses.[10] All three, like Lakatos, attempt to escape problems associated with both the logical positivism of Popper and the relativism of some of Kuhn's successors. Perhaps due to their complexity, these three schools of thought are not addressed in any detail in the other chapters of this volume (except for Stephen Walker's interesting use of Laudan's approach in Chapter 7). While these schools do indeed complicate the issues at hand, they also merit attention because they provide useful perspectives on the role of heuristic and background novelty. Thus, while I expect that many readers will have little patience for these complexities and may prefer to skip over my brief and inexpert summary of them, I hope that some will find useful insights. Like that of Lakatos, these three approaches attempt to provide a rational basis for the theory choices made by practicing scientists, but in contrast to Lakatos, they are more rigorous in their references to the historical evolution of scientific theories and more willing to defer to the actual practitioners of various sciences when philosophical logic seems to contradict scientific practice.

THE BAYESIAN APPROACH TO THEORY CHOICE

The Bayesian approach attempts not to confirm or reject theories, but to assign to them high or low probabilities of truth or degrees of belief, and to update these degrees of belief continually in the light of new evidence. This approach builds upon Bayes's theorem, one form of which states the following: if H is the hypothesis at issue, K is the background knowledge, and E is new evidence, then:

$$\frac{Pr(H/E\&K) = Pr(H/K) \times Pr(E/H\&K)}{Pr(E/K)}$$

---

10. This is sometimes referred to as the "underdetermination" thesis, as it argues that evidence never conclusively points only to one theory as being true. It is also at times termed the Quine-Duhem problem; Quine and Duhem did not write on this subject together, but their respective writings on it are often cited together. See Pierre Duhem, *The Aim and Structure of Physical Theory* (originally published in 1906), trans. P. Wiener (Princeton, N.J.: Princeton University Press, 1954), pp. 180ff; and Willard Van Orman Quine, "Two Dogmas of Empiricism," *The Philosophical Review*, Vol. 60 (1951), pp. 20–43.

In other words, the probability of hypothesis H being true equals the prior probability assigned to H, or Pr(H/K), multiplied by the probability of observing evidence E if H is true, divided by the prior probability of E.[11] To take the concrete example above, since GTR "explained" Mercury's orbit, we might assign it a prior probability of 50 percent. Then, with the eclipse experiment, we might have a high probability of observing the curvature of light if GTR were true, and a very low probability of witnessing this curvature given the extant Newtonian background knowledge. Thus, the finding that light in fact appeared to curve around the sun gives us a high numerator and low denominator in Bayes's theorem and greatly increases the probability we assign to the truth of GTR.

This approach to theory confirmation has become a leading school of thought in contemporary philosophy of science, and it addresses many of the same issues that concerned Lakatos, whose distinction between the hard core and outer belt is unconvincing to the Bayesians. Bayesianism allows for incremental confirmation of theories and avoids the pitfall of "naive falsification."[12] Some Bayesians claim also to have helped resolve the Duhem-Quine problem by, in effect, giving the benefit of the doubt to whichever of the two theoretical assertions—the main hypothesis in question or the auxiliary hypotheses—had the strongest prior probability going into a test.[13] This is the Bayesian analogue to Lakatos's distinction between highly probable hard core assumptions and less probable outer belt assertions,[14] and to the Bayesians' critics it is no more convincing.

---

11. This presentation is from Earman, *Bayes or Bust?* p. 33.

12. Earman, *Bayes or Bust?* pp. 64–65.

13. Earman argues that this claim is at best a very qualified success story for Bayesians; Earman, *Bayes or Bust?* pp. 84–85, 99–101.

14. Geoffrey Hellman, "Bayes and Beyond," *Philosophy of Science*, Vol. 64, No. 2 (June 1997), p. 199. Hellman is more confident than Earman that Bayesians can resolve the Duhem-Quine problem, but he acknowledges they have to do more to explain "the hard cases of theory choice in which an entrenched old theory, fairly successful in its domain, confronts anomalies and a rival new theory which may overcome some of these but which is itself still in a rather

At the same time, the Bayesian approach suffers from sharp limitations. A full accounting of the strengths and limits of Bayesianism is beyond the present task, but one key problem for Bayesians is that of "objectifying the priors," or giving a defensible basis for the prior probability assigned to a hypothesis for the purpose of applying the Bayesian theorem. The most promising solution to this problem is the argument that over the long run, even researchers who begin with vastly different subjective estimates of the prior probability of a hypothesis should converge toward a consensual probability estimate for that hypothesis as new evidence accumulates. Differences in prior probability estimates, in other words, "wash out."[15] This suggests that the convergence of scientific communities around agreed-upon theories that Kuhn describes is not merely a sociological phenomenon, but perhaps has a rational basis in the washing out of scientists' different prior probabilities as evidence mounts.[16]

Bayesian logic leads to an ambivalent view of heuristic or use novelty. John Earman quotes John Worrall's argument that "it is unlikely that the theory would have got this phenomenon precisely right just 'by chance'," only if we can rule out "that the theory was engineered or 'cooked up' to entail the phenomenon in question." Earman then argues that "insofar as Worrall's rationale is a good one, it can be given a Bayesian reading, since information about the genesis of a theory is clearly relevant to the assessment of its prior probability ...

---

nascent state." Ibid., p. 202. In such cases, it is not clear which theory deserves a higher prior probability.

15. Earman, *Bayes or Bust?* pp. 58–59. The remaining limitation, Earman notes, is that this solution does not address the short or medium-run time frame. Another Bayesian result, analogous to the washing out of prior probabilities, is the conclusion that a wide variety of different kinds of evidence is conducive to increasing confidence in a theory, as this allows for successive applications of Bayes's theorem.

16. The Bayesians would note that scientists should never have a hundred percent confidence in a theory, however, and they would also expect some diversity of opinion to remain. See Earman, *Bayes or Bust?* pp. 192–194. For a critique of efforts to reconcile Kuhnian and Bayesian views, see Deborah Mayo, *Error and the Growth of Experimental Knowledge*, pp. 112–127.

[but] since the assignment of priors is a tricky and subjective business, the Bayesian reading of [use novelty] gives a much less firm status than it was intended to have."[17] Earman adds that this result is appropriate since use novelty is controversial among scientists and philosophers of science. Moreover, he notes that other aspects of use novelty are inconsistent with Bayesian logic. Specifically, if a theory T entails two pieces of evidence, E1 and E2, and the former is used to construct T but the latter is not, then E2 must provide stronger support for the theory. In Bayes's equation, however, this is possible only if the probability of E2's occurrence is less than that of E1, and it would be illogical to think that the prior likelihood of evidence should depend on whether it was used in constructing T. After raising this issue, Earman states that he leaves it to the reader to judge the usefulness of use novelty by considering historical examples.[18] While partly tongue-in-cheek, this statement illustrates that at least some Bayesians do not privilege their relentless logic when it conflicts with extant and pragmatically successful scientific practices.

A related problem for Bayesians is that of "old" evidence. For evidence E to bear on the probability that a hypothesis is true, the probability of that evidence occurring must be less than one; otherwise, there is no new information and the hypothesis is not put "at risk." In the GTR example above, however, Mercury's orbit was well known before Einstein devised GTR, so Bayesian theory prohibits Mercury's orbit from having any value in updating the probability of GTR's truth. Yet as Earman points out, according to the most careful empirical study of the history, most physicists found Mercury's orbit to provide stronger confirmatory evidence of GTR than the bending of light around the sun.[19] Earman's proposed solution is to pose a counterfactual that imagines the researcher is "empirically deficient" and "didn't know E and asks what, in these circumstances, the agent's degree of belief in T would have been when T was introduced, and

---

17. Earman, *Bayes or Bust?* pp. 115–116.
18. Earman, *Bayes or Bust?* pp. 115–116.
19. Ibid., p. 119.

then it compares that number with what the agent's subsequent degree of belief in T would have been had he then learned E."[20] Interestingly, this "counterfactual" parallels closely the actual story of the physicist who was unaware of the constancy of mammalian blood pressure, which is perhaps why this confirmation seems so compelling.

The Bayesians also make life complicated on the issue of background novelty. For them, background novelty is reflected in the elusive "K" in Bayes's theorem. The probability of evidence E, given this background knowledge, is sometimes referred to as the "catchall factor" (another way to express it is as the probability of E given not H, or the probability of observing E even if H is not true). Background novelty also relates to eliminative induction: if all competing hypotheses can be eliminated, then the probability of the one remaining hypothesis approaches unity.[21] The problem with the Bayesian catchall factor is that it is unclear which and how many background theories should be taken into consideration, and in particular, whether one needs to include only extant hypotheses proposed by actual scientists or also the infinite number of possible hypotheses that have not yet been articulated. Wesley Salmon proposed at one point that we should limit comparisons to rival theories that have actually been proposed, but for complex reasons that need not be outlined here, this undercuts the ability of Bayesian theory to make judgments about which kinds of evidence have the greatest confirmatory value.[22] A better approach, Earman argues, is not to aspire to eliminate all but one hypothesis, but to eliminate piecemeal as many hypotheses or "chunks of the possibility space" as possible.[23] Earman wants to cast the net of alternative hypotheses more widely than Salmon, to theories that might reasonably be proposed, without making it infinitely wide. In this view, an alternative hypothesis only becomes relevant when it is explicitly stated and when it indicates a

---

20. Ibid., p. 134.
21. Ibid., p. 163.
22. Ibid., pp. 84, 171–172.
23. Ibid., p. 165.

type of observation for which it makes a different prediction than the hypothesis of interest.[24] Earman adds that "in some instances, our grasp of the space of alternatives may seem firm.... Firmly entrenched background theories rather than artifice may supply the grasp."[25] Later, however, he concedes that "there can be no noncircular inductive justification for circumscribing the possibility space in the fashion presupposed by the program. I am thus committed to a kind of epistemic relativism where enquiry is conducted relative to a frame for local induction."[26]

In short, only a pragmatic answer is possible on the question of how widely to cast the net for alternative explanations. Only extant theories and variations on them that the researcher can develop are viable candidates, and we cannot know all the possible alternatives. This is one reason why, for Bayesians, we are never one hundred percent confident in our theories.

THE "ERROR-STATISTICAL" APPROACH TO THEORY CHOICE

The "error-statistical" approach to theory testing is most fully articulated in the work of Deborah Mayo.[27] Mayo raises to a new level of sophistication the common criticism of the Bayesians' reliance on subjective prior probabilities. In her view, the Bayesian solution to the Duhem-Quine problem "just returns as the problem of justifying the correctness of the probabilities in the Bayesian equations."[28] At the same time, Mayo finds Lakatos's methodology of scientific research programs too permissive in keeping potentially false research programs alive indefinitely.[29] Yet she joins in Lakatos's rejection of Popper's falsificationism because it also fails to address the Duhem-

---

24. Ibid., p. 169, quoting Harold Jeffreys.

25. Ibid., p. 172.

26. Ibid., p. 184.

27. Deborah Mayo, *Error and the Growth of Experimental Knowledge*. As Mayo notes, her work builds on that of a group she calls the "new experimentalists," including Ian Hacking, Nancy Cartwright, and Ronald Giere. Ibid., p. 58.

28. Ibid., p. 104.

29. Ibid., pp. 2–3.

Quine problem and is too quick to blame anomalies on the theories being tested rather than on auxiliary assumptions. Instead, Mayo seeks to resolve the Duhem-Quine problem by probing the standard sources of error in scientific experiments, such as mistakes in measurement or insufficient statistical control of the variables.[30] Mayo argues that "if we just ask ourselves about the specific types of mistakes we can and do make, and how we discover and avoid them—in short, how we learn from error—we would find that we have already taken several steps beyond the models of both Popper and Lakatos."[31] It is the probing for error in experimental settings, in her view, that helps us localize the blame for anomalous findings.

This approach leads Mayo to a specific view on what constitutes a "severe test." While for Popper a hypothesis passed a severe test by explaining outcomes that rival hypotheses failed to explain (background novelty), for Mayo a severe test is one that is capable of assessing the many ways in which a misleading result might arise in a given experimental setting.[32] Put another way, *"a passing result is a severe test of hypothesis H just to the extent that it is very improbable for such a passing result to occur, were H false.... To* calculate this probability requires considering the probability a given procedure has for detecting a given type of error."[33] In contrast to Bayesian accounts that begin with the evidence already established and seek a relationship between the evidence and the hypothesis, Mayo's notion of severity "refers to a method or procedure of testing, and cannot be assessed without considering how the data were generated, modeled, and

---

30. Ibid., p. 63. Mayo lists the "canonical sources of error" as mistaking experimental artifacts or chance effects for genuine correlations, mistaking the value of a parameter, "mistakes about a causal factor" such as errors in specifying the form of a model, and "mistakes about the assumptions of experimental data." Mayo, *Error and the Growth of Experimental Knowledge*, pp. 18, 140.

31. Mayo, *Error and the Growth of Experimental Knowledge*, p. 4.

32. Ibid., p. 9.

33. Ibid., p. 178 (emphasis in original).

analyzed to obtain relevant evidence in the first place."[34] Building on renewed attention to historical narratives on the role of experiments and instruments in science, Mayo argues that in order to resolve the Duhem-Quine problem, one should look "to the already well worked out methods and models for designing and analyzing experiments that are offered in standard statistical practice," such as statistical significance levels and tests.[35] Thus, theories of experimental instruments help justify which data constitute accepted observations; efforts at establishing experimental controls help eliminate auxiliary factors as possible explanations for anomalies; and standard statistical tests help falsify statistical or probabilistic claims.[36]

In contrast to the Bayesian approach, Mayo argues that the same evidence provides differential confirmation of competing hypotheses not because of differences in these hypotheses' prior probabilities, but because the same experimental procedure has different error probabilities for different hypotheses and can provide a more severe test of one hypothesis than another. Mayo gives the example of an extremely sensitive medical probe that has a high chance of finding a rare disease when it is present, but also a fairly high chance of indicating a person has a disease when the person is healthy. Such a probe poses a severe test for the hypothesis that a disease is present: an indication of no disease is strong evidence of good health. But such a

---

34. Ibid., p. 11. The Bayesians could try to appropriate Mayo's severe tests by arguing that scientists' understanding of the experimental context and the sources of error enter into their probability estimates of the truth of the central and auxiliary hypothesis. As with many other Bayesian fixes, however, this raises the question of whether Bayes's theorem is merely an "accounting device" for keeping track of more fundamental processes.

35. Ibid., p. 12.

36. Ibid., p. 13. This view is similar to those expressed in Gary King, Robert O. Keohane, and Sidney Verba, *Designing Social Inquiry: Scientific Inference in Qualitative Research* (Princeton, N.J.: Princeton University Press, 1994), though the correspondence of views between these two books is not necessarily complete and neither book refers to the other (the King, Keohane, and Verba book was published in 1994, and the Mayo book in 1996, though several of Mayo's relevant articles appeared in the early 1990s).

probe poses a less severe test of the hypothesis that the person is ill: an indication that a disease is present is likely to be wrong since very few individuals have the disease and most of those whom the test shows to have the disease will be "false positives."[37]

These views lead Mayo to distinct interpretations of the issues of background novelty and use novelty. For Mayo, a hypothesis that passes the test of background novelty has not necessarily passed a severe test; this depends on whether the test procedure itself is severe in the sense of ruling out probable errors that could lead to accepting a false hypothesis.[38] Conversely, the existence of alternative hypotheses that are also consistent with the evidence does not mean that a hypothesis H has not passed a severe test: Mayo argues that an experiment may pose a more severe test for H than for the alternatives.[39] On this point, Mayo maintains that her emphasis on

---

37. Mayo, *Error and the Growth of Experimental Knowledge*, p. 184. This relates to the standard discussion in statistics of "Type 1" errors (rejecting true hypotheses) and "Type 2" errors (accepting false hypotheses). For an illustration of the differences between the Bayesian and error-statistical approaches on how to use error probabilities, see the divergent interpretations of a hypothetical example presented by Colin Howson, "A Logic of Induction," *Philosophy of Science*, Vol. 64, No. 2 (June 1997), pp. 279–281; and Deborah Mayo, "Response to Howson and Laudan," *Philosophy of Science*, Vol. 64, No. 2 (June 1997), pp. 326–329. Essentially, Howson argues that one can combine prior probabilities observed in a population with the error probabilities of a particular test to interpret the test outcomes for individuals. Thus, if a student from a population that is almost universally poorly educated passes an admissions exam, we might still be skeptical of the student's readiness for college. Mayo argues instead that combining population parameters and the error probabilities of a test is illegitimate. In this view, the error probabilities of the test itself may provide more reliable results for individuals, even though Howson's approach might give sensible average losses in repeated tests. Thus, if the entrance exam is highly reliable in rejecting unprepared students, certain students who pass the exam may be ready for college even if most of their peers are not. This disagreement appears to involve differences over whether unit homogeneity assumptions apply to the population or to the test itself.

38. Mayo, *Error and the Growth of Experimental Knowledge*, p. 212.

39. Ibid., p. 175.

error probabilities is superior to the Bayesians' use of the "catchall factor," or the probability assigned to the large or even infinite range of alternative hypotheses that might be consistent with the observed evidence. Recalling a remark from Wesley Salmon, Mayo notes that assigning a low value to this catchall factor requires that we "predict the future course of the history of science," or assess the probability of hypotheses not yet articulated.[40]

Similarly, Mayo argues that her concept of severe testing supersedes the issue of use novelty. In Mayo's view, the use of data to construct a hypothesis guarantees that the hypothesis will fit the data, but this does not rule out that the data may constitute a severe test of the hypothesis.[41] For example, she argues, in an opinion poll where the margin of error (estimated using normal assumptions) is low, it is unlikely that the poll would estimate a particular result if the actual population proportion was outside the margin of error, even though the proportion reported in the poll is constructed by the poll itself.[42] In this case, the poll result has passed a severe test even though it is use-constructed and has zero chance of being falsified in this single poll. "What matters is not whether passing is assured," Mayo states, "but whether erroneous passing is."[43]

Although Mayo agrees that many use-constructed theories may be badly constructed and badly tested, the lack of severe testing arises from the testing procedure itself, and not the use-construction of the theory.[44] Novelty, she argues, "was not the real issue in the first place":

---

40. Ibid., p. 188.

41. Ibid., p. 266.

42. Ibid., pp. 272–273.

43. Ibid., pp. 274–745.

44. Mayo critiques the views of those Bayesians who dismiss use novelty out of hand, arguing that "for Bayesian philosophers of science, just as with earlier 'logicist' approaches, there is no slot in which to take into account the novelty of the data.... Finding UN [use novelty] unnecessary ... the Bayesian declares the arguments in favor of UN wrong.... I differ from the Bayesian and concur with the UN proponent in holding that when a difference in appraisal is warranted, the fault lies in the testing process and not in our priors." Ibid., p. 260. On the Bayesian rejection of use novelty, she cites Colin Howson and

What lay behind the intuition that novelty mattered is that severe tests matter. What underlies the basic intuition that if the data are not novel, then they fail to test or support a hypothesis are the various impediments to severity that correlate with violating novelty of one sort or another. But this correlation is imperfect. Novelty and severity do not always go hand in hand: there are novel tests that are not severe and severe tests that are not novel. As such, criteria for good tests that are couched in terms of novelty wind up being either too weak or too strong, countenancing poor tests and condemning excellent ones. I believe that our notion of severe tests captures pronovelty intuitions *just where those intuitions are correct.*"[45]

A key limitation in light of the issues raised herein is that Mayo's resolution of the Duhem-Quine problem comes at the cost of sacrificing the generalizability of test results. In the error-statistical view, the results of experiments apply only to the very narrow aspects of a theory being specifically tested in the experiment. In this view, for example, the eclipse experiment of GTR only tested the specific prediction GTR made on the deflection of light around the sun against "alternative values of the deflection, not alternatives to the general theory of relativity." The results of the experiment thus had few or no implications for other aspects of GTR, such as its predictions about gravity waves or black holes.[46] Mayo recognizes that in this respect her approach runs counter to those of Lakatos, Laudan, and others who have tried to resolve the Duhem-Quine problem by "going bigger," or looking for standards for judging entire complexes of theories and sequences of theory shifts, such as research programs (Lakatos) or research traditions (Laudan). Mayo instead consciously chooses to "go smaller," to specific experiments and the local tests of "normal science."[47] Her focus is on piecemeal tests in the puzzle-solving

---

Peter Urbach, *Scientific Reasoning: The Bayesian Approach* (La Salle: Open Court, 1989), rather than Earman, who as noted above is more equivocal on use novelty.

45. Ibid., pp. 252–253 (emphasis in original).

46. Ibid., p. 188.

47. Ibid., pp. 19–20, 57.

tradition, and she argues that although we can only take baby steps, we can "take those baby steps severely."[48]

Two additional limitations on Mayo's approach are worth noting. The first is the problem of deriving the error probabilities of particular experiments, procedures, and instruments. Mayo relies on "frequentist" probabilities, or observed probabilities, but this requires strong assumptions on "unit homogeneity" between the entities or tests observed and those not yet observed. Careful experimental controls and random assignment to treatment and control groups might increase our confidence in the necessary unit homogeneity assumptions, but this is of little help when experimental research designs are not possible. This highlights the second limitation, which is that it is unclear in general whether and how Mayo's framework applies to non-experimental settings, historical explanation, and case studies, as distinct from statistical and experimental studies. As is evident in the section that follows, a third post-Lakatosian school, the naturalists, is critical of Mayo on these issues, providing a rejoinder to Mayo's critique of the Bayesians.

THE NATURALIST APPROACH TO THEORY CHOICE

Like other post-Lakatosian philosophies of science, the "naturalist" school admits of no easy or entirely consensual definition. Broadly conceived, however, it includes both Larry Laudan and Philip Kitcher, who agree on most fundamental points even though they disagree on several specific issues. In Kitcher's view, naturalism is an effort to chart a pragmatic course between the logical empiricists, such as Popper, and the post-Kuhnian relativists, such as Paul Feyerabend, without falling prey to the logical blind alleys of the former or the "anything goes" claims of the latter. Kitcher attempts to draw on the insights of biology, cognitive science, and sociology in understanding scientists and scientific progress. He argues that the growth of science is "a process in which cognitively limited biological entities combine their efforts in a social contest," and he adds that "placing the knowing subject firmly back into the discussion of epistemological problems

---

48. Ibid., pp. 191–192.

seems to me to be the hallmark of naturalistic epistemology."[49] Yet in drawing upon social and cognitive science to understand how scientists function, Kitcher remains broadly within the camp of scientific realists, agreeing that scientists probe a world that exists independently of human cognition.[50] Laudan's naturalism is similarly pragmatic, focusing on science as problem-solving, downplaying (as Kitcher does) the problem of underdetermination, and giving an important role to long-lived sets of guiding theoretical assumptions—Laudan calls these "research traditions" and Kitcher terms them "consensual practices"—without attempting to define them as rigidly as Lakatos tries to do in his discussion of the hard core assumptions of research programs.

At the heart of Laudan's view of scientific progress is his assertion that "science progresses just in case successive theories solve more problems than their predecessors."[51] Laudan elaborates on this by

---

49. Philip Kitcher, *The Advancement of Science: Science without Legend, Objectivity without Illusions* (New York: Oxford University Press, 1993), p. 9. One possible example of how cognitive science helps undergird epistemological and methodological reasoning, although Kitcher does not raise it, is that use novelty is one means of addressing the problem of confirmation bias. This is the bias, demonstrated in numerous psychology experiments, toward fitting incoming evidence to existing theories or schema. Thus, being aware of the cognitive biases in how our brains function provides a justification for use novelty that is separate from any logical justification. This helps explain part of the intuitive appeal of the heuristic novelty criterion. One example of an effort by scientists to avoid confirmation bias concerns work in particle physics, in which physicists intentionally hid key information from themselves. See James Glanz, "New Tactic in Physics: Hiding an Answer," *The New York Times*, August 8, 2000, p. D1. Researchers also need to guard against other cognitive biases distorting causal inference, such as over-confidence in one's causal theories, a preference for monocausal explanations, and the tendency to assume that causes resemble consequences in terms of scope, scale, and complexity. Richard Nisbett and Lee Ross, *Human Inference: Strategies and Shortcomings of Social Judgment* (Englewood Cliffs, N.J.: Prentice-Hall, 1980), pp. 97–101, 116, 128.

50. Ibid., p. 127.

51. Larry Laudan, *Beyond Positivism and Relativism: Theory, Method, and Evidence* (Boulder, Colo.: Westview Press, 1996), p. 78.

arguing that theories can progress by addressing either empirical problems or conceptual problems. Empirical problems include potential problems, or descriptive observations as yet lacking an explanation. The various empirical findings on the "democratic peace" described in James Lee Ray in Chapter 6, for which there are not yet accepted theories, are a good example of a potential problem. Empirical problems also include what Laudan terms "solved problems," or findings putatively explained by a theory, and "anomalous problems," or problems that rival theories claim to solve but that the theory of interest does not. Conceptual problems include internal inconsistencies, ambiguous postulates on causal mechanisms, conflicts with other theories, empirically unwarranted claims, and assumptions that violate the "research tradition" of which the theory is a part.[52] The elimination of a theory's conceptual problems, Laudan argues, can constitute progress, just as increasing empirical support does.

Kitcher critiques Laudan's emphasis on puzzle-solving for its failure to specify whether a puzzle is "solved" when enough members of a community think it is solved, which raises the problem of relativism, or when the solution is warranted on some logical basis, which raises the logical positivists' problem of how to make such a warrant.[53] He introduces a slightly different approach to resolving theoretical or empirical inconsistencies, though he acknowledges that it does not fully address the dilemma faced by Laudan's puzzle-solving approach. Kitcher argues that scientists resolve problems by adding further statements to a theory that are consistent with the remaining statements in the original theory, that compensate for the resulting explanatory losses in the original theory, and that conform to the constraints derived from consensus practices within the field in question.[54] Scientists consider modifying the constraints of consensus practices only when less radical theory shifts continue to create their

---

52. Ibid., p. 79.
53. Kitcher, *Advancement of Science*, p. 130, note 4.
54. Ibid., pp. 256–263.

own inconsistencies. Kitcher argues that the process of deciding how to resolve inconsistencies, and how to choose among alternative resolutions, is simple in outline, but complex in practice, and he suggests that we may be able to achieve only methodological exemplars rather than general rules about this process.[55]

The naturalists are perhaps more content with (or resigned to) incomplete standards of progress because of their pragmatic approach to the problem of underdetermination. In his chapter on "demystifying underdetermination," Laudan critiques the various versions of the underdetermination problem, including the Duhem-Quine thesis, and argues that their implications are overstated. While acknowledging that for some rules of theory choice, and for some pairs of alternative theories, theory choice is underdetermined for some sets of evidence, Laudan rejects blanket claims that all rules underdetermine theory choice for all evidence, or that all theories can be made equally consistent with any set of evidence.[56] Similarly, Kitcher circumscribes the problem of "infinite" alternative hypotheses, arguing that "there are any number of *logically* possible hypotheses ... however, the *serious* hypotheses are relatively few in number." As for the Duhem-Quine version of the underdetermination problem, he also argues that not all modifications to a theory, or to the background setting, are equally viable. In both instances, the formation of alternative hypotheses and modifications of theories are constrained by prior practices that recognize "certain kinds of processes as occurring in nature and not others."[57] In a statement that echoes similar remarks by both Lakatos and Mayo, Kitcher notes that scientists cannot merely circumscribe generalizations to exclude anomalies one at a time because "a claim that there is a local error in investigating things of a very special type needs to be integrated with our background ideas about the potential sources of error."[58] While agreeing with Laudan that the real problem

55. Ibid., p. 263, note 57.
56. Laudan, *Beyond Positivism and Relativism*, pp. 29–53.
57. Kitcher, *Advancement of Science*, pp. 247–249.
58. Ibid., p. 251.

of underdetermination arises when there are alternative ways of revising beliefs that are equally consistent with methodological constraints, Kitcher suggests that such situations may be temporarily inconclusive, and that they are "ultimately resolved through the provision by the victor of successes in the terms demanded by the rival."[59]

This perspective leads in turn to a pragmatic view on the issue of background novelty. With regard to the Bayesians' concern over the "catchall factor" problem of comparing a theory to alternative hypotheses not yet devised, Kitcher simply states that "since we do not know how to state the unknown rivals, it is impossible to proceed systematically to eliminate them. We simply cast our net as widely as we can."[60] Here again, the prior state of scientific practices selects which candidate theories are to be included in the comparison. Similarly, Laudan agrees that theory choice is a relative issue of comparing theories to "extant rivals," not all logically possible alternatives, and he states that a theory is more persuasive if it can solve empirical difficulties confronting rival theories.[61]

Laudan and Kitcher both argue that use novelty should not be a strict requirement, but they do accord it at least some relevance. Laudan states that the discovery of anomalies can lead to non–use-novel but progressive theories, because it is difficult to explain anomalies without at the same time decreasing the ability of the theory to explain the many other puzzles or problems it had already appeared to solve.[62] Similarly, Kitcher notes that "accommodating the evidence is often *not* an easy game, because the constraints from prior practice are so powerful that they make difficult the genesis of even one hypothesis that will fit accepted findings." He adds, however, that when there is

59. Ibid., p. 252.

60. Ibid., p. 245.

61. Larry Laudan, *Progress and Its Problems: Towards a Theory of Scientific Growth* (Berkeley: University of California Press, 1977), pp. 1–3, 18, 124; Larry Laudan, *Science and Values: The Aims of Science and Their Role in Scientific Debate* (Berkeley: University of California Press, 1984), pp. 27–28.

62. Larry Laudan, *Progress and its Problems*, p. 116.

low confidence in the completeness of prior scientific practices, then hypotheses that merely accommodate anomalies are suspect. He thus locates the problem of use novelty not with the practice of accommodation itself, but with the weakness of prior practices and the failure to explore fully the space of reasonable rival explanations of the anomaly: "surprising novel predictions may be striking, but the touchstone of their evidential force is the ability to reduce the space of rivals sanctioned by prior practice."[63]

Like Lakatos, the naturalists give a central role to enduring theoretical assumptions in constraining the numbers of rival theories to be compared and the ways in which these theories can be legitimately modified. However, the naturalists define these guiding assumptions somewhat differently from Lakatos's notion of a "hard core." Kitcher, in particular, distinguishes between the practices of individual scientists and the consensus practices of scientific fields. He defines consensus practices to be constituted by:

a language; an (impersonal) assessment of significant questions; a set of accepted statements with a (partial) justificatory structure; a set of explanatory schema; a set of paradigms of authority and criteria for identifying authorities; a set of exemplary experiments, observations, and instruments and justificatory criteria; and, finally, a set of methodological exemplars and methodological principles.[64]

Both Laudan and Kitcher argue that these practices, or Laudan's equivalent of "research traditions," change more continually and incrementally than is suggested by Lakatos's notion of research programs or Kuhn's concept of paradigms. Moreover, Kitcher argues that "traditional conceptions of the units of change"—in which he includes Kuhn's paradigms, Lakatos's research programs, and Laudan's research traditions—conflate "things that belong to the daily psychological lives of individuals, things that count among their more stable commitments, and things that are the property of the

---

63. Kitcher, *Advancement of Science*, p. 246.
64. Ibid., p. 87.

community rather than of any single member."[65] He thus allows for a more differentiated range of shared commitments than Lakatos, who argues that the hard cores of research programs are sharply delineated and widely shared.

Finally, the naturalists have critiqued the error-statistical and Bayesian schools, though they share some views with both. Laudan and Kitcher agree with Mayo that in many cases, shared rules about experimental design and theories on the sources of error help scientists to resolve disputes between competing theories.[66] Kitcher also finds common ground with Earman's emphasis on eliminative induction, and Kitcher and Laudan agree with Earman on the need to limit background theory comparisons to extant rival hypotheses.[67] Laudan, however, critiques the Bayesians for short-circuiting the Duhem-Quine problem by relegating it to whether a hypothesis or its background assumptions had higher prior probabilities. Instead, he argues, scientists should confront anomalies by examining whether modifications to the hypothesis of interest and/or its background assumptions prove fruitful in terms of generating and corroborating new evidence and explaining most of the domain of their predecessors. Laudan also critiques Mayo's proposed solution to the Duhem-Quine problem for appearing "to fall back on the statisticians' equivalent of the probability theorists' catchall hypothesis." He adds that:

if there are difficulties ... with the Bayesians' hope of calculating the value of the catchall hypothesis (viz., the probability of E, explained by H, if H is false), Mayo appears to run squarely into the same problems with her demand that we must calculate the probability that H would pass test T *if H were false*. With the Mayo-ists, as with the Bayesians, we seem to be

---

65. Ibid., p. 89.

66. Laudan, *Science and Values*, pp. 25–30.

67. Kitcher, *Advancement of Science*, p. 192.

confronted by a probability calculation involving an indefinitely long disjunction of rival hypotheses to H.[68]

Also, in Laudan's view Mayo is too narrow in her approach in arguing that the light-bending experiments have no bearing on GTR's general claims, such as those about gravity waves or black holes.[69] If so, then "Duhemian ambiguities return with a vengeance" in the form of the inability to use tests to assess general theories. Laudan argues that it is instead necessary to "drop the pretense, dear to the hearts of both Bayesians and error-statisticians, that our evaluations of hypotheses are absolute. Instead, let us say explicitly what scientific practice already forces us to acknowledge, viz., that the evaluation of a theory or hypothesis is relative to its *extant* rivals.... A theory has been severely tested provided that it has survived tests its known rivals have failed to pass (and not vice versa)."[70]

SUMMARIZING POST-LAKATOSIAN APPROACHES TO THEORY CHOICE

The brief and admittedly dense review above of three post-Lakatosian approaches does not allow for any easy summary. Nor can we readily treat the three approaches discussed above as complementary; despite acknowledging some bridges to Bayesianism, for example, Mayo devotes an entire chapter of her book to the topic of "Why You Cannot Be Just a Little Bit Bayesian."[71] Yet the three approaches do bear directly on the issues raised by Lakatos, the Elmans, and Dessler, and there are

68. Larry Laudan, "How About Bust? Factoring Explanatory Power Back into Theory Evaluation," *Philosophy of Science*, Vol. 64, No. 2 (June 1997), p. 312 (emphasis in original).

69. Ibid. See also Mayo's rejoinder in Mayo, "Response to Howson and Laudan," pp. 329–330. In her view, the original Duhem-Quine problem was that of localizing blame for an anomaly in a specific test, and Laudan and others have preemptively given up on this problem and "gone bigger" to try to assess research traditions instead of specific hypotheses. Mayo argues that the error approach can resolve the more specific variant of the problem without having to refer to larger theories such as research programs.

70. Ibid., p. 314.

71. Mayo, *Error and the Growth of Experimental Knowledge*, chap. 10; for her references to possible bridges to Bayesianism, see pp. 86, 360.

several points worth emphasizing. First, like the methodology of scientific research programs, all three approaches have significant limitations, and none has completely resolved the problems of theory choice. The Bayesians have the problems of the catchall factor and the objectification of prior probabilities. Mayo has the problem of justifying error probabilities; her metatheory is unable to assess the wider implications of theories; and it is unclear how her metatheory applies to non-statistical methods and non-experimental settings. The naturalists are vague on what constitutes successful puzzle-solving, and on how to decide the toughest cases of theory choice. This suggests that no single metatheory is likely to be appropriate for all the sciences, for all kinds of theories at all levels of generality, or for all epistemic aims. As John Earman has argued:

the philosophy of science is littered with methodologies of science, the best known of which are associated with the names of Popper, Kuhn, Lakatos, and Laudan.... I have two common complaints. The first stems from the fact that each of these methodologies seizes upon one or another feature of scientific activity and tries to promote it as the centerpiece of an account of what is distinctive about the scientific enterprise. The result in each case is a picture that accurately mirrors some important facets of science but only at the expense of an overall distortion. The second common complaint is that these philosophers, as well as many of their critics, are engaged in a snark hunt in trying to find The Methodology of Science.[72]

The absence of any single convincing metatheory should engender healthy skepticism regarding categorical methodological injunctions, such as making heuristic novelty an absolute requirement, prohibiting the testing of a theory in the same case from which it was derived, or forbidding selection on the dependent variable. These methods may be inappropriate in some instances, for some theories, and for some epistemic aims, but they may be appropriate for others.

Second, in contrast to the Elmans' essay, the three approaches give a limited and problematic role to heuristic novelty. All three agree, though for very different reasons, that theories which are not

---

72. Earman, *Bayes or Bust?* pp. 203–204.

heuristically novel may still be progressive. The verdict on background novelty is more mixed: the Bayesians and naturalists give background novelty an important role, whereas Mayo argues that a theory may have been severely tested even when the evidence is also consistent with rival theories. On the issue of which background or rival theories to consider, the Bayesians and naturalists make a convincing argument for a pragmatic approach of considering broadly the extant hypotheses that various schools of thought have proposed. In IR research, this should include not only the theoretical literature, but also implicit theories proposed by regional and functional experts and historians, and those articulated by participants in the events being studied. As both schools remind us, we cannot consider all hypotheses that might eventually be articulated, so our results remain provisional.

Third, IR theory has arguably made progress no matter which of these approaches we find most convincing in providing standards for theory choice. The clearest example of this is the research on the democratic peace discussed by James Lee Ray in Chapter 6. The Bayesians would recognize this research as progressive because researchers beginning with widely divergent prior expectations on the existence of the democratic peace have converged toward a consensus, though they have not reached a unanimous one, that democracies fight other democracies less often than they fight other types of regimes. Mayo would recognize progress in that successively more sophisticated statistical tests have ruled out possible sources of error that could undermine this judgment: the results have proven robust in statistical tests using many different definitions of "war" and "democracy" and have emerged even after controlling for other variables. The naturalists would recognize progress in terms of successful (although still incomplete) problem-solving in the increasingly detailed empirical record, and increasingly sophisticated (although still contested) concepts proposed to explain the democratic peace.

The Schism on "Isms" in IR Theory: By What Units Should We Judge Theoretical Progress?

As we move from abstract discussions of the philosophy of science to the assessment of progress in international relations theory, one underlying issue that comes to the fore concerns the relevant theoretical unit for judging progress: is it the broad schools of thought, or is it the "isms" in IR theory—(neo) realism, (neo) liberalism, and constructivism—that correspond best to Lakatos's conception of the hard core assumptions of research programs? Or should we focus on the "outer belt" theories of these schools, such as neoclassical realism, offensive realism, and defensive realism? Or perhaps we should judge progress in terms of problem-driven or puzzle-driven research, such as research on the democratic peace, alliance behavior, two-level games, deterrence, and international regimes? Most of the attention in judging progress in IR theory has focused on the first two approaches, but other fields in political science and the naturalist view of the philosophy of science outlined above suggest that puzzle-driven research deserves increased attention in assessing progress.

After the publication of Thomas Kuhn's famous study of scientific revolutions, political scientists rushed to define their own paradigms and stake claims to having achieved scientific revolutions.[73] Similarly, as the Elmans' Chapter 2 notes, after reading Lakatos, many IR theorists have focused on defining the hard core assumptions and outer belt arguments of their theories. This focus on the "isms" through the last two decades has usefully clarified IR theories and debates, helped make the views of many scholars commensurable, and made it easier to teach IR theory to our students. To the extent that the focus on "isms" has diverted attention from empirical puzzle-solving and problem-driven research, however, the field has suffered. Lakatos's methodology of scientific research programs focuses on judging progress over periods of years or even decades, and it is less useful in assessing the more incremental shifts of most theory

73. Thomas S. Kuhn, *The Structure of Scientific Revolutions* (Chicago: University of Chicago Press, 1962).

development. Moreover, a single-minded focus on the "isms" runs up against the lack of any nonarbitrary way to delineate the hard core of a research program. Worse, most articles presuming to adopt a Lakatosian stance focus on comparisons between the hard core "isms," and too few have addressed tests between outer-belt theories such as offensive versus defensive realism, or theories of bipolar versus multipolar stability. Many articles have also adopted decidedly non-Lakatosian language on theory testing, implying that an "ism" could be easily discredited by "disconfirming" examples.[74] Much research has become almost formulaic in "tests," pitting neorealism versus neoliberalism or constructivism as if the hard core of any of these programs could be unseated by a single book or article, and their results are too often reported in terms of the explanatory power rather than the scope conditions of rival theories.

Other scholars have noted that the field of comparative politics has not been organized around broad "isms," but has focused instead on problem-driven research programs, such as those focused on transitions to democracy, party structure, voting behavior, the implications of alternative types of domestic regimes, and so on.[75] IR theory can benefit by increasing the relative attention devoted to problem-driven research programs, though this does not require entirely bypassing the "isms" as tools in guiding research and pedagogy and facilitating communication within the field. In the last several decades we have developed progressively better explanations of international relations research programs on the democratic peace, alliance behavior, military innovation, military intervention, deterrence theory, and the roles of absolute and relative gains.

---

74. For example, Michael Desch poses the question of whether cultural theories "merely supplement realist theories or actually threaten to supplant them." This creates a straw man argument—the idea that a major research program such as realism could be fully supplanted—and it also privileges realism, rather than constructivism, as the research program to be supplemented. Michael Desch, "Culture Clash: Assessing the Importance of Ideas in Security Studies," *International Security*, Vol. 23, No. 1 (Summer 1998), p. 141.

75. Peter Katzenstein, "The Role of Theory in Comparative Politics: A Symposium," *World Politics*, Vol. 48, No. 1 (October 1995), p. 10.

Another level of theorizing that deserves increased attention is that of individual-level causal mechanisms. The causal mechanisms of rational choice theory have been the focus of intense research and debate, but this debate has not been as clearly brought into discussions of theoretical progress as the debate over the "isms"; the causal mechanisms of cognitive theories at odds with rational choice assumptions demand attention as well. Finally, we can judge progress in terms of typological theories that bring together conjunctions of causal mechanisms, and that integrate variables from the "isms."

In general, if we take a cue from the naturalists, move away from Lakatos's rigid and ultimately unsuccessful attempt to delineate hard core and outer belt theories, and recognize more diverse theoretical units, ranging from causal mechanisms to typological theories to puzzle-driven research agendas to broad schools of thought, we can develop more diverse and sophisticated means of judging theoretical progress. Scholars need to keep continually focused on the question of what different parts of our field need at their current stage of development: re-articulation of the "isms," problem-focused research, a better understanding of causal mechanisms, or contingent generalizations. Chapter 3 by Robert Keohane and Lisa Martin, for example, is an excellent illustration of how to identify and address the research that a particular program, in this case institutional theory, needed in order to resolve specific shortcomings and move forward.

What Kind of Science is Political Science?

A final issue that demands attention is the question of how political science, or the social sciences generally, differ from the natural sciences that are the focus and basis of both the methodology of scientific research programs and its successors, and of how any differences affect the application of these metatheories to a field for which they were not designed. The Elmans' Chapter 2 points out that Lakatos was less dismissive of the social sciences than is often assumed, yet he was still rather skeptical of the social sciences in some of his writings. He worked to apply his methodology of scientific research programs to economics, but economics is the social science with the most ambitious claims to epistemologies patterned after those in the physical sciences (to some extent psychology is another such social science, and socio-biology occupies a middle ground as well). This leaves unclear what Lakatos thought of political science and sociology. It also leaves unclear how the methodology of scientific research programs or other metatheories might have to be adapted for use in political science.

The obvious difference between the social and physical sciences, as constructivists have emphasized, is that human social agents and social structures are mutually constitutive, and social change can proceed causally in both directions, from agents to structures and from structures to agents. As David Dessler has persuasively argued, this constructivist ontology entirely encompasses structuralist ontologies because it takes into account social as well as material structures and the intended as well as the unintended consequences of social interaction.[76] This ontological formulation does not necessarily privilege constructivist theories over structuralist theories such as neorealism. It could still be true that key social structures, such as the "state" or the realpolitik version of "anarchy," are sufficiently recursive that the ability of agents to change structures is tightly circumscribed and neorealism is the best way to theorize about world politics *as currently constituted.*[77] The mutual constitution of agents and structures does require, however, that the post-modernist or hermeneutic critiques of post-positivism be given a more serious hearing in the social sciences than in the physical sciences. Social science research programs can change not only through discovery of unexplained empirical facts, but through changes in the very nature of the objects under study, such as the emergence of capitalism or of state sovereignty. This dictates that all social generalizations are necessarily contingent and time-bound. Here again, however, to acknowledge this fact is not to concede fully to the post-modernist critique of social theory.

---

76. David Dessler, "What's at Stake in the Agent-Structure Debate," *International Organization*, Vol. 43, No. 3 (Summer 1989), pp. 441–474.

77. The prominent constructivist theorist Alexander Wendt, for example, has acknowledged that many neorealist assumptions may be fairly accurate for world politics as currently constituted. See Alexander Wendt, "Constructing International Politics," *International Security*, Vol. 20, No. 1 (Summer 1995), p. 72.

Important social structures such as sovereignty or capitalism clearly are sufficiently recursive and long-lived that social scientists can usefully and cumulatively generate theories upon them over meaningful periods of time, sometimes even hundreds or thousands of years.[78]

These factors give theories in the social sciences a different "life-cycle" from those in the physical sciences. In the social sciences, much cumulation takes the form of increasingly narrow and more contingent but also more valid generalizations.[79] As the Elmans note, virtually every work in neorealism subsequent to Kenneth Waltz's 1979 *Theory of International Politics* has added variables to Waltz's spare theory.[80] The same is arguably true of neoliberalism since its early formulation by Robert Keohane and others.[81] At the same time, although most social science problemshifts are toward more contingent generalizations, inter-program problemshifts are more frequent in the social sciences than in the physical sciences, not just because of the "faddishness" or "subjectivity" of the social sciences, but because the objects of study change in reflexive ways.

The reflexivity of social subjects constrains social science theorizing in a variety of ways. Strategic interaction, self-fulfilling and self-

---

78. Moreover, the proposition that observation is theory-laden does not imply that observation is theory-determined, so social science theorists subscribing to the post-Lakatosian metatheories described above need not necessarily cede ground to those post-modernists who challenge the "scientific realist" view that social realities exist independently of particular observers and can be fruitfully and cumulatively studied.

79. On the other hand, the effort to build theories on the basis of individual-level causal mechanisms, whether these mechanisms are rational choice, cognitive, or socio-biological, does move toward more universal generalizations.

80. Kenneth Waltz, *Theory of International Politics* (Reading, Mass.: Addison-Wesley, 1979).

81. Robert O. Keohane, *After Hegemony: Cooperation and Discord in the World Political Economy* (Princeton, N.J.: Princeton University Press, 1984). Similarly, comparativists have been developing sub-types of democracy, or "democracy with adjectives." David Collier and Steven Levitsky, "Democracy with Adjectives: Conceptual Innovation in Comparative Research," *World Politics*, Vol. 46, No. 3 (April 1997), pp. 430–451.

denying prophecies, "moral hazard," selection effects, and a range of other phenomena make the development of predictive theories far more difficult in the social sciences than in the physical sciences.[82] It is useful to distinguish here between theories that can explain and predict both processes and outcomes, which are common in the physical sciences, and those that can explain processes and outcomes but not predict them. The latter kinds of theories, common in the social sciences, are not unknown in the physical sciences. Theories of evolutionary biology, for example, explain processes and, post-facto, outcomes, but they do not predict outcomes.

This raises David Dessler's important point that in many domains the most appropriate epistemic aim for the social sciences is historical explanation rather than development of general laws. As Dessler notes, the two are linked, in that historical explanation uses theoretical generalizations to argue why under specified historical conditions certain outcomes were to be expected.[83] But the logic of historical explanation does differ from that of nomological generalization. For example, contrary to a widespread view, it is possible to devise a theory from a case and still test the theory in that same case without violating heuristic novelty. It is necessary only that the theory's prediction be tested against data in the case that are different from and sufficiently independent of the data that gave rise to the theory. In the example used above regarding schizophrenia, even if there were only one schizophrenic in the world, we might find that schizophrenic's chain-smoking to be a heuristically novel corroboration of the brain chemistry theory of schizophrenia. Indeed, in explaining a particular historical case, it is often more convincing to develop a theory from data in that case and then to test the theory against other data in the same case, rather than testing the theory against predictions it makes regarding another case and arguing that the results help explain the

---

82. Robert Jervis, *Systems Effects: Complexity in Political and Social Life* (Princeton, N.J.: Princeton University Press, 1997).

83. In addition to Dessler's Chapter 11 herein, see Clayton Roberts, *The Logic of Historical Explanation* (University Park: Pennsylvania State University Press, 1996).

original case. Homicide detectives, scientists studying mass dinosaur extinctions, and political scientists studying historical cases engage in this kind of reasoning all the time.[84]

Historical explanation has the added virtue of drawing the field's attention away from a single-minded focus on the "isms," as it naturally encourages the use of many variables and theories from multiple levels of analysis and schools of thought. One striking development at the Arizona conference that led to the present volume is that as the discussion moved from assessing the "isms" to explaining particular historical cases or phenomena, scholars began to borrow from schools of thought not ordinarily emphasized in their works. Stephen Krasner explicitly offered a neoliberal institutionalist explanation of how states might engage in self-binding behavior to give weaker states the confidence to enter into mutually beneficial regimes; Robert Keohane noted the realist inputs into post–Cold War European institutions; and Kenneth Waltz acknowledged that his theories allowed for agents to shape structures as well as the reverse.

Conclusions: Going Beyond Lakatos

The introduction to this volume argues that even political scientists who proclaim their indifference to the philosophy of science have a stake in metatheoretic issues. One recent and prominent book of political science methods, for example, states in its second paragraph that it is not "a work in the philosophy of the social sciences," but then proceeds to offer methodological advice based on implicit epistemological assumptions, such as use novelty, that are hotly contested in the

---

84. Extremely useful here is William Wohlforth's suggestion that social scientists should make clear predictions on what we should expect to find as new sources of historical information become available through interviews with policy makers and the gradual declassification of documents and opening of archives. Such predictions, although focusing on past processes, can forestall confirmation biases. William Wohlforth, "Reality Check: Revising Theories of International Politics in Response to the End of the Cold War," *World Politics*, Vol. 50, No. 4 (July 1998), pp. 650–680.

philosophy of science, as this chapter indicates.[85] The contributors to the present volume, therefore, set about the tasks of explicating Lakatos's metatheory, evaluating its usefulness for judging progress in IR theory, and examining what other insights from the philosophy of science might help us understand and judge the progressivity of IR theory. This chapter has concentrated on the second and third tasks, and it concludes that Lakatos's novel facts criteria are useful, even though his distinction between the hard core and outer belt of research programs insufficiently differentiates the two. This distinction can be given a Bayesian reading, but it is not fully warranted or defensible. Still, until the hard core versus outer belt distinction is superseded by a better metatheory it will remain a useful metaphor for addressing the complex issues of theory choice. Yet Lakatos alone is not enough, even though the post-Lakatosian metatheories in the philosophy of science also face sharp limitations. The most challenging question that remains, given that Lakatos's metatheory is fairly useful and (with the Elmans' clarifications) relatively simple compared to his successors, is the following: Why should we go beyond Lakatos when many in the field have had trouble enough as it is faithfully implementing Lakatos's metatheory, and when his successors are also flawed or incomplete?

The answer is that going beyond Lakatos helps inform our research methods and theory choices and guides us toward an answer, or rather many answers, to the nagging question of whether IR has progressed and how we would know if it has. From the naturalists, we can gain an appreciation for the many different forms that theories and research agendas can take, from causal mechanisms to just plain "isms." This can rescue us from one-sided emphasis on the "isms," where progress is evident mostly over long periods of time, and it allows us to recognize progress on many levels of theory. From David Dessler, we can learn that historical explanation is a worthy epistemic aim that characterizes much of our research, and we can demonstrate substantial progress in terms of increasingly complete theory-based explanations of important historical events. From the Bayesians, we can gain insight into some of

85. King, Keohane, and Verba, *Designing Social Inquiry*, p. 3.

the methods used in case study research, such as the focus on deviant cases, most-likely cases, and least-likely cases. These cases can have more influence on our confidence in the theories being tested than cases that are more representative of wider populations. This alerts us to progress in terms of clearer scope conditions for our theories and narrower but more valid contingent generalizations. From Deborah Mayo, we have a firmer philosophical basis for statistical methods, and a clearer understanding of their strengths and limitations. This allows us to measure progress in terms of increasingly sophisticated statistical instruments that represent more complex functional forms and are less prone to recognizable forms of error.

Drawing on these diverse metatheories and avoiding the temptation toward any single view of science, we can discern a discipline that is more diverse and progressive than perhaps we realize. We need not see ourselves as the poor relations of the physical sciences; indeed, another advantage of reading the philosophy of science is the realization that the physical sciences, too, have problematic accounts of scientific progress. Rather, we are a different science, where the changing and reflective nature of our subject renders our theories more provisional but does not prevent cumulative and progressive theorizing over long periods of time. Most of our theories may remain explanatory rather than predictive, but our progress is most evident in our puzzle-driven research programs and our historical explanations. Who would have thought fifteen years ago that the long list of correlates James Lee Ray provides from the democratic peace program would enjoy a widespread consensus today? Who then would have anticipated that this program would generate numerous and increasingly complete (though still conflicting) case studies of the Fashoda crisis of 1898?

One of the Bayesians' favorite arguments is that theory choice is ultimately a practical question of how we choose to spend the time and resources we have available for research. This is a kind of wager on which we are staking our professional lives, and thus it is the most serious epistemic commitment we undertake. It is more than a mere sociological fad that we are spending our time very differently from Thucydides, or even from ourselves as of a decade or two ago.

About the Contributors

Andrew Bennett is Associate Professor of Government at Georgetown University, and co-author, with Alexander L. George, of *Case Studies and Theory Development*, forthcoming with MIT Press.

David Dessler is Associate Professor of Government at the College of William & Mary. He has had fellowships at the Center for International Affairs at Harvard University and the Center for International Security and Cooperation at Stanford University. Dessler's primary research interests include the philosophy of social science, research methodology, and international relations theory, and he continues to work on a project concerning positivism in the study of world politics.

Jonathan M. DiCicco is a Ph.D. candidate in Political Science at Rutgers, the State University of New Jersey. His research focuses on the causes of interstate conflict and on the coercive uses of military power, and he has published articles in the *Journal of Conflict Resolution* and the *Naval War College Review*. His dissertation explores the sources of persistent rivalries in international relations.

Colin Elman is Assistant Professor of Political Science at Arizona State University. His work has appeared in the *American Political Science Review, International Security, Security Studies*, the *International History Review*, and *International Studies Quarterly*; he is also the co-editor of *Bridges and Boundaries: Historians, Political Scientists and the Study of International Relations* (with Miriam Fendius Elman) and *Realism and the Balancing of Power: A New Debate* (with John Vasquez). Elman is Executive Director of the Consortium on Qualitative Research Methods.

Miriam Fendius Elman is Associate Professor of Political Science at Arizona State University. She is the editor of *Paths to Peace: Is Democracy the Answer?* and co-editor of *Bridges and Boundaries: Historians, Political Scientists and the Study of International Relations* (with Colin Elman). Her work has appeared in the *American Political Science Review*, the *British Journal of Political Science, International Security*, the

International History Review, Security Studies, and other scholarly journals.

Robert Jervis is Adlai E. Stevenson Professor of International Politics at Columbia University and served as President of the American Political Science Association in 2000–01. His most recent book is *System Effects: Complexity in Political and Social Life.*

Robert O. Keohane is James B. Duke Professor of Political Science at Duke University, and was Stanfield Professor of International Peace at Harvard University. His books include *After Hegemony: Cooperation and Discord in the World Political Economy* (1984); *International Institutions and State Power: Essays in International Relations Theory* (1989); *Power and Interdependence: World Politics in Transition* (with Joseph S. Nye, Jr., 1977, 1988); and *Designing Social Inquiry: Scientific Inference in Qualitative Research* (with Gary King and Sidney Verba, 1994). His newest book, *Power and Governance in a Partially Globalized World,* was published by Routledge in 2002. He has edited *International Organization* (1974–80), and served as president of the International Studies Association (1988–89). He is a fellow of the American Academy of Arts and Sciences.

Jack S. Levy is Board of Governors' Professor of Political Science at Rutgers University. He is author of *War in the Modern Great Power System, 1495–1975* and numerous articles and book chapters. His research interests focus on the causes of war and on foreign policy decisionmaking.

Lisa L. Martin is a Professor of Government at Harvard University, and is a member of the Executive Committee of the Weatherhead Center for International Affairs. Her books include *Democratic Commitments: Legislatures and International Cooperation* (2000), and *Coercive Cooperation: Explaining Multilateral Economic Sanctions* (1993).

Andrew Moravcsik is Professor of Government and Director of the European Union Center at Harvard University. He is the author of *The Choice for Europe: Social Purpose and State Power from Messina to Maastricht.*

James Lee Ray is a Professor of Political Science at Vanderbilt University. He is author of *Democracy and International Conflict* (1995), *Global Politics*, 7th ed. (1998); his articles have appeared in the *British Journal of Political Science, International Organization, International Studies Quarterly, Journal of Peace Research, Journal of Theoretical Politics,* and the *Political Research Quarterly.*

Randall Schweller is associate professor in the Department of Political Science at Ohio State University. He is the author of *Deadly Imbalances: Tripolarity and Hitler's Strategy of World Conquest;* his articles have appeared in such journals as *International Security, American Journal of Political Science, Security Studies, World Politics,* and *International Studies Quarterly.*

Roslyn Simowitz is an associate professor of political science at University of Texas at Arlington. Her interests include theories of international relations and philosophy of science. Her work has appeared in the *American Political Science Review, Journal of Peace Research, Journal of Economic Issues and Teaching Political Science,* and *Peace Research Society Papers (International).*

Jack Snyder is the Robert and Renée Belfer Professor of International Relations in the political science department and Institute of War and Peace Studies at Columbia University. His books include *From Voting to Violence: Democratization and Nationalist Conflict* (2000).

John Vasquez is Professor of Political Science at Vanderbilt University. His books include *The Power of Power Politics: From Classical Realism to Neotraditionalism, The War Puzzle, What Do We Know about War?* (editor), and most recently, *Realism and the Balancing of Power: A New Debate* (co-edited with Colin Elman). His scholarly articles have appeared in *International Studies Quarterly, World Politics, Security Studies, American Political Science Review, Journal of Peace Research, International Organization, Journal of Politics, International Political Science Review, Millennium, British Journal of Political Science,* and others. He has been President of the Peace Science Society (International) and the International Studies Association.

Stephen Walker is a Professor of Political Science at Arizona State University. His recent journal publications dealing with the psychological sources of foreign policy decisions are in *International Studies Quarterly*, *Journal of Conflict Resolution*, and *Political Psychology*.

Kenneth N. Waltz is an Adjunct Professor at Columbia University, and is a Fellow of the American Academy of Arts and Sciences. He served until 1994 as Ford Professor of Political Science at the University of California at Berkeley, and was President of the American Political Science Association in 1987–88. His books include *Man, the State, and War: A Theoretical Analysis* (1959), *Foreign Policy and Democratic Politics: The American and British Experience* (1967, 1992), *Theory of International Politics* (1979) and, with Scott Sagan, *The Spread of Nuclear Weapons: A Debate* (1995). He is also co-editor and co-author, with Robert Art, of *The Use of Force*. He received the 1999 James Madison Award for "distinguished scholarly contributions to political science" from the American Political Science Association.

Index

BCSIA Studies in International Security

Published by The MIT Press

Sean M. Lynn-Jones and Steven E. Miller, series editors
Karen Motley, executive editor
Belfer Center for Science and International Affairs (BCSIA)
John F. Kennedy School of Government, Harvard University

Allison, Graham T., Owen R. Coté, Jr., Richard A. Falkenrath, and Steven E. Miller, *Avoiding Nuclear Anarchy: Containing the Threat of Loose Russian Nuclear Weapons and Fissile Material* (1996)

Allison, Graham T., and Kalypso Nicolaïdis, eds., *The Greek Paradox: Promise vs. Performance* (1996)

Arbatov, Alexei, Abram Chayes, Antonia Handler Chayes, and Lara Olson, eds., *Managing Conflict in the Former Soviet Union: Russian and American Perspectives* (1997)

Bennett, Andrew, *Condemned to Repetition? The Rise, Fall, and Reprise of Soviet-Russian Military Interventionism, 1973–1996* (1999)

Blackwill, Robert D., and Michael Stürmer, eds., *Allies Divided: Transatlantic Policies for the Greater Middle East* (1997)

Blackwill, Robert D., and Paul Dibb, eds., *America's Asian Alliances* (2000)

Brom, Shlomo, and Yiftah Shapir, eds., *The Middle East Military Balance 1999–2000* (1999)

Brom, Shlomo, and Yiftah Shapir, eds., *The Middle East Military Balance 2001–2002* (2002)

Brown, Michael E., ed., *The International Dimensions of Internal Conflict* (1996)

Brown, Michael E., and Šumit Ganguly, eds., *Government Policies and Ethnic Relations in Asia and the Pacific* (1997)

Carter, Ashton B., and John P. White, eds., *Keeping the Edge: Managing Defense for the Future* (2001)

de Nevers, Renée, *Comrades No More: The Seeds of Political Change in Eastern Europe* (2003)

Elman, Colin, and Miriam Fendius Elman, eds., *Bridges and Boundaries: Historians, Political Scientists, and the Study of International Relations* (2001)

Elman, Miriam Fendius, ed., *Paths to Peace: Is Democracy the Answer?* (1997)

Falkenrath, Richard A., *Shaping Europe's Military Order: The Origins and Consequences of the CFE Treaty* (1994)

Falkenrath, Richard A., Robert D. Newman, and Bradley A. Thayer, *America's Achilles' Heel: Nuclear, Biological, and Chemical Terrorism and Covert Attack* (1998)

Feaver, Peter D., and Richard H. Kohn, eds., *Soldiers and Civilians: The Civil-Military Gap and American National Security* (2001)

Feldman, Shai, *Nuclear Weapons and Arms Control in the Middle East* (1996)

Feldman, Shai, and Yiftah Shapir, eds., *The Middle East Military Balance 2000–2001* (2001)

Forsberg, Randall, ed., *The Arms Production Dilemma: Contraction and Restraint in the World Combat Aircraft Industry* (1994)

Hagerty, Devin T., *The Consequences of Nuclear Proliferation: Lessons from South Asia* (1998)

Heymann, Philip B., *Terrorism and America: A Commonsense Strategy for a Democratic Society* (1998)

Kokoshin, Andrei A., *Soviet Strategic Thought, 1917–91* (1998)

Lederberg, Joshua, *Biological Weapons: Limiting the Threat* (1999)

Shaffer, Brenda, *Borders and Brethren: Iran and the Challenge of Azerbaijani Identity* (2002)

Shields, John M., and William C. Potter, eds., *Dismantling the Cold War: U.S. and NIS Perspectives on the Nunn-Lugar Cooperative Threat Reduction Program* (1997)

Tucker, Jonathan B., ed., *Toxic Terror: Assessing Terrorist Use of Chemical and Biological Weapons* (2000)

Utgoff, Victor A., ed., *The Coming Crisis: Nuclear Proliferation, U.S. Interests, and World Order* (2000)

Williams, Cindy, ed., *Holding the Line: U.S. Defense Alternatives for the Early 21st Century* (2001)

The Robert and Renée Belfer Center for Science and International Affairs

Graham T. Allison, Director
John F. Kennedy School of Government
Harvard University
79 JFK Street, Cambridge, MA 02138
Tel: (617) 495-1400; Fax: (617) 495-8963
http://www.ksg.harvard.edu/bcsia   bcsia_ksg@harvard.edu

The Belfer Center for Science and International Affairs (BCSIA) is the hub of research, teaching and training in international security affairs, environmental and resource issues, science and technology policy, human rights and conflict studies at Harvard's John F. Kennedy School of Government. The Center's mission is to provide leadership in advancing policy-relevant knowledge about the most important challenges of international security and other critical issues where science, technology, and international affairs inter-sect.

BCSIA's leadership begins with the recognition of science and technology as driving forces transforming international affairs. The Center integrates insights of social scientists, natural scientists, technologists, and practitioners with experience in government, diplomacy, the military, and business to address these challenges. The Center pursues its mission in four complementary research programs:

- The **International Security Program** (ISP) addresses the most pressing threats to U.S. national interests and international security.

- The **Environment and Natural Resources Program** (ENRP) is the locus of Harvard's interdisciplinary research on resource and environmental problems and policy responses.

- The **Science, Technology and Public Policy** (STPP) program analyzes ways in which science and technology policy influence international security, resources, environment, and development, and such cross-cutting issues as technological innovation and information infrastructure.

- The **WPF Program on Intrastate Conflict, Conflict Prevention and Conflict Resolution** analyzes the causes of ethnic, religious, and other conflicts, and seeks to identify practical ways to prevent and limit such conflicts.

The heart of the Center is its resident research community of more than 140 scholars: Harvard faculty, analysts, practitioners, and each year a new, interdisciplinary group of research fellows. BCSIA sponsors frequent seminars, workshops and conferences, maintains a substantial specialized library, and publishes books, monographs, and discussion papers.

The Center's International Security Program, directed by Steven E. Miller, publishes the BCSIA Studies in International Security, and sponsors and edits the quarterly journal *International Security*.

The Center is supported by an endowment established with funds from Robert and Renée Belfer, the Ford Foundation and Harvard University, by foundation grants, by individual gifts, and by occasional government contracts.